RENÉ BOSEWITZ / ROBERT KLEINSCHROTH

BETTER THAN THE BOSS

BUSINESS ENGLISH FÜRS BÜRO

Rowohlt
rororo

Wir danken Frau Ortrud Grimm vielmals
für ihre Hilfe bei der Erstellung des Manuskripts.
Ohne sie hätten wir es wohl nicht geschafft.

14. – 16. Tausend Januar 2000

Originalausgabe
Veröffentlicht im Rowohlt Taschenbuch Verlag GmbH, Reinbek bei Hamburg, September 1996

Umschlaggestaltung Barbara Hanke (Illustration: Cathrin Günther)
Gestaltung Anne Drude und Alexander Urban
Satz OCRA und Stone sans, PostScript Linotype Library, QuarkXPress 3.31 (Dolev 800)
Druck und Bindung Clausen & Bosse, Leck
Printed in Germany
ISBN 3 499 60138 9

Inhalt

Vorwort

Business English fürs Büro kann unterhaltsam sein. James Kelly ist ein englischer *trainee*, der die Abteilungen von Low Valley Photocopiers kennenlernen soll. Für James gibt es viel zu belächeln, aber auch zu bewundern. Manchmal ist er *better than the boss* – zum Beispiel, wenn es darum geht, das Wohlwollen trinkfester russischer Kunden zu erhalten.

Wie in vielen Firmen, die multinational denken, so ist auch in Low Valley Photocopiers Englisch Verkehrssprache. Begleiten Sie James Kelly auf seinem Gang durch die Etagen des Betriebs, und frischen Sie dabei Ihr Business English auf. Damit der Stoff gut verdaulich ist, haben wir ihn mit viel Witz zubereitet.

Und so ist ein typisches Kapitel aufgebaut:

- Business Frame: Eine mehr oder weniger ernste Situation in der Firma bildet den Rahmen für Wortschatz, Grammatik und Übungen. Kurze Multiple-choice-Tests überprüfen das Textverständnis. Der präsentierte Wortschatz wird in kurzen Übungen gefestigt.
- **Grammar Rhymes:** Damit Sie sich einen Reim auf Grammatik machen können, sind die wichtigsten Regeln in kurze Merkverse gefaßt.
- **Grammar Jokes:** Witze, Graffiti oder pfiffige Lebensweisheiten machen das Üben zu einem Lern- und Lesespaß.
- **Business Words:** Sie erweitern den Wortschatz der Business Frames und wiederholen ihn in kurzen, übersichtlichen Übungen.
- **Business Culture** ist ein Knigge für den Umgang unter Kollegen und mit Geschäftsfreunden. Hier finden Sie die Redemittel, die für das Abschirmen des Vorgesetzten oder die Behandlung von Beschwerden nützlich sind.

Noch ein Wort an die Leserinnen. Als wir dem Computer sagten, er solle *man* und *woman* durch das moderne *person* ersetzen, erhielten wir für *manpower* und *manager* das neutrale *personpower* und *personager*. Aus stilistischen Gründen haben wir die Zweigeschlechtlichkeit teilweise aufgegeben. Wo immer wir *milkman* oder *manager* geschrieben haben, waren wir in Gedanken bei der *milkwoman* und *womanager*.

Wir wünschen Ihnen viel Spaß und Erfolg mit diesem Band aus der Reihe Business English.

Hire and fire

CONTENTS

Business Frame:	**Low Valley Photocopiers need a new trainee**
Grammar Rhymes:	**Conditional sentences**
Grammar Jokes:	**Practising if-clauses**
Business Words:	**They talk about it in the personnel department**
Plus:	**Business English jokes and some useful exercises**

Let's start with a smile: How to fire somebody

"Dobson," said the boss one morning, "I just don't know how we are going to get along[1] without you – but starting Monday[2], we're going to try."

1 auskommen 2 ab Montag

Personnel matters

The name of the company is Low Valley Photocopiers (Hollerberg, somewhere in Germany). Let's eavesdrop at the door of the personnel department. The people working there are responsible for all the matters connected with the staff in the company. They think they know best about salary, promotion, further education and training – and usually they do.

Let's listen at the door! Director Block (**B**) is speaking to Mr Seba (**S**). Mr Seba is the man who really has to do the work, but since he is not the boss he has to implement the will of his superior, Mr Block.

B: Could you come into my office for a moment, Mr Seba?
S: Of course, Mr Block, I'll be along in a minute.
B: Not in a minute, now, Mr Seba. I mean immediately.
S: Yes, sir.
(*In the office*)
B: Now Seba, the company needs a trainee to work in the various departments. Then, if he's the right man for the job, he'll get the position of personal assistant to the advertising director, Mr Tal.
S: If I might interrupt a minute, Mr Block, I think you mean we need a "management trainee". That means the candidate has already attended a university or other institution of higher education.
B: Do you think I would be where I am, if I didn't know what a trainee was?
S: Sir, if we call it by the wrong name, we'll get the wrong type of candidate.
B: If we get the wrong type of applicants, I'll have to ask myself why we employ you. He should be about 25 years old ...
S: Sir, I really have to draw your attention to something. If we talk about "he" in the advertisement, we'll get problems about "sexual" discrimination.
B: Of course we're interested in a man for this position. It's a position of responsibility. We can't have some young woman running off for family reasons after three years of training here.
S: Mr Block, I feel I have to point out to you that we cannot proceed in this way. If I were you ...

B: You aren't, Seba. Please keep in mind that I am your boss and I am the boss of the Human Resources Department. Do you think you know things better than your boss?

So Mr Seba prepares the advert for the newspaper. He decides to do it in a way which will cause fewer problems for the company and which will probably find the right "person" for the job.

Low Valley Photocopiers

Centre of the world · Germany · Europe.

We are looking for a
management trainee
to take part in a rotation programme
inside our company.

Your training

will last 18 months and will involve work in advertising, finance, production, R&D, quality control, etc. etc. and personnel. Chances of promotion are excellent if you show the right motivation. We require a degree in business administration or equivalent, knowledge of two foreign languages, six months practice in industry.

Salary

by negotiation. After 18 months, re-negotiable depending on success. Trial period: 3 months. We are an equal opportunities employer.

Contact

B. Sparler ext. 68 2317.

These words will help you to understand the text

advert, advertisement	(Zeitungs-)Anzeige
advertising director	Direktor der Werbeabteilung
advertising	Werbung
applicant	Bewerber
apply	bewerben, sich ~
attend a university	eine Universität besuchen
business administration	Betriebswirtschaft
contact partner	Ansprechpartner
decide	entscheiden
degree	Hochschulabschluß
depending on	abhängig von
attention, draw ~ to	Aufmerksamkeit lenken auf
eavesdrop	lauschen, horchen
education	Ausbildung
employ	anstellen, beschäftigen
equivalent	Gleichwertiges
further education	Aus- / Weiterbildung
Human Resources Department	Personalabteilung
immediately	sofort
implement a plan	ausführen, einen Plan ~
interrupt	unterbrechen
involve	beinhalten, umfassen
keep in mind	nicht vergessen
matters connected with ...	Dinge, die mit ... zusammenhängen
office	Büro
personal assistant (P.A.)	persönlicher Assistent
personnel department	Personalabteilung
point out	hinweisen auf, erklären
position	Stelle, Position, Posten
position of responsibility	verantwortungsvolle Stelle
prefer	vorziehen
proceed	verfahren

promotion	Beförderung
quality control	Qualitätskontrolle
re-negotiable, be ~	erneut zu verhandeln sein
require	erfordern, verlangen
responsible for	verantwortlich für
salary by negotiation	außertarifliches Gehalt (AT)
sex discrimination authority	Behörde für Gleichstellung von Mann und Frau
staff	Personal
take part in	teilnehmen an
the right man for the job	der richtige Mann für den Job
trainee	Azubi
management trainee	Trainee
trial period	Probezeit
various departments	verschiedene Abteilungen

EXERCISE 1: Memory Test. Tick off the right answers

(More than one answer is possible)

1. *The personnel department is responsible for?*

☐ *promotion*
☐ *salary*
☐ *public relations*

2. *They are looking for a(n)*

☐ *personal assistant*
☐ *trainee*
☐ *applicant*

3. *They don't talk about "he" in the advert because they*

☐ *prefer a woman*
☐ *want to avoid problems*
☐ *'re offering a secreterial job*

4. *The applicant should*

☐ *have a university degree*
☐ *speak a foreign language*
☐ *have 18 months practice*

Grammar Rhymes

Conditional sentences

Ihnen sind sicher die vielen Bedingungssätze mit *if* aufgefallen. Bei genauem Hinsehen werden Sie zwei Typen unterscheiden.

Erster Grundtyp

Der Sprecher glaubt als Optimist,
Daß die Bedingung erfüllbar ist.

erfüllbare Bedingung (wenn)	**sichere Folge** (dann)
If an experiment *works*	something *has gone* wrong.
If anything *can* go wrong	it *will*.
Gegenwart / Present tense	**sinngemäße Verbform**

Zweiter Grundtyp

Die Bedingung ist nur Theorie,
Erfüllt sich selten oder nie

theoretische Bedingung	**mögliche Folge**
If wise men never *erred*[1]	fools *would* despair[2]. (Goethe)
If I *owned* all the cows in Arabia	*would* I then *be* a milk sheikh?
Vergangenheit	**Bedingungsform 1 (*would* + Infinitiv)**
Past tense	**Conditional 1**

MERKE:	Schriftsprache:	If I *were* king
	Umgangssprache:	If I *was* king

I had und *I would* werden in der gesprochenen Sprache zu I'd.

1 irren 2 verzweifeln

Grammar Jokes

EXERCISE 2:

A. Put the verb in brackets[1] in the right form

❶ In a tourist guide to English restaurants you can read:
If it's hot, it (*be*) soup.
If it's cold, it (*be*) beer.

❷ Army recruit: What happens if this parachute[2] (*fail*[3]) to open?
Army instructor: If you (*bring*) it back, you (*get*) a new one.

❸ A lot of husbands (*leave*) their wives
if they (*know*) how to pack their suitcases[4].

❹ In a shop window I once saw the following sign:
If you (*not/know*) what you want, come in, we have got it.

❺ Security[5] officer: Look, in this bottle there is poisonous[6] gas.
Now, what steps[7] (*you/take*), if I dropped this bottle?
Young Scientist: Very large ones, sir!

B. Do you remember these conditionals in our dialogue?

1. If he (*be*) the right man for the job, he (*get*) the position.
2. If we (*call*) it by the wrong name, we (*get*) the wrong type of candidate.
3. Chances of promotion (*be*) excellent if you (*be*) the right candidate.
4. If we (*talk*) about "he" in the advertisement, we (*get*) problems with the sex discrimination authorities.
5. If I (*not/know*) what a trainee was, I (*not/be*) where I am, would I?

1 Klammern 2 Fallschirm 3 nicht öffnen 4 Koffer 5 Sicherheit 6 giftig 7 Schritte

They talk about it in the personnel department

abziehen	*deduct*
Abzüge	*deductions*
Altersversorgungsplan	*pension scheme*
Anfangsgehalt	*starting salary*
Angestellter	*clerk*
Anstellung	*employment*
Arbeitgeber	*employer*
Arbeitnehmer	*employee*
Arbeitsplatzbewertung	*job evaluation*
besuchen, die Universität ~	*attend university*
Bewerber	*applicant*
Bezahlung	*payment*
Bruttogehalt	*gross pay*
Büropersonal	*clerical staff*
Einkommen	*income*
einstellen	*hire*
einstellen	*employ*
entlassen	*dismiss*
entlassen (feuern), jdn. ~	*fire s.o., sack s.o.*
Entlassung	*dismissal*
freie Stelle	*vacancy, vacant post*
Gewerkschaft	*union, trade ~*
Grundlohn	*basic wage*
kündigen	*give in one's notice*
kündigen, zurücktreten von	*resign from*
Kündigung	*resignation*
Lohnliste	*payroll*
Lohnpolitik	*wages policy*
Lohnskala	*wage scale*
Lohnsteuerabzug vor Auszahlung des Lohns	*PAYE (Pay As You Earn)*
Lohntüte	*wage packet*

Nettogehalt	*net pay*
Personalführung	*personnel management*
Personalvertreter	*staff representative*
Personalwesen	*human resources*
Rente	*pension*
Sozialversicherung	*national insurance*
Steuer	*taxes*
steuerpflichtiges Einkommen	*taxable income*
Untergebener	*subordinate*
Verantwortung	*responsibility*
Verhandlungen	*negotiations*
Vorgesetzter	*superior*

EXERCISE 3: What are the opposites (Gegenteile)

fire	*h . . .*
dismiss	*e . . . . y*
employee	*e . . . . . . r*
superior	*s . . . .*
hire	*s . . .*

EXERCISE 4: Find words that have almost the same meaning

human resources department	*. . . . . department*
boss	*s . . . .*
personnel	*s . . . .*
clerk	*e . . . . . . e*
vacant post	*v . . . . . .*

EXERCISE 5: Wordbuilder's corner. Find the nouns.

verb	noun
advertise	*advertisement*
employ	....
deduct	....
resign	....
be responsible	....
promote	....
dismiss	....

A Biblical conditional Type II

Our modern world is so full of problems that *if* Moses *came* down from Mount Sinai again, the two tablets[1] he was carrying *would be* aspirins.

The difference between salary and wages

Pupil: What's the difference between wages and salaries, sir?
Teacher: Well, *if you get* a wage, *you get paid* once a week. *If you get* a salary, *you are paid* once a month. For example, I get a salary, I'm paid once a month.
Pupil: Please, sir, where do you work?

1 Tafeln, Tabletten

Once a boss, always a boss

CONTENTS

Time for a smile

The personnel manager of a chemical company was looking the applicant up and down[1]. Finally he said: "What we're looking for is a man with initiative, drive[2], enthusiasm and determination[3]. A man with leadership qualities; a man who can inspire[4] others. In short, a man who can pull the company's football team up from the bottom of the league[5].

Sign[6] that can be found in almost all companies

In our company all colleagues are equal[7] – only the salaries aren't.

1 von Kopf bis Fuß betrachten 2 Schwung, Elan 3 Entschlossenheit 4 inspirieren, motivieren 5 der letzte Platz in der Liga 6 Schild 7 gleich

Preparing the CV

A young post-graduate student, James, sees an advertisement for a management trainee at a copier manufacturer in Germany in the newspaper and prepares his job application. His father, a boss who knows better than everybody, gives him paternal advice. His idea of a CV and James' own notion are far apart. Will James follow his own ideas through?

Old Mr Kelly, the Father (**F**), James Kelly, the son (**J**)

F: So you've finally decided to apply for a job. Well, it's about time, that's for sure. Now when I was your age I'd already decided what I wanted to do and I'd planned all the qualifications for it, too. I ...

J: Now look father, times have changed. You're nothing nowadays if you haven't got a university degree.

F: If you'd taken my advice you'd have done a training as a commercial clerk. Just two or three years and you'd have had money coming in and a steady job. If I'd have known that it'd take so long,
I would have told you to ...

J: Father, it only took four years and it didn't cost you anything. Anyhow, I have to concentrate on my CV. I want to do it as well as I can so that I have the chance of a real shot at this job.

F: Okay, well, if you listen to me you'll make a table of all the things you've done in chronological order. Then you list where you've had work experience and at the end state your hobbies.

J: Actually, I've already written it. I didn't write it in tabular form. I just put the date and a description of what I did in one sentence after each date.

F: If you'd let me do it, it would've been better. You've no experience in these matters. Let me see your CV. Where are your hobbies? You've forgotten to mention them.

J: No, I haven't forgotten. I simply don't think the company would be interested. It's not appropriate.

F: Listen, James, I've been reading these resumés for years. I didn't become boss of John Stag Tractors for nothing. Take my advice! You can't do it better than the boss!

J: (*to himself*) You're always bossing everybody around, that's for sure.

F: What did you say, James?

J: Nothing that you'd understand. See you later.

James Kelly's CV (short version)

Name:	James Kelly
Age:	23
Place of birth:	Notts, England
Address:	7, Birchwood Avenue, Notts
Education:	1988 – 1992 attended Manchester University, Second Class Degree in Economics. 1992 – 1993 attended Manchester Business School, Diploma in Business Studies. 1993 – 1994 M.B.A. (Manchester)
Practical experience:	1993 (4 months) job placement at ICI, England 1994-1995 Practical year at Esselte Meto, Germany.
Extra qualifications:	London Chamber of Commerce and Industry Advanced German, Advanced English for Business, LCCI Marketing Diploma.

These words will help you to understand the text

advice	Rat(schlag)
advanced German	fortgeschrittenes Deutsch
age	Alter
application	Bewerbung
appropriate	angemessen
attend university	besuchen, die Universität ~
boss around	herumkommandieren
Chamber of Commerce and Industry	Industrie- und Handelskammer
commercial training	kaufmännische Ausbildung
commercial clerk	Industriekaufmann
copier manufacturer	Hersteller von Photokopierern

CV (curriculum vitae)	Lebenslauf
description	Beschreibung, Schilderung
have a real shot	einen ernsthaften Versuch machen
job placement	Praktikum
mention	erwähnen
notion	Idee, Vorstellung
paternal advice	väterlicher Rat
place of birth	Geburtsort
post-graduate student	etwa: Doktorand
practical experience	praktische Erfahrung
state	angeben, behaupten
steady job	feste Anstellung
table	hier: Tabelle
tabular form	tabellarisch
take long	lange brauchen
work experience	Arbeitserfahrung

Exercise 1: Test your memory. Tick off the right answers

(Sometimes there is more than one possibility)

1. *How many years did James attend university?*
   - ☐ *two years*
   - ☐ *three years*
   - ☐ *four years*

2. *James wrote his CV*
   - ☐ *in tabular form*
   - ☐ *in chronological order*
   - ☐ *stating only date and descriptions of what he had done*

3. *James did not state his*
   - ☐ *hobbies*
   - ☐ *his work experience*
   - ☐ *his third foreign language*
   - ☐ *his job placement*

4. *James attended*
   - ☐ *Manchester University*
   - ☐ *ICI Business School*
   - ☐ *Meto Highschool*
   - ☐ *Manchester Business School.*

Grammar Rhymes

Conditional sentences

Sie haben sicher gemerkt, daß die Konditional- beziehungsweise Bedingungssätze in diesem Dialog etwas anders aussehen. Hier ein Merkvers zur Einstimmung:

Dritter Grundtyp

Die Kondition erfüllt sich nie,
Sie ist meist reine Utopie.

nicht erfüllbare Bedingung	mögliche Folge
If Columbus *hadn't discovered* America	he *would have spared* us a lot of trouble.
Vorvergangenheit	**Bedingungsform 2**
Past perfect	**Conditional 2**

Merken wollen wir
Uns der Wörter vier,
Die in Bedingungssätzen
oft das *if* ersetzen:

1. *unless*: wenn nicht	Unless he drives slowly he'll be killed.
2. *providing*: vorausgesetzt	Providing you pay the bill, you'll get no trouble.
provided: vorausgesetzt	Man is master of the universe, provided nothing happens.
2. *in case*: falls	In case I don't have enough money, I'll phone you.

VORSICHT FALLE:
I had und *I would* werden in der gesprochenen Sprache zu *I'd*.

Grammar Jokes

EXERCISE 2:

A Put the verb in brackets in the right form

❶ If I'd been the Virgin Mary[1], I (*say*) "No!"

❷ God (*never/give*) us the bicycle, if he (*want*) us to walk.

❸ A husband is someone who will share[2] with you all the troubles which you (*not/have*) had if you (*not/marry*[3]) him.

❹ Eve was unhappy in Paradise because she couldn't tell Adam about all the wonderful lovers she (*have*) if she (*not/marry*) him.

❺ First girl: Why don't you leave your husband if you're so fed up[4] with marriage[5]?
Second girl: I (*do*) it if I had found a way without making him happy.

B Do you remember these conditionals in our dialogue?

1. If you (*take*) my advice you (*do*) a commercial training as a clerk.
2. If I (*know*) that it'd take so long, I (*tell*) you ...
3. If you (*let*) me do it, it would've been better.

1 Jungfrau Maria 2 teilen 3 heiraten 4 die Nase voll haben 5 Ehe

Business words for applications and interviews

Akademiker	*graduate*
Arbeitsamt	*labor office, (US) job centre*
Arbeitsbedingungen	*working conditions*
Arbeitsplatzbeschreibung	*job description*
Arbeitswoche	*working week*
Arbeitszeit	*working hours*
Ausbildung	*education, training*
Ausbildung am Arbeitsplatz	*on the job training*
ausführliche Bewerbung	*application with full particulars*
Aushilfspersonal	*temporary personnel*
Auswahl	*selection*
auswählen	*select*
Belegschaft	*work force*
Berufsausbildung	*vocational training*
besetzen, eine Stelle ~	*fill a job*
beurteilen, jdn. ~	*assess s.o.*
Bewerber "sieben"	*screen candidates*
Bewertung	*assessment*
Dienst nach Vorschrift	*work-to-rule*
Diplom	*diploma*
einstellen, jdn. ~	*recruit, take on s.o.*
Einstellung	*recruitment*
Einstellungsbedingungen	*conditions (of employment)*
Empfehlungen, Referenzen	*references*
engere Wahl (der Bewerber)	*short list*
Facharbeiter	*skilled worker*
Handelsschule	*business school*
höhere Handelsschule	*commercial college*
in Ruhestand treten	*retire*
Krankenurlaub	*sick leave*
Laufbahn	*career*
Lehre	*apprenticeship*

Lehrgang	*training course*
Leistung	*performance*
offenes Zeugnis	*testimonial*
Prämie	*bonus*
Probezeit	*probationary period*
Prüfungskomitee	*interview panel*
Qualifikationen, Zeugnisse	*qualifications*
Stellenvermittlung	*employment agency*
Überstunden	*overtime*
umschulen	*retrain*
ungelernter Arbeiter	*unskilled worker*
Urlaub	*holiday, vacation*
Verdienst	*earnings*
Vergütung	*remuneration*
Vorarbeiter	*foreman*
Vorstellungsgespräch	*interview*

EXERCISE 3: Do you remember the correct Business English word?

Period of time ...	
1. for students to get practical experience	*j . . p . . . .*
2. to learn basic skills necessary for a job	*a . . . . p*
3. to see if somebody is the right person	*p . . . . y p . . . . .*
4. to play golf on the Bahamas	*h . . . . . .*
5. working hours after 6 o'clock p.m.	*o . . . .*

EXERCISE 4: The steps to employment

Here are the German words to help you:

Vertrag, Anzeige, engere Wahl, Auswahl, Vorstellungsgespräch, Sichtung (der Bewerberlage)

a . . . . -
. . . t

i . . . .

s . . . . g

s . . . . l . . .

s . . . . . ion

c . . . .

EXERCISE 5: Documents the applicant must not forget

c . . . .
v . . . .

qu . . . . . -
c . . . . . s

application

d . . . .

r . . . . s

test . . . . . . s

Extra Reading

A personnel manager knows how to interprete CVs

The candidate writes:	A personnel manager thinks:
Objective[1]**:**	**Objective:**
I want to find a position that utilises[2] my abilities and challenges[3] my intellect. I am willing to relocate[4].	He's looking for a position that enables him to day-dream for as much of the day as possible; wants to move to another country to avoid arrest warrants[12].
Experience:	**Experience:**
1991 – 1992 News Presenter, at BBC	He was a newspaper delivery boy[13] at Bulls & Beef Company
1990 – 1991 Transportation Executive[5], C & C Distribution.	Van Driver, Curry & Chips Delivery.
1989 – 1990 Landscape[6] Technician, UK Attitudinal Adjustment Centre[7].	Gardener[14] in a prison.
1988 – 1989 Comestibles[8] Allocation Expediter[9], FB Foods.	1988 – 1989 fast food server, Funky Burger.
Other interests:	**Other interests:**
Studying chance vector variables[10].	Gambler[15], drinking beer
References:	**References:**
J. Rape, Guidance Counsellor[11].	J. Rape, Probation Officer[16]

Adapted from David Westwood. The Office Manual. Kingston, UK. 1993

1 Ziel 2 nutzen 3 herausfordern 4 Wohnort wechseln 5 leitender Angestellter 6 Landschaft 7 Zentrum zur Anpassung von Neigungen 8 Nahrungsmittel 9 Spediteur 10 Wahrscheinlichkeitsrechnung 11 Berufsberater 12 Haftbefehl 13 Zeitungsausträger 14 Gärtner 15 Glücksspieler 16 Bewährungshelfer

Getting grilled[1] at the interview

CONTENTS

Business Frame:	**At the interview**
Grammar Rhymes:	**Simple past tense**
Grammar Jokes:	**Test your simple past tense**
Business Words:	**Words for the personnel department**
Business Culture:	**The encounter**
Plus:	**Useful exercises and a lot of jokes**

Let's start with a smile

Once I heard Director Block say to an applicant[2]:
"If you want to work here, young man, there are two things you should know. First, we are very keen on[3] cleanliness[4]. By the way, did you wipe your feet on the mat[5] before you came in?"
"Yes, of course, sir," replied the applicant.
"And there's another thing you should know," he went on, "we're very keen on honesty[6], too. There is no mat!"

1 in die Mangel nehmen 2 Bewerber 3 Wert legen auf 4 Sauberkeit 5 Fußabstreifer 6 Ehrlichkeit

Exchanging proverbs

James Kelly goes to his interview. He's already on the short list. So far, so good! He meets Director Block and Mr Seba. Director Block has a more critical and aggressive attitude; he feels he must give a clear picture of what he thinks. Mr Seba has a more constructive one and tries to smooth things over. He wants to find out what the candidate knows and could offer to the company. He is looking for a positive and efficient colleague.

Director Block (**B**), Mr Seba (**S**), James Kelly (**K**)

B: Well, Mr Kelly, we're happy to welcome you here to our company. I hope you had a good journey. Please permit me to introduce Mr Seba, our specialist in personnel affairs.

S: How do you do?

K: How do you do?

B: Let's come straight to the point. We want a good man. We want to find out if you're up to our requirements.

S: What Mr Block means in other words is that we'd like to find out if you would fit into our team.

K: Well, I'm sure I'll do my best.

S: Mr Kelly, you mention in your CV that you attended Manchester University. You studied economics. What did these courses include, I mean what did you study there?

K: I did courses in business administration, business calculation, economy, management, civil service ...

B: Thank-you, Mr Kelly. That's almost the same as our curriculum here in Germany. But, of course, you only studied it for four years so your qualification cannot be as high as ours.

K: I beg your pardon, but our university only took the top five per cent of pupils. I ...

S: If I could break in, I think Mr Block only wanted to point out that your course must have been very compact to include so much material in only four years. By the way, we were very impressed that you took the trouble to obtain extra qualifications in languages and marketing.

K: Yes, I did several evening courses over two years to get more practical experience.

S: What did you feel was the greatest advantage from this extra work?

K: There are a lot of things not taught at university. The extra courses were very practical and they gave us tips about how business really works.

B: Very impressive! But you seem to do nothing but work the whole time. In your resumé you give no information about your private life. Have you no hobbies?

S: You seem to be a very busy person. Do you find time for sport etc.?

K: Of course I do. I play squash three times a week, swim regularly. I train weights twice a week.

B: Aha! The body beautiful! So outward appearance plays an important part in your life? Well, you know we say in German: "Kleider machen Leute." Mr ... Kelly, perhaps you'll excuse me now. I have another more important meeting. Do your best and maybe we'll meet again. Sie machen ohne mich weiter, Seba? Guten Tag.

K: We also have a proverb in England. "Manners make the man." Do you know it, Mr Seba?

S: Yes, I do. Good. Now that's over. Perhaps I could ask you a few rather more relevant questions?

K: I shouldn't ask, but can you do it better than your boss?

S: Just wait and see ... only one sentence: He's in cloud cuckoo land, as we say. But you never heard me say that! Now, let me see ...

Personnel assessment form: Candidate J. Kelly

	Excellent	Good	Average
Education:			x[1]
Professional experience:			x
Foreign experience:		x[2]	
Knowledge of English:		x[3]	
Knowledge of German:			x[4]
Initiative:		x	
Motivation:			x
Behaviour:			x

1 took place in England. Not sure of equivalents · 2 in Germany · 3 has a strong accent (not school English) · 4 has a slight foreign accent

Vocabulary to help you with the dialogue

advantage	Vorteil
appearance	Erscheinung
attitude	Einstellung
average	durchschnittlich
business calculation	Wirtschaftskalkulation
by the way	übrigens
C.V. (Curriculum Vitae)	Lebenslauf
civil service	öffentlicher Dienst
course, a compact ~	ein intensiver Studiengang
curriculum	Lehrplan
economics	Volkswirtschaft
efficient	tüchtig
fit into the team	passen, in die Mannschaft ~
grill s.o.	ausquetschen, jdn. ~
impressed, be ~	beeindruckt sein
include	beinhalten, umfassen
interview	Vorstellungsgespräch
introduce s.o.	vorstellen, jdn. ~
obtain	erzielen, erreichen
outward appearance	äußere Erscheinung
permit me to	gestatten Sie, daß ...
personnel affairs	Personalwesen
personnel assessment	Personalbeurteilung
relevant questions	wichtige Fragen
requirements, be up to our ~	Anforderungen, unseren ~ genügen
resumé	Lebenslauf
short list	engere Wahl
smooth things over	die Wogen glätten
straight to the point, let's come ~	direkt zur Sache, kommen wir ~
take the trouble to ...	s. die Mühe machen, zu ...
tip	Hinweis (auch Trinkgeld)
weights, train ~	Gewichtstraining machen

Grammar Rhymes

Simple past tense

1. Vergangenes Allgemeinwissen

Simple past muß stehen,
Wenn wir vergangenes Geschehen
Als abgeschlossen sehen.

The last charter flight was so crowded that the pilot *went* by boat.
Amateurs *built* Noah's Ark – Professionals *built* the Titanic.

2. Handlungsketten

Simple past nehme man,
Wenn man die Frage stellen kann:
Was trat neu ein? Was geschah wann?

I was a war baby. My parents *took* one look at me and *started* fighting.

3. Zeitangaben der Vergangenheit

Ein Zeitpunkt der Vergangenheit
Ist oft Signal für diese Zeit.
zum Beispiel:
last week; yesterday; two days ago; the other day (neulich); *when* (als)

My brother had a terrible accident *the other day*.
He had the right of the way [1] but the other guy [2] had the truck[3].

VORSICHT FALLE: In der Umgangssprache nehmen Deutsche das Perfekt:
Amateure *haben* Noahs Arche *gebaut* ...

1 Vorfahrt 2 Bursche 3 Lastwagen

Grammar Jokes

EXERCISE 1: Translate:

❶ Lehrer: Ich habe niemals gelogen[1], als ich ein Kind war.
Schüler: Wann haben haben Sie (damit) angefangen?

❷ Seba: Ich bin letztes Jahr im Zoo gewesen.
Block: In welchem Käfig[2] waren Sie?

EXERCISE 2: Put the verb in brackets in the right form

❶ There was a young lady from Riga,
Who (*ride*) with a smile on a tiger.
They (*return*[3]) from the ride
With the lady inside
And the smile on the face of the tiger.

❷ Graffiti:
I (*not/believe*) in reincarnation[4] the last time either[5].

❸ God (*be*) a woman until she (*change*) her mind.

EXERCISE 3: Do you remember these sentences in our dialogue?

1. Ich hoffe, Sie hatten eine gute Reise.
2. Sie haben Volkswirtschaft studiert?
3. Sie haben nur vier Jahre lang studiert.
4. Was hatten die Kurse zum Inhalt?

There's another past, of course – the past progressive

more about that in chapter 4

"Waiter[6], what was this fly doing in my soup?"
"Breast-stroke[7], I suppose."

1 lie 2 cage 3 zurückkehren 4 Wiedergeburt 5 not ... either: auch nicht 6 Kellner 7 Brust-schwimmen

Words for the personnel department

ablehnen, ein Angebot ~	*turn down, ~ an offer*
Arbeitgeber, ehemaliger ~	*former employer*
Arbeitsbedingungen	*conditions of employment*
Arbeitsplatzbeschreibung	*job description*
Arbeitsvertrag	*contract of employment*
Begeisterung zeigen	*show enthusiasm*
bekommen, die Stelle ~	*land the job*
Bewerbung	*application*
deutlich darstellen	*give a clear picture*
Eindruck, einen guten ~ machen	*impression,make a good ~*
Einführungskurs	*induction course*
einladen (zum Vorstellungsgespräch)	*call for (an interview)*
Firmenkultur	*corporate culture*
Gehaltserhöhung	*increments, salary rise*
Gehaltserhöhung	*raise in salary (auch rise)*
Gehaltserhöhung, ~ bekommen	*rise, get a ~ (auch raise in salary)*
Gehaltsniveau	*salary level*
Gesprächspartner	*interviewer*
Kandidat	*interviewee*
Leistungsanreize	*perks*
Meinung, ~ äußern	*opinion, voice an ~*
nehmen Sie Platz	*take a seat*
offenes Zeugnis	*open testimonial*
Schwäche	*weakness*
Stelle, jdm. eine ~ anbieten	*post, offer s.o. a ~*
Stenographie	*shorthand*

EXERCISE 4: Test your memory. Tick off the right answers

(Sometimes there is more than one possibility)

1. *What did James Kelly's studies at university not include?*

- ☐ *business calculations*
- ☐ *management*
- ☐ *data processing*
- ☐ *business administration*
- ☐ *foreign languages*

2. *According to Kelly, which courses were not taught at university?*

- ☐ *business administration*
- ☐ *management*
- ☐ *economy*
- ☐ *marketing*

3. *Mr Block and Mr Seba want to find out if James*

- ☐ *has the qualifications required for the job*
- ☐ *fits into their team*
- ☐ *has qualifications which are as high as the German ones*

EXERCISE 5: The ABC of our Business words

answer to a job advertisement	*a . . . . n*
mathematics for managers	*b . . . . tions*
government employment	*c . . . . ce*

EXERCISE 6: Find the partners to these words

husband	*wife*
employer	. . . .
interviewer	. . . .

EXERCISE 7: Wordbuilder's Corner

Verb	*Noun*
apply	....
describe	....
appear	....
impress	....
require	....

EXERCISE 8: Increase your word power

Two English words for one German word

bekommen

. . t a job | **. . . d a job**

Lebenslauf

. . . . . é | **. .**

wichtige Fragen

. . . . nt questions | **. . . . . . . nt questions**

Gehalts-erhöhung

. . . . . y r . . . | **. . . . . . ent**

Time for a smile

Boss: Now, Dobson, we are giving you a raise in salary because we want your last week to be a happy one.

Business Culture: The encounter[1]

Believe it or not, this is the advice[2] old Mr Kelly, former boss of John Stag Tractors, gave his son. First impressions are most important. Sometimes it is decided in the first minute if an applicant gets the post or not.

Names, names, names

1. Don't forget the names of persons you are introduced to.
2. Repeat them immediately: "Good morning Mr Block, Good morning Mr Seba."
3. When you introduce[3] yourself, give your first and last name. If you are a man, don't introduce yourself as "Mr James Kelly". James Kelly is enough.
4. If it is of interest to know if a lady is married or not, then of course she introduces herself as Mrs Armbruster.
5. "How do you do?" is not the first question in the interview, but a greeting. You answer with the same question: "How do you do?"
6. When you meet a second time, you say "How are you?" The normal reaction is: "Fine, thank you."

Do the English shake hands[4]?

1. Yes, they do! It all starts with a handshake.
2. Normally your future boss will stretch out his or her hand first.
3. If he or she does not, then you take the initiative, no matter whether you are man or woman.
4. Don't squeeze[5] the other person's hand. Your handshake should be firm, dry and warm.
5. How long does the proper handshake last? About three seconds is more than enough.
6. And do not pull the other person towards your body – not yet. Keep a polite distance of about one metre between you.
7. Do not look the other person straight[6] into his or her eyes.
8. Keep smiling.

Let's see if James follows this paternal advice.

1 Begegnung 2 Ratschläge 3 sich vorstellen 4 Hände schütteln 5 quetschen 6 gerade, direkt

Meeting key people

CONTENTS

Business Frame:	**Getting to know new colleagues**
Business Culture:	**Meetings and greetings**
Business Words:	**The language of introduction**
Grammar Rhymes:	**Tense and aspect**
Grammar Jokes:	**Past tense – simple and progressive**
Plus:	**Useful exercises and some nice jokes**

Let's start with a smile

When the boss came into the office fifteen minutes early one morning, he surprised[1] the office manager locked in fond embrace[2] with his personal secretary. "Dobson!" thundered[3] the boss. "You're not paid to do this, you know!" – "I know, sir," replied Dobson. "But I don't mind[4]."

1 überraschen 2 innig umschlungen 3 donnern 4 es macht mir nichts aus

Getting to know the new colleagues

So James got a job working for a German company. The money's not so brilliant. But it's part of his training. He's a "management trainee". That means he's going to do job rotation; he will move from one department to another. In each department he "learns the ropes". He will get a practical background in business. But first he is introduced to a few key people in the company. By the way, the official company language is English. The company is trying to live up to its name as a multi-national.

Mr Seba (**S**), Mr Fatter (**F**), Mr Kelly (**K**), Dr. Rope (**R**)

S: So, Mr Kelly, if you'll follow me, I'll just introduce you to a few people on your first day. Through here is the security lodge, we call it the "porter's" lodge. You get your identity pass from here, so they have a lot of power. Ha, ha, ha. Just a joke. Can I introduce you to Mr Fatter?

F: How do you do? My name's Fatter.

K: How do you do? James Kelly.

S: Mr Fatter is the man to speak to if you need to get in or out of the company out of working hours. Right, we'll have to be going, Mr Fatter. Okay, let's move on to the finance department. I want you to meet the department head straight away since it's the department you'll be working in first.
(*They take the lift to the first floor and go through the glass doors into the finance department*).
Here's Dr. Rope's room. Hello, Dr. Rope, may I present Mr Kelly from England?

R: Pleased to meet you. I hope you'll enjoy your time with us doing accounts. Can you add up? I hope you can do it better than some of your fellow countrymen. They don't seem able to get their figures right when they do business with the European Community, ha,ha. Just my black sense of humour. You could say my British sense of humour. Ha, ha.

K: I guess my sense of humour is better than my sense of mathematics, anyway.

R: That's good because the invoices are a bit of a joke, too, ha, ha. By the way, where is Mr Block? I think he wanted to introduce Mr Kelly.

S: Oh, he didn't manage to arrive for the appointment. He's very busy, you know.

R: But if you can't keep appointments, you shouldn't make them. Well, as far as I can see you're doing the introductions with Mr Kelly better than your boss, anyway. He's always so stressed.

S: Well, thanks for your time, Dr. Rope, but we'll really have to be leaving you now. We've got a tight schedule. Good-bye.

Some vocabulary to help with the dialogue

accounts, do ~	Buch führen
department head	Abteilungsleiter
finance department	Finanzwesen
get one's figures right	seine Zahlen in Ordnung bringen
schedule, have a tight ~	Terminplan, einen engen ~ haben
identity pass	Firmenausweis
invoice	Rechnung
job rotation	Rotation in der Firma
keep an appointment	Termin einhalten
key person	Schlüsselfigur, jd. in Schlüsselstellung
learn the ropes	sich einarbeiten
live up to one's name	seinem Namen Ehre machen
make an appointment	Termin vereinbaren
management trainee	Trainee
move on to	weitergehen zu
pleased to meet you	sehr erfreut
present s.o.	vorstellen, jdn. ~
security lodge	Pförtnerhäuschen
working hours	Arbeitszeit

EXERCISE 1: Test your memory. Tick off the right answers

1. *Job rotation means that James*
- ☐ *will take over from employees in other departments*
- ☐ *will move from department to department*
- ☐ *will be trained by managers from other departments*

2. *What is James' first job?*
- ☐ *He will help Mr Fatter in the security department*
- ☐ *He will have to add up numbers*
- ☐ *He will learn how to invoice customers*

3. *The key personnel of company*
- ☐ *is responsible for the keys in the company*
- ☐ *gives you your identity pass and the office keys*
- ☐ *takes the important decisions.*

EXERCISE 2: Where do these prepositions belong?

up, with, on, from, for		
We're looking forward	**to**	*meeting you.*
They try to live		*to their name.*
Let's move		*to the next room.*
He managed to arrive		*the appointment.*
Mr Kelly is		*England.*
You'll enjoy your time		*us.*

EXERCISE 3: Are you flexible?

Find words that have almost the same meaning	
arrange a meeting	....
keep the books	....
bill (you send it your customers)	....
top management	....
I have little time	....

Business Culture: Meetings and Greetings

James meets key people at Low Valley's. His father had told him:
"How do you do?" is a greeting, not a question,
so don't tell your boss about your indigestion.[1]

How James meets Mr Fatter and Dr. Rope

Mr Seba	**Mr Fatter**	**Mr Kelly**
Mr Kelly, may I introduce you to Mr. Fatter? This is Mr. Kelly.	How do you do? My name's Fatter.	How do you do? James Kelly.
Mr Seba	**Dr. Rope**	**Mr Kelly**
Dr. Rope, may I present Mr Kelly from England?	Pleased to meet you, Mr Kelly.	The pleasure is mine.

What else could they have said?

Mr Seba	**Dr. Rope**	**Mr Kelly**
Let me introduce you to Dr. Rope.	Welcome to Low Valley, Mr Kelly.	Thank you, Dr. Rope.
Mr Kelly, I'd like you to meet Dr. Rope. Paul, This is Mr Kelly.	Nice to meet you. How do you do, Mr Kelly.	How do you do, Dr. Rope?

Informal meetings and greetings

Paul, I'd like you to meet Peter. Peter, this is Paul.	How do you do?	How do you do?
Paul, have you met James? James, this is Paul.	Hi, James.	Hi.

Sollten die Gastgeber der Party Sie vergessen haben, spielen Sie nicht das Mauerblümchen. Stellen Sie sich selber vor, vielleicht so: Excuse me, I don't think we've met. My name's James Kelly. Oder: I'd like to introduce myself. I'm James Kelly, the new trainee.

1 Verdauungsschwierigkeiten

The language of introduction

ansprechen, jdn. ~	*address s.o.*
Aufsichtsrat	*supervisory board*
Ausbildungsabteilung	*training department*
Ausbildungsleiter	*head of training*
bekanntmachen, darf ich Sie mit Herrn X ~?	*may I introduce you to Mr X?*
duzen, Sie können mich ~	*you can call me by my first name*
eintreten in eine Firma	*join a company*
kennenlernen, neue Kollegen ~	*meet new colleagues*
Leiter der Produktion	*production head*
Leiter der Finanzen	*head of finance*
Leiter der Buchhaltung	*head of accounts*
Personalleiter	*head of personnel*
Projektleiter	*project leader*
Tätigkeitsbeschreibung	*job specification*
übrigens	*by the way*
und das hier ist Herr X	*and this is Mr X*
verantwortlich, sie ist für ~	*she's responsible for*
Vornamen, Sie dürfen mich mit meinem ~ anreden	*you can call me by my first name*
Vorsitzender	*chairman*
Vorstand	*board of management*
Vorstandsmitglied	*member of the board*
vorstellen, darf ich Ihnen X ~?	*may I introduce you to X?*
Vorstellung, die ~ übernehmen	*make the introductions*
zuständig sein für	*be in charge of*

EXERCISE 4: Fill the empty heads

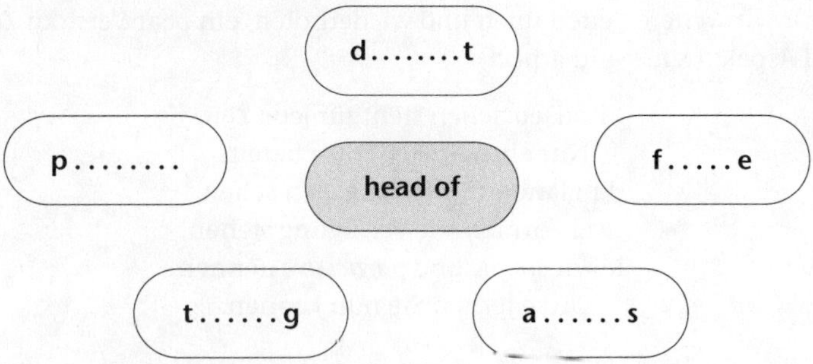

EXERCISE 5: Flexibility training

Find a second expression that means almost the same.

she's responsible for security.	*she is in ...... of security.*
may I introduce you to Mr Rope?	*may I .... Mr Rope?*
Here's the porter's lodge.	*Here's the .... lodge.*
Let's go to the next department.	*Let's .... .. to the next department.*

EXERCISE 6: Please repair the dialogue. It´s in the wrong order.

Put numbers next to these sentences

(Number one has already been done for you)

- ☐ *Nice to meet you.*
- ☐ *Paul, this is Mr Kelly.*
- ☐ *How do you do?*
- 1 *Mr Kelly, I'd like you to meet Dr. Rope.*
- ☐ *How do you do?*

Grammar Rhymes

Bevor wir weitere Zeiten üben und wiederholen, ein paar Verse zu Zeit und Aspekt (tense and aspect):

Im Deutschen steht für jede Zeit
Nur eine einzige Form bereit.
Engländern, wie Sie gleich sehen,
Zwei Formen zur Verfügung stehen,
die wir *simple* und *progressive* nennen.
Diese lernen Sie nun kennen.

Bildung der Formen:

Simple Aspect	Tense	Progressive Aspect
He *brings* the little babies	**Present**	a bird *is standing*
she *explained* to Betsy	**Past**	they *were visiting*
they *have found*	**Perfect**	she *has been watering*

Und so sehen diese Formen in unseren Grammar Jokes aus:

Little Betsy and her mother *were visiting* London Zoo."Look," *explained* her mother, "that bird there that *is standing* on one leg is a stork. He brings all the little babies." A little later they were looking at some enormous elephants. "Mother, where do the elephants come from? But don't give me that story about the stork again."

Graffiti: No Easter this year. They *have found* the body.

Snobbish? She *has been watering* her flowers with Perrier water.

Die Regeln wiederholen und üben wir im Zusammenhang mit den einzelnen Zeiten. Eine globale Regel für alle Zeiten gibt es nicht.

Grammar Rhymes

Past progressive – Die Verlaufsform der Vergangenheit

Wir nehmen past progressive,

❶ wenn zu einem Zeitpunkt der Vergangenheit
noch ablief die Begebenheit

Policeman: Miss, *you were driving* 150 kilometers per hour when you crossed this street.

Young lady: Really? That's great. And I only learned to drive yesterday.

❷ wenn man in Erzählung und Bericht von
Begleitumständen spricht

An old Indian *was observing*[1] his teenage daughter's party and was fascinated by the modern dances the young people *were enjoying*. Scratching[2] his head, he said to his wife, "Well, if that doesn't bring rain, nothing will."

❸ Legt man die Betonung auf
Die Handlung selbst, ihren Verlauf,
Wenn also nicht das Ergebnis wichtig,
Dann ist *past progressive* richtig.

Two flies *were playing* football in a saucer[3]. Said one: "We'll have to do better than this – we're playing in the cup[4] next week."

1 beobachten 2 kratzen 3 Untertasse 4 Pokal, Tasse

Grammar Jokes: Past – progressive or simple?

EXERCISE 7: Put the verbs in brackets in the right form

❶ One day two Austrians (*hunt*) in a valley. High up in the air two hang-gliders[1] (*circle*) above their heads. "Look! two eagles[2]," said the first, "Quick! shoot them!"
"I (*hit*) one?" asked the second after his third shot.
"I don't know, but it (*drop*) its prey[3]."

❷ Churchill was not one of G.B. Shaw's admirers[4]. He sent him the following note:
I (*buy*) a copy[5] of your new play. Who (*write*) it for you?
Shaw replied: Who (*read*) it to you?

❸ Two East Friesians[6] (*hunt*) in the marshes[7], when one of them (*see*) a rabbit[8], which (*disappear*[9]) after a few seconds. "What the hell you (*wait*) for? Why you (*not / shoot*)?" shouted the first.
"Sorry," replied the other, "but my gun (*not / load*[10])."
"Well," said the first, "you know that, and I know that, but the rabbit didn't."

❹ Tourist: Last time I (*visit*) the Shetland Islands there were a lot of ponies around. Where are they?
Farmer: They (*drown*[11]) when we tried to train them for surf-riding.

❺ Two fishermen (*fish*) in the Rhine. One had a bite and (*pull*) in the most beautiful mermaid[12]. He freed her from the hook, (*look*) her up and down, (*shake*) his head and threw her back into the water.
"But why?" asked his friend.
"Well, how?" was the reply.

1 Drachenflieger 2 Adler 3 Beute 4 Bewunderer 5 Exemplar 6 Ostfriese 7 Marsch 8 Kaninchen 9 verschwinden 10 laden 11 ertrinken 12 Meerjungfrau

Office Vocabulary: Things on our desks

Bleistift	*pencil*
Briefbeschwerer	*paper weight*
Briefkorb	*letter tray*
Brieföffner	*letter opener*
Briefumschlag	*envelope*
Büroklammer	*paper clip*
Bürolocher	*punch, hole punch*
Diaprojektor	*slide projector*
Dias	*slides*
Einschreiben	*registered post*
Etikette, Aufkleber	*label*
Farbband	*typing ribbon*
Folien	*foils / transparencies*
Füller	*fountain pen*
Hefter	*stapler*
Heftklammern	*staples*
Kartei	*card index*
Klebeband	*adhesive tape*
Klebstoff	*glue*
Kugelschreiber	*biro, ball pen*
Leinwand	*screen*
Lineal	*ruler*
Magnettafel	*magnet board*
Marker	*highlighter*
Overheadprojektor	*OHP projector*
Post, ausgehende, eingehende ~	*outgoing, incoming mail*
Radiergummi	*rubber*
Schere	*scissors*
Schlagschere	*guillotine*
Schreibmaschine	*typewriter*
Schreibmaschinenpapier	*typing paper*
Schreibset	*writing set*

Spitzer	*pencil sharpener*
Stempel	*stamp*
Telefonbuch	*telephone book*
Tesafilm	*cellotape*
Textmarkierer	*marker*
Tinte	*ink*
Tippex flüssig	*liquid paper*
Trennblatt	*divider*
Verstärkerring	*reinforcement ring*
Visitenkarte	*business card / visiting card*
Telefaxpapier	*telefax paper*

Time for a smile

Greetings and meetings at the Kanzleramt

A visitor from the planet Mars landed in Bonn in front of the Kanzleramt. "Excuse me, I'm from Mars. Please take me to your leader,[1]" the man from Mars said to the security officers.
He was taken to the German chancellor, Helmut Kohl, and introduced to the ministers of his cabinet. "I'm pleased to meet you, gentlemen. I've a message for your leader."
"The pleasure is ours," replied Helmut Kohl. "And please tell your company how much my wife and I enjoy your chocolate bars[2]."

1 Führer 2 Schokoladenriegel

A tour of the plant

CONTENTS

Time for a smile

Mr Block's definition of his right hand: A right hand is a man or a woman who asks you every morning "How are you today?" and who is disappointed[1] when you answer: "Thank you. I'm in the best of health[2]".

1 enttäuscht 2 mir geht es blendend

Director Block seems confused

Sometimes it is really necessary to delegate tasks to one's subordinates. It seems to be difficult as many bosses really think they have to do everything themselves. That means they have no time to carry out the responsibilities that they were employed for. In the next dialogue Director Block takes it on himself to show people around the factory. It's not really his task. So he gets it wrong. Employees on lower levels have to put him right.

Director Block (**B**), James Kelly (**K**), Mr Seba (**S**), one of the customers; Mr Taylor (**T**)

B: I'd like to welcome you three trainees here today for our "tour" around the company. Now my name's Block, as you already know.

K: Excuse me, Mr Block. I think there's some confusion here. I'm the only management trainee here today. I think the other two gentlemen are customers.

T: Yes, that's right young man. I'm from Pronto Print in Scotland.

B: Well, there must be something I don't know about, gentlemen.

K: Eh, Mr Block, I think I heard Mr Seba say that he wanted to put two tours together to save time.

B: It's a good thing that somebody knows what's going on around here. Ha, here comes Mr Seba now.

S: Sorry I'm late. Somebody ordered all the electronic identity passes to be blocked. What a stupid situation!

B: That was my instruction, actually. Pink for a manufacturing company is nonsense. I had all the colours changed. Now, if we could proceed. Gentlemen, we are now in the works where the actual manufacturing takes place. On the right there is the training department for the technical trainees. A lot of high precision work goes on there. As you see the training centre is larger than any of our competitors' centres.

K: Mr Block. Something is worrying me. Why does the sign above the door say "canteen"?

B: Yes, there must be a good reason for that.

S: Of course there is, Mr Block. It's because it actually is the canteen. You moved the departments around six months ago. Excuse me, gentlemen. Mr Block has more important strategic matters to deal with. He's not so well informed about the operational level.

B: Absolutely! Now, if you'd come through this doorway, gentlemen, in front of you there is the cylinder and roller manufacturing. We're extremely proud of this technology.

K: I'm a bit confused, Mr Block. Mr Seba told us yesterday that these parts were manufactured in another town.

B: Hm ... Eh, actually I haven't been in this part of the plant for quite a while ... Mr Seba ...

S: Well, gentlemen, there are only some special parts which are really produced here. It's all very top secret, you know, that is why this workshop looks like an ordinary store.

T: Listen, are we going to see a bit of the factory, or not? I've come a long way.

B: Of course, Mr Taylor. If my two colleagues here would stop splitting hairs we could move on to the next department. Mr Seba would you please take over from me? I'm expecting an important visitor. Gentlemen, I wish you good-day. See you at the banquet tonight.

T: Well, Mr Seba, perhaps you could tell us a bit about the company. You seem to have a better idea of it than your boss ...

Some vocabulary to help with the dialogue:

competitor	Wettbewerber, Konkurrent
confusion	Verwirrung
customer	Kunde
deal with	zu tun haben mit
delegate	delegieren
high precision work	Präzisionsarbeit
identity pass	Betriebsausweis
instruction	Anweisung
manufacture	herstellen, produzieren
manufacturing company	Produktionsfirma
operational level	Betriebsebene, innerbetrieblicher Bereich
pink	rosa
plant, works	Werk, Anlage
proceed	fortfahren, weitermachen

proud	stolz
roller	Walze
save, ~ time	sparen, Zeit ~
show people around	Leute herumführen
split hairs	Haarspalterei betreiben
store	Lager
strategic matters	strategische Angelegenheiten
subordinate	Untergebener
workshop	Werkstatt

EXERCISE 1: Test your memory

Director Block confused

t . . . . c		**canteen**
c . . . . s	**a n d**	**tr . . . . . s**
w . . . . . . p		**store**

and he had all the identity passes changed.

EXERCISE 2: Another memory test

(Choose the alternatives used in the dialogue)

1. *How did Mr Block greet the group?*

- ☐ *Welcome to Low Valley.*
- ☐ *I'd like to welcome you here today for our tour around the company.*
- ☐ *Good morning. I'd like to invite you to a "tour" of the plant.*

2. *How did Mr Block introduce himself?*

- ☐ *Now, I'm director Block.*
- ☐ *I'd like to introduce myself. I'm Block.*
- ☐ *Now, my name's Block.*

3. *Mr Seba didn't get into the plant at once. Why?*

- ☐ *He had forgotten his identity pass.*
- ☐ *His identity pass was not valid (gültig).*
- ☐ *His identity pass was pink.*

4. *How did Mr Block say goodbye to the group?*

- ☐ *Gentlemen, I wish you good-day.*
- ☐ *Gentlemen, I wish you goodbye.*
- ☐ *Gentlemen, I wish you a nice day.*

EXERCISE 3: Prepositions have to be learnt in the phrase

Why does the sign	. . . .	*the door say "canteen"?*
There must be a good reason	. . . .	*that.*
He's not so well informed	. . . .	*operational matters.*
Would you please take	. . . .	*from me?*
See you	. . . .	*the banquet tonight.*

Business Culture: Hello and Goodbye

"How are you?" ist weniger eine Frage nach dem Wohlbefinden als ein Gruß. Sie sollte von durchtrainierten dynamischen Geschäftsleuten mit einer Variante von "Fine, thank you" beantwortet werden, ganz gleich, wie miserabel sie sich fühlen. Mit der Gegenfrage "And how are you?" wird der Partner zu einer ähnlichen Notlüge aufgefordert.

Kombinierbare Fragen und Antworten für alle, die gesund sein müssen	
How are you this morning?	*I'm feeling great / fine.*
How are you these days?	*I feel on top of the world.*
How are things with you today?	*Oh, not too bad.*

Einen Plausch anbahnen	
Wie geht es dir so?	*How's life been treating you?*
Ich habe Sie ja schon lange nicht mehr gesehen.	*I haven't seen you for ages.*
Ich habe dich seit Jahren nicht gesehen.	*I haven't seen you for years.*
Was hast du die ganze Zeit gemacht?	*What have you been doing all the time?*

Das Goodbye vorbereiten	
Ich glaube, das wär's einstweilen.	*I think that's it for now.*
Ich glaube, das wäre im Moment alles.	*Well, I guess that's all for now.*
Gibt es sonst noch etwas (zu besprechen)?	*Is there anything else (to discuss)?*
Ich störe Sie nun nicht mehr weiter in Ihrer Arbeit.	*I'd better let you get on with your work.*
Ich würde mich freuen, wieder von Ihnen zu hören.	*I'm looking forward to hearing from you again.*
Wir müssen jetzt gehen.	*We've got to be leaving now.*
Wir müssen uns jetzt verabschieden.	*We have to say goodbye. We have to leave now.*
Einen schönen Tag noch!	*Have a good day!*
Bis heute abend.	*See you tonight.*

Strange Encounters

EXERCISE 4: Fill in the speech functions

1. *On a bus an absent-minded[1] professor looked at the lady next to him and exclaimed[2]:" Hello, Lydia Preston. How . . . . . . ? I haven't . . . . you . . . . How you've changed! You used to weigh[3] 75 kilos and now you are nothing but skin and bones[4]. Why Lydia, you've changed your hairstyle, too. You used to have grey hair and now you are blond..."*
"I beg your pardon,"said the lady, "but I'm not Lydia Preston."
"Fancy that[5]," replied the professor, "You've changed your name as well."

2. *Two elderly ladies met at a banquet[6] after not seeing each other for three weeks. Said the first, "Good gracious, Elizabeth, I . . . . you . . . quite a while. You certainly look a lot older."*
"You look much older, too, Dorothy, dear. I wouldn't have recognized[7] you except for[8] the dress and hat."

3. *What . . . . you . . . . all the time?*
Tom: Six months. Cheating on the taxes[9].

1 zerstreut 2 ausrufen 3 früher hast du ... gewogen 4 nur noch Haut und Knochen 5 also so was 6 Galadiner 7 wiedererkennen 8 ohne das Kleid und den Hut 9 Steuerhinterziehung

Some more words about the Low Valley plant

Auftrag	*order*
Baustoffe, Rohstoffe	*materials*
Dienstleistungen	*services*
Einrichtung	*facilities*
Entwurf	*design*
Fabrik	*factory*
Fertigungsstraße	*production line*
herstellen, fertigen	*produce*
Hersteller	*manufacturer*
Herstellung / Fertigung	*manufacturing*
Ingenieur	*engineer*
Komponenten	*components*
konkurrieren mit	*compete with*
Konstrukteur	*designer*
leistungsfähig, effizient	*efficient*
Maschinenbau	*engineering*
Montage	*assembly*
Parkplatz	*car park*
Planung	*planning*
Produktion	*production*
Produktionssteuerung	*production control*
rechts / links	*on your right / left*
Standort	*location*
unterbringen	*house*
Verantwortung	*responsibility*
Verfahren	*process*
Wartung	*service*
zusammenbauen	*assemble*

EXERCISE 5: Word builder's corner

Verb	*Noun*
proceed	....
assemble	....
compete	....
produce	....
plan	....

Food for Thought: Stranger in his own company

'What is going on at Low Valley Photocopiers?' you might have wondered. There is a director who changes the passes without telling his assistants and doesn't know the first thing about his company ("There must be something I don't know about"). He confuses[1] canteen, store and trainees with training centre, workshop and customers. And everybody seems to know better than the boss. What a strange working climate! What a ridiculous[2] figure, this director Block!

However, you could see the situation from a different point of view[3]. Sure, Mr Block is not informed. But who is to blame[4]? Mr Seba, I think. A good assistant would always make sure that the boss knows what is going on, especially in other departments. He could simply mention things when he sees Mr Block. And when his boss has not got the time, there are notes, memos and reports[5] to keep him in the picture. This will prevent[6] him from making a fool of himself[7] in the presence of subordinates[8] and clients.

1 verwechseln 2 lächerlich 3 Standpunkt 4 wer ist schuld? 5 Bericht 6 verhindern 7 sich lächerlich machen 8 Untergebene

Office Vocabulary:

Things you can see in your office

Ablage	*tray*
Aktenschrank	*filing cabinet*
Beistelltisch	*side table*
Büromöbel	*office furniture*
Drehkartei	*rotary index*
Drehstuhl	*swivel chair*
elektronische Waage	*electronic scales*
Frankiermaschine	*franking machine*
Großraumbüro	*open plan office*
Hängeordner	*suspension file*
Kalender	*calendar*
Konferenztisch	*conference table*
Papierkorb	*wastepaper basket*
Regal	*shelves*
Reißwolf	*shredder*
Schreibtisch	*desk*
Schreibtischgarnitur	*desk set*
Schreibtischlampe	*desk lamp*
Schublade	*drawer*
Teppich	*rug, carpet*
Trennwand	*partition*

Adding things up

CONTENTS

Business Frame:	**Joining the financial department**
Business Words:	**Words accountants use**
Speech Functions:	**Dr. Rope assigns duties**
Business Words:	**Words from the accounts department**
Business Culture:	**The accountant's dos and don'ts**
Plus:	**Words, words words, jokes and a lot of useful exercises**

Time for a smile

An accountant is a man hired to explain that you didn't make the money you did.

Cutting down expenses[1] is something you must do while you're in the black[2]. When you are in the red[3], it's too late.
Paul Getty

1 Ausgaben kürzen 2 schwarze Zahlen schreiben 3 in den roten Zahlen sein

Joining the financial department

Mr Kelly has joined the financial department at Low Valley Photocopiers. He is shown around by the department head, Dr. Rope. Of course, James Kelly is a bit nervous about his first day. He has learnt some things at university but nothing very practical. Dr. Rope is a typical boss. See why in the following dialogue.

Dr. Rope (**R**), Mr Kelly (**K**), Mr Pinter (**P**)

R: Good morning, Mr Kelly. Today I'd like to describe some of the tasks you'll have to cope with in the next six months with us here in finances. First of all, don't worry! You'll get the hang of things very quickly.

K: Calculating wasn't my strongest point when I was at college. I hope there are some calculating machines in the department.

R: It wasn't my best subject, either. And look at me now! Ha, ha. Well, here we don't do much calculating ourselves. Every workplace is equipped with a PC which has several types of software on it.

K: Oh, does the company have Lotus 1, 2, 3? I'm used to working with that.

R: I'm sorry, Mr Kelly. I personally haven't used the software for several years. Mr Pinter! Could you come here for a moment? What's our calculation software?

P: I think you mean spreadsheet software, Dr. Rope. We've got a couple of them. Excel, Lotus 1, 2, 3. Let me show you Excel, Mr Kelly. Start the program by clicking into ...

R: Just a minute! You can do all that later. I'm just assigning Mr Kelly his duties. Now, so first you'll do some calculating and some checking of invoices. But the most interesting part will be work which is actually new for our department. That is cost accounting of a whole photocopier.

K: That sounds interesting. So we have to analyse the costs of parts, production and working hours. All the expenditure necessary for the construction of the copier.

R: Yes, it's all to do with value analysis.

P: Talking about value and time, Dr. Rope, you have a meeting with me to discuss employee assessments at 11 o'clock.

R: Never mind, Mr Pinter. I'm sure you know the quality of the employee's work better than I do. Do it without me and I'll introduce Mr Kelly to his new tasks.

P: *(to himself)*. What do we need a boss for, if we can do everything better than him? Just another cost.

Some vocabulary to help with the dialogue

accounts department	Finanzabteilung
analyse	analysieren
assign duties	Aufgaben zuweisen
calculating machine	Rechenmaschine
check	prüfen
click into	anklicken
construction	Aufbau
cope with	zurechtkommen mit
cost accounting	Kostenrechnung
do it without me	machen Sie es ohne mich
employee assessment	Mitarbeiterbeurteilung
equip	ausrüsten
expenditure	Ausgaben, Aufwendungen
get the hang of things	den Dreh herausbekommen
join a department	in eine Abteilung eintreten
spreadsheet software	Tabellenkalkulationsprogramm
subject	Fach
task	Aufgabe
use a special software	eine spezielle Software benutzen
used to, be ~ working with a computer	daran gewöhnt sein, mit einem Computer zu arbeiten
value analysis	Wertanalyse
workplace	Arbeitsplatz

Speech Functions: How does Dr. Rope give instructions?

Er benutzt die Befehlsform, den Imperativ, für seine Anweisungen:

Den Imperativ hat man im Nu,
Nimmt man die Grundform ohne *to*.

Start the program by clicking into...
Do it without me and I'll introduce Mr Kelly to his new tasks.

•

Die bejahte Form drückt aus
Befehl, Wunsch, Forderung, Gebot.
Für Warnung, Rat und für Verbot
Geht der Befehlsform *don't* voraus.

Save water. Shower with a friend!

Dr. Rope: First of all, *don't worry*!

Advice to students before a test:
Don't believe in miracles[1]. Rely[2] on them.

•

Um Befehle höflich auszudrücken,
Genügt es, *will you*? nachzuschicken.
Beziehst du dich in den Befehl mit ein,
Sollte es ein *shall we*? sein.

Doctor to Lady:
And if these pills don't cure[3] your kleptomania,
try and *get* me a video-recorder, *will you*?

will + infinitiv hat Dr. Rope für folgende Anweisung verwendet:

First *you'll do* some calculating and some checking of invoices.

1 an Wunder glauben 2 sich verlassen auf 3 heilen

EXERCISE 1: Test your memory

Which task is not part of James' duties?

- ☐ *cost-accounting of a whole photocopier*
- ☐ *employee assessments*
- ☐ *checking of invoices*
- ☐ *analysing the costs of production*

EXERCISE 2: Let's have a look at the word list

Which word from the text or the word list fits the definition?

1. *part of a company or organization*	*de . . . . . . n t*
2. *tasks an employee has to do*	*d . . . . s*
3. *software used in accounting*	*s . . . . ts*
4. *explain or give duties to a person*	*a . . . . n duties*
5. *another word for costs*	*e . . . . e*
6. *be able to manage*	*c . . . w . . .*
7. *task that is new to Dr. Rope's department.*	*c . . . a . . . .*

EXERCISE 3 : Find the missing part and translate

English: two words	**deutsch: zusammengesetzte Wörter**
c . . . . machine	. . . .
. . . . . analysis	. . . .
. . . . assessment	. . . .
. . . . software	. . . .

More words you'll hear in the accounts department

Absatzpreis	*selling price*
Anschaffung, Beschaffung	*purchasing, procurement*
bei einer Firma anfangen	*join a company*
Beschaffung, Einkauf	*acquisition*
Bestände	*inventories, stocks*
beurteilen; bewerten	*assess*
Bilanz	*balance sheet*
Buchhalter	*accountant*
einen Kredit eröffnen	*open a credit*
Fertigungskosten	*manufacturing costs*
Gemeinkosten	*overhead costs, overheads*
Gesamtbetrag der Rechnung	*invoice total*
in Rechnung stellen	*invoice*
Ist-Kosten	*actual cost*
Kostenrechnung	*cost accounting*
Kostenstelle	*cost centre*
Mengenrabatt	*quantity discount*
netto Kasse	*net cash*
Preispolitik	*pricing policy*
Ratenzahlung	*pay by installment*
Rechnung	*bill*
Rechnungsbegleichung	*payment of invoices*
Rechnungsdatum	*date of invoice*
Selbstkostenpreis	*cost price*
variable Kosten	*variable costs*
Wechsel	*bill of exchange*
Wiederverkäuferrabatt	*trade discount*
Zahlungsweise	*method of payment*

EXERCISE 4: Complete the "cost words"

	cost	
p . . . e	**c . . . . e**	**a . . . . g**
	v . . . . . . e	
a l	**costs**	**. . . . . . . d**
	m . . . -	

EXERCISE 5: The ABC of our wordlists

person who keeps the books	*a*	. . . .
you have to pay it	*b*	. . . .
you do it with a mouse	*c*	. . . .
analyse the value of persons or things	*a*	. . . .
the English for "Bilanz"	*b*	. . . .
you do it on a computer	*c*	. . . .

Business Culture: The accountant's dos and don'ts

What an accountant should not do

get into the red	rote Zahlen schreiben
manipulate figures	die Zahlen manipulieren
cook the books	die Konten frisieren
fiddle the taxes	Steuern hinterziehen
go bankrupt	Bankrott machen

What an accountant should do

watch the cash-flow	den Kapitalfluß beobachten
audit the books	die Bücher prüfen
balance the books	die Bücher abschließen
pay debts	Schulden bezahlen
get into the black	schwarze Zahlen schreiben

Extra activities at the airport

CONTENTS

Business Frame:	**Meeting Boris at the airport**
Grammar Rhymes:	**Simple present perfect**
Grammar Jokes:	**Becoming perfect with perfects**
Business Words:	**Airport vocabulary**
Extra Reading:	**At the airport**
Plus:	**Words, jokes and a lot of useful exercises**

Let's start with a smile

The boss was addressing[1] a meeting of the firm's senior executives[2] and sales staff[3]. "Now, when my son starts to work here tomorrow," he said, "I want you to treat[4] him just as you would treat any other employee who was going to take over the company[5] in two year's time."

1 eine Ansprache halten 2 leitender Angestellter 3 Verkaufspersonal 4 behandeln
5 die Firma übernehmen

Meeting Boris at the airport

Sometimes in a company we have to perform some tasks or duties which are outside our normal range of work. In this case there are some extra responsibilities for James Kelly. After his first three weeks in the company, he has a task which could well test his competence: a visitor from distant lands. And all Kelly has from his boss is a name!

Dr. Rope (**R**), James Kelly (**K**), Mr Zhukov (**Z**)

R: Mr Kelly, I've got a special job for you this week.

K: Oh, that's good, Dr. Rope. I was beginning to get a little bit bored sitting in front of the computer. It's been three weeks already.

R: Three weeks? My dear boy, most employees have to do the same old job all their lives and for a pittance, too.

K: Oh, I'm sorry, Dr. Rope. I didn't mean it like that. It's just that it has tired me out looking at figures on a screen for so long.

R: I understand, but training is training. Okay, I'd like you to fetch an important person from the airport for us. It's the boss of our agency in Russia. And he's their company controller, too. So we have to take care of him in our department. And you're volunteering to fetch him and introduce him to the company.

K: But I've only just joined the company. I don't know enough about it. And I certainly didn't volunteer.

R: "Volunteer" is one of those special words which don't have a meaning. We have every confidence in you. Now, he's arriving at Frankfurt at 10:12 a.m. on the 4012 from Moscow. The name's Zukovski. Good luck!

(*At the airport*)

K: Sir, is your name Zukovski, by any chance?

Z: Actually, my name is Zhukov. I'm here to visit Low Valley Photocopiers. But why do you have the wrong name?

K: Oh, I'm sure there's a simple explanation.

Z: I feel your superior should know the names of his important visitors.

K: Please excuse the misunderstanding, Mr Zhukov. Actually, I myself made the mistake with the spelling when I was preparing the meeting. I really must apologise.

Z: Aha, I see. Very good. I accept your apology. How long have you worked for the company?
K: Oh, not so long. A few weeks, I suppose.
Z: You suppose. Do you not know if you work there or not, or for how long? Well, never mind, I have met many employees and I'm sure you will be among the best in the future. You are already doing your job, perhaps better than your boss. Mr Kelly, let's go to your company. I'm pleased to meet you! Call me Boris!

Vocabulary to help you with the dialogue

apologise	sich entschuldigen
apology	Entschuldigung
bored	gelangweilt
boring	langweilig
chance; by any ~	Zufall; zufällig
company controller	Leiter des Rechnungswesens (US. Leiter der Buchhaltung)
competence	Tüchtigkeit, Fähigkeit
confidence	Vertrauen
distant lands	ferne Lande
explanation	Erklärung
fetch from the airport	abholen vom Flugplatz
perform a task	eine Aufgabe erfüllen
pittance	Hungerlohn, "paar Pfennige"
range of work	Arbeitsgebiet
responsibilities	Pflichten
screen	Bildschirm
spell	buchstabieren
superior	Vorgesetzter
tire somebody out	jdn. erschöpfen, ermüden
volunteer	sich freiwillig melden
wear out	ermüden, erschöpfen

Grammar Rhymes

Simple present perfect

Typ A

Einfaches Perfekt wird gewählt,
Wenn einzig das Ergebnis zählt.
Die Frage "Wann ist es passiert?"
Hier überhaupt nicht interessiert.

An adult[1] is somebody who *has ceased*[2]
to grow[3] vertically but not horizontally.

Der Zeitpunkt, der ist unbekannt,
Oder er wird nicht genannt.

Typ B

Die Handlung begann irgendwann
Und reicht zur Gegenwart heran.

Graffiti:
After man came woman,
And she *has been* after him ever since[4].

Bob: *Have you been* to a zoo?
René: You mean as a visitor?

Signalwörter, nach denen man
Typ A und B oft finden kann:
already, just, since, never
so far, for, yet und *ever.*

1 Erwachsener 2 aufhören 3 wachsen 4 seit damals

Grammar Jokes: Simple past or simple perfect?

EXERCISE 1:

A Put the verb in (...) in the right form

❶ Director Block to his new secretary: "The chief qualities we need in this company are intelligence and energy." – "I know, sir. I only (*be*) here for two weeks, but I (*already/find*) that out.

❷ Patient: Doctor, doctor, everybody hates me.
Psychiatrist: Nonsense! You (*not/meet*) everybody yet.

❸ Before the Kohl government came to power, we (*be*) on the edge[1] of an economic precipice[2]. Since then we (*take*) a great step forward.

❹ Saving is a fine thing, especially when your parents (*do*) it for you.

❺ Bob: How you (*get*) that splinter[3] in your finger?
René: I don't know. All I (*do*) was scratch[4] my head.

❻ Ronny: Do you believe in free love?
Anne: I (*ever/send*) you a bill[5]?

B Now let's do the same with some sentences from the dialogue:

1. It's (*be*) three weeks already.
2. It (*tire out*) me looking at figures on a screen for so long.
3. But I only just (*join*) the company.
4. Actually, I myself (*make*) the mistake with the spelling when I was preparing the meeting.
5. How long you (*work*) for the company?

1 am Rande 2 Abgrund 3 Spreißel 4 kratzen 5 Rechnung

EXERCISE 2: Test your memory

1. How long has James been sitting in front of the computer?
2. Why did James mispronounce Mr Zhukov's name?
3. Where is Mr Zhukov from?

EXERCISE 3: If you know one, then you know the other

Can you find the noun **(Hauptwort)***?*		
responsible	....	Pflicht
apologise	....	Entschuldigung
explain	....	Erklärung
distant	....	Entfernung

EXERCISE 4: The ABC of our wordlists

Before you do this exercise you should have a look at the Airport Words on page 74.

Do it when you mispronounce a name.	*a*	....
You wait there for your luggage.	*b*	....
The feeling that you can trust a person.	*c*	....
Place that a passenger would like to get to.	*d*	....

The act of apologising.	*a*	....
It's the opposite of exciting.	*b*	....
What kind of job has Mr Zhukov got?	*c*	....
We measure it in metres and kilometres.	*d*	....

Extra Reading: At the airport

Customs formalities are simple at international airports. In most cases you have to go through the passport control first and wait for your luggage at the baggage claim, which means that you have to find the conveyor belt at which your flight number is indicated. The suitcases, bags and boxes come out of a tunnel right in front of you, and it is important for you to identify your luggage as quickly as possible so that you can take it away from the conveyor belt before other people push you aside.

If you have nothing to declare, you may pick up your suitcase and bag and pass through the customs control without being stopped. Very often, however, spot checks are made by the customs officers, which means that your luggage is searched for dutiable goods.
If you yourself have bought something in a foreign country that has cost more than £ 300, you have to indicate this at the customs and pay a certain percentage of its original price as duty.
Lost and Found: Sometimes it can happen that you don't get your luggage at the baggage claim because it has been put onto a plane with a different destination. So it may be that you are in London and your suitcase arrives in Madrid, Rome, or elsewhere.
Experienced travellers put some of the things they need most in their hand luggage and take it with them on board, which certainly is helpful if your luggage is only likely to appear in a few days' time.

If your luggage is lost, you have to go to the desk with the sign "Lost and Found" and indicate what you are missing on a special form. From this time on the staff will do everything possible to find your luggage again and with the help of modern computer they very often succeed within a relatively short time. In case they are not able to find your property, the airline pays up to a certain sum as compensation, which, however, will never be the whole sum you would need to buy everything again. This is the reason why a lot of people prefer to take out insurance policies for everything they take with them on a journey.

Airport words

appear	erscheinen, auftauchen
baggage label	Gepäckanhänger
baggage claim	Gepäckausgabe
be missing	fehlen
boarding pass	Bordkarte
check-in counter	Abfertigungsschalter
competence, within the ~ of	Zuständigkeit, in der ~ von
conveyor belt	Förderband
customs	Zoll
customs formalities	Zollformalitäten
declare sth., pay duty,	etw. verzollen
destination	Reiseziel
distance	Entfernung
dutiable	zollpflichtig
excess baggage	Mehrgepäck
experienced	erfahren
hand luggage	Handgepäck
have competence in	kompetent sein in
indicate	angeben
insurance policy	Versicherungspolice
likely	wahrscheinlich
Lost and Found	Fundbüro
passenger lounge	Warteraum
passport control	Paßkontrolle
property	Eigentum, Besitz
queue	Schlange, Reihe, Warteliste
security check	Sicherheitskontrolle
spot check	Stichprobe

EXERCISE 5: Check the signs

Below there are some definitions for airport signs. Now, which sign belongs to which definition?

1. *An office where you can get foreign currency and change your money.*
2. *A place where you can get snacks and drinks but not full meals.*
3. *A place where you can do your shopping, especially for food and drink.*
4. *A small room which carries five or six people from one level to the other.*

a 

b 

c 

d 

EXERCISE 6: Give terms for the following airport signs:

1 

2 

3 

4 

1. .... **3.** ....

2. .... **4.** ....

EXERCISE 7: A little translation training

We give you the German and the sign. You give us the English. Don't despair, there's a key to this exercise.

1  *Babyraum*

2  *Information*

3  *Gepäck-träger*

4  *Eisenbahn*

5  *Telefon*

6 

Toiletten

7 

Flug-steige

8 

Zoll

9  *Bad*

10  *Friseur*

11 

Veranstal-tungsräume

12  *Restaurant*

13  *Bus*

14  *Taxi*

15  *Autoverleih*

16  *Rendevous*

17  *Abflug*

18  *Post*

1	2 ....
3	4 ....
5	6 ....
7	8 ....
9	10 ....
11	12 ....
13	14 ....
15	16 ....
17	18 ....

Pointing out the facts

CONTENTS

Business Frame:	**Good advice from Mr Stein**
Grammar Rhymes:	**Pitfalls[1] in English tenses**
Grammar Jokes:	**Becoming perfect with present, past and perfect**
Speech Functions:	**Passing on good advice**
Business Words:	**Vocabulary for presentations**
Advice for presenters:	**Aida and the magic seven**
Plus:	**Jokes and useful exercises**

Time for a smile

Advice for managers from Arthur Bloch (Murphy's Laws adapted):

1. Always try to look very important.
2. Try to be seen with important people.
3. Keep out of sight and out of the limelight[2].

1 Falle 2 Rampenlicht

Good advice from Mr Stein

James is getting into his new job by now. Of course, there are some practical things he doesn't know about. He turns to his colleagues for help and is pleasantly surprised that they are willing to assist. Read on!

Mr Stein (**S**), James Kelly (**K**)

S: Well, how are things going with the new job? Are you getting on top of it?

K: In general everything's fine. The only problem is that I've been given a task to do but I'm not quite sure what I'm expected to do.

S: Perhaps I can help you. What assignment did the boss give you?

K: I've got to make a presentation. Dr. Rope told me to compile information about the history of the company. It'll be one of my jobs to show visitors and customers around the plant.

S: So where's the problem?

K: Actually, I've not spoken in public before. I don't know if I'm confident enough. I'm already getting butterflies in my stomach about standing in front of so many people.

S: Oh, I've had to make a lot of presentations in the last few years. You just speak up and project your voice to the back of the group. Why don't you try to make a few jokes? Do it in a relaxed way! Can I give you another piece of advice? It's all a matter of the three "S"s. Stand up, speak up and shut up! – when you've finished, of course.

K: The other day, Dr. Rope gave me a few transparencies about the company but I think they're a bit boring somehow.

S: Just a minute. Let me have a look at them. Hmm. Well, you're right. They're not very professional.

K: Can I improve them in any way?

S: I guess so. In fact there are some principles to keep in mind when preparing OHP transparencies. Let's rework them. I'm sure you'll be able to design them better than your boss.

K: Look at this one, for example. There are four diagrams on it. It's confusing!

S: So there you have it. One of the most important principles is not to overload the audience. So you should take one transparency for each table. And place the table in the centre. You should also make sure you've got the appropriate equipment to work with. You need a glass pointer. If you have a flipchart you should also stand to one side of it. And never turn your back to the audience! Let's practise it a bit.

K: Great! I'll soon be up to the mark at this rate. I really appreciate this.

Words to help with the dialogue

appropriate equipment	passende Ausrüstung
assignment	Aufgabe
audience	Publikum, Zuhörer
compile	zusammenstellen
confident	selbstsicher, selbstbewußt
get on top of	fertig werden mit, beherrschen
get butterflies in one's stomach	ein flaues Gefühl in der Magengegend bekommen
guess, I guess	annehmen, ich nehme es an
improve	verbessern
keep in mind	nicht vergessen, bedenken
mark, be up to the ~	der Sache gewachsen sein
overload	überladen, überlasten
pass on good advice	guten Rat weitergeben
pleasantly surprised	angenehm überrascht
pointer	Zeigestab
presentation	Vortrag; Präsentation
public, in ~	Publikum, vor ~
rate, at this ~	Tempo, bei diesem ~
rework	überarbeiten, umgestalten
shut up	den Mund halten
speak up	laut und deutlich sprechen
table	Tabelle
the other day	neulich
transparency	Folie
turn one's back on s.o.	jdm. den Rücken kehren

Grammar Rhymes

Present, Past and Perfect

Wir Deutsche gehn fast alle
In folgende Grammatikfalle:
Als Beispiel nehmen wir
Diese beiden Sätze hier.

"*Waren* Sie mal in Ankara?"
"Ja, wir *waren neulich* da."
Auf Englisch ist mit diesem *waren*
Ganz unterschiedlich zu verfahren:

"*Have you been* to Ankara (yet)?"

Weil es egal, wann es geschehen,
Muß das *Present perfect* stehen.

"Yes, we *were* there the other day."

Past tense müssen wir immer haben
Mit vergangnen Zeitangaben.

Simple past nehme man,
Auf die Frage "Was war wann?"
Und auch dann, wenn unser Blick
Auf Vergangnes geht zurück:

I remember Jack – he *died* with his boots on[1].
One *was* on the accelerator[2].

Anmerkung:
Nach einleitendem *Present perfect* fährt man oft im *Past tense* fort.

1 er starb in seinen Stiefeln 2 Gaspedal

Grammar Jokes

EXERCISE 1:

A. Put the verb in brackets in the right form

❶ "Doctor, doctor, I (*lose*) my memory[1]."
"When this (*happen*)?"
"When what (*happen*)?"

❷ I (*join*) the navy[2] to see the world and (*spend*) five years in a submarine.

❸ Doctor: This is your first visit. So tell me your problems.
Patient: Shall I start at the beginning?
Doctor: Please do so.
Patient: Well ... In the beginning I (*create*[3]) Heaven and Earth.

❹ In six days God (*make*) Heaven and Earth.
He (*be*) self-employed[4].

B. Present perfect or past tense?

Can you translate these sentences taken from our dialogue?

1. Man hat mir eine Aufgabe gestellt, aber ich bin nicht sicher, was man von mir erwartet.
2. Dr. Rope hat mir gesagt, ich solle Informationen über die Geschichte der Firma sammeln.
3. Dann hat er mir zwei Folien über die Firma gegeben. (Siehe Anmerkung Seite 80)
4. Ich habe noch nie vor Publikum gesprochen.

1 Gedächtnis 2 zur Marine gehen 3 erschaffen 4 selbständig

Speech Functions: Giving advice

So wird James Kelly von Mr Stein beraten	
Why don't you try to make a few jokes?	Warum machen Sie nicht ein paar Witze?
May I give you another piece of advice?	Darf ich Ihnen noch einen Rat geben?
I think you should use the right equipment.	Sie sollten das richtige Gerät dafür benutzen.

Was hätte Mr Stein noch sagen können?	
Well, if you ask me, I'd not overload the transparency.	Wenn Sie mich fragen, ich würde die Folie nicht überladen.
If I were you, I'd do it in a relaxed way.	An Ihrer Stelle würde ich es locker machen.
If I had to do it, I'd use a glass pointer.	Wenn ich es tun müßte, würde ich einen Zeigestab aus Glas nehmen.
I advise you to practise it in front of a mirror.	Ich rate Ihnen, es vor dem Spiegel zu üben.
I recommend you never to turn your back on the audience.	Ich empfehle Ihnen, dem Publikum nie den Rücken zuzukehren.
The best thing to do is to record your presentation on tape.	Am besten nehmen Sie Ihre Präsentation auf Tonband auf.
Wouldn't it be better if ...?	Wäre es nicht besser, wenn ...?
You'd better ...	Sie täten gut daran ...

Food for thought

The only thing to do with good advice is to pass it on.
It is never of any use to oneself.

Oscar Wilde

Nothing that is worth knowing can be taught.

George Bernhard Shaw

Advice with a Smile

EXERCISE 2: Fill in the correct speech function of advice

❶ *René: I hate paying my income-tax[1]*
Bob: Be a good citizen[2]. Why .... pay with a smile?
René: I'd like to but they insist on[3] money.

❷ *Driving instructor: ....if you slowed down?*
Young Lady: But I'm allowed to drive 50 miles an hour in this area.
Driving instructor: Yes, but not on the pavement[4].

❸ *Mr Block: So you want to marry my daughter? I think you .... see my wife first.*
René: I have, sir, but I´d prefer to marry your daughter.

❹ *"Now that you are married, may I give ....?*
Take out some insurance[5]."
"But why? My wife isn't dangerous."

❺ *A two-sentence message received by Vice-President Lyndon Johnson came from an Indian reservation: " .... better be careful with your immigration laws[6]. We were careless with ours."*

❻ *Bob: I've lost my dog.*
René: If .... put an advertisement in the paper.
Bob: Rubbish! You seem to forget that my dog can't read.

❼ *"Doctor, doctor, do you think I'll live after this operation?"*
"Sure. But I wouldn't .... it."

1 Einkommensteuer 2 Bürger 3 bestehen auf 4 Gehsteig 5 Versicherung 6 Einwanderungsgesetze

The Language of presentations

auf der Folie	***on the transparency***
durchgehende Linie	*continuous line*
gestrichelte Linie	*dashed line*
Punkt	*dot*
punktierte Linie	*dotted line*
Zeichnung	*drawing*
Abbildung, Ziffer	*figure*
Graphik, Diagramm	*graph*
Abbildung	*illustration*
Präsentation, eine ~ machen	*presentation, make a ~*

Ausrüstung	***equipment***
Laserstab	*laser pointer*
Monitor	*monitor / screen*
Tageslichtfolie	*OHP foil / OHP sheet*
Plakat	*poster*
Diaprojektor	*slide projector*
Dia	*slide*

erläutern	***explaining***
Einführung	*introduction*
rechts unten	*bottom right*
links oben	*top left*
veranschaulichen, erläutern	*illustrate*
betrachten wir die Alternativen	*let's consider the options*
gehen wir die Möglichkeiten durch	*let's go through the possibilities*
zusammenfassen	*sum up*
zusammengefaßt	*in summary*
letzten Endes	*in the final analysis*
Abschluß	*conclusion (of a presentation)*

EXERCISE 3: Find expressions with almost the same meaning

on the monitor	....
graphic	....
let's consider the options	....
OHP transparency	....
diagram	....

EXERCISE 4: Find expressions with almost the opposite meaning

bottom right	....
on the right	....
conclusion	....
continuous line	....
shut up	....

EXERCISE 5: The ABC of our wordlists

people who listen to a presentation	*a* ....
it's the opposite of top right	*b* ....
to collect (information for example)	*c* ....

EXERCISE 6: And a few prepositions to finish with

1.	*Is Kelly*	....	*to the mark?*
2.	*Never pass*	....	*bad advice.*
3.	*Keep that*	....	*mind.*
4.	*I've never spoken*	....	*public.*

More advice for presenter James Kelly:

The Magic Seven

"Don't overload the audience" advised Mr Stein. There are golden rules to be observed. They all have to do with the figure seven. Why? For some genetic reason our short term memory cannot store and process more than seven pieces of information properly at the same time.

Therefore the ideal transparency is as follows:

- no more than **seven lines**
- each line should have between **seven and fourteen syllables**

Hint on presenting:

- you should not speak more than **seven minutes** about one transparency
- if you prepare **seven transparencies** then your presentation will last about 45 minutes – that's the limit.

The AIDA principle

Attention[1]: attract the attention of your audience by using jokes, cartoons, body language[2] or other effects.

Interest: your subject, the problem or a question should not only arouse their interest[3]. In the course of your talk they should feel that a solution[4] is in their own interest.

Decision: your aim[5] is to convince[6] the audience so that they take the decision you want them to take.

Action: a decision is not enough, it should be put into practice. In the last part of your presentation you show the road from decision to action and you rally your supporters[7].

1 Aufmerksamkeit 2 Körpersprache 3 Interesse wecken 4 Lösung 5 Ziel 6 überzeugen
7 Befürworter/Anhänger um sich sammeln

Hollerberg hotel scandal

CONTENTS

Time for a smile: A Russian in Hollerberg (1)

The first night in the Europahotel in Hollerberg, Boris Zhukov had a nasty experience[1]. He walked into the wrong room in his hotel, and surprised[2] a young girl who was just undressing[3]. He was so embarrassed[4], that he stood in the doorway[5] for almost an hour, apologising[6] in Russian.

1 unangenehmes Erlebnis 2 überraschen 3 sich ausziehen 4 verwirrt 5 auf der Türschwelle 6 sich entschuldigen

One Russian too many!

Sometimes there are some extraordinary situations which the staff have to deal with. In the following dialogue James is confronted by a problem of this sort. Read on to see how he copes with it:

Dr. Rope (**R**), James Kelly (**K**), Hotel receptionist (**H**)

R: Mr Kelly, can I have a word with you?

K: Certainly, Dr. Rope. Is anything wrong?

R: Just another little problem to test our patience. All this trouble with foreigners. I'm sorry, Mr Kelly ... present company excepted, of course.

K: How can I be of assistance?

R: You remember Mr Zhukov, the gentleman from Russia?

K: You mean the fellow I fetched from the airport?

R: Yes. Well, he's been causing problems at his hotel.

K: What's he been doing?

R: He's been getting himself drunk. He does it every evening.

K: Actually, I don't see anything wrong with that. He's old enough to know what he should do in his leisure time.

R: Unfortunately he doesn't seem to know. At least he has different social habits. He's been pushing his attentions onto the female guests in the hotel. The manager has just been on the phone. Mr Zhukov is obliged to vacate his room by lunch today. And I'd like you to find another hotel for him. Can you get on the phone right away?

K: Yes, sir!

(*5 minutes later*)

H: Punta Hotel. Can I help you?

K: Yes, I'd like a room for a customer of ours.

H: Yes sir, just a moment. I'll check reservations. Yes, we have some vacant rooms. What facilities do you require?

K: Well, he certainly requires a shower and bathroom with running water.

H: Actually, all our rooms have running water nowadays – for more than 40 years in fact. So a single room with shower.

K: Well, perhaps it might be better if he had a double room with a bar in it.

H: Oh, sir is expecting the client with his little wife?

K: Well, I'm not sure it's a matter of wife or of size. Actually, there may be several ...

H: More than one wife. That's bigamy, sir!!

K: Look, I think we've been misunderstanding each other in the last five minutes. Mr Zhukov isn't married. At least his wife isn't with him in Germany.

H: Oh, I see. He didn't want to bring his wife. Well, sir, perhaps this hotel isn't quite the sort of institution that you ... or rather your client needs.

K: Oh, I think I'll forget the whole affair. I probably didn't express myself correctly.

H: Oh, on the contrary. I think I've understood you perfectly well.

Vocabulary to help with the dialogue

accommodation	Unterkunft, Unterbringung
assistance, how can I be of ~ ?	Hilfe, wie kann ich Ihnen behilflich sein?
attention	Aufmerksamkeit
obliged, be ~ to	müssen
cause problems	Probleme machen, verursachen
client	Kunde
confront	konfrontieren, gegenüberstellen
cope with	fertig werden mit
deal with	sich befassen mit, sich beschäftigen mit
excepted, present company ~	ausgenommen, Anwesende ~
extraordinary	außergewöhnlich
facilities in a room	Zimmerausstattung
fellow	Kerl, Zeitgenosse, Bursche
foreigner	Ausländer(in), Fremde(r)
get on the phone	sich ans Telephon setzen
habit	(An-)Gewohnheit
increase	vergrößern, erhöhen

leisure time	Freizeit
on the contrary	im Gegenteil
patience	Geduld
push one's attentions on to ...	aufdringlich werden
receptionist	Empfangsdame/-herr
require	verlangen, benötigen
size	Größe
staff	Belegschaft
vacant rooms	freie Zimmer
vacate	räumen, frei machen
vacancy	Zimmer frei, freie Stelle

EXERCISE 1: Test your memory. How did they say it?

1. *How does Dr. Rope open the conversation with James?*
2. *How does James offer to help Dr. Rope?*
3. *What are the receptionist's first words?*
4. *What are Kelly's last words?*

Time for a smile: A Russian in Hollerberg (2)

The pretty bell girl[1] of the Europahotel in Hollerberg showed Mr Boris Zhukov to his room[2]. He asked what the rates[3] were. "Eighty marks," said the girl. – "That's wonderful, I'll pay eighty marks ... with pleasure[4]." – "With pleasure," replied the girl, "it will be five hundred."

1 Lauf-, Zimmermädchen 2 aufs Zimmer bringen 3 Preis, Tarif 4 Vergnügen

Grammar Rhymes

Present perfect progressive

Typ A

Die Handlung begann irgendwann
Und reicht zur Gegenwart heran.
Das Augenmerk richten wir auf
Handlungsdauer und Verlauf.

A much-worried mother once said
"My dear, *you've been kissing* young Fred
since six; it's now ten.
Do it just once again
And then think of going to bed."

Signalwörter, nach denen man
Den Typ A oft finden kann:

all the time, for years / weeks,
so far, for the last three days / months,
since six o'clock

Typ B

Wenn etwas Ärgernis, Panne, Zufall war,
Mach es mit *perfect* im *progressive* klar.
Zeitpunkt ist wieder unbekannt,
Oder er wird nicht genannt.

"What a mess! Why are you so dirty?"
"I'*ve been repairing* the TV."

ACHTUNG: Sowohl *he is* und *he has* werden in der
Umgangssprache zu *he's*.

Grammar Jokes: Test your simple and progressive perfects

EXERCISE 2:

A Put the verb in (...) in the right form

❶ Psychiatrist: So, you(*suffer*)[1] from loss of memory[2]. Well, in your case[3] my fee is $200 in advance[4].

❷ Letter of complaint to a laundry: Dear sirs, we (*just /receive*) some buttons with no shirts on them. Would you please return the shirts as well?

❸ Jone's Third Law of TV Programmes:
The show you (*look forward to*) all week will be cancelled.

❹ Salesman: Nothing is impossible for me, sir.
Mr Block: I know. You (*do*) nothing *for years*.

❺ Tramp: I (*not/ eat*) for three days.
Lady: I wish I had your willpower.

❻ I (*be*) in love with the same man for twenty years. If my husband finds out, he'll kill me.

B. Do you remember these sentences in our dialogue?

1. Well, the Russian (*cause*) problems at his hotel.
2. What has Mr Zhukov (*do*)? What's the problem?
3. He (*get*) himself drunk.
4. The manager (*just/be*) on the phone.
5. We (*misunderstand*) each other in the last five minutes.
6. I think, I (*understand*) you perfectly well.

1 leiden an 2 Gedächtnisschwund 3 in Ihrem Fall 4 im voraus

Expand your hotel vocabulary

Auftrag, im ~ von	*on behalf of*
Aufzug	*lift / elevator (US)*
ausgebucht	*fully-booked*
äußern, sich ~, erklären	*express oneself*
Ausstattung, Einrichtungen,	*facilities*
bestätigen, eine Buchung ~	*confirm a booking*
buchen, ein Zimmer, Hotel ~	*book a room/hotel*
Buchung, eine ~ vornehmen	*booking, make a ~*
deponieren, hinterlegen	*deposit*
Hotelkosten	*hotel charges*
Komfort, Annehmlichkeiten	*conveniences*
Konferenzzimmer	*conference room*
Parkmöglichkeiten	*parking facilities*
Portier, Empfangsdame	*receptionist*
Rechnung an … ausstellen	*bill, make a bill out to …*
reservieren, ein Zimmer ~	*reserve a room*
Reservierung, eine ~ vornehmen	*reservation, make a ~*
stornieren, könnten Sie mein Zimmer ~?	*cancel, could you ~ my room?*
Telefon, ans ~ holen	*phone, fetch somebody on the ~*
unterbringen, können Sie 5 Personen ~?	*accommodate, can you ~ 5 people?*
Unterkunft, für ~ sorgen	*arrange accommodation*
verbinden, ich verbinde Sie mit der Rezeption	*put through, I'll ~ you ~ to reception*
verfügbar, erhältlich	*available*
Wertsachen, Wertgegenstände	*valuables*

EXERCISE 3: The ABC of our word lists

Any kind of room to sleep in	*a*	....
I'm phoning on ... of Dr Rope	*b*	....
Another word for customer	*c*	....
It means 'handle, look after' sth.	*d*	....
How can I be of ... ?	*a*	....
It tells you how much to pay	*b*	....
A room for meetings	*c*	....
You do it with your valuables	*d*	....

EXERCISE 4: Say it with a noun (Hauptwort)

book a room	*make a ....*
reserve a room	*make a ....*
bill a person	*make a .... out to a person*
accommodate five people	*....... .... for five people*

Time for a smile: An Indian in Hollerberg

The receptionist[1] of the Europahotel in Hollerberg stared[2] at the red-skinned[3] guest from the USA and asked: "Do you have a reservation[4]?" The guest answered: "Sure have, heap big place near Rio Grande."

EXERCISE 5: A difficult customer

a difficult customer

First he b . . . . . a room

Finally he c . . . . the booking

Then he c . . . . . . the booking

1 Hotelportier 2 starren 3 rothäutig 4 Reservierung, Reservat

EXERCISE 6: Fill in the booking form

Sie reisen mit Ihrer Freundin oder Frau. Sie buchen ein Doppelzimmer mit Dusche für vier Nächte. Sie kommen am 12.7. an. Sie haben Sonderwünsche: ein ruhiges Zimmer zum Hof. Von den drei angebotenen Hotels ist das Sheraton Ihre erste, Holiday Inn Ihre zweite Wahl. Ferner buchen Sie die Zugfahrkarte zweiter Klasse Glasgow – London. Vergessen Sie nicht, die Anzahlung anzugeben.

Please book .... persons for
3 days (2 nights) arriving .... (Date)
or
5 days (4 nights) arriving .... (Date)
or
.... days (....... nights) arriving .... (Date)

Splits .... (1st Date) .... (2nd Date)

ANY SPECIAL REQUIREMENTS ....

ACCOMMODATION REQUIRED - Enter the number of rooms required in the relevant box
(All supplements per person per night - plus V.A.T.)

Telephone Reference Number:

Double or Twin without bath	☐	Double or Twin with bath or shower	☐
Single without bath	☐	Single with bath or shower	☐
Three bedded (3 seperate beds or double large & single) without bath	☐	Three bedded (3 seperate beds or double large & single) with bath or shower	☐

Preferred Hotel: If first choice is full - similar grade will be booked.

1st choice ....

2nd choice ....

3rd choice ....

Detailed hotel descriptions - see pages 6-9.
Hotel and single room supplements - see pages 4-5.

Second Class Return Rail tickets are required from .... Station (............ county) to London
Your rail tickets are included in the price. Ask your travel agent for details of train timings.

Please book Excursion Numbers .... Number of persons ....

SURNAMES (All members in party)	Initials	Mr. Mrs Miss	**Address and telephone number** of first named member of party to whom all tickets etc. will be sent.	Ages of Children

Member of Association of British Travel Agents

Member of The London Tourist Board

I enclose remittance of £ .... being a deposit of £7.50 per person, plus £1.50 or £1.90 per person Insurance (if required) as detailed, and agree to accept the booking conditions as stated.

Signature .... Date ....

Please debit my credit card: Access/Barclaycard

☐☐☐☐☐☐☐☐☐☐☐☐☐☐☐

£ .... Signed ....

Agent's ABTA number: ____________

Agent's V.A.T. Reg number: ____________

Advice to bosses

The best boss is the one who has sense enough[1] to pick good men to do what he wants done, and self-restraint[2] enough to keep from meddling with[3] them while they do it.

Theodore Roosevelt

I am always looking for people who can do a job better than I can.

T. Boone Pickens

Hire people who are smarter than you are.

Lew Wasserman

Never hire your client's children

David Ogilvy

Time for a smile

Assistant manager:	Whose idea was it to hang up this ghastly[4] picture in my office?
Secretary	It was the boss's idea, sir.
Assistant manager:	Doesn't it look nice?

1 der klug genug ist 2 Selbstbeherrschung 3 sich einmischen 4 gräßlich

Tell the whole world

CONTENTS

Business Frame:	**Eavesdropping[1] in the advertising office**
Grammar Rhymes:	**The simple present**
Grammar Jokes:	**Present – simple and progressive**
Business Words:	**Words you might hear in the advertising office**
Business Culture:	**Sometimes silence[2] is golden**
Plus:	**Jokes and useful exercises**

Let's start with a smile

Advertisement in an East-Friesian Newspaper: Will the person who forgot a shopping bag containing[3] fish and other seafood in our new bus last Tuesday please report to the police. He can have the bus.

1 lauschen 2 Schweigen 3 enthalten

James Kelly in the advertising office

After six weeks in the finance department, James Kelly is moved to his second department. Being a trainee gives him a lot of practical experience. This time it's in the advertising department. They consider themselves responsible for the company's image. The department is also responsible for public relations. The boss here is Mr Hill.

Mr Hill (**H**), James Kelly (**K**), Mr Bucker (**B**)

H: So you're going to do a stint in my department. Well, I'm absolutely certain you'll find the work more interesting and much more useful than what you were doing in the last office.

K: Oh, the jobs I had in Dr. Rope's department were also quite interesting. I can't complain.

H: I'm sure you can't, but we all know how disorganised they are over there. I shouldn't really tell you this but ... well, here you'll have a chance to be creative, especially since you're a native speaker of English.

K: Yes, sir. Exactly what is done here in Advertising?

H: Just a brief overview and then I'll pass you to Mr Bucker. He'll explain something about the office itself. So here we prepare the formal advertising. That means we compile the actual sheets of information for our potential customers. We make the masters for brochures and bulletins. And we prepare all articles about the company that should appear in the press; that's not advertising directly, it's more PR, public relations. Ah, here's Mr Bucker. Talk of the devil. May I present Mr Kelly, Mr Bucker? Now I'll leave you two alone. I have to chair a meeting. So long!

B: So you've met Mr Hill. He's a boss of the old school. He likes discipline. But don't worry about him. Look, we've got a very modern office, an open plan office. That's your desk over there.

K: There certainly are a lot of machines here. What do they all do?

B: Next to your desk you have a fax machine with multi-feed. You've got a phone on your desk with your own answering machine. In the middle of the room we've got a CPU with four workstations located around it. So when you want to use the computer you move to those PCs. One's an Apple Mackintosh. They are served by a laser printer.

K: What sort of applications do you use?

B: We need a mixture of text and graphics to prepare our originals for printing. So we use Pagemaker, QuarkXpress, CorelDraw, Freelance. Look, I've got your first job. We've just received this leaflet from a translator. Could you check it and prepare it for print? Mr Hill has already corrected it but I'm not sure if it's okay.

K: You don't want me to seem to be better than my new boss, do you?

B: Well, who's the native speaker, you or him?

Vocabulary to help you with the dialogue

advertising department	Werbung, Werbeabteilung
answering machine	Anrufbeantworter
application	Anwendung, Software
brief	kurz
brochure	Broschüre
bulletin	Mitteilungsblatt, Bulletin
chair (a meeting)	den Vorsitz haben
compile	zusammenstellen
complain	beklagen, sich beschweren
CPU (central processing unit)	Zentralrechner
creative	kreativ, schöpferisch
device	Gerät, Anlage, Einrichtung
disorganised	desorganisiert, unordentlich
graphics	Graphiken
image	Image
laser printer	Laserdrucker
leaflet	Flugblatt, Prospekt, Merkblatt
masters	Druckvorlagen, Originale
meeting; chair a ~	Besprechung, eine ~ leiten
move to the next department	umziehen, zur nächsten Abteilung ~
multi-feed fax	Fax mit automatischem Einzug
native speaker	Muttersprachler
open plan office	Großraumbüro
overview	Überblick, Übersicht

pamphlet	Broschüre
potential customer	potentieller Kunde
practical experience	praktische Erfahrung
printed matters	Drucksachen
public relations (PR)	Öffentlichkeitsarbeit
stint	Pensum, Schicht
talk of the devil!	Wenn man den Teufel nennt ...!

EXERCISE 1: Test your memory (There is no key to this exercise)

1. *What are the main activities of the department?*
   a) A . . . . *b) P . . . .*

2. *What is the department responsible for?*
   It's responsible for the company's . . . . . .

3. *What kind of printed matters do they produce here?*
   a) leaflets *b) b . . . . s* *c) b . . . . s* *d) a . . . . . . s*

4. *What kind of office have they got?*
   They have got a modern . . . .

5. *Why does Mr Hill have to leave James Kelly?*
   He has to . . . . . a . . . .

Grammar Rhymes

Simple Present[1]

Typ A

Für alles, was sich jeden Tag
Jederzeit ereignen mag,
Für alles was du immer tust,
Du *simple present* nehmen mußt.
Über Hobby, Job, Gewohnheit
Spreche nur in dieser Zeit.

"Waiter, have you got frogs' legs[2]?"
"No, sir. I *always walk* like this."

Simple present nach sich haben
Gewöhnlich diese Zeitangaben:

always, never, often, sometimes,
every day, usually, regularly.

Typ B

Simple present steht auch fürs Futur,
Jedoch mit Zeitangaben nur:
Man glaubt, daß nach festem Plan geschieht,
Was höhere Instanz vorsieht.

The Glasgow train *leaves at 17.18*.

Type C

Simple present sollte stehen,
Wenn einer vormacht, was wir sehen.

I *take* three whites of an egg.
Then I *whip* them foamy[3] and add some sugar ...

1 einfache Gegenwart 2 Froschschenkel 3 schaumig schlagen

Grammar Jokes: Simple and progressive

(see also chapter 4 and chapter 15)

EXERCISE 2:

A. Put the verb in brackets in the right form

❶ James Kelly: How can you (*make*) money selling[1] your photocopiers so cheap?
Director Block: No problem. We (*make*) a profit repairing them.

❷ Italians (*make*) the best lovers[2], but the Japanese (*make*) them smaller and cheaper.

❸ Character is what you have got when nobody (*look*).

❹ A true gentleman is someone who (*know*) how to play the trumpet[3] and doesn't.

❺ Policeman: Get out of the lake; there is no bathing allowed here!
Tourist: I (*not / bathe*[4]). I (*drown*[5])

❻ Patient: Doctor, doctor, my hand won't stop shaking[6].
Doctor: you (*drink*) a lot?
Patient: No, I (*spill*[7]) most of it.

❼ People who (*say*) nothing is impossible should try gargling[8] with their mouths shut.

B. Can you translate these sentences from our dialogue?

1. Hier bereiten wir die Werbung vor.
2. Wir stellen die Informationsblätter für unsere Kunden zusammen.
3. Wir machen die Druckvorlagen für die Broschüren und Mitteilungsblätter.

1 selling ist Gerund, nicht Teil des *present progressive* 2 Liebhaber 3 Trompete 4 baden 5 ertrinken 6 zittern 7 verschütten 8 gurgeln

Words you may hear in the advertising office

Firmenimage	*corporate image*
für ein Produkt werben	*promote a product*
in der Zeitung werben	*insert ads in the press*
inserieren, annoncieren	*place an ad/advert*
Katalog, Verzeichnis	*catalogue*
Kaufanreiz	*sales appeal*
Produkteigenschaft	*product feature*
Produktvorteil	*product advantage*
Rundschreiben	*circular*
TV-Spot / Fernsehwerbung	*TV slot / spot*
Verkaufs-/Absatzförderung	*promotion*
Verkaufsargument, das konkurrenzlose ~	*Unique Selling Proposition (USP), the unique ~*
Verkaufsbotschaft	*selling message*
Verkaufsziel	*sales goal*
Werbekampagne	*advertising campaign*
Werbeleiter	*advertising manager*
Werbespot	*advertising slot / spot*
Werbung, Annonce, Anzeige	*ad / advert / advertisement*

Advice from the experts

Doing business without advertising is like throwing kisses to a lovely girl in the dark: you know what you are doing, but she doesn't.

Edgar Watson Howe.

Advertising may be described[1] *as the science of arresting* [2] *the human intelligence long enough to get money from it.*

Stephen Leacock

1 hier: bezeichnen 2 hier: gefangenhalten

EXERCISE 3: Do you remember the devices in Mr Hill's office?

Die deutschen Bezeichnungen werden Ihnen helfen: PC, Zentralcomputer, Fax mit automatischem Einzug, Telefonbeantworter, Laserdrucker

Devices in the office

- a . . . . g m . . . . . .
- p . . . . . l c . . . . . . r
- . . s . . . . . n . . .
- c . . . . . . p . . . . u . . .
- m . . . i- f x

EXERCISE 4: What do they produce in the advertising office?

masters for

- . . . . . . gues
- a . . . . - m . . . .
- . . . . . lets
- . . . . hics
- . . . . . ures
- . . . . . tins

EXERCISE 5: Three times "annonce" in English

ad

a . . . . .

a . . . .

Business Culture: Sometimes silence[1] is golden

Mr Hill to James Kelly: "Well, I'm absolutely certain you'll find the work more interesting and much more useful than what you were doing in your last office ... we all know how disorganised they are over there. I shouldn't really tell you this ..."
Why does Mr Hill behave that way? Maybe he envies[2] Dr. Rope, maybe he feels inferior[3]. Maybe what he says is even true. However, he should never have spoken about it to a complete newcomer to the company.
What is wrong at Low Valley Photocopiers? A director who is not informed, a head of department who makes disparaging remarks[4] about the head of department next door. And everybody thinks that he or she is better than the boss.
Obviously, loyalty and discretion[5] are virtues[6] that are the basis of mutual[7] understanding and respect.

1 Schweigen 2 beneiden 3 unterlegen 4 verächtliche Bemerkungen 5 Diskretion, Verschwiegenheit 6 Tugenden 7 gegenseitiges Verständnis

Office Vocabulary:
Some devices you can see in an office

Anrufbeantworter	*answering machine*
Arbeitsspeicher	*RAM (Random Access Memory)*
Bildschirm	*screen*
Datenbank	*database*
Diktiergerät	*dictaphone*
Diskette	*floppy disk*
elektronisches Telefonverzeichnis	*electronic telephone directory*
Faxgerät	*fax*
Festplatte	*hard disk*
Handy	*hands-free telephone, cellphone*
Kassette	*cassette*
Kopierer	*photocopier*
Laserdrucker	*laser printer*
Lesespeicher	*ROM (Read Only Memory)*
Mobiltelefon	*mobile phone*
Nadeldrucker	*impact printer*
Piepser	*pager*
schnurloses Telefon	*cordless telephone*
Taschenrechner	*pocket calculator*
Tastatur	*keyboard*
Textverarbeitung	*word processor*
Tintendrucker	*ink-jet printer*
Tischrechner	*desk calculator*

Put it on display[1]

CONTENTS

Time for a smile

The other day[2], my boss told me that he'd welcome an exchange of opinion[3]. What he meant by that is that I should come with my opinion and go away with his.

1 etwas ausstellen 2 neulich 3 Meinungsaustausch

Preparing the trade fair

It often happens that the new person is thrown in at the deep end. In the advertising department with Mr Hill James is given a priority task. Probably nobody else had time to do it. Let's see how he copes in the following scene:

Mr Hill (**H**), James Kelly (**K**), Mr Bucker (**B**)

H: Mr Kelly, one of our tasks here in advertising is to prepare trade fairs. And you know we've got one in front of us in a few weeks' time.

K: That sounds great. In what way will I be involved?

H: In every way! You'll be responsible for all the general preparations.

K: But Mr Hill, I've never done anything like this before. This sort of thing wasn't offered at university.

H: We have every confidence in your abilities. You'll be given every assistance by Mr Bucker. He did the same work four years ago. Good luck and remember we're counting on you.

(*In Mr Bucker's room*)

K: Listen, I've no idea what I'm expected to do really.

B: It's okay. Don't get in a panic! Mr Hill is always exaggerating. When you were told that you had full responsibility he only meant the tasks on the operational level, timing, size of the stand at the trade fair. Budget for the exhibition and the contents have already been decided at board level. That's like a skeleton for the whole exercise. And the flesh must be put on it by us.

K: Well, that's a relief! So what's the order of priorities?

B: First you've got to telephone the trade fair centre to make sure that they've reserved the right location in the fair, and the correct number of square metres. Things can go wrong. And phone up the exhibition contractor to make sure that the stand is being erected in the right way.

K: What about all the promotional material?

B: We've already composed the text and graphics. The photograph of the mechanical parts and the aerial photograph of the plant will be delivered to us this afternoon. Your job is to fit all these parts together like a jigsaw puzzle. And you'll certainly have to go to the exhibition site to check that everything's in place locally.

K: And I won't have any problems with arranging payment for any of this, will I?

B: Of course not. The board and Mr Hill have authorised all the budgets. There's just one thing. Everybody makes a mistake occasionally. You might, too. But don't make it with the director's opening speech! When you correct it, make sure it's really correct!

K: Hmmph! If I'm writing and correcting the speech, I might as well make it.

B: Now you're beginning to learn. We do all the work and the bosses get the glory.

Vocabulary to help you with the dialogue

abilities	Fähigkeiten
aerial photograph	Luftaufnahme
assistance	Hilfe, Unterstützung
authorise the budget	den Etat genehmigen
board level	Vorstandsebene
confidence, have ~ in	Vertrauen haben zu
cope with a problem	fertig werden mit einem Problem
count on s.o.	zählen, vertrauen auf jdn.
display, be on ~	Auslage, ausgestellt werden
don't get in a panic!	regen Sie sich nur nicht auf!
erect / put up a stand	aufstellen, einen Stand ~
exaggerate	übertreiben
exhibition contractor	Firma für Messebedarf, Ausstellungsausstatter
exhibition site	Ausstellungsgelände
fit together	zusammensetzen
flesh	Fleisch (lebendes ~)
glory	Ruhm, Ehre
involve	betreffen, einbeziehen
location	Standort, Lage, Platz
operational level	Betriebsebene

priority task	vorrangige Aufgabe
promotional material	Reklame-, Werbematerial
relief, that's a ~!	Trost, ich bin erleichtert!
skeleton	Skelett, Gerüst
square metres	Quadratmeter
throw s.o. in at the deep end	jdn. ins tiefe Wasser werfen
trade fair	Handelsmesse

EXERCISE 1: Test your prepositions

We've confidence	. . . .	*your abilities.*
I can't cope	. . . .	*the problem.*
This wasn't offered	. . . .	*university.*
We're counting	. . . .	*you, Kelly.*
The budget has been decided	. . . .	*board level.*
You won't have any problems	. . . .	*arranging payment.*

EXERCISE 2: Test your memory

1. *What job is given to James?*

   James has to prepare a t . . . . f . . .

2. *Which decisions have already been taken at board level?*

   a) t . m . . g *b) s . . e of stand*
   c) b . . g . .t *d) c . . t . . . s*

3. *Why does James have to phone the trade fair centre?*

   He has to make sure that they reserved
   a) the right l . . . . . . n and
   b) the correct number of s . . a . . m . . . . .

Grammar Rhymes

Passive and Active

Je nachdem, wie Sie die Handlung sehen,
Wird Aktiv oder Passiv stehen.
Ist Ihnen Tat und Täter wichtig,
Dann ist ein Satz im Aktiv richtig.
They didn't teach us that sort of thing at university.

Wenn man in erster Linie sieht,
Was mit dem Tatopfer geschieht,
Dann wird das Passiv angewandt.
Der Täter ist oft unbekannt,
Oder er bleibt ungenannt.
Nothing that is worth learning can *be taught*
(George Bernhard Shaw).

Wenn man den Täter kennt,
Stellt man ihn mit *by* ans End.
High heels[1] *were invented*[2] *by a woman*
who didn't like to be kissed on her forehead[3].

Formen

Die Zeiten bilden Sie mit einer Form des Verbs *to be*.
Nun hängen Sie daran ein Partizip des Perfekts an.

Simple present:	Hamburgers *are* not *served* in this hotel.
Present progressive:	A new car *is being developed* by Mercedes.
Simple past	*Were* you *treated* well in prison?
Past progressive:	*He was being interviewed* when I arrived.
Present perfect:*	I *have often been asked* this question.
Past perfect:*	He *had been hired* before Kelly arrived.
Will-future:*	You *will be fired* by director Block.

* Diese Zeiten haben ein Passiv, aber ohne ein *progressive*

1 hohe Absätze 2 erfinden 3 Stirn

Grammar Jokes

EXERCISE 3: Put the verb in brackets in the right form

❶ A man who steals a handful of gold (*put*) into prison;
a man who steals a whole country (*make*) king.

❷ An executive is a man who hires others to do what he (*hire*) to do.

❸ "When I was seven years old I (*take*) to London Zoo."
"You (*accept*)?"

❹ There was a young fellow from Bristol
Who shot three old maids with a pistol.
When it (*know*) what he'd done
He (*give*) a gun
By all the bachelors of Bristol.

❺ A pessimist is a man who (*force / present perfect*) to live with an optimist.

EXERCISE 4:

Can you change these sentences from our Business Frame back into the passive? (The example has been done for you)

	Subject	***Verb***	***Object***
Active:	*Mr Bucker*	*helps*	*James*
Passive:	*James*	*is helped by*	*Mr Bucker*

1. I've no idea what *they expect* me to do.
2. Phone up the exhibition contractor to make sure that *they are erecting* the stand the right way.
3. They didn't offer this sort of thing at university.
4. *They have already decided* the budget for the exhibition at board level.
5. *Mr Bucker will give you* every assistance.

Business Words you might need for trade fairs

Anlaufkosten	*launching costs*
aufstellen, einen Messestand ~	*assemble a stand*
Ausstellung	*exhibition / exposition (US)*
Ausstellungsfläche, sich um ~ bewerben	*exhibition space, apply for ~*
Ausstellungskatalog	*exhibition catalogue*
besuchen, eine Messe ~	*visit, attend a fair*
Einführung (eines Produkts)	*launching*
Einführungstermin	*launching date*
erschließen, neue Märkte ~	*open up new markets*
Fachmesse	*specialised fair*
Fachpresse	*trade press*
Marke, Sorte, Klasse	*brand*
Messe	*fair*
Messebesucher	*visitor to a fair*
Messegebäude	*exhibition building*
Messeleitung	*exhibition board*
Messestand	*exhibition stand / booth*
Pressekonferenz	*press conference*
Pressemitteilung	*press release*
Produkte auf den Markt bringen,	*launch products*
Produktmanager, Markenbetreuer	*brand manager / product manager*
veranstalten, eine Messe ~	*hold a fair*
Verbraucher, Konsument	*consumer*
Verbraucherumfrage	*consumer survey*
Verbrauchsgüter	*consumer goods*
Weltausstellung	*world fair*
Werbekampagne	*publicity campaign*

EXERCISE 5: Do you remember the right word?

1. area where an exhibition is held	*exhibition s . . .*
2. hall where the exhibition booths are	*exhibition b . . . . . . g*
3. it is measured in square metres	*exhibition s . . . .*
4. another word for exhibition booth	*exhibition s . . . .*
5. firm that erects exhibition booths	*exhibition c . . . r . . . . r*
6. it tells you who is who at the fair	*exhibition c . . . . e*
7. the American word for fair	*ex . . . .*
8. a big international exhibition	*w . . . .*

EXERCISE 6: The ABC of business words

Another word for "help"	*a . . . . e*
He is responsible for a product	*b . . . . m . . . . . r*
It tells you what customers need	*c . . . . . . r s . . . . y*
Something like a shop window	*. . . . . . y*

EXERCISE 7: Activities around the fair

ask for a location for your stand	*. . . . . for exhibition s . . . e*
visit a fair	*. . . . . . a fair*
organise a fair	*. . . . a fair*
erect a stand	*. . . . . a stand*

Selling your grandma

CONTENTS

Food for thought[1]

In Oxford Steet a ragged[2] street-salesman selling lipsticks and nylon stockings was surrounded[3] by four men – his accountant[4], his bank manager, his chief buyer[5] and the Income Tax inspector.[6]

1 Stoff zum Nachdenken 2 zerlumpt 3 umgeben 4 Buchhalter 5 Einkaufschef 6 Finanzbeamter

At the sales department

James moves along through the departments. Now he has arrived at the sales department. Mr Haid is the department leader of sales for large-size copiers. He is the kind of salesman who would sell his grandma if the price were right. Selling can take place in many ways and in many situations. Sometimes scoring a hit with a potential customer can be quite a surprise. You never know when you might hit the mark.

Mr Haid (**H**), James Kelly (**K**), Mr Zhukov (**Z**)

H: So your role here will be more supportive than actually doing any selling. We don't expect somebody straight from school to know how to sell products.

K: Actually I attended university and business school, Mr Haid. So I'm not a complete beginner.

H: Of course not, of course not! Now there are some things you are going to have to learn. It's not just a matter of persuading some potential customer to buy something. You'll have to deal with the sales contracts. The delivery conditions and terms of business, prices, discounts, margins etc. will have to be fixed and we have rules about that. But don't worry! As I mentioned before you'll hardly be selling anything with your experience.

K: You might be right but I'm willing to learn. What are these special rules you were talking about?

H: Okay, I'll give you an example and then you'll have a different task to cope with. I'll come back to that later. So when you negotiate a sale with a prospect, that's what we call a potential customer, you must talk about transport charges, the insurance or taxes like VAT. If you quote the price without these extras it is called the net price. With them it's the gross price. We've got some special terms which explain what charges the customer must pay and what costs we must cover. Terms like ex-works or f.o.b. But Mr Hartmann will explain all that to you later.

Now to the other little matter. That impossible Russian is coming to visit the company tomorrow. He arrives on the five o'clock train from Frankfurt. I had a discussion with him but I found him to be unbearable to be with. He made a lot of trouble last time he was here. So

I'm not going to see him again, if I can help it. Now, I heard from a colleague that you get on quite well with him.

K: I wouldn't put it like that. I went for a drink with him when he was thrown out of his hotel.

H: I'm sure you'll manage very well. See you later.

(In the bar at the hotel with Mr Zhukov):

Z: So James, I must say I'm pleased that you were able to accept my invitation today.

K: That's alright, Boris. I'm glad to see you back in Germany so quickly. It's only about six weeks since you left, isn't it?

Z: Yes, that's right. And I was glad to leave. You were the only person who found some time for me and my Russian passions. Now what are we going to do tonight? By the way, my brother is inviting us for dinner. He owns one of those new printshops in Moscow. ... Ah, here he comes. Leo, please meet James from England. Let's sit down together. I have a little liquid something in my pocket. (*To be continued*).

Vocabulary to help you with the dialogue

charges	Gebühren
delivery conditions	Lieferbedingungen
discounts	Rabatte
ex-works	ab Werk
get on well with s.o.	gut mit jdm. auskommen
gross price	Bruttopreis
hit the mark	ins Schwarze treffen
I wouldn't put it like that	das würde ich nicht so nennen
invitation	Einladung
it's not just a matter of...	es geht nicht nur um ...
liquid	flüssig
margins	Margen, (Gewinn-)Spannen
passion	Leidenschaft
persuade	überzeugen

potential customer	potentieller Kunde
prospect	potentieller Kunde
quote	Angebot, Kostenvoranschlag
rule	Regel
sales contract	Kaufvertrag
sales department	Verkauf, Verkaufsabteilung
sales negotiation	Verkaufsverhandlung
salesman	Verkäufer
score a hit	einen Treffer landen
subsidiary	Tochtergesellschaft
supportive	unterstützend
terms of business / trade	Geschäftsbedingungen
unbearable	unerträglich
VAT (value added tax)	Mehrwertsteuer
willing, I'm ~ to ...	bereit, ich bin ~ zu ...

EXERCISE 1: Memory test. Tick off the correct answers

1. *James' job is to*
   - ☐ *sell copiers*
   - ☐ *deal with sales contracts*
   - ☐ *make sales negotiations*

2. *James has attended*
   - ☐ *business school*
   - ☐ *high school*
   - ☐ *university*

3. *Mr Haid*
   - ☐ *is going to see Mr Zhukov*
   - ☐ *is avoiding the Russian*
   - ☐ *has an appointment with him*

4. *Leo Zhukov*
   - ☐ *arrives on the 5 o'clock train*
   - ☐ *is offering James some Vodka*
   - ☐ *is inviting him for dinner*

Grammar Rhymes:

The Future

How do the English speak about the future?

Wir Deutsche haben nur
Drei Möglichkeiten fürs Futur,
Ganze fünfe an der Zahl
Stehn dem Engländer zur Wahl.

❶ *Will Future* nimmt der Engländer für:

1. Entscheidungen, spontan gefällt,
2. Zukunftsprognosen, die man stellt,
3. Ereignisse nach fremdem Plan,
   den man nicht verändern kann.

Drinking *will not stop* your problems but it *will give* you lots of interesting new ones.

❷ *Going-to Future* nimmt der Engländer

1. Wenn er in die Zukunft sieht
   Und voll Gewißheit Schlüsse zieht,
2. Wenn er über Plan und Absicht
   Mit dem Blick aufs Morgen spricht.

After Christmas the department stores were crowded with people trying to exchange the Christmas presents they didn't like. A disgusted[1] husband shouted to his wife: "*Are you* at least *going to* keep the baby?"

1 angewidert

Grammar Rhymes

The Future

❸ Wann nehmen wir *will-future progressive*?

Wenn wir in die Zukunft sehen
Und sagen wollen, daß ein Geschehen
Begonnen hat, aber nicht geendet,
Wird diese Zukunftsform verwendet.

"Lovely weather we're having," said one fortune-teller[1] to the other. "Yes, indeed," said the other, "it reminds[2] me of the summer we'*ll be having* in the year 2015"

❹ *Simple present* mit Zukunftszeitangaben
Für Pläne, auf die wir keinen Einfluß haben.

Graffiti:
Eat, drink and be happy
for *tomorrow we diet.*

❺ *Present progressive* (mit Zeitangabe in der Zukunft)

Für Programme, die *wir* selbst gewählt,
Für Pläne, die wir aufgestellt,
Und die wir ändern, wenn es uns gefällt.

A young nun was talked into[3] a moonlight walk by a young priest. Out in the romantic night he took her into his arms and gave her a long kiss. When he let her go, she started to cry: "Oh Lord, forgive me, I have sinned twice!" Astonished[4] he asked "What do you mean, twice?" "*You aren't stopping* with just one kiss, are you?" was the reply.

1 Wahrsager 2 jdn. erinnern an 3 überreden zu 4 erstaunt

Grammar Jokes

EXERCISE 2:

A Put the verbs in brackets into the right form

❶ An actor was offered $ 5,000 a week to work on a new film. "What is it called?", he asked. "The One-Legged[1] Transvestite of Dartmoore Prison," replied the director. "Be sure to be on the set[2] Tuesday, at 8 o'clock."
"For that money I don't mind starting on Sunday."
"Not on Sunday. But on Monday you (*have*) your operations."

❷ Doctor: I can't see anything wrong with you. It must be the drink.
Patient: Never mind, doctor, I (*come*) back when you are sober[3].

❸ Voice on telephone:
"Give us $ 50,000 or you (*not see*) your husband again."
"I (*not / give*) you the money. But I'm interested in your offer[4]."

B. In our Business Frame these sentences refer[5] to the future

1. You (*have to*) deal with the sales contracts.
2. I (*come*) back to that later.
3. That impossible Russian (*come*) to visit us tomorrow.
4. He (*arrive*) on the five o'clock train from Frankfurt.
5. I (*not / see*) him again, if I can help it.
6. Now what we (do) tonight?

1 einbeinig 2 am Drehort 3 nüchtern 4 Angebot 5 verweisen auf

Extend your allround sales vocabulary

abschließen, einen Vertrag ~	*conclude a contract*
Auftrag	*order*
aushandeln, Bedingungen ~	*negotiate conditions*
Barzahlungsrabatt	*cash discount*
bestätigen, einen Auftrag ~	*confirm an order*
brechen, eine Vertrag ~	*break a contract*
Exporteur	*exporter*
frei an Bord	*f.o.b. (free on board)*
frei längsseits Schiff	*f.a.s. (free alongside ship)*
Handelsrabatt	*trade discount*
Kosten und Fracht	*c.&f. (cost and freight)*
Kosten, Versicherung, Fracht	*c.i.f. (cost, insurance, freight)*
Kostenvoranschlag, ein verbindlicher ~	*quote, a firm ~*
Ladekosten	*loading costs*
Lieferant	*supplier*
Liefervertrag	*supply contract*
Lieferzeit	*delivery time*
Mengenrabatt	*quantity discount*
Mengenrabatt	*bulk discount*
Preisliste, gültige ~	*price list, current ~*
Scheck, per ~	*by cheque (check – US)*
Skonto	*prompt payment discount*
Spedition, Spediteur	*forwarder, forwarding agent, carrier*
Überweisung, per ~	*by transfer*
Verpackungskosten	*packing costs*
Versand	*despatch*
Versandkosten	*shipping costs*
Vertragsbedingungen	*terms of contract*
Vertragsbruch	*breach of contract*
Zahlungsbedingungen	*terms of payment*

EXERCISE 3: Arrange the following expressions in chronological order

Vertrag ➔ *Auftrag* ➔ *Lieferung*

payment

quote

EXERCISE 4: They all begin with sales

sales

c . . . . . . t

m . .

d . . . .

n . . . t . . t . . . s

EXERCISE 5: Verbs around a contract

n . g . . . . . e

. . . a k

a contract

c . . . l . . e

s . . n

EXERCISE 6: Terms you should know

t....

p.....t

terms of

b.......

c......t

Oh, these salesmen!

A monologue is a conversation between you and a motor-car salesman.

"There's a salesman waiting outside, sir. He's got a big blonde woman with him."
"Get rid of him, Miss Child. Tell him I've already got one."

Enjoying food and drink

CONTENTS

Our Business Frame:	**Explaining the menu**
Grammar Prose:	**Let's repeat a few structures**
Speech functions:	**Entertaining business friends**
Business Words:	**The menu**
Business Culture:	**Doing business with Russians and how to toast with them**
Plus:	**Some more exercises to test your grammar and vocabulary**

Let's start with a smile

We had been waiting for ages[1] for the waiter. "Gentleman," said my father, raising[2] an empty glass, "I rise to toast[3] absent friends, among whom I include[4] the waiter of this table."

"Waiter! Look at that! You've brought me a lobster[5] with only one claw[6]."
"I'm ever so sorry, sir, but it lost its claw in a fight."
"Never mind! Take it away and bring me the winner."

1 eine Ewigkeit warten 2 ein leeres Glas erheben 3 ich erhebe mich, um anzustoßen auf ...
4 einbeziehen 5 Hummer 6 Schere

Explaining the menu

Sometimes in our professional lives we have to mix business with pleasure. In this case it is dinner with visitors from abroad. See how James handles this in the following dialogue:

James Kelly (**K**), Boris Zhukov (**B**), Leo Zhukov (**L**)

B: So, Jamie, let's go together into the town to a typical restaurant with local food. This stuff here in the hotel is boring. It's the same all over the world. Do you know a good place?

K: Well, I've not been in Germany very long myself but I have got a favourite place. It's called "Zur Traube".

L: What does that mean? It sounds awful.

K: Actually it means "The Grape" in English. They serve typical country food. And large portions of it.

B: And they've got good vodka, I hope.

K: Well, they serve very good wines from this region. I don't know about vodka. And another good thing. They speak English to the guests there. They have a lot of Americans.

(In the Traube)

B: Waitress, could you bring us the menu, please? Thank you. What would you recommend, Jamie?

K: I suggest we stay with wine. It'd be ...

L: No, no, no! First we must drink an aperitif, a pernod from France. Three pernods, please waitress.

B: Okay, what about the first course?

K: There are several things worth eating here. You could have baked Camembert or Brie with berries, ham and melon or prawn salad.

B: I'll take the Brie.

L: Me, too.

K: And I'll have the prawns for a change. Now to the main course.

B: It's a long menu. Suggest your favourites. Waitress, a round of schnapps.

K: They do very good local meat dishes. You can get steaks, pork chops and pork leg.

L: Ugh! Pork leg. That's nothing for me.

K: The tastiest thing in my opinion is the game.

B: What's game? I haven't the slightest idea what that might be.

K: It's all the meat or poultry we get by hunting. They serve very good venison, wild boar, rabbit and duck. It comes with potatoes or croquettes and vegetables. Things like red cabbage, broccoli, beans and carrots. You should drink a dry red wine with it.

L: Hmm! My mouth's beginning to water. I'll take the venison. What about you, brother?

B: I've never eaten wild boar, so that'll be my choice.

K: Good, and I'll take the duck. Excuse me, waitress!

(Two hours later: very merry and all very good friends)

L: And that's the reason for my trip to Germany this time. We weren't really sure whether to purchase from your company, especially since we didn't have a good feeling about your boss. But now we've made our decision. The only condition is that we'd like you to complete the sale and the contract with us. We consider you personally have tipped the balance in favour of a purchase.

K: Really, I don't know what to say.

B: The word is na zdoroviya! Prost. And three more vodkas!

Vocabulary to help you with the dialogue

appetiser	Vorspeise
awful; it sounds ~	schrecklich, es klingt ~
choice	Wahl
course; first ~	Gang, erster ~
decision	Entscheidung
from abroad	aus dem Ausland
I'll take the Brie	Ich nehme den Brie
it's worth doing	es lohnt sich zu tun
local food	heimische Küche
main course / main meal	Hauptgang
menu	Speisekarte
merry	fröhlich
recommendation	Empfehlung
purchase from a company	von einer Firma kaufen

serve, they ~ meat dishes	sie haben Fleisch auf der Karte
starter	Vorspeise
stay, ~ with the wine	bleiben, beim Wein ~
suggest	vorschlagen
suggestion	Vorschlag
they do good fish here	sie haben guten Fisch hier
tip the balance	den Ausschlag geben
waiter	Kellner, Ober
waitress	Fräulein, Kellnerin

(see also the food list on page 129f)

EXERCISE 1: Memory test. Tick off the correct answers
(more than one correct answer is possible)

1. What is "game"?
- ☐ *beef*
- ☐ *pork*
- ☐ *venison*
- ☐ *poultry*

2. They eat at the Traube because
- ☐ *it is Leo's favourite pub*
- ☐ *it is James' favourite pub*
- ☐ *hotel food is boring*
- ☐ *Boris likes country food*

3. Mr Zhukov is in Germany
- ☐ *to see Mr Haid*
- ☐ *to help his brother*
- ☐ *to buy photo copiers*
- ☐ *to complete a contract*

4. Leo buys from Low Valley
- ☐ *because he likes James*
- ☐ *because he likes Mr Haid*
- ☐ *because the price is right*
- ☐ *because Boris works for Low Valley Copiers*

EXERCISE 2: Wordbuilder's Corner. Find the nouns

start	*starter*
suggest	....
choose	....
recommend	....
decide	....

EXERCISE 3: Are you flexible?

They have almost the same meaning

main course	**main m . . .**
buy	**p . . . .**
serve game	**. . game**

A short list of what you might eat

Starters

ham and melon	Melone mit Schinken
prawn cocktail	Krabbencocktail
smoked salmon	Räucherlachs
lobster	Hummer

Main course

***mutton* – Hammel**

lamb	Lamm
lamb chops	Lammkoteletts
lamb roast	Lammbraten

pork – **Schwein**	
cutlet	Kotlett
bacon	Speck

beef – **Rind**	
beef burgundy	Burgunderbraten
brains	Hirn
veal	Kalb
minced meat	Hackfleisch

poultry – **Geflügel**	
roast duck	gebratene Ente
roast chicken	gebratenes Hähnchen
partridge	Rebhuhn
turkey	Pute

game – **Wild**	
wild boar	Wildschwein
venison	Reh, Hirsch
rabbit	Kaninchen

fish – **Fisch**	
trout	Forelle
perch	Barsch
pike	Hecht
salmon	Lachs
plaice	Scholle
sole	Seezunge

vegetables – **Gemüse**	
boiled vegetables	gekochtes Gemüse
stir-fried vegetables	Wok-Gemüse
peas	Erbsen
cabbage	Kohl
cauliflower	Blumenkohl
sprouts	Rosenkohl

fried potatoes	Bratkartoffeln
chipped potatoes, chips	Pommes frites
mashed potatoes	Kartoffelbrei

salad – Salat

mixed salad	gemischter Salat
cucumber salad	Gurkensalat
lettuce	grüner Salat

dessert – Nachspeise

pancake	Pfannkuchen
stewed fruit	Kompott
fruit salad	Obstsalat

Time for a smile

In Russia everything is bigger.
Boris Zhukov: In our country they serve steaks that are so big you can milk them.

A tourist saw an advertisement for a restaurant which claimed that any dish requested[1] could be served. The man decided to test this restaurant. He entered and ordered an elephant on toast. The waiter took the order[2] and went away into the kitchen. A few minutes later, he returned and said calmly: "We do apologize[3], sir, but we have run out of bread[4]".

1 jedes verlangte Gericht 2 Bestellung aufnehmen 3 um Entschuldigung bitten 4 uns ist das Brot ausgegangen

Speech functions: Entertaining business friends

Is there a good restaurant here?	
Do you know a good pub?	Kennen Sie eine nette Kneipe?
Which restaurant would you recommend?	Welches Restaurant würden Sie empfehlen?
They do good meals there.	Die haben eine gute Küche.
What would you recommend?	Was würden Sie empfehlen?

Recommending and suggesting	
They serve very good wines from this region.	Sie haben sehr gute Weine aus der Gegend.
There are several dishes worth eating here.	Es gibt einige empfehlenswerte Gerichte / Speisen.
They do very good local meat dishes.	Sie machen sehr gute regionale Fleischgerichte
You can get excellent pork knuckle.	Sie bekommen hier ausgezeichnete Schweinshaxe.
The tastiest thing here in my opinion is the game.	Meiner Meinung nach schmeckt Wild hier am besten.
They serve very good venison.	Der Rehbraten ist hier sehr gut.
I suggest we stay with wine.	Ich schlage vor, wir bleiben beim Wein.
You should drink a dry red wine with it.	Sie sollten einen trockenen Rotwein dazu trinken.

Talking to the waiter	
A table for three, please.	Einen Tisch für drei, bitte.
Have you reserved/booked a table?	Haben Sie einen Tisch reserviert?
Sorry, we're full this evening.	Tut mir leid, wir sind heute voll besetzt.
Excuse me please, can I have the menu?	Entschuldigen Sie, kann ich bitte die Speisekarte haben?
What are your specialities?	Was sind Ihre Spezialitäten?

Is there anything special today?	Gibt es heute etwas Besonderes?
What's the chef's special?	Was ist die Spezialität des Kochs?

Making up your mind

I've never eaten wild boar. That'll be my choice.	Ich habe noch nie Wildschwein gegessen. Das nehme ich.
And I'll take the duck.	Und ich nehme die Ente.
I'll try the lamb.	Ich versuche mal das Lamm.
I'll have the pork chop.	Ich nehme das Schweinekotelett.

Paying the bill

Can I pay by card?	Kann ich mit der Karte bezahlen?
Do you accept cheques?	Nehmen Sie Schecks?
Do you take credit cards?	Nehmen Sie Kreditkarten?
I think there's something wrong with the bill.	Ich glaube, mit der Rechnung stimmt etwas nicht.
Could I have a receipt, please?	Könnte ich bitte einen Beleg haben?
Keep the change.	Behalten Sie das Wechselgeld.

Old jokes at the restaurant

"Waiter! What is this fly doing in my soup?"
"Looks like breast-stroke[1], doesn't it?"

"Waiter! What is this fly doing in my soup?"
"I'm most awfully sorry, sir. Would you prefer[2] it to be served separately[3]?"

1 Brustschwimmen 2 vorziehen 3 getrennt serviert

Grammar Prose: Let's repeat a few structures

EXERCISE 4: What's your choice?

Was drückt das will-future hier aus? *(see chapter 12)*

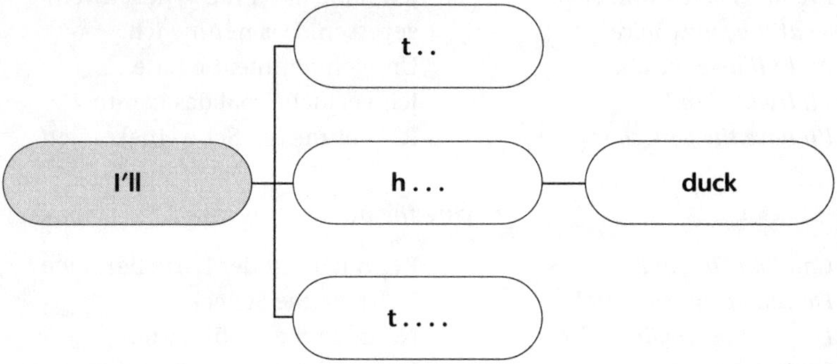

EXERCISE 5: Simple or progressive?

Here are some sentences from the conversation in the restaurant.

Put the verb in brackets into the right form

1. They (*serve*) very good venison here.
2. My mouth (*begin*) to water.
3. We consider you (*tip*) the balance in favour of a purchase.
4. We (*not/be*) sure whether to purchase from your company.
5. But now we (*make*) our decision.

Business Culture: Doing business with Russians

Russians make up no more than 50 per cent of the former USSR. It is not easy to do business in Russia, especially with ministries, because there is still a lot of red tape[1] to overcome[2] before a contract is signed.

Meetings and greetings

Shake hands when first meeting people and leaving. Introductions are informal and direct. Russians are still very title-conscious[3]: use titles and show respect. Russians think of themselves as being honest and trustworthy[4]. So don't show distrust[5]. Like most nations they are proud[6] of their country. Don't tell them that in your country everything is bigger, cleaner and better organised.

Negotiating contracts

Russian negotiators[7] tend to be sentimental. However, they plan and prepare thoroughly[8]. Presentations should be strictly factual and full of technical detail.

Entertainment[9]

Dinner is eaten early. If you are invited to a Russian home, it is customary[10] to bring flowers and liquor. Toasts[11] are common, and the guest must be prepared to return toasts.

Adapted from Copland, L., Griggs: Going International. How to make Friends and Deal Effectively in the Global Marketplace. New York, 1986

1 Papierkrieg 2 überwinden 3 titelbewußt 4 vertrauenswürdig 5 Mißtrauen 6 stolz 7 Unterhändler 8 gründlich 9 Bewirtung 10 üblich 11 Trinksprüche

Business Culture: Toasts

Russians are fond of toasts and expect you to return them. The following might come in handy[1] during your next business trip to Novosibirsk or Vladivostock.

For all occasions	
Good health!	Auf Ihr Wohl!
Cheers!	Prost!

… or you simply say na zdorovija!

For special occasions	
Here's to our contract!	Trinken wir auf den Vertrag!
I'd like to make a toast to our new chairman.	Ich würde gerne auf das Wohl unseres neuen Vorsitzenden anstoßen.
I'd like to propose a toast to the merger of our firms.	Ich würde gerne auf die Fusion unserer Firmen anstoßen.
Let's raise our glasses to the future of your country.	Erheben wir unsere Gläser, und stoßen wir auf die Zukunft Ihres Landes an.

Time for a smile

The newly-wed husband stood up and raised his glass: "Here's to the lovely creature that has become my wife. Her voice is like a warm breeze[2] in May. Her bright sunshine has dispelled the dark clouds[3] of my depression …" Here his father-in-law[4] interrupted him: "Is this a toast or the weather forecast[5]?"

Bob: Let's raise our glasses to our host's[6] excellent health. May he live to be one hundred years old and twenty days.
Host: Thank-you very much. But why the twenty days?
Bob: I certainly don't want you to die suddenly.

1 nützlich sein 2 Brise 3 die Wolken auflösen 4 Schwiegervater 5 Wetterbericht 6 Gastgeber

The company work-horse

CONTENTS

Time for a smile

"You're late," said the boss to his secretary when she strolled[1] in at 10 a.m. "I'm not really late, sir," she said. "I just took my coffee break[2] before I came in."

1 schlendern 2 Kaffeepause

The company work-horse or the secretary

About the same time as James Kelly joined the company there was an advertisement for the post of secretary to the director of the purchasing division.

Time for a smile: Guess who got the job?

They've given the job to Miss Reed
She's just the person they need.
She's pretty and slim[1]
And her figure is trim[2]
And she hits[3] the right keys[4] at great speed[5].
(From English for Secretaries, Oxford University Press, 1978)

1 schlank 2 schmuck, adrett 3 treffen 4 Tasten 5 Geschwindigkeit

Sally Reed's secretary power

Sally Reed from Nottingham in the Midlands of England got the job. She settled in quickly and was soon dealing with the callers who phoned in almost every day, wanting to sell something or other.

As mentioned earlier the secretary can protect her boss. Very often it is necessary to screen incoming calls. The secretary can be extremely polite and positive. Nevertheless she is an obstacle to an unwanted outsider reaching her boss. Let's analyse a typical case. The salesperson, Andrew Dobson, wants to get an appointment with a boss. He has to get past the secretary.

Sally Reed, the secretary (**S**), Andrew Dobson (**D**)

S: Hello, this is Low Valley Photocopiers, can I help you?

D: Hello. Could I speak to Mr Stein, please?

S: Who's calling, please?

D: Andrew Dobson

(*The caller gives as little information as possible. He hopes the secretary will make an appointment perhaps thinking he is a friend. She might put him through immediately*).

S: From which company?

(*Obviously that strategy did not work. She does not recognise this name and therefore asks for more details*).

D: I'm from New Age Documentation.

(*The salesperson does not go into more detail. He still hopes the secretary will put him straight through*).

S: Can I ask what it concerns?

(*This secretary is a hard case. Now the sales person must show that his call is necessary or, at the very least, that it will not delay or inconvenience the boss*).

D: Yes, of course, I need to speak to Mr Stein for a couple of minutes about the range of manuals we produce. In fact, I just want to introduce myself and ask him a couple of questions about the manuals he normally uses. I'll only be a moment.

(*The salesperson does not "want" to speak to Mr Stein. He "needs" to. He also stresses that it will not take too much time. The secretary must decide if she can handle this matter. If she thinks it is not important enough she will fall back on the famous line ...:*)

S: I'm very sorry, Mr Stein is busy just at the moment. And he isn't to be disturbed. Maybe I can help you?

D: Well, actually I really needed to speak to Mr Stein personally. (*He tries again*).

S: I'm terribly sorry but his schedule is completely full. Perhaps you could write a letter.
(*The salesperson has more or less lost the battle*).

Vocabulary to help you with the dialogue and texts

appointment	Termin
approximately	circa, ungefähr
battle, lose a ~	Schlacht, eine ~ verlieren
call, take a ~	Anruf, einen ~ entgegennehmen
caller	Anrufer
case	Fall
Chamber of Commerce	Handelskammer
computer literate, be ~	Computererfahrung, ~ haben
concern	betreffen, gehen um
disturb s.o.	stören, jdn. ~
fall back on	zurückgreifen auf
famous	berühmt
go into detail	eingehen, auf Einzelheiten ~
handle a matter	erledigen, eine Sache ~
hard case	harter Fall
immediate	sofort
include	umfassen, beinhalten
inconvenience s.o.	jdm. Umstände machen
lose the battle	den Kampf verlieren
manual	Handbuch

medical insurance	Krankenversicherung
nevertheless	trotzdem
obstacle	Hindernis
obviously	offenbar
p.a. (per annum)	pro Jahr
pension	Pension, Rente
polite	höflich
put somebody through	verbinden, jemanden ~
recognise	erkennen
schedule	Zeitplan, Terminkalender
screen	abschirmen
senior management	Führungskräfte
settle in	einziehen in
stress	betonen
task	Aufgabe

✔ **EXERCISE 1: Memory test. Tick off the correct answers**

(More than one correct answer is possible)

1. *Which tasks are not mentioned in the advertisement?*
   - ☐ *dealing with correspondence in English and German*
   - ☐ *entertaining business friends*
   - ☐ *writing advertisements*
   - ☐ *managing the telephone in the two languages*
   - ☐ *arranging schedules and meetings for senior management*

2. *Why does Mr Dobson want to speak to Mr Stein?*
   - ☐ *he wants to buy a photocopier*
   - ☐ *he is applying for a job*
   - ☐ *he wants to sell him manuals*

Telephone Tactics: Identifying the caller and screening the boss

How to identify the caller	**Den Anrufer identifizieren**
May I have your name, please?	Dürfte ich Sie um Ihren Namen bitten?
Sorry, I didn't catch your name.	Entschuldigen Sie, ich habe Ihren Namen nicht verstanden.
Could I ask your name, please?	Darf ich Ihren Namen erfahren?
May I ask who is calling?	Darf ich um Ihren Namen bitten?
Who shall I say is calling?	Wen darf ich bitte melden?

Why are they calling?	**Der Grund des Anrufs**
What's the reason for your call?	Was ist der Grund Ihres Anrufs?
May I ask the purpose of your call?	Darf ich nach dem Zweck Ihres Anrufs fragen?
What's it in connection with?	Um was geht es bitte?
Who would you like to speak to?	Wen möchten Sie sprechen?
I'm not to put through any unidentified callers.	Ich darf keine anonymen Anrufer verbinden.

How to excuse the boss	**Den Chef entschuldigen**
I'm afraid he's very busy at present.	Ich fürchte, er ist gerade sehr beschäftigt.
He left strict instructions that he was not to be disturbed.	Er hat strenge Anweisung gegeben, nicht gestört zu werden.
I'll check if he can take the call.	Ich frage nach, ob er Ihren Anruf entgegennehmen kann.
He is out on business at the moment.	Er ist gerade geschäftlich unterwegs.
I suggest you try again tomorrow.	Ich schlage vor, Sie versuchen es morgen noch einmal.
Could his secretary help you?	Könnte Ihnen vielleicht seine Sekretärin weiterhelfen?

EXERCISE 2: The receptionist's hitlist of excuses

Here are nine frequently used excuses if the boss can't take a call. Can you complete them?

I'm afraid Mr Brain is not a . . . . able at the moment.
I'm sorry, but Mr Brain is on h . . . . . . this week.
I'm afraid she is o . . o . the office this week.
Mr Brain is away . . b . . . . . s s .
I'm sorry, Mr Brain is at a m . . . ing .
He left strict instructions not to be d . . . . d .
He's in the middle of an i . . . . w .
He has got an important v . . . . . r .
Dr. Brain is very . . . y at the moment.

EXERCISE 3: Translate the dialogue between secretary and client

R: Scheider, SIP Computers. Guten Tag.
A: Guten Tag. Verbinden Sie mich bitte mit dem *Leiter des Kundendiensts.* — *head of the customer service*
R: Wie war bitte Ihr Name?
A: Anton Sparbier. Ich bin ein *Stammkunde.* — *regular client*
R: Um was handelt es sich bitte?
A: Ich möchte Sie auf einen *Fehler* in einem ihrer neuen *Modelle* hinweisen. — *defect*, *model*
R: Einen Moment, ich verbinde.

Time for a smile

It was the annual general meeting[1] and the managing director was in the middle of his opening address[2] when the door opened and his secretary came in with a worried look[3] on her face. "Excuse me, sir," she whispered, "the chief accountant[4] wants to give his report. He's calling from the Bahamas."

1 Jahreshauptversammlung 2 Eröffnungsrede 3 besorgter Blick 4 Buchhalter

Tips for the Boss: How (not) to get on with the secretary

1. Never start work early in the morning – the secretary really prefers a terrific rush in the afternoon.
2. Please smoke when dictating; it helps pronunciation.
3. Hours for dictating: during the lunch hour or at any time between 4.30 and 5.30 p.m.
4. If work is required urgently (a most unusual occurrence) it helps if you rush in at intervals of 30 seconds to see if it is done.
5. When the secretary staggers out carrying a pile of files, please don't open the door for her. She has learned to open it with her teeth or crawl under it.

Tips for the Secretary: How to handle the boss

She's not a department in the company. Maybe she's every department. She's almost certainly in every department. Exactly what is a secretary? This can be best summarised by the comment that "the more effective the secretary, the more productive her boss". She deals with the routine and administrative matters. A true PA helps her boss to concentrate on his proper job. What does this include? What should she do?

- organise the day of her boss so well that he can make the best use of his working day;
- set his priorities, but not in a bossy way;
- deputise for him and handle his problems in a sensible way when he is out of town;
- screen him from unnecessary callers and problems;
- act as a valve when he is under pressure.

Of course, every secretary knows that she must get along with her boss. And the clever secretary can identify the "boss stereotypes". When she can identify the type, she can deal with his strange habits more easily. The astute secretary has identified the following stereotypes. Here's some advice:

The workaholic

Never allow yourself to become upset by workaholics. They experience a perverse pleasure in pushing things along at their crazy pace. Work peacefully in a relaxed way. Even they should appreciate your calming influence.

The "arroganto"

Some bosses can be arrogant because everybody bows and scrapes to the "bossman". So don't be rude to him, and never creep around this sort of boss. All you can do is be efficient and keep smiling.

The "superior"

This sort of person will frustrate you because he will treat you as if you have no brain. When you feel yourself beginning to burn because of his attitude, just keep your sense of humour. But be totally reliable and efficient. In the course of time this boss will soften towards you.

In this way you will gradually become "better than your boss".
(Adapted from S. Tomkins: The Secretary's Survival Manual. Kogan Page, London)

EXERCISE 4: Complete the Joke

The telephone rings. Dr. Rope's secretary answers the phone[1].

Sec: It's your wife, Dr. Rope. Are you going to t . . e the c . . l[2]?

Rope: Oh no, not now. Tell her that I've got a v . . . . . r and that I'll be home late from the office because of an unexpected[3] conference. (Smiling) You know what I mean, don't you?
(The secretary does as she is told and hangs up[4].)

Rope: How did my wife react? Was she very angry?

Sec: Not at all[5]. She only wanted to know if she could absolutely rely on[6] your coming home late.

1 den Hörer abnehmen 2 den Anruf entgegennehmen 3 unerwartet 4 auflegen 5 keineswegs 6 sich verlassen auf

Vocabulary to help you with the text

administrative matters	Verwaltungsangelegenheiten
appreciate	schätzen, zu ~ wissen
astute	schlau
attitude	Einstellung, Haltung
bossy	herrisch
bow and scrape	katzbuckeln und kriechen
crawl	kriechen
creep around	herumschleichen
deputise	vertreten
file	Aktenordner
gradually	allmählich
occurrence	Ereignis
p.a.	persönlicher Vorstands-Assistent
pace	Tempo
pile	Stapel
pressure	Druck, Streß
priorities, set ~	Prioritäten setzen
pronunciation	Aussprache
push things along	etwas vorantreiben
reliable	zuverlässig
rush	Hetze, hereinstürzen
sensible	vernünftig
soften towards s.o.	weich werden, sich erweichen
stagger out	hinaustaumeln
summarise	zusammenfassen
treat s.o. badly	jdn. schlecht behandeln
upset	aufgeregt
urgent, urgently (adverb)	dringend
use, make ~ of	Gebrauch machen von
valve	Ventil

In the purchasing department

CONTENTS

Time for a smile

Two bosses met in a bank one morning to conclude their business[1] when a gang of masked men burst in[2]. Their leader shouted, "This is a hold up! We want all the money in the safe – and you people, empty[3] your pockets and hand over your wallets[4]!"
One of the bosses whispered[5] to the other, "Jim – you know that I owe[6] you $ 5000. Well, here's the money, take it!"

1 ein Geschäft abschließen 2 hereinstürmen 3 leeren 4 Brieftaschen 5 flüstern 6 schulden

Buy it but buy it cheaper

James' next port of call is the purchasing department. The staff here deal with buying the components and subassemblies from external suppliers. These parts are then further manufactured and assembled into copiers at the factory in Kleindorf. The chief buyer is Herr Stumpf.

James Kelly (**K**), Sally Reed (**S**), Mr Reitbaier (**R**)

K: Hi, my name's James Kelly. I've heard you're from England.

S: Yes, from Nottingham originally. I'm Sally Reed. I finished working there three months ago.

K: How long have you been here at the centre of the world?

S: About ten weeks. It was a bit difficult at first but I'm getting used to living here now.

K: Well, what sort of problems have you been having exactly?

S: What I don't understand is why so many people keep telling me that everything here is better than everywhere else. I dislike hearing that sort of thing.

K: Oh, don't worry about that! They're not all like that. There are some friendly ones as well. Tell me, what happens here in general in the purchasing department? I'm joining a meeting with a supplier later this week.

S: Basically there are twenty clerks here, each one taking care of a field of purchasing.

K: What exactly do they buy?

S: All the parts to be assembled into photocopiers. Electronic parts for the control system, the frames of the copiers, plastic parts, packing materials for the copier. They have a purchasing budget of more than sixty million. It's very responsible work. They also purchase parts that are produced within the company here.

K: Yes, I've heard something about that. There's a big discussion about "make" or "buy" here at the moment.

S: Yes, the company has to decide whether it's cheaper to buy most parts from suppliers. The problem seems to be to maintain the quality if they use external suppliers.

K: If they start outsourcing surely a lot of people employed here will risk losing their jobs,won't they?

S: Of course, that's the big question mark. Ha, here comes Mr Reitbaier. He'll be able to tell you more.

R: Hello, my name's Reitbaier. You must be Mr Kelly? How are you?

K: Fine thanks. I was just asking about how your department works.

R: Oh, I see. In a nutshell we get an order from the director of the plant to order something he needs from a supplier, internal or external. Our boss, Mr Stumpf delegates the task to the responsible clerk. He or she then contacts likely suppliers who are asked to give us a quote for the parts. We check these offers, look at the production facilities of the supplier and then come together for a price negotiation. Sometimes the results are reported to Mr Stumpf to get his okay. If he's not satisfied he will call the supplier for another discussion. Sometimes suppliers even try to delay sending the components as a weapon against us.

K: So, the work is actually done twice. Does he ever get better conditions?

R: Very frequently.

K: Well, this is a case of the employees really not being better than their boss then?

R: Yes, and be careful with him. He's as sharp as his name is blunt, as it were. Ha, ha. Just my shining sense of humour.

EXERCISE 1: Memory test. Tick off the correct answers

1. *Which parts are assembled into photocopiers?*

☐ *frames*
☐ *plastic parts*
☐ *wheels*

2. *Outsourcing means*

☐ *producing all parts in the company.*
☐ *buying from external suppliers.*
☐ *maintaining the quality*

3. *Suppliers delay sending the components*

☐ *to get better conditions*
☐ *to negotiate directly with Mr Stumpf*
☐ *because they wait until Mr Stumpf gives his okay*

Vocabulary to help you through the dialogue

assemble	zusammenbauen
basically	im Grunde genommen
blunt	stumpf
chief buyer	Einkaufsleiter
components	Komponenten
control system	Steuerung
delay	verschieben, verzögern
frame	Gestell, Rahmen
frequently	häufig
get used to (+ gerund) to sth.	sich an etwas gewöhnen
likely suppliers	mögliche, potentielle Lieferanten
negotiation	Verhandlung
nutshell, in a ~	kurz gesagt
okay, get an ~	grünes Licht bekommen
originally	ursprünglich
outsource	Produktion von Teilen an Fremdfirmen vergeben
packing	Verpackung
production facilities	Produktionseinrichtungen
purchasing	Einkauf
question mark	Fragezeichen
quotation, give a ~	Preisangebot, ein ~ machen
responsible clerk	zuständiger Sachbearbeiter
subassembly	Baugruppe
supplier	Lieferant
take care of	betreuen
weapon	Waffe

EXERCISE 2: Test your memory again.

What are the exact terms for the following definitions?

head of the purchasing department	c . . . . b . . . .
elements or parts of a photocopier	c . . . .
company you buy your parts from	s . . . .
put the parts of a copier together	a . . . .
it keeps the parts of the copier together	f . . . .
it ensures that all parts work properly	c . . . . . . s . . . . .
guns, pistols and knives are ...	w . . . . . s

EXERCISE 3: Let's repeat tense and aspect

A. Here are a few sentences taken from the dialogue. Put the verb in brackets into the right form.

1. It was a bit difficult at first but I (*get*) used to living here now.
2. Well, what sort of problems you (*have*) recently?
3. I (*join*) a meeting with a supplier later this week.
4. I (*finish*) working there two months ago.

B. Und nun fügen Sie bitte die richtige Satznummer in die folgenden Behauptungen ein:

Satz Nummer ...... bezieht sich auf die Zukunft.
Satz Nummer ...... bezieht sich auf die Gegenwart.
Satz Nummer ...... bezieht sich auf den Zeitraum bis zur Gegenwart.
Satz Nummer ...... bezieht sich auf die Vergangenheit.

C. Ergänzen Sie zum Schluß zwei if-Sätze aus dem Gespräch:

1. If they start outsourcing surely a lot of people employed here (*risk*) losing their jobs.
2. If he (*be*) not satisfied he will call the supplier for another discussion.

Grammar Rhymes

Das Gerund – die andere "ing-Form"

1. Formen

An die Grundform hänge man
Einfach *ing* als Silbe an.
Je nachdem wie wir die Handlung sehen,
Kann es im Aktiv oder Passiv stehen.

Form: learn + ing = learning
Passiv: Being married to a woman means
Aktiv: *seeing* her in the morning instead[1] of in the evening.

2. Häufigkeit und Stellung des Gerunds

Sehr oft nimmt Gerund im Satz
Nach Verhältniswörtern[2] Platz.

"Do you have trouble[3] *in* making up your mind[4]?"
"Well, yes and no."

3. Funktionen des Gerunds

Im Satz kann es die Aufgaben
Von Hauptwort und von Zeitwort haben,
Als Satzteil kann es obendrein
Mal Subjekt und mal Objekt sein

Planning means replacing[5] chance by error[6].
Credit cards have made *buying* easier but *paying* harder.

1 anstatt 2 Präpositionen 3 Schwierigkeiten haben 4 sich entscheiden 5 ersetzen 6 Irrtum

Grammar Rhymes and Grammar Jokes

Das Gerund verwenden wir
Nach dieser Verbengruppe hier:

enjoy, reject[1], keep on,
escape, delay, postpone[2],
consider, finish, justify[3]
imagine, give up und deny[4],
appreciate[5], avoid[6] und miss,
mention, mind, admit, practise.
Auch fancy[7], dislike und include
Sind immer für ein Gerund gut.

EXERCISE 4: Gerund oder kein Gerund? Aber was dann?

A. Put the verb in brackets into the right form

❶ Leave the most difficult problems for the laziest managers[8] (*solve*). They will come up with the quickest solutions.

❷ No wife minds her husband (*be*) a dreamer as long as he isn't a snorer[9].

❸ Nothing is illegal if 100 businessmen decide (*do*) it.

❹ Sometimes I think that God in (*create*) man somewhat overestimated[10] his ability. (Oscar Wilde)

❺ I dislike (*feel*) at home when I am abroad[11]. (George Bernhard Shaw)

B. Do you remember these sentences from our story?

1. I finished (*work*) there two months ago.
2. I dislike (*hear*) that sort of thing.
3. What I don't understand is why so many people keep (*tell*) me that everything here is better than everywhere else.
4. Sometimes suppliers even try (*delay*) (*send*) the components as a weapon against us.

1 zurückweisen 2 aufschieben 3 rechtfertigen 4 leugnen 5 schätzen 6 vermeiden 7 gerne mögen 8 der faulste Manager 9 Schnarcher 10 überschätzen 11 im Ausland

Business Words used in the purchasing department

Angebot, ein ~ abgeben	*tender, to make a ~*
Bedingungen festlegen	*lay down terms*
Entlassung	*lay-off*
Garantie, Gewährleistung	*guarantee, warrantee*
Geschäftsbedingungen	*terms of business*
Güter, Artikel	*goods*
Kostenvoranschlag machen	*give an estimate*
Lagerbestand	*stock level*
Lagerkontrolle	*stock control*
Lieferbedingungen	*delivery conditions*
Lieferzeit	*delivery period*
Markenartikel	*brand name*
Materialkosten	*material cost*
Preisangebot machen	*submit a quotation*
Produktionsstillstand	*production stoppage*
Rabatt	*discount*
schriftlich	*in writing*
sofortige Lieferung	*prompt delivery*
Spezifizierung, Spezifikation	*specification*
Stückkosten	*cost per item*
Stückpreis	*price per item*
übliche Bedingungen	*standard conditions*
Verhandlung, eine ~ führen	*negotiation, lead a ~*
Warenzeichen, Handelsmarke	*trade mark*
Zahlungsbedingungen	*terms of payment*
Zusicherung, vertragliche ~	*warranty*

EXERCISE 5: The ABC of our business words

put the parts of a copier together	*a . . . .*
something like a trade mark	*b . . . . n . . .*
parts of a machine	*c . . . . s*
time you have to wait for the goods	*d . . . . p . . . . d*

EXERCISE 6: What are negotiations about?

You fix...

- **g . . . . e**
- **d . . . . . . t**
- **terms of p . . . . . t**
- **t . . . . of business**
- **d . . . . conditions**
- **p . . . . p . . item**

EXERCISE 7: What's the right verb?

to l . . .	*a negotiation*
to s . . . . t	*a quotation*
to m . . .	*a tender*
to l . . down	*terms*

EXERCISE 8: Let's 'assemble' a limerick

In this limerick there is one gerund in the passive and one infinitive; all the other verbs are in the simple past:

There (*be*) a young lady of Leek
Who (*have*) fifty proposals[1] a week.
Though she never (*grow*) tired
Of (*admire*),
She (*be*) often too sleepy (*speak*).

Business Culture

To err is human – and in case of error you have to apologise. Here is a message pad[2] with a variety of excuses to choose from.

The Official Office Excuse Pad

☐ I was too busy	☐ Nobody told me
☐ I didn't know	☐ I thought that you knew
☐ I forgot	☐ I didn't know it was important
☐ It's not my job	☐ I thought someone else was doing it

MESSAGE

From:

1 Heiratsantrag 2 Block

The language of meetings

CONTENTS

Let's start with a smile

Parkinson's Law of Triviality:
The time spent on any item of the agenda[1] will be in inverse proportion[2] to the sum involved[3].

The chairperson was pretty smug[4];
He slapped[5] his brief and cried "Hey presto[6]!"
Then missed his footing[7], slipped and fell
And wrecked his entire manifesto[8].

1 Punkt auf der Tagesordnung 2 im umgekehrten Verhältnis 3 die Geldsumme, um die es geht 4 geschniegelt, blasiert 5 (hin)klatschen 6 Simsalabim 7 den Halt verlieren 8 Programm, Rede

Meet them on their own terms

In a typical company there are indeed a large number of meetings. Some people would say far too many. If you have to go to a meeting it should be prepared in advance. You should keep to the points on the agenda and it is very important to arrive on time. It is disrespectful of others to turn up late, unless there is a very good reason. The following meeting takes place at Low Valley Photocopiers in the purchasing department. Our hero, James Kelly, is present, too.

Mr Stumpf (**S**), James Kelly (**K**), Mr Reitbaier (**R**), Mr Maiser (**M**), supplier of components

S: Well, I'm happy to welcome all of you here today to our meeting on quantities and prices for the plastic guards for our copiers. Mr Maiser, may I introduce Mr Kelly from England? He's learning the art of negotiation with us. Mr Reitbaier seems to have been held up by an act of God or something. Can I apologise for him being late?

R: (*with red face, puffing*). Sorry, I'm late. I was kept at another appointment.

S: Well, when I began at the company punctuality used to be a virtue! Now, perhaps we could begin.

M: As Mr Reitbaier will verify we've already fixed the quotations for the guards for next year and the cost per item. And as far as I know all quality standards have been met for this part.

R: Well, there were one or two questions concerning the quality ...

S: If I could just break in a moment here, gentlemen, I'm afraid this is all a bit too quick for me. Could we talk about the quantities first?

M: Yes, the requirement for next year is only 3,300. As you will appreciate this is hardly enough to justify any bigger discount than the three per cent we discussed last week.

S: I think it's not quite as simple as that, Mr Maiser. What we are giving you is a guarantee to purchase or place orders with you for the next three years. In other words "stability". That's worth a reduction of five per cent. Let's call it a stability discount, shall we?

M: Well, we also have our overheads in the company, you know and they are rising all the time.

R: With all respect, Mr Maiser, your overheads would be the same with or without our order for the guards.

S: Of course. In fact, with our order we are reducing your fixed costs. Now if nobody objects I'd like to return to the question of quality. That's point two on my list. Mr Reitbaier, would you care to fill us in on the background concerning our incoming goods quality inspection?

(*One hour later in the coffee break*)

R: Well, old Stumpf was certainly in form today. I wouldn't like to be in the supplier's shoes.

K: You've hit the nail on the head there. There's no question of trying to be better than the boss in his department. He's really on top of the job of purchasing.

Vocabulary to help you through the dialogue

act of God	höhere Gewalt
appreciate, as you will ~	verstehen, Sie werden ~
art of negotiation	Kunst der Verhandlung
be on top of one's job	sein Geschäft verstehen
break in	unterbrechen
concern	betreffen
disrespectful	unhöflich, respektlos
fill in on	aufklären, unterrichten über
fixed costs	Fixkosten
guard	Schutz
hardly	kaum
hold up, be held up	aufhalten, aufgehalten werden
hit the nail on the head	den Nagel auf den Kopf treffen
I wouldn't like to be in his shoes	ich möchte nicht in seiner Haut stecken
in advance	im voraus
incoming goods, goods inward	eingehende Waren, Wareneingang
justify	rechtfertigen

meet standards	Normen erfüllen
object	Einwand erheben
overheads	allgemeine Betriebskosten
part	Teil
place an order	bestellen
puff	schnaufen
quality inspection	Qualitätsprüfung
quantities	Mengen
requirement	Bedarf, Anforderung
terms, on their own ~	Bedingungen, zu ihren ~
verify	überprüfen
virtue	Tugend

EXERCISE 1: Memory test. Tick off the correct answers

1. Mr Reitbaier is late because

- ☐ *he was held up by an act of God*
- ☐ *he was kept at another appointment*
- ☐ *punctuality is no longer a virtue at the company*

2. Mr Stumpf asks for a higher discount because

- ☐ *he is dissatisfied with the quality*
- ☐ *he is placing orders for the next three years*
- ☐ *the price per item is too high*

3. Kelly thinks that Mr Stumpf

- ☐ *has hit the nail on the head*
- ☐ *was in bad form on that day*
- ☐ *is on top of his job*

Speech functions: The language of meetings

Starting the meeting	
I'd like to begin by ...	Ich würde gerne mit ... anfangen.
I'd like to mention briefly ...	Ich möchte kurz erwähnen, ...
There are some points I'd like to make.	Ich würde gerne einiges klarstellen.

Introducing a new point	
I'd now like to move to another matter.	Ich würde jetzt gerne zu einem anderen Thema übergehen.
I want to turn to the problem of ...	Ich würde mich gerne dem Problem ... zuwenden.
The next matter I'd like to discuss is ...	Die nächste Angelegenheit, die ich gerne besprechen würde, ist ...

Adding something extra	
In addition, I'd like to ...	Zusätzlich würde ich gerne ...
Here one might add that ...	An dieser Stelle könnte man noch anfügen, daß ...
On the other hand ...	Andererseits ...
Moreover ...	Darüber hinaus ...

Giving an example	
Let me give you an example.	Darf ich Ihnen ein Beispiel geben?
To illustrate this point I'd like to ...	Um diesen Punkt zu veranschaulichen, würde ich gerne ...
A typical case of this sort is ...	Ein typischer Fall, der ähnlich gelagert ist, wäre ...

Making a general point	
On the whole ...	Im großen und ganzen ...
Generally speaking ...	Im allgemeinen kann man sagen ...
All in all ...	Alles in allem ...

Concluding the meeting

I'd like to call it a day now.	Lassen wir es für heute genug sein.
Let me conclude by saying ...	Lassen Sie mich mit diesen Worten schließen ...
In conclusion I would like to say ...	Zum Abschluß möchte ich sagen ...
Finally it is time to ...	Es ist nun an der Zeit, zu ...
I'd now like to bring this meeting to an end by saying that ...	Ich würde diese Konferenz nun gerne mit den Worten schließen ...

Exercise 2: Verbs that go with "meeting"

planen, leiten, vorbereiten, kontrollieren, teilnehmen, beenden

Meetings are

pre . . . ed

m . . . . . . ed

pl . . . ed

con . . . . . ed

at . . . . ed

ch . . red

They might come in handy – sie könnten nützlich sein

You need...

- **overhead projector**
- **trans-parencies**
- **slides**
- **white-board**
- **video recorder**
- **flipchart**

"Meetings, Bloody Meetings"

(The following scene has been taken from Meetings, Bloody Meetings, Video Art Books, an excellent management training video by and with John Cleese, one of Britain's greatest comedians – a video that should be on the shelves of all company training centres).

Being at cross purposes

Tim: Right. Everyone got the agenda? Item One. Improving company communications. I think we all understand the problem. Ron?
Ron: It's a problem all right. It'll cost a lot of money to solve it.
Jack: You mean staff costs?
Ron: No, not staff. Equipment.
Tim: Surely it's management time at the root of it?
Ron: No. Equipment. At least six more video display units.
Tim: What?
Ron: Well, if you want Sales and Accounts to have direct access to data, the...
Tim: Look, Ron, we may be able to deal with this later or if there's time, but can we take Item One now?

Ron: I am taking Item One. Improving company communications.
Jack: No, no, Ron, it's not the computer, it's the telephones. Look, every time we try to get through down there, they're engaged.
Tim: No it isn't.
Ron: What?
Tim: I'm talking about the staff briefing sessions. How we brief the staff on this year's company results.
Jack: The company results? I thought you wanted an automated switchboard. You know the hold-ups we've been having down there.
Tim: Look, I'm talking about company communications.
Ron: So am I.
Jack: So am I. How can we communicate if the phone's always busy?
Tim: Look, the whole point of this is to get ideas on how to brief staff on this year's company results.
Ian: Well, why didn't you say so?
Tim: I mean hasn't anyone done any thinking about this ...?

Vocabulary to help you with the text

agenda	Tagesordnung
at the root	im Grund, letztlich
automated switchboard	vollautomatische Telefonanlage
brief s.o.	jdn. informieren
busy, the phone is ~	das Telefon ist besetzt
company communications	Kommunikation innerhalb der Firma
cross purposes, be at ~	aneinander vorbeireden
direct access	direkter Zugang
engaged, the line is ~	besetzt, die Leitung ist belegt

equipment	Gerät, Ausrüstung
improve	verbessern
item one	Punkt eins
staff briefing session	Personalbesprechung
staff costs	Personalkosten
video display units	Bildschirme

Business Culture: Five rules

Having served on various committees I have drawn up a list of rules:

- Never arrive on time: this stamps[1] you as a beginner.
- Don't say anything until the meeting is half over: this stamps you as wise.
- Be as vague as possible: this avoids[2] irritating the others[3].
- When in doubt[4], suggest a subcommittee be appointed[5].
- Be the first to move for adjournment[6]: this will make you popular[7] – it's what everyone is waiting for.

  Harry Chapmas

Time for a smile

The managing director of a big manufacturing company was well-known for his dominating[8] way of handling meetings[9]. At the end of a meeting he used to[10] look round and say: "Let's have a vote[11] and call it a day. All those who are against my suggestions raise[12] their hands and say: I resign[13]".

1 abstempeln 2 vermeiden 3 die anderen verärgern 4 im Zweifelsfall 5 einen Unterausschuß ernennen 6 Vertagung beantragen 7 beliebt 8 herrische Art 9 Konferenzen führen 10 er pflegte 11 stimmen wir ab 12 die Hand heben 13 ich trete zurück, ich kündige

Checklist: How to plan meetings

Before the meeting

- Is the meeting really necessary?
- What are the objectives[1] of the meeting?
- Who is needed to ensure[2] that these objectives are achieved[3]?
- What will the pay-off from achieving the objectives be?
- What will the meeting cost?
- What equipment[4] is needed for the meeting?
- If an agenda[5] is required[6], has it been prepared and distributed[7]?

The first questions in the meeting

- Are all the participants[8] clear about the start time and location of the meeting?
- Have attendees[8] received all the relevant background information?
- Do all the participants need to be present for the whole meeting?

After the meeting

- How much did the meeting cost?
- Were the costs of attending a meeting greater than the benefits[9] gained?
- How many meetings were delayed because of latecomers?
- Did the meetings often last longer than expected?
- Did I make worthwhile contributions[10] to the meeting?
- Did other participants make worthwhile contribution?
- Did the meetings tend to[11] wander away from the agenda?
- Were decisions taken during the meeting followed up[12]?

1 Ziele 2 gewährleisten 3 (Ziel) erreichen 4 Ausrüstung 5 Tagesordnung 6 erforderlich sein 7 verteilen 8 Teilnehmer 9 Vorteile 10 lohnende Beiträge 11 neigen zu 12 nachbereiten

Chapter 17

Made in Germany

CONTENTS

Business Frame:	**At the quality control department**
Grammar Rhymes:	**Indirect speech**
Grammar Jokes:	**Let's practise indirect speech**
Business Words:	**Extra vocabulary for quality control**
Plus:	**Jokes and useful exercises**

Let's start with a smile

Mr Groß, the head of Quality Control, was not satisfied[1] with the quality of their photocopiers. So he called a meeting of the works staff. "We've got to improve[2] efficiency," he said. "We've got to work harder. From now on, whenever I come down to the factory floor, I want to see every man hard at work. I'm installing a Suggestions Box[3] and if anyone has any ideas as to how to improve quality, will he please put them in the box." The next day there was just one suggestion in the box. It read: "Take the rubber heels[4] off your shoes."

1 zufrieden 2 verbessern 3 Briefkasten für Verbesserungsvorschläge 4 Gummiabsätze

At the quality control department

After a pleasant six weeks in purchasing, James moves over to the quality control department. The people working there are responsible for checking to see if the quality is good enough on both the suppliers' parts and parts manufactured internally. Mr Groß is explaining some of the activities in quality control.

Mr Groß (**G**) head of QC, James Kelly (**K**)

G: So you see we have to ensure that all these parts and components come up to the required standard.

K: How can you be sure that a part meets requirements?

G: Well, we've got several ways of testing using computer systems nowadays. Quality control is based on the idea that in mass production no two units are identical but that it is possible to mass-produce almost identical units. We can do this at least within certain tolerances. A customer can accept his product within these tolerances but not outside them.

K: So quality control sets the standards which are acceptable to the customers? But it seems to me that these QC activities could be very costly indeed. They're very time-intensive, aren't they?

G: In fact, you're right. We're an extra overhead in the production department but we're necessary. We'd like our suppliers to carry out all quality inspections for us but they don't seem to be able to do it.

K: Yes, I noticed that. I was at a meeting with a supplier last week and there were problems about quality. I was surprised since everybody's always telling me there are no problems with quality in Germany. It's no different than anywhere else.

G: Don't say things like that! That will be considered as high treason. Can you remember who the supplier was and what he said?

K: Yes, it was Mr Maiser. He was of the opinion that the department had accepted the quotations for the guards and that his company had met the quality standards required.

G: And what was Mr Stumpf's reply to that?

K: Well, he said he wanted to postpone the question of quality and preferred to discuss prices. He mentioned that things weren't quite clear for him.

G: Yes, I can imagine things weren't clear. In fact, I explained to Mr Stumpf two days ago that the quality wasn't up to specs on the guards. I showed him that the tolerances weren't narrow enough.

K: So your departments actually work close together, as I see.

G: Especially at the higher levels. Of course, the top men like to compete with each other to see who's the better boss. But it doesn't matter. A little competition is a healthy thing.

Vocabulary to help you with the dialogue

at least	wenigstens
check quality	überprüfen, die Qualität ~
compete with	rivalisieren
competition	Wettbewerb
component	Bauelement
ensure	sicherstellen, gewährleisten
high treason	Hochverrat
mass production	Serienproduktion
mass-produce	in Serie herstellen
matter, it doesn't matter	ausmachen, es macht nichts
meet requirements	erfüllen, Anforderungen ~
narrow	eng
opinion, be of the ~	Meinung, der ~ sein
overheads	Betriebskosten
postpone	verschieben
quality inspection	Qualitätsprüfung
quality control department (QC)	Abteilung für Qualitätskontrolle
quotation	Kostenvoranschlag
required standards	geforderte Normen
requirements	Anforderungen
set standards	bestimmen, Normen ~
specs, be up to ~	Spezifikationen, den ~ entsprechen
standards, up to ~	Anforderungen, den ~ genügen
supplier	Lieferant
tolerance	Toleranz
unit	Einheit

✔ EXERCISE 1: Memory test. Tick off the right answers

Sometimes there are two correct answers

1. *Quality control*

- ☐ *sets standards for the customer*
- ☐ *sets standards for the supplier*
- ☐ *sets standards for their own production*

2. *According to Mr Groß, mass-produced components*

- ☐ *must be identical*
- ☐ *are never identical*
- ☐ *differ from each other within acceptable tolerances*

3. *Mr Stumpf did not want to discuss the question of quality because*

- ☐ *the question of prices was more important*
- ☐ *the specifications were not quite clear to him*
- ☐ *the components did not meet the required standards*

EXERCISE 2: Do you remember these abbreviations?

QC	....	Qualitätskontrolle
CV	....	Lebenslauf
PC	....	Persönlicher Computer
USP	....	konkurrenzloses Verkaufsargument
fob	....	frei an Bord

EXERCISE 3: Guess what I mean?

(The first one has been done for you)

man who sells you the components you need	*supplier*
you get it when you assemble the components	*u . . .*
to deal with a question at a later date	*. . . . . one*
manufacture in large quantities	*. . . . – . . . . . ce*
the costs of running a company	*. . . . . . . ds*

Grammar Rhymes

Indirect speech

Indirect speech ist zum Erzählen,
Was andre sagen, fragen und befehlen.

Aussagesätze A patient tells his doctor (that) he often feels like killing himself ...

Fragesätze ... and he asks him what to do (what he should do).

Befehlssätze The doctor told the man to leave that problem to him.

Indirekte Aussagesätze nach Verben
des Sagens, Denkens oder Schreibens:

Vor der indirekten Rede steht
Das Vorschaltverb mit oder ohne *that*.
Vorschaltverben sind zum Beispiel
tell, think, write, know, hope und feel.

Some East-Friesians[1] still *think that* a transistor is a priest[2]
who likes wearing women's clothes.

1. Das Vorschaltverb steht im Präsens oder Perfekt

Steht im Präsens oder Perfekt der Bericht,
Ändern sich die Zeiten nicht.
Nur die Pronomen gleiche man
Dem Standpunkt des Erzählers an.

So wird es gesagt:	So wird es berichtet:
I can't find my glasses.	He says *he* can't find *his* glasses

2. Das Vorschaltverb steht in der Vergangenheit

Bericht in der Vergangenheit
Ändert auch beim Verb die Zeit.

1 Ostfriese 2 Pfarrer

Grammar Rhymes

Das hat Prof. Farnart gesagt:	**So wurde es berichtet:**
"Today, I *have performed* my first appendix transplant."	He *said* yesterday that he had *performed* his first appendix transplant.

Inscription on a tombstone[1] of a hypochondriac[2]:
"See – I *told* you (that) I *was* ill."

Direkte Rede		**Indirekte Rede**	
present	"I'*m* ill."	past	He *told* us he *was* ill
present perfect	"I'*ve been* ill."	past perfect	He *told* us he *had been* ill before.
past	"I *was ill* that day."	past prefect	He told us he *had been* ill that day.

Entsprechendes gilt für die Verlaufsformen der Zeiten.

Bei den Hilfsverben ändern wir
Die Zeiten lediglich bei vier:

Direct speech	***Indirect speech***
I *cannot* come	He said he *could not* come
What *shall* I do?	He didn't know what he *should* do.
It *will* rain tonight.	He said it *would* rain that evening.
May I leave earlier?	He asked if he *might* leave earlier.

Auch Ort und Zeit passe man
Der Perspektive des Erzählers an.

Direct speech	***Indirect speech***	***Direct speech***	***Indirect speech***
today	the following day	now	then
tomorrow	the next day	one week ago	one week before
here	there	yesterday	the day before

1 Grabstein 2 Hypochonder

Grammar Jokes

EXERCISE 4:

A. Put the verbs in brackets into the correct tense

❶ He has just been elected salesman of the year. In Africa he sold sheets of sandpaper to tourists for $ 10 each. He (*tell*) them that it (*be*) a map[1] of the Sahara.

❷ There was a young lady of Kent
Who (*say*) that she (*know*) what it meant
When men asked her to dine
Upon lobster[2] and wine.
She knew! Oh, she knew! But she went.

❸ There was an old man of Peru
Who (*dream*[3]) he (*be eating*) his shoe.
He awoke in the night
With a terrible fright[4]
And found it was perfectly true.

❹ When I was young I (*think*) that money (*be*) the most important thing in life. Now that I am old I (*know*) that it (*be*). Oscar Wilde

❺ A worried father asked his daughter about her first sex lesson at school. He was hoping that the teacher (*not/go*) too far. The girl replied with an innocent[5] smile that the first lesson (*be*) quite useless because they had only done the theory.

B. Now try to complete these lines from our dialogue

1. K: He was of the opinion that he (*agree*) quotations for the guards and that his company (*meet*) the quality standards required.
2. K: Well, he (*say*) he (*want*) to postpone the question of quality. He (*mention*) that things (*not / be*) quite clear for him.
3. G: In fact I (*explain*) to Mr Stumpf two days ago that the quality (*not / be*) up to specs on the guards.

1 Landkarte 2 Hummer 3 Traum 4 Angst, Furcht 5 unschuldig

Grammar Rhymes

Indirekte Fragesätze

"Weißt du, ob ...?" "Kannst du mir sagen ...?"
So beginnen indirekte Fragen.

So wurde gefragt:	So wurde berichtet:
"Do you *drink* whisky?" "Well, what else *can* you do with whisky?"	He *asked* me *if* I *drank* whisky. I *wondered what* else one *could* do with whisky.

Für die Zeiten gelten die Regeln der indirekten Aussagesätze

Dem Verb des Fragens füg hinzu
Ein Fragewort wie *what, why, who.*
Und fehlt ein Fragewort im Satz,
Nimmt *if* und *whether* deren Platz.
if, whether = ob

Indirekte Befehlssätze

Struktur 1: Infinitiv + to	
"Don't believe in miracles. Rely on them." (Finagle's rule, Murphy's laws)	Finagle *tells* students *not to believe* in miracles. He *advises them to rely* on them.

Struktur 2: (that) + should	
Graffiti: Visitor, *try* the famous echo in the German Bundestag.	A graffiti *suggested that* tourists *should try* the famous echo in the German Bundestag.

Ronny: How did you have this terrible accident, Bob?
Bob: Well, the driving instructor *told me to look and listen.* And while I did, the train hit me.

Grammar Jokes

EXERCISE 5: Put the verbs in brackets into correct tense:

❶ The ecologists want us (*say*) no to fast breeders[1], because the only safe fast breeder is a rabbit[2].

❷ Mark Twain was asked what he (*think*) about Heaven and Hell[3]. He replied that didn't want to express an opinion because he had friends in both places.

❸ A diplomat is a man who can tell you (*go*) to hell in such a way that you actually look forward to the trip.

❹ For a while we pondered whether (*take*) a vacation[4] or get a divorce[5]. We decided that a trip to Bermuda would be over in two weeks but a divorce is something you always have.
Woody Allen

Extra vocabulary for quality control

ablehnen, zurückweisen	*reject*
Abweichung	*deviation*
Altmaterial, Schrott	*scrap*
Ausschußware	*reject*
Ersatzteillager	*central stock, component centre*
Fließbandfertigung	*assembly line work*
Handarbeit	*manual work*
Kontrolle	*check*
Kontrolleur, Prüfer	*inspector*
Meßinstrument	*measuring instrument*
Muster, Probe, Warenprobe	*sample*
Prüfbank	*test bench*
Prüfbericht	*test report*
prüfen, Werkstücke ~	*test workpieces*

1 schneller Brüter 2 Kaninchen 3 Hölle 4 Urlaub 5 Scheidung

Prüfingenieur	*testing engineer*
Prüfstand	*test stand,*
Serie, Stapel, Stoß	*batch*
Serienfertigung	*serial production*
ständige Stichproben	*continuous sampling*
Stapelverarbeitung	*batch-processing*
Stichprobe	*random sample*
Überarbeitung	*re-working*
verschrotten	*scrap*

EXERCISE 6: Words that have almost the same meaning

control	**. . . ck**
component centre	**central . . . . .**
test stand	**test . . . . .**
serial production	**m . . . p . . . . on**

EXERCISE 7: Words around test

	test	
. . . . d	**. . . . ch**	**. . . ort**

EXERCISE 8: Do you know what I mean?

samples that do not meet the standards . . . .
parts that are thrown away . . . .
person who tests the quality of a batch . . . .
deviation that is acceptable . . . .

Time for a smile

Lord Grey had ordered a new suit[1] for a banquet at Buckingham Palace. After three weeks he phoned the tailor[2] to ask when his suit would be ready. "In six weeks, sir," replied the tailor. "Six weeks! I really can't accept that!" shouted Lord Grey. "It took only six days to make the whole world." – "Yes, indeed, sir – but have you noticed the shape[3] it is in?"

1 Anzug 2 Schneider 3 Zustand

Limericks for the office:

Mister Gray loves his secretary dearly[1],
So one day he dictated quite clearly:
"We make a good pair,
Let us have an affair."

I've given the job to Miss Reed.
She is just the person I need.
She is pretty and slim
And her figure is trim
And she hits the right keys at great speed.

There once was a typist called Shirley,
Who worked for a boss who was surly[2].
He was stingy[3] and bitter,
And would never permit[4] her
To come late or go away early.

"I loathe[5] filing[6]," said Joan, "it's a bore.
Like tidying up, it's a chore.
I must start, I suppose,
'Cos[7] these drawers just won't close,
And reports lie all over the floor."

Said the auditors[8] sadly, "It looks,
As though Schweibur's been hoodwinked[9] by crooks[10].
We've discovered the ruse[11],
We have proof[12] and accuse[13]
Mr Flügel of cooking the books."[14]

From: English for Secretaries. Oxford University Press O.U.P. 1978

1 von Herzen lieben 2 mürrisch 3 geizig 4 erlauben 5 hassen 6 archivieren 7 because: weil 8 Buchprüfer 9 täuschen, betrügen 10 Schurken 11 List 12 Beweis 13 anklagen 14 die Bücher frisieren

In the customer complaints department

CONTENTS

Business Frame: An angry customer
Speech Functions: The language of complaints
Business Words: Customer relations
Special Test: Do you phone efficiently?
Plus: Words, jokes and exercises of course

Time for a smile

Alf was in hospital. There was a chart[1] over his bed with a series of complaints[2]. Nearly all the nurses[3] had written something.

1 Karte 2 eine Reihe von Beschwerden 3 Krankenschwester

An angry customer

James' last department on his rotation programme is the customer complaints department. This office is very well equipped; they need the best tools to deal with customers' complaints as fast as possible. However, all the equipment can't help in the face to face (or rather ear to ear) confrontation with an angry customer.

Mr Frogger (**F**), James Kelly (**K**), Mr Bronson (**B**), an angry customer; Operator (**O**)

F: So, basically we have all the latest equipment in this section. We're "electrified", as it were.

K: So what sort of electric stuff have you got in the customer complaints?

F: Well, it starts with the incoming phone-calls. We're a very large department. We've thirty-two employees taking care of customers world-wide.

K: My goodness! That's a big operation. And what about the slogan "made in Germany"? Are there so many defects in the copiers and systems?

F: No, don't worry about that! Of course there are many new electronic components which are very sensitive to the different climatic conditions etc. But that's not the reason. We have a policy of offering our customers first-class after-sales service all over the world within 24 hours. So we make use of a switchboard here in the office.
(*Phone rings*)
Oh, I'll take that. I'm expecting a call from a customer in Australia. ...Yes, Frogger speaking. Can I help you?

B: Mr Frogger, I'd very much like to complain. I know that you're responsible for the Copiomatic. Now this copier has cost me...

F: Hello, hello, ...are you there? ... Damn, we've been cut off. ...

B: Mr Frogger, I've got a serious complaint to make. Can you hear me? ... What a service!

F: Operator, first there was a bad connection and then we were cut off completely.

O: I'm sorry, sir. There's nothing we can do about it. You'll have to wait for the caller to phone again.

F: Okay. Nothing we can do about it.

(*Phone rings again*)

F: Frogger speaking, ... ah, it's you, Mr Bronson.

B: Mr Frogger. I really must complain most strongly. When I purchased your copier the agreement included a guarantee that the copier would continue to run at full production. I needed this condition to make my costings for the bank.

F: Yes, you're quite right. I remember our negotiation. I'm awfully sorry to hear that. So what exactly has happened?

B: My copier has been down for three days. And no service on the hot-line, no service call. It's costing me thousands.

F: That's a real nuisance. I can understand that you are dissatisfied. I'll get the department leader onto it immediately. Could you fax your number and a short description of the problem?

B: Okay, but I want a reply within the hour.

F: Certainly, Mr Bronson. We'll look into it immediately. ... Yes, Mr Bronson ... We owe you more than an apology, sir. Goodbye. Well, Kelly, you see how it is. We have to react quickly. That's why we need modern technical equipment. I'll just make a note of this.

Telephone Message Form

Date: June 7, 1997 **Time:** 15.00 (urgent)/ **non-urgent**
Name of caller: Bronson, Charles
Firm: Photo Print **Tel.No.** ?
Message for: Mr Steiner

Customer very angry, copier down three days,
no contact from side of Low Valley;
Copier type: Copiomatic

Taken by: Frogger

K: What other devices do you have here?

F: Well, look around. Over there there's a telex, although nowadays we prefer e-mail. And all the section leaders also have mobile phones, because they're often on the road. Here's mine!

K: I'm very impressed with all this. I'm not surprised the company's so successful. Very dynamic! I'll be sorry to leave. You know I'm coming to the end of my contract with Low Valley.

F: Oh, that reminds me. There was a call from the Personnel Director, Mr Block.

K: Ugh! I wonder what I've done wrong. See you!

Vocabulary to help you with the dialogue

after-sales service	Kundendienst
agreement	Vereinbarung
although	obwohl
caller	Anrufer
climatic conditions	klimatische Bedingungen
complain	reklamieren, sich beschweren
costings	Kalkulation
customer complaint	Kundenbeschwerde, Reklamation
cut off	unterbrechen
defect	Fehler
device	Gerät
e-mail	E-Mail, elektronische Post
equipment	Ausrüstung
equipped	ausgerüstet
hotline	Notruf
impressed	beeindruckt
include	einschließen
manual	Handbuch
mobile phone	Handy
section	Abteilung
sensitive to	empfindlich gegen

slogan	Schlagwort
successful	erfolgreich
surprised	überrascht
switchboard	Telefonzentrale
tool	Werkzeug

EXERCISE 1: Memory test. Tick off the right answers

(More than one answer might be correct)

1. Customers in Asia have problems with copiers because

- ☐ *customers don't understand the manuals*
- ☐ *copiers are sensitive to climatic conditions*
- ☐ *they are not made in Germany*

2. Mr Bronson complains because

- ☐ *the hotline has broken down*
- ☐ *his copier has broken down for three days*
- ☐ *it's costing him too much*
- ☐ *there have been no service calls*

Speech functions you will hear in customer services

The language of complaints	
I've got a serious complaint to make.	Ich habe eine schwerwiegende Reklamation.
I'd very much like to complain.	Ich möchte mich beschweren.
I really want to complain most strongly.	Ich möchte mit allem Nachdruck reklamieren.
I really can't accept this kind of thing again.	Ich kann so etwas einfach nicht noch mal hinnehmen.

What to say to the angry customer	
I'm awfully sorry to hear that.	Das tut mir furchtbar leid.
What is the reason for your complaint?	Was ist der Grund für Ihre Beschwerde?
In this case your complaint seems to be justified.	In diesem Fall scheint Ihre Reklamation gerechtfertigt.

Something has obviously gone wrong.	Da ist offensichtlich etwas schiefgelaufen.
We'll look into it immediately.	Wir werden es sofort überprüfen.
That's a real nuisance.	Das ist wirklich ärgerlich.
I can understand why you are dissatisfied.	Ich kann verstehen, daß Sie unzufrieden sind.
We owe you more than an apology, sir.	Wir schulden Ihnen mehr als nur eine Entschuldigung.
How can we make up for the inconvenience?	Wie können wir Sie für die Unannehmlichkeiten entschädigen?
I assure you that this sort of thing won't happen again.	Ich versichere Ihnen, daß so etwas nicht wieder vorkommt.

✔ EXERCISE 2: Let's practise the language of complaint

(More than one answer is possible)

1. *Which speech functions of complaint did Mr Bronson not use?*

☐ *I'm afraid I have to register a serious complaint.*
☐ *Mr Frogger, I'd very much like to complain.*
☐ *I've got a serious complaint to make.*
☐ *I really want to express my dissatisfaction about your customer service.*

2. *How did Mr Frogger show his sympathy?*

☐ *I'm awfully sorry to hear that.*
☐ *That's a real nuisance.*
☐ *I can understand that you are dissatisfied.*
☐ *Now, what is the reason for your complaint?*
☐ *We owe you more than an apology.*
☐ *In this case your complaint seems to be more than justified.*

3. *How does Mr Frogger offer his cooperation?*

☐ *How can we make up for the inconvenience?*
☐ *I'll get the department leader onto it immediately.*
☐ *We'll look into it immediately.*
☐ *I assure you that this sort of thing won't happen again.*

Extra vocabulary on customer relations

Abhilfe schaffen	*remedy a situation*
Ausrede	*excuse*
ausspannen, Kunden ~	*alienate customers*
beschädigte Waren	*damaged goods*
besorgt	*concerned, worried*
bestätigen	*confirm*
Bestätigung	*confirmation*
erklären, den Hintergrund ~	*explain the background*
Ersatzwaren	*replacement goods*
kundenfeindlich	*against the interest of customers*
Kundeninformationsdienst	*customer relations*
Produktqualität	*product quality*
reklamieren	*make complaints*
schlecht verpackt	*badly packed*
sich entschuldigen	*make an apology, apologise*
treuer Kunde	*faithful customer*
unempfindlich gegenüber	*insensitive to*
verlieren, seine Kunden ~	*lose one's customers*
verlorene Waren	*lost goods*

Time for a smile

"It says here on the card there that if customers have any complain they should tell the manager."

"That's right, sir"

"Well, I thought I'd just let you know I suffer pretty badly from[1] rheumatics and pains[2] in the head."

1 ziemlich leiden unter 2 Schmerzen

EXERCISE 3: Guess what I mean

to say that you are sorry	*. . . . . . . se*
another word for handbook	*. . . . al*
if you lose your caller then you are	*. . . . ff*
saying that you are not satisfied	*. . . . . ain*
customers you have had for years	*. . . . . . ul customers*

EXERCISE 4: Wordbuilder's corner

The first example has been done for you.

Verb	*Noun*
apologise	*apology*
complain	. . . .
confirm	. . . .
copy	. . . .
agree	. . . .

EXERCISE 5: Grammar in review

Here are a few sentences taken from our dialogue.

Fill in the correct verb form. Try to explain why (see key).

1. I'm (*expect*) a call from a customer in Australia (in the next five minutes).
2. So what exactly (*happen*)?
3. My copier (*be*) down for three days.
4. There (*be*) a call from the Mr Block (two hours ago).
5. We (*look*) into it immediately

SPECIAL TEST: Do I know how to phone efficiently?

Do I ...	*Some-times*	*Always*	*Never*
rush to answer the phone as soon as it rings?			
spend longer on calls than is really necessary?			
have to make calls twice because there was something I forgot to say?			
allow telephone calls to interrupt my meetings?			
dial numbers and then forget who I called?			
drop what I'm doing when I remember a call I need to make?			
not screen my calls even when there is someone available to do so?			
spend more than 30 seconds dealing with unsolicited sales callers?			
finish calls without covering the topics I want to discuss?			
scatter my calls randomly throughout the day?			
forget to pass telephone messages on to others?			

For each "sometimes" answer, we should score ourselves one point, for each "always" answer, three points, and zero points for each "never" answer.

A score of 16 or more puts us into the telephone junkie category and we need to sit back and evaluate how we are using the telephone. Why are we not using it productively? What needs to change before we can gain control over the telephone? Even *a score of less than 16* means that the telephone probably rules our lives from time to time.

The questionnaire will have helped in identifying those areas we specifically need to work on today and in the future. We should use our score as a benchmark to gauge our improvement over the coming weeks and months.

Vocabulary to help with the test

benchmark	Meßlatte, Maßstab
dial a number	eine Nummer wählen
drop what one is doing	alles stehen- und liegenlassen
evaluate	beurteilen, bewerten
gauge	abschätzen
interrupt meetings	Besprechungen unterbrechen
make calls twice	Anrufe zweimal machen
pass messages on to	Nachrichten weitergeben
randomly	zufällig
rule s.o.'s life	jds. Leben beherrschen
rush	Eile
scatter	zerstreuen
score	erzielen
spend time on calls	Zeit auf Anrufe verwenden
unsolicited callers	ungebetene Anrufer

Time for a smile

Mrs Brain rang up the laundry[1]: "I'd very much like to complain. You've just sent back some buttons[2] with no shirts[3] on them. Would you please send the shirts as well?"

1 Wäscherei 2 Knöpfe 3 Hemd

Epilogue
All's well that ends well

CONTENTS

Time for a smile

Boss: What a lazy[1] worker you are. Is there anything you can do quickly?
Clerk: Let me see. Yes, there is something. I get tired[2] quickly.

1 faul 2 müde werden

"Do you mean you're offering me a job?"

This time there is no background. James was in such a hurry to reach Mr Block's room he didn't have time to tell us anything:

Mr Block (**B**), James Kelly (**K**)

B: Hello, come in please. Don't waste time outside! Time is money, you know.

K: Oh, thank you very much, Mr Block. There isn't anything wrong, is there?

B: Well, there were a few things you could have done better. I heard you got your figures wrong in the accounts department a few times.

K: Well, I'm used to working with electronic media, so I'm a bit out of practice.

B: Yes, that's as may be but attention to detail is important if you want to rise in the company. Look at me, for example, you'd never see me getting my details wrong.

K: Actually, sir, I seem to remember you had a misunderstanding about the canteen.

B: That wasn't a detail! Now to your case. We've decided that you're quite dynamic and creative. Perhaps we can find a use for you on a regular basis.

K: Do you mean you're offering me a job?

B: I prefer to say we're offering you a chance. A chance to show what you are capable of. And you'll be happy to know that it's in my department. In the training section. You'll like that, won't you? You like explaining things to people, don't you? We think it's right up your street.

K: What does it actually involve?

B: Here you are. I've prepared a diagram. Our work is at the level of training objectives. And your task is to formulate training plans of action to achieve our targets. Do it well and you'll do well but remember there's always somebody, some boss who might do it better. So don't rock the boat! Find Mr Seba. He'll get the contract of employment organised. Good luck!

K: (*to himself*). Block by name, but not by nature. I never would've guessed it.

Director Block had spent the whole morning to make this plan on his laptop:

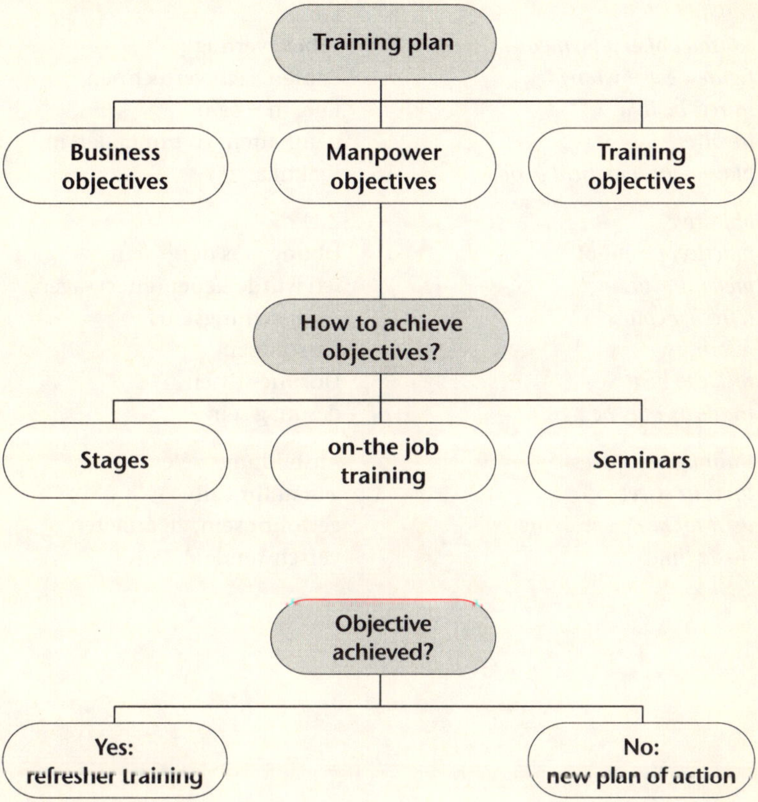

The last vocabulary list to help you with the dialogue

achieve a target	ein Ziel erreichen
capable	fähig
contract of employment	Arbeitsvertrag
figures, get ~ wrong	Zahlen, sich verrechnen
hurry, be in a ~	Eile, in ~ sein
involve	beinhalten, zu tun haben mit
placement, practical period	Praktika
objective	Ziel
practice, be out of ~	Übung, aus der ~ sein
prefer, I ~ to say	ich würde lieber (eher) sagen
refresher course	Auffrischungskurs
resources	Ressourcen
rock the boat	Unruhe stiften
that's as may be	das mag sein
training objectives	Ausbildungsziele
up your street	genau Ihr Fall
used to, be ~ ~ working	gewohnt sein, zu arbeiten
waste time	verschwenden, Zeit ~

Grammar Rhymes: Question tags

Form

Ein Hilfsverb, das im Satz verneint,
Bejaht im *question tag* erscheint.
Doch wenn es bejaht im Satze steht,
Dann ist es gerade umgekehrt.

Satz verneint	Question tag bejaht
We aren't late,	*are we?*
Tom couldn't win,	*could he?*
He didn't hurt you,	*did he?*

Satz bejaht	Question tag verneint
You *have* got a car,	*haven't you?*
Tina *is* Irish,	*isn't she?*
You *will* help me,	*won't you?*

MERKE: Was steht im *question tag*?

1. Namen werden durch Pronomen ersetzt (*Tom – he*)
2. Hilfsverben (*have, do*) und modale Hilfsverben (*could, must* etc.) werden wieder aufgenommen.
3. Vollverben werden durch *do* oder *did* ersetzt.

We all *make* mistakes, *don't* we?

Gebrauch

Question tags, eine Nebensache,
Gibt es nur in der gesprochenen Sprache.
Wo wir *oder*? und *nicht wahr*? verwenden,
Tun Engländer den Satz mit *tags* beenden.

Warum tun sie das?

a) Damit wir ihnen Beifall zollen,
b) wenn sie bestätigt werden wollen.

Grammar Jokes

EXERCISE 1: Complete the jokes using a question tag

❶ *A hedgehog[1], finding himself on top of a scrubbing brush[2]:*
"We all make mistakes, ... we?"

❷ *Architect: The acoustics in our new concert hall are fantastic,*
.... they?
Karajan: Pardon?

❸ *Office manager to a new cleaning woman:*
Look at all that dust[3] on the shelves[4]! It seems as if they haven't been cleaned for a month! – "You're not going to blame[5] me, sir, ...? I've only been here for a week, haven't I?"

❹ *"Are you innocent[6] or guilty[7]?" MacTavish was asked by the judge.*
"I can't tell until I've seen the evidence[8], ...?" replied MacTavish.

❺ *The oldest joke I know is when Eve asked Adam "You love me, darling, ...?" and he replied "Who else?"*

EXERCISE 2:

You remember the question tags in our dialogue, don't you?

There isn't anything wrong, ... there?
You'll like that, ...?
You like explaining things to people, ...?

1 Igel 2 Schrubber 3 Staub 4 Regale 5 die Schuld geben 6 unschuldig 7 schuldig 8 Beweise

Glossary: The complete ABC of our Business Words

n. = noun = Substantiv *v.* = verb = Verb *adj.* = Adjektiv *adv.* = Adverb
US = amerikanisches Englisch

A

abilities	Fähigkeiten
accommodate, can you ~ five people?	unterbringen, können Sie fünf Personen ~ ?
accommodation	Unterkunft, Unterbringung
accountant	Buchhalter
accounts department	Finanzabteilung
accounts, do ~	Buch führen
achieve a task	einen Auftrag erfüllen
acquisition	Beschaffung, Einkauf
act of God	höhere Gewalt
actual costs	Ist-Kosten
ad / advert / advertisement	Werbung, Annonce, Anzeige
address s.o.	jdn. ansprechen
adhesive tape	Klebeband
administrative matters	Verwaltungsangelegenheiten
advanced German	fortgeschrittenes Deutsch
advantage	Vorteil
advert, advertisement	(Zeitungs-)Anzeige
advertising	Werbung
advertising campaign	Werbekampagne
advertising manager	Werbeleiter
advertising slot / spot	Werbespot
advertising department	Werbung, Werbeabteilung
advertising director	Direktor der Werbeabteilung
advice	Rat(schlag)
aerial photograph	Luftaufnahme
after-sales service	Kundendienst
against the interest of customers	kundenfeindlich
age	Alter
alienate customers	Kunden ausspannen
although	obwohl
analyse	analysieren
and this is Mr X	und das hier ist Herr X

answering machine	Anrufbeantworter
apologise	sich entschuldigen
apology	Entschuldigung
appear	erscheinen, auftauchen
appetiser	Vorspeise
applicant	Bewerber
application	Anwendung, Software, Bewerbung
application with full particulars	ausführliche Bewerbung
application	Bewerbung
apply	sich bewerben
appointment	Termin
appreciate	schätzen, zu ~ wissen
appreciate, as you will ~	verstehen, Sie werden ~
apprenticeship	Lehre
appropriate	angemessen
appropriate equipment	passende Ausrüstung
approximately	circa, ungefähr
arrange accommodation	Unterkunft, für ~ sorgen
art of negotiation	Kunst der Verhandlungsführung
ashtray	Aschenbecher
assemble	zusammenbauen
assemble a stand	einen Messestand aufstellen
assembly	Montage
assembly line work	Fließbandfertigung
assess s.o.	jdn. beurteilen
assessment	Beurteilung, Bewertung
assign duties	Aufgaben zuweisen
assignment	Aufgabe
assist	helfen
assistance	Hilfe, Unterstützung
assistance, how can I be of ~?	Hilfe, wie kann ich Ihnen behilflich sein?
at least	wenigstens
attend university	besuchen, die Universität ~
attention	Aufmerksamkeit
attention, draw ~ to	Aufmerksamkeit lenken auf
attitude	Einstellung, Haltung
audience	Publikum, Zuhörer
authorise the budget	genehmigen, den Etat ~
available	verfügbar, erhältlich

average	durchschnittlich
awful, it sounds ~	schrecklich, es klingt ~

B

bacon	Speck
badly packed	schlecht verpackt
baggage label	Gepäckanhänger
baggage claim	Gepäckausgabe
balance sheet	Bilanz
basic wage	Grundlohn
basically	im Grunde genommen
batch	Serie, Stapel, Stoß
batch-processing	Stapelverarbeitung
battle, lose a ~	Schlacht, eine ~ verlieren
be in charge of	zuständig sein für
be up to the mark	der Sache gewachsen sein
be on top of one's job	sein Geschäft verstehen
be missing	fehlen
beef	Rind
beef burgundy	Burgunderbraten
behalf, on ~ of	Auftrag, im ~ von
behave	sich benehmen
benchmark	Meßlatte, Maßstab
bill	Rechnung
bill of exchange	Wechsel
bill, make a ~ out to ...	Rechnung für ... ausstellen
biro, ball pen	Kugelschreiber
bloody	verdammt
blunt	stumpf
board of management	Vorstand
board level	Vorstandsebene
boarding pass	Bordkarte
boiled vegetables	gekochtes Gemüse
bonus	Prämie
book a room/hotel	ein Zimmer buchen
booking, make a ~	Buchung, eine ~ vornehmen
bored	gelangweilt
boring	langweilig

boss s.o. around	jdn. herumkommandieren
bossy	herrisch
bottom right	rechts unten
bow and scrape	katzbuckeln und kriechen
brains	Hirn
brand manager	Produktmanager, Markenbetreuer
brand	Marke, Sorte, Klasse
brand name	Markenartikel
breach of contract	Vertragsbruch
break a contract	einen Vertrag brechen
break in	unterbrechen
brief	kurz
brochure	Broschüre
bulk discount	Mengenrabatt
bulletin	Mitteilungsblatt, Bulletin
business administration	Betriebswirtschaft
business card / visiting card	Visitenkarte
business school	Handelsschule
business calculation	Wirtschaftskalkulation
by the way	übrigens
by cheque (US: check)	per Scheck
by transfer	per Überweisung

C

c.&f. (cost and freight)	Kosten und Fracht
c.i.f. (cost, insurance, freight)	Kosten, Versicherung, Fracht
C.V. (Curriculum Vitae)	Lebenslauf
cabbage	Kohl
calculating machine	Rechenmaschine
calendar	Kalender
call for (an interview)	einladen (zum Vorstellungsgespräch)
call, take a ~	Anruf, einen ~ entgegennehmen
caller	Anrufer
cancel, could you ~ my room?	stornieren, könnten Sie mein Zimmer ~?
capable	fähig
car park	Parkplatz
card index	Kartei
career	Laufbahn

carrier	Spedition, Spediteur
case	Fall
cash discount	Barzahlungsrabatt
cassette	Kassette
catalogue	Katalog, Verzeichnis
cauliflower	Blumenkohl
cause problems	Probleme machen, verursachen
cellotape	Tesafilm
cellphone	Handy
central stock	Ersatzteillager
chair (a meeting)	den Vorsitz haben
chairman	Vorsitzender
Chamber of Commerce	Handelskammer
Chamber of Commerce and Industry	Industrie- und Handelskammer
charges	Gebühren
check (n.)	Kontrolle
check (v.)	prüfen
check quality	die Qualität überprüfen
check-in counter	Abfertigungsschalter
chief buyer	Einkaufsleiter
chipped potatoes	Pommes frites
choice	Wahl
circular	Rundschreiben
civil service	öffentlicher Dienst
clerical staff	Büropersonal
clerk	Angestellter
click into	anklicken
client, customer	Kunde
commercial college	höhere Handelsschule
commercial clerk	Industriekaufmann
commercial training	kaufmännische Ausbildung
company controller	Leiter des Rechnungswesens (US: Leiter der Buchhaltung)
company, present ~ excepted	Anwesende ausgenommen
compete with	konkurrieren mit
competence	Tüchtigkeit, Fähigkeit
competence, within the ~ of	Zuständigkeit, in der ~ von
competence, have ~ in	Kompetenz haben in
competition	Wettbewerb

competitor	Mitbewerber, Konkurrent
compile	zusammenstellen
complain	beklagen, sich beschweren, reklamieren
complaint	Reklamation, Beschwerde
component centre	Ersatzteillager
component	Bauelement
components	Komponenten
computer literacy	Computererfahrung, -kenntnisse
concern	betreffen, gehen um
concerned	besorgt
conclude a contract	einen Vertrag abschließen
conclusion (of a presentation)	Abschluß
conditions of employment	Arbeitsbedingungen
conference room	Konferenzzimmer
conference table	Konferenztisch
confidence	Vertrauen
confidence, have ~ in	Vertrauen haben zu
confident	selbstsicher, selbstbewußt
confirm an order	bestätigen, einen Auftrag ~
confirm a booking	eine Buchung bestätigen
confirmation	Bestätigung
confront	konfrontieren, gegenüberstellen
confusion	Verwirrung
construction	Aufbau
consumer	Verbraucher, Konsument
consumer survey	Verbraucherumfrage
consumer goods	Verbrauchsgüter
contact partner	Ansprechpartner
continuous line	durchgehende Linie
continuous sampling	ständige Stichproben
contract of employment	Arbeitsvertrag
contrary, on the ~	Gegenteil, im ~
control system	Steuerung
conveniences	Komfort, Annehmlichkeiten
conveyor belt	Förderband
cooling system	Kühlsystem
cope with	zurechtkommen mit
cope with a problem	fertig werden mit einem Problem

cordless telephone	schnurloses Telefon
corporate culture	Firmenkultur
cost accounting	Kostenrechnung
cost centre	Kostenstelle
cost price	Selbstkostenpreis
cost per item	Stückkosten
costings	Kalkulation
count on s.o.	zählen, vertrauen, auf jdn. ~
course, first ~	Gang, erster ~
course, a compact ~	ein intensiver Studiengang
CPU (central processing unit)	Zentralrechner
crawl	kriechen
creative	kreativ, schöpferisch
creep around	herumschleichen
cucumber salad	Gurkensalat
curriculum	Lehrplan
curriculum vitae	Lebenslauf
customer	Kunde
customer complaint	Kundenbeschwerde, Reklamation
customer relations	Kundeninformationsdienst
customs	Zoll
customs formalities	Zollformalitäten
cut off	unterbrochen
cutlet	Kotelett
CV (curriculum vitae)	Lebenslauf

D

damaged goods	beschädigte Waren
dashed line	gestrichelte Linie
database	Datenbank
date of invoice	Rechnungsdatum
deal with	sich befassen mit, sich beschäftigen mit, zu tun haben mit
decide	entscheiden
decision	Entscheidung
declare sth.	etw. verzollen
deduct	abziehen
deductions	Abzüge

degree	Hochschulabschluß
delay	verschieben, verzögern
delegate	delegieren
delivery conditions	Lieferbedingungen
delivery time	Lieferzeit
delivery period	Lieferzeitraum
department head	Abteilungsleiter
depending on	abhängig von
deposit	deponieren, hinterlegen
deputise	vertreten
description	Beschreibung, Schilderung
design	Entwurf
designer	Konstrukteur
desk calculator	Tischrechner
desk set	Schreibtischgarnitur
desk lamp	Schreibtischlampe
despatch (dispatch)	Versand
dessert	Nachspeise
destination	Reiseziel
deviation	Abweichung
device	Gerät, Anlage, Einrichtung
diagram	Diagramm
dial a number	eine Nummer wählen
dictaphone	Diktiergerät
diploma	Diplom
discounts	Rabatte
dismiss	entlassen
dismissal	Entlassung
disorganised	desorganisiert, unordentlich
display, be on ~	Auslage, ausgestellt werden
disrespectful	unhöflich
distance	Entfernung
distant lands	ferne Lande
disturb s.o.	jdn. stören
divider	Trennblatt
do it without me	machen Sie es ohne mich
don't get in a panic!	regen Sie sich nicht auf!
dot	Punkt
dotted line	punktierte Linie

drawer	Schublade
drawing	Zeichnung
drop what one is doing	alles stehen- und liegenlassen
dutiable	zollpflichtig

E

e-mail	E-Mail, elektronische Post
earnings	Verdienst
eavesdrop	lauschen, horchen
economics	Volkswirtschaft
education	Ausbildung, Erziehung
efficient	leistungsfähig, effizient, tüchtig
electronic telephone directory	elektronisches Telefonverzeichnis
electronic scales	elektronische Waage
employ	anstellen, beschäftigen, einstellen
employee	Arbeitnehmer
employee assessment	Mitarbeiterbeurteilung
employer	Arbeitgeber
employment	Anstellung
employment agency	Stellenvermittlung
engineer	Ingenieur
engineering	Maschinenbau
ensure	sicherstellen, gewährleisten
envelope	Briefumschlag
equip	ausrüsten
equipment	Ausrüstung
equipped	ausgerüstet
equivalent	Gleichwertiges
erect, ~ a stand	aufstellen, einen Stand ~
estimate, give an ~	Kostenvoranschlag machen
evaluate	beurteilen, bewerten
ex-works	ab Werk
exaggerate	übertreiben
excepted, present company ~	Anwesende ausgenommen
excess baggage	Mehrgepäck, Übergepäck
excuse	Ausrede
exhibition building	Messegebäude
exhibition stand / booth	Messestand

exhibition / exposition	Ausstellung
exhibition space, apply for ~	Ausstellungsfläche, sich um ~ bewerben
exhibition site	Ausstellungsgelände
exhibition board	Messeleitung
exhibition catalogue	Ausstellungskatalog
exhibition contractor	Firma für Ausstellungsbedarf
expenditure	Ausgaben, Aufwendungen
experienced	erfahren
explain the background	den Hintergrund erklären
explanation	Erklärung
exporter	Exporteur
exposition (US)	Ausstellung
express oneself	äußern, sich ~, erklären
extraordinary	außergewöhnlich

F

f.a.s. (free alongside ship)	frei längsseits Schiff
f.o.b. (free on board)	frei an Bord
facilities	Ausstattung, Einrichtungen,
factory	Fabrik
failed, a ~ meeting	mißlungen, eine ~e Konferenz
fair	Messe
faithful customer	treuer Kunde
fall back on	zurückgreifen auf
famous	berühmt
fax	Faxgerät
fellow	Zeitgenosse, Bursche, Mensch
fetch from the airport	abholen vom Flugplatz
figure	Abbildung, Ziffer
figures, get ~ wrong	Zahlen, falsche ~ haben
file	Aktenordner
filing cabinet	Aktenschrank
fill s.o. in on	aufklären, unterrichten, jdn. ~ über
fill a job	eine Stelle besetzen
finance department	Finanzwesen
fire	entlassen, feuern
first name, you can call me by my ~	Vorname, Sie können mich duzen
fit together	zusammensetzen

fit into the team	passen, in die Mannschaft ~
fixed costs	Fixkosten
flesh	Fleisch (lebendes ~)
floppy disk	Diskette
foil, transparency	Folie
foreigner	Ausländer(in), Fremde(r)
foreman	Vorarbeiter
former employer	ehemaliger Arbeitgeber
forwarder	Spedition, Spediteur
forwarding agent	Spedition, Spediteur
fountain pen	Füller
frame	Gestell, Rahmen
franking machine	Frankiermaschine
frequently	häufig
fried potatoes	Bratkartoffeln
from abroad	aus dem Ausland
fruit salad	Obstsalat
fully-booked	ausgebucht
further education	Aus- / Weiterbildung

G

game	Wild
gauge	abschätzen
get used to (+ gerund)	gewöhnen, sich an etwas ~
get the hang of things	den Dreh herausbekommen
get one's figures right	richtig rechnen, buchen
get butterflies in one's stomach	ein flaues Gefühl in der Magengegend bekommen
get on well with so.	auskommen, gut mit jdm. ~
get on the phone	sich ans Telephon setzen
get on top of	fertig werden mit, beherrschen
give in one's notice	kündigen
give a clear picture	deutlich darstellen, Probleme ~
glory	Ruhm, Ehre
glue	Klebstoff
go into detail	auf Einzelheiten eingehen
goods	Güter, Artikel
goods inward	eingehende Waren

gradually	allmählich
graduate	Akademiker
graph	Graphik, Diagramm
graphics	Graphiken
grill s.o.	jdn. ausquetschen
gross pay	Bruttogehalt
gross price	Bruttopreis
guarantee	Garantie, Gewährleistung
guard	Schutz
guess, I guess	annehmen, ich nehme es an
guillotine	Schlagschere

H

habit	(An-)Gewohnheit
ham and melon	Melone mit Schinken
hand luggage	Handgepäck
handle a matter	sich um eine Sache kümmern
hands-free telephone	Handy
hard disk	Festplatte
hard case	harter Fall
hardly	kaum
head of finance	Leiter der Finanzabteilung
head of accounts	Leiter der Buchhaltung
head of personnel	Personalleiter
head of training	Ausbildungsleiter
high treason	Hochverrat
high precision work	Präzisionsarbeit
highlighter	Marker
hire	einstellen
hit the nail on the head	den Nagel auf den Kopf treffen
hit the mark	ins Schwarze treffen
hold a fair	veranstalten, eine Messe ~
hold up, be held up	aufhalten, aufgehalten werden
holiday, vacation (US)	Urlaub
hotel charges	Hotelkosten
hotline	Notruf
house	unterbringen
Human Resources Department	Personalabteilung

human resources	Personalwesen
hurry, be in a ~	Eile, in ~ sein

I

I wouldn't like to be in his shoes	ich möchte nicht in seiner Haut stecken
I wouldn't put it like that	das würde ich nicht so nennen
I'll take the Brie	Ich nehme den Brie
identity pass	Firmenausweis
illustrate	veranschaulichen, erläutern
illustration	Abbildung
image	Image
immediate (adj.)	sofort
immediately (adv.)	sofort
impact printer	Nadeldrucker
implement a plan	einen Plan ausführen
impressed, be ~	beeindruckt sein
impression, make a good ~	Eindruck, einen guten ~ machen
improve	verbessern
in summary	zusammengefaßt
in writing	schriftlich
in advance	im voraus
in the final analysis	letzten Endes
include	umfassen, beinhalten
income	Einkommen
incoming goods	eingehende Waren
inconvenience s.o.	Umstände, jdm. ~ machen
increase	vergrößern, erhöhen
increments	Gehaltserhöhung
indicate	angeben
induction course	Einführungskurs
ink	Tinte
ink-jet printer	Tintendrucker
insensitive to	unempfindlich gegenüber
insert ads in the press	in der Zeitung werben
inspector	Kontrolleur, Prüfer
instructions	Anweisungen
insurance policy	Versicherungspolice
interrupt meetings	Besprechungen unterbrechen

interview	Vorstellungsgespräch
interview panel	Prüfungskomitee
interviewee	Kandidat
interviewer	Gesprächspartner
introduce s.o.	jdn. vorstellen
introduction	Einführung
inventories, stocks	Bestände
invitation	Einladung
invoice total	Gesamtbetrag der Rechnung
invoice (n.)	Rechnung
invoice (v.)	in Rechnung stellen
involve	beinhalten, umfassen, einbeziehen, zu tun haben mit
it is within the competence of	Zuständigkeit, in die ~ fallen von
it is likely to …	es wird wahrscheinlich …
it's worth doing	es lohnt sich zu tun

J

job specification	Tätigkeitsbeschreibung
job description	Arbeitsplatzbeschreibung
job evaluation	Arbeitsplatzbewertung
job production (single items)	Auftrag
job placement	Praktikum
job rotation	Rotation in der Firma
join a company	eintreten in eine Firma
justify	rechtfertigen

K

keep in mind	nicht vergessen, bedenken
keep an appointment	Termin einhalten
key personnel	Personal in Schlüsselpositionen
keyboard	Tastatur

L

label	Etikette, Aufkleber
labor office (US), job centre	Arbeitsamt

lamb	Lamm
lamb roast	Lammbraten
lamb chops	Lammkoteletts
land the job	die Stelle bekommen
laser pointer	Laserstab
laser printer	Laserdrucker
launch products	Produkte auf den Markt bringen
launching	Einführung (eines Produkts)
launching date	Einführungstermin
launch costs	Anlaufkosten
lay-off	Entlassung (vorübergehende)
leaflet	Flugblatt, Prospekt, Merkblatt
learn the ropes	sich einarbeiten
leisure time	Freizeit
let me introduce you to Mr X	bekannt machen, darf ich Sie mit Herrn X ~?
let's consider the options	betrachten wir die Alternativen
let's go through the possibilities	gehen wir die Möglichkeiten durch
letter tray	Briefkorb
letter opener	Brieföffner
lettuce	grüner Salat
lift / elevator (US)	Aufzug
likely suppliers	mögliche, potentielle Lieferanten
likely	wahrscheinlich
liquid	flüssig
liquid paper	Tippex flüssig
live up to one's name	seinem Namen Ehre machen
loading costs	Ladekosten
lobster	Hummer
local food	heimische Küche
location	Standort, Lage, Platz
lose one's customers	seine Kunden verlieren
lose the battle	den Kampf verlieren
Lost and Found	Fundbüro
lost goods	verlorene Waren

M

magnet board	Magnettafel
mail, outgoing / incoming ~	Post, ausgehende / eingehende ~

main course / main meal	Hauptgang
main course	Hauptgericht
make an apology	sich entschuldigen
make an appointment	Termin vereinbaren
make calls twice	Anrufe zweimal machen
make the introductions	die Vorstellung übernehmen
make complaints	reklamieren
management trainee	Trainee
manual work	Handarbeit
manual	Handbuch
manufacture	herstellen, produzieren
manufacturer	Hersteller
manufacturing cost	Fertigungskosten
manufacturing	Herstellung / Fertigung
manufacturing company	Produktionsfirma
margins	Margen, (Gewinn-)Spannen
marker	Textmarkierer
mashed potatoes	Kartoffelbrei
mass production	Serienproduktion
mass-produce	in Serie herstellen
masters	Druckvorlagen, Originale
material cost	Materialkosten
materials	Baustoffe, Rohstoffe
matter, it doesn't matter	ausmachen, es macht nichts
matter, it's not just a ~ of	Angelegenheit, es geht nicht nur um ...
matters connected with ...	Dinge, die mit ... zusammenhängen
may I introduce you to X?	vorstellen, darf ich Ihnen X ~?
measuring instrument	Meßinstrument
medical insurance	Krankenversicherung
meet standards	erfüllen, Normen ~
meet requirements	erfüllen, Anforderungen ~
meet new colleagues	neue Kollegen kennenlernen
meeting, chair a ~	Besprechung, eine ~ leiten
member of the board	Vorstandsmitglied
mention	erwähnen
menu	Speisekarte
merry	fröhlich
method of payment	Zahlungsweise
minced meat	Hackfleisch

mixed salad	gemischter Salat
mobile phone	Handy, tragbares Telefon
monitor / screen	Monitor
move to the next department	zur nächsten Abteilung umziehen
move on to	weitergehen zu
multi-feed fax	Fax mit automatischem Einzug
mutton	Hammel

N

narrow	eng
national insurance	Sozialversicherung
native speaker	Muttersprachler
negotiate conditions	Bedingungen aushandeln
negotiation, lead a ~	Verhandlung, eine ~ führen
net pay	Nettogehalt
net cash	netto Kasse
nevertheless	trotzdem
night shift	Nachtschicht
notion	Idee, Vorstellung
nutshell, in a ~	kurz gesagt

O

object	Einwand erheben
objective	Ziel
obliged, be ~ to	müssen
obstacle	Hindernis
obtain	erzielen, erreichen
obviously	offenbar
occurrence	Ereignis
office	Büro
office furniture	Büromöbel
OHP foil / sheet /transperency	Tageslichtfolie
OHP projector	Overheadprojektor
okay, get an ~	grünes Licht bekommen
on the job training	Ausbildung am Arbeitsplatz
on your right / left	rechts / links
open up new markets	neue Märkte erschließen

open a credit	einen Kredit eröffnen
open plan office	Großraumbüro
open testimonial	offenes Zeugnis
operational level	innerbetriebliche Ebene, Bereich
opinion, be of the ~	Meinung, der ~ sein
order	Auftrag
originally	ursprünglich
outsource	Teile kaufen statt zu produzieren
outward appearance	äußere Erscheinung
overhead costs, overheads	Gemeinkosten
overheads	allgemeine Betriebskosten
overload	überladen, überlasten
overrun, a meeting overruns	überziehen, eine Konferenz wird überzogen
overtime	Überstunden
overtime rates (of money)	Überstundengeld
overview	Überblick, Übersicht

P

p.a. (per annum)	pro Jahr
pace	Tempo
packing	Verpackung
packing costs	Verpackungskosten
pager	Piepser
pamphlet	Broschüre
pancake	Pfannkuchen
paper clip	Büroklammer
paper weight	Briefbeschwerer
parking facilities	Parkmöglichkeiten
part	Teil
partition	Trennwand
partridge	Rebhuhn
pass messages on to ...	Nachrichten weitergeben an ...
pass on good advice	guten Rat weitergeben
passenger lounge	Warteraum
passion	Leidenschaft
passport control	Paßkontrolle
paternal advice	väterlicher Rat

patience	Geduld
pay by installment	Ratenzahlung
pay duty	Zoll zahlen, verzollen, etwas ~
PAYE (Pay As You Earn)	Lohnsteuerabzug vor Auszahlung
(Pay As You Go – US)	des Lohns
payment	Bezahlung
payment of invoices	Rechnungsbegleichung
payroll	Lohnliste
peas	Erbsen
pencil sharpener	Spitzer
pencil	Bleistift
pension	Pension, Rente
pension scheme	Altersversorgungsplan
perch	Barsch
perform a task	eine Aufgabe erfüllen
performance	Leistung
perks	Leistungsanreize, zusätzliche ~
permit me to ...	gestatten Sie, daß ...
personal assistant (P.A.)	persönlicher Assistent
personnel assessment	Personalbeurteilung
personnel affairs	Personalwesen
personnel department	Personalabteilung
personnel management	Personalführung
persuade	überzeugen
phone, get somebody on the ~	Telefon, ans ~ holen
photocopier	Kopierer
pike	Hecht
pile	Stapel
pink	rosa
pittance	Hungerlohn, "paar Pfennige"
place of birth	Geburtsort
place an ad/advert	inserieren, annoncieren
place an order	bestellen
placement	Praktikum
plaice	Scholle
planning meeting	Planungskonferenz
planning	Planung
plant	Werk, Anlage
pleasantly surprised	angenehm überrascht

pleased to meet you	sehr erfreut, Sie kennenzulernen
pocket calculator	Taschenrechner
point out that ...	darauf hinweisen, daß ...
point, is there any ~ in ...?	Sinn, hat es überhaupt ~, zu ...?
pointer	Zeigestab
polite	höflich
position	Stelle, Position, Posten
position of responsibility	verantwortungsvolle Stelle
post, offer s.o. a ~	Stelle, jdm. eine ~ anbieten
post-graduate student	etwa: Doktorand
poster	Plakat
postpone	verschieben
potential customer	potentieller Kunde
poultry	Geflügel
practical experience	praktische Erfahrung
practice, be out of ~	Übung, aus der ~ sein
prawn cocktail	Krabbencocktail
prefer, I ~ to say	ich würde lieber (eher) sagen
present s.o.	jdn. vorstellen
presentation	Vortrag, Präsentation
presentation, make a ~	Präsentation, eine ~ machen
press conference	Pressekonferenz
press release	Pressemitteilung
pressure	Druck, Streß
pretty sharpish	ziemlich pünktlich, schnell
price per item	Stückpreis
price list, current ~	Preisliste, gültige ~
pricing policy	Preispolitik
printed matters	Drucksachen
printing press manufacturer	Druckmaschinenhersteller
priorities, set ~	Prioritäten setzen
priority task	vorrangige Aufgabe
probationary period	Probezeit
proceed	fortfahren, weitermachen
process	Verfahren
procurement	An-, Beschaffung
produce	herstellen, fertigen
product feature	Produkteigenschaft
product advantage	Produktvorteil

product quality	Produktqualität
production	Produktion
production facilities	Produktionseinrichtungen
production head	Leiter der Produktion
production stoppage	Produktionsstillstand
production control	Produktionssteuerung
production line	Fertigungsstraße
project leader	Projektleiter
promote a product	für ein Produkt werben
promotion	Verkaufs-/Absatzförderung, Beförderung
promotional material	Reklame-, Werbematerial
prompt payment discount	Skonto
prompt delivery	sofortige Lieferung
pronunciation	Aussprache
property	Eigentum, Besitz
prospect	potentieller Kunde
proud	stolz
public relations (PR)	Öffentlichkeitsarbeit
public, in ~	Publikum, vor ~ , öffentlich
publicity campaign	Werbeaktion
puff	schnaufen
punch, hole punch	Bürolocher, Aktenlocher
purchase	kaufen
purchasing	Anschaffung, Beschaffung, Einkauf
push one's attentions onto ...	aufdringlich werden
push things along	etwas vorantreiben
push aside	zur Seite schubsen, wegstoßen
put s.o. through	durchstellen, jdn. ~
put through, I'll ~ you ~ to reception	verbinden, ich verbinde Sie mit der Rezeption
put up a stand	einen Stand aufstellen

Q

qualifications	Qualifikationen, Zeugnisse
quality control	Qualitätskontrolle
quality control department (QC)	Abteilung für Qualitätskontrolle
quality inspection	Qualitätsprüfung
quantities	Mengen

quantity discount	Mengenrabatt
question mark	Fragezeichen
queue	Schlange, Reihe, Warteliste
quotation	Kostenvoranschlag
quotation, give a ~	Angebot, ein ~ machen
quote	Angebot, Kostenvoranschlag
quote, a firm ~	Kostenvoranschlag, ein verbindlicher ~

R

R & D	F & E, Forschung und Entwicklung
rabbit	Kaninchen
raise in salary (auch rise)	Gehaltserhöhung
RAM (Random Access Memory)	Arbeitsspeicher
random sample	Stichprobe
randomly	zufällig
range of work	Arbeitsgebiet
rate, at this ~	Tempo, bei diesem ~
re-negotiable	erneut zu verhandeln
re-working	Überarbeitung
receptionist	Portier, Empfangsdame, -herr
recognise	erkennen
recommendation	Empfehlung
recruit/take on s.o.	jdn. einstellen
recruitment	Einstellung
references	Empfehlungen, Referenzen
refresher course	Auffrischungskurs
registered post	Einschreiben
reinforcement ring	Verstärkungsring
reject (v.)	ablehnen, zurückweisen
reject (n.)	Ausschußware
relevant questions	wichtige Fragen
relevant clerk	zuständiger Sachbearbeiter
reliable	zuverlässig
relief, that's a ~!	Trost, das ist ein ~!
remedy a situation	Abhilfe schaffen
remuneration	Vergütung
replacement goods	Ersatzwaren
require	verlangen, benötigen, erfordern

required standards	geforderte Normen
requirement	Bedarf, Anforderung
requirements, be up to our ~	Anforderungen, unseren ~ genügen
reservation, make a ~	Reservierung, eine ~ vornehmen
reserve a room	reservieren, ein ~ Zimmer
resign from	zurücktreten von, kündigen
resignation	Rücktritt
resources	Ressourcen
responsibility	Verantwortung
responsible for	verantwortlich für
resumé	Lebenslauf
retire	in Ruhestand treten
retrain	umschulen
rework	überarbeiten, umgestalten
rise, get a ~ (auch raise in salary)	Gehaltserhöhung, ~ bekommen
roast duck	gebratene Ente
roast chicken	gebratenes Hähnchen
rock the boat	für Unruhe sorgen
roller	Walze
ROM (Read Only Memory)	Lesespeicher
rotary index	Drehkartei
rubber	Radiergummi
rug	Laufer, Teppich
rule s.o.'s life	jds. Leben beherrschen
rule	Regel
ruler	Lineal
rush (n.)	Eile
rush (v.)	eilen

S

sack s.o.	jdn. entlassen (feuern)
salary by negotiation	außertarifliches Gehalt (AT)
salary level	Gehaltsniveau
sales negotiation	Verkaufsverhandlung
sales contract	Kaufvertrag
sales goal	Verkaufsziel
sales department	Verkauf, Verkaufsabteilung
sales appeal	Kaufanreiz

salesman	Verkäufer
salmon	Lachs
sample	Muster, Probe, Warenprobe
save time	Zeit sparen
scatter	zerstreuen
schedule	Zeitplan, Terminkalender
schedule, have a tight ~	Terminplan, einen engen ~ haben
scissors	Schere
score a hit	einen Treffer landen
score	erzielen (Punkte, Tore z. B.)
scrap (n.)	Altmaterial, Schrott
scrap (v.)	verschrotten
screen	Bildschirm, Leinwand
screen one's boss	seinen Chef abschirmen
screen candidates	Bewerber "sieben"
section	Abschnitt
security lodge	Pförtnerhäuschen
security check	Sicherheitskontrolle
select	auswählen
selection	Auswahl
selling proposition (USP), the unique ~	Verkaufsargument, das konkurrenzlose ~
selling price	Absatzpreis
selling message	Verkaufsbotschaft
senior management	Führungskräfte
sensible	vernünftig
sensitive to	empfindlich gegen
series production	Serienfertigung
serve, they ~ meat dishes	sie haben Fleisch auf der Karte
service	Wartung
services	Dienstleistungen
set standards	bestimmen, Normen ~
settle in	einziehen in
sex discrimination authority	Behörde für Gleichstellung von Mann und Frau
she's responsible for	verantwortlich, sie ist ~ für
shelves	Regal
shipping costs	Versandkosten
shop floor	Werkstatt
short list	engere Wahl (der Bewerber)

shorthand	Stenographie
shot, have a real ~	einen ernsthaften Versuch machen
show people around	Leute herumführen
show enthusiasm	Begeisterung zeigen
shredder	Reißwolf
shut up	den Mund halten
sick leave	Krankenurlaub
side table	Beistelltisch
size	Größe
skeleton	Skelett, Gerüst
skilled worker	Facharbeiter
slide	Dia
slide projector	Diaprojektor
slogan	Schlagwort
smoked salmon	Räucherlachs
smooth things over	die Wogen glätten
soften towards s.o.	weich werden, sich erweichen
sole	Seezunge
speak up	laut und deutlich sprechen
specialised fair	Fachmesse
specification	Spezifizierung, Spezifikation
specs, be up to ~	Spezifikationen, den ~ entsprechen
spell	buchstabieren
spend time on calls	Zeit auf Anrufe verwenden
split hairs	Haarspalterei betreiben
spot check	Stichprobe
spreadsheet software	Tabellenkalkulationsprogramm
sprouts	Rosenkohl
square metres	Quadratmeter
staff	Belegschaft, Personal
staff representative	Personalvertreter
stagger out	hinaustaumeln
stamp	Stempel
standard conditions	normale Bedingungen
standards, up to ~	Anforderungen, den ~ genügend
standby	Vertretung
stapler	Hefter
staple	Heftklammer
starter	Vorspeise

starting salary	Anfangsgehalt
state (v.)	angeben, behaupten
stay, ~ with the wine	bleiben, beim Wein ~
steady job	feste Anstellung
stewed fruit	Kompott
stint	Pensum, Schicht
stir-fried vegetables	Wok-Gemüse
stock levels	Lagerbestand
stock control	Lagerkontrolle
stocks	Bestände
store	Lager
straight to the point, let's come ~	direkt zur Sache, kommen wir ~
strategic matters	strategische Angelegenheiten
stress	betonen
subassembly	Baugruppe
subject	Fach
submit a quotation	ein Preisangebot unterbreiten
subordinate	Untergebener
subsidiary	Tochtergesellschaft
successful	erfolgreich
suggest	vorschlagen
suggestion	Vorschlag
summarise	zusammenfassen
superior (adj.)	überlegen
superior (n.)	Vorgesetzter
supervisory board	Aufsichtsrat
supplier	Lieferant
supply contract	Liefervertrag
supportive	unterstützend
surprised	überrascht
suspension file	Hängeordner
switchboard	Telefonzentrale
swivel chair	Drehstuhl

T

table	Tabelle, Tisch
tabular form	tabellarisch
take care of	betreuen

take a seat	nehmen Sie Platz
take part in	teilnehmen an
take long	lange brauchen
talk of the devil!	Wenn man den Teufel nennt!
task	Aufgabe
taxable income	steuerpflichtiges Einkommen
taxes	Steuer
telefax paper	Telefaxpapier
telephone book	Telefonbuch
temporary personnel	Aushilfspersonal
tender, to make a ~	Angebot, ein ~ abgeben
terms of payment	Zahlungsbedingungen
terms of contract	Vertragsbedingungen
terms of business / trade	Geschäftsbedingungen
terms, lay down ~	Bedingungen festlegen
terms, on their own ~	Bedingungen, zu ihren eigenen ~
test report	Prüfbericht
test workpieces	Werkstücke prüfen
test bench	Prüfbank
test stand	Prüfstand
testimonial, open ~	Zeugnis, offenes ~
testing engineer	Prüfingenieur
that's as may be	das mag sein
the right man for the job	der richtige Mann für den Job
they do good fish here	sie haben guten Fisch hier
throw s.o. in at the deep end	jdn. ins tiefe Wasser werfen
tip	Hinweis (auch Trinkgeld)
tip the balance	den Ausschlag geben
tire somebody out	jdn. erschöpfen, ermüden
tolerance	Toleranz
tool	Werkzeug
top left	links oben
trade discount	Wiederverkäuferrabatt
trade press	Fachpresse
trade discount	Handelsrabatt
trade mark	Warenzeichen, Handelsmarke
trade fair	Handelsmesse
trainee	Azubi
training	Ausbildung

training course	Lehrgang
training department	Ausbildungsabteilung
training objectives	Ausbildungsziele
transparency	Folie
tray	Ablage
treat s.o. badly	jdn. schlecht behandeln
trial period	Probezeit
trout	Forelle
turkey	Pute
turn one's back on s.o.	jdm. den Rücken kehren
turn down, ~ an offer	ablehnen, ein Angebot ~
TV slot / spot	TV-Spot / Fernsehwerbung
typewriter	Schreibmaschine
typing ribbon	Farbband
typing paper	Schreibmaschinenpapier

U

unbearable	unerträglich
union, trade ~	Gewerkschaft
unit	Einheit
unskilled worker	ungelernter Arbeiter
unsolicited callers	unerwünschte Anrufer
up your street	genau Ihr Fall
upset	aufgeregt
urgent, urgently (adv.)	dringend
use a special software	eine spezielle Software benutzen
use, make ~ of	Gebrauch machen von
used to, be ~ working with a computer	daran gewöhnt sein, mit dem Computer zu arbeiten

V

vacancy	Zimmer frei, freie Stelle
vacant post	freie Stelle
vacant rooms	freie Zimmer
vacate	räumen, frei machen
valuables	Wertsachen, Wertgegenstände
value analysis	Wertanalyse

valve	Ventil
variable costs	variable Kosten
various departments	verschiedene Abteilungen
VAT (value added tax)	Mehrwertsteuer
veal	Kalb
vegetables	Gemüse
venison	Reh, Hirsch
verify	überprüfen
virtue	Tugend
visit/attend a fair	besuchen, eine Messe ~
visitor to a fair	Messebesucher
vocational training	Berufsausbildung
voice an opinion	äußern, Meinung ~
volunteer	sich freiwillig melden

W

wage packet	Lohntüte
wage scale	Lohnskala
wages policy	Lohnpolitik
waiter	Kellner, Ober
waitress	Fräulein, Kellnerin
warranty	Zusicherung, vertragliche ~
waste (v.) time	verschwenden, Zeit ~
waste (n.) of time	Zeitverschwendung
wastepaper basket	Papierkorb
weakness	Schwäche
weapon	Waffe
wear out	ermüden, erschöpfen
weights, train ~	Gewichte, Gewichtstraining machen
wild boar	Wildschwein
willing, I'm ~ to ...	bereit, ich bin ~, zu ...
word processing	Textverarbeitung
work force	Belegschaft
work experience	Arbeitserfahrung
work-to-rule	Dienst nach Vorschrift
working hours	Arbeitszeit
working conditions	Arbeitsbedingungen
working week	Arbeitswoche

workplace	Arbeitsplatz
works	Werk
workshop	Werkstatt
world fair	Weltausstellung
worried	besorgt
writing set	Schreibset

Key to the exercises

CHAPTER 1

Exercise 1:
1. The personnel department is responsible for promotion and salary. 2. They are looking for a trainee. 3. They don't talk about "he" in the advert because they want to avoid problems. 4. The applicant should have a university degree and speak a foreign language

Exercise 2A:
1. If it's hot, it'*s* soup.If it's cold, it'*s* beer.
2. What happens if this parachute *fails* to open? If you *bring* it back, you'*ll get* a new one.
3. A lot of husbands *would leave* their wives if they *knew* how to pack their suitcases.
4. If you *don't* know what you want, come in, we have got it.
5. Now, what steps *would* you *take*, if I dropped this bottle?

Exercise 2 B:
1. If he *is* the right man for the job, he *will get* the position.
2. If we *call* it by the wrong name, *we'll get* the wrong type of candidate.
3. Chances of promotion *are* excellent if you *are* the right candidate.
4. If we *talk* about "he" in the advertisement, *we'll get* problems with the sex discrimination authorities.
5. If I *didn't know* what a trainee was, I *wouldn't be* where I am, would I?

Exercise 3:
hire; employ; employer; subordinate; sack

Exercise 4:
personnel department; superior; staff; employee; vacancy

Exercise 5: Wordbuilder's corner
employment; deduction; resignation; responsibility; promotion; dismissal

CHAPTER 2

Exercise 1:
1. Four years. 2. James stated only date and descriptions of what he had done.
3. James did not state his hobbies and his third foreign language. 4. James attended Manchester University and Manchester Business School.

Exercise 2 A:
1. If I'd been the Virgin Mary, I'*d have said* "No!"
2. God *would never have given* us the bicycle if he *had wanted* us to walk.

3. A husband is a someone who will share with you all the troubles which you *wouldn't have had* if you *hadn't married* him.
4. Eve was unhappy in Paradise because she couldn't tell Adam about all the wonderful lovers she *would have had* if she *hadn't married* him.
5. I *would have done* it if I had found a way without making him happy.

Exercise 2 B:
1. If you*'d taken* my advice you*'d have done* a commercial training as a clerk.
2. If I'*d have known* that it'd take so long, I *would have told you* ...
3. If you'*d let* me do it, it would've been better.

Exercise 3:
1. job placement 2. apprenticeship 3. probationary period 4. holiday 5. overtime

Exercise 4:
advertisement; interview; screening (of the applicants); short list; selection; contract

Exercise 5:
curriculum vitae; qualifications; references; testimonials; diplomas

CHAPTER 3

Exercise 1:
1. I never lied when I was a child. – So, when did you start, sir?
2. I was at the zoo last year. – Which cage were you in?

Exercise 2:
1. Who *rode* with a smile on a tiger. They *returned* from the ride.
2. I *didn't believe* in reincarnation the last time, either.
3. God *was* a woman until she *changed* her mind.

Exercise 3:
1. I hope you had a good journey.
2. You studied economics? Did you study economics?
3. You only studied for four years.
4. What did these courses include?

Exercise 4:
1. Kelly's studies at university did not include data processing and foreign languages.
2. Marketing was not taught at university.
3. Mr Block and Mr Seba want to find out if James fits into their team.

Exercise 5:
application; business calculations; civil service

Exercise 6
employee; interviewee

Exercise 7
application; description; appearance; impression; requirement

Exercise 8:
get a job / land a job; salary rise / increment; resumé / CV;
important questions / relevant questions

CHAPTER 4

Exercise 1:
1. Job rotation means that James will move from department to department.
2. James will learn how to invoice customers.
3. The key personnel takes the important decisions.

Exercise 2:
They try to live *up* to their name. Let's move *on* to the next room.
He managed to arrive *for* the appointment. Mr Kelly is *from* England.
You'll enjoy your time *with* us.

Exercise 3:
make an appointment; do the accounts; invoice; key personnel; I have a tight schedule

Exercise 4:
head of department; head of finance; head of accounts; head of training; head of personnel

Exercise 5:
in charge of ; present; security lodge; move on to

Exercise 6:
1 Mr Kelly, I'd like you to meet Dr. Rope. 2 Paul, this is Mr Kelly. 3 How do you do?
4 How do you do? 5 Nice to meet you.

Exercise 7:
1 were hunting; were circling; did I hit; dropped 2 have bought; wrote; read
3 were hunting; saw; disappeared; were you waiting; didn't you shoot; is not loaded 4 visited; drowned 5 were fishing; pulled; looked; shook

CHAPTER 5

Exercise 1:
training centre – canteen; customers – trainees; workshop – store

Exercise 2:
1. I'd like to welcome you here today for our tour around the company. 2. Now, my name's Block. 3. His identity pass was not valid. 4. Gentlemen, I wish you good-day.

Exercise 3:

Why does the sign	above	the door say "canteen"?
There must be a good reason	for	that.
He's not so well informed	about	operational matters.
Would you please take	over	from me?
See you	at	the banquet tonight.

Exercise 4:
1. How are you? I haven't seen you for ages / for years. 2. I haven't seen you for almost two years. 3 What have you been doing all the time?

Exercise 5:
procedure; assembly; competition; production; planning

CHAPTER 6

Exercise 1:
employee assessments

Exercise 2:
1. department 2. duties 3. spreadsheet 4. assign duties 5. expenditure 6. cope with 7. cost accounting

Exercise 3:
calculating machine: Rechenmaschine; value analysis: Wertanalyse; employee assessment: Mitarbeiterbeurteilung; spreadsheet software: Tabellenkalkulationsprogramm

Exercise 4:
cost price; cost centre; cost accounting;
variable costs; overhead costs; manufacturing costs; actual costs

Exercise 5:
accountant; bill; click; assess; balance sheet; calculate

CHAPTER 7

Exercise 1 A:
1. I know, sir. I' *ve only been* here for two weeks, but I'*ve found* that out already. 2. Nonsense! You *haven't met* everybody yet. 3. ... we *were* on the edge ... Since then we'*ve taken* a great step forward. 4. Saving is a fine thing, especially when your parents *have done* it for you. 5. Bob: How *did* you *get* that splinter in your finger? René: I *don't know*. All I *did* was scratch my head. 6. Anne: *Have* I ever *sent* you a bill?

Ecercise 1 B:
1. It's *been* three weeks already.
2. It *has tired* me out looking at figures on a screen for so long.
3. But I*'ve* only just *joined* the company.
4. Actually, I myself *made* the mistake with the spelling when I was preparing the meeting.
5. How long *have* you *worked* for the company?

Exercise 2:
1. James has been sitting in front of the computer for three weeks.
2. Because Dr. Rope had pronounced it the wrong way.
3. He is from Moscow.

Exercise 3:
responsibility; apology; explanation; distance

Exercise 4:
apologise; baggage claim; confidence; destination;
apology; boring; controller; distance

Exercise 5:
1d, 2a, 3c, 4b
Here are the English expressions: a) snack b) lift c) supermarket d) exchange

Exercise 6:
1 left luggage 2 baggage claim 3 arrivals 4 Lost and Found

Exercise 7:
nursery 2 information 3 porter 4 railway 5 telephone 6 toilets 7 gates 8 customs 9 bath 10 hairdresser 11 function rooms 12 restaurant 13 bus 14 taxi 15 car rental 16 meeting point 17 departure 18 post

CHAPTER 8

Exercise 1A:
1. I*'ve lost my* memory. When *did* this *happen*? When *did* what *happen*?
2. I *joined* the navy to see the world and *spent* five years in a submarine.
3. In the beginning I *created* Heaven and Earth.
4. In six days God *made* Heaven and Earth. He *was* self-employed.

Exercise 1B:
1. I've been given a job to do but I'm not quite sure what I'm expected to do.
2. Dr. Rope told me to compile information about the history of the company.
3. Then he gave me two foils/transparencies about the company.
4. (Actually) I've never spoken in public before.

Exercise 2:

1. Be a good citizen. *Why don't you* pay with a smile?
2. Driving instructor: *Wouldn't it be better* if you slowed down?
3. I think you *should* see my wife first.
4. ... may I give you a piece of advice /some advice?
5. *You'd* better be careful with your immigration laws.
6. If *I were you I'd* put an advertisement in the paper.
7. Sure. But *I wouldn't advise it.*

Exercise 3:

on the screen; illustration; let's go through the possibilities; OHP sheet; graph

Exercise 4:

top left; on the left; introduction; dashed line / dotted line; speak up

Exercise 5:

audience; bottom left; compile

Exercise 6:

1. up 2. on 3. in 4. in

CHAPTER 9

Exercise 1:

1. Mr Kelly, can I have a word with you?
2. How can I be of assistance?
3. Can I help you?
4. I probably didn't express myself correctly.

Exercise 2 A:

1. So, you'*ve been suffering* from loss of memory.
2. Dear sirs, we'*ve just received* some buttons with no shirts on them.
3. The show you'*ve been looking forward to* all week will be cancelled.
4. You'*ve been doing* "nothing" for years.
5. I'*ve not eaten* for three days.
6. I'*ve been* in love with the same man for twenty years.

Exercise 2 B:

1. Well, the Russian *has been causing* problems at his hotel.
2. What *has* Mr Zhukov *been doing*? What's the problem?
3. He'*s been getting* himself drunk.
4. The manager *has just been* on the phone.
5. We'*ve been misunderstanding* each other in the last five minutes.
6. I think I'*ve understood* you perfectly well.

Exercise 3:
accommodation; behalf; client, deal with; assistance; bill; conference room; deposit

Exercise 4:
make a booking; make a reservation; make a bill out to a person; arrange accommodation for five people.

Exercise 5:
First he booked a room, then he confirmed the booking, finally he cancelled the booking

Exercise 6:

Please book .... 2 .... persons for
3 days (2 nights) arriving .... (Date)
or
5 days (4 nights) arriving .... 12/7 .... (Date)
or
.... days (....... nights) arriving .... (Date)

Splits .... (1st Date) .... (2nd Date)

ANY SPECIAL REQUIREMENTS ....
quiet room looking to the yard

ACCOMMODATION REQUIRED - Enter the number of rooms required in the relevant box.
(All supplements per person per night - plus V.A.T.)

Telephone Reference Number:

Double or Twin without bath		Double or Twin with bath or shower	✗
Single without bath		Single with bath or shower	
Three bedded (3 seperate beds or double large & single) without bath		Three bedded (3 seperate beds or double large & single) with bath or shower	

Preferred Hotel: If first choice is full - similar grade will be booked.
1st choice ....
2nd choice ....
3rd choice ....
Detailed hotel descriptions - see pages 6-9.
Hotel and single room supplements - see pages 4-5.

Second Class Return Rail tickets are required from .... Glasgow .... Station (........ 2 .... county) to London
Your rail tickets are included in the price. Ask your travel agent for details of train timings.

Please book Excursion Numbers .... Hyde Park .... Number of persons ....

SURNAMES (All members in party)	Initials	Mr. Mrs Miss	**Address and telephone number** of first named member of party to whom all tickets etc. will be sent.	Ages of Children
Bosewitz	R.	Mr	Belfortstr. 1, 69172 Heidelberg	
Loren	S.	Mrs		

I enclose remittance of £ 10:50 ... being a deposit of £7.50 per person, plus £1.50 or £1.90 per person Insurance (if required) as detailed, and agree to accept the booking conditions as stated.
Signature R. Bosewitz ... Date 18/May 96
Please debit my credit card: Access/Barclaycard
£ .... Signed ....
Agent's ABTA number:
Agent's V.A.T. Reg number:

Member of Association of British Travel Agents
Member of The London Tourist Board

CHAPTER 10

Exercise 2A:

1. How can you *make* money selling your photocopiers so cheap? We *make* a profit repairing them.
2. Italians *make* the best lovers, the Japanese *make* them smaller and cheaper.
3. Character is what you have got when nobody *is looking.*
4. A true gentleman is someone who *knows* how to play the trumpet and doesn't.
5. I'*m not bathing*. I'*m drowning*.
6. Doctor: *Do* you *drink* a lot? Patient: No, I *spill* most of it.
7. People who *say* nothing is impossible should try gargling with their mouths shut.

Exercise 2B:

1. Here we prepare the advertising. 2. We compile the sheets of information for our customers. 3. We make the masters for brochures and bulletins.

Exercise 3:

personal computer; central processing unit; multi-feed fax; laser printer; answering machine

Exercise 4:

catalogues; advertisements; graphics; bulletins; brochures; pamphlets

Exercise 5:

advert; advertisement

CHAPTER 11

Exercise 1:

We've confidence *in* your abilities. I can't cope *with* the problem. This wasn't offered *at* university. We're counting *on* you. The budget has been decided *at* board level. You won't have any problems *with* arranging payment.

Exercise 2:

Sorry, no key available. Have a look at the text.

Exercise 3:

1. A man who steals a handful of gold *is put* into prison; a man who steals a whole country *is made* king.
2. An executive is a man who hires others to do what he *is hired* to do.
3. When I was seven years old I *was taken* to London Zoo. – *Were* you *accepted*?
4. When it *was known* what he'd done he *was given* a gun.
5. A pessimist is a man who *has been forced* to live with an optimist.

Exercise 4:

1. I've no idea what *I'm expected* to do.
2. Phone up the exhibition contractor to make sure that the stand *is being erected* the right way.
3. This sort of thing *wasn't offered* at university.
4. The budget for the exhibition *has already been decided* at board level.
5. *You'll be given* every assistance by Mr Bucker.

Exercise 5:

1. exhibition site 2. exhibition building 3. exhibition space 4. exhibition stand 5. exhibition contractor 6. exhibition catalogue 7. exposition 8. world fair

Exercise 6:

assistance; brand manager; consumer survey; display

Exercise 7:

apply for exhibition space; attend a fair; hold a fair; assemble a stand

CHAPTER 12

Exercise 1:

1. deal with sales contracts 2. university, business school 3. he is avoiding the Russian 4. is inviting him for dinner

Exercise 2 A:

1. Not on Sunday. But on Monday *you'll be having* your operations.
2. Never mind, doctor, *I'll come* back when you are sober.
3. Give us £ 50,000 or you *will not see* your husband again. – *I'm not going to give* you the money.

Exercise 2B:

1. You'*ll have* to deal with the sales contracts.
2. I'*ll come* back to that later.
3. That impossible Russian *is coming* to visit us tomorrow.
4. *He arrives* on the five o'clock train from Frankfort.
5. *I'm not going to see* him again, if I can help it.
6. Now what *are we going* to do tonight?

Exercise 3:

quote > contract > order > delivery > payment

Exercise 4:

salesman; negotiations; department; contract

Exercise 5:
negotiate, conclude, sign, break a contract

Exercise 6:
terms of trade, business, contract, payment

CHAPTER 13

Exercise 1:
1. venison 2. They eat at the Traube because it is James' favourite pub, hotel food is boring and because Boris likes country food. 3. Zhukov is in Germany to buy photocopiers 4. Leo buys from Low Valley because he likes James and because Boris works for Low Valley Photocopiers

Exercise 2:
suggestion; choice; recommendation; decision

Exercise 3:
main course – main meal; buy – purchase; serve game – do game

Exercise 4:
I'll try / I'll have /I'll take the duck.
Will-future drückt eine spontane Entscheidung aus.

Exercise 5:
1. They *serve* very good venison here.
2. My mouth *is beginning* to water.
3. We consider you *have tipped* the balance in favour of a purchase.
4. We *were not* sure whether to purchase from your company.
5. But now we *have made* our decision.

CHAPTER 14

Exercise 1:
1. Entertaining business friends and writing advertisements
2. He wants to sell him manuals

Exercise 2:
I'm afraid Mr Brain is not *available* at the moment.
I'm sorry, but Mr Brain is on *holiday* this week.
I'm afraid she is *out of* the office this week.
Mr Brain is away *on business.*
I'm sorry, Mr Brain is at a *meeting.*
He left strict instructions not to be *disturbed.*

He's in the middle of an *interview.*
He has got an important *visitor.*
Dr. Brain is very *busy* at the moment.

Exercise 3:
R: Schneider SIP Computers. Good morning. What can I do for you?
A: Good morning. Put me through to the head of customer services, please.
R: What did you say your name was?
A: Anton Sparbier. I'm one of your regular clients.
R: What's it in connection with, please?
A: I'd like to draw your attention to a defect in one of your models.
R: One moment, please, I'm putting you through.

Exercise 4
Are you going to take the call? Tell her that I've got a visitor.

CHAPTER 15

Exercise :
1. frames and plastic parts 2. buying from external suppliers 3. Suppliers delay sending the components to get better conditions

Exercise 2:
chief buyer; components; supplier; assemble; frame; control system; weapons

Exercise 3 A:
I'm getting used to living here now.
Well, what sort of problems *have* you *been having* recently?
I'*m joining* a meeting with a supplier later this week.
I *finished* working there two months ago.

Exercise 3 B:
Satz Nummer 3 bezieht sich auf die Zukunft.
Satz Nummer 1 bezieht sich auf die Gegenwart.
Satz Nummer 2 bezieht sich auf den Zeitraum bis zur Gegenwart.
Satz Nummer 4 bezieht sich auf die Vergangenheit

Exercise 3 C:
1. If they start outsourcing surely a lot of people employed here *will risk* losing their jobs.
2. If he *is* not satisfied he will call the supplier for another discussion.

Exercise 4 A:

1. Leave the most difficult problem for the laziest managers *to solve*.
2. No wife minds her husband *being* a dreamer as long as he isn't a snorer.
3. Nothing is illegal if 100 businessmen decide *to do* it.
4. Sometimes I think that God in *creating* man somewhat overestimated his ability.
5. I dislike *feeling* at home when I am abroad.

Exercise 4 B:

1. I finished *working* there two months ago.
2. I dislike *hearing* that sort of thing.
3. What I don't understand is why so many people keep *telling* me that everything here is better than everywhere else.
4. Sometimes suppliers even try *to delay sending* the components as a weapon against us.

Exercise 5:

assemble; brand name; components; delivery period

Exercise 6:

discount; terms of business; price per item; delivery conditions; terms of payment; guarantee

Exercise: 7

to lead ; to submit ; to make; lay down

Exercise 8:

There *was* a young lady of Leek
Who *had* fifty proposals a week.
Though she never *grew* tired
Of *being admired*,
She *was* often too sleepy *to speak*.

CHAPTER 16

Exercise 1:

1. he was kept at another appointment 2. he is placing orders for the next three years 3. is on top of his job

Exercise 2:

meetings are prepared, concluded, planned, chaired, monitored, attended

CHAPTER 17

Exercise 1:
1. sets standards for the supplier and for their own production 2. differ from each other within acceptable tolerances 3. his components did not meet the required standards

Exercise 2:
QC: quality control; CV: curriculum vitae; PC: personal computer; USP: unique selling point; fob: free on board

Exercise 3:
unit; postpone; mass-produce; overheads

Exercise 4 A:
1. He *told* them that it *was a* map of the Sahara.
2. There was a young lady of Kent / Who *said* that she *knew* what it meant
3. There was an old man of Peru / Who *dreamt* he *was eating* his shoe.
4. When I was young I *thought* that money *was the* most important thing in life. Now that I am old I *know* that it *is*.
5. He was hoping that the teacher *hadn't gone* too far. The girl replied that the first lesson *had been* quite useless because they had only done the theory.

Exercise 4 B:
1. K: He was of the opinion that he *had agreed* quotations for the guards and that his company *had met* the quality standards required.
2. K: He *said* he *wanted* to postpone the question of quality. He *mentioned* that things *weren't* quite clear for him.
3. G: I *explained* to Mr Stumpf two days ago that the quality *wasn't* up to specs on the guards.

Exercise 5:
1. The ecologists want us *to say* no to fast breeders.
2. Mark Twain was asked what he *thought* about Heaven and Hell.
3. A diplomat is a man who can tell you *to go* to hell in such a way that you actually look forward to the trip.
4. For a while we pondered whether *to take* a vacation or get a divorce.

Exercise 6:
check; central stock; test bench; mass production

Exercise 7:
test stand; test bench; test report

Exercise 8:
rejects; scrap; inspector; tolerance

CHAPTER 18

Exercise 1:

1. copiers are sensitive to climatic conditions 2. his copier has been down for three days and there have been no service calls.

Exercise 2:

1. I'm afraid I have to register a serious complaint.
   Mr Frogger, I'd very much like to complain. I've got a serious complaint to make.
2. I'm awfully sorry to hear that.
   I can understand that you are dissatisfied. That's a real nuisance.
   We owe you more than an apology.
3. I'll get the department leader onto it immediately.
   We'll look into it immediately.

Exercise 3:

apologise; manual; cut off; complain; faithful customers

Exercise 4:

complaint; confirmation; copier, agreement

Exercise 5:

1. I'*m expecting* a call from a customer in Australia ...
   (nicht abgeschlossen zum Zeitpunkt des Sprechens)
2. So what exactly *has happened*?
   (Das Wann interessiert nicht, nur das Was)
3. My copier *has been* down for three days.
   (Zustand, dauert zum Zeitpunkt des Sprechens immer noch an)
4. There *was* a call from the Mr Block.
   (Abgeschlossen in der Vergangenheit. Frogger erinnert sich, daß vor zwei Stunden ein Anruf kam.)
5. We'*ll look* into it immediately.
   (Kein Futur, sondern ein spontanes Versprechen bzw. Angebot)

CHAPTER 19

Exercise 1:

1. We all make mistakes, *don't we*? 2. Architect: The acoustics in our new concert hall are fantastic, *aren't they*? 3. You're not going to blame me, sir, *are you*? 4. I can't tell until I've seen the evidence, *can I*? 5. You love me, darling, *don't you*?

Exercise 2:

1. is there? 2. won't you? 3. don't you?

3667/1

Personen

Die historischen Personen sind mit einem * gekennzeichnet.

Eine Aufstellung der wichtigsten Personen:

Willem Dirks Bakker*, Hotelier
Klaas Willems Bakker*, sein ältester Sohn
Dirk Willems Bakker*, sein zweitältester Sohn
Adeline Bakker*, Dirks Ehefrau
Jann Willems Bakker*, dritter Sohn
Eildert Willems Bakker*, vierter Sohn
Jakob Willems Bakker*, fünfter Sohn
Hieltje Bakker*, Jakobs Ehefrau
Geeske Willems Bakker*, jüngstes Kind von Willem Dirks und einzige Tochter
Wilhelm Bakker*, Geeskes Ehemann; trägt ebenfalls den Geburtsnamen Bakker, ist jedoch nicht blutsverwandt
Hermine Flessner, Zimmermädchen
Luise Menninga, Hausdame
Georg Köhler*, Hotelier und Bürgermeister
Georg Köhler Junior*, sein Sohn
Johann Fischer*, erster Sparkassenchef auf Borkum

6

Prolog

Borkum, 7. Juli 1887

Liebe Hermine!

Nun geht der Sommer bald zu Ende und ich komme endlich dazu, dir zu schreiben. Deine Mutter hat meiner erzählt, dass es euch immer schlechter geht, auch wenn deine Mutter das nicht wahrhaben will. Du weißt, es gibt eine Lösung. Wir haben oft genug darüber gesprochen und ich sage es dir noch einmal. Du verdienst nirgends mehr Geld als auf den Inseln. Die Arbeit als Borkum-Mädchen ist die gleiche, die du zu Hause auch tun musst, nur hier bekommst du Geld dafür. Einen guten Lohn, das verspreche ich dir. Gerne rede ich mit Herrn Köhler und sage ihm, daß du ein fleißiges Mädchen bist. Er wird ganz bestimmt eine Arbeitsstelle für dich haben. Überlege es dir, du hast ja noch etwas Zeit. Vor dem kommenden April wird sowieso niemand eingestellt. Und es sind ja nur fünf Monate, die wirst du sicherlich überstehen.

Liebe Grüße
Deine Cousine Bertha.

PS: Verrate deiner Mutter nicht, was ich dir geschrieben habe. Sie möchte sicher nicht, dass alle Welt erfährt, wie schlecht es euch geht.

Hermine ließ den Brief sinken. Sie hatte ihn oft gelesen. Er hatte ihr so manche schlaflose Nacht bereitet.

„Rück mal ein Stück", sagte ihre jüngere Schwester Hedwig. Beide teilten sich ein Bett. Im gegenüberliegenden schliefen Mutter und die neunjährige Hildegard. Vater und ihre drei Brüder teilten sich das Zimmer auf der anderen Seite des Flures. Eigentlich sollten sie schon vor drei Jahren in ein größeres Haus umziehen, doch dann wurde Vater krank. Er konnte nur noch stundenweise im Kontor aushelfen, und wenn er nicht schon so lange dort beschäftigt wäre, hätte sein Arbeitgeber ihn sicherlich längst entlassen. Seither drehten sie jeden Pfennig dreimal um, ehe er ausgegeben werden konnte.

„Glaubst du, ich bekomme zum Geburtstag ein Geschenk?"

Die Frage brach Hermine das Herz. „Ganz bestimmt", log sie.

Hermine legte den Brief zurück in die Nachttischschublade und blies das Lampenlicht aus. Im kommenden Jahr sollte Hedwig auf jeden Fall eines bekommen. Ihr Entschluss stand fest. Sie würde Berthas Angebot annehmen.

Kapitel 1

Borkum, April 1888

„Sie sind ganz blass im Gesicht, junges Fräulein. Kommen Sie, setzen Sie sich zu mir."

Genau das hätte sie gerne vermieden. Lieber wäre ihr eine Sitzgelegenheit an einem Tisch mit Frauen oder einer Familie, statt einem allein reisenden Herrn gegenüber Platz zu nehmen. Doch auf dem Schiff war jede Sitzbank dicht besetzt. Der honorige Herr wirkte freundlich, dennoch klangen Hermine Großmutters Worte in den Ohren: „Meide die feinen Pinkel, die sind nichts für unsereiner."

Das mussten die anderen Mitreisenden auch gedacht haben, warum sonst saß er allein am Tisch? Seine Kleidung war edel. Er wirkte, als käme er von einem Empfang zu Ehren des niederländischen Königs Wilhelm III. von Oranien-Nassau. In der Zeitung stand, der habe gestern stattgefunden. Hermine blickte zum Bullauge hinaus. Die Küstenlinie des holländischen Festlands war nur noch als schmaler Streifen zu erkennen.

„Sind Sie seekrank?" Der alte Herr klang mitfühlend, dennoch meinte sie den Schalk in seinen Augen zu entdecken. Hermine schüttelte den Kopf.

„Dann ist Ihnen oben an Deck kalt geworden. Der April kann an der Nordsee lausig sein."

Hermine nickte. Doch das war nicht der einzige Grund ihrer Flucht ins untere warme Deck. Über die Reling gebeugt hingen gleich zwei Reisende, obwohl nur kleine Wellen die See bewegten. Die Gerüche des Erbrochenen und die würgenden Geräusche hatten Hermine den Magen umgekrempelt.

„Ich bestelle Ihnen ein schönes heißes Schokoladengetränk." Der alte Herr hob seinen Spazierstock, um die Bedienung auf sich aufmerksam zu machen. Der silberne Griff in Form eines Seehundes blitzte im Sonnenlicht, das durch die salzverkrusteten Scheiben der Bullaugen fiel.

„Nein. Bitte nicht."

„Sie mögen keine Schokolade? Das ist ungewöhnlich für ein junges Mädchen." Sein Lachen klang freundlich.

Ich liebe Schokolade, dachte Hermine. Nur reichte ihr Geld für diese Köstlichkeit kaum aus. Vom Vater hatte sie drei Mark Reisegeld zugesteckt bekommen. „Für Notfälle", hatte er gesagt.

„Oh, entschuldigen Sie bitte! Meine Manieren lassen zu wünschen übrig. Ich habe mich gar nicht vorgestellt." Er lüftete leicht den Hintern von der Sitzbank, als wolle er aufstehen, und deutete eine Verbeugung an. Hermine war unangenehm berührt, dass ein so feiner und offensichtlich reicher Herr sie so höflich behandelte. Im Nacken spürte sie die Blicke der Mitreisenden.

„Mein Name ist Willem Dirks Bakker. Schiffer und Hotelier." Viele kleine Lachfältchen umgaben seine Augen. Er schien ein netter Herr zu sein.

Ihr Unwohlsein schwand. „Hermine Flessner."

„Nett, Sie kennenzulernen, Fräulein Flessner. Ich frage mich, woher Sie kommen?"

„Aus Leer."

„Eine schöne Stadt. Mit vielen Reedereien. Ich kenne sie gut. Beide, die Stadt und die Reedereien. Reisen Sie das erste Mal nach Borkum?"

Hermine nickte. „Ich war niemals dort."

„Ich schon mein ganzes Leben lang. Nur gelegentlich verlasse ich die Insel. Früher öfter. Greetsiel, Emden, Borkum." Sein Zeigefinger wies nach links und nach rechts. „Als Schiffer kommt man herum. Gerade komme ich von einer Badekur zurück. Aber alte Leute sollten in Gegenwart von jungen Menschen nicht über Krankheiten sprechen, das ist langweilig." Sein Lächeln hatte etwas Freches. „Und das interessiert Sie sicherlich nicht."

Er schaute zum Fenster hinaus. Die Insel kam nach fünfstündiger Seereise endlich an Steuerbordseite in Sicht. „Ah, sehen Sie!" Willem Dirks Bakker deutete darauf. „Das ist Borkum. Der Kapitän der *Augusta* hat vermutlich ein paar Schüppen Kohle zusätzlich aufgelegt, um schnell heimzukommen."

„*Augusta?*"

„Der Name des Raddampfers, auf dem wir fahren."

Er muss mich für eine dumme Gans halten, wenn ich das nicht mitbekommen habe, dachte Hermine. Eine Weile sahen beide schweigend aufs Meer hinaus.

„Darf ich raten?", nahm Bakker das Gespräch wieder auf. „Sie haben eine Anstellung auf der Insel bekommen."

Hermine nickte, dann schüttelte sie den Kopf. „Ich hoffe auf eine Arbeitsstelle. Meine Cousine, sie ist Zimmermädchen in

Köhlers Dorfhotel, hat mir geschrieben, dass dort immer Personal gesucht wird."

„Sie reisen auf gut Glück zur Insel? Sie sind eine mutige junge Dame, das muss ich schon sagen." Willem Dirks Bakker klang, als habe sie sich auf ein Räuberabenteuer eingelassen.

Hermine bekam rote Wangen und fühlte sich plötzlich elend. Sie schaute zum Bullauge hinaus, dann senkte sie den Blick und betrachtete ihre Hände. In Gedanken überflog sie ihre Barschaft. Drei Mark Reisegeld von Papa, zwei Mark und fünfundachtzig Pfennige hatte sie gespart und jeweils eine Mark von Oma und Opa. Wenn sie die Anstellung nicht bekommen sollte, würde es hoffentlich ausreichen, um irgendwo preiswert zu übernachten und die Rückreise bezahlen zu können. Sie hob den Kopf, weil sie sich von ihm beobachtet glaubte, und fasste den Mut zu fragen: „Wie meinen Sie das?"

Wie hatte sie nur so dumm sein und sich auf die Briefe von Cousine Bertha verlassen können? Es wird keine Arbeit geben. Sie hatte die beschwerliche und teure Reise umsonst angetreten. Dabei hatte Bertha bei ihrem letzten Besuch in Leer behauptet, auf allen Inseln suchten sie händeringend Personal. Zugegeben, das war Monate her. Im vergangenen Jahr mochte das so gewesen sein, doch schien es sich in der Zwischenzeit geändert zu haben.

Hermine wurde angst und bange. Ein zusätzlicher Gedanke kam ihr. Was, wenn kein Zimmer zu mieten war und sie die kommende Nacht unter freiem Himmel verbringen musste? Doch dann beruhigte sie sich. In Cousine Berthas Kammer in *Köhlers Dorfhotel* konnte sie sicherlich Quartier nehmen. Auch wenn das bedeutete, dass sie gemeinsam in einem Bett schlafen mussten.

„Es erfordert Courage“, sagte Bakker in die Stille hinein.

Tränen traten Hermine in die Augen. Sie zwinkerte sie fort.

„Ich vermute, der Herr Köhler weiß gar nicht, dass Sie anreisen, um bei ihm zu arbeiten?“

Hermine nickte, unfähig einen Ton herauszubekommen.

Bakker griff in seine Westentasche und reichte ihr ein gebügeltes Herrentaschentuch. Hermine lehnte ab und Willem Dirks Bakker steckte es wieder ein.

„Wissen Sie was?“ Er klang, als sei ihm eben etwas eingefallen. „Das scheint mir eine Fügung Gottes zu sein, dass wir beide uns begegnet sind. Sie kommen mit zu mir.“

Was fällt dem alten Kerl ein?

„Ich rede von meinem Gästehaus. Wie es der Zufall will, hat Frau Luise, das ist der gute Hausgeist in meinem Hotel, sich den Arm gebrochen. Sie ist beim Gardinenaufhängen von der Leiter gestürzt. Eine zusätzliche Hilfe im Hotel könnte sie gebrauchen. Oh, ich sehe schon, Sie haben Angst, dass ihre Arbeit beendet ist, sobald Frau Luise wieder gesund ist. Aber dem ist nicht so. Sie müssen wissen, dass ich expandiere. Im Vertrauen gesagt“, er beugte sich ein wenig vor und schaute zum Nachbartisch herüber, ob jemand lauschte, „ich besitze zwei Logierhäuser auf der Insel. Da benötige ich immer helfende Hände. Und Sie, junges Fräulein, sehen aus, als könnten Sie anpacken.“

Hermine nickte. Ja, das war so. Alles, was Cousine Bertha über die Arbeit im Hotel erzählt hatte, konnte sie. Hausarbeit eben.

Willem Dirks Bakker schaute sie an. Er erwartete eine Antwort. Hermine schwitzte und lockerte ihr Halstuch. Wenn sie das Angebot annahm, hatte sie die erhoffte Anstellung. Aber konnte sie einem Fremden vertrauen? Einem, der so mir nichts, dir nichts auf der Heimreise jemanden einstellte? Sein erwartungsvolles Lächeln erinnerte sie an ihren Großvater. So schaute Opa, wenn Hermine seine Pfeife suchen sollte, die Großmutter gern versteckte, damit er weniger rauchte. Und wenn Hermine die Augen leicht zusammenkniff und sich Bakkers Bart ein bisschen voller und weißer vorstellte, hätten die beiden sogar Brüder sein können.

„Das Gehalt wäre das übliche. Zusätzlich freie Verpflegung und Unterkunft im Haus. Probezeit bis …", er schaute zur Backbordseite aufs Meer hinaus, als müsse er kurz überlegen, „sagen wir bis Pfingsten."

Das hörte sich verlockend an.

„Sie werden sich eine Dachkammer mit ein oder zwei Mitarbeiterinnen teilen. Was meinen Sie?"

Hermine sollte ablehnen. Behaupten, dass Cousine Bertha sie erwartete. Zudem würde Bertha enttäuscht sein, wenn sie in einem anderen Haus eine Arbeit annahm. Andererseits hatte sie von Bertha seit Wochen keine Nachricht bekommen. Sollte es in *Köhlers Dorfhotel* nicht klappen, wäre Hermines Chance auf sofortige Anstellung vertan. Sie musste Herrn Bakker die Wahrheit sagen. Dass sie Zeit zum Überlegen brauchte und vorher mit Bertha sprechen möchte. Doch ihre Stimme sagte was anderes, als ihr Hirn ihr riet. „Einverstanden. Das hört sich gut an."

„Dann sind wir uns einig." Bakker wirkte zufrieden. Über den Tisch hinweg reichten sie sich die Hände. „Schauen Sie, wir sind fast da. Ich sehe schon die Kutschen."

Hermine rückte auf der Sitzbank näher ans Bullauge heran und traute ihren Augen kaum. Was für ein schöner Anblick!

Einige Hundert Meter entfernt lag ein weißer Sandstrand. Dahinter konnte man zwischen den Dünen eine imposante Villa und ein paar kleinere Häuser erkennen.

„Wo ist denn die Anlegestelle?" In Hermines Heimatstadt Leer gab es einen Hafen mit gemauerten Kaianlagen und eisernen Pollern, an denen die Schiffe festmachten. Auch Emden besaß betonierte Anlegeplätze. Es war keine sechs Stunden her, als dieses Schiff dort abgelegt hatte.

„Die ist noch nicht fertiggestellt. Genießen Sie das Ausschiffen, denn das wird es bald nicht mehr geben. Spätestens im kommenden Jahr werden alle Schiffe im Borkumer Hafen anlegen. Aber keine Bange, Fräulein Flessner, wir kommen trockenen Fußes an Land. Sehen Sie die Kutschwagen?"

Hermine sah sie. Gleich drei vierrädrige hohe Kutschen, gezogen von jeweils zwei Pferden, die bis zum Bauch im Wasser standen, näherten sich dem Raddampfer. Schweres Rasseln zeigte an, dass der Kapitän der *Augusta* den Befehl zum Ankerauswerfen gegeben hatte.

Die Reisenden machten sich zum Ausstieg bereit.

„Ist das Ihr Gepäck?" Bakker deutete auf Hermines Tasche. Sie nickte. In diesem Moment kam ein Mann an ihrem Tisch vorbei. Bakker hob seinen Gehstock, um ihn aufzuhalten.

„Tischlermeister Buse, wie gut, Sie anzutreffen! Wären Sie so freundlich und würden Sie mein Köfferchen und die Reisetasche dieser jungen Dame mit an Land nehmen?"

Ehe Hermine sich versah, entschwand ihre Tasche und Bakker hakte sich bei ihr unter. Jetzt gab es kein Zurück mehr.

Am Ausgang standen die Reisenden und warteten darauf, dass ihnen die Matrosen beim Ausstieg aus dem Schiff und Übertritt in die Kutschen eine helfende Hand reichten.

„Ah, Köhler, mein Freund", sprach Willem Dirks Bakker einen etwa sechzigjährigen Herrn an, der durch seinen runden Kopf auffiel. Die Melone, die sein spärliches Haar bedeckte, stand ihm gar nicht. Bakkers Worte „mein Freund" klangen alles andere als freundlich. Köhler lehnte mit dem Rücken an der Reling und schien auf jemanden zu warten.

„Wie geht es Ihnen, Köhler? Was machen die Geschäfte?"

„Alles bestens, Bakker. Wie war die Kur und wie geht es Ihrer Frau? Sie sehen gut gelaunt aus. Haben Sie wieder jemanden übers Ohr gehauen?"

„So ist es, Köhler. So ist es!"

Das musste Berthas Arbeitgeber sein, dachte Hermine. Ein kleiner untersetzter Mann, und ein unverschämter noch dazu – in aller Öffentlichkeit anzudeuten, Bakker hätte jemanden übers Ohr gehauen! Doch ehe sie weiter darüber nachdenken konnte, reichte Tischlermeister Buse einem Matrosen Hermines Reisetasche sowie Bakkers Gepäckstück, der sie unter der Sitzbank der Kutsche verstaute. Und schon griff der Seemann nach Hermines Hand, um ihr vom Schiff hinüberzuhelfen. Zum Glück schwankte die *Augusta* nur wenig. Hermine hätte es allein geschafft. Wie ihr Begleiter Willem Dirks Bakker, der seine Seemannsbeine trotz Gehstock nicht verloren hatte.

Als der Wagen voll war, kletterte der Kutscher auf seinen Platz und lenkte die Pferde durchs Meerwasser an den Strand. Seine Fracht, die aus jeweils zehn Personen mit Gepäck bestand, brachte er trockenen Fußes an Land. Keine hundert Meter weiter, am Rand der Dünen, rief der Kutscher: „Endstation."

Die Tiere blieben stehen und der Fuhrmann half seiner Kundschaft die vier Stufen der eisernen Kutschentreppe hinunter. Sobald sein Gefährt leer war, fuhr er zurück zur *Augusta*, um weitere Passagiere an Land zu bringen. Hermine schaute einen Augenblick hinterher, und als sie sich zur Insel umwandte, sah sie Meister Buse mit langen Schritten Richtung Dorf eilen. Er hatte Bakkers Gepäck dabei.

„Reichen Sie mir Ihren Arm?" Bakker griff nach Hermines Reisetasche und ließ sich von ihr unterhaken. Es war ihr unangenehm, dass der Hotelier ihre Tasche trug. Sie folgten einem schmalen Weg durch die Dünen hoch zu einer unbefestigten Straße. Rechts und links gab es jedoch gepflasterte Gehsteige.

Bakker war offensichtlich ein geachteter Insulaner. Fast jeder, der ihnen begegnete, grüßte höflich. Ein Mann zog zum Gruß seine Kappe vom Kopf und drei junge Frauen in schlichten Kleidern deuteten einen Knicks an. Sie kamen an kleinen Inselhäuschen, zwei Baustellen, einer Bäckerei, einem Schlachter und anderen Läden vorbei. In der Ferne sah Hermine einen viereckigen Leuchtturm, auf den Bakker zusteuerte. Vor einem großen Gebäude hielt er an. *Hotel Bakker Senior* stand über dem Eingang zu lesen. Das Hotel schien aus zwei Haupthäusern mit einem Verbindungsbau dazwischen zu bestehen. Die Veranda, die vom rechten Gebäude über den Zwischenbau bis zum linken Haus reichte, zählte viele Fenster.

In der ersten Etage gab es jeweils drei große Fenster, sicherlich die Gästezimmer. Die zweite Etage lag unter dem Dach. Vermutlich waren dort die Kammern des Personals, dachte Hermine. Kurz keimte die Hoffnung in ihr auf, dass sie unter den kleineren Rundbogenfenstern Quartier finden würde. Dann hätte sie eine Aussicht, die sie an zu Hause erinnerte. Die dem *Hotel Bakker Senior* gegenüberliegende Straßenseite war mit kleinen Häusern bebaut. Vor dem linken Teil des Hotels standen ein paar Bäume, deren Äste zur Straßenseite hin fast vollständig abrasiert waren. Die Blätter zeigten ein zartes Grün. Die Natur schien im Vergleich zum Festland vier Wochen hinterherzuhinken.

„Kommen Sie?"

Hermine folgte Herrn Bakker um das Haus herum zum Hintereingang.

Über einen gepflasterten Seitengang gelangten sie in einen großen Hinterhof. Aus der Backstube der angrenzenden Bäckerei duftete es verführerisch. Durch eine hölzerne, grün gestrichene Tür betraten sie das Haus. Der Fußboden war mit schwarz-weißen Fliesen ausgelegt. Aus einer offen stehenden Tür kamen ihnen Dampfschwaden entgegen. Es roch nach Kochwäsche. Bakker führte sie an der Waschküche vorbei in einen großen Raum: die Hotelküche. Die hintere Front wurde von drei Öfen eingenommen. Daneben und an den Seitenwänden gab es Arbeitsflächen, ein großes Waschbecken und eine Pumpe. Unter der Decke am *Wiemstock* hingen jeder Menge Küchenutensilien. Eine hochgewachsene dürre Frau stand am Herd. Sie rührte emsig in einem Topf. Es roch nach Eintopf. Das Wasser lief Hermine im Mund zusammen. Mutters Reiseproviant hatte sie bereits in Emden, kurz bevor das Schiff abgelegt hatte, aufgegessen.

Die dürre Frau schien sie gehört zu haben und wandte sich mit erhobenem Kochlöffel in der Hand um.

„Ach, Sie sind es. Willkommen daheim", grüßte sie Willem Dirks Bakker. „Ich hoffe, Sie hatten eine angenehme Reise."

„Danke, Gertrud."

„Und wie geht es der Frau Gemahlin?"

„Sie wird noch einige Wochen in der Kur bleiben."

„Oh, das habe ich befürchtet. Erst heute Morgen ..."

Bakker hatte keine Lust, sich anzuhören, was die abergläubische Gertrud heute Morgen erlebt hatte und weshalb seine Frau die Kurverlängerung angeblich hatte verlängern müssen. „Was gibt es Leckeres zum Essen?", unterbrach er sie.

„Ihr Lieblingsessen, Herr Bakker. *Updrögte* Bohnen."

Auf einem Band aufgefädelte luftgetrocknete Bohnen. Zusammen mit Kartoffeln und Speck gekocht, war es auch Hermines Leibgericht. Ihr Magen knurrte. Sie legte vor Schreck eine Hand darauf.

„In einer halben Stunde, Herr Bakker, kann ich es servieren lassen."

„Ah, da kommt ja meine Schwiegertochter." Willem Dirks Bakker ließ Hermines Tasche fallen und begrüßte eine junge Frau, etwa Mitte dreißig, mit schwarzem Haar, Mittelscheitel, strengem Haarknoten und rundem Bauch. „Adeline, wie schön dich gesund und munter zu sehen! Wie geht es dir und dem Kind?"

Adeline fuhr sich über den Bauch. „Es strampelt."

„Wunderbar! Das ist Fräulein Hermine Flessner." Mit einem Nicken deutete er auf Hermine, hängte sich den Knauf des Stockes an den Arm und zog eine goldene Taschenuhr aus seiner Westentasche. Er warf einen Blick darauf und schien erschrocken, wie spät es war. „Ich muss los", verkündete er.

Seine Schwiegertochter Adeline schaute ihm kopfschüttelnd hinterher. Erst als er verschwunden war, wandte sie sich an Hermine.

„Und was machen Sie hier?"

„Herr Bakker hat mich eingestellt."

„Soso. Der Herr Schwiegervater hat Ihnen Arbeit versprochen. Darf ich fragen, als was?“

Ja, als was genau? Spontan sagte sie: „Zimmermädchen.“

„Von denen habe ich genug.“ Adeline Bakker fuhr erschrocken herum, als ein hysterisches Kreischen über ihnen zu hören war. Kinder, die sich heftig stritten. Adeline raffte ihren Rock und eilte die Treppe empor.

Das war es dann wohl mit der Anstellung. Hermine hätte statt „Zimmermädchen“ einfach „Mitarbeiterin“ oder „Mädchen für alles“ sagen sollen. Doch nun war es zu spät. Sie verließ das Hotel auf dem gleichen Weg, den sie gekommen war. Auf der Straße erkundigte sie sich nach dem Weg zu *Köhlers Dorfhotel.*

„Hier um die Ecke und dann immer geradeaus.“

Hermine bog an der nächsten Straßenecke rechts ab, an deren Bürgersteig ein hüfthoher eiserner Pfahl stand. Dem Flachbau, *Fischers Basar*, mit seinen Schaufenstern schenkte sie keine Beachtung. Hundert Meter Vogelfluglinie vom *Hotel Bakker Senior* entfernt stand das *Hotel Bakker Junior*. Das musste das zweite Logierhaus sein, von dem der alte Herr gesprochen hatte. Dieses Haus war zweistöckig, mit spitzem Dach. Die Giebelwand lag quer zur Straße. In der Tiefe hatte das Haus ein Dutzend Fenster auf jeder Etage. Hermine vermutete, dass es ein wenig kleiner war als das *Bakker Senior*.

Die dem Hotel gegenüberliegende Straßenseite war unbebaut. Auf einer großen Fläche erstreckte sich ein Nutzgarten. Hermine erkannte Kartoffeln, die eben ihre ersten Blätter aus dem Boden streckten.

Etwa zweihundert Meter vom *Hotel Bakker Junior* entfernt, am Fuße des viereckigen Leuchtturmes, stand *Köhlers Dorfhotel.*

Hermine brauchte für die Strecke keine Minute. Das *Dorfhotel* war von einem eisernen Zaun umgeben. Am offen stehenden Tor stand ein Page, gut an der Uniform zu erkennen.

„Entschuldigen Sie bitte", sprach sie ihn an. „Ich möchte zu Bertha Flessner."

Der Page musterte sie. Er erkannte an ihrer Kleidung, dass sie kein Gast sein konnte. „Bertha? Die ist nicht da."

„Wann kommt sie wieder?"

„Keine Ahnung. Vielleicht gar nicht."

„Heißt das, sie ist nicht mehr auf der Insel?"

„Davon können Sie ausgehen."

„Und woher wissen Sie das?"

„Wenn sie noch hier wäre, hätte ich sie irgendwann getroffen. Hab ich aber nicht."

„Seit wann ist sie fort?"

„Ein paar Wochen werden es schon sein."

„Danke." Hermine machte auf dem Absatz kehrt. *Zurück ins Bakker Senior?,* fragte sie sich. Ihr blieb keine Wahl, denn in der Aufregung hatte sie ihre Reisetasche zurückgelassen.

Als sie ein zweites Mal durch den Hintereingang das Haus betrat, schien die Situation unverändert. Von oben war Kindergeheul zu hören, in der Küche klapperte Köchin Gertrud mit Töpfen. Und plötzlich stand Willem Dirks Bakker hinter ihr.

„Fräulein Flessner, was stehen Sie hier noch herum?"

„Ich …"

„Ah, Frau Menninga", grüßte Bakker eine kleine dralle Frau etwa Mitte dreißig, die ihnen den langen Flur aus Richtung des Haupteinganges entgegenkam. „Das ist Hermine Flessner, eine neue Mitarbeiterin. Fräulein Hermine, das ist die gute Seele in unserem Hause, Hausdame Luise Menninga. Frau Luise, wie wir alle sagen. Würden Sie der jungen Dame bitte ihr Zimmer zeigen."

„Sehr wohl, Herr Bakker. Darf ich fragen, wie es Ihnen geht?"

„Gut, Frau Luise."

„Und der Frau Gemahlin?"

„Sie wird noch einige Wochen in der Kur bleiben."

„Ich hoffe, das wird ihre Lunge auskurieren."

„Das hoffen wir alle, Frau Luise."

„Welchen Posten soll die junge Dame hier bekleiden?"

„Als Zimmermädchen."

„Oh. Davon haben wir genug." Luise schien sein Stirnrunzeln zu bemerken und fügte hinzu: „Aber es gibt immer Arbeit im Haus. Wir werden schon etwas finden." Sie warf einen schnellen Blick auf Hermine. „Dann wollen wir mal."

Hermine suchte ihre Tasche. Sie war fort. Sie schaute sich danach um, doch sie war nirgends zu sehen. Frau Luise Menninga war schon einige Schritte auf der Treppe vorausgegangen. Auf der vierten Stufe blieb sie stehen. „Kommen Sie, Fräulein Flessner?"

Hermine folgte ihr.

„Wenn es keinen wichtigen Grund gibt, benutzt das Personal die Hintertreppe", informierte sie Frau Luise. „Die Dienstboten sollen von unseren Gästen kaum zu sehen sein." Luise Menninga, die ihren Arm in einer Stoffschlinge vor dem Bauch trug, eilte in die zweite Etage. Von hier aus führte eine wesentlich schmalere Treppe hinauf ins Dachgeschoss.

Bis hierher hatten Malereien die Wände bedeckt. Bunte Vögel und exotische Pflanzen. Der Flur zu den Dienstkammern hinauf war weiß getüncht, ohne jegliche Verzierungen. Es war dunkel. Durch eine offen stehende Kammertür fiel ein wenig Tageslicht herein.

„Hier hinein." Frau Luise öffnete eine Tür. Hermine musste in dem Zimmerchen den Kopf beugen, um nicht gegen die schrägen Seitenwände zu stoßen. Unter den Dachneigungen standen die Betten, und wenn man an einen der Nachtschränke kommen wollte, musste man den Rücken krümmen. „Dort schläft Mathilde Remmers, das da ist mein Bett. Aber nur so lange, bis die Kammer", Luises gesunder Arm deutete über ihre Schulter, „bezugsfertig ist. Ich hoffe, Tischlermeister Buse wird heute die restlichen Holzarbeiten fertigstellen."

„Wie lange arbeiten Sie schon für die Familie Bakker, Frau Menninga?"

„Einige Jahre. Aber sag Frau Luise zu mir, das machen alle. Wenn man mich mit Frau Menninga anspricht, fühle ich mich so …"

Wie Frau Luise sich dabei fühlte, sollte Hermine nicht erfahren, denn in diesem Moment kam ein dürres Mädchen mit langen Beinen und fettigem Haar herein.

„Ah, Fräulein Remmers. Das ist unsere Neue. Sie heißt Hermine."

Mathildes Begrüßung fiel mürrisch aus. Sie warf sich auf ihr Bett, griff nach der Decke, um sich zuzudecken, und drehte sich zur Wand.

„Sie hat vermutlich wieder die halbe Nacht in *Köhlers Giftbude* verbracht." Luises Stimme klang missbilligend mit einem Unterton, als würde sie sich so etwas nicht mehr lange gefallen lassen.

„*Köhlers Giftbude?*" Das hörte sich schrecklich gefährlich an. Hermine brachte den Namen sofort mit dem untersetzten kleinen Mann, der bei ihrer Ankunft mit Willem Dirks Bakker einen kurzen Schlagabtausch gehabt hatte, zusammen.

Vermutlich hatte sie großes Glück gehabt, Bakker auf dem Schiff getroffen zu haben. Mit einem Mann, der eine *Giftbude,* was immer das sein mochte, betrieb, wollte sie nichts zu tun haben. Cousine Bertha hatte kein Wort davon erwähnt. Wo mochte sie wohl sein?

„Hört sich schlimmer an, als es ist", knurrte Mathilde unter ihrer Bettdecke.

„Wie man's nimmt", sagte Frau Luise. „Ich finde, es ist kein geeigneter Umgang für ein junges Mädchen."

„Gerade für junge Mädchen", raunte Mathilde, drehte sich wieder um und blickte hinauf zur Decke.

„Ich dachte, wir brauchen keine neuen Mitarbeiter mehr." Mathilde nickte zu Hermine hinüber.

„Eine Entscheidung des Seniors", sagte Frau Luise und Hermine berichtete ausführlich, wie sie an die Anstellung gelangt war.

„Und da wundern Sie sich, dass der alte Herr Ihnen die ganze Zeit die Tasche getragen hat?", fragte Frau Luise. Ganz so dumm, wie die Hausdame glaubte, war Hermine nicht. Mittlerweile war ihr klar, dass Bakker Köhler eine Angestellte abgejagt hatte. Und damit sie ihm nicht davonlief, hatte er ihre Tasche quasi als Pfand getragen.

„Schlitzohr!" Luise strich über ihren in der Schlinge liegenden Arm und lächelte verschmitzt. Hermine hätte ihr Reisegeld darauf verwettet, dass die Hausdame mit dem Ausgang dieser Geschichte zufrieden war. Ja, ein unterschwelliger Hauch von Stolz klang in dem einen Wort mit. Darauf, dass der Chef es fertiggebracht hatte, seinem Mitbewerber eins auszuwischen.

„Einen zusätzlichen Punkt für uns“, sagte Mathilde.

„Die Zankerei und das gegenseitige Übers-Ohr-Hauen geht schon seit einiger Zeit“, vertraute Frau Luise Hermine an. „Dabei waren die Herren noch vor Monaten die dicksten Freunde.“

Mathilde war derweil eingeschlafen und schnarchte leise. Sie grunzte kurz auf und schmatzte ein wenig, sodass sich Hermine wieder an den Grund der Müdigkeit ihrer neuen Kollegin erinnerte. „Und was ist mit der *Giftbude*?“

„Die werden Sie schon kennenlernen.“ Und etwas leiser, als wolle sie nicht, dass Mathilde sie höre, fügte sie hinzu: „Es ist ein beliebter Treffpunkt der Saisonarbeiter. Vom Knecht bis zum Zimmermädchen. Mathilde übertreibt es gerne. Sie ist eine, die …“ Luise tat, als ob sie trinken würde. „Ich frage mich, wie lange die Bakkers sich das noch gefallen lassen.“

Frau Luise deutete Hermines Gesichtsausdruck richtig.

„Keine Angst, die hört uns nicht. Sie schläft jetzt wie ein besoffener Seemann und sägt dabei ganze Schiffsmasten ab, wenn sie erst einmal in Fahrt kommt.“ Wie aufs Stichwort wurde Mathildes Schnarchen lauter.

„Lassen Sie Ihre Tasche hier“, sagte Frau Luise.

„Die ist fort.“

„Man hat sie gestohlen?“ Frau Luise klang, als sei so etwas in diesem Hause unmöglich.

„Ich weiß es nicht. Zuletzt stand sie im Flur in der Nähe der Hotelküche.“ Hermine überlegte, ob sie Luise von dem kurzen Abstecher zu *Köhlers Dorfhotel* erzählen sollte.

„Ach, dann hat Waldemar, er ist unser Page, sie bestimmt in der Rumpelkammer abgestellt. Sie wissen, was eine Rumpelkammer ist?“

„Ein Raum, in den alles Mögliche hineinkommt."

„Richtig. In unserem Fall sind es die Gepäckstücke der Gäste. Kommen Sie, ich zeige es Ihnen. Dann können Sie gleich den Rest des Hauses anschauen."

„Sind denn keine Gäste da?"

„Die ersten werden am kommenden Samstag erwartet."

Nach der Hotelbesichtigung, die privaten Räume der Familie Bakker ausgenommen, wollte Hermine über ihre Aufgaben sprechen.

„Frau Luise, werde ich als Zimmermädchen arbeiten? Frau Bakker sagte, Sie hätten genug."

Die hübsche Uniform würde ihr gefallen und die weiße Haube ihr sicherlich stehen. Sie sah sich schon in den schicken Gästezimmern elegante und teure Kleidung wegräumen und in den Schrank hängen. Aus der Nähe edlen Schmuck, exklusive Wäsche und Taschen anschauen zu dürfen, wäre sicherlich spannend. Und sie freute sich auf den guten Ruf, den diese Anstellung mit sich brachte.

„In den kommenden Tagen werden Sie meinen Part auf den Zimmern übernehmen. Bis die ersten Gäste kommen, müssen alle Räume hergerichtet sein. Danach sehen wir weiter. Den Verband", sie hob den Arm, um auf ihren Gips aufmerksam zu machen, „bekomme ich nächste Woche abgenommen. Dann übernehme ich wieder und Sie werden überall dort aushelfen, wo jemand gebraucht wird. In der Küche und bei der Wäsche. Können Sie mit Kindern umgehen?"

„Ich habe fünf Geschwister."

„Sehr schön. Die Chefin ist hochschwanger. Da werden Sie sich auch um die Bakker-Kinder kümmern. Wo kommen Sie her, Fräulein Flessner?"

„Aus Leer."

„Soso." Frau Luise verzog kurz das Gesicht, als würde ihr das missfallen.

„Kennen Sie Leer?"

Die Frage schien ihr noch weniger zu behagen.

„Dann ab mit Ihnen nach oben, Fräulein Flessner. Packen Sie Ihre Tasche aus und wecken Sie Mathilde. In wenigen Minuten erwarte ich Sie zum Essen in der Küche."

***

Hermine war es nicht gelungen, ihre Zimmerkollegin zu wecken. Jetzt saß sie allein am großen Küchentisch und schaute der Köchin Gertrud und dem Küchenmädchen Dina beim Hantieren zu.

„Soll ich Ihnen wirklich nicht helfen, Frau Dirksen?"

„Nein. – Pass doch auf!", ermahnte die Köchin Dina.

„Entschuldigung, Frau Dirksen." Dina stellte den umgeworfenen Becher mit dem Salz wieder auf und begann, die weißen Kristalle mit dem Handrücken vom Tisch zu streichen.

Es war bereits für acht Personen eingedeckt. Neben Tellern und Besteck standen Teetassen. Erst jetzt bemerkte Hermine ihren Durst, wagte jedoch nicht, um ein Glas Wasser zu bitten.

„Vergiss nicht, dir etwas über die Schulter zu werfen, sonst bringt es Unglück." Gertrud Dirksen stellte dampfende Töpfe auf den langen Tisch und schüttelte angesichts der Langsamkeit, mit der Dina das Salz zusammenstrich, den Kopf.

„Und du kannst weiß Gott ein wenig Glück gebrauchen, so tollpatschig, wie du bist. Ich werde froh sein", schalt die Köchin, „wenn du wieder in der Küche im *Bakker Junior* dein Unwesen treibst."

Die etwa dreizehnjährige Dina knickste und erweckte nicht den Eindruck, die herben Worte der Köchin würden sie verletzen.

„Können Sie servieren, Fräulein Flessner?"

„Ja, Frau Dirksen", behauptete Hermine.

„Schön, dann kann ich ja sicher sein, dass die Herrschaften ihr Essen bekommen, ohne dass es in einer Katastrophe endet." Frau Dirksen stellte eine große Schüssel mit gekochten Kartoffeln und eine weitere mit den Bohnen auf ein Tablett. Daneben kam ein Teller mit fettem Speck und ein zweiter mit geräucherten Würsten.

„Meine Mutter kocht immer alles in einem Topf", bemerkte Hermine. Dina riss erschrocken die Augen auf. Ihr Blick wanderte zur Köchin. Die nickte.

„Ich mache das normalerweise auch so, doch Frau Bakker mag das nicht." Die Köchin verstummte für einen Moment. „Dina? Ist der Tisch für die Herrschaften ordentlich eingedeckt?"

„Jawohl, Frau Dirksen." Dina knickste erneut.

„Dann bringt das Essen rüber, bevor es kalt wird. Du gehst voran und hältst für Fräulein Flessner die Türen auf."

So servierte Hermine Willem Dirks Bakker, seiner Schwiegertochter und einem Mann, der Bakker ein wenig ähnelte, aber gut zwanzig Jahre jünger war, das Essen. Fünf Kinder saßen kerzengerade mit am Tisch. Das kleinste schätzte Hermine auf drei Jahre, das älteste Kind, ein Junge, musste etwa zwölf sein. Also drei Jahre jünger als sie. Hoffentlich gab das keine Probleme beim Kinderhüten.

„Guten Appetit!“, wünschte Hermine. „Dürfen wir Ihnen sonst noch etwas bringen?“

Hermine sah, wie Dina entsetzt die Hand vor den Mund schlug.

„Wir haben alles“, sagte die Schwiegertochter.

„Danke, Fräulein Flessner.“ Der Senior zwinkerte ihr zu.

„Frau Bakker sah böse aus“, petzte Dina, als sie zurück in die Hotelküche kamen.

„Was ist passiert?“ Frau Luise saß am Kopf des Küchentisches. An den Längsseiten hatten andere Personen Platz genommen.

„Sie hat gefragt, ob wir sonst noch etwas bringen sollen.“ Es klang wie eine Todsünde.

„Frau Bakker hat es nicht gerne, bei Tisch angesprochen zu werden. Es ist unsere Pflicht, ehe die Herrschaften Platz nehmen, alles, was für die Mahlzeit benötigt wird, bereitzustellen. Zu fragen, ob etwas fehlt, bedeutet, wir haben beim Tischeindecken nicht aufgepasst.“

„Das wäre ein falscher Fehler“, sagte ein junger Mann. Er saß in der Mitte der langen Seite des Tisches und lächelte Hermine an.

„Das ist Waldemar. Unser Page.“

„Und Bartender“, erklärte er mit geschwellter Brust.

„Und ich bin Margret. Borkum-Mädchen im zweiten Jahr.“ Sie knuffte Waldemar am Arm. „Waldemar sagt immer so komische Wörter.“

„Und das ist Sabine, ebenfalls im zweiten Jahr hier tätig“, stellte Margret die Kollegin vor.

Dina nahm gegenüber der Köchin Platz und Hermine setzte sich wieder dorthin, wo sie eben schon gesessen hatte.

„Fräulein Remmers liegt in Sauer?", erkundigte sich die Köchin. Frau Luise nickte ergeben.

„Dass die das darf", meinte Dina, schüttelte den Kopf und reichte Hermine den Topf mit den Kartoffeln.

„Das geht dich nichts an", mahnte Frau Luise.

„Die war wieder in *Köhlers Giftbude*", maulte Dina und fügte leise hinzu: „Weiß gar nicht, warum ich da nicht hindarf."

„Darfst du schon, Dina. Nur solltest du die Finger vom Alkohol und von Män..."

Frau Luise hüstelte künstlich und die Köchin verstummte.

„Guten Appetit."

„Trinken Sie nicht *den* Tee." Frau Dirksen hielt Hermines Arm fest, die eben nach einer der beiden Teekannen greifen wollte. „Dinas Tee ist dünner als ich. Richtige Ostfriesen können etwas Stärkeres vertragen." Sie nahm Hermines Tasse und schenkte ihr aus der zweiten Kanne ein.

„Vorsicht!", mahnte Margret. „Im Tee unserer Frau Dirksen bleibt der Löffel senkrecht stehen."

Hermine blickte in ihre Tasse. Margret hatte ein wenig übertrieben, dennoch schwamm ein Ölfilm auf der Oberfläche.

Da half nur viel Sahne und Kluntjes, sonst würde ihr Magen rebellieren.

***

Der untersetzte Mann mit kleinem Bauchansatz bahnte sich in großer Hast seinen Weg durch die fast leeren Straßen. Er fand es unklug, am helllichten Tag im Haus des selbstständigen Kaufmanns und Fuhrunternehmers zusammenzukommen. Der Hotelier schüttelte den Kopf. Warum musste man sich auf diese Weise treffen? Er war ein wenig zu spät und wollte auf keinen Fall etwas von der Besprechung versäumen. Im Grunde seines Herzens traute er allen bis auf einen über den Weg. Das war der Kaufmann. Nicht wegen seiner Fähigkeiten als Selbstständiger, sondern eher, weil dessen Spleen langsam Auswüchse annahm.

Dennoch waren sie eine Zweckgemeinschaft. Was sie zusammenführte, war ein gemeinsames Ziel.

Der Hotelier eilte an dem neuen Leuchtturm vorbei, den das Bauunternehmen Schumacher aus Leer in nur neun Monaten Bauzeit hochgezogen hatte. Bewundernswert. Sollte er mit seinen Plänen Erfolg haben, würde er diese Firma für sich arbeiten lassen. Doch da musste er schnell sein, andere hatten sicherlich den gleichen Gedanken.

Vor der Tür des Hauses, in dem das Treffen stattfand, wurde er von einem Jungen aufgehalten.

„Parole?“, fragte der Knabe und sah sich dabei um, als wolle er von niemandem mit dem Hotelier gesehen werden. Er kannte den Elfjährigen seit dem Tag seiner Geburt, so wie er jeden auf der Insel kannte. Dass der Kaufmann das Kind mit in die Sache hineingezogen hatte, bestätigte dem Hotelier sein ungutes Gefühl.

„Strandhotel“, antwortete er.

Der Junge schaute ihn fragend an. „Das ist die falsche Parole.“

„Willst du mich jetzt nicht reinlassen?“ Seine Stimme klang schneidend.

„Natürlich. Entschuldigung, Herr Bakker. Sie dürfen eintreten.“ Er öffnete für ihn die Tür und schloss sie sofort wieder. Im Hausflur war es dunkel, doch Bakker kannte den Weg. Er ging bis zum Ende des Flures und klopfte an die letzte Tür rechts. „Wer ist da?“, hörte er Pieter Akkermanns Stimme.

Dieses geheimnisvolle Treffen war auf seinem Mist gewachsen, ebenso wie die Vorsichtsmaßnahmen.

„Ich bin es“, rief Bakker und die Tür wurde aufgerissen.

„Nicht so laut.“ Akkermann zog ihn in den Raum und blickte den Flur hinunter bis zur Haustür, als ob er sichergehen wollte, dass niemand sah, wie er Willem Bakker einließ.

„Wir haben auf dich gewartet“, sagte Georg Köhler, der einzige Mann in der Runde, den Willem Bakker als guten Freund bezeichnet hätte. Neben dem, was sie in dieser Zweckgemeinschaft vorhatten, würden die beiden Männer zusätzlich ihr eigenes Ding drehen, um an ihr Ziel zu gelangen.

Bakker zog an der Kette seiner Taschenuhr. Sie glitt aus der Westentasche in seine Hand. Er ließ den Deckel aufspringen und schaute auf das Ziffernblatt. Er war noch nicht zu spät. Wie von ihm vermutet, waren die anderen aus Nervosität zu früh gekommen. Er steckte die Uhr wieder ein und nickte dem dicken Wybrands zu, der bereits mit Mitte vierzig schon eine Glatze hatte. Er wollte gerade seinen Namen sagen, damit er ein Stückchen rücken würde, um an den einzigen noch freien Stuhl zu gelangen. Weiter als bis: „Rücken Sie ein Stückchen, Herr Wyb…“, kam er nicht.

„Wir sollten uns Decknamen zulegen“, sagte Akkermann.

„Warum das denn?“

„So kann man unter Folter die wahre Identität des anderen nicht verraten", meinte Pieter Akkermann im Brustton der Überzeugung.

„Erstens kenne ich alle eure Namen, bis zu euren Großeltern kann ich die Daten aufzählen –, und zweitens gibt es hier niemanden, der foltert."

Jedermann wusste, dass Akkermann sich für die Geschichten des Grafen von Monte Christo und den Pinkerton-Express-Agenten aus Amerika interessierte. Bei jeder sich bietenden Gelegenheit bemerkte er, was jene Abenteurer in dieser Situation gemacht hätten.

„Setzen Sie sich endlich", sagte Akkermann. „Unser Herr Bürgermeister dachte schon, Sie hätten es sich anders überlegt."

Willem Bakker tauschte einen schnellen Blick mit seinem besten Freund Georg Köhler. Der lächelte, als wolle er sagen: „Zeig Nachsicht, wir brauchen ihn."

Doktor Schmidt hob seinen Zeigefinger.

„Hier muss sich niemand zu Wort melden, Doktor."

„Wie Sie meinen, Bürgermeister."

Bürgermeister Georg Köhler grinste Pieter Akkermann an. „Das sind keine Abenteuerspielchen. Es geht hier um unser aller Zukunft, meine Herren!"

„Können wir jetzt anfangen? Ich muss noch zum Frachtschiff. Heute bekomme ich neue Gästebetten", sagte Pensionswirt Behrends und strich sich sein viel zu langes Haar hinters Ohr.

Willem Bakker setzte sich auf den freien Stuhl und blickte in die Runde. Mit ihm waren sie sechs Männer. Alles wohlsituierte Insulaner, die sich finanziell und ideell das würden leisten können, was diese Gruppe erreichen wollte.

Ihnen allen ging es darum, bei der Ausschreibung der Inselgemeinde eines der angebotenen zwanzig Grundstücke zu erwerben. Alle sechs wollten sie dieses Geschäft machen und gleichzeitig verhindern, dass Fremde vom Festland kamen, die begehrten Grundstücke erwarben und den Einheimischen Konkurrenz machten. Allen Männern war es zuwider, wenn Zugereiste mit bloßen Versprechen und blendenden Worten die Welt der Insulaner durcheinanderbrachten, alles besser wussten, ihnen auf Jahre das Geldverdienen erschwerten und ihre Betriebe dann, weil sie keine Ahnung von Saisonvermietung hatten, pleitegingen.

„Sie kommen mit einem Pappkarton und gehen wieder mit einem. Alles schon mehrfach da gewesen." Oft hinterließen sie einen Scherbenhaufen, den die Insulaner dann wieder aufkehren durften.

„Dem wollen wir entgegenwirken", stellte Akkermann noch einmal für alle fest. „Deswegen ist es wichtig, dass wir uns gegenseitig unterstützen. Sei es mit Geld, Informationen oder sonst etwas."

„Absprachen sind wichtig", meinte Behrends und rieb sich die lange Nase. „Nun rücken Sie schon mit den ersten Bedingungen heraus."

Alle blickten Georg Köhler an. Als Bürgermeister wusste er welche Voraussetzungen der Gemeinderat für die Vergabe der Grundstücke beschlossen hatte.

„In zwei Wochen wird die Ausschreibung in der Zeitung bekannt gegeben. Bewerben kann sich jeder."

Drei der Männer stöhnten. „Wäre es nicht für alle einfacher gewesen, wenn der Rat gleich beschlossen hätte, nur Borkumer zuzulassen?"

„Das verstößt gegen das Gleichheitsgesetz."

„Aber als Bürgermeister können Sie doch sicherlich etwas an den Vorgaben drehen", meinte Doktor Schmidt.

„Wenn das so wäre, müssten wir uns hier nicht heimlich treffen, Doktor. Zumal ich als befangen gelte, sobald ich mein Angebot abgegeben habe."

„Bedeutet das, Sie werden dann keine Interna mehr erfahren?"

„So ist es. Deswegen sitzen wir ja hier, um die Vorteile unserer persönlichen Beziehungen zu bündeln."

„Wenn sich alle daran halten und alles nach Plan läuft, werden wir den anderen gegenüber im Vorteil sein", versicherte Köhler. „Nur diese geheimen Treffen machen mir Sorgen. Ich möchte wetten, dass es trotz aller Heimlichtuerei einige bemerken werden. Die Leute werden sich fragen, was wir denn so zu besprechen haben, und dann …"

„Ich werde Abhilfe schaffen", versprach Willem Bakker. „Bis zur öffentlichen Bekanntmachung bleiben noch vierzehn Tage. In dieser Zeit werde ich meine liebe Frau in ihrer Kur besuchen." Und schon mal mit einem Architekten und dem Leeraner Bauunternehmer Kontakt aufnehmen. Doch das verriet er den anderen nicht. „Und wenn ich zurück bin, habe ich jemanden, der für uns Informationen hin- und herbringen wird."

„Wer soll das sein?"

„Jemand, den keiner von uns kennt."

„Ein Fremder fällt doch sofort auf. Die Insel ist klein, wir haben keine tausend Einwohner."

„Das ändert sich in den kommenden Wochen. Wenn erst die Saison beginnt und die Gäste zusammen mit dem Sommerpersonal anreisen, brauchen die Insulaner lange, bis sie sich die Gesichter und Namen aller neuen Mitarbeiter merken und sie wissen, wer für wen arbeitet. Bis dahin habe ich jemanden gefunden." Noch ehe er es ausgesprochen hatte, wusste Bakker, dass er den Mund zu voll genommen hatte. Wo sollte er so einen Mann finden? Einen, dem man vertrauen konnte, ohne ihn überhaupt näher zu kennen, und das von Anfang an. Zudem sollte so ein Mann sich durchsetzen können. Bei dem, was er plante, sollte die Person auch entscheidungsfreudig sein. Ein blitzschneller Verstand wäre ebenfalls von Vorteil. Unmöglich so jemanden auf die Schnelle zu finden. Ihm blieben ja nur ein paar Wochen.

„Und woran erkennen wir den Spion?", fragte Pieter Akkermann.

Tja, wenn ich das nur wüsste. „Das werden Sie dann schon merken, meine Herren. Ach, und eines noch ..." Willem Bakker war aufgestanden und schon halb zur Tür hinausgegangen. Er deutete mit dem Finger auf Akkermann. „Zu niemandem ein Wort. Das gilt auch für Ihren Filius."

Akkermann wirkte pikiert, die anderen versuchten erst gar nicht, sich ein Grinsen zu verkneifen.

„Und mit dir, Georg Köhler", Bakker stand in der offenen Tür und deutete mit finsterer Miene auf seinen besten Freund, „habe ich noch ein Hühnchen zu rupfen."

Mit den letzten Worten hatte Bakker einen weiteren Grundstein im Wettstreit um die begehrten Grundstücke gelegt. Er konnte sicher sein, dass Köhler da mitmachen würde.

Dieses Treffen war jetzt drei Wochen her und Willem Bakkers Entscheidung, wer als Spion geeignet war, ist auf Fräulein Flessner gefallen. Zugegeben, ein spontaner Entschluss. Nicht im

Traum wäre ihm bis zur Heimreise eingefallen, den Posten mit einem fünfzehnjährigen Borkum-Mädchen zu besetzen. Aber er hatte ein gutes Gefühl dabei. Hermine Flessner hatte ihn beeindruckt. Ohne feste Anstellung auf die Insel zu reisen bewies Mut. Und niemand, nicht einmal seine fünf Mitstreiter, würden auf die Idee kommen, dass der Posten des Spions nicht von einem Mann besetzt werden würde. Schon hörte er die Herren laut aufschreien. „Ein Weibsbild? Sind Sie verrückt geworden, Bakker? Die kann doch nie und nimmer den Mund halten."

Doch das traute er ihr zu. Es gab sehr wohl Frauen, die schweigen konnten. Blieb nur noch eines zu tun. Er musste es Hermine Flessner sagen.

Am nächsten Morgen nach seiner Heimreise bat er seinen zweitältesten Sohn Dirk Willems Bakker auf ein Wort ins Kontor. Vor acht Jahren hatte er die Führung des Hotels Bakker Senior an Dirk übertragen. In den privaten Räumlichkeiten trieb Adeline, Dirks Ehefrau, die Kinder an, sich zu beeilen.

„Damit die Quengelei aufhört", teilte sie den Männern mit, „gehe ich mit ihnen an den Strand."

„Darf ich an der Segelbuhne ...", hörten sie den Ältesten fragen, da waren sie zur Tür hinaus.

„Adeline sagt, du hast ein neues Mädchen eingestellt." Die Worte seines Sohnes klangen neutral, dennoch wusste Willem Dirks Bakker, dass Adeline ihm deswegen zugesetzt hatte. Ihr gefielen seine Einmischungen im Betrieb immer weniger und Dirk, der Ärmste, versuchte, den Balanceakt zwischen Ehefrau und Vater zu halten, ohne selbst dabei an Würde zu verlieren. Selten schlug er sich offen auf die Seite von einem der beiden.

„Sie hat uns gestern das Essen serviert und macht auf mich einen kompetenten Eindruck. Zudem hatte ich dabei das große Glück, sie Georg Köhler abzuwerben."

„Musste das sein Vater? Dieser Zank zwischen euch ist unwürdig. Ihr wart jahrzehntelang Freunde. Setz eurer Fehde endlich ein Ende! Ich hatte gehofft, der Aufenthalt bei Mutter hätte dich versöhnlicher gestimmt."

„Du meinst, weil sie dem Tode eben so von der Schippe gesprungen ist?"

„Wir wissen beide, dass das gelogen ist. Wie geht es Mutter?"

„Den Umständen entsprechend. Die Klinik ist hervorragend, dennoch wird es eine Weile dauern, bis sie wieder gesund ist." Bakker Senior grinste. „Es macht Spaß, dem alten Köhler eins auszuwischen. Ich konnte nicht widerstehen."

„Verrätst du mir, was euch auseinandergebracht hat?"

„Das geht dich nichts an. Und sag mir nicht, dass du keine zusätzliche helfende Hand im Haus gebrauchen kannst."

„Schon. Nur ist es Adelines Aufgabe, Personal einzustellen. Du weißt, dass sie sich da ungern hereinreden lässt."

„Wie geht es ihr?", wechselte Bakker Senior das Thema.

„Gut. Das Kind kommt erst in ein paar Wochen."

„Dennoch sollte sie sich schonen."

„Mein Reden. Doch sie meint, beim siebten Mal habe sie genug Erfahrung im Kinderkriegen. Sie wüsste am besten, was ihr guttut und was nicht. Aber du hast recht, Vater", kam Dirk auf das ursprüngliche Thema zurück. „Ein zusätzliches Borkum-Mädchen im Familienbetrieb ist immer willkommen."

Borkum-Mädchen nannte man die jungen Frauen, die im Frühjahr auf die Insel reisten, um für die Sommersaison zu arbeiten. Im Herbst verließen sie das Eiland wieder, denn im

Winter war kein einziger Gast auf der Insel und es gab für Hotelpersonal keine Arbeit.

Viele dieser Saisonkräfte kamen wie die Zugvögel im darauffolgenden Frühling zurück. Einige von ihnen seit Jahren. Gelegentlich kam es vor, dass die eine oder andere junge Frau für immer auf der Insel blieb. Sei es, weil sie eine ganzjährige Beschäftigung gefunden hatte, so wie Luise Menninga, oder sie in eine Borkumer Familie hineinheiratete. Was die Inzucht, wie Bakker Senior gerne beteuerte, auf der Insel in annehmbaren Schranken hielt.

„Sie heißt Hermine, fast so wie deine Mutter. Hermine – Harmina. Ich finde, das ist ein gutes Omen."

„Dein Wort in Gottes Ohr."

„Du hörst dich schon wie deine Mutter an. Dennoch sollten wir für sie beten."

Bakker Senior konnte der strengen Gläubigkeit seiner Frau Harmina nichts abgewinnen, erst recht nicht, seit dieser Wahn zu ihrem Aufenthalt in der Nervenklinik geführt hatte.

„Beten? Und das aus deinem Mund, Vater?"

Sie schwiegen eine Weile, was keinem peinlich war.

„Ach, ehe ich es vergesse", nahm Dirk das Gespräch wieder auf. „Tischlermeister Buse hat gestern dein Gepäck gebracht. Ich hatte den Eindruck, dass er ein wenig pikiert war."

Willem Dirks Bakker nickte in Gedanken an die Situation auf der *Augusta*. Hermine Flessner hatte sein Stellenangebot angenommen, doch er hatte gemerkt, wie unwohl sie sich dabei gefühlt hatte. Damit sie ihm nicht davonlief, hatte er zu einem Trick greifen müssen. Ihre Tasche zu tragen, war nicht nur höflich gewesen, es hatte sie gezwungen, an seiner Seite zu bleiben. Nur hatte er dabei Hilfe gebraucht, denn sein eigener Koffer, die

Reisetasche der jungen Dame und der Handstock, da hatte er ganz klar eine Hand zu wenig gehabt. Ohne den Gehstock war er schlecht zu Fuß. Erst recht auf einem rollenden Dampfer. Da war Tischlermeister Buse die Lösung gewesen.

„Apropos Tischlerarbeiten. Seine sind einwandfrei. Noch gestern Abend hat er die Dachkammer für Frau Luise fertiggestellt. Seine Rechnung habe ich sofort bezahlt."

„Schön. Und was macht Fräulein Remmers?"

Dirk Willems Bakker stieß verächtlich die Luft aus. Das Zimmermädchen Mathilde Remmers kannte das Familiengeheimnis. Die Seniorchefin Harmina Bakker war keineswegs lungenkrank und eben dem Tod von der Schippe gesprungen, wie der Öffentlichkeit gegenüber von der Familie behauptet wurde. Sie steckte aufgrund ihrer religiösen Wahnvorstellungen in einer Nervenheilanstalt.

Mathilde nutzte ihr Wissen um das Familiengeheimnis, um bevorzugt behandelt zu werden. Erpressung. „Ihr Schlendrian wird immer dreister", verriet Dirk. „Und gelegentlich schlägt sie über die Stränge."

„Köhlers Giftbude?"

„Ja. Die hat seit einer Woche wieder geöffnet."

„Ich hatte gehofft, dass einer der Winterstürme ihr den Garaus macht, doch da oben auf der Düne steht die Bude sicher."

„Vater!" Dirks Stimme klang entsetzt. „Wie kannst du so was sagen? Ihr solltet Frieden schließen!"

„Du musst etwas dagegen unternehmen."

„Gegen Köhler? Niemals. Zieht mich nicht in euren Streit hinein."

„Ich rede von Fräulein Remmers. Es ist nur eine Frage der Zeit, bis es zu Unstimmigkeiten unter dem Personal kommt.

Du kannst ihr nicht alles durchgehen lassen. Sieh zu, dass du das in den Griff bekommst."

„Du hast gut reden, Vater. Wir können nur hoffen, dass Mutter bald wieder gesund ist. Dann schmeiß ich Mathilde raus."

***

Adeline Bakker hätte die konsequente Aussage ihres Mannes gefallen. Dirk war in ihren Augen zu kompromissbereit, um ein Hotel mit strenger Hand zu führen. Gut, dass er sie hatte.

Borkum im Frühling war ein wundervoller Anblick. Die wenigen Obstbäume, die es seit ein paar Jahren auf der Insel gab, knospten und in den Dünen blühten winzig kleine blaue Veilchen. Auf den Salzwiesen vor dem Wattenmeer blühte die Strandnelke. Ihr Lila war von Weitem zu sehen.

Das Borkum-Mädchen Margret hatte Adelines Kinder unter ihre Obhut genommen und so konnte sie in aller Ruhe einen ausgedehnten Spaziergang machen. Sie hob den Rocksaum, damit er im feuchten Wattgrund nicht nass wurde, und wünschte, Gott würde ihr ein Zeichen geben. Sie war zum siebten Mal schwanger und der Arzt hatte ihr versichert, dass es keine leichte Geburt werden würde. Aber was wussten Männer schon mehr über Niederkünfte als Frauen, die bereits einige hinter sich hatten? Dennoch hegte Doktor Schmidt schwere Bedenken und bat sie inständig, sich zu schonen. „Das sollte die letzte Schwangerschaft sein", mahnte er. „Sie werden große Probleme bekommen, an denen Sie sterben könnten." Das Kind hatte sich nicht gedreht, doch Adeline war zuversichtlich, dass es das in den kommenden Tagen tun würde. Bis zur Geburt war noch reichlich Zeit.

Ärzte! Sie fand es unmöglich, Angst und Schrecken zu verbreiten. Ihrer Erfahrung nach war alles genauso wie bei den vergangenen Schwangerschaften.

Die vernichtenden Worte ihrer Schwägerin Geeske Bakker kamen ihr in den Sinn. Sie war die einzige Tochter und jüngstes Kind ihrer Schwiegereltern und nahm selten ein Blatt vor den Mund. Erst vorgestern hatte Geeske lautstark verkündet, dass Doktor Schmidt ihr anvertraut habe, er hielte Frauen über fünfunddreißig fürs Kinderkriegen zu alt. Vermutlich stimmte es, doch musste Geeske es ja nicht laut in die Welt hinausposaunen!

Ein Kind ist von Gott gegeben, versuchte Adeline sich einzureden, also würde der HERR auch über sie beide wachen. Da konnte sie unmöglich …

Adeline mochte den Gedanken nicht zu Ende denken. Besorgt streichelte sie den gewölbten Bauch und hoffte im Stillen, dass es ein Mädchen werden würde. Jungen hatte sie drei. Petra, ihre hübsche kleine Tochter, war vor einigen Jahren im zarten Alter von nicht einmal zwei Lenzen gestorben. Seither verbrachte Adeline schlaflose Nächte, wenn eines ihrer Kinder kränkelte. Ihre beiden jüngsten Töchter entwickelten sich gut. Adeline flüsterte ein Ave-Maria für ihr verstorbenes Baby. Ja, dachte sie, ein drittes Mädchen würde ihr gefallen.

„Du hörst dich an wie meine Mutter."

Adeline fuhr erschrocken herum.

„Wofür betest du nun schon wieder?" Schwägerin Geeske, die eine ganze Weile gut hundert Meter hinter ihr hergelaufen war, hatte unbemerkt aufgeschlossen.

„Verflixt, was für ein Schreck!"

„Entschuldige, Adeline. Wofür betest du?"

„Für Beistand und Fügung in unserer Angelegenheit." Adeline würde lieber tot umfallen, als vor ihrer Schwägerin eine körperliche Schwäche zu zeigen oder sie gar in private Sorgen einzuweihen.

„Von welcher Angelegenheit sprichst du?" Geeskes Hut saß keck auf ihren blonden Locken und wirkte bei einem Spaziergang fehl am Platze. Eben tupfte sie sich mit einem Spitzentaschentuch ihre markante Nase. Auch wenn die Adlernase ein wenig zu groß für ihre zarten Gesichtszüge war, machte sie Geeske dennoch sehr attraktiv.

„Die Angelegenheit, die unser aller Zukunft entscheidet. Mein Gott, Geeske, denk doch mal an etwas anderes als nur an dich."

Die beiden Frauen waren grundverschieden, im Aussehen wie im Geiste.

Adeline musste den Kopf ein wenig anheben, um ihrer Schwägerin direkt in die Augen sehen zu können. Sie schnaufte, denn sie war um einiges fülliger als diese. Auch wenn sie nicht gerade schwanger war.

„Du bist gereizt, liebste Adeline. Du hättest einen Sonnenhut aufsetzen sollen." Adeline strich sich über den Kopf. Ihr schwarzes Haar, in der Mitte gescheitelt und nach hinten zu einem straffen Knoten zusammengebunden, fühlte sich in der Sonne heiß an.

„Gegen Sonnenstich hilft auch kein Beten."

Adeline wunderte sich oft über die fehlende Gottesfurcht ihrer Schwägerin. Vermutlich hatte Geeskes Mutter, die selbst Adeline mit ihrer Frömmigkeit auf die Nerven ging, es in der Erziehung ihrer Kinder mit der Religion übertrieben.

Von dem vielen Geld, das die Schwiegermutter in die Kirche steckte, was schon gelegentlich zu finanziellen Engpässen in der Familie geführt hatte, einmal abgesehen.

„Außerdem – wenn *ich* nicht an mich denke, tut es keiner." Geeske bückte sich, um einige Strandnelken zu pflücken.

„Was willst du, Geeske? Warum folgst du mir?"

Die Schwägerin ließ die eben gepflückten Pflanzen achtlos wieder fallen und schenkte ihr einen treuherzigen Augenaufschlag.

„Schau nicht wie ein weidwunder Seehund. Damit kannst du Vater oder deine Brüder um den Finger wickeln. Bei mir zieht das nicht. Es hat doch einen Grund, dass du mir hinterherläufst. Spazieren war noch nie deine Stärke."

Geeske liebte den Trubel, der mit dem Frühling und der Anreise der Gäste auf der Insel einsetzte. Musik, Tanz, den Besuch von Cafés oder Kurkonzerten zog Geeske immer einer Wanderung querfeldein durch Dünen und Salzwiesen vor. Zumal in Begleitung von Adeline, die sich nicht scheute, nach einem Querfeldeinspaziergang mit schmutzigen Röcken nach Hause zu kommen oder gar an einer vorwitzigen Brombeerranke hängen blieb und sich den Stoff zerriss.

„Ich frage mich, liebste Schwägerin …"

Liebste Schwägerin? Die Angelegenheit musste für Geeske wichtig sein. Adeline blieb stehen, stemmte die Hände in die Hüften und streckte den Rücken gerade. Mit dem Gesicht zur Sonne schloss sie die Augen und holte tief Luft. Dieser Geruch nach Frühling, durchmischt mit einer salzigen Meeresbrise, war herrlich.

„Wilhelm und ich möchten noch in diesem Jahr mit dem Bau einer weiteren Apotheke beginnen." Geeske war mit dem

Apotheker Wilhelm Bakker verheiratet. Er trug den gleichen Namen wie sein Schwiegervater, nur dass der eine Willem und der andere Wilhelm hieß. Trotz gleichen Familiennamens waren sie nicht miteinander verwandt. Somit wurde nach Geeskes Heirat aus Fräulein Bakker Frau Bakker geborene Bakker. Um den Alten und dessen Schwiegersohn auseinanderzuhalten, gaben ihm die Insulaner den Spitznamen Pillen-Bakker.

„Ich weiß, ihr redet ja kaum von etwas anderem."

„Stimmt. Aber Vaters Zusage fehlt."

„Und du weißt, warum."

„Wegen dem blöden Projekt. Alles dreht sich nur noch um den Bau des Luxushotels. Als ob wir nicht schon genug Gästebetten hätten." Sie hörte sich an wie ein Kind, dem der Nachtisch verweigert wurde.

„Wir haben auch genug Pillen, Zäpfchen, Cremes und Wässerchen."

„Aber die Gästezahlen steigen, wenn man den Mannsbildern Glauben schenken darf. Da wird eine zweite Apotheke auf Borkum eine Goldgrube werden."

„Das gleiche Argument hat Vater auch." Adeline blieb stehen, um Atem zu holen.

„Dass wir eine weitere Apotheke brauchen?"

„Nein, dass wir bei steigenden Gästezahlen mehr Betten brauchen."

„Dachte ich's mir doch. Du bist auch gegen ein neues Hotel?" Geeske klatschte wie ein kleines Mädchen in die Hände. „Dann unterstütze mich und meine Apotheke."

„Deine Apotheke?"

Geeske reagierte immun auf jede Ironie. Sie selbst konnte ein Zäpfchen nicht von einer Pille unterscheiden.

„Dann habe ich deinen Beistand?“

„Den wirst du nicht brauchen. Die Entscheidung liegt bei den Männern.“

Geeske lachte. „Aber *wir* sagen ihnen, welche Meinung sie haben.“

Auch in dieser Hinsicht gab es einen Unterschied zwischen den Schwägerinnen. Während Adeline versuchte, ihren Mann in den eigenen vier Wänden von ihrer Meinung zu überzeugen, tat Geeske es in aller Öffentlichkeit.

„In der Bibel steht, die Frau sei dem Mann untertan. Also werden sie bestimmen, wo es langgeht.“

„Gerade in deinem Zustand, liebste Adeline, kannst du es schwerlich von der Hand weisen, dass eine weitere Apotheke für die gesamte Familie von Vorteil ist. Wir sollten es anpacken, ehe jemand uns zuvorkommt.“

„Konkurrenz belebt das Geschäft, Geeske.“

„Das Gleiche gilt für Papas geplantes Luxushotel. Als ob ein paar neue Möbel in den Zimmern es nicht auch täten.“

„Das musst du gerade sagen.“

„Was soll das denn heißen?“

„Du und Hieltje seid doch stets die Ersten, wenn es darum geht, sich mit Luxus zu umgeben.“

„Zugegeben, elektrisches Licht und fließendes heißes Wasser würden mir gefallen.“

„Wie geht es Schwiegermama?“, fragte Adeline, um das Thema zu wechseln.

„Keine Ahnung. Sie sitzt vermutlich immer noch in der Klapsmühle und kommt so schnell nicht wieder nach Hause.“

„So spricht eine liebende Tochter!“ Adelines Sarkasmus prallte an Geeske ab.

„Solange sie in einer Zwangsjacke steckt, kann sie wenigstens der Kirche kein neues Dach kaufen."

„Wo du doch das Geld viel dringender benötigst."

„Ich frage mich, warum wir alle so ein Geheimnis um Mutters Krankheit machen."

„Weil die Leute komisch auf verwirrte Frauen reagieren. Sie redet doch dauernd vom Weltuntergang und hält mehr mahnende Predigten über die Verführungskünste des Teufels als zehn Pastoren zusammen. Und was glaubst du, sagen unsere Gäste, wenn sie durchs Hotel schleicht und jeden fragt, ob er einen Engel gesehen hat? Das ist auch für eine Apotheke keine gute Reklame." Adeline blieb stehen und griff nach dem Arm ihrer Schwägerin, um sich festzuhalten.

„Was ist?"

„Senkwehen."

„Der Spaziergang war zu anstrengend", mahnte Geeske. „Soll ich Hilfe holen?"

„Nein. Es geht schon wieder." Adeline rieb ihren Bauch. „Lass mich bei dir untergehakt bleiben. Aber nur bis zum Pfahl an der Ecke, dann gehe ich allein."

Vor dem Hoteleingang grüßte Waldemar, indem er sich leicht verbeugte, ehe er für Adeline Bakker die Eingangstür aufhielt. Die Hausdame, Frau Luise, kam ihr entgegengeeilt und berichtete, dass sie ihre neue Kammer bezogen habe und Mathilde und Hermine jetzt die große Dachkammer für sich alleine hätten. Luises Kommentar, froh über die zusätzliche neue Hilfskraft zu sein, half keineswegs gegen Adelines miese Laune. Eigentlich hätte sie aufgrund ihrer komplizierten Schwangerschaft über jede zusätzliche anpackende Hand im Hotel froh sein sollen.

„Die Neue soll zu mir kommen", trug sie missmutig Frau Luise auf. „Ich erwarte sie in der Personalküche."

Keine drei Minuten später stand Hermine Flessner vor ihr und grüßte mit einem Knicks. Das blutjunge Mädchen bereitete ihr neben ihrer gesundheitlichen Verfassung zusätzliche Kopfzerbrechen. Dass die Borkum-Mädchen aber auch immer hübscher und jünger wurden, dachte Adeline, wohl wissend, dass sie da übertrieb. Doch Hermine Flessners zauberhafte braune Locken, die zu winzig waren, um sie um den kleinen Finger wickeln zu können, verstärkten ihre innere Unruhe. Die fahlblauen Augen, die wie blasse Veilchen wirkten, erzählten von einem wachen Verstand. Älter als fünfzehn konnte sie kaum sein. Ein prüfender Blick auf Hermines schmale Hände verriet ihr, dass das Mädchen fest zupacken konnte. Wenigstens etwas.

Adeline seufzte. Sie würde in Zukunft noch mehr darauf achten müssen, ihren Schwager aus dem *Hotel Bakker Senior* und von den weiblichen Angestellten fernzuhalten.

Innerlich verfluchte sie die verdammte Fehde, die zwischen Georg Köhler und Schwiegerpapa seit Monaten herrschte. Nur ihr hatte sie die neue Hilfskraft zu verdanken. Sie sollte dafür beten, dass die beiden alten Herren wieder Freunde wurden. Sobald sie an den Schwiegervater dachte, spukte ein weiterer lästiger Gedanke durch ihren Kopf. Es wurde Zeit, dass der alte Herr sich aus den Familiengeschäften komplett zurückzog. Kaum war er vom Festland zurück, mischte er sich in die Leitung der Betriebe ein. Warum, fragte sie sich, hatte er die Prokura für dieses Hotel schon vor Jahren seinem Sohn überschrieben, wenn er sich weiter einmischte? Dirks Befugnisse waren in dieser Hinsicht keinen Pfifferling wert, von der Untergrabung ihrer Autorität einmal ganz zu schweigen.

Hermine Flessner blickte sie erwartungsvoll an. Adeline seufzte erneut. Der Rücken schmerzte und das Kind trat heftig gegen die Blase. Sie strich sich über den Bauch, in der Hoffnung, das Baby zu beruhigen. Sicherlich spürte es Adelines innere Aufregung.

„Wie heißen Sie?" Die Frage klang barsch, die Antwort kannte sie bereits.

„Hermine Flessner." Das Mädchen knickste erneut und schaute ihr direkt in die Augen.

Benehmen konnte sie sich. „Frau Luise hat Ihnen Ihre Verpflichtungen aufgezählt?"

„Jawohl." Abermals knickste Hermine. „Das hat sie, Frau Bakker." Und schon listete sie all die Tätigkeiten, die von ihr in Zukunft erwartet wurden, auf.

„Ich erwähnte es bereits: Zimmermädchen habe ich genug. Also machen Sie sich da keine Hoffnungen. Zunächst werden Sie sich bei der Wäsche nützlich machen." Adeline sah, dass dies dem jungen Mädchen nicht gefiel. Gut so. „Zudem werden Sie in der Küche unserer Köchin zuarbeiten. Kartoffeln schälen können Sie?"

„Selbstverständlich, Frau Bakker."

„Gut. Sie arbeiten überall dort, wo eine helfende Hand vonnöten ist. Ich erwarte von meinen Mitarbeitern, dass sie fleißig sind, auch dann, wenn sie sich unbeaufsichtigt wähnen. Die Arbeit sehen und sie erledigen, ist die Maxime unseres Hauses."

„Sehr wohl, Frau Bakker. Das hat Frau Luise bereits erwähnt."

„Der Gast ist König, merken Sie sich das."

„Ja, Frau Bakker."

„Nun, Fräulein Flessner, da mein Schwiegervater Sie eingestellt hat", die Verärgerung darüber versuchte sie nicht zu verbergen, „habe ich ein paar Fragen."

Hermine nickte, wirkte weniger eingeschüchtert als erhofft.

„Erzählen Sie von sich. Woher kommen Sie?"

„Aus Leer, Frau Bakker."

Adeline musterte sie schweigend.

Schnell fügte Hermine hinzu: „Mein Vater ist Bürovorsteher in einer Anwaltskanzlei."

Demnach kein Bauerntrampel. Erleichtert holte Adeline tief Luft. Das hörte sich nach einer ordentlichen Herkunft an. Der Vater Bürovorsteher, da durfte man gute Umgangsformen erwarten. Sie überlegte, ob sie Hermine die Betreuung ihrer Kinder anvertrauen sollte, zu der sie selbst in den kommenden Wochen kaum Zeit finden würde. „Und Ihre Mutter?"

„Mutter ist ein wenig ängstlich, weil ich alleine hier bin", sagte Hermine. „Aber es ist ja nur für sechs Monate."

Adeline musste lächeln. „Ich meinte, was macht Ihre Mutter?"

„Oh, ja. Entschuldigung. Mama ist zu Hause."

„Haben Sie Geschwister?"

Hermine nickte. „Drei Brüder und zwei Schwestern. Ich bin die Älteste."

Da wird sie mit Kindern umgehen können und vermutlich ihren kompletten Lohn nach Hause schicken. Vom Gehalt eines Bürovorstehers wird die Familie keine großen Sprünge machen können. Adeline musste sich eingestehen, dass ihr Schwiegervater ein gutes Auge bei der Einstellung bewiesen hatte.

Hermine wirkte wie ein ordentliches Mädchen. Ganz anders als Mathilde, die man, seit sie bereits im Februar angereist war, kaum zu etwas gebrauchen konnte. Sie bereute den Fehler, Mathilde überhaupt wieder eingestellt zu haben.

Sie seufzte. All die vielen Angestellten, um die man sich kümmern musste! Für ihren Geschmack war der Familienbetrieb Bakker schon jetzt zu groß. Zwei Hotels, das *Bakker Junior* und das *Bakker Senior.* Dann die Restaurants, Bars und Bierkneipen in jedem Haus. Nicht zu vergessen die Krämerläden, die ihr Schwiegervater von dessen Vater geerbt hatte und längst hatte abstoßen wollen. Dann die Frachtschiffe und Fuhrbetriebe, die ebenfalls aus der Ära des Großvaters ihres Mannes stammten und neben guten Erträgen jede Menge Ausgaben für die Mitarbeiter erforderten. Doch mit letzteren drei Betrieben hatte ihr Ehemann Dirk Willems Bakker zum Glück nur selten etwas zu schaffen. Darum kümmerten sich sein älterer Bruder Klaas und die jüngeren Brüder Jann und Eildert. *Ich schweife ab,* dachte sie.

„Wie alt sind Sie?"

„Fünfzehn."

Adeline bemerkte das kurze Zögern. Vermutlich war sie erst vierzehn.

„Wann ist denn der fünfzehnte Geburtstag?" Adeline bekam ihren Verdacht bestätigt. Hermine Flessner wurde rot und senkte kurz den Kopf, ehe sie ihn wieder hob und ihr fest in die Augen schaute.

„In drei Tagen."

***

„He, das ist meine Kleiderstange!“ Mathilde klang wie Hermines Großvater, wenn der zu viel geraucht hatte.

„Und wo soll ich meine Sachen hinhängen?“

Mathilde quälte sich von ihrem Bett hoch, fuhr sich durch die Haare und gähnte, dass man zwei angefaulte Backenzähne sehen konnte. Ihre langen Beine wirkten wie Stöcke. Die Hände in die Hüften gestemmt, blickte sie Hermine herausfordernd an.

„Warum kann ich mein Kleid nicht an die Stange hängen?“

„Weil da Frau Luises Sachen hängen.“

„Die ist doch ausgezogen.“ Hermine deutete mit dem Daumen über ihre Schulter. „Ihre eigene Kammer ist fertig.“

„Gott sei Dank! Da sind wir den Drachen los. Waldemar muss uns helfen, das dritte Bett rauszuschmeißen.“

Hermine tat, als hätte sie das nicht gehört, und hängte ihr Kleid an die Stange. Auf dem Flur waren Schritte zu hören.

„Beeil dich!“, mahnte Mathilde. „Die Köchin mag es gar nicht, wenn wir zu spät zum Frühstück kommen.“

Ihren zweiten Vormittag auf der Insel verbrachte Hermine in der hoteleigenen Waschküche. Die Wäscherin, Frau Kolbe, zeigte ihr die Waschmaschinen. Drei große Holzbottiche, in denen die Wäsche mit einer Kurbel bewegt wurde. Auch standen Gestelle mit je zwei Walzen, ebenfalls mit einer Kurbel daran, im Raum.

„Die Wäschemangeln“, erklärte die Waschfrau, während sie ihre Hand auf eines der Räder legte. An einer Wand reihten sich Körbe aneinander. Nur einer von ihnen war voll schmutziger Wäsche, was, so vermutete Hermine, sich in den Wochen, wenn das Hotel belegt war, ändern würde.

„Und hier ...“, Frau Kolbe führte sie zu einer Tür, öffnete sie und ließ Hermine einen Blick in den Nebenraum werfen. Regale mit schrankfertiger Bettwäsche, Stapeln von Handtüchern, Geschirrtüchern, Tischdecken und mehr füllten die Wände. „Hier lagern wir die saubere Wäsche.“ Frau Kolbe schloss die Tür und nickte Hermine zu. Offensichtlich hatte sie ihr erstauntes Gesicht bemerkt.

„Ganz schön viel, nicht wahr?“

„Das kann man wohl sagen.“ Hermine half, seit sie ein kleines Mädchen war, ihrer Mutter bei der Wäsche. Doch die Mengen, die sich in den beiden Räumen stapelten, hatten Dimensionen, die sie sich bis gestern nicht hätte vorstellen können. Sie dankte stumm ihrer Mutter und Großmutter, dass sie sich bei der zukünftigen Arbeit in der Waschküche nicht anstellen würde, als habe sie noch niemals in ihrem Leben Wäsche gewaschen.

„Na, dann hol mal Wasser.“ Frau Kolbe deutete auf die Pumpe. „Bald bekommen wir fließendes Wasser“, verkündete sie, als Hermine den ersten gefüllten Eimer in einen Kessel goss, der auf einem großen Herd stand. Frau Kolbe schürte das Feuer im Ofen und sobald das Wasser heiß war, schüttete sie es in die hölzerne Waschtrommel, in der bereits die schmutzige Wäsche und die Seife lagen. Sie schloss die Trommel und Hermine musste die Kurbel drehen. In der Zwischenzeit brachten die Köchin, die Zimmermädchen Margret und Sabine und die Chefin mehr Schmutzwäsche.

„Wenn es so weit ist, kommt deine eigene Wäsche auch hier hinein“, sagte Frau Kolbe, nachdem die vierte Partie fertig durchgekurbelt war und sie die private Kleidung der Herrschaften hineingefüllt hatte. „Jeden Mittwoch waschen wir die Unterwäsche unserer Mitarbeiter. Die Wäsche der Familie Bakker natürlich immer. Bei den feinen Sachen von Geeske und Hieltje müssen wir gut aufpassen. Die beiden Damen haben sehr hohe Ansprüche."

Frau Kolbe musste Hermines fragenden Blick bemerkt haben. „Was, die kennst du noch nicht? Das wird sich sicher bald ändern."

„Inwiefern?"

„Die herrschaftlichen Damen wohnen zwar nicht in diesem Haus, lassen aber hier waschen."

Man musste kein Hellseher sein, um zu erkennen, wie sehr es der Waschfrau missfiel.

Nach drei Stunden standen die beiden in eigener nasser Kleidung und mit roten aufgeweichten Händen auf dem Hof, um eine kleine Verschnaufpause einzulegen. Vor ihnen flatterten auf den gespannten Leinen Betttücher und Tischdecken, die vorhin noch im Bottich vor sich hin geköchelt hatten, in der Trommel gedreht oder durch die Mangel gequetscht worden waren, damit das Wasser herauskam. „Du kannst tüchtig anpacken", lobte Frau Kolbe. „Das kann man nicht von jedem hier im Hause behaupten."

„Danke, Frau Kolbe."

„Wenn ich dir einen guten Rat geben darf, Mädchen …"

Hermine nickte.

„Solltest du zusammen mit deiner Zimmerkollegin hier zum Waschen eingeteilt werden, sieh zu, dass sie dich nicht die ganze Arbeit machen lässt."

Mittagessen. Allein der Gedanke daran ließ Hermines Magen knurren. Seit sie auf der Insel angekommen war, hatte sie ständig Hunger. „Das liegt an der schweren Arbeit“, meinte Frau Kolbe. Doch Köchin Gertrud behauptete, es läge am Hochseeklima und würde sich mit den Tagen einpendeln. „Geh rasch nach oben und zieh die nassen Sachen aus“, empfahl Gertrud.

Minuten später folgte Hermine Mathilde die Treppenstufen hinunter in die Hotelküche. Drei der zehn Stühle am langen Tisch waren besetzt.

Der Duft, der Hermine bereits auf der Hintertreppe in die Nase gestiegen war, ließ ihr das Wasser im Munde zusammenlaufen.

„Waldemar hat frische Muscheln besorgt“, verkündete Köchin Gertrud, bei deren Figur niemand erriet, wie gut sie kochen und essen konnte.

„Lang und dürr wie eine von des Pharaos Kühen“, flüsterte Mathilde ihr zu, als habe sie Hermines Gedanken erraten. „Und abergläubisch noch dazu. Sieh bloß zu, dass du in ihrer Gegenwart niemals das Salz umkippst.“

„Ein bisschen davon über die Schulter werfen, und alles ist wieder gut“, meinte Hermine in Erinnerung an gestern.

„Pass bloß auf, was du hier sagst“, flüsterte Mathilde.

„Wie bitte?“

„Wenn die Alte wieder da ist, solltest du dir so ein abergläubisches Geschwafel verkneifen.“

„Welche Alte?“, flüsterte Hermine. Die Köchin war damit sicherlich nicht gemeint. Hermine schätzte Gertrud Dirksen jünger als ihre Mutter.

„Die Seniorchefin. Sie ist frommer als der Papst.“ Mathilde blickte zur Küchentür und erhob die Stimme. „Unsere allseits vermisste Seniorchefin. Wie man hört, ist sie immer noch in

Kur. Hermine folgte ihrem Blick und erkannte Adeline, die sich sofort abwandte.

Gertrud trat mit einem Kochtopf an den Tisch. Um Platz dafür zu machen, schob Waldemar die Körbchen mit Schwarzbrot und zwei Schalen mit Butter beiseite. Gertrud platzierte den Topf in der Mitte des Tisches. Hermine erkannte Miesmuscheln. Gekocht in einem Sud aus Weißwein, Karotten und Gewürzen waren alle, wie es sich gehörte, aufgeplatzt. Das Muschelfleisch, hellbeige und dicker als ein Männerdaumennagel, duftete herrlich.

„Dina!" Gertrud deutete auf zwei Schüsseln, die neben dem Herd standen. „Heute bringst du sie den Herrschaften."

„Die Familie Bakker speist im Restaurant", informierte Mathilde.

„Ich weiß", sagte Hermine.

„Wo hast du die geerntet?", wollte eine dunkelhaarige Frau von etwa dreißig Jahren wissen.

„Das ist Renate. Heute angekommen", verriet Waldemar. „Dritte Saison." Renate schenkte Waldemar ein Lächeln. „Ich teile mit Margret die Kammer am Ende des Ganges."

„Waldemar? Wo haben Sie die herrlichen Muscheln gefunden?"

„Er verrät niemandem, wo die besten Miesmuscheln zu ernten sind", murmelte Renate.

„An den Buhnen am Strand", erwiderte Waldemar.

Dina kam zurück und setzte sich an den Tisch. Mit einem Nicken gab sie der Köchin zu verstehen, dass ihr das Servieren geglückt war und sie selbst mit dem Essen beginnen konnten. Alle langten zu.

Sie aßen schweigend. Hermine half beim Abräumen. Die im leichten Wind getrocknete Wäsche musste abgenommen, zusammengefaltet und weggeräumt werden. Tischwäsche und diverse Oberhemden verlangten nach einem Bügeleisen und so verging auch der Nachmittag mit Arbeit.

Nach dem Abendessen – Gertrud hatte die übrig gebliebenen Muscheln mit Käse überbacken, dazu gab es Brot und Aufschnitt – konnte Hermine jeden einzelnen Knochen spüren.

Sie wünschte Gute Nacht und ging in ihre Dachkammer. Mathilde war nicht da. Durch die Dachluke schien das Licht der untergehenden Sonne herein. Der Himmel war lila, orange und glutrot und erinnerte Hermine an eine der vielen Geschichten, die Großvater bei leuchtenden Sonnenuntergängen gerne erzählte. „Wenn der Abendhimmel so glüht", spann er sein Seemannsgarn, „kommt das von den riesigen Heringsschwärmen in den Meeren, die sich im Himmel widerspiegeln." Ein anderes Mal hatte er erklärt, die Lichter seien die Fackeln der Götter, die die Seelen der Verstorbenen ins Paradies geleiteten. Sicherlich würden diese Geschichten der abergläubischen Köchin gefallen.

Ernst nachdem Hermine ihren Erdkundelehrer gefragt hatte, wusste sie, dass, wenn Großvater von den Fackeln der Götter sprach, von Polarlichtern die Rede war, die im ostfriesischen Raum selten zu sehen waren. Und die glühenden Heringsschwärme waren seine Erklärung für Meeresleuchten. Hermine hoffte, eines Tages solch ein Leuchten zu sehen.

Sie lächelte bei dem Gedanken und legte ihren Rock und die Bluse auf den einzigen Stuhl in der Kammer. Sie hatte eben ihr Nachthemd übergezogen, als sie draußen Stimmen hörte. Sie warf ihre Kleidung aufs Bett, raffte das Hemd bis über die Knie und stieg auf den Stuhl, um aus dem halb offenen Dachfenster auf die Straße sehen zu können.

Ein Mann und eine Frau stritten sich. Beide groß und schlank. Sie schienen jung zu sein. Mit einer Hand umfasste er ihr linkes Handgelenk, mit der anderen knallte er ihr eine. Sie schrie auf, hielt sich die Wange, riss sich los und lief davon. Er blickte sich um und Hermine meinte zu spüren, wie er erleichtert aufatmete, da die Szene seiner Meinung nach niemand mitbekommen hatte. Einerseits hoffte Hermine, dass er hochblickte, um sein Gesicht zu erkennen, andererseits fürchtete sie sich davor. So ein Kerl war imstande, auch ihr gegenüber handgreiflich zu werden, um zu verhindern, dass sie über die Angelegenheit sprach. Zum Glück schaute er nicht hinauf.

Hastig stieg sie vom Stuhl und wollte das Fenster schließen. Im letzten Augenblick fiel ihr ein, dass der Mann das Geräusch hören würde. Mit dem verblassenden Licht der untergehenden Sonne entzündete Hermine die Talglampe, faltete ihre Kleidung zusammen und legte diese in die Schublade und sich ins Bett.

Gut eine Stunde später flog die Kammertür auf und schlug gegen die Wand. Wie vom Blitz getroffen, saß Hermine aufrecht im Bett, die Decke bis unter das Kinn gezogen.

„Verflixt, ist das kalt hier." Mathilde benötigte keinen Stuhl, um die Dachluke zu schließen.

„Das eine sage ich dir …" Mathilde öffnete ihren Haarknoten und Hermine dachte, dass sie selten so fettiges Haar gesehen hatte. „Ich schlafe nicht bei Licht." Mathilde deutete auf die Talglampe, die auf der Kommode stand. „Bei uns zu Hause ist mal so eine Lampe mitten in der Nacht runtergefallen. Am kommenden Tag war nur noch ein Aschehaufen zu sehen, wo vorher Haus und Hof standen."

„Ich hätte es schon ausgepustet", versicherte Hermine.

„Das erwarte ich. Frau Luise würde dir die Hammelbeine langziehen." Mathilde breitete die Arme aus und tat, als stände sie in einem großen Saal. „Ich hoffe, wir bekommen nicht wieder ein drittes Bett hier rein." Sie ließ sich auf ihr Lager fallen und zog sich aus. Die Kleidungsstücke warf sie achtlos auf den Boden. Hermine wandte sich ab.

„Brauchst nicht an die Wand zu starren. So etepetete bin ich nicht." Mathilde lachte. Es klang nicht nett. „Ich hörte, die Chefin hat mit dir gesprochen?"

„Ja."

„Weiß sie, dass er dich dem Köhler abgejagt hat?"

„Ja."

„Erzähl mal, wie ist das gelaufen."

„Bei der Chefin?"

„Nee. Mit dem Alten."

Aber das habe ich doch schon, dachte Hermine. Dennoch fasste sie die Ereignisse der Überfahrt, das Zusammentreffen mit Willem Dirks Bakker und den Abschluss des Arbeitsvertrages durch Händeschütteln kurz zusammen.

„Das wird seiner Schwiegertochter nicht gefallen haben."

Damit verriet Mathilde nichts Neues.

„Sieh dich vor!", warnte Mathilde und kroch unter die Bettdecke. „Die Alte kann gemein sein."

Kurz darauf hörte Hermine Mathildes gleichmäßiges Atmen. *Hoffentlich bin ich eingeschlafen, bevor sie anfängt zu schnarchen.* Doch der Schlaf wollte nicht kommen. Die gebratenen und mit Käse überbackenen Miesmuscheln setzten sich in ihrem Magen noch lange der Verdauung zur Wehr und Hermine musste an Cousine Bertha denken. Wo war sie? Erst drei Tage vor Hermines Abreise aus Leer hatte die

Schwester ihrer Mutter, Tante Frieda, eine Postkarte von Bertha erhalten. Die kam von Borkum. Der Text war kurz. Bertha ginge es gut, das Wetter sei schön und sie freue sich auf die Saison.

Wie konnte Bertha auf der Insel eine Postkarte schreiben und abschicken, wo doch der Page von *Köhlers Dorfhotel* behauptet hatte, sie seit Wochen nicht mehr gesehen zu haben? Da passte irgendetwas nicht zusammen.

Sie versuchte sich einzureden, dass die Karte einfach vom vergangenen Jahr stammte und im Postamt verschlampt worden war. Jemand hatte ihr mal erzählt, ein Brief wäre hinter einen Schrank der Poststelle gefallen und erst Jahre später gefunden und ordnungsgemäß zugestellt worden.

Über die grübelnden Gedanken und das Magengrummeln schlief Hermine ein.

Kapitel 2

„Los, aufstehen!“

Mathilde rüttelte Hermine am kommenden Morgen wach. „Raus aus den Federn, sonst ist das heute dein letzter Arbeitstag!“

„Wer sagt das?“

„Ich. Wer zu spät zum Frühjahrspicknick kommt, hat ganz schlechte Karten.“

„Warum hast du mich nicht eher geweckt?“

„Ich bin nicht dein Kindermädchen.“

Hermine hatte Muskelkater von der schweren Arbeit mit der Wäsche und quälte sich aus dem Bett. Nach der ersten Tasse von Dinas Blümchentee und einer Scheibe Brot ging es ihr in Bezug auf ihren Hunger besser. Blümchentee nannte sie Dinas dünnes Gebräu, weil man durch die Flüssigkeit die gemalte Blume auf dem Tassenboden sehen konnte.

Der Ausflug begann gleich nach dem Frühstück.

„Schnell raus mit euch“, mahnte Köchin Gertrud. „Niemand hat gemerkt, dass ihr verschlafen habt.“ Hermine eilte durch den Hintereingang, um über den Hof zur Straße zu gelangen. Vom gestrigen Waschtag tat ihr jeder einzelne Knochen weh.

„Damit du es weißt", hörte Hermine Gertrud zu Mathilde sagen, „für dich habe ich das nicht getan." Dann standen die Frauen auf der Straße.

Vor dem *Hotel Bakker Senior* warteten drei Kutschen. Normalerweise transportierten diese Fahrzeuge vom Bierfass bis zum Mauerstein alles, was mit den Schiffen an- und auf der Insel ausgeliefert werden musste. Für heute war der Stauraum mit Sitzbänken ausgestattet, damit die Mitarbeiter aus beiden Hotels eine ordentliche Sitzgelegenheit vorfanden. Die Personenkutschwagen wurden heute für den Einsatz am Strand gebraucht.

Neben dem Kutscher des ersten Fahrzeuges saß der Senior Willem Dirks Bakker. Er delegierte mit dem Zeigefinger, wer auf welchem Kutschwagen Platz nehmen sollte.

Mathilde stieß Renate in die Rippen. Mit dem Kopf deutete sie auf einen Mann.

„Was macht der denn auf dem Kutschbock?", wollte Mathilde wissen. Renate kniff die Lippen zusammen und tat, als habe sie nichts gehört.

„Wer ist das?", fragte Hermine leise.

„Jakob Willems Bakker", flüsterte Renate und bekam knallrote Wangen.

Schneidig sah der etwa 35-Jährige in seiner Reiterkleidung aus. Für einen Betriebsausflug viel zu schick gekleidet. Seine Kleidung erinnerte Hermine an eines jener englischen Ölgemälde, auf denen Herrschaften an einer Treibjagd teilnahmen. Mit hocherhobenem Kinn zupfte er an seinem Halstuch und strich das dunkle Haar zurück. Ein Mann, der sich seiner Wirkung auf Frauen bewusst war.

„Sieh dich vor!", flüsterte Renate. „Er ist der größte Casanova, den es je auf der Insel gegeben hat."

„Was ist ein Casanova?"

Mathilde rümpfte die Nase über die Unwissenheit ihrer Kollegin, ließ sich jedoch herab, es zu erklären. Es fielen Worte wie umgarnen, untreu, attraktiv und schön.

Interessiert betrachtete Hermine den Mann, den sie alles andere als schön fand.

„Glotz doch nicht so!" Sie erhielt einen heftigen Stoß mit dem Ellenbogen. „Das bringt nur Ärger. Oh, oh. Und da kommt er schon."

„Wer?"

„Der Ärger."

Hermine folgte Mathildes Blick. Eine blasse Frau mit rötlichen Haaren und üppigem Busen drängte sich zwischen die wartenden Hotelangestellten hindurch. Vor der zweiten Kutsche blieb sie stehen, um sich von Jakob hinaufhelfen zu lassen. Er ergriff ihre Hand und Waldemar, der Page, fasste ihren Ellenbogen, um ihr die drei eisernen Stufen hinaufzuhelfen. Ihr schickes Kleid war für ein Picknick unpassend. Es eignete sich eher für einen Tanzabend.

„Hieltje – Jakobs Frau." Mathildes Gesichtsausdruck verriet eine Mischung aus Missfallen, Verachtung und Erheiterung.

„Angeblich soll er mehrere Liebschaften haben", flüsterte Renate. „Deswegen passt sie höllisch auf. Ich wette, sie hat gar keine Lust zu diesem Ausflug. Aber sie lässt ihn ungern aus den Augen."

Was Jakob nicht vom Flirten in Hieltjes Gegenwart abhielt. Sein kurzes Augenzwinkern galt Renate. Es brachte sie endgültig zum Glühen. Er schien Spaß daran zu haben, was man von Hieltje nicht behaupten konnte. Ihr finsterer Blick ließ Renate auf der Stelle erblassen.

„Sie ist eifersüchtiger als ein Straßenköter auf den Knochen eines anderen", raunte Mathilde. „Pass bloß auf, dass du immer weit genug von ihm entfernt bleibst."

„Auf, auf, die jungen Damen!" Frau Luise stand hinter ihnen. „Was trödelt ihr so herum? Bitte einsteigen!"

Sie saßen noch nicht auf den Bänken, da reichten Gertrud Dirksen und ihr Küchenmädchen Dina Körbe hinauf, die unter den Sitzbänken verstaut wurden. Proviant fürs Picknick, wie der aufsteigende Duft Hermine verriet. Ihr Magen knurrte schon wieder.

***

Adeline Bakker trat aus dem Haus. Sie hatte sich entschieden, hierzubleiben. Das Schütteln in der Kutsche würde ihrer Schwangerschaft schlecht bekommen. Ehemann Dirk Willems Bakker, der im ersten Kutschwagen saß, warf ihr einen Handkuss zu und Adeline hob den Arm, um zum Abschied zu winken. Schon schnalzte der Kutscher des vorderen Wagens und die Pferde zogen an. In dem trockenen Sand hatten sie anfangs Mühe, doch als die Räder rollten, ging es flott voran. Sie bogen um die Ecke, fuhren an *Köhlers Dorfhotel* und dem viereckigen Leuchtturm vorbei.

„Er wird jetzt der alte Leuchtturm genannt", erklärte Bakker Senior, der in letzter Sekunde vom Kutschbock abgestiegen war und sich Hermine gegenüber hingesetzt hatte. „Seit neun Jahren gibt es den neuen, der den Schiffen mit seinem Licht den Weg weist. Der alte Turm, er stammt aus dem Jahr 1576

…" Bakker deutete darauf. „Fast drei Jahrhunderte lang loderte nachts oben ein Feuer. Die Leuchtturmwärter verbrachten jede Nacht dort oben, damit es ja nicht ausging. Erst 1857 bekam der Turm einen Fresnel'schen Glaskuppelapparat. Dadurch hat sein Turmlicht erstmals über die niederländische Nachbarinsel Rottum hinaus und weit auf Borkum Riff hinausgestrahlt. Im Februar vor neun Jahren kam es zur Katastrophe. In einer Sturmnacht brannte er vollkommen aus. Durch den Kamineffekt loderte das Feuer lichterloh, und weil es so windig war, konnte es unmöglich gelöscht werden. Im gleichen Jahr wurde der neue Leuchtturm, er ist gut zwanzig Meter höher als dieser, erbaut. Keine neun Monate haben sie gebraucht, um den Turm hochzuziehen."

Sie umfuhren das jetzt außer Dienst gestellte Seezeichen, an dem eine kleine Kirche angebaut war und um das rundherum ein Friedhof lag.

Hermine meinte, den Brandgeruch zu riechen, doch das war nur Einbildung.

Da Hermine aus ihrem Hotel schon fast alle Kollegen, aber aus dem *Hotel Bakker Junior* noch niemanden kannte, versuchte sie anhand der Kleidung zu erkennen, wer zur Bakker-Familie und wer zum Personal gehörte. So wie es aussah, waren bis auf drei Personen alle Mitarbeiter der Gästehäuser.

Jeder schien sich auf den Ausflug zu freuen. Köchin Gertrud strahlte übers ganze Gesicht, als habe man ihr mit dieser Landpartie eine besondere Freude gemacht.

Die Sonne schien. Ein paar kleine Wolken verzogen sich nach Süden. Man merkte, dass der Tag warm werden würde.

Hinter dem alten Leuchtturm bogen die Kutschen in einen Weg ein, der am Upholmhof vorbeiführen würde. Hier erfuhr

Hermine, warum der Turm auf der Nordseite keine Uhr besaß. Als die Uhren eingebaut worden waren, hatte nach Norden hin nur eine einzige Familie gewohnt: der Konter-Clan. Der Gemeinderat hatte beschlossen, aus finanziellen Gründen auf eine vierte Turmuhr zu verzichten. Also keine Uhr nach Norden. Herr Konter hatte sich darüber beschwert und moniert, ob er ein Mensch zweiter Klasse sei. Er hatte so lange geklagt, bis die Gemeinde ihm eine Taschenuhr geschenkt hatte, damit er Ruhe gab.

Alle Kutschinsassen lachten, obwohl Hermine vermutete, dass Gertrud, Mathilde und Renate die Geschichte schon oft und immer bei dieser Gelegenheit gehört hatten.

Am Upholmhof herrschte am frühen Vormittag bereits hektisches Treiben. Neben der bäuerlichen Tätigkeit hatte der Eigentümer den vorderen Teil des Gebäudes als Ausflugslokal hergerichtet. Mitarbeiter rückten auf der Terrasse Stühle und Tische zurecht, der erste Sonnenschirm wurde aufgespannt.

Bis die Kutschen im Ostland ankamen, verging eine Stunde. Der Senior unterhielt seine Angestellten mit alten Borkumer Geschichten. Weit und breit gab es nur karge Dünen. Kein einziges Haus war zu sehen.

„Herr Bakker?“ Gertrud hob den Zeigefinger wie in der Schule. „Erzählen Sie uns von den Franzosen!“

Hermine bekam das Gefühl, als habe der Senior nur auf die Aufforderung gewartet. Mathilde verdrehte die Augen und Renate klatschte in die Hände. „Oh, ja! Die Geschichte höre ich so gerne.“

Sichtlich geschmeichelt strich Willem Dirks Bakker seinen Bart glatt, die Finger glitten gedankenverloren über den silbernen Knauf seines Gehstocks.

„Die Geschichte ist aus erster Hand, Fräulein Flessner." Hermine erschrak, weil er sie direkt ansprach. Renate kicherte albern und Mathilde grinste teuflisch.

„Aber ich ...", stotterte Hermine.

„Nicht, dass Sie glauben, ich erzähle hier nur Seemannsgarn."

„Niemals, Herr Bakker!" Jetzt war es Hermine, die rote Wangen bekam.

„Es war mein Stiefvater, der die Franzosen das Fürchten lehrte. Sie wissen, dass die Franzmänner hier gewesen sind?"

Hermine kannte einige Geschichten über die Franzosen, die sich in ganz Ostfriesland breitgemacht hatten. Auch ihr Großvater konnte einige Erlebnisse aus der Zeit erzählen. Sie nickte.

„Aber wussten Sie, dass Napoleons Truppen hier auf der Insel gewesen sind? Es ist gerade mal etwas über siebzig Jahre her, als sie unser Eiland besetzten. Das war eine schlimme Zeit, dennoch muss ich ehrlich zugeben, dass die Familie Bakker dem kleinen Kaiser seine Besitztümer zu verdanken hat."

Bakker erzählte, wie sein Stiefvater mit dem Fährschiff, der *Vriendschap,* Napoleons Kontinentalsperre umfahren und mit Schmuggelwaren ein Vermögen gemacht hatte. „Er hat nicht nur geschmuggelt, sondern die Ware gleich in seinen eigenen Läden verkauft. Damals galt für jedes Schiff, das auf der Nordsee fuhr, die Vorschrift, immer einen französischen Soldaten an Bord zu haben. Damit dieser die Einhaltung des Embargos überwachen konnte. Mein Stiefvater hat sich eine Uniform besorgt, sie mit Stroh ausgestopft, ihr eine Flinte in den Arm gedrückt und sie vorne an Deck festgebunden. So sah es von Weitem aus, als wäre alles rechtens."

Ähnliche Schilderungen kursieren in ganz Ostfriesland, deshalb vermutete Hermine, dass einiges davon mit einem Hauch von Seemannsgarn gesponnen worden war. Willem Dirks Bakker konnte gut erzählen, wie etwa die Geschichte von zwei Borkumern, die für Napoleon in den Krieg ziehen mussten. Der französische Kaiser zwang gerne Ostfriesen in seine Armee, da sie gute Seeleute waren. Die beiden Insulaner fuhren auf Napoleons Kriegsschiff und das Schiff wurde von den Engländern gekapert und die Männer gefangen genommen. Vor die Wahl gestellt, Gefängnis oder Kriegsmarine, entschieden sie sich für Letzteres. Eines Tages lag die englische Brigg vor Borkum. Die beiden nutzten die Gelegenheit und desertierten. Um sie weiter zum Kriegsdienst zu zwingen, nahmen die englischen Soldaten den Borkumer Bürgermeister als Geisel. Zudem drohten sie, den Familien etwas anzutun, wenn die Deserteure nicht zurückkämen. Auf Fahnenflucht stand der Tod durch den Strang, dennoch gingen die beiden zurück an Bord der Brigg. Später gab es ein glückliches Ende.

„Denn sie kamen nach Ende des Krieges zurück. Warum man sie nicht gehängt hat, bleibt bis heute ein Geheimnis", sagte Bakker. „Ebenso, was die feigen Froschfresser in den vier Tagen taten", endete Bakkers Geschichte immer gleich, „als die englische Korvette im Hopgraben lag. Vermutlich haben sie sich in ihrer Schanze verkrochen und so getan, als wären sie nicht da."

Die Zeit verging schnell, die ersten Ostlandhöfe kamen in Sicht.

Hier liefen die gleichen Vorbereitungen wie zuvor auf dem Upholmhof. Die Ausflugsziele bereiteten sich auf ihre Gäste vor. An diesem warmen, sonnigen Tag erwarteten die Cafébesitzer die ersten Urlauber dieser Saison. Hermine nahm sich vor, an einem ihrer freien Tage hierher zu kommen, um bei einer Tasse heißem Kakao die bäuerliche Stimmung zu genießen. Gerüche nach Kuhfladen, Pferdemist und frisch gebackenem Kuchen stiegen ihr in die Nase und verflogen, als sie weiterfuhren.

Der Weg führte an den Ostlandhöfen vorbei und endete vor einer Sanddüne.

Die Kutschen hielten und wie der Schwarm Gänse, der eben über ihren Köpfen hinweg Richtung Osten geflogen war, schwärmten die Ausflügler aus.

„Wir sollten Vogelkojen aufstellen", rief Dirk Willems Bakker seinem Vater zu und schaute den Tieren hinterher.

„Vogelkojen? Was ist das denn?" Frau Luise Menninga, den einen Arm in der Schlinge, am anderen hing ein Picknickkorb, stand noch in der Kutsche. Hermine nahm ihr den schweren Korb ab und half ihr die Stufen hinunter. Aus dem Augenwinkel sah sie einige Kolleginnen in die Dünen laufen. Sie blieb jedoch stehen, denn sie wollte unbedingt wissen, was Vogelkojen waren. Vor ihrem inneren Auge sah sie Federvieh in Bettdecken gekuschelt in einer Koje liegen, den Kopf unter die Flügel gesteckt, und schlafen.

„Das sind Fangnetze, Frau Luise. Ähnlich wie Fischreusen. Man lockt die Tiere, meistens sind es Enten, auf eine Wasserfläche herunter, indem man darauf hölzerne Vögel treiben lässt. Mit einer Tröte macht man Lockgeräusche, und Futter verführt die Tiere, in die Netze zu schwimmen, die, wie gesagt, wie eine Aalreuse nach hinten immer enger werden. Da kommen die Vögel dann nicht mehr heraus."

„Die armen Tiere!", sagte Mathilde.

„Das habe ich gerne", maulte die Köchin. „Mitleid haben, aber wenn es Entenbraten mit Rotkohl gibt, gleich zwei Portionen vertilgen."

Die Ausflügler folgten dem Senior die Düne hinauf und auf der anderen Seite wieder hinunter.

Die Kutscher blieben bei den Pferden. In einer großen Dünendelle wurden Decken ausgebreitet und die Proviantkörbe ausgepackt.

In der Sonne war es angenehm warm, der leichte Wind wehte über das Dünental hinweg. Alle fanden einen Platz auf den Decken und ließen sich die Köstlichkeiten schmecken.

Die hartgekochten Eier gab es in zwei Sorten. Weiße und grüne mit dunklen Flecken. „Das sind Möweneier", erklärte Gertrud. „Nicht jedermanns Geschmack. Sie sind leicht fischig. – Dina?"

„Ja, Frau Dirksen."

„Wie lange müssen Möweneier gekocht werden?"

„Mindestens zwanzig Minuten, Frau Dirksen."

„Sehr gut aufgepasst. Und warum, Dina?"

„Wegen der Bakterien. Sanellen oder so."

„Salmonellen. Sie wurden 1880 entdeckt und nach dem Herrn Salmon benannt."

„Nun ist aber Schluss mit dem Unterricht, Frau Dirksen." Mathilde schaute der Köchin in die Augen. Es dauerte nur wenige Momente, ehe Gertrud den stummen Zweikampf aufgab und nach einem Hühnerei griff.

„Wusstet ihr", versuchte Renate die peinliche Situation zu überspielen, „dass es Hühneraugen auch am Kopf gibt?"

„Ich hätte nicht gedacht, dass du so einen Quatsch glaubst", knurrte Mathilde.

„Doch, die gibt es. Bei Hühnern." Renate lachte laut über ihren eigenen Witz.

Hermine erschrak, als eine Männerstimme dicht an ihrem Ohr fragte: „Wussten Sie, dass Borkum vor einiger Zeit noch aus zwei Inseln bestand?"

Plötzlich saß Jakob Willems Bakker auf der karierten Decke dicht hinter ihr. Über die Schulter hinweg blickte sie in himmelblaue Augen, die für ihren Geschmack viel zu nah waren. Jakob bemerkte ihren erschrockenen Gesichtsausdruck und rückte ein wenig ab. Hermine tauschte mit Mathilde einen schnellen Blick. Deren Miene verriet einiges. „Ich habe dich gewarnt", schien sie zu sagen. Doch war da noch etwas. Neid – Eifersucht? Ehe sie sich weiter Gedanken darüber machen konnte, erklärte Jakob, dass es früher eine östliche und eine westliche Insel gegeben habe und man nur bei Ebbe von der einen zur anderen habe gelangen können. „Tatkräftig anpackenden Insulanern", dabei zeigte er auf seinen Bizeps, „ist es gelungen, den Wasserdurchlauf zu schließen. Heute sieht man kaum noch etwas davon. Aber es muss ungefähr an dieser Stelle gewesen sein, wo das Meer hindurchströmte."

„Jakob?" Hieltjes Stimme klang ungnädig. „Ich brauche deine Hilfe." Sie schwenkte eine Flasche Sekt, die geöffnet werden sollte.

„Oh, oh!", flüsterte Mathilde, als Jakob aufstand und zu seiner Frau hinüberging. „Da hast du dir ja in Sekundenschnelle eine Feindin gemacht."

„Sie kann nichts dafür", nahm Gertrud Hermine in Schutz. Und Dina fügte hinzu: „Nur nicht neidisch werden, liebe Mathilde."

„Als ob ich mir etwas aus Sekt machen würde", maulte Mathilde.

Dina grinste frech und steckte sich eines der Käsehäppchen in den Mund, gefolgt von einem halben hartgekochten Ei mit einer Senffüllung und einer Scheibe Räucherlachs.

„Schling nicht so, Dina! Du bist keine Möwe!" Gertrud reichte dem Küchenmädchen einen Becher mit frischer Kuhmilch und Mathilde reckte den Hals, als ob sie durch bloßes Herüberschauen einen Schluck Sekt angeboten bekommen würde.

Die Hotelküche hatte ihr Bestes gegeben. Die Mitarbeiter schwelgten in Köstlichkeiten, die normalerweise nur den Hotelgästen serviert wurden.

Keine zehn Minuten später waren die Picknickkörbe leergefuttert. Dirk Willems Bakker, der zwei Decken weiter saß, erhob sich und klatschte in die Hände. „Wie wäre es mit einem Spaziergang?"

Viele standen auf und folgten ihm im Gänsemarsch in die Dünen hinein.

„Gehen Sie nicht mit?", fragte Hermine Gertrud.

„Nein. Sie spazieren bis an den Strand. Das ist mir zu weit. Ich bleibe lieber hier sitzen und genieße die Sonne. Aber Sie haben junge Beine. Laufen Sie."

Hermine stellte ihren Milchbecher in den Sand und wollte aufstehen. Ein schneller Blick auf Jakob zeigte ihr, wie er unnötig irgendetwas an seinen Schuhen richtete. Doch Hermine und seiner Ehefrau konnte er nichts vormachen. Er wartete darauf, dass Hermine sich erhob und der Gruppe folgte.

Hieltje Bakker hatte eben noch laut verkündet, nicht mitzugehen, da sie Angst um ihre Garderobe habe. Die Beerenranken, die überall in den Dünen zu finden waren, könnten ihrem Kleid schaden. Jetzt ließ sie das Sektglas achtlos in den Sand fallen und sprang von ihrer Decke auf. Vier, fünf Schritte nur, und sie packte die Hand ihres Ehemannes, zog ihn hoch und hakte sich bei ihm ein. Den giftigen Blick, den Hermine erhielt, würde sie so schnell nicht vergessen.

„Ich bleibe bei Ihnen, Frau Gertrud", sagte sie laut, damit alle es hörten. Schade, dachte Hermine, die Wanderung zum Strand hätte sie gerne mitgemacht.

Keine fünf Minuten später zeigte ein gleichmäßiges Atmen an, dass die Köchin auf der Picknickdecke eingeschlafen war. Hermine legte sich ebenfalls hin, verschränkte die Arme hinter dem Kopf und betrachtete den Himmel. Fast wäre auch sie eingedöst, wurde jedoch vom Ruf eines Kuckucks wach gehalten. Es würde bald Zeit werden, aufzubrechen. Und da kamen die Spaziergänger schon angelaufen. Auch wenn sie auf den Kutschwagen unter Planen sicher geschützt vor dem Regen sitzen würden, mahnte Jakob Willems Bakker, sich zu beeilen. Zu Hermines Erleichterung nahmen er und seine Ehefrau wieder in der ersten Kutsche Platz, sodass sie die Rückfahrt unbeschwert genießen konnte. Auf halber Strecke begann es zu regnen. Und einen Kilometer, bevor sie den alten Leuchtturm erreichten, prasselte es und die Pferde wurden unruhig.

„Sie wittern den Stall", erklärte der Kutscher und nahm die Zügel fester in die Hand.

Als der Wagen am *Hotel Bakker Junior* vorbeikam, wieherte eines der Zugpferde. Beim Einbiegen aus der Großen Straße in die Neue Straße schnitt der Fuhrmann die Kurve und blieb mit dem Hinterrad an dem hüfthohen Metallpfahl, an dem sich abends die Dorfjugend traf, hängen. Das Rad riss ab, der Kutschwagen kippte leicht und Hermine, die am Ende der Sitzbank saß und die rückseitige Wagentür schon geöffnet hatte, fiel hinaus.

Zwei kräftige Arme fingen sie auf. Jakob Bakker.

„Alles in Ordnung?"

„Danke für Ihre Hilfe." Hermine befreite sich aus seinen Armen, die sie länger als schicklich festhielten. Sie richtete ihr Kleid und sah auf. Ihr Blick traf den von Hieltje.

„Ich sag es noch mal", raunte Mathilde ihr wenige Sekunden später zu. „Pass auf dich auf! Heute hast du dir eine Feindin gemacht."

***

Hieltje kochte vor Zorn. Warum nur um alles in der Welt, stellte ihre Schwägerin blutjunge und hübsche Borkum-Mädchen ein? Sie grollte ihr, obwohl sie wusste, dass es nicht an Adeline lag, schließlich konnte niemand bei den schriftlichen Bewerbungen der jungen Frauen sehen, ob sie hässlich oder hübsch waren.

Bevor sie Jakob geheiratet hatte, kannte Hieltje keine Eifersucht. Als Kinder hatten sie sich bereits gekannt, doch dann war sie zur Ausbildung aufs Festland gezogen. In Hannover hatte sie zwei Jahre verbracht, ehe sie auf ihre Heimatinsel zurückgekehrt war. Die Monate in der Großstadt waren glückliche gewesen und kein Vergleich mit dem Leben auf einer kleinen Insel mit weniger als tausend Einwohnern. Hieltje war es schwergefallen, sich in die Inselgemeinschaft, in die sie hineingeboren worden war, erneut einzufügen. Sie hielt sich aufgrund ihrer Lebenserfahrung in der großen Stadt für etwas Besseres und hatte die Insel nochmals verlassen. Dieses Mal war sie nach Wiesbaden gezogen. Im Nachhinein war das keine gute Idee gewesen, denn gerade in der Fremde hatte sie Jakob Bakker erneut kennengelernt. Der war für sechs Monate in der großen Stadt, um eine Ausbildung zum Kaufmann bei einem der Stammgäste des Vaters zu absolvieren. Der Zufall hatte es gewollt, dass sie im Stadtpark aufeinandertrafen. Er war ihren flammendroten Haaren verfallen und dem üppigen Busen, und weil Jakob nicht nur ein Schwerenöter war, sondern auch jemand, der sich keine Gesichter merken konnte, blieb es nicht aus, dass er sie ansprach. Hieltje hatte sofort gewusst, wer er war, bei ihm hatte es einige Zeit gedauert, bis er herausfand, dass sie Borkumerin war. Zu dem Zeitpunkt hätte es für Hieltje noch ein Zurück gegeben, denn sein schlechter Ruf, was Frauenbekanntschaften anging, war ihm schon damals vorausgeeilt. Doch er hatte den Eindruck erweckt, sich geändert zu haben. Sie hatte sich in ihn verliebt und seinen Schwüren, ihr treu ergeben zu sein, geglaubt. Wenige Wochen später hatte es eh kein Zurück mehr gegeben.

„Aus der schlichten Insulanerin ist in der Großstadt eine schicke, selbstbewusste junge Dame geworden", antwortete Jakob heute gerne, wenn sich jemand nach der Geschichte ihres Kennenlernens erkundigte. „Sicherlich habe ich sie deswegen nicht sofort wiedererkannt." Danach erzählte Jakob, wie er sie im Park angesprochen und in ein Café eingeladen hatte. „Und innerhalb der kommenden Tage erlag sie meinem Charme."

Seinen Kaufmannsabschluss hatte er bis heute nicht gemacht.

Als Hieltje bemerkte, dass sie schwanger war, war Jakob bereits seit drei Wochen wieder auf der Insel. In dem Textilgeschäft, in dem sie Brautmoden verkaufte, durfte sie nicht bleiben. Ihr blieb nichts anderes übrig, sie musste zu ihren Eltern nach Borkum zurückkehren. Hier zeigte Jakob sein wahres Gesicht, indem er abstritt, der Vater zu sein. Doch seine Eltern wussten es besser und gemeinsam mit Hieltjes Vater und Mutter drängten sie ihn zur Heirat. Keine gute Voraussetzung für eine Ehe, dachte Hieltje oft. Doch sie liebte ihn und sie redete sich ein, dass sie nicht die Erste und nicht die Letzte sein würde, die heiraten musste, weil etwas Kleines unterwegs war. Bei den meisten war es ja gut ausgegangen. Mittlerweile war sie Mutter zweier Kinder und nach Eifersuchtsanfällen fand sie großen Gefallen daran, Jakobs Geld mit vollen Händen auszugeben. Doch all die schönen Kleider und der Schmuck verschafften ihr nur für eine kurze Weile inneren Frieden. Die Eifersucht fraß sie auf und sorgte für eine anhaltende Trauermiene. Damit machte sie sich wenig Freunde, das wusste sie, und doch konnte sie nicht anders. In ihrer Verdrossenheit rümpfte sie gerne die Nase über die Rückständigkeit der Insulaner und ließ die Menschen ihren Zorn spüren. Sie kränkte Nachbarn, die sie für Hinterwäldler hielt, und sie war dumm genug, es ihnen ins Gesicht zu sagen. *Warum nur,* fragte sie sich oft im Nachhinein, *ist meine Zunge schneller als das Hirn?*

Kein Wunder, wenn die Angestellten in beiden Hotels der Familie Bakker sich hinter ihrem Rücken lustig machten, ihre Stimme und Körperhaltung nachäfften und sie „die Gräfin" nannten.

In ihrem Frust verbreitete Hieltje Unruhe unter den Mitarbeitern der Hotels. Hinzu kam der Umstand, dass Ehemann Jakob im Familienbetrieb wohl mit anpackte, jedoch in keinem der Betriebe eigenständig verantwortlich war. Im Gegensatz zu seinen Brüdern war er nirgends der Chef.

Er galt allgemein nur als Sohn des Hauses und sie war sein teures Anhängsel. Dass sie aufgrund der beiden Kinder selbst keine Zeit fand, sich in den Betrieben einzubringen, war für sie selbstverständlich, hinderte sie jedoch nicht daran, Angestellte herumzukommandieren.

„Du musst sie in ihre Schranken weisen", forderte Dirk Willems Bakker seinen Bruder Jakob auf, „wenn du den Frieden in meinem Haus nicht gefährden willst. Frau Luise hörte, wie Hieltje verkündete, dafür zu sorgen, dass die Neue rausgeworfen wird. Wer in diesem Hotel rausfliegt, entscheide immer noch ich."

„Bist du dir sicher, Brüderchen?"

Dirk winkte ab. Jakob wusste genauso gut wie er, dass ihr Vater, auch wenn er die Leitung der beiden Hotels an Dirk abgegeben hat, immer noch das letzte Wort hatte.

„Lenk nicht vom Thema ab. Die Hausdame im *Junior* soll angedroht haben zu kündigen, wenn deine Ehefrau weiter so tut, als sei sie die Herrin im Haus. Vielleicht solltet ihr aus dem Hotel ausziehen und in irgendein kleines Häuschen übersiedeln. Auf jeden Fall sieh zu, dass du sie von meinen Mitarbeitern fernhältst."

Dirk sah, dass die Angelegenheit seinen Bruder kaum interessierte. Ob nun die Dickmamsell aus der Hotelküche oder die Hausdame des *Bakker Junior* kündigen wollten, war Jakob egal, und die Zankereien seiner Hieltje noch mehr. Jakob hatte nur Frauen im Kopf. Um ihn wenigstens ein wenig aufzurütteln, griff Dirk zur Notlüge und setzte noch eins drauf. „Und die Elisabeth will ebenfalls gehen."

„Das niedliche blonde Zimmermädchen mit den langen Zöpfen, das täglich unsere Betten macht?"

Kurz spürte Dirk Mitleid mit seiner Schwägerin. Kein Wunder, dass Hieltje ständig mit einer Trauermiene durch die Gegend lief. Dennoch blieb Jakobs Schürzenjägerei auch Dirks

Problem, denn alles, was er anstellte, fiel auf die ganze Familie zurück. Vielleicht sollte Dirk Jakob nochmals auffordern, genauer darüber nachzudenken, was er mit seinem Laster auslöste und wem er alles damit schadete. Gut möglich, dass Hieltje ihre Sauertöpfigkeit aufgab, wenn sie sich der vollen und ungeteilten Aufmerksamkeit ihres Mannes endlich sicher sein konnte.

„Ich werde mit ihr reden." Das süffisante Lächeln seines Bruders ließ Dirk ahnen, dass er vermutlich von dem Zimmermädchen sprach.

„Reiß dich einfach am Riemen und lauf nicht jedem Rock hinterher."

„Kann ja nicht jeder so ein Saubermann sein wie du." Jakob warf seinem älteren Bruder einen spöttischen Blick zu.

***

„Er ist schon ein fescher Bursche." Mathilde stupste Hermine mit dem Ellenbogen an.

„Findest du?" Hermine fand es lästig, dass Mathilde auf dem Thema herumritt. Ihrer Meinung nach war Jakob Willems Bakker alles andere als fesch. Nachdem er sie beim Sturz aus dem Kutschwagen aufgefangen und länger als notwendig an sich gedrückt hatte, empfand sie im Nachhinein nur peinliches Unwohlsein.

„Alle finden ihn appetitlich", ließ Mathilde nicht locker.

Dieses Wort im Zusammenhang mit einem erwachsenen Mann hatte Hermine niemals zuvor gehört. Sie schüttelte den Kopf. „Ich nicht."

„Auf jeden Fall ist er auf dich aufmerksam geworden.“ Mathildes Stimme hatte einen neiderfüllten Unterton.

„Darauf kann ich gerne verzichten.“

„Die Leute werden reden und seine Ehefrau wird nicht eher Ruhe geben, bis sie dich entlassen haben.“ Mathilde warf ihr ein Ende des Bettbezuges zu. Gemeinsam zogen sie die Wäsche lang und traten dicht zusammen, damit die eine der anderen ihr Teilstück übergeben konnte. Einmal zusammengefaltet, reckten und streckten sie es erneut, bis Hermine es Mathilde aus den Händen nahm, nochmals faltete und in den Korb legte. Mathilde zupfte derweil das nächste Wäschestück von der Leine.

„Willst du gar nicht wissen, was die Leute reden?“

Schweigend bereiteten sie das Wäschestück vor. Als Hermine es zu dem ersten in den Korb legte, seufzte sie. „Nun erzähl schon. Du gibst ja doch keine Ruhe.“

„Ich will nur, dass du weißt, auf wen du dich da einlässt.“

„Ich lasse mich auf niemanden ein. Der Mann kann mir gestohlen bleiben.“

„Es wird gemunkelt, dass der Kutscher das extra gemacht hat.“

„Was? Wovon sprichst du?“

„Es heißt, er habe mit Absicht den Pfahl umgefahren.“

„Damit ich hinausfalle und Jakob mich auffangen kann? Blödsinn.“

Mathilde ignorierte ihren Einwand. „Wusstest du“, sagte sie, „dass der Kutscher andauernd Unfälle baut. Es vergeht kein Monat, in dem er keinen Schaden bei den Bakkers anrichtet. Und wusstest du, dass er Hieltjes älterer Bruder ist?“

Nein, woher sollte Hermine das wissen. Sie schüttelte den Kopf und zog ein Bettlaken von der Leine.

„Und ich verrate dir noch etwas." Mathilde nahm ihr Ende des Lakens, machte jedoch keine Anstalten, mit dem Ziehen zu beginnen. „Die Bakkers lassen dem tollpatschigen Kutscher alles durchgehen."

„Sicherlich, weil er zur Familie gehört."

„Nein. Sie sind ihm was schuldig. Deswegen kann er sich erlauben, was er will."

„Und was hat das jetzt mit mir zu tun?"

„Das …"

„Seid ihr endlich fertig?" Adeline Bakkers Stimme hallte über den Hof.

„Nur noch drei Teile, Frau Bakker. Dann können wir mit dem Bügeln beginnen."

Das Geheimnis um den Kutscher Teerling sollte Hermine erst später erfahren.

***

Vier seiner Enkelsöhne hießen Willem. Willem Jannsen Bakker, der Sohn seines Sohnes Jann; Willem Eilderts Bakker, der Sohn von Eildert; Willem Jakobs war der Erstgeborene von Jakob und Willem Dirks der von Dirk.

Letzterer wurde Willi genannt, da er trotz Zwischennamen genauso hieß wie sein Großvater. Schließlich musste man sie ja irgendwie auseinanderhalten.

Der Senior konnte nur hoffen, dass eines Tages einer seiner Nachfahren auf die Idee käme, sich der patronymischen Namensgebung zu widersetzen und sein Kind nicht nach dem

Vorfahren benannte, sondern ihm den Vornamen gab, der den Eltern gefiel. Zumindest würde es verhindern, einen Menschen mit gleichem Namen „den Alten" oder „den Jungen" zu nennen oder ihm einen anderen treffenden Spitznamen zu geben. Wie Esel-Willi, Klaas-Barbier oder Flaschen-Dirk.

Seine Frau wäre entsetzt gewesen, wenn sie von diesem Gedanken gewusst hätte. *Und mich halten sie für altmodisch,* dachte Willem Dirks Bakker der Alte und grinste.

„Was lächelst du so zufrieden, Großvater?" Willi saß ihm gegenüber und blickte vom Schachbrett auf. Als der Junge fünf Jahre alt geworden war, hatte er ihm das Schachspiel geschenkt. „An einem Ball hätte Willi sicherlich mehr Gefallen gefunden", hatte damals seine Schwiegertochter Adeline gemeint, doch da hatte sie sich getäuscht. In den Wochen nach Willis fünftem Geburtstag brachte er seinem Enkel das Spiel bei und kein Jahr später musste er nicht mehr so tun, als würde er verlieren, er verlor wirklich. Jetzt wurde Willi bald dreizehn, dachte er, und dennoch nahm der Junge sich gelegentlich Zeit, um mit seinem Opa eine Partie zu spielen.

„Ich musste gerade an deinen sechsten Geburtstag denken, Willi."

„Du hast mir das hier geschenkt und alle glaubten, ich sei zu dumm, um es zu lernen."

„Nun, ganz so war es nicht. Aber deine Mutter und deine Oma hätten es lieber gesehen …"

Willi nickte, machte den nächsten Zug und nahm einen Springer vom Feld. „Für Fußball interessiere ich mich bis heute nicht", murmelte er und deutete auf den schwarzen Turm.

„Übrigens hatte Fräulein Flessner Geburtstag." Willis Stimme klang gleichgültig, doch sein Opa kannte ihn gut.

„Soso. Das wusste ich gar nicht. Ich hoffe, du hast ihr im Namen der Familie gratuliert.“

Willi hatte ihr einen kleinen Strauß Strandnelken überreicht und nur die Worte „Herzlichen Glückwunsch zum Geburtstag“ herausbekommen. Doch das verriet er nicht.

„Habe ich, Großvater. Pass auf deine Dame auf.“

„Das mache ich immer.“

„Apropos Dame, Großvater. Was schreibt Großmutter?“

Der Senior lächelte. Sein Enkel Willi war der Einzige, der sich regelmäßig nach Harminas Gesundheit erkundigte. „Es geht ihr gut. Sie lässt euch alle grüßen.“

„Wird sie bald wiederkommen?“

„Du vermisst sie, oder?“

„Natürlich vermisse ich sie, auch wenn es bedeuten würde, dass ich wieder öfter in die Kirche muss, wenn sie da ist.“

„Ich denke …“ Seine Hand schwebte über dem Schachspiel und er bewegte die Finger, als wolle er Klavier spielen.

„Lass es, Großvater!“

„Was denn?“

„Wenn du so machst“, Willi wiederholte seine Fingerspiele, „bist du dir unsicher und machst einen falschen Zug.“

Erneut musste er lächeln. Sein Enkel kannte ihn besser als seine Kinder.

„Ich denke“, wiederholte er, „dass deine Großmutter Ende des Monats, spätestens Mitte kommenden Monats wieder zu Hause sein wird. Aber …“ Er machte seinen Zug, den er sofort bereute, da Willi ihm, ohne nachzudenken, seinen Läufer wegnahm.

„Aber was?“

„Sie wird von ihrem religiösen Wahn nicht vollkommen geheilt sein.“

„Das habe ich auch nicht erwartet, Großvater. Sie war immer gläubig und hat sich für die Kirche engagiert …"

„Nur dass sie es am Ende übertrieben hat." Die zwei schauten sich kurz gegenseitig an. Beide dachten an die letzten Tage, bevor Doktor Kock und Doktor Schmidt gemeinsam entschieden hatten, dass Frau Bakker in ein Sanatorium gehörte, um von ihren Wahnvorstellungen, sie sei die Verkörperung des Satans und müsse alles wiedergutmachen, herunterzukommen. Wie war sie nur auf die Idee gekommen, dachte der Senior nicht zum ersten Mal. Seine Ehefrau war jemand, der sich für andere einsetzte, sich um die Belange der Kirche, der Armen und wer weiß wen noch kümmerte und die ihr letztes Hemd dafür hergab. Als sie ihren Ehemann aufgefordert hatte, er solle die Kosten für ein neues Gotteshaus aufbringen, damit ihrer aller Seelenheil gerettet werde, war das der letzte Tropfen gewesen, der das Fass zum Überlaufen gebracht hatte.

„Aber jetzt ist sie wieder die Alte, ich meine gedanklich und so?"

„Das ist sie, Willi. Obwohl wir alle wohl weiterhin jeden Sonntag in die Kirche müssen, doch das ist nicht so tragisch, oder?"

Willi schüttelte den Kopf und der Senior wusste nicht, ob er die Großmutter oder die Schachpartie meinte.

„Vorsichtig, Großvater!", mahnte Willi, dabei hatte er sich noch gar nicht entschieden, welchen Zug er machen wollte.

„Und wie steht es um deinen besten Freund?"

„Georg Köhler?"

„Hast du noch mehr beste Freunde, Großvater?"

„Jede Menge. Köhler geht es offensichtlich gut." Er machte seinen nächsten Zug und sah, wie sein Enkel traurig den Kopf schüttelte.

„Was denn? Bin ich schachmatt?“

„Nein, noch nicht. Sagst du mir, wann ihr wieder gute Freunde seid?“

„Bald, Willi.“

„Das habe ich mir gedacht. Spätestens an dem Tag, an dem die Ausschreibung zu Ende ist, habe ich recht?“

Willi kannte ihn und seinen besten Freund, den der Junge Onkel Köhler nannte, gut. Der Senior lächelte. Sein Enkel war viel zu altklug für sein Alter, dachte er und bewegte die Dame.

„Bist du sicher, dass du das durchziehen willst, Großvater?“

Erneut war der Senior unsicher, ob sein Enkel den Zug der Dame oder die Aufrechterhaltung des Schwindels mit seinem guten Freund Georg Köhler meinte.

„Sicher.“

„Wie du meinst, Großvater. Schachmatt.“

***

„Du hast mir immer noch nicht erzählt, warum der Kutscher mit Absicht den Pfeiler gerammt haben soll.“

„Du hast mir ja auch nicht verraten, von wem du die trockenen Blumen bekommen hast.“

„Ein Geschenk zum Geburtstag von dem kleinen Willi.“

Mathilde grinste spöttisch. „Du machst dir genauso viele Freunde wie Feinde. Gratulation nachträglich!“

„Was ist nun mit dem Kutscher?“

„Du redest von Hieltje Bakkers Bruder?“

„Keine Ahnung. Sind denn hier alle auf der Insel miteinander verwandt?"

„Die meisten. Was dazu führt", Mathilde wedelte mit der Handfläche vor ihren Augen, „dass die hier allesamt langsam verblöden. Wir sind es, die hier frisches Blut reinbringen."

„Und was hat das jetzt mit dem Kutscher, der Absicht und dem Pfeiler zu tun? Mit dem Rad am Pfahl hängen zu bleiben kann jedem Fuhrmann mal passieren."

„Aber nicht andauernd", sagte Mathilde. „Wenn es auf Borkum zu einem Unfall kommt, ist garantiert der Kerl daran beteiligt."

„Dann sollte er nicht mehr auf dem Kutschbock sitzen."

„Da bin ich deiner Meinung. Doch egal, was passiert, die Bakkers halten ihm die Hände vor den Arsch."

Hermine hasste es, wenn Mathilde sich so derbe ausdrückte. Am liebsten hätte sie gesagt: „So wie bei dir", doch sie ließ es bleiben.

„Und ich sage dir auch, warum das so ist." Mathilde kroch unter ihre Bettdecke und schüttelte sich. „Abends ist es ganz schön frisch. Mann, ich hoffe, dass es bald wärmer wird."

Die Bettdecken waren ein wenig klamm. Sobald draußen die Temperaturen stiegen, sollte sich das legen. Einen Ofen gab es in der Dachkammer nicht. Mathilde beugte sich über ihr Nachtschränkchen, zog die Schublade auf und nahm eine Flasche heraus. „Möchtest du einen Schluck?"

„Was ist das?"

„Das hält dich warm."

Alkohol. Hermine schüttelte den Kopf. Wie Schnaps schmeckte, hatte sie mal bei ihrem Opa probiert und scheußlich gefunden. Was er bewirkte, wusste sie auch. Mathilde nahm einen Schluck, schraubte den Flachmann zu, legte ihn zurück und schloss die Schublade.

„Was ist nun mit dem Kutscher?“ Hermine wollte endlich schlafen. „Nun erzähl schon.“ Sie zog die Bettdecke bis zum Kinn hoch und lauschte der Geschichte, wie der Sohn vom Alten, Dirk, als kleiner Junge auf einer Buhne gestanden hatte, um zu angeln. Plötzlich war er ausgerutscht, hatte sich den Kopf am Holz des Wellenbrechers aufgeschlagen und war ins Wasser gefallen. Der Kutscher Hendrik Teerling hatte es vom Strand aus gesehen. Wie die meisten Insulaner konnte Teerling nicht schwimmen und war niemals tiefer als bis zu den Knien im Meerwasser gewesen. Dennoch war er ins Wasser gerannt, das ihm nach einigen Metern bis an den Hals gereicht hatte, und hatte den ohnmächtigen Jungen an Land gezogen. „Seither ist er bei den Bakkers beschäftigt“, schloss Mathilde.

Hermine fand, dass er es sich verdient hatte, und sagte es auch. Sie schwiegen eine Weile und Hermine glaubte schon, ihre Zimmergenossin sei eingeschlafen.

„Ich kann dir helfen“, sagte Mathilde.

„Wobei?“

„Dass Hieltje und Adeline dich in Ruhe lassen.“

An Mathildes rasante Themenwechsel musste sie sich erst gewöhnen. „Und wie willst du das machen?“

„Das lass mal meine Sorge sein. Aber es kostet dich etwas.“

„Geld habe ich keins. Du weißt, dass ich den Monatslohn an meine Familie schicke. Vater ist krank und …“

„Verschone mich mit deiner Sippschaft. Es muss ja nicht immer Geld sein. Wenn ich dir helfe, dass die Weiber dich in Ruhe lassen, schuldest du mir etwas. Irgendwann kommt die Zeit, da wirst du mir den Gefallen erwidern. Eine Hand wäscht die andere."

Warum habe nur ich so ein ungutes Gefühl dabei, dachte Hermine.

„Was ist nun?" Mathilde setzte sich auf und klopfte ihr Kopfkissen zurecht. „Haben wir eine Abmachung?"

„Ich weiß nicht …"

„Vertrau mir."

Genau das tat Hermine nicht. Sie schwieg.

„Ich kann dir versprechen", sagte Mathilde, „dass Adeline Bakker dir die Stelle eines Zimmermädchens geben wird. Oder willst du die ganze Sommersaison lang immer nur Hilfsarbeiterdienste machen?"

Ein verlockendes Angebot. Doch Hermine witterte Unannehmlichkeiten. Davon hatte sie bereits genug. Mathilde musste etwas über die Bakkers wissen, womit sie sie unter Druck setzte. Da wollte sie auf keinen Fall mit hineingezogen werden.

„Ich weiß nicht …", wiederholte sie.

„Aber ich weiß es. So eine kleine Erpressung …" Mathilde schlug sich eine Hand vor den Mund. Doch Hermine wusste, dass der Versprecher Absicht war. „Jetzt ist es heraus. Die Bakkers werden tun, was ich will, glaube mir. Was denn? Schau nicht so ungläubig. Die feinen Herrschaften sind auch nicht besser als ich. Deren Vermögen ist auf Lug und Betrug, Schmuggel und Piraterie begründet. Was ist da schon eine winzig kleine Erpressung?"

„Unter Napoleon waren viele ehrbare Bürger Schmuggler. Das ist etwas anderes als eine Seeräuberei."

„Steuern haben sie allemal hinterzogen."

„Da war Krieg, das ist doch was ganz anderes."

„Ach ja? Durch den Schwarzhandel ist Bakkers Stiefvater ein reicher Knilch geworden."

„Mein Opa kann Tausende solcher Geschichten erzählen."

„Mag sein. Aber wurden die auch alle Millionäre?"

„Nein."

„Und wenn ich bedenke", Mathilde klang verächtlich, „dass der Kerl sogar vom König von Hannover für seine Schmuggelei eine Verdienstmedaille bekommen hat, dann wird mir schlecht."

Wegen passiven Widerstands – so hatte es Willem Dirks Bakker allen beim Ausflug erzählt. Ebenso, dass van Dyk, so hatte Bakkers Stiefvater geheißen, ein schlauer Kerl gewesen sein musste. Er hatte nicht nur Waren unter den Nasen von Napoleons Soldaten vorbeigeschmuggelt, sondern hatte sie auch gleich in eigenen Läden verkauft und den Schnaps und den Wein in seiner Schankwirtschaft. Sogar der Transport zu Wasser und an Land war in seiner Hand gelegen. Schiffe, Pferde und Wagen waren sein Eigentum gewesen und hatten sich stetig vermehrt. Doch so einfach, wie Mathilde glaubte, konnte es für Klaas van Dyk nicht gewesen sein. Mit dem Schmuggeln hatte er tagtäglich sein Leben riskiert.

„Muss ein toller Mann gewesen sein, dieser van Dyk", flüsterte Hermine.

„Findest du? Dann höre und staune, wie der Kerl sich die beiden Bakker'schen Hotels einverleibt hat. Es ist Jahrzehnte her, da heiratete er die Mutter unseres Seniors. Sie war damals eben erst Witwe geworden."

„Aber das ..."

„... war nett von ihm? Wolltest du das sagen?"

„Ja."

„Sie war zehn Jahre älter als er.“

„Ist das so schlimm? Vielleicht hat er sie geliebt!“

„Pah. Sie hatte drei Kinder.“

Kann dennoch Liebe gewesen sein, dachte Hermine, schwieg jedoch.

„Jedenfalls ist dann unser Senior als kleiner Junge bei ihm an Bord mitgefahren.“

„Er hat ihn seemännisch ausgebildet. Das ist doch gut.“

„Du bist naiv. Eher war unser Senior damals eine kostenlose Arbeitskraft für ihn.“

„Das weißt du doch gar nicht.“

„Willst du jetzt hören, wie es damals war, oder nicht?“

„Ich bin ja schon still.“

„Jedenfalls hat die Witwe, also die Mutter unseres Seniors, zwei große Gästepensionen mit in die Ehe gebracht, die dann zu Hotels umgebaut wurden.“ Mathilde machte eine raumgreifende Bewegung. Doch Hermine verstand auch so, dass das *Hotel Bakker Junior* und das *Bakker Senior* damit gemeint waren.

„Und dann kam die Katastrophe. Die Mutter unseres Seniors, ich glaube, sie hieß Geeske, wie die Schwester vom Baas. Sie starb. Und was macht der alte Stiefvater?“ Mathilde schaute Hermine herausfordernd an, als läge die Antwort auf der Hand.

„Er nahm sich eine neue Frau. Seine Haushälterin. Die war ganze siebenundvierzig Jahre jünger als er und hat natürlich sofort ein Kind bekommen. Wie es heißt, sind noch zwei weitere Blagen gefolgt, und du kannst dir vorstellen, dass die Bakkers da Angst um ihr Erbe hatten. Es ging um das, was ihre Mutter mit in die Ehe gebracht hatte. Natürlich gehörte das jetzt alles dem Stiefvater, Klaas van Dyk. Es heißt, es kam zu Unstimmigkeiten, aber ich kann mir denken, dass die ordentlich gestritten haben. Und wie man sieht, mit Erfolg. Für die Bakkers ist alles gut gelaufen."

„Dann hat unser Senior Halbgeschwister?"

„Ach, Hermine, denk doch mal nach! Wenn van Dyk sein Stiefvater war, können dessen Kinder mit einer fremden Frau nicht mit den Bakkers verwandt sein. So. Nun weißt du, wo der Reichtum herkommt. Ist sicher nicht alles koscher abgelaufen, das garantiere ich dir. Also, was ist jetzt? Die Alte und die Eifersüchtige wollen dich lieber heute als morgen vor die Tür setzen. Haben wir eine Vereinbarung?"

„Ich überlege es mir." Hermine löschte das Talglicht. „Gute Nacht."

***

Die kommenden Tage verliefen ereignislos. Hermine wurde dort zur Arbeit eingeteilt, wo eine helfende Hand benötigt wurde. Sie lernte ihre Kollegen näher kennen und freundete sich mit Gertrud an, obwohl die Köchin vom Alter her ihre Mutter hätte sein können. Sie merkte, dass Mathilde sich einiges an Unverschämtheiten herausnehmen durfte, mit denen andere Kollegen nicht durchgekommen wären. Gertrud verriet ihr, dass sie vermutete, es gäbe irgendein Geheimnis, das Mathilde von den Bakkers wusste. Doch um was es ging, wusste sie nicht.

Jetzt saß Hermine in ihrer Dachkammer. Sie hatte ihrer Mutter versprochen, regelmäßig Briefe zu schicken. In der Nachttischschublade lag griffbereit das Briefpapier. Heftiges Möwengeschrei ließ sie ihr Vorhaben auf später verschieben. Durch das Fenster hörte sie, wie die Vögel sich zankten. Die Ratten der Lüfte stritten um eine Beute. Hermine war neugierig genug, um sich zu fragen, was es war.

Abermals schob sie den Stuhl unter das Dachfenster und stieg hinauf. Sie öffnete die Luke, konnte die Vögel aber nirgends entdecken. In nördlicher Richtung sah sie den neuen Leuchtturm. Gertrud hatte beim Geschirrabräumen wiederholt, was der Senior erzählt hatte. Der Turm sei vor einigen Jahren innerhalb von neun Monaten errichtet worden. „Unglaublich!", hatte sie geschimpft. „Mein Mann und ich bauen unser Häuschen ein wenig um. Die Maurer sind schon seit Monaten dabei und haben nicht einmal die erste Etage des Anbaus fertiggestellt."

Hermine fragte sich, ob die Geschichte vom schnellen Turmbau in den Bereich des Seemannsgarns gehörte.

Richtung Norden, gleich hinter dem rundgemauerten Leuchtturm, sah sie das Meer. Ein Segelboot fuhr vorbei. Sicherlich eines der Ausflugsboote, von denen Mathilde beim Frühstück gesprochen hatte. Sie boten Ausflüge zu den Seehundsbänken an oder fuhren für einen Tag zur Nachbarinsel Juist.

Hermine schaute in die andere Richtung. Im Osten standen einige Häuser mit kleinen Gärten, überwiegend Gemüseanbauflächen. Einige hatten Bohnenstangen in den Grund gesetzt. Vermutlich krochen die zarten Pflanzen bereits aus dem Boden und begannen am Stock emporzuwachsen. Hinter den Gemüsegärten erhoben sich graue, braune und grüne Dünen. Nach Süden hin blickte sie am alten viereckigen Leuchtturm vorbei. Ganz im Hintergrund war das Land zu erkennen. Die niederländische Küste lag der Insel näher als die deutsche. Ihr Blick ging nach Westen, über die Dächer der Häuser hinweg bis zu zwei kleinen Inseln. Das mussten Rottum und Rottumeroog sein. Die Eilande, bis auf Rottum, gehörten ebenfalls zu den Niederlanden und waren unbewohnt. Da sollte angeblich ein einzelner Mann leben, der über die Insel wachte.

Hermine hörte, wie jemand in die Hände klatschte. Gleich darauf kamen aus dem Hotelhof drei Möwen geflogen. Sie zeterten und schrien, als wollten sie sich über die Störung beschweren. Jemand hatte vergessen, den Deckel aufzulegen, und die Vögel hatten sicherlich die Mülltonne geplündert. Hermine stieg vom Stuhl, nahm das Schreibzeug aus der Schublade, setzte sich an den winzigen Tisch und schrieb den Brief.

Borkum, 05. Mai 1888

Lieber Vater, liebe Mutter!

Borkum ist sehr schön. Es gefällt mir gut. Ich habe eine Kammer unter dem Dach, die ich mit einer Kollegin teile. Wenn ich aus dem Fenster schaue, kann ich das Meer sehen. Heute kommen die ersten Sommergäste, dann geht die Arbeit richtig los. Das Wetter ist schön und die Kollegen sind nett.

Ich umarme Euch.

Eure Hermine

Sie hätte noch so viel mehr schreiben können, davon, dass sie nicht wie geplant in *Köhlers Dorfhotel* untergekommen war, dass sie ein eigenes Bett hatte und sich Freunde, aber schon genauso viele Feinde geschaffen hatte und vor allem, dass Bertha verschwunden war. In den vergangenen Tagen hatte sie jede Gelegenheit genutzt, um sich nach ihrer Cousine zu erkundigen. Doch niemand wusste, wo sie abgeblieben war. Mit schlechtem Gewissen, so viel den Eltern zu verschweigen, steckte sie den

Brief in ein Kuvert. Sie fügte den Wochenlohn hinzu und fragte sich mit Unbehagen, ob die Post auch sicher ankommen würde. Ehe sie den Umschlag verschloss, nahm sie die Hälfte des Geldes wieder heraus. Sie wusste nicht, was die Briefmarken kosteten. Und sie wollte sich am Strand mitten unter den Touristen etwas gönnen. Sich in den freien Stunden zwischen den Urlaubern so zu fühlen, als sei sie selbst in den Ferien. Sich ein Eis schmecken lassen, eine Tasse Kaffee oder einfach nur eine Limonade zusammen mit den neuen Kolleginnen genießen. Ihr schlechtes Gewissen, weil sie kein Geld sendete, hielt nur einen Moment an. Es war ihres, und dass Vater nur noch halbe Tage arbeiten konnte, war nicht ihre Schuld. Den kommenden Wochenlohn würde sie schicken. Versprochen.

Die Poststation lag nur wenige Schritte entfernt, wie alles hier auf der Insel schnell zu erreichen war. Im Erdgeschoss von *Köhlers Dorfhotel* war die Post untergebracht. Als sie aus dem Postkontor wieder herauskam, sah sie ein Zimmermädchen in den Köhler'schen Hoteluniformfarben auf dem Bürgersteig stehen. Die Gelegenheit, um nach Cousine Bertha zu fragen. „Tut mir leid", sagte die junge Frau. „Ich bin erst vor einer Woche angekommen. Ich kenne keine Bertha und habe nie etwas von ihr gehört."

Dennoch machte sie Hermine Mut. „Komm doch in *Köhlers Giftbude.* Heute Abend treffen sich dort alle Köhler'schen Borkum-Mädchen. Vielleicht weiß eine von ihnen, was aus deiner Cousine geworden ist."

Kapitel 3

Geeske Willems Bakker, einzige Tochter von Willem Dirks Bakker, sah missvergnügt an sich herab. „Was um alles in der Welt soll das sein?"

„Ein blaues Kleid."

„Das sehe ich selber. Gibt es in diesem Laden nichts, was der neuesten Mode entspricht?" Geeskes Augen funkelten böse. „Überall nur Bauerntrampel!", fügte sie hinzu, als wäre sie wie ihre Schwägerin Hieltje jemals selbst in der großen weiten Welt gewesen.

Die Ladeninhaberin und ihre Angestellte tauschten einen spitzbübischen Blick. Geeske bemerkte ihn nicht.

„Erika, bring der Frau Bakker den Hut."

„Jawohl, Frau Karsten."

Ehrfürchtig, als trage sie eine Königskrone auf einem roten Samtkissen, ging Erika gemessenen Schrittes mit dem Hut in den Händen auf Geeske zu. Der Hut war in dem gleichen Blau wie das Kleid, das Geeske anprobiert hatte und ihrer für unwürdig hielt.

„Das Neueste aus Berlin", verkündete Frau Karsten.

„Dieses alberne Ding? Muss die Feder so lang sein?"

„Das ist der allerletzte Schrei auf dem Kurfürstendamm, Frau Bakker." Ohne zu fragen, setzte sie Geeske den Hut auf den Kopf. „Erika, bring die Federboa!“, befahl Frau Karsten. Das Mädchen stob davon, um kurz darauf mit dem Gewünschten zurückzukehren.

„Die ist grün!“, protestierte Geeske, ließ aber zu, dass Frau Karsten sie ihr um die Schultern legte und zurechtzupfte.

„Das gleiche Grün finden Sie an der Spitze der Hutfeder wieder“, bemerkte Frau Karsten. „Wie gesagt: Es ist der allerneueste Schrei. Ich beziehe sie von einer der Topschneidereien aus Berlin.“

Geeske streckte den Rücken und drehte sich mehrmals vor dem Spiegel hin und her. Sie hob die Hände und schob den Hut ein wenig schräger.

„Die passenden Schuhe dazu haben wir auch. – Erika!“

Schon stand Erika mit hochhackigen Lederpumps in der Hand hinter ihnen. Frau Karsten fasste Geeske leicht am Arm, als müsse sie die Kundin zu dem Stuhl geleiten, auf dem sie zur Anprobe der Pumps Platz nehmen sollte. Als sei sie Wilhelmina von Oranien-Nassau, die blutjunge Königin aus den Niederlanden, setzte Geeske sich und hob den rechten Fuß. Flink kniete Erika sich nieder und tauschte den flachen Schuh gegen den hochhackigen aus. Das Gleiche tat sie mit dem linken. Ein wenig wie der Storch im Salat stakte Geeske auf den hohen Absätzen zum Spiegel. Drehte sich mehrmals und hob den Kleidersaum an, um die Schuhe genauer zu betrachten. Sie nickte. „Ich nehme das Kleid“, meinte sie gnädig und verschwand in der Umkleidekabine.

Frau Karsten und Erika tauschten einen zufriedenen Blick. Sie nickten sich zu. *Geht doch!*

„Hilft mir mal jemand?“, kam es anklagend aus der Kabine.

„Das Inseläffchen sputet sich“, flüsterte Erika ihrer Chefin zu.

Geeskes Ehemann Wilhelm Lüpkes Bakker blickte finster, als er seine Frau nach Hause kommen sah. Sie war einkaufen gewesen und hatte sicherlich wieder einmal ein kleines Vermögen ausgegeben. Nicht, dass sie Einkaufstaschen mit sich führte. Er erkannte es daran, dass der Page ihres Bruders ihr schwer beladen folgte. Wilhelm Lüpkes Bakker seufzte. Sie gab mehr Geld aus, als seine Apotheke abwarf. Doch hatte er es aufgegeben, sie darauf aufmerksam zu machen. Sie würde ihm nur wieder vorhalten, er sei geizig oder müsse eben mehr verdienen. Und überhaupt könne er sich glücklich schätzen, dass er erstens eine eigene Pharmazie von ihrem Vater bekommen habe und zweitens sie als Ehefrau.

Wilhelm Lüpkes Bakker trug fast den gleichen Namen wie sein Schwiegervater. Jedoch waren er und die Bakker-Familie seiner Frau nicht miteinander verwandt. In ganz Ostfriesland war der Nachname keine Seltenheit. Wilhelm kam aus Klein-Midlum. Vogelfluglinie keine siebzig Kilometer entfernt. Doch mit dem Meerwasser dazwischen konnte die Reise dorthin schon mal einen ganzen Tag dauern.

Als er das erste Mal Borkum besucht hatte, um auszukundschaften, ob sich eine Apotheke auf der Insel lohnen würde, war er Geeske begegnet. Sie hatten gemeinsam über die Ähnlichkeit der Namen gelacht und es hatte nicht lange gedauert, bis Wilhelm sich in sie verliebt hatte. Glücklicherweise hatte das auf Gegenseitigkeit beruht, sodass sie sich schnell verlobt und geheiratet hatten. Das war jetzt sechs Jahre her. Wilhelm bereute keinen einzigen Tag. Auch wenn Geeske sein sauer verdientes Geld mit vollen Händen ausgab.

Sobald sie eine weitere Apotheke bauen könnten, hätte er es geschafft. Finanziell gesehen. Und wenn sein Instinkt ihn wie damals nicht trog, würde das zweite Standbein goldrichtig sein. Die Küstenbadeorte, allen voran die Inseln, waren im Aufbruch. Allein was in den letzten Jahren auf Borkum gebaut worden war, versprach eine glorreiche Zukunft. Medizinische und technische Drogen, Pillen, Zäpfchen, Verbandstoffe, Toilettenseifen und Sonnenbrandcreme brauchten die Menschen immer und Urlauber machten da keine Ausnahme. Er würde sein Sortiment an Fruchtsäften, diätischen Nährstoffen und Mineralwässern erweitern. Und dem Pyrola-Parfüm mehr Raum geben. Davon konnte er gar nicht so viel heranschaffen, wie die Gäste verlangten.

„Hallo, Schatz!", begrüßte er Geeske, die wie eine Königin zur Tür seiner Apotheke hereingerauscht kam.

„Moin, mein Lieber!" Sie umrundete den Apothekentresen und eilte in die hinteren Räume. Dicht gefolgt vom Pagen seines Schwagers.

Das erneute Klingeln der Glöckchen über der Apothekentür hinderte ihn an einem Kommentar zu Geeskes Neuerwerb. Vermutlich war seine Frau aus diesem Grund hierhergekommen, anstatt die Einkäufe nach Hause zu bringen.

„Guten Tag, Frau Teerling", grüßte er seine Kundin. „Womit kann ich dienen?"

Frau Teerling, Ehefrau von Hendrik Teerling, dem Kutscher und Schwager seiner Ehefrau, war eine Stammkundin. Im Gegensatz zu Hendrik, für den sie oft Franzbranntwein zur Kühlung blauer Flecken, Salbe für Schürfwunden und gelegentlich Bandagen und Gips für Knochenbrüche besorgte, war sie kerngesund. Dennoch kam sie wenigstens einmal die Woche und hegte und pflegte ihr eingebildetes Zipperlein. Sie war gerne krank. In Absprache mit den beiden Inseldoktoren Schmidt und Kock, die es abwechselnd übernahmen, Hendriks Brüche fachmännisch einzugipsen, war sie die Hauptabnehmerin seiner selbstgedrehten Pillen, die zu hundert Prozent aus Traubenzucker bestanden.

„Die rosa Tabletten von neulich …"

„… helfen besser als die gelben?", unterbrach er sie.

„So ist es, mein lieber Herr Bakker. Da frage ich mich, weswegen sie mir erst jetzt verschrieben wurden."

Bakker murmelte etwas von Labor, Entwicklung und neuesten medizinischen Erkenntnissen und bückte sich, um eine silberne Dose aus einer der Schubladen zu nehmen. Mit einer Pinzette zählte er zehn Pillen in eine winzige Papiertüte. Frau Teerling schob ihm das Geld über den Tresen und sagte: „Haben Sie schon gehört?"

„Was denn?"

„Sie sind dabei, die Schienen auf dem Bahnhof zu verlegen. Ein Bahnhof mitten auf der Insel, hat man so was schon gehört? Und warum, frage ich Sie, Herr Bakker. Warum fangen die mit den Arbeiten an, wenn die ersten Gäste anreisen? Kann man so etwas nicht im Winter machen? Und außerdem …"

Bakker verschloss die Ohren vor weiteren bissigen Bemerkungen. An jeder noch so kleinen Erneuerung auf der Insel hatte sie etwas auszusetzen, anstatt sich über den Fortschritt zu freuen. Das traf bei ihr nur in einem einzigen Punkt zu: wenn es neue Mittelchen gab.

Bakker legte den Zeigefinger auf seine Lippen und sie verstummte. Zuerst besagte ihr Blick, seine Geste wäre eine Unverschämtheit, war aber doch neugierig. „Wenn Sie es niemandem verraten, Frau Teerling", flüsterte er, obwohl kein weiterer Kunde in der Apotheke stand, „ich habe da ganz was Neues. Frisch aus Amerika. Diätische Nährstoffe", wisperte er noch ein wenig leiser. Als würde er verbotene Drogen verkaufen wollen, blickte er zum Fenster hinaus, ob nicht jemand sie beobachtete. Er zog eine der vielen Schubladen hinter seinem Rücken auf, entnahm ihr einen Riegel und schob ihn über den Verkaufstresen. „Etwas Feines aus …" Das letzte Wort nuschelte er. „Nur für spezielle Kunden. Hilft gegen fast alles. Ist aber nicht ganz billig."

„Was ist da drin?"

„Neben Nüssen und Honig sehr geheime Zutaten. Die Hersteller verraten es natürlich nicht, sonst könnte es ja jeder nachmachen."

„Ich nehme das Kleid."

Eine Minute später ertönten erneut die Türglöckchen.

„Ich werde Vater bitten, seinem Kutscher das Gehalt zu erhöhen", sagte Geeske.

Das ist einer der Gründe, dachte der Apotheker, *warum ich sie liebe.* Sie küsste ihm die Wange. Ihr Lächeln war spöttisch, gleichzeitig nachsichtig und gedankenvoll.

***

Wegen eines fast umgefahrenen Pfahls und des Radschadens am Kutschwagen Hendrik zu entlassen, kam Klaas Willems Bakker, der für die Fuhrgeschäfte der Familie verantwortlich war, nicht in den Sinn. „Die Dankbarkeit für ein Leben darf man nicht wegen einer leichten Havarie fallen lassen", sagte der Vater stets. Klaas vertrat die gleiche Meinung. Für Hendrik würde es immer ein Auskommen bei den Bakkers geben.

„Hendrik?" Klaas Willems Bakker fand den Kutscher im Stall. Niemand konnte so gut mit Pferden umgehen wie er.

„Hier hinten."

Klaas lehnte sich mit den Armen auf den unteren Teil der Boxentür. Die Stute lag im Stroh, ihr Atem ging heftig und der gewölbte Bauch bewegte sich.

„Das Fohlen kommt bald." Hendrik wedelte mit den Händen, als wolle er Klaas wegscheuchen. Mit der Geburt würde er allein klarkommen, da brauchte er die Hilfe eines Kapitäns, der sich nur widerwillig mit den Fuhrgeschäften seiner Familie beschäftigte, nicht.

„Ich brauche dich am Abend." Klaas wandte sich ab, als sich zwei kleine Hufe unter dem Schweif der Stute zeigten.

„Bis dahin sind wir hier fertig", rief Hendrik ihm hinterher. In der offenen Stalltür musste Klaas erst einmal Luft holen. Geburten waren nichts für einen Seemann. Meterhohe Wellen konnten ihn nicht schrecken, doch wenn er ein wenig Blut sah, wurde Klaas mulmig im Magen.

Zwei zusätzliche Fuhrleute hatten sich krankgemeldet und Klaas benötigte bei der Ankunft des Raddampfers mehrere Kutschwagen. Zwei, um die anreisenden Gäste an Land zu bringen. Und wenigstens drei weitere für die Waren, die sofort zur Kundschaft transportiert werden sollten.

Es wurde langsam Zeit, dass der Hafen und die Gleisstrecke bis in den Ort fertig wurden. Es hieß, sie wären bereits im Ort angelangt. Seit dem Bau des neuen Turmes vor ein paar Jahren gab es die Gleise. Doch es sollte noch dauern, bis sie so weit wären und sie auch für den Transport von Personen verwendet werden konnten und bis eine Bahnstation gebaut werden würde. Jetzt fehlten noch immer die Waggons und einige Bauarbeiten für einen anständigen, fest gepflasterten Bereich für den Einstieg am Hafen und am Bahnhof.

Der Bürgermeister und die Firma Habicht und Goth, denen der Hafen und die Gleisanlagen gehören, hatten versprochen, dass noch in diesem Jahr alles fertiggestellt sein würde. Dann würde das lästige Ausschiffen endlich ein Ende haben. Da konnte seine Schwester noch so herumjammern, dass durch die Gleistrasse die Eislauffläche zerstört würde, er fand die Erneuerung gut.

„Wir sind immer am langen Wasser Schlittschuh gelaufen, soll das jetzt alles wegfallen?" Als ob es nicht genügend andere Flächen gäbe, auf denen man im Winter eislaufen konnte. Doch die waren Madame ja zu weit weg.

Klaas blickte zum Himmel. Die Geschwindigkeit der Wolken verriet ihm, dass die *Augusta* heftig schaukeln würde und sicherlich einige Reisende seekrank sein würden. Vermutlich würde sich dadurch und durch den hohen Wellengang die Ankunftszeit verschieben und ihm bliebe Zeit, andere Männer als Kutscher zu organisieren, bevor er es selbst machen musste. Doch die verspätete Ankunft des Dampfers brachte auch Probleme. Bei Dunkelheit war es schwieriger, Reisende und Waren an Land zu bringen als bei Tageslicht. Die Gäste würden beim Übertritt auf die Kutschen unsicher sein, da sie nur wenig würden sehen können. Im vergangenen Jahr hatte einer der Matrosen eine Dame wie einen Sack Kartoffeln über die Schultern nehmen müssen, da sie sich nicht vom Schiff heruntergetraut hatte und hysterisch geworden war. Wenn möglich, wollte Klaas solche Situationen vermeiden.

Missgelaunt verließ er den Stall und das Gelände. Er nahm sich vor, seinen Vater erneut zu bitten, jemand anderem die Leitung der Fuhrbetriebe zu übertragen. Jakob zum Beispiel. Immer noch von Beruf Sohn, der gelegentlich als Gastwirt in einem der beiden Bierlokale, die Vater nicht aufgeben wollte, aushalf. Hieltje beschwerte sich dauernd, dass ihr Jakob keine führende Aufgabe im Familienbetrieb innehatte. *Keine gute Idee,* dachte Klaas. Dann wäre Jakob der Chef seines Schwippschwagers Hendrik. Die beiden konnten überhaupt nicht miteinander auskommen.

Klaas' Sehnsucht, endlich wieder auf große Fahrt zu gehen, schnürte ihm den Brustkorb zu. Batavia, das Mittelmeer oder einfach nur auf Ostseefahrt nach Danzig schippern. Das war doch etwas anderes, als in den Sommermonaten mit der *Tjalk* regelmäßig Emden, Leer oder Greetsiel zu fahren, um Waren zu transportieren.

Er sollte abhauen, seinen Traum vom Kapitän auf großer Fahrt wieder wahr werden lassen. Erst vor einigen Wochen hatte der Vater in einem Gespräch gemeint: „Ich bin zwar alt, aber lebe nicht hinter dem Mond. Es ist kurzsichtig zu denken, dass nach der Fertigstellung der Gleise weniger Fuhrwerke gebraucht werden. Die Insel wächst. Schau dich um. Überall schießen Hotels, Gasthäuser und Pensionen wie Pilze aus dem Boden. Haben wir heute tausend Einwohner, können es in zehn Jahren schon dreimal so viel sein. Ich mache mir um die Zukunft unserer Kutschen keine Sorgen. Ein stetiger Anstieg von Urlaubern bedeutet mehr Versorgungsmaterial. Die Bahn kann nur vom Hafen in den Ort transportieren. Der Transport auf den Wegen und Straßen wird weiter durch Pferdefuhrwerke erfolgen. Ich glaube, wir werden in Zukunft sogar mehr Kutscher, Pferde und Fahrzeuge brauchen."

Ja, er sollte einfach seinen Seesack packen und verschwinden.

Kapitel 4

Acht Wochen waren seit Hermines Ankunft vergangen und es gab keinen Tag, an dem sie nicht an Bertha dachte. Inzwischen kannte sie alle Mitarbeiter beider *Bakker-Hotels* und einige aus *Köhlers Dorfhotel.* Doch niemand wusste etwas über den Verbleib ihrer Cousine zu berichten. Auch hatte Hermine *Köhlers Giftbude* besucht. Allerdings nur ganz kurz, denn sie hatte kein Geld dabei gehabt. Jedoch hatte das, was sie gesehen hatte, dem Namen der Gaststätte seinen Schrecken genommen. Ein hölzernes Gebäude hoch oben auf einer Düne, in dem Kaffee und Tee ausgeschenkt und Kuchen serviert wurde. Dort verkehrten Urlauber wie Einheimische gleichermaßen und gönnten sich ein paar erholsame Stunden mit Blick auf den weiten Strand und das Meer. Und bei jedem Sonnenuntergang, so hatte man ihr erzählt, waren alle Fensterplätze besetzt. Sie hatte sich vorgenommen, bald wiederzukommen.

„Post für Sie." Mit gerunzelter Stirn überreichte Frau Luise ihr einen Brief. „Die Adresse ist falsch, Fräulein Flessner. Der Umschlag wurde an *Köhlers Dorfhotel* geschickt. Sie können von Glück sagen, dass der Portier dort Sie zu kennen scheint." Frau Luise Menninga klang, als missbillige sie eine Freundschaft zwischen den Angestellten beider Häuser. Die Geschichten über Zwistigkeiten der Hoteliers Bakker und Köhler, die einstmals beste Freunde gewesen waren, hatten Hermine schon am Tag ihrer Anreise erreicht.

„Sehen Sie zu, dass Ihre Post in Zukunft an die richtige Adresse geschickt wird!“

„Sehr wohl, Frau Luise.“ Hermine knickste und streckte die Hand nach dem Brief aus. Mutters Schrift erkannte sie sofort.

Ich muss Mama Berthas Verschwinden beichten, dachte Hermine, steckte den Brief in die Schürzentasche und griff nach dem gefüllten Wäschekorb, um die Weißwäsche auf dem Hof an die Leinen zu hängen. Als sie mit der Arbeit fertig war, setzte sie sich auf die hölzerne Bank am Ende des Grundstücks. Die Sonne schien, es war ein warmer Tag. Die Sitzbank durfte das Personal nutzen, um kurze Pausen einzulegen. Hermine hatte schon manch eine Freistunde hier verbracht. Ein herrlicher Rückzugsort, um in Ruhe ihre Post zu lesen. Sie nahm Mutters Brief aus der Tasche und öffnete ihn.

Am Datum erkannte sie, dass er einige Tage unterwegs gewesen war.

Leer, 25. Juni 1888

Mein liebes Kind!

Wir sind glücklich, daß es Dir gut geht und Dir die Arbeit gefällt. Sag, Minchen, bekommst Du auch genug zu essen? Und denke daran, immer schön fleißig zu sein! Schreib uns, wie Dir die Arbeit als Zimmermädchen gefällt. Sicherlich lernst Du viele interessante Menschen kennen. Wir danken Dir recht herzlich für das Geld. Vater konnte vergangene Woche gar nicht zur Arbeit gehen, aber seit gestern fühlt er sich etwas besser. Leider kann er nur zwei Stunden am Tag ins Kontor. Deinen Geschwistern geht es gut. Dein Bruder will jetzt Kapitän werden. Schauen wir mal. Erst muss er die Schule beenden. Tante Käthe sagt, sie habe lange nichts von Bertha gehört. Rede mit ihr und bitte sie, ihrer Mutter zu schreiben. Vielleicht kannst Du uns ja mitteilen, wie es ihr geht, damit ich Käthe beruhigen kann. Du kennst sie doch. Sie regt sich immer so schnell über alles auf. Denk nur, Hildegard hat in ihrer Mathematikarbeit eine Vier geschrieben. Langsam begreift sie, wie das mit dem Rechnen funktioniert. Leider hast Du Herberts Einschulung verpasst. Er war so stolz auf seine Schultüte und den Tornister, den er von Müllers ältestem Sohn überlassen bekommen hat. Die Müllers lassen herzlich grüßen. Hedwig meint, sie möchte im kommenden Jahr auch als Borkum-Mädchen arbeiten. Aber sie soll erst die Schule beenden. Schreib uns bald, wie Deine Tage aussehen und was Du erlebst. Einen dicken Kuss von uns allen.

In Liebe, Deine Mutter

P.S.: Jetzt haben wir schon den dritten Kaiser in diesem Jahr. Ich weiß nicht, ob ihr es auf der Insel mitbekommen habt. Am 15. Juni starb der zweite Kaiser. Ich überlege, ob es sich lohnt, sich seinen Namen zu merken.

„Er heißt Wilhelm, Mama", sagte Hermine laut. „Genauso wie die meisten hier in meiner Umgebung. Einer von ihnen ist der Inselkaiser. Oder zumindest ein ungekrönter König."

Hermine faltete den Brief zusammen, hob den Kopf und schloss die Augen. Jetzt wusste sie, wie es Vater, den Geschwistern und Nachbarn ging. Mutter schrieb aber kein Wort über sich selbst. Hermine war klar, dass ihre jüngere Schwester Hedwig nun mehr im Haushalt helfen musste als vorher. Sie konnte nur hoffen, dass es Papa gesundheitlich bald besser ging, dann hätte die Familie auch wieder mehr Geld.

Doch wo um alles in der Welt mochte Cousine Bertha stecken? Rina, eines der Köhler'schen Zimmermädchen, hatte behauptet, sie hätte gewechselt und wäre als Norderney-Mädchen in diesem Jahr zur Nachbarinsel gereist. Doch warum teilte Bertha es ihren Eltern nicht mit? Für sie würde es keinen großen Unterschied machen, ob Bertha auf Borkum, Juist oder Norderney arbeitete. Hauptsache, sie hatte eine Beschäftigung und verdiente Geld.

Hermine sollte Rinas Hinweis ihrer Mutter schreiben. Andererseits war da das Gespräch mit Hubert gewesen. Er war Hoteldiener in *Köhlers Dorfhotel*. Er hatte von Bremerhaven, einem Auswandererschiff, streng geheimen Passagen und etwas von einem undurchsichtigen Mann berichtet. Aber Hubert erzählte viel, wenn der Tag lang war. Außerdem hatte er es in *Köhlers Giftbude* gesagt und war angeblich schon stark angetrunken gewesen. Und Wissen aus zweiter oder dritter Hand war immer mit Vorsicht zu genießen.

Sobald sie ihren nächsten Wochenlohn bekäme, würde Hermine der *Giftbude* erneut einen Besuch abstatten. Aber diesmal wollte sie sich einen Platz an einem der Fenster suchen, um bei einem Eis die flanierenden Gäste am Strand zu beobachten. Erst seit Tagen wusste sie, dass die meisten von ihnen gut betucht waren und sogar mit eigenem Kindermädchen anreisten. Es war eine Freude, dachte sie, sich diese Menschen anzuschauen. Sie alle wirkten, als hätten sie keine Sorgen. Der Gedanke brachte sie zurück zu Berthas Verschwinden. In der *Giftbude* würde sie hoffentlich noch mehr Saisonkräfte kennenlernen. Die Logierhäuser, Cafés, Läden und wer weiß was noch beschäftigten genug davon. Irgendjemand musste doch etwas über den Verbleib ihre Cousine wissen.

„Fräulein Flessner?" Willem Dirks Bakker fing sie am Fuß der Hintertreppe ab. Sie hatte den Seniorchef seit Tage nicht gesehen. Es freute sie, dass seine Blässe, die ihn bei ihrer ersten Begegnung auf dem Dampfer kränkelnd hatte aussehen lassen, durch Sonnenbräune ersetzt worden war. Sie war versucht, ihn nach der Gesundheit seiner Frau zu fragen, ließ es jedoch bleiben.

„Schön, dass ich Sie treffe."

Hermine hatte den Eindruck, als habe er sie abgepasst. „Guten Tag, Herr Bakker. Was kann ich für Sie tun?"

„Mein Anliegen ist …", er trat einen Schritt näher an sie heran, „von delikater Art."

Hermine, eben erst fünfzehn Jahre alt geworden, wusste durchaus, was mit *delikat* gemeint war. Sollte sie sich so in dem alten Herrn getäuscht haben?

Bakker griff in seine Westentasche und holte einen Briefumschlag heraus. War er auf Freiersfüßen, jetzt, da seine Ehefrau weit weg war? Und sie sollte den Postillon d'Amour spielen? Sie versuchte, ihre Vermutung mit einem neutralen Gesichtsausdruck zu verschleiern. Es gelang ihr nicht.

Sein Lächeln verriet, dass er ahnte, was sie dachte. „Keine Bange, Fräulein Flessner. Ich verlange nichts Unschickliches. Dennoch möchte ich Sie bitten, Stillschweigen zu bewahren."

Hermine griff nach dem Umschlag, den er ihr hinhielt. Ein flüchtiger Blick auf die Adresse ließ ihr Herz höherschlagen. Nicht unschicklich? Warum schrieb er dann im Geheimen an eine Dame? Gesine Köhler? Da wunderte es sie nicht, dass die beiden Hoteliers keine Freunde mehr waren, wenn …

„Schnell, stecken Sie ihn ein!"

Aus der nahen Hotelküche erklangen Stimmen.

„Unnötig zu erwähnen, dass …"

„Auf mich können Sie sich verlassen", hörte Hermine sich selbst sagen und steckte den Brief in ihre Rocktasche. Sie knickste und wollte zum Haupteingang hinaus, doch da stand Frau Luise mit einem der Hotelgäste. Sie wandte sich um, doch zur Hintertür kam Bakkers Schwiegertochter Adeline herein. Beiden Vorgesetzten mochte sie später nicht erklären müssen, warum sie ohne triftigen Grund jetzt das Haus verließ. Sie eilte die Treppenstufen des Hinterhauses empor. Erst nachdem sie die Tür ihrer Dachkammer hinter sich geschlossen hatte, holte sie den Umschlag heraus. Ein erneuter Blick auf den Empfänger ließ ihr die Röte ins Gesicht schießen. *Gesine Köhler* hatte sie gemeint, vorhin gelesen zu haben, doch dort stand *Georg Köhler*. Laut stieß sie die Luft aus. Einerseits eine Erleichterung, dass sie ihren Chef zu Unrecht der Untreue verdächtigt hatte, andererseits warf der Vorname von Bakkers Erzfeind, wie Mathilde behauptete, neue Überlegungen auf. Was mochte der eine Hotelier dem anderen wohl heimlich mitteilen?

Das geht dich nichts an!, ermahnte sich Hermine. Kurz darauf schlich sie die Treppenstufen hinunter und verließ ungesehen das Hotel. Auf den paar Metern bis zu *Köhlers Dorfhotel* begegnete ihr kein Mensch, den sie kannte. Sie lief über den schmalen Gang zwischen Dorfhotel und dem alten Leuchtturm und klopfte an die Hintertür.

Niemand öffnete, also pochte sie lauter. Hubert, Köhlers Hoteldiener, riss die Tür auf. Sie musste ihn bei irgendetwas gestört haben. Beim Versuch, die Uniformjacke anzuziehen, hatte er sich offenbar in einem Ärmel verheddert. Sein pickliges Gesicht hellte sich auf, als er sie erkannte. „Fräulein Hermine, was treibt Sie in der Mittagsstunde hierher?"

Hermine hatte überlegt, wie sie den Brief heimlich zustellen konnte, ohne dass es irgendjemand mitbekam. Vor dem Hotel auf Georg Köhler zu warten, verwarf sie sofort. Zum einen hatte sie dazu keine Zeit, zum anderen war es zu auffällig. Und was, wenn er überhaupt nicht das Gebäude verließ? Jemanden einweihen? Friederike vielleicht? Auch ein Köhler'sches Zimmermädchen, das sie kennengelernt hatte. Hermine kannte sie erst seit Kurzem und wusste nicht, ob man ihr ein Geheimnis anvertrauen konnte oder ob sie ein Mädchen war, das alles brühwarm weitererzählte. Sich ins Hotel hineinzuschmuggeln, war ebenfalls keine Option, da Hermine den Weg zu Köhlers Privaträumen oder seinem Kontor nicht kannte. Ihre ganze Hoffnung lag auf Hubert, einem jungen Mann, der hoffentlich genauso naiv war, wie er ausschaute.

„Kann ich reinkommen?" Ohne eine Antwort abzuwarten, schob sie sich an ihm vorbei ins Hinterhaus. Endlich hatte er seine Jacke richtig an und knöpfte sie zu. Ehe er fragen konnte, was sie wollte, setzte sie ein verlegenes Lächeln auf. „Es ist ein wenig heikel", begann sie.

„Aha?" Seine Jacke war falsch zugeknöpft. Unten und oben blieb jeweils ein Knopf beziehungsweise ein Loch übrig. Hermine deutete mit einem Nicken darauf.

Hubert bekam rote Wangen und knöpfte alles wieder auf. „Ich kann mich doch auf deine Verschwiegenheit verlassen?", sprach sie ihn einfach mit du an.

Sein Blick verklärte sich, als habe sie ihn bei irgendetwas Verbotenem ertappt. „Können Sie, Fräulein Hermine. Ich schweige wie ein Grab."

„Dann lass mich rein. Ich muss unbedingt mit Friederike sprechen."

Unzufrieden hantierte er an der Knopfleiste. Zwölf silberne Knöpfe, da konnte man schon durcheinanderkommen.

„Komm her, ich helfe dir."

Das schien Hubert noch mehr aus dem Konzept zu bringen, trotzdem ließ er sich von ihr die Jacke zuknöpfen.

„So, jetzt siehst du perfekt aus. Wenn du mir jetzt noch sagst, wo ihre Kammer ist, finde ich es schon allein." Sie zupfte Huberts Jacke nach unten, so wie sie es oft bei ihren jüngeren Brüdern tat, wenn ihre Kleidung unordentlich saß. „Tadellos", versicherte sie ihm.

Doch sein Blick war skeptisch. „Es ist immer das Gleiche", maulte er ungehalten. „Du behauptest, du willst zu Friederike und in Wirklichkeit willst du zu *ihm*. Was hat er nur, dieser eitle Fatzke, dass alle Mädchen ihm nachstellen?"

Von wem, um Himmels willen, sprach er?

„Du brauchst nicht so überrascht zu tun. Von dir hätte ich etwas anderes erwartet! Aber wenn du darauf bestehst …" Hubert deutete mit dem Zeigefinger nach oben. „Ich warne dich. Der feine Herr Hotelier-Sohn ist keinen Deut besser als euer Jakob. Er verdreht vielen Frauen den Kopf, aber heiraten tut er keine."

Hermine hatte gehört, dass es einen Georg Köhler Junior gab, ihn jedoch noch nie gesehen.

Verflixt, dass die Leute in ostfriesischen Familien auch alle gleich hießen! War der geheimnisvolle Brief etwa für den Junior gedacht? Nein, dann würde es draufstehen. Ihr wurde heiß bei dem Gedanken, einen Fehler zu machen, wenn der Umschlag den falschen Köhler erreichte.

„Was ist hier los?“ Eine dunkle Stimme ließ Hermine und Hubert erschrocken herumfahren.

„Ähem“, räusperte Hubert sich verlegen.

„Ab an die Arbeit! Ich kümmere mich um die junge Dame.“

Georg Köhler Senior, sie sah ihn zum ersten Mal seit ihrer Anreise, wartete, bis von Hubert nichts mehr zu sehen war.

„Fräulein Flessner, schön, Sie wiederzusehen. Sie haben eine Nachricht für mich?“ Georg Köhler fuhr sich mit der Hand über die Wange, eine Wolke von Rasierwasser hüllte ihn ein. Sein Gesicht verriet, dass er gerne viel und ungesund aß.

Hermine zog den Brief aus ihrer Rocktasche und überreichte ihn. Ein schneller Knicks und schon wandte sie sich zum Gehen.

„Moment, junge Dame.“

Er hielt ihr seine geschlossene rechte Hand entgegen. Zwei Münzen wechselten den Besitzer. Erneut knickste Hermine und verschwand.

Auf dem Weg zurück betrachtete sie die Münzen und ihr Herz machte einen Sprung. Zwei Fünf-Mark-Münzen. So viel Geld! Köhler hatte sich bestimmt versehen. Für dreiunddreißig Mark konnte man eine Woche im *Hotel Dabelstein* an der Bahnhofsbaustelle logieren. Und zwei Mark kostete ein *table d'Hôte á couvert* hier im *Dorfhotel*, wie ein Schild an der Straße anpries.

Eines bedeuteten die Münzen auf jeden Fall: Sie verpflichteten zu absolutem Stillschweigen.

Am nächsten Morgen erwachte Hermine, weil ein Sonnenstrahl ihre Nase kitzelte. Noch im Halbschlaf merkte sie, dass etwas nicht stimmte. Von Mathildes Seite her kam kein Schnarchen. Sie wandte den Kopf zum Nachbarbett. Es war leer. Wie spät mochte es sein? Hermine befürchtete, verschlafen zu haben. Sie schwang die Beine aus dem Bett und trat an den Waschtisch. Verflixt, Mathilde hatte das Wasser aufgebraucht und vergessen, die Kanne wieder zu füllen! Das Stück Seife in der Porzellanschüssel war feucht. Na, immerhin hatte sie sich gewaschen. Ein Blick auf den Eimer verriet, dass Mathilde das Abwasser heruntergetragen und den geleerten Eimer wieder zurückgebracht hatte. Dann musste es eben ohne Gesichtswäsche gehen. Hermine zog sich schnell an und schaute in den Spiegel, der an der Wand gleich neben der Kammertür hing. Durch die Stockflecke hindurch erkannte sie, wie struppig ihre Haare abstanden. Sie musste sich in der Nacht ordentlich herumgewälzt haben. Kein Wunder. Neben den Sorgen um Bertha und der Neugier, was in dem geheimnisvollen Brief gestanden haben mochte, plagte sie die Not, wo sie die Münzen verstecken sollte. Wenn Mathilde sie entdeckte, würde sie so lange auf sie einreden, bis Hermine ihr das Geheimnis verriet. Zudem war ihrer Zimmerkollegin zuzutrauen, dass sie die Münzen an sich nahm und in *Köhlers Giftbude* oder nachts bei irgendeiner Tanzveranstaltung ausgab.

Hermine bändigte die kleinen widerspenstigen Locken zu einem Haarknoten und kam zu dem Schluss, dass sie mit dem Häubchen eines Zimmermädchens, der passenden Schürze über der hellblauen Bluse und dem gleichfarbigen Rock recht ansprechend aussah. Das Hotel war voll belegt und Sabine, eines der Zimmermädchen, war krank geworden. Deshalb sollte Hermine in den kommenden Tagen bei der Reinigung der Gästezimmer helfen. Bluse und Rock der Bakker'schen Arbeitskleidung passten hervorragend zu ihren fahlblauen Augen. Sie drehte sich vor dem Spiegel. Perfekt! Luise, die Hausdame, achtete mit Argusaugen darauf, dass die Mitarbeiter ordentlich aussahen. „Immer einen guten Eindruck hinterlassen", betonte sie oft, „ist unser Motto. Wir sind das erste Haus am Platz und haben einen Ruf zu verlieren."

Hermine fuhr glättend mit der Hand über die Schürze. Erst vorgestern hatte sie in der Wäschekammer einen ganzen Stapel davon gebügelt und kaum noch zu hoffen gewagt, selbst eine anziehen zu dürfen.

Kurz kam ihr der Verdacht, dass Mathilde ihr den Aufstieg zum Zimmermädchen nicht gönnte und sie deshalb nicht geweckt hatte.

Sie setzte sich auf die Bettkante, um die Schuhe anzuziehen. Sie waren neu, vom Hotel gestellt und drückten ein wenig. „Na dann", murmelte sie. „Auf, auf! Die Arbeit ruft."

Hermine eilte die Hintertreppe hinunter. Noch ehe sie die Hotelküche betreten konnte, um zu sehen, ob Gertrud ein Scheibchen Brot für sie hatte, wurde sie von Luise Menninga aufgehalten. „Ah, Hermine. Schon so früh auf den Beinen?"

„Wie spät ist es denn?"

„Kurz vor sechs."

So früh! Hermine brauchte unbedingt eine Uhr.

„Ist Mathilde auch schon wach?" Eine Antwort schien Frau Luise Menninga nicht zu erwarten. Sie hatte es eilig. „Herr Bakker will Sie sprechen. Er ist in seinem Kontor."

„So früh am Morgen?"

„Er hat gestern Abend bereits nach Ihnen gefragt, aber da schliefen Sie schon." Es klang, als wäre es etwas Anstößiges. Hermines Herz klopfte heftig. Den Brief hatte sie ordnungsgemäß abgeliefert und niemandem etwas gesagt. Hubert war der Einzige, der sie in *Köhlers Dorfhotel* gesehen hatte. Sollte der sich verplappert haben? Oder hatte Adeline Bakker einen Grund gefunden, um Hermine rauszuwerfen? Warum Bakkers Schwiegertochter ihr das Leben schwer machte, konnte Hermine nicht verstehen. *An meinem Fleiß kann es nicht liegen,* dachte sie. *Im Vergleich zu Mathilde bin ich die reinste Arbeitsbiene.* Apropos Mathilde. Wo mochte sie stecken?

Vor Bakkers Bürotür blieb sie stehen. Sich mit beiden Händen über die Haare fahrend und die Schürze zurechtrückend, holte sie einmal tief Luft. Mit pochendem Herzen, den knurrenden Magen ignorierend, klopfte sie zwei Mal an die Tür.

„Herein."

Hermine öffnete die Tür und trat ein. Das Arbeitszimmer war vollgestellt mit Büchern und Aktenordnern. Vor dem linken Fenster stand eine dunkelbraune Kommode mit vielen Schubladen, darauf ein Globus, ein ausziehbares Fernglas und ein Sextant. Die rechte Fensterbank füllten üppige Pflanzen. Hermine war überrascht, Dirk Willems Bakker statt des Seniors zu sehen. Sie trat an den eichenen Schreibtisch und deutete einen Knicks an. „Guten Morgen, Herr Bakker."

„Ah, Fräulein Flessner." Dirk Willems Bakker sah seinem Vater recht ähnlich. Die gleiche lange Nase, nur nicht so schmal. Wie beim Senior bedeckte ein Vollbart Oberlippe und Kinn und reichte bis zum Haaransatz hinauf. Von Mathilde wusste sie, dass er die Leitung des *Hotels Bakker Senior* vor einigen Jahren übertragen bekommen hatte. Warum das *Bakker Junior* von der dortigen Hausdame geleitet wurde, würde Hermine sicherlich noch herausfinden.

„Haben Sie sich ein wenig eingelebt?"

„Ja, Herr Bakker. Es gefällt mir sehr."

„Wenn Sie …“ Seine Hand fuhr durch die Luft, als wolle er eine Fliege verscheuchen. Hermines Herz klopfte wie wild. Seine Ehefrau würde dafür gesorgt haben, dass sie entlassen würde. Was hatte die Frau nur gegen sie? Hermine war sich keiner Schuld bewusst.

„Sie wurden in *Köhlers Dorfhotel* gesehen.“

Hermine nickte. Sie war beim Feind gewesen. Sicherlich würde Adeline Bakker das zum Grund nehmen, um sie loszuwerden. Hermine senkte den Kopf und schwieg.

„Hubert, der Page …“ Das Gespräch schien ihm ebenfalls unangenehm zu sein. „Sein Vater und ich sind zusammen zur Schule gegangen.“

Er schweift ab, dachte Hermine. Beide schwiegen eine Weile. Bakker räusperte sich und strich mehrmals über seinen Bart.

„Sie haben es sicherlich gehört, Fräulein Flessner. Unsere Hotels sind in einen Konkurrenzkampf verwickelt.“

Eher einen Wettstreit. Aus einer alten Freundschaft war eine Feindschaft geworden, so viel hatte Hermine schon mitbekommen. Unter dem Personal schlossen sie bereits Wetten ab, wer dem anderen als Nächstes einen Streich spielte und damit die Nase vorne hat. Niemand wusste den Grund der Fehde und sie schien die Einzige zu sein, die ahnte, dass alles nur vorgetäuscht war. Blieb die Frage – warum?

„Ich weiß, Herr Bakker. Aber ich suche meine Cousine.“

Bakker blickte sie an. Er wirkte, als falle ihm ein Stein vom Herzen.

„Sie heißt Bertha Flessner und ist verschwunden. In den letzten drei Jahre war sie als Borkum-Mädchen in *Köhlers Dorfhotel* tätig. Ich habe den Hoteldiener befragt und auch mit ein paar Zimmermädchen gesprochen.“

„Und da wollten Sie …“ Dirk Bakker war ein Meister der unvollendeten Sätze.

„Niemand weiß, wohin sie gegangen ist. Die Familie und ich, wir machen uns große Sorgen.“ Hermine blickte hinab auf ihre Hände. Sie sprach die Wahrheit. Ein Glück. Wenn sie log, konnte es ihr jeder ansehen.

„Sie sollten Georg Köhler direkt fragen. Vielleicht hat er sie entlassen, oder …“

„Danke, Herr Bakker. Das ist eine gute Idee. Das werde ich tun.“ Erneut knickste sie, und da er keine Anstalten machte, noch etwas zu sagen, verließ sie das Kontor.

Kapitel 5

Die Suche nach Hermines Cousine Bertha blieb weder dem Personal der Häuser Bakker und Köhler noch den Eigentümern der Hotels verborgen. Gerüchte, dass Hermines Cousine in den auslaufenden Sommermonaten des vergangenen Jahres etwas mit Jakob Willems Bakker gehabt haben sollte, hielten sich hartnäckig. Man munkelte, sie sei in Ungnade gefallen, wobei die Erzähler mit der Hand eine wölbende Bewegung vor dem Bauch machten.

Und was tat man gegen üble Gerüchte, die die Familie betrafen? Man musste ihnen etwas entgegensetzen. Am besten ein weiteres Gerücht in Umlauf bringen. Die zweite Klatschgeschichte sollte auf jeden Fall die erste übertreffen. Sie musste schöner, gruseliger oder gemeiner sein als die vorherige. Nicht einfach.

Wenn also die Leute behaupteten, dass Jakob dem Mädchen zu nahe getreten sei, dann würde Adeline Bakker ihrem Schwager beistehen. Sie erzählte einer Nachbarin, dass im Dunkeln Köhlers Sohn und Jakob sich verdammt ähnlich sahen.

Einer Bekannten berichtete sie hinter vorgehaltener Hand, dass unter dem Personal in *Köhlers Dorfhotel* die Geschichte die Runde mache, besagter Georg Junior sei öfter im Dachgeschoss gesehen worden.

„Das ist der Bereich, der den weiblichen Dienstboten vorbehalten ist."

Einer dritten Person erzählte sie, ihre Hausdame habe gesehen, wie der Sohn von Georg Köhler in den Posträumen, die im Erdgeschoss von *Köhlers Dorfhotel* lagen, entdeckt worden sei. Obwohl er dort nichts zu suchen habe. Die Räume seien schließlich vermietet. Angeblich habe man beobachtet, wie er heimlich etwas in den Stapel der ausgehenden Post geschoben hätte. Das wäre zwar nichts Ungewöhnliches, es dürfe ja jeder Briefe oder Postkarten verschicken, aber wenn sie mit einem Herz versehen seien, gäbe es doch Anlass zum Nachdenken.

All die Lügen beflügelten die Fantasie der Leute. Sie bekamen die Möglichkeit, die Informationen miteinander zu verknüpfen und auszuschmücken.

Zum Abschluss flüsterte Adeline einer Bäckereiverkäuferin eine weitere Lüge zu.

Jakob habe in besagter Zeit, als die beiden angeblich ein Verhältnis miteinander gehabt hätten, mit dem Segelboot die sieben Ostfriesischen Inseln abgefahren. Was bekanntlich mehrere Wochen gedauert habe. Es musste also einen anderen Grund für Bertha Flessners Verschwinden geben.

„Ich wusste", murmelte Adeline, „dass das Mädchen Ärger machen würde."

Nun blieb ihr nur noch abzuwarten, ob die Insulaner wie gewünscht das Puzzle zusammensetzten und berauscht von ihrem neuen Wissen es gleich unter die Leute brachten.

Ihr schlechtes Gewissen beruhigte Adeline mit der Kenntnis, dass Georg Köhler Junior seit August vergangenen Jahres auf dem Festland lebte, um in Hamburg in einem noblen Haus das Handwerk eines Hotelkaufmanns zu vertiefen. Zudem beruhigte sie die Tatsache, dass Schwiegerpapa mit seinem besten Freund Köhler Senior gebrochen hatte. Die Last der Beschmutzung engster Freunde berührte sie deshalb nicht.

Es wurde Zeit, dass Schwager Jakob endlich ein treuer Ehemann wurde. Dass er Hieltje geheiratet hatte, war zu ertragen, denn Jakob liebte seine Frau nicht. Doch wenn er andere Frauen begehrte, litt sie wie ihre Schwägerin. Heftige Eifersucht war ein mieses Gefühl, doch sie kannte keinen Weg, wie Jakob zur Treue gezwungen werden konnte.

„Geht es dir gut, meine Liebe?" Dirk Willems Bakker war besorgt.

Gut, dass er nichts von ihrer geheimen Schwärmerei ahnte. Ihn zu heiraten, hatte sie nicht bereut. Auch wenn sie damals nach dem Motto „Wenn ich Jakob nicht bekommen kann, dann wenigstens seinen Bruder" gehandelt hatte. In all den Jahren war die Zuneigung zu Dirk stetig gewachsen, doch das heiße Brennen, das den ganzen Körper in Flammen setzte, spürte sie in seiner Gegenwart nicht.

Ihre Liebe zu Dirk war eben von einer anderen Art.

Sie lächelte ihn an. Seine Fürsorge rührte sie. Ihre Probleme während dieser Schwangerschaft blieben ihm nicht verborgen. Dabei hatte er weiß Gott genügend andere Sorgen. Schwiegerpapas Pläne, den Familienbetrieb zu erweitern, lösten große Befürchtungen bei ihm aus. Der Senior hatte sich, ohne mit seinen Kindern Rücksprache zu halten, um eines der Grundstücke, die die Gemeinde ausschrieb, beworben. Direkt am Hauptbadestrand sollten hochmoderne Hotels mit fließend Wasser, Kanalisation, Elektrizität und Gasanschluss entstehen. Zugegeben, ein guter Gedanke für die Zukunft der Insel. Doch Dirks Meinung nach sollten die Bakker'schen

Familienbetriebe sich da heraushalten. So ein Neubau verschlang ein Vermögen. Wie sollten sie sich einen solch gewaltigen Kredit leisten können, wenn Geeske das Geld mit vollen Händen ausgab? Mehr, als mit der Apotheke zu verdienen war.

„Es geht mir gut." Adeline reckte sich ein wenig und stopfte sich das Sofakissen fester in den Rücken.

„Und dir? Du hast vorhin etwas von Zu-viel-Geld-Ausgeben gemurmelt." Dirk fiel fast vor Schreck die Pfeife aus der Hand. „Habe ich das laut gesagt?"

Adeline nickte. „Manchmal führst du Selbstgespräche."

„Geeske hat wieder …" Den Rest ließ er offen und wandte seine Aufmerksamkeit der Pfeife zu. Sicherlich, um nicht Adelines wütenden Gesichtsausdruck sehen zu müssen. Viele Rechnungen für neue Kleider, Pelze und Schmuck bekamen sie gar nicht zu sehen, denn sie liefen normalerweise über Vaters und später über Eilderts Schreibtisch. Dirk gestattete sich gelegentlich einen Blick in die Bücher des Familienbetriebes, die Eildert führte. Doch Adeline war nicht blind. Die neuen Kleider, der Schmuck und die anderen schönen Dinge waren für jedermann sichtbar.

Sollte der Schwiegervater ein Luxus-Strandhotel bauen, würde die Verschwendungssucht der beiden in der Zukunft zu einem Problem werden.

„Du musst mit deinem Vater reden. Ich verstehe gar nicht, warum der Herr Apotheker nicht selbst für die Ausgaben seiner Frau aufkommt."

„Du weißt, sie ist Vaters Liebling …"

„… und die einzige Tochter. Ich kenne die alte Leier. Wenn alle Frauen aus der Familie wie Geeske das Geld mit vollen

Händen zum Fenster hinauswerfen würden, können wir uns bald einen Platz im Armenhaus suchen."

Adelines Beispiel war schlecht gewählt. Das Armenhaus in der Süderstraße war eine Herzensangelegenheit von Dirks Mutter Harmina. Ohne ihre finanzielle Unterstützung hätte die Gemeinde das Armenhaus schließen müssen. Zumindest wäre es in einem erbärmlichen Zustand und die Bewohner würden in den Wintermonaten vermutlich ohne Feuerholz und Kohle in der Kälte sitzen. Ein Fass ohne Boden, sagte Dirk oft, fand diese Geldausgabe aber sinnvoller als Geeskes neue Kleider.

Adeline musste ihm den Gedanken angesehen haben. „Sollte Mutter noch länger in der Heilanstalt bleiben, werde ich wohl das Armenhaus unterstützen. Was ich gerne tue. Und wenn unser siebtes Kind in Sack und Asche gehen muss ..."

„Übertreibe nicht, mein Lieber."

Es klopfte an der Tür. „Herein", rief Dirk.

Ganz langsam öffnete sich die Wohnzimmertür. Das konnte nur Karl-Gustav sein. Dirk kannte ihn sein Leben lang. Wie alt Karl-Gustav war, wusste vermutlich nur er selbst. Er arbeitete seit Ewigkeiten als Hausmeister für die Familie. Seit er nicht mehr so fit auf den Beinen war, taten alle so, als arbeite er noch genauso fleißig wie früher. Vater hatte ihm angeboten, eine Rente für ihn zu entrichten, doch Karl-Gustav wollte nicht allein zu Hause herumsitzen. Die Arbeit im Hotel, auch wenn es manchmal nur ein Tag in der Woche war, sei sein Leben. Ihn könne man nur mit den Füßen voran hier herausbekommen.

„Es ist wichtig", betonte Karl-Gustav und trat ein. Feierlich, als würde er eine Urkunde überreichen, gab er Dirk eine Mappe. „Mit freundlichen Grüßen Ihres Herrn Vaters."

Bauzeichnungen, erkannte Dirk.

„Aber die habe ich schon gesehen, Karl-Gustav."

„Diese nicht. Es sind die neuesten, was das Projekt Ihres Herrn Vater angeht."

„Danke, Karl-Gustav."

Der alte Herr nickte und an Adeline gewandt: „Ich hoffe, dass es Ihnen gut geht, Frau Bakker."

Adeline lächelte. Karl-Gustav war einer der wenigen Menschen, über die sie noch nie ein übles Wort verloren hatte. „Danke, Karl-Gustav."

Der alte Mann wandte sich zum Gehen. Die Tür fiel nur ganz langsam hinter ihm zu und so konnten sie hören, wie er sagte: „Mir scheint die Notwendigkeit, zwei neue Hotels zu erbauen, ein wenig übertrieben."

Zwei Hotels?

Dirk faltete die Bauzeichnung auseinander. Karl-Gustav hatte recht. Diese Unterlagen waren andere als die, die er bereits gesehen hatte.

Seine Befürchtung wuchs. Bei genauerer Betrachtung erkannte er, dass Lage, Größe und Ausrichtung ebenfalls eine andere waren.

Adeline stand schwerfällig auf, stellte sich hinter ihn, legte die Hände auf seine Schultern und betrachtete den Plan.

„Er will doch nicht etwa …?", fragte Dirk.

„Sieht so aus", antwortete Adeline.

Wie vom Sohn und der Schwiegertochter erkannt worden war, hatte Willem Dirks Bakker zwei Baupläne anfertigen lassen.

Bei der Vielzahl der ausgeschriebenen Grundstücke versprach er sich damit einen größeren Vorteil gegenüber anderen Bewerbern.

Nur die Finanzierung bereitete ihm Sorgen. Auf dem Weg zu seiner Bank gingen ihm die morgendlichen Grußworte an Freunde, Verwandte, Bekannte und Geschäftspartner automatisch über die Lippen. Je nach Zuneigung, Höflichkeit oder Respekt fiel das schlichte Wort „Moin" unterschiedlich aus. „Mohoin!" mit einem „H" dazwischen ausgesprochen und gleichzeitig erhobener Stimme verriet, dass man den Angesprochenen mochte. Ein knappes kraftvoll ausgestoßenes „Moin!" zeigte an, dass man sich nicht gerade sympathisch war, aus Höflichkeit und Respekt dennoch grüßte. Und das langgezogene „Mooooooin!" verriet gegenseitige Freundschaft. Daneben gab es einige Varianten, deren Bedeutung nur die sich grüßenden Personen kannten. An diesem Morgen ging er in Gedanken versunken grußlos seinen Weg, was bei den Borkumern für Irritationen sorgte.

„Geht es ihm nicht gut?", fragten sich gute Bekannte besorgt. „Jetzt ist er arrogant genug geworden, um überhaupt nicht mehr zu grüßen", vermutete ein anderer. Oder: „Sicherlich in Gedanken bei seiner kranken Harmina."

„Moin, Bakker!", sprach ihn Johann Fischer von der Ostfriesischen Sparkasse an. Der Bankdirektor stand in der offenen Tür seines Kreditgeschäftes und paffte eine Zigarre. „Wollen Sie zu mir?"

„Moin, Fischer."

„Sie scheinen mit den Gedanken woanders zu sein."

„Wie kommen Sie darauf?"

„Sie wirken, als wäre Ihnen so eine fette Laus über die Leber gelaufen." Fischer deutete mit den Händen die Größe eines Kätzchens an.

„Eher eine fette Ratte." Bakker schaute sich um, ob niemand in der Nähe stand. „Haben Sie einen Moment Zeit für mich?"

„Für Sie, lieber Herr Bakker, doch immer! Kommen Sie, wir gehen in mein Büro."

„Die neuen Bauzeichnungen sind gestern mit der Post gekommen."

„Lassen Sie mich raten: Der angesetzte Betrag des Bauvorhabens übersteigt Ihr Budget."

„Nein, nein. In dieser Hinsicht bleibt alles unverändert."

„Dann weiß ich nicht, warum Sie so ein besorgtes Gesicht machen."

„Nun, ich muss Ihnen etwas gestehen."

Fischer lachte. „Ich kann mir schon denken, was."

„Ach, ja?"

„Nun, mein lieber Herr Bakker. Wie Sie wissen, bin ich nicht nur Vertreter in der Gemeindeverwaltung, sondern auch in der *Badekommission.* Außerdem pfeifen es die Spatzen von den Dächern. Oder haben Sie geglaubt, es bleibt in der Gemeindeverwaltung unter dem Deckel, dass Sie sich gleich zweimal, allerdings für unterschiedliche Flurstücke, beworben haben?" Rauchkringel stiegen gegen die Zimmerdecke, Fischer blickte ihnen hinterher.

„Löchrige Geheimhaltung im Amt. Wie das Netz eines Krabbenschiebers."

„Was erwarten Sie? Die Leute reden. Das Objekt verändert nicht nur das Leben derjenigen, die dort investieren. Es betrifft ganz Borkum. Wenn alles glattläuft, wird die Insel in fünf Jahren dreimal so viele Gäste beherbergen können wie heute. Und um Sie zu beruhigen, Bakker …" Fischer deutete auf einen der Sessel, die in seinem Büro standen. „Es ist legitim, sich auf mehrere Grundstücke zu bewerben. Sie sind da nicht der Einzige, der auf die Idee gekommen ist."

„Wie stehen meine Chancen? Wie man hört, ist der Ansturm von Kandidaten vom Festland enorm."

„So ist es." Fischer bot seinem Gast eine Zigarre an, doch Bakker lehnte ab. Lieber hätte er die Auskunft bekommen, was Fischer über die anderen Bewerber wusste, doch da konnte er vermutlich lange warten. Fischer war für seine Verschwiegenheit bekannt. Ein Grund, weswegen er hier Kunde war. Nur eines konnte er Fischers Tonfall entnehmen. Dem Banker missfiel die Vergabe an Spekulanten vom Festland ebenso wie ihm. Im Falle einer Grundstücksvergabe an Fremde, also diejenigen, die bislang keinen Wohnsitz auf der Insel hatten, wären weder die Borkumer Sparkasse noch hiesige Firmen involviert. Das Kreditgeschäft würde auf dem Festland gemacht werden und die Fremden brächten eigene Handwerker mit.

„Sie tun gut daran, Bakker, sich auf zwei Plätze zu bewerben." Fischer schloss die Zigarrenkiste und legte sie beiseite. „Aber", er hob mahnend den Zeigefinger, „sollten Sie zwei Zuschläge erhalten, benötigen Sie auch zwei Finanzierungspläne."

Bakker nickte. Kurz kam ihm der Gedanke, auch bei der Volksbank vorzusprechen, doch dafür müsste er nach Emden fahren.

„Deswegen bin ich hier."

„Bringen Sie die neuen Unterlagen vorbei. Bauzeichnungen, Kostenberechnungen des Architekten, Statik und so weiter. Sie kennen das ja." Fischer öffnete beide Hände und lächelte breit.

Es klopfte an der Bürotür. Frau Wybrands, Kassiererin, Sekretärin und Buchhalterin in einem, steckte den Kopf herein.

„Herr Fischer, Ihr Zehn-Uhr-Termin ist da."

Fischer nickte. „In zwei Minuten." Und an Bakker gewandt: „Machen Sie sich keine Sorgen, mein Lieber! Sie sagen mir, was Sie brauchen, alles andere regle ich."

Damit war Bakker entlassen. Auf dem Weg nach draußen traf er Doktor Schmidt. Die Herren tauschten ein freundschaftliches „Moin!", nickten sich zu und grinsten beide wissend.

Es stimmte also, dachte Bakker, der liebe Herr Doktor bewarb sich ebenfalls um einen Baugrund.

***

Das war wieder typisch für Mathilde, dachte Hermine. Sie war auf dem Weg ins Wohnzimmer der Herrschaften. Die empfindliche Kälte von gestern Nacht und der Wind, der durch die Flügelfenster pfiff, machten es in der Wohnstube ungemütlich. Adeline hatte ein Feuer im Kamin entfachen lassen und Mathilde hatte an diesem Morgen den Auftrag bekommen, alles wieder sauber zu machen. Doch das hatte Mathilde nicht getan. Und gleich erwartete Adeline Bakker ihre Freundinnen zu Besuch. Die Chefin sah es gerne, wenn alles picobello sauber war, wie sie sich ausdrückte. Das war vermutlich Italienisch und hieß blitzblank und rein, überlegte Hermine. Wie auch immer, sie konnte jetzt Mathilde hinterherputzen, die sich womöglich irgendwo am Strand zwischen den Urlaubsgästen herumdrückte. Wenn ihre Kollegin so weitermachte, war sie die Arbeit bald los. Wenigstens standen schon zwei Eimer und Lappen bereit. Etwas Gutes hatte es: Hermine betrat zum ersten Mal das Wohnzimmer der Herrschaften – das Allerheiligste, wie die Hausdame, Frau Luise, sich ausdrückte.

Hermine klopfte. Als niemand antwortete, öffnete sie die Wohnzimmertür und trat ein. Vor Überraschung hätte sie fast einen Laut von sich gegeben. Über dem Sofa hing ein Ölgemälde mit herrschaftlich aussehenden Menschen darauf. Die komplette Familie Bakker in Öl gemalt. Im Hintergrund waren Dünen, das Meer und ein wolkenverhangener Himmel zu sehen. Hermine trat etwas näher heran. Bei genauerer Betrachtung fiel ihr die Ähnlichkeit zweier Männer auf. Klaas, der Seemann, und sein Bruder Jann, der Bäckermeister von nebenan, hätten Zwillingsbrüder sein können. Doch soweit sie wusste, lagen fünf Jahre zwischen den beiden Brüdern. Allesamt wirkten die Personen auf dem Ölgemälde, als hätten sie – wie Mathilde sagen würde – einen Stock im Arsch.

„Gefällt es Ihnen?"

Erschrocken wirbelte Hermine herum. Sie hatte Jakob Bakker nicht kommen hören. Was wollte er hier? Seine privaten Räumlichkeiten befanden sich im anderen Hotel. „Nicht wirklich", verriet sie.

„Na, wenigstens sind Sie ehrlich." Jakob lächelte, fasste sie von hinten an den Schultern und schob sie ein wenig nach vorn. „Gehen Sie näher ran!", meinte er und ließ sie wieder los. „Sehen Sie, wie der Maler meine Augen getroffen hat?"

Hermine hatte keine Ahnung, worauf er hinauswollte. Jakobs Augen in Öl starrten sie von der Wand her an, seinen Atem spürte sie im Nacken. Ein unangenehmer Schauder überfiel sie. Am liebsten wäre sie fortgelaufen.

„Und jetzt gehen Sie drei Schritte nach links. Aber immer den Blickkontakt zu den Augen halten!"

Hermine tat wie befohlen. Jakobs Ölpupillen auf dem Bild schienen mitzuwandern.

„Und jetzt sechs Schritte nach rechts!" Auch den Befehl erfüllte Hermine und erneut folgten die gemalten Augen ihrer Bewegung.

„Wie kann das sein?" Hermine fand es gruselig, probierte es aber noch einmal aus. Sie wanderte hin und her, wobei sie diesmal in andere Augen blickte, doch diese blieben bewegungslos.

„Eine ganz besondere Malweise. Das kann nicht jeder Künstler."

Hermine ging noch zweimal hin und her, um zu sehen, was die Augen aller anderen taten. Nichts. „Warum ist das nur bei Ihnen so?", fragte sie und eine Kälte kroch ihr in den Magen.

Er trat ganz dicht von hinten an sie heran. Viel zu nah. Ihr Herz schlug so heftig, als rüttele der Wind mit Stärke neun am Strandhafer. Das Gerede der Kollegen war keine übertriebene Spinnerei. Sie behaupteten, jede, die einen Rock trug und unter dreißig war, solle sich in Sicherheit bringen, wenn Jakob in die Nähe kam. Erneut legte er seine Hände auf ihre Schultern. Wenn er sie herumdrehte, würden sie Nase an Nase beisammenstehen. Hermine erstarrte bei dem Gedanken. Sie mochte Jakob Willem Bakker nicht. Auch wenn er das Leben leicht zu nehmen schien, meistens lächelte, jeden vom Küchenmädchen bis zum Bürgermeister grüßte und gleichermaßen nett und zuvorkommend war. Seine Nähe war ihr unangenehm, machte ihr Angst.

„Weil ich etwas ganz Besonderes bin", antwortete er, die Lippen nur wenige Zentimeter von ihrem Ohr entfernt.

Hermine lief erneut ein kalter Schauer den Rücken hinunter.

„Das glaubst nur du", sagte eine Männerstimme von der Tür her. Der Senior.

„Jakob, lass die Finger von dem Mädel!"

„Wie du meinst, Vater."

Schnell machte Hermine sich an die Reinigung des Kamins, froh darüber, nicht mehr mit Jakob allein in dem Zimmer zu sein. Als wolle Willem Dirks Bakker auf sie achtgeben, setzte er sich aufs Sofa, direkt unter das Ölgemälde, entfaltete die Tageszeitung und begann zu lesen. Entweder las er jede einzelne Zeile besonders langsam oder er tat nur so, denn er blätterte nicht ein einziges Mal um. Jakob verschwand, sein Vater blieb. Endlich war Hermine mit der Reinigung des Kamins fertig. Sie nahm den Eimer mit Wasser und den Ascheeimer in beide Hände, die Lappen klemmte sie sich unter die Achsel. Sie deutete einen leichten Knicks vor dem Senior an und sagte: „Danke."

„Gern geschehen. Ach, Fräulein Flessner!"

„Ja, Herr Bakker?"

Seine Finger glitten in die kleine Tasche seiner Weste. Hervor kam ein Blatt Papier, mehrmals zusammengefaltet. „Wenn ich Sie erneut um einen Gefallen bitten dürfte."

„Gerne, Herr Bakker."

„Es muss aber unter uns bleiben."

„Versprochen, Herr Bakker." Hermine stellte ihre Last ab und trat näher. Er überreichte ihr den Zettel und sie steckte ihn sofort in ihre Schürzentasche. Ein schneller Blickkontakt und Hermine wusste, dass Willem Dirks Bakker sich darauf verließ, dass sie keinen Blick auf das gefaltete Blatt werfen würde. Ein stillschweigendes Abkommen, beruhend auf Vertrauen. Sie deutete ein schwaches Nicken an. Der Handel war beschlossen.

„Soll wieder *er* es bekommen?", flüsterte sie.

„Sie sind eine kluge junge Dame", lobte Bakker. Es klang, als wäre er stolz auf sie. „Schaffen Sie es, dass niemand etwas davon mitbekommt?"

„Ich versuche es." Sie knickste erneut, griff nach Eimer und Aschebacke und verließ den Wohnraum. Diesmal nahm sie sich vor, es geschickter anzustellen, wenn sie *Köhlers Dorfhotel* betrat.

„Mein Stiefvater, Klaas Klaassen van Dyk, hat mir einiges beigebracht." Willem Dirks Bakker hielt im Garten des Upholmhofes eine Ansprache. Die Familie feierte die Taufe des dritten Kindes von Eildert Willems Bakker, einem der Söhne des Seniors. Der nutzte die Taufe seines Enkels, um eine Rede zu halten. Normalerweise tat er das nur zu seinem eigenen Geburtstag, wenn er dem Gemeinderat etwas vortrug oder vor mehreren Geschäftsfreunden sprach. Niemals begannen seine Vorträge mit der Namensnennung seines Stiefvaters.

„Ihr wisst", sagte er, „dass mir mein Ziehvater vieles beigebracht hat. Als Knabe und später als junger Mann habe ich ihn sehr verehrt."

Jedes Familienmitglied kannte die Geschichte. Erst mit dem Tod seiner Mutter war ihr familiäres und freundschaftliches Verhältnis zerbrochen. Der Leichnam von Willems Mutter war praktisch eben erst unter der Erde, da hatte van Dyk seine Haushälterin geheiratet, eine siebenundvierzig Jahre jüngere Frau. Van Dyk hätte ihr Großvater sein können.

Es waren lange Jahre des Streites um die Häuser gefolgt, die Willems verstorbene Mutter mit in die Ehe gebracht hatte. Van

Dyk hatte die *Hotels Bakker Senior* und *Junior* nicht herausrücken wollen. Der Machtkampf hatte fast zehn Jahre gedauert.

„In dieser Zeit sind van Dyk und seine junge Ehefrau drei Mal Eltern geworden. Bis der alte Seeräuber den restlichen Teil von Mutters Vermögen endlich herausrückte." Die Immobilien sowie neuntausend Mark in bar hatte van Dyk herausrücken müssen. Vom Gericht hatte Willem beide Hotels und einen großen Teil an Ländereien zugesprochen bekommen.

„In den Jahren, als ich auf das Gerichtsurteil über das mir zustehende Erbe wartete", sagte Bakker, „hatte ich meine Hände nicht untätig im Schoß liegen."

Seine Familie nickte, einige schienen sich zu fragen, warum er gerade heute die alten Kamellen aufwärmte. Sie alle wussten, dass Bakkers Stiefvater durch seinen Unternehmergeist nicht nur Fährschiffe angeschafft hatte, er hatte auch seinen Handel ausgebaut, indem er mehr eigene Läden geschaffen und sich Schankwirtschaften zugelegt hatte, die sein Stiefsohn nach van Dyks Tod vor vier Jahren allesamt übernommen hatte. Bei den meisten Unternehmen war er grundbuchmäßig schon vor van Dyks Tod Miteigentümer gewesen. Den Rest hatten van Dyks junge Ehefrau und die drei Kinder geerbt. Bakker hatte es ihnen zu einem ordentlichen Preis abkaufen können.

„Und nun, meine Lieben, fragt ihr euch sicherlich, warum ich diese alten Geschichten aufwärme. Ganz einfach." Bakker blickte in die Runde auf seine fünf Söhne, seine Tochter und Schwiegerkinder. Er lächelte einige seiner vierzehn Enkelkinder an. Vier seiner Enkelsöhne hießen Willem, wie es die patronymische Namensgebung verlangte. Willem Dirks Bakker,

Willem Jannsen Bakker, Willem Eilderts Bakker, der heute getauft und noch kein Jahr alt war, und Willem Jakobs Bakker. Der liebste war ihm Willem Dirks, genannt Willi, doch das würde er niemals öffentlich zugeben.

Er hatte wohl ein wenig zu lange geschwiegen, denn gleich zwei seiner Kinder nickten ruckartig mit dem Kopf, um anzuzeigen, dass er endlich sagen möge, warum.

„Die Familie Bakker wird immer größer", zögerte er die Antwort hinaus und blickte auf Adeline und Hieltje, die beide guter Hoffnung waren. Adeline schon kugelrund, bei Hieltje konnte man noch nichts sehen. „Und deswegen müssen sich auch unsere Betriebe vergrößern, wenn wir wollen, dass alle auch noch in zwanzig oder dreißig Jahren einen eigenen Betrieb und ein eigenes Einkommen haben sollen."

„Hört, hört!", rief sein einziger Schwiegersohn.

„Wenn alles gut läuft, bauen wir ein neues Hotel."

„Das wissen wir schon, Vater", sagte Jakob.

„Stichwort Strandhotel", rief Geeske und rückte ihren Hut zurecht, der für eine Familienfeier viel zu pompös wirkte.

„Stimmt, ihr Lieben. Neu ist, dass ich beschlossen habe, auf gleich zwei Grundstücke ein Angebot abzugeben. Das erhöht unsere Chancen …"

„Hab ich's gewusst!", sagte Adeline. Ihr Kommentar ging im allgemeinen Stimmengewirr unter. Da keiner an einer eingehenden Erklärung interessiert schien, widmete er sich seinem Kuchen. *Olderwetze Cremeschnitte*, sein Lieblingskuchen. Auf Hochdeutsch – altmodische Creme-Schnitte. Bakker kippte das Stück um fünfundvierzig Grad. Ein Trick, um zu verhindern, dass der feste Blätterteigdeckel die Puddingfüllung herausquetschte, wenn man mit der Gabel hineinstach.

„Was, Großvater …“, fragte Willi, sein Lieblingsenkel, „was machst du denn, wenn beide Bewerbungen angenommen werden?“

***

Die Stube des Hausherrn lag im ersten Stock, am Ende des Flurs. Die Fenster nach Süden und mit Blick in Hof und Garten. Hinterm Haus, an der Grenze zum Nachbargrundstück, hatte der Eigentümer Apfel- und Birnbäume gepflanzt.

Der Mann deutete auf zwei bequem aussehende Sessel. Auf einem winzigen Tischchen zwischen diesen Sesseln standen einige Karaffen mit Spirituosen. „Rum oder Cognac?“

„Cognac.“

Der Mann schenkte ein.

„Hat dich jemand kommen sehen?“

„Nein.“

Der Gastgeber nahm Zunderdose, Stahl und Stein aus einer Schublade. Ebenso kam ein Fässchen mit feinstem Tabak auf den Tisch.

„Seit über sechzig Jahren gibt es Streichhölzer“, sagte Willem Dirks Bakker. Sein Gastgeber lächelte.

„Erinnerst du dich, als dein Stiefvater uns zeigte, wie man damit Feuer macht?“

„Natürlich.“

„Dazu hatte er uns eine Schauergeschichte erzählt, bei der er sich nur retten konnte, weil er wusste, wie man das macht. Seither liebe ich die alte Art, ein Feuerchen zu entfachen.“ Schon bald stiegen die ersten Schwaden blauen Rauchs aus ihren Pfeifen gegen die Zimmerdecke.

„Zum Wohl!“, sagte Willem Dirks Bakker und die großen Schwenker gaben einen tiefen Ton von sich, als sie aneinanderstießen.

„Auf gute Geschäfte!“, meinte der andere. Dabei sah er Bakker verschmitzt lächelnd an. Der trank langsam sein Glas aus und paffte an seiner Pfeife. Es war schön, mit seinem Gegenüber eine Weile zu schweigen, ohne dass es einem von ihnen unangenehm wäre.

„Ich habe deinen Zettel bekommen“, sagte Köhler. „Was gibt es denn Wichtiges?“

Bakker trank den Rest aus seinem Glas, ehe er dem alten Freund verriet, was er sich ausgedacht hatte.

„Sollte sie das jemals herausbekommen, wird sie mir nie verzeihen.“

„Frau Wenke ist nicht nachtragend. Und sie wird mir nur Geheimnisse anvertrauen, wenn sie dir dadurch schaden kann.“

„Hätte niemals gedacht, dass Jakobs Eskapaden einmal zu etwas gut sein würden. Also behalten wir die Finte bei?“

„Besser ist es.“

Kapitel 6

Pfingsten war längst vorbei und Hermines vereinbarte Probezeit somit beendet. Um dieses Ereignis zu feiern, gönnte sie sich ein Eis, das sie auf einer der Bänke, die um den runden Musikpavillon herumstanden, schleckte. Vor drei Tagen hatte sie ihr erstes eigenes Konto bei der Ostfriesischen Sparkasse eröffnet und den letzten Wochenlohn und das fürstliche Trinkgeld eingezahlt. Den größten Teil des Wochenlohnes überwies sie an die Familie. Gestern hatte sie sich drei Mark auszahlen lassen und fühlte sich wunderbar. Ihr erstes Konto. Nicht einmal Mutter hatte eines.

„Ich habe den Verdacht", sagte eine heisere männliche Stimme, „dass Köhler und Bakker nur so tun, als wären sie sich spinnefeind."

„Warum sollten sie das machen?", fragte eine hoch klingende Stimme, die jedoch ganz klar einem Mann gehörte.

„Für stille Absprachen."

„Ich kann Ihnen nicht ganz folgen, Akkermann", meinte die hohe Stimme.

„Nicht so laut!"

„Wieso nicht? Weit und breit ist niemand zu sehen und hören kann uns auch keiner."

Falsch, dachte Hermine. Was der Mann nicht bedachte, war, dass sie am Fuße des runden hölzernen Musikpavillons saßen. Sie konnten sich nicht gegenseitig sehen, aber hören. Ganz leise rückte sie bis ans Ende der Parkbank, um besser lauschen zu können.

„Was ich Ihnen jetzt sage, Wybrands, muss unter uns bleiben."

„Abgemacht. Wenn es um Köhler und Bakker geht, sollten wir anderen zusammenhalten."

„So ist es, mein Freund. Ich habe den Verdacht, dass die zwei stille Absprachen halten."

„Köhler und Bakker? Niemals. Die beiden sind sich spinnefeind."

„Das lassen sie uns glauben. Aber stimmt das wirklich?"

Kurz schwiegen die Männer. „Und was sollen die beiden besprechen, egal, ob jetzt Freund oder Feind?"

„Dinge, die ihnen Vorteile uns gegenüber bringen, mein lieber Wybrands."

„Das können sie als beste Freunde doch viel besser."

„Das ist ja eben der Casus knacksus."

„Der was?"

„Der Trick. Die List, mit der sie alle täuschen."

„Das müssen Sie mir genauer erklären."

„Nun, wir beide, ebenso wie Bakker und Köhler und ein paar andere Insulaner haben sich um die Parzellen beworben."

Es ging um die Grundstücke am Strand, das war Hermine sofort klar. Bei den Arbeitskollegen gab es bald kein anderes Gesprächsthema mehr. Wer einen der Bauplätze ergatterte und ein Hotel darauf baute, war für die Zukunft ein gemachter Mann. Die Nachfrage nach Hotelzimmern stieg stetig, das wusste jeder. Wer jetzt auf der Insel investierte, konnte sich gesundstoßen. Soviel Hermine mitbekommen hatte, vergab die Gemeinde die begehrten Flächen. Jedermann konnte sich bewerben, musste nur ein Angebot abgeben. Was, bitte schön, konnte da abgesprochen werden? Die Antwort erhielt Hermine prompt.

„Wenn jetzt Köhler und Bakker sich mit dem Preis absprechen, kann es sein, dass sie uns überbieten."

„Dann wissen die beiden immer noch nicht, was uns anderen Bewerbern die Grundstücke wert sind. Also, was wir für den Grund bieten."

„Stimmt. Ich habe jedoch von …", Akkermann machte eine Pause, als überlege er, „ist ja egal, von wem, gehört, dass Köhler andere Interessenten gegen Bakker einnimmt. Er sagt: ‚Wir müssen unbedingt verhindern, dass Bakker noch mehr an sich reißt.' Und anschließend fragt er jeden, welche Summe er in seinem Angebot angeben will."

„Dann sind sie blöd, wenn sie es ihm verraten. Ich verstehe immer noch nicht, was er damit erreichen will."

„Angenommen Köhler weiß, was Bewerber A bieten wird. Dem versichert er, dass die Summe reichen wird, um den Zuschlag zu erhalten, weil er gehört hat, dass Bakker nicht mehr als die Summe X anbieten kann."

„Woher weiß Köhler das, wenn sie angeblich Feinde sind?"

„Das ist doch egal. Die Leute werden es ihm glauben, da jeder weiß, dass sie sich eben spinnefeind sind. Jedenfalls führt Köhler das gleiche Gespräch mit Bewerber B und C. Was denn?" Akkermanns Stimme stockte und Hermine befürchtete schon, sie wäre entdeckt worden. „Hat er Sie etwa auch gefragt?"

„Hat er. Und Sie meinen, Bakker macht das Gleiche mit den Bewerbern D, E und F und bis wer weiß wohin?"

„Kann ich mir gut vorstellen. Und da der eine oder andere denkt: ‚Köhler ist ein netter Kerl, dem kann ich es ja verraten, und Bakker möchte ich eins auswischen, der wird es ja nie erfahren', und andersrum. Und so wissen beide, was ihre Konkurrenz auf die Grundstücke bietet."

„Perfide."

Hermine fand das alles unlogisch, konnte sich jedoch vorstellen, dass sowohl Bakker als auch Köhler Feinde beziehungsweise Neider hatten.

„Sie sagen es. Ah, da kommt mein Schwiegersohn. So wie er aussieht, hat er Neuigkeiten. Schauen Sie nicht so, Wybrands. Ich habe Köhler beschatten lassen. Wenn wir Glück haben, sitzen die beiden jetzt zusammen und wir überraschen sie in flagranti."

Hermine hatte genug gehört. Sie sprang auf, umrundete den Pavillon auf der entgegengesetzten Seite, um nicht gesehen zu werden, überquerte die Kaiserstraße und eilte von der Strandstraße kommend hinunter ins Dorf und bog in die Große Straße ein. Wenn Willem Dirks Bakker und Georg Köhler sich heimlich trafen, dann sicherlich im *Hotel Bakker Junior*. Da konnte man ungesehen von der Parallelstraße aus über das mit einer schmucken Villa bebaute Grundstück des ältesten Bakker-Sohnes an die Hintertür des Hotels gelangen. Den gleichen Weg schlug Hermine ein. Aus dem Augenwinkel erkannte sie, wie drei Herren, vermutlich Akkermann, Wybrands und dessen Schwiegersohn, den etwas längeren Weg zum Hotelhaupteingang einschlugen. Heftig atmend erreichte Hermine den Hintereingang. Sie stürmte die Treppe in die erste Etage hinauf und öffnete, ohne nachzudenken oder anzuklopfen, die Tür zum Kaminzimmer. Da saßen sie, wie von Akkermann vermutet.

„Fräulein Flessner?“, rief Willem Dirks Bakker erstaunt und wollte sich erheben.

„Keine Zeit für Erklärungen, Herr Bakker. Bleiben Sie sitzen.“ Sie deutete auf den Funkenschutz des Kamins. Der stand in der Ecke des Raumes, da er im Sommer nicht benutzt wurde. „Und Sie, Herr Köhler, schnell, verstecken Sie sich dahinter.“

„Aber …“

„Kein Aber!“, sagte sie barsch. „Ich erkläre es später.“ Sie löste mit einem schnellen Handgriff ihren Haarknoten, ließ sich in den freigewordenen Sessel fallen und griff nach einem der beiden Gläser, die auf dem Tisch standen. Keine Sekunde zu früh, denn in diesem Augenblick wurde erneut die Tür aufgerissen. Herein stürmten die Herren Akkermann und Wybrands.

Hermine, vollkommen aufgelöst durch das schnelle Laufen und mit hochrotem Kopf, stellte das Glas auf den Tisch und band sich mit zittrigen Fingern einen Haarknoten. Dabei schaute sie verschämt zu Boden. Das war knapp gewesen.

„Oh, entschuldigen Sie die Störung, Herr Bakker“, rief Akkermann. „Nichts für ungut“, fügte er mit einem ungläubigen Blick auf Hermine hinzu. „Wir werden schweigen wie ein Grab.“

„Versprochen“, bestätigte Wybrands, der ebenfalls die falschen Schlüsse zog. Und schon stoben die Männer hinaus und schlossen die Tür von außen.

Die drei im Kaminzimmer Zurückgebliebenen verharrten noch einige Sekunden.

„Woher wussten Sie das, Fräulein Flessner?", flüsterte Willem Dirks Bakker während Georg Köhler mit einem breiten Grinsen aus seinem Versteck hervorkam.

„Junges Fräulein", wisperte er, „wir stehen in Ihrer Schuld."

Warum nur hatte sie das getan, fragte sich Hermine. Mit klopfendem Herzen und hochrotem Kopf verließ sie die beiden Herren im Kaminzimmer. Mit ihrer unüberlegten Handlung hatte sie ihren Ruf ruiniert. Und den des alten Bakkers gleich mit. Wie in Trance hatte sie das Hotel verlassen, um ins andere hinüberzugehen. Sie war die Treppen hoch bis unters Dach gestürmt und hatte sich auf ihr Bett geworfen. Die Männer würden das Gesehene herumerzählen. Sie würden behaupten, Hermine habe mit dem Senior ein Verhältnis. In Gedanken hörte sie die Kommentare: „Die ist hinter seinem Vermögen her, jetzt, da seine Ehefrau auf dem Festland in einem Krankenhaus liegt." Oder: „Man kennt das ja. Bakkers Stiefvater hatte auch so eine blutjunge Frau, die seine Enkeltochter hätte sein können."

Was würden ihre Eltern sagen und Bakkers Kinder und Schwiegerkinder? Sicherlich würden die nicht stillhalten. Ihre Anstellung wäre sie bald los. Auch wenn der Senior weiter seine schützende Hand über sie hielte, würde ihre Zukunft im *Hotel Bakker* keine rosige sein. Und dann die Kommentare der Kollegen, allen voran Mathilde! Hermine meinte, Gertruds bedauernden Blick zu sehen. Die Meinung der Köchin über sie war ihr sehr wichtig. Dennoch war ihr klar, dass sie die alten Freunde nicht verraten würde.

Und das alles nur, weil Willem Dirks Bakker sie an ihren Großvater erinnerte? Nein, daran mochte es kaum liegen. Hermine konnte sich ihre spontane Reaktion nicht erklären. Zugegeben, sie mochte den alten Herrn, begeisterte sich für seine Hinterlist, seit er sie vor wenigen Wochen dem angeblichen Kontrahenten Köhler abgeworben hatte.

„Bakker, Sie sehen aus, als hätten Sie wieder jemanden übers Ohr gehauen", meinte sie Köhlers Stimme immer noch im Ohr zu haben. Es hatte so echt geklungen, als Bakker geantwortet hatte: „So ist es, Köhler, so ist es."

Ob sie schon damals gespürt hatte, wie viel Spaß es den alten Herren machte, sich gegenseitig zu ärgern. Alles nur Theater. Und aus welchem Grund? Sie befürchtete, die Herren Akkermann und Wybrands hatten recht. Je länger sie darüber nachdachte, desto besser gefiel ihr der Gedanke.

Die Worte ihres Opas gingen ihr durch den Kopf. *„De beiden bünt sik einag as Schkapelusen"*, hätte er dazu gesagt und herzlich gelacht. Ja, wie zwei Schafsläuse, die sich einig waren, sahen die Herren Köhler und Bakker aus.

„Woher wussten Sie, dass wir hier zusammensitzen?", hatte Willem Dirks Bakker sie gefragt.

„Ich wusste es nicht", hatte sie geantwortet. „Es war mehr eine Ahnung." Dann hatte sie von dem belauschten Gespräch der Herren Akkermann und Wybrands erzählt.

„Sie sind ein schlaues junges Fräulein und werden es weit bringen", hatte Köhler gemeint. „Wenn Sie einmal Hilfe benötigen, lassen Sie es mich wissen."

„Die brauche ich. Ich suche meine Cousine. Bertha Flessner ist ihr Name."

Leider hatte Georg Köhler nur zu berichten gewusst, dass Bertha gekündigt und die Insel verlassen habe. Er versprach, sich zu erkundigen.

Hermines Sorgen häuften sich. Ihr Ruf war ruiniert, Bertha weiterhin verschwunden, ihr Ansehen bei der Chefin und den Kollegen auf null gesunken, wenn sie nicht gar entlassen würde, und noch immer hatte sie Mutter nichts von Berthas Verschwinden geschrieben.

Es konnte kaum schlechter werden.

Doch es wurde schlimmer.

Am nächsten Vormittag stand Köhlers Page mit einer großen Schachtel Pralinen im Hotelflur.

„Für Frau Bakker?", fragte die Hausdame Frau Luise und nahm ihm das Präsent ab.

„Nein. Es ist für Fräulein Flessner."

„Bist du dir sicher, Hubert?"

„So steht es auf der Karte." Um zu beweisen, dass er die Wahrheit sagte, zeigte er ihr die Grußkarte. Unter Hermines Namen stand nur ein Wort: Danke.

Beide tauschten einen vielsagenden Blick, ließen sich aber zu keinem Kommentar hinreißen.

Hubert hatte längst das Hotel verlassen, als Frau Luise Hermine in einem der Gästezimmer in der zweiten Etage fand.

„Auf ein Wort, Fräulein Flessner." Frau Luise winkte sie auf den Flur hinaus und schloss die Zimmertür. „Für Sie ist etwas abgegeben worden." Frau Luises Gesichtsausdruck wirkte bedrückt.

„Was ist es?"

„Etwas, das mir zu den umlaufenden Gerüchten zusätzliches Kopfzerbrechen bereitet. Ich habe es in Ihrer Kammer unter die Bettdecke gelegt." Luise legte eine Hand auf Hermines Oberarm und streichelte sie kurz. „Passen Sie auf sich auf, Kind!"

„Was wollte sie?" Mathilde schüttelte ein Kopfkissen auf, knallte es aufs Bett und verpasste ihm mit der Handkante einen Schlag in der Mitte.

„Ich soll heute Abend in der Küche helfen."

Mathildes Blick war lauernd. „Und um dir das zu sagen, befiehlt sie dich auf den Flur und schließt die Zimmertür?"

Hermine zuckte die Schultern und verbrachte die kommenden Stunden damit, zu grübeln, was unter ihrer Bettdecke so Geheimnisvolles liegen mochte.

Erst nachdem sie mit der Arbeit fertig war und wusste, dass Mathilde das Haus verlassen hatte, sah sie nach.

Pralinen. Was für ein schönes Geschenk! Sie liebte Schokolade. Doch ebenso wie Frau Luise zog sie die gleiche Schlussfolgerung: Diese Schachtel trug dazu bei, ihren Ruf, den sie selbst angeschlagen hatte, noch mehr zu ruinieren. Die drei Männer hatten längst das, was sie meinten gesehen zu haben, herumgetratscht. Da war es wenig hilfreich, jetzt auch noch eine Schachtel Pralinen geschickt zu bekommen. Das musste Herrn Köhler doch klar sein.

Die Zimmertür wurde aufgerissen und schlug gegen die Wand.

„Stimmt es, was die Leute sagen?" Mathilde knallte die Tür wieder zu, nahm ihr die Schachtel aus der Hand und ließ sich damit auf ihr Bett fallen. „Es stimmt also."

Hermine konnte nicht erkennen, ob Mathilde missgestimmt war, weil Hermine angeblich einen alternden Liebhaber hatte oder weil sie nichts davon gewusst hatte.

„Wer ist es?"

„Niemand."

„Aha. Niemand schickt dir Konfekt." Mathilde zerrte die Verpackung auf. „Dann kann ich ja das hier …"

„Gib es mir zurück!“ Hermine riss ihr die Pralinen aus der Hand und stopfte sie unter ihre Bettdecke.

„Schon gut“, maulte Mathilde. „Es heißt, Hubert hat die Schachtel abgegeben. Sie kommt also von Köhler. Hast du was mit dem Alten oder dem Jungen?“

Den Sohn hatte Hermine noch nie gesehen. Wie sie hörte, war er in Hamburg. Und dass Mathilde ihr zutraute, mit dem kleinen knubbligen Mann, der ihr Vater oder sogar ihr Großvater hätte sein können, etwas anzufangen, empörte sie.

„Mit keinem von beiden.“

„Dann hat Johanna recht. Sie arbeitet im Gästehaus Wybrands. Da reden sie nur noch über dich und …“ Mathildes Zeigefinger deutete nach unten.

„Wen?“, fragte Hermine, obwohl sie es wusste.

„Den Senior. Mann, Hermine! Der Alte ist immer noch verheiratet. Auch wenn seine Frau in der Klapsmühle sitzt, ist er noch lange kein Witwer.“

„*Wo* steckt sie?“

Mathildes Blick verriet, dass sie verärgert war. Zornig auf sich selbst. „In der Irrenanstalt. Wenn du das jemandem erzählst“, drohte sie, „dann lernst du mich von meiner schlechten Seite kennen.“

Hermine nickte und zog die Schachtel unter der Bettdecke hervor. Da sie halb aufgerissen war, konnten sie genauso gut etwas naschen. Sie öffnete den Deckel, steckte sich eine der Köstlichkeiten in den Mund und bot ihrer Zimmergenossin ein Teil an. Ihr war bewusst, dass sie das Geheimnis entdeckt hatte, mit dem Mathilde die Familie Bakker erpresste.

„Gehe ich recht in der Annahme“, fragte Mathilde, „dass du mit keinem der alten Säcke ein Verhältnis hast? Hätte ich dir auch nicht zugetraut. Verrätst du mir, warum du dennoch Geschenke bekommst. Nicht? Das habe ich mir gedacht. Aber ich warne dich, Hermine. Ich werde es herausbekommen.“

Die gesamte Wäsche beider Hotels wurde im Hinterhaus des Hauses *Bakker Senior* in der Hotelwaschküche gewaschen. Zu den Bergen von Bettlaken, Handtüchern und Tischwäsche gesellte sich die Leibwäsche der Hausangestellten, von derjenigen der Familie Bakker ganz zu schweigen. Die saubere nasse Wäsche kam anschließend an die Leinen, die über den gesamten Hof gespannt waren. Die Windeln der Kinder flatterten ebenso im Wind wie die Nachthemden der Frauen und die Unterhosen der Männer. Hermine war für die kommenden Tage zur Arbeit in der Waschküche eingeteilt. Eines der Mädchen, die Frau Kolbe zur Hand gingen, war erkrankt. Eben begann Hermine die Herrenhemden in den Zuber zu stopfen. Im letzten Moment konnte sie aus einem der Oberhemden einen Zettel retten, der in der Brusttasche steckte. Ohne weiter einen Gedanken daran zu verlieren, stopfte sie ihn in die Schürzentasche. Erst drei Stunden später, als alle Leinen voll hingen und die Teile im Wind flatterten, erinnerte sie sich daran. Schon als sie ihn entfaltete, überfiel sie ein schlechtes Gewissen. Zu Hause war ihr beigebracht worden, persönliche Dinge anderer zu achten. Sie selbst und jede ihrer Schwestern und jeder ihrer Brüder besaß eine Zigarrenkiste, in der sie Kleinigkeiten sowie kleine Geheimnisse aufbewahrten. Niemandem wäre eingefallen, in die Kiste eines seiner Geschwister zu schauen, und soweit sie sich erinnern konnte, hatte keiner gegen diese Regel verstoßen.

Es geht dich nichts an, was jemand anderes geschrieben hat, dachte sie. Andererseits musste sie wissen, wer von den Männern den Zettel in seinem Hemd vergessen hatte, um ihn zurückgeben zu können. Das ginge nur, wenn sie einen Blick darauf würfe. „Mein Geliebter …", las sie und etwas davon, dass ein Termin verschoben werden muss.

Hätte sie nur auf ihr Gewissen gehört, dachte sie ein paar Sekunden später. Was sollte sie jetzt damit anfangen? Den Zettel beim Eigentümer abgeben? Unmöglich. Dann wüsste er, dass sie Bescheid wüsste. Einfach wegwerfen – vielleicht in der Waschküche hinter einen Zuber fallen lassen? Nein, dann bekäme jemand anderes das Problem aufgehalst, und wenn ihn ein Mensch mit Mathildes Charakter in den Fingern hielte, könnte es für den Eigentümer schlecht ausgehen. Mit dem schlüpfrigen Inhalt des Briefes war der Mann erpressbar.

Hermine könnte den Zettel in Wäschelauge tauchen, alles, was draufstand, unleserlich machen und ihn in die Brusttasche des Hemdes zurückstecken. Diese Lösung erschien ihr die beste. So wurde jedermanns Gesicht gewahrt und nur Hermine, die Zettelschreiberin und *er* würden davon wissen.

Hermine verbrachte zwei unruhige Tage und Nächte in Gedanken an das pikante Zusammentreffen, die Pralinenschachtel und die daraus folgenden Gerüchte. Doch nichts geschah. Einige Kollegen schienen sie komisch anzusehen und das eine oder andere Mal bildete sie sich ein, aus Gesprächen in ihrer Nähe Zweideutiges herauszuhören. Einmal hatte Adeline sie zu sich zitiert, aber nur, damit sie auf die Kinder aufpasste. Die Hochschwangere hatte vermutlich im Augenblick andere Probleme, als sich um unangebrachte Geschenke, die eine ihrer Angestellten erhielt, zu sorgen. Gestern war sie Hieltje im Hotelflur begegnet. Sie kam selten ins *Hotel Bakker Senior*. Auf der Suche nach ihrem Ehemann hatte sie gefragt: „Haben Sie meinen Mann gesehen?" Ihre Stimme hatte neutral geklungen.

„Nein, Frau Bakker", hatte Hermine mit dem Gefühl geantwortet, Frage und Antwort wären vollkommen wertfrei. Vielleicht, so hoffte Hermine, hatte der Beginn der Baumaßnahmen für die neue Schule ihre Geschichte in den Schatten gestellt. Keine zweihundert Schritte von hier, direkt gegenüber dem Dorfhotel, war der Grundstein gelegt worden. Bei dem trockenen Wetter staubten sowohl die Bauarbeiten als auch der rege Materialtransport gewaltig. Da regten der durch die Luft wirbelnde Staub und Sand die Gemüter mehr auf als die schnöden Gerüchte um eine Saisonarbeiterin.

„Ah, Fräulein Flessner." Frau Luise stand plötzlich hinter ihr. „Gut, dass ich Sie treffe. Schnell, gehen Sie und ziehen Sie sich um! Wir haben eine kleine musikalische Veranstaltung und beim Servieren wird Ihre Hilfe benötigt."

Hermine hatte sich bereits abgewandt, um dem Befehl zu folgen, doch Frau Luise hielt sie zurück. „Und wenn Sie so nett wären", eine Hand fasste Hermine am Arm, „und das hier Herrn Jakob Bakker geben würden."

„Der ist nicht im Haus, oder?"

„Natürlich ist er das. Sonst hätte ich Sie hinüber ins *Junior* geschickt." Frau Luise hielt ihr einen Briefumschlag hin. Hermines widerwilligen Gesichtsausdruck deutete die Hausdame falsch. „Er ist nicht von mir, sondern von der Sängerin, die später auftreten wird", fügte Frau Luise schnell hinzu. „Sie ist sehr berühmt und kommt aus Berlin."

„Aber ich soll beim Servieren helfen."

„Dann werden Sie ja Herrn Bakker antreffen." Frau Luises Kopf deutete in Richtung Kaminzimmer. „Nun?" Sie wedelte mit dem Umschlag. „Hierin steht vermutlich die Reihenfolge der Lieder, die sie singen wird."

Widerwillig nahm Hermine den Briefumschlag entgegen. „Ich sollte mich bei der Post bewerben", grummelte sie. Hermine machte sich auf den Weg ins Dachgeschoss. Sie musste sich umziehen.

Keine fünf Minuten später durchquerte Hermine das Hotelrestaurant, um in die Hotelbar zu gelangen. Dahinter lag das Kaminzimmer, das von den rauchenden Gästen gerne genutzt wurde. Dichte Schwaden von Zigarren-, Zigaretten- und Pfeifenrauch verräucherten den Raum. Hier würde sie Jakob am ehesten antreffen.

Wie erwartet saßen Männer in Anzügen an einzelnen Tischen, qualmten Zigarren oder Pfeifen und sprachen mit gedämpften Stimmen miteinander. Einige Damen hatten ihre Hüte nicht abgenommen oder sie auf dem Schoß liegen. Sie nippten am Sekt und blickten gelangweilt. Die Gespräche der Männer wurden lauter.

Zwei Herren sprachen über die Baulokomotive *Melitta*, die den Zug von der hölzernen Anlegestelle durch das Watt zum fast fertiggestellten Bahnhof ziehen sollte. Und sie diskutierten den Vorteil, wenn weitere Gleisanschlüsse das Gaswerk und den Wasserturm erreichten. Letzterer wurde mit der Zeit zu klein und sie sprachen darüber, an welcher Stelle ein geeigneter Punkt wäre, um einen neuen Wasserturm zu bauen. „Auf jeden Fall sollte er auf einer hohen Düne stehen", meinte einer und drückte seine Zigarette im gläsernen Aschenbecher aus. „Wie sonst soll das Wasser in die vierte oder fünfte Etage der zukünftigen Hotels gelangen?"

Die Frauen sprachen über das Parfüm, das der Herr Apotheker aus den in den Dünen wachsenden *Pyrola* selbst herstellte.

Die einen fanden den Duft herrlich und frisch, anderen war er zu blumig. Eine bezweifelte, ob er die Mengen wirklich selbst herstellte oder einen Lieferanten hatte. Doch die Damen, das blieb Hermine nicht verborgen, als sie ihnen die Getränke servierte, schienen auf etwas zu warten.

Es hieß, ein Stehgeiger solle heute Abend sein Können zum Besten geben. Vermutlich neben der Sängerin auch ein berühmter Mann, dessen Vortrag nervöse Erwartung hervorrief. Dann fielen Hermine Frau Luises Worte ein, die etwas von einer Sängerin und der Reihenfolge ihrer Lieder gesagt hatte.

Um keinen weiteren Ärger zu bekommen, sollte sie, dachte Hermine, vor Beginn der Aufführungen den Umschlag abgeben.

Hermine spürte ihn eher, als dass sie ihn sah. Sie konnte an den Reaktionen der Damen erkennen, dass die Person, die erwartet wurde, eingetroffen war. Und dabei handelte es sich nicht um den Stehgeiger oder die Sängerin. Hermine brauchte sich nicht umzudrehen, an der Stimme erkannte sie ihn: Jakob Willems Bakker. Er betrat den Raum wie ein gefeierter Künstler. Hermine hätte es nicht gewundert, wenn er beide Arme in die Höhe gestreckt und sich einmal um sich selbst gedreht hätte und Applaus aufgebraust wäre.

Was in aller Welt veranlasste die Frauen, sich wegen des Mannes zum Affen zu machen? Sie reckten die Hälse, zupften an ihren Frisuren oder wedelten sich heftig mit ihrem Fächer Luft zu. Zugegeben, Jakob Willems Bakker war attraktiv, doch es gab viele, die Hermines Meinung nach besser aussahen. Und dennoch besaß er eine magische Präsenz, die die Herzen der Frauen höherschlagen und die Augen der Herren schmaler werden ließ. Sein Lächeln konnte man allgemein als spitzbübisch bezeichnen. Hermine erschien es eher hinterlistig, doch sie war wohl eine der wenigen weiblichen Menschen, die so dachten.

Jakob Willems Bakker hatte sich in Schale geworfen. Sein schwarzer, seidener Anzug schimmerte im Lampenlicht. Er ging von Tisch zu Tisch, sagte hier „Guten Abend, Frau Kommerzienrat!“ und dort „Küss die Hand, Madame!“. Oder: „Wie geht es Ihrer Tochter? Susanne heißt sie, soweit ich mich erinnern kann. Was, sie ist schon in der Schule? Dabei sehen Sie, gnädige Frau, so aus, als hätten Sie erst letztes Jahr selbst die Schulbank verlassen.“ In diesem Ton ging es weiter mit den Schmeicheleien. Auch den Herren gönnte er honigsüße Worte. „Fabrikant Schuster aus Berlin, wenn ich mich recht erinnere!“ Er schüttelte einem dickbäuchigen Herrn die Hand und zwinkerte seiner spindeldürren Ehefrau zu. „Kochtöpfe und Pfannen, nicht wahr? Wie laufen die Geschäfte?“ Schusters Antwort schien Jakob nicht zu hören, denn er blickte ständig in die Runde, als erwarte er jemanden. Seine Unachtsamkeit schien nur Hermine aufzufallen, die zurückhaltend mit einem Tablet in der Hand gleichsam mit der dunklen Wandverkleidung verschmolz.

„Immer unauffällig unbemerkt im Verborgenen bleiben“, hatte Waldemar in seiner umständlichen Art ihr schon vor Tagen eingeschärft. Servieren hatte Hermine zuerst gar nicht gelegen. Ihre Hände hatten gezittert und sie hatte Angst gehabt, etwas zu verschütten. Doch mittlerweile fand sie Gefallen daran. Während der Arbeit gab es Momente, in denen nichts zu tun war, und sie konnte wunderbar die Menschen beobachten. Dabei hatte sie festgestellt, dass der Gast einen Kellner nur wahrnahm, wenn er benötigt wurde. Und auf ein

Serviermädchen achteten sie noch weniger. Sie blieb praktisch unsichtbar.

Erneut wandelte sich die Atmosphäre im Raum von einer Sekunde zur anderen. Eine junge Frau, das Kleid in einem glitzernden Kastanienbraun, betrat das Kaminzimmer. Den Ausschnitt des Kleides bis zum Hals mit einem Unterblüschen hochgeschlossen. Die vielen Ketten erinnerten Hermine an einen Pfingstochsen. Sie trug ihr Haar kunstvoll hochgesteckt und voller glitzernd goldener Spangen. Wie etwa zehn Minuten zuvor bei Jakobs Erscheinen galt ihr die gleiche ungeteilte Aufmerksamkeit. Diesmal waren es die Männer, denen der Auftritt der Dame besonders gefiel. Doch im Gegensatz zu den eben noch eifersüchtigen Herren merkte man es den Frauen an, dass ihnen die Konkurrenz missfiel.

Ein günstiger Augenblick, um den Brief, den Frau Luise ihr gegeben hatte, noch vor Beginn der musikalischen Unterhaltung der Sängerin an Jakob zu übergeben. Hermine zog ihn aus ihrer Rocktasche und warf einen Blick auf den Umschlag. Die Schrift kam ihr bekannt vor. Dieselbe wie auf dem Zettel, den sie beim Wäschewaschen gefunden, unleserlich gemacht und zurück in die Herrenhemdtasche gesteckt hatte. Das musste sie sein, die Schreiberin. Dass es Jakobs Hemd gewesen war, hatte sie sich denken können, doch dass eine angeblich so berühmte Sängerin sich für ein Abenteuer mit einem verheirateten Mann hergab, war kaum zu glauben.

Hermine würde einen Wochenlohn darauf wetten, dass der Umschlag alles andere als eine Liste der vorzutragenden Lieder enthielt.

Hermine bemerkte aus dem Augenwinkel, dass Waldemar ihr Zeichen gab. Sie löste sich von der Wand, um an die Bar zu gehen. Für die Übergabe des Umschlages war es jetzt zu spät. Genau genommen hatte Hermine überhaupt keine Chance gehabt, den Brief zu übergeben.

„Ich habe schon dreimal mit der Hand gewedelt und gewunken", beschwerte sich Waldemar. „Du wirst nicht fürs Herumstehen und Leute-Anstarren bezahlt."

„Ich starre nicht."

„Nein, natürlich nicht."

„Den sarkastischen Tonfall kannst du dir sparen."

„Pass bloß auf!", warnte Waldemar.

„Nur weil mir einmal ein Glas heruntergefallen ist, heißt das noch lange nicht …"

„Davon rede und spreche ich nicht", unterbrach sie Waldemar. „Mathilde soll es dir sagen."

„Was denn, Waldemar?"

„Es geht und handelt sich um seine Frau." Waldemar nickte zu Jakob hinüber. „Sie hat wohl Unfeines und wenig Schönes über die singende Sängerin gesagt. Und jetzt starrst du …" Weiter kam er nicht.

Jakob klatschte in die Hände, um auf sich aufmerksam zu machen. „Meine Damen und Herren, Ladys and Gentlemen", rief er und deutete quer durch den Raum. Mit schnellen Schritten erreichte er die Dame im kastanienbraunen Kleid, ergriff ihre Hände und hauchte einen Kuss auf ihren rechten Handrücken.

„Frau Kammersängerin Charlotte Sommer aus Berlin gibt sich heute am Klavier die Ehre." Galant führte er sie ans Piano, rückte den Schemel unter ihrem Hintern zurecht und applaudierte, noch ehe sie ihre Finger auf die Tasten gelegt und einen Ton gespielt hatte.

Der Stehgeiger würde wohl nicht kommen, dachte Hermine eine Stunde später. Das Konzert war zu Ende, einige Gäste blieben aber noch. Sie wollte ein Tablett mit leeren Gläsern in die Hotelküche bringen und wählte den längeren Weg durch den Hotelflur, weil hier niemand war und sie ungehindert das zu voll gestellte Tablett zu Dina tragen konnte. Hermine war schon einen Schritt an der offen stehenden Tür zum Frühstücksraum vorbei, als sie ein Frauenlachen hörte. Neugierig blieb sie stehen.

„Ich habe mich bisher nur einmal in meinem Leben verliebt, und das ist lange her."

Hermine erkannte Jakobs Stimme und trat zwei Schritte zurück, um zu erkennen, mit wem er sprach.

„Seither habe ich keine andere Frau mehr angesehen. Doch was ich jetzt fühle …"

Durch den Spalt zwischen Türblatt und Türzarge erkannte Hermine das kastanienbraune, schillernde Kleid der Sängerin und sah, wie er ihre Hand ergriff und dieses Mal einen viel zärtlicheren Kuss darauf hauchte.

„Was ist mit Ihrer Ehefrau?", flüsterte die Sängerin. Der Brief fiel Hermine wieder ein und sie musste über ihren spontanen Gedanken grinsen: Sie sollte ihn jetzt übergeben, doch das wagte sie nicht.

„Sie ist die, von der ich sprach. Doch unsere Liebe ist erkaltet und ich dachte schon, es würde nie wieder eine Frau mein Herz erwärmen können. Doch als ich Sie sah, war es um mich geschehen."

„Mir geht es ebenso, deswegen schrieb ich …"

Ein wachsendes Unbehagen überfiel Hermine. Sie schlich einige Schritte vorwärts und versuchte, Jakobs Worte mit dem

Mann in Einklang zu bringen, den sie seit ein paar Wochen kannte und der den Spitznamen Inselcasanova trug. Jakobs Beschwörungen klangen sogar in ihren Ohren, als spräche er die Wahrheit. Arme Hieltje! Und das jetzt, da die Kollegen behaupteten, sie sei erneut schwanger.

Als Hermine sich weit genug entfernt wähnte, lief sie schneller. Ein paar Gläser klirrten heftig aneinander und schon war sie in der Hotelküche verschwunden.

Den Brief gab sie am nächsten Morgen Frau Luise zurück, mit der Behauptung, es vergessen zu haben. Komischerweise schien die Hausdame deswegen nicht böse zu sein.

„Du solltest auf dich achtgeben!" Mathilde lag auf ihrem Bett, die Hände hinter dem Kopf verschränkt, und schaute zu Hermine hoch, die ein wenig Wasser in die Waschschüssel goss, um ihr Gesicht zu waschen.

„Ist etwas mit dem Kleid?" Hermine versuchte ihre Rückseite im Spiegel zu betrachten, doch der war zu klein, zu fleckig und hing zu hoch, um alles darin erkennen zu können.

„Dein Kleid ist in Ordnung. Dennoch musst du aufpassen, dass sie dich nicht rausschmeißen."

„Was soll ich jetzt wieder angestellt haben?" Vor Schreck hätte sie fast die Kanne mit dem Wasser umgestoßen. „Du bist doch diejenige, die sich Dinge herausnimmt, die andere nicht dürfen." Den Grund dafür kannte Hermine, seit Mathilde sich verplappert hatte, dennoch hatte keine von ihnen seither das Bakker'sche Familiengeheimnis erwähnt.

„Ich kann es mir leisten, du nicht."

„Aber was habe ich jetzt schon wieder getan, dass sie mich entlassen wollen?"

„Du meinst, weil du so ein fleißiges Bienchen bist, kannst du bleiben?“ Mathilde lächelte und es sah nicht so aus, als sei diese Bemerkung bösartig von ihr gemeint. „Es ist Jakobs Ehefrau, die darauf drängt.“

Hermine trocknete Gesicht und Hände, hängte das Handtuch an den Haken und ließ sich schwer auf ihr Bett fallen.

„Mach nicht so große Augen, Minchen! Es ist nur so, dass Hieltje Angst hat, du hättest etwas mit Jakob angefangen.“

Da war sie auf dem falschen Dampfer, dachte Hermine. „Niemals.“

„Du weißt das, ich weiß das und die Köchin, glaube ich, auch. Aber die Gräfin denkt da anders. Vermutlich weil sie sich selbst den Sohn eines Hoteliers geangelt hat, geht sie davon aus, dass andere Frauen das Gleiche planen. Reich einheiraten.“

„Aber Jakob ist doch verheiratet und …“ Fast hätte sie sich verplappert.

„Die Köchin hat recht, du bist ein dummes Schaf! Schon mal das Wort Mätresse gehört?“

„Das ist eine Liebhaberin.“

„Eher eine Bettgenossin.“ Mathilde grinste anzüglich.

„Niemals könnte ich mit Jakob unter einer Decke …“

„Du schauderst ja richtig! Dann wird dich die andere Variante noch mehr gruseln.“

Hermine glaubte, in Mathildes Augen Belustigung zu erkennen.

„Was kann es Gruseligeres geben als den Gedanken, mit … Du weißt schon, was ich meine.“

„Dass Adeline Bakker jetzt fest davon überzeugt ist, du seist nicht hinter ihrem Schwager, sondern hinter dem Schwiegervater her.“

Mathilde wartete einige Sekunden. Als keine Reaktion kam, stand sie auf, setzte sich neben Hermine und legte einen Arm um ihre Schultern.

Hermine hatte Schwierigkeiten, nicht in Tränen auszubrechen. Fürchterlich genug, dass das Gerücht immer noch die Runde machte, und abscheulich, dass man ihr so etwas zutraute. Doch viel schlimmer war, dass sie die Arbeit verlieren würde. Ihre Familie war auf das Geld, das sie verdiente, angewiesen. Wenn man ihr kündigte, würde sie auf der Insel bestimmt keine andere Anstellung finden. Personalmangel hin oder her, bei dem Ruf stellte sie niemand ein.

„Willst du gar nicht wissen, warum Adeline das glaubt?"

Hermine schüttelte den Kopf, doch dann nickte sie.

„Zum einen, weil er dich mitgebracht hat …"

„Mitgebracht? Von woher?"

„Vom Festland."

„Aber wir haben uns auf dem Schiff kennengelernt und …"

„Mir brauchst du das nicht noch mal zu erklären. Ich glaube dir. Aber die Leute erzählen, ihr hättet Händchen gehalten."

„*Was*? Das ist nicht wahr!"

Mathilde ließ ihre Schulter los und stupste ihr freundschaftlich mit dem Ellenbogen gegen die Hüfte. „Und die Geschichte im *Junior*? Wybrands erzählt überall, er habe euch in flagranti erwischt. Ganz zu schweigen von den Pralinen."

„Aber die kamen doch von Georg Köhler."

„Soso." Mathilde setzte sich zurück auf ihr Bett. „Mit dem hast du also auch zu tun. Eines Tages wirst du mir alles verraten. Ich schwöre dir, ich bekomme die Wahrheit heraus. Mach das Licht aus."

Hermine löschte die Lampe.

„Sieh es positiv." Es klang, als wäre Mathilde kurz vorm Einschlafen.

„Was soll an all dem positiv sein?"

„Dass man dich wie eine erwachsene Frau behandelt und nicht mehr als kleines Mädchen wahrnimmt." Ein leises Schnarchen zeigte, dass die Angelegenheit für Mathilde vorerst erledigt war.

***

Ein schlechtes Gewissen gegen ein anderes einzutauschen, hob nicht gerade seine Stimmung. Dennoch war er sicher, das Richtige getan zu haben. Er konnte nicht zulassen, dass seine Schwiegertöchter Fräulein Flessner entließen. Da Hieltje sowieso tat, was Adeline ihr einredete, musste er mit Adeline sprechen. Er hatte sie gewarnt. Wenn sie Fräulein Flessner entlassen sollte, würde er seinem Sohn ihr Geheimnis verraten. Er musste nicht erst erwähnen, um welches es sich handelte, sie ahnte schon seit Jahren, dass er um ihre „Schwärmerei" für den Schwager, wie er sich ausdrückte, Bescheid wusste.

Willem Dirks Bakker versuchte seine Gedanken auf andere, wichtigere Dinge zu lenken. Mit seinem Banker hatte er ein weiteres Mal gesprochen und die Zusage erhalten, dass, sollte der unwahrscheinliche Fall eintreten und Bakker auf seine beiden Bewerbungen zwei Zuschläge bekommen, die Bauten auch zu finanzieren wären.

„Nicht sofort", meinte Johann Fischer, der Sparkassendirektor. „Einer nach dem anderen. Soviel ich weiß, muss mit dem

Bau nicht gleich begonnen werden. Im Zweifelsfall bauen Sie erst das eine Luxushotel, und wenn die Einnahmen fließen, beginnen Sie mit dem nächsten Bau."

Fischer war für seinen Optimismus bekannt, Bakker war da eher Realist. Als erfolgreicher Geschäftsmann wusste er, dass man hier und da nachhelfen musste, wenn man ans Ziel gelangen wollte. Nur deswegen veranstalteten sein Freund Köhler und er das Theater. Um an mehr Informationen heranzukommen.

Wie im Fall der Gemeindeangestellten Frau Wenke. Sie mochte Köhler gut leiden und hasste die Familie Bakker. Wegen eines Zwischenfalls aus der Vergangenheit, den sie Jakob zu verdanken hatten.

Zugegeben, Bakker zweifelte mittlerweile daran, ob das Theater, das Köhler und er den anderen vorspielten, weiterhin einen Wert hatte. Wenigstens machte es den beiden Spaß. Als er Köhler eine Lieferung geräucherter Wurstwaren abspenstig gemacht hatte und sein Küchenpersonal umdisponieren musste … Es war lustig anzusehen gewesen, wie Hubert umständlich die Angebotstafel zum *table d'hôte* abwischen und eine neue Variante aufschreiben musste. Als Gegenzug hatte Köhler ihm eine Lieferung Fassbrause versaut. Seither ging das Gerücht um, in keinem Bakker'schen Ausschank gäbe es mehr dieses wohlschmeckende Getränk. Und dann die Maus, die Gertrud Dirksen in der Küche entdeckt hatte. Köhler war es nicht gewesen. Das Tierchen hatte allein den Weg in die Hotelküche gefunden. Dennoch kam es auf der Liste auf Köhlers Habenseite. Und dass Jakob die Kammersängerin abgeworben hatte, war zum Pluspunkt der Bakker-Betriebe geworden.

Er freute sich schon auf den Anfang des kommenden Monats. Ab dann würde das Post- und Telegrafenamt vom *Dorfhotel* in die Apotheke seines Schwiegersohnes verlegt werden. Nur Georg Köhler, er selbst und natürlich sein Schwiegersohn wussten bisher davon. Alle drei würden behaupten, dass Bakker Köhler die Poststelle abgenommen habe. In Wahrheit brauchte Köhler die Räumlichkeiten in seinem Hotel für andere Zwecke und sein Schwiegersohn versprach sich durch das Postamt einen Anstieg im Verkauf seiner Arzneien. „Zur Post gehen die Leute regelmäßig", sagte der Apotheker, „zu mir nur, wenn es ihnen schlecht geht. Ich hoffe auf einen Verkaufsanstieg bei den Cremes, Duftwässerchen und Tees. Frei nach dem Motto: Wenn ich schon mal hier bin, kann ich gleich etwas für meine Gesundheit tun."

Er lächelte bei der Vorstellung, wie seine und Köhlers Mitarbeiter diesen Coup verbuchen würden. Für beziehungsweise gegen ihren eigenen Betrieb. Ein weiterer Vorteil dieser Täuschung. Beide Hoteliers wussten, dass ihre Angestellten hinter ihnen standen und mitfieberten.

***

Adeline verstand es meisterhaft, allen anderen als ihrem Schwager die Schuld an seinem Verhalten zu geben. Jede hübsche Frau schmiss sich an Jakob heran. Einerseits in der Hoffnung, in eine reiche Familie einzuheiraten, andererseits, weil er ein schmucker Kerl war. Da war Fräulein Flessner keine Ausnahme, nur dass die es bei den älteren Herren versuchte. Wie sonst war die Drohung ihres Schwiegervaters anders zu deuten? Er hatte ihr unmissverständlich klargemacht, dass er erwarte, Adeline solle sie in Ruhe lassen.

„Die Frauen haben heutzutage keinen Anstand mehr“, hätte sie ihm gerne entgegengeschleudert. Flirteten ungeniert und schmissen sich in aller Öffentlichkeit an Hotelbesitzer oder ihre Söhne heran. Ebenfalls lag ihr der Kommentar auf der Zunge, alternde Männer seien blind für solche Sachen, doch das verkniff sie sich. Momentan machte ihr die Kammersängerin aus Berlin mehr Sorgen als die kleine Angestellte.

Innerlich verfluchte sie die Anfälle von Eifersucht. Mit Dirk hatte sie einen guten und treuen Ehemann und jetzt, da sie das siebte Kind von ihm erwartete, wäre es wünschenswert, endlich über die Schwärmerei für Jakob hinweg zu sein. Doch der Geist denkt und das Herz lenkt, wie ein alberner Spruch treffend sagt.

„Wenn du mich fragst …“ Adeline saß auf dem Sofa und ließ die Stricknadeln klappern. Ihre geschickten Finger führten den Faden und reihten Masche für Masche aneinander. Jetzt nur noch abketteln, dann wäre das Teil fürs neue Baby fertig. Seufzend legte sie die Strickarbeit beiseite.

„Alles in Ordnung?“ Dirk blickte von seiner Zeitung auf.

„Nein. Die Geschichte mit der Sängerin hast du gehört?“

„Jakob hat sie Köhler abgeworben. Ein Pluspunkt für uns.“ Dirks Stimme klang müde, so als habe er die Worte aus der Borkumer Zeitung vorgelesen.

„Das auch. Aber er hat was mit ihr.“

Verärgert schlug Dirk die Zeitung zusammen und warf die zerknautschten Blätter auf den Tisch.

„Es wird Zeit“, sagte Adeline, „dass dein Bruder mehr Verantwortung bekommt. Sollte Vater den Zuschlag für eines der Grundstücke erhalten, wäre es sinnvoll, Jakob die Leitung zu übergeben.“

„Was versprichst du dir davon?“

„Dass er seine ganze Energie in die Arbeit steckt und keine Zeit mehr findet, um …“ Sie griff nach dem Strickzeug und wickelte den Faden um den linken Zeigefinger, ehe sie die letzten Maschen strickte.

„Ich denke nicht, dass so eine große Verantwortung ihn von seinem Treiben abhalten würde. Was genau schwebt dir denn vor, meine Liebe?“

„Er soll all das übernehmen, was mit einem Zuschlag auf uns zukommt. Vom Bau des neuen Hotels angefangen, bis später zur Leitung des Hauses.“

„Er wird uns in den Ruin treiben.“

„Jetzt übertreibst du aber. Denk darüber nach. Oder willst du das etwa alles selbst machen?“

„Noch steht es nicht fest, ob wir einen Zuschlag bekommen werden.“

„Nein. Aber ich will vorbereitet sein.“

„Ich denke nicht, dass Jakob dazu in der Lage sein wird.“

„Weil ihr ihm nie etwas anvertraut habt, heißt das nicht, dass er es nicht kann.“

Dirk lachte, doch er klang nicht belustigt. „Hat Hieltje dich dazu überredet?“

„Das brauchte sie nicht, ich mache mir meine eigenen Gedanken, wie du weißt.“

„Und setzt sie durch.“

Lautes Stricknadeln-Geklapper bekam er zur Antwort.

„Du hast recht. Wir beide haben mit diesem Haus und der Familie“, er blickte auf ihren gewölbten Bauch, „genug Arbeit. Aber alles zu seiner Zeit. Noch reden wir über ungelegte Eier.“ Dirk griff nach seiner Pfeife, nahm sie in den Mund und saugte kurz daran, um anschließend den Porzellanpfeifenkopf, der am Ende eines langen Stiels hing, zu betrachten. Ein Geschenk, das sie ihm zu Weihnachten überreicht hatte. Der Porzellankopf trug die Aufschrift: *Zu diesem Feste wünsch' ich heut' alles, was dein Herz erfreut.*

Der Tabak war verbraucht. Adeline beobachtete schweigend, wie ihr Mann die Delfter Porzellandose mit dem hölzernen Deckel öffnete, ihr ein wenig Tabak entnahm und damit die Pfeife stopfte. Sie hasste es, wenn er den Tisch vollkrümelte, sagte jedoch nichts. Dass er so umständlich hantierte, verriet ihr, dass er über den Vorschlag nachdachte. Als er die Dose schloss und ein sanftes Ploppen des Deckels zu hören war, trafen sich ihre Blicke. Adeline verkniff sich ein Lächeln. Dirk hatte ihre Überlegung angenommen.

„Hoffen wir, dass Hieltje die Belastung als Hotelchefin aushält." Damit besiegelte er ihren Vorschlag. „Dann kann sie dicke und hässliche Zimmermädchen einstellen, so viel sie will", murmelte er leise und griff nach der Streichholzschachtel.

Adeline biss den Faden ab, legte das fertige Strickjäckchen auf den Tisch und erhob sich schwerfällig. „Dann will ich mal nach dem Rechten sehen." Dabei strich sie mit beiden Händen über den gewölbten Bauch.

Die Tür war schon längst hinter Adeline ins Schloss gefallen, als Dirk murmelte: „Viel wichtiger scheint mir die Frage, ob wir uns Vaters Visionen leisten können."

Kapitel 7

„Ich spürte, dass ein Unglück vor der Tür steht." Köchin Gertrud, das Küchenmädchen Dina, Mathilde und Hermine arbeiteten in der Hotelküche. Dina wischte mit langen, langsamen Bewegungen die Fettspritzer von den Delfter Fliesen, die an der Wand hinter dem Herd klebten.

Gertrud hatte sich mit ihrer Kochkunst am Mittag selbst übertroffen. Ihre Scholle mit Kartoffelsalat nach Borkumer Art verschlangen die Gäste zur Mittagszeit am *table d'hôte* restlos, sodass nichts mehr für die Mitarbeiter übrig geblieben war. Deshalb mussten für das bevorstehende Abendessen neuer Salat angemacht und zusätzliche Fische eingekauft werden.

Table d'hôte boten die Bakkers im Hotelrestaurant mittags und abends ihren Hausgästen und auch anderen Besuchern der Insel gerne an. Es war für die Küche einfacher zu handhaben und weniger personalintensiv, als nach Speisekarte zu kochen. Beim *table d'hôte* aßen alle Gäste zusammen zur selben Zeit und die gleichen Speisen. Dabei war es üblich, an aneinandergereihten Tischen zu sitzen. Sehr beliebt bei den Gästen. Es kam eine familiäre Stimmung auf, man lernte sich kennen oder traf alte Bekannte aus dem letzten Urlaub wieder.

„So schlimm ist das Unglück nun auch nicht", meinte Dina. „Der Salat hat genügend Zeit, um durchzuziehen, und die Fische kann ich doch holen."

„Wie konnte ich mich nur in der Menge so verschätzen?" Gertrud überhörte Dinas Worte.

Hermine ahnte, dass die Köchin von einem anderen Unglück sprach. Ihrer Meinung trafen ihre abergläubischen Vorhersagen in gut zur Hälfte ein. Wenn es nur ein Ja oder Nein gab, war das keine große Kunst.

„Sie werden alt", maulte Mathilde hinter Gertruds Rücken. Sie hatte schlechte Laune, weil ihr und Hermine der freie Nachmittag gestrichen wurde, um zu helfen, die Schieflage in der Küche geradezubiegen.

Zuerst galt es, neuen frischen Fisch zu besorgen. Ohne den bräuchten sie auch keinen Kartoffel- und Gurkensalat zu machen.

„Hermine, Sie schnappen sich den Korb und gehen in den Damenpfad. Sie wissen schon, die Straße mit den vielen Geschäften. *Altonaer Seefischhandlung* steht groß über der Ladentür. Das ist das Fischgeschäft. Hier, ich habe Ihnen aufgeschrieben, wie viel ich brauche. Aber lassen Sie sich keinen alten Kram andrehen! Das macht Teerling gerne, wenn er glaubt, jemanden vor sich zu haben, der keine Ahnung hat. Sie wissen, wie frischer Fisch aussehen muss?"

„Die Augen dürfen nicht trüb sein und meine Mutter hat mir gezeigt, wie die Haut reagieren soll, wenn man mit dem Finger draufdrückt."

„Braves Mädchen! Fünfzig Schollen, von etwa dieser Größe." Gertrud zeigte es mit den Händen. „Und denken Sie daran: Fisch, der nach Fisch riecht, ist alt."

„Teerling? Ist er verwandt mit Hieltje Bakker?“ Mathildes Frage klang in Hermines Ohren, als wüsste sie die Antwort bereits.

„Das hört sie gar nicht gerne und das wissen Sie genau.“ Gertrud drückte Hermine den Korb und einen Zettel in die Hand. Sie winkte mit den Fingern, Hermine solle losgehen.

„Alle Teerlings, Akkermanns und Bakkers sind miteinander verwandt“, kommentierte Dina.

„Bekomme ich Geld?“ Hermine stand schon in der Tür, drehte sich jedoch noch einmal um.

„Sie bekommen Ihren Lohn am Ende der Woche.“ Gertrud wedelte stärker mit der Hand, sie solle endlich gehen.

„Geld, um den Fisch zu bezahlen.“

„Lassen Sie es ins Kontobuch des Hotels anschreiben. Aber achten Sie darauf, dass es auch unser Buch ist.“

Nicht mit dem *Bakker Junior* zu verwechseln. Hermine verstand nicht, warum die Familie keine gängigeren Namen wie *Seestern* oder *Dünenblick* für ihre Häuser erfand, die weniger zu Verwechslungen führten.

„Wozu ist der Zettel? Fünfzig Schollen kann ich mir merken.“

„Teerling kennt Sie nicht. Das da“, Gertrud deutete auf das Stück Papier, „ist meine Erlaubnis, dass Sie für mich einkaufen.“

Hermine war noch keine zehn Sekunden fort, als Dina fragte: „Stimmt es, dass Hermine Pralinen bekommen hat?“

Gertrud musterte sie wie eine Katze ihre Beute. Schweigend trank sie ein Glas Milch in aller Ruhe aus, wischte sich mit dem Handrücken die Lippen und schnalzte mit der Zunge. Sie schaute Mathilde mit halb zusammengekniffenen Augen an. „Wussten Sie, dass es nichts Besseres als handwarme

Kuhmilch vom Ostlandbauern Lübben gibt? Von dem gekühlten Kram bekomme ich Sodbrennen. Und wissen Sie, was mir Magenschmerzen bereitet? Wovon mir so richtig speiübel wird?"

„Was sehen Sie mich so an?" Mathildes Empörung wirkte aufgesetzt.

„Weil ich ahne, wer die alte Kamelle wieder aufgewärmt und Dina zugeflüstert hat."

„Wovon wird Ihnen denn speiübel?" Dina schien ihre vorherige Frage vergessen zu haben.

„Von Leuten, die es ärgert, nicht alles zu wissen, und die ihre Kollegen anschwärzen."

„Pah." Mit einem kräftigen Ruck warf Mathilde eine halb geschälte Kartoffel in den Pott mit Wasser, schob ihren Stuhl zurück und verließ mit erhobenem Kopf die Küche.

Keine dreißig Minuten später kam Hermine in Begleitung des jungen Mannes, der im Fischladen aushalf und für sie den schweren Korb trug, zurück. Ein prüfender Blick der Köchin auf die Ware, ein Nicken in Hermines Richtung und ein Danke an den jungen Mann, und schon bearbeiteten die Frauen, jetzt nur noch zu dritt, die Schollen. Gertrud schlitzte sie auf und entfernte die Innereien. Hermine betätigte die Wasserpumpe, damit Dina die Fischleiber unter fließendem Wasser abwaschen und die Bauchhöhle von den Resten säubern konnte. Anschließend schnitten sie gemeinsam mit Scheren großzügig die Flunken, wie hier die kleinen Gräten an den Rändern des platten Fischlaibes genannt wurden, ab. Niemand sollte beim Essen die winzigen Fischknochen aussortieren müssen.

„Ach, Frau Dirksen", kam Dina auf Gertruds anfängliche Prophezeiung zurück. „Jetzt haben wir Ihr angekündigtes Unglück glücklicherweise abgewendet."

„Die blöden Fische habe ich doch gar nicht gemeint, Dina. Erst gestern", Gertrud schlug die alte Zeitung zusammen, auf der sie die Fischinnereien gesammelt hatten, „habe ich gesehen, wie der Seniorchef auf seinem Weg ins Kontor fast über einen umgefallenen Besen gestolpert wäre."

„Ich war das nicht", rechtfertigte sich Dina.

„Das sagt ja keiner."

Hermine nahm ihr den Fischmüll ab, um ihn im Abfalleimer zu entsorgen.

„Jedenfalls hat Bakker den Besen aufgehoben und mit der Bürste nach oben hinter die Tür gestellt."

Dina schlug die Hand vor den Mund. „Ach du Schreck!", flüsterte sie.

„Du sagst es! Als Insulaner und ehemaliger Seemann sollte er es besser wissen", bestätigte Gertrud.

„Was denn?" Hermine kannte einigen Aberglauben. Nicht einer hatte etwas mit einem Besen zu tun.

„Solange ein Mann auf See ist, darf seine Frau keinen Besen mit den Borsten nach oben hinter die Tür stellen. Das bringt dem Ehemann den Tod oder zumindest großes Unglück."

„Aber der Senior fährt nicht zur See." Hermine war verwirrt.

„Umgekehrt kann so etwas auch gelten."

Hermine fand es an den Haaren herbeigezogen. Dennoch kam ihr Bakkers Ehefrau in den Sinn. Die war seit Monaten auf dem Festland in einer Nervenklinik untergebracht, was als Familiengeheimnis galt. „Sie glauben, der Seniorchefin passiert etwas?"

„Man kann nie vorsichtig genug sein. Jedenfalls", sagte Gertrud und zupfte ihre Schürze, die ihr an der mageren Taille hing, zurecht, „habe ich schnell den Besen umgedreht. Doch vermutlich war es schon zu spät, um das Unglück abzuwenden."

Mathilde betrat die Küche. „Das ist sogar für Sie, Frau Dirksen, weit hergeholt. Verschonen Sie uns mit Ihren Lügengeschichten!"

„Mein Opa", sagte Hermine, „spinnt auch gerne Seemannsgarn."

„Noch einer, der Spaß daran hat, anderen Angst einzujagen."

„Sie müssen es ja nicht glauben." Gertrud hantierte laut mit einigen Töpfen. Sie hatte genügend Wasser aufgesetzt, um die Kartoffeln zu kochen. „Aber wenn ich bedenke, dass erst gestern ein Brief angekommen ist, der von einer Klinik auf dem Festland stammt, befürchte ich, dass es unserer Seniorchefin gar nicht gut geht."

„Ich jedenfalls", Dina wischte sich mit dem Handrücken eine Strähne aus der Stirn, „mache mir jetzt große Sorgen. Was, wenn's nicht die alte Frau Bakker trifft, sondern dieses Haus?"

„Dummes Mädchen!", schalt Mathilde Dina.

„Weil mir niemand auf meine Fragen eine Antwort gibt", maulte Dina. „Wie mit den Pralinen."

Gertruds Zeigefinger deutete auf den zweiten Herd. „Halt den Mund und stell die Pfannen auf."

Hermine schaute die Köchin fragend an. Gertrud Dirksen hielt dem Blick stand, gab dann aber auf. Sie seufzte. „Ich will gar nicht wissen, von wem die Pralinen sind. Doch ich gebe Ihnen einen guten Rat, Fräulein Flessner. Sehen Sie sich vor!"

„Es ist nur ein Geschenk, weil ich jemandem einen Gefallen getan habe."

„Das muss ein großer Gefallen gewesen sein", meinte Gertrud. „Pralinen sind teuer."

„Mathilde hat gesagt, die Leute sagen, Sie sind darauf aus, sich einen reichen Hotelier zu angeln." Dina hatte das Butterfass aus der Vorratskammer geholt.

„Dina!", warnte Gertrud. „Das sind alte Kamellen und sie stimmen nicht."

„Ich frage mich", überlegte Dina, „ob ich das auch versuchen sollte." Für die träge und naive Dina eine Herausforderung und ein Ding der Unmöglichkeit.

Gertrud und Hermine lachten, bis ihnen die Tränen kamen. „Spaß beiseite", wandte Gertrud sich flüsternd an Hermine, „wie gesagt, ich persönlich glaube kein einziges Wort davon. Dennoch mehren sich die Gerüchte. Wie Jakob Ihnen beim Ausflug den Hof machte, habe ich selbst gesehen." Gertrud wehrte Hermines geplanten Protest mit einer Handbewegung ab. „Aber das kenne ich von ihm, es ist nichts Neues. Doch etwas anderes macht mir Sorgen." Gertrud nahm Hermines Hände in die ihren und schaute auf sie hinab. „Diese Geste", sie nickte mit dem Kopf auf die sich haltenden Hände, „kann in vielerlei Hinsicht gedeutet werden. Es heißt, auf der Überfahrt zur Insel habe der Seniorchef Ihre Hände genauso gehalten."

„Ich kann mich daran nicht erinnern", sagte Hermine und machte sich von Gertrud los.

„Ich glaube es. Aber erschwerend kommt hinzu, dass Sie hier arbeiten, obwohl Sie nicht angekündigt wurden. Ich weiß", Gertrud hob die Hand, „das hat der Senior gemacht, um Köhler eins auszuwischen. Und wir alle haben auf der Liste Bakker gegen Köhler auf unserer Seite einen fetten Strich machen können. Dennoch sieht es im Licht betrachtet zusammen mit dem Geld …“

„Welches Geld?“

„Man hat Sie beobachtet, wie Sie zwei Fünf-Mark-Münzen bei der Sparkasse eingezahlt haben.“

„Aber das war Lohn für …“

„Ich glaube Ihnen das, Kind. Doch da ist noch etwas. Man hat Sie mehrmals in *Köhlers Dorfhotel* gesehen. All das zusammengenommen, ergibt ein schlechtes Bild.“

„Ein schiefes Bild.“

„Jedenfalls wird es den Söhnen vom Senior nicht gefallen.“

„Was haben die damit zu tun?“

„Ich erzähle es dir, Hermine. Ich sage einfach du, einverstanden?“

Hermine nickte.

„Um es dir verständlich zu machen, muss ich weiter ausholen. Der Stiefvater von Willem Dirks Bakker, Klaas van Dyk hieß er, hat nach dem Tode von Willems Mutter seine Haushälterin geheiratet. Sie war siebenundvierzig Jahre jünger als van Dyk. Er hätte ihr Großvater sein können. Anschließend hat er mit seiner blutjungen Frau noch drei Kinder bekommen. Es gab Erbstreitigkeiten um die Hotels, die Bakkers Mutter damals mit in die Ehe eingebracht hatte. Also …“ Köchin Gertrud sah zu Dina hinüber, die sich mit dem Anfachen des Herdfeuers Zeit ließ. Dann sah sie Hermine direkt in die Augen und hob die Augenbrauen. Doch bei Hermine war der Groschen noch nicht gefallen.

„Ach, ich sehe schon. Du weißt wirklich nicht, worauf ich hinauswill. Also …“ Sie rückte ein wenig näher an Hermine heran. „Es ist gut vorstellbar, dass Bakkers Kinder annehmen könnten, dass du es darauf anlegst, dass der Alte dich nach dem Tod seiner Frau heiraten will. Und ich meine vor allem Geeske Bakkers Stimme jetzt schon zu hören, wie sie ein Wort andauernd wiederholt: Erbschleicherin."

Hermine starrte Gertrud entsetzt an.

„Ja, Kind. Die Bande befürchtet, das ganze Familiendrama von damals könnte sich wiederholen. Sie haben Angst um ihr Erbe. So, jetzt ist es raus." Gertrud schien zufrieden. Hermine war erschüttert.

„Ich und der Senior? Nie im Leben!", rief sie. „Ich bin eben erst fünfzehn geworden. Er könnte mein Großvater sein."

„Wie gesagt. Alles schon vorgekommen."

„Das ist doch …", stotterte Hermine.

„Alles Quatsch, vollkommener Humbug?"

„Genau."

„Ich glaube dir, Hermine. Aber sieh dich vor!"

Kapitel 8

Fünf Briefe und ein dicker, großer Umschlag lagen auf seinem Schreibtisch. Er nahm den silbernen Brieföffner zur Hand.

Zwei Umschläge trugen Briefmarken, kamen demnach vom Festland. Der erste schmale Brief enthielt eine Einladung seines Weinhändlers, Firma Vissering aus Leer. Er veranstaltete im kommenden Monat eine Verköstigung und bot dabei griechische Weine wie den Mavrodaphné und weißen Malvasier zu zwei Mark die große Flasche an. Versand: franco. Ein Angebot, das er überdenken würde.

Der zweite Umschlag, ohne Marke, enthielt eine Information an alle Hotels zur geflissentlichen Bekanntgabe an ihre Gäste: *Die Lesehalle in der Nähe des Leuchtturms neben der Villa Schumacher ist geöffnet von morgens acht Uhr bis abends acht Uhr, mit Ausnahme der Table-d'hôte-Zeit auf eine Stunde.*

Das Blatt legte er zur Seite. Frau Luise sollte es im Flur ans Schwarze Brett heften.

Im dritten Brief teilte man ihm auf einem Sonderblatt mit, dass ein Männergesangsverein aus Oldenburg, unterstützt von einem Herrn Windel aus Hamburg (Tenor) und Herrn Stammer (Bariton), vortragen möchten. Gefolgt vom Programm.

Von *Tannhäuser* über *der Studenten-Nachtgesang* bis hin zu *Schlaf ein, du holdes Kind* war alles dabei. Auch etwas, worüber er nachdenken wollte.

Der vierte Brief enthielt eine Einladung zur Vorstandssitzung seines Turnvereines, gefolgt von zwei Bitten. Er würde postwendend zusagen, Geld für die Anschaffung neuer Turngeräte zu spenden, und absagen, weil er nicht gewillt war, auf der geplanten Vollversammlung eine Rede zu halten oder gar einen Posten anzunehmen. Das konnten andere viel besser.

Der letzte Brief trug ebenfalls keine Briefmarke, war also im Hotel abgegeben worden. Er kam von einer Frau Auguste Flöge. Sie hatte in der Süderreihe 7 eine Dampf-Wäscherei eingerichtet und sah sich imstande, die ihr übergebene Wäsche innerhalb von drei bis vier Tagen zurückzuliefern.

Dirk würde mit seiner Frau darüber sprechen, ob es Sinn machte, den Hotelwäschebetrieb auszulagern.

Der dickere Umschlag kam von einem Architekten. Er enthielt die Aufstellung all der ermittelten Kosten für das erste Projekt am Strand, das, sollte er den Zuschlag bekommen, den Namen *Strandvilla Bakker* tragen würde.

Da wusste der Mann schon mehr als er.

Zudem lag eine Schätzung der Kosten für das zweite Objekt vor, das der Konstrukteur nur grob umriss, um es zu gegebener Zeit weiter auszuarbeiten. Zeichnungen, Statiken und einiges mehr. Er überflog es kurz, um es sich später genauer anzusehen, ehe er es an den Vater weitergäbe.

Der letzte Briefumschlag trug als Absender den Namen der Klinik, in der seine Mutter untergebracht war. Da die Anschrift nur auf Herrn Bakker lautete, durfte er auch diesen Brief öffnen. Mit einem unguten Gefühl in der Magengegend setzte er den Brieföffner an. Er verharrte einen Augenblick, ehe er ihn aufschlitzte.

Bakker kannte die allgemeinen Vorstellungen der Insulaner, wie es in einer Nervenheilanstalt zuging. Unruhige und aggressive Kranke steckten in Tollkisten, als ob man sie lebendig einsargen würde, damit sie sich beruhigten. Die meisten Borkumer dachten, dass psychisch Kranke irgendwo angekettet an einer Wand oder gefesselt und zitternd auf einer Pritsche lagen, mit Schaum vor dem Mund schrien und an ihren Fesseln rüttelten. Schuld daran war die alte Geschichte über die *Maale Geertje*, die verrückte Geertje, die ihnen im Kopf herumspukte.

Angeblich war die arme Frau vierzig Jahre lang im Borkumer Armenhaus angekettet gewesen, weil sie als Wahnsinnige gegolten hatte. Vollkommener Quatsch. Doch die Geschichte hielt sich hartnäckig. Vor seinem inneren Auge sah er eine arme Frau vor sich, die gelegentlich Depressionen hatte und dann Gefahr lief, ins Wasser zu gehen.

Sein Vater erinnerte sich gut an sie, auch wenn er damals noch ein Kind gewesen war. Da hatte sie wohl oft mittags am Tisch seines Stiefvaters Klaas van Dyk gesessen, um mitzuessen. Er konnte sich nicht erinnern, dass der Vater jemals erwähnt hatte, sie sei ständig wirr gewesen. Nicht so, wie seine Mutter es über Monate gewesen war, bevor sie in die Klinik gekommen war. Mama war überzeugt, vom Teufel besessen zu sein, und das, obwohl es kaum jemanden auf der Insel gab, der mehr für die Kirche und die Armen tat als sie.

Bakker beschloss, am kommenden Sonntag den Gottesdienst zu besuchen, um für seine Mutter ein Gebet zu sprechen. Er glaubte zwar nicht daran, dass es helfen würde, doch Mama würde es gefallen. Einmal tief Luft geholt, dann entfaltete er den Brief der Klinik.

Was der Arzt schrieb, ließ sein Herz schneller schlagen.

***

„Mathilde Remmers, du sollst sofort zur Chefin kommen."

„Was will sie?"

„Keine Ahnung."

„Wo ist sie?"

„In der Küche."

Mathilde schubste Dina beiseite. „Verräterin!"

„Was soll ich denn verraten haben?"

„Nichts. Weil du nichts weißt." Mathilde musste sofort ihren Frust loswerden, ehe sie auf die Chefin traf. Dina zu erschrecken, ihr einen Vorwurf zu machen oder vorzugeben, böse auf sie zu sein, half.

Ihr war klar, dass das Küchenmädchen zu loyal war, um überhaupt jemanden bei der Chefin anzuschwärzen. *Nicht einmal mich,* dachte sie. Und zu dumm, um sich eine Lügengeschichte auszudenken, mit der sie Mathilde loswerden konnte, war sie allemal. Da Mathilde sich in den vergangenen Tagen nichts zuschulden hatte kommen lassen, konnte es nur eines bedeuten. Es musste mit dem Brief aus der Klinik zu tun haben, den Gertrud erwähnt hatte. Das Unglück, das die abergläubische Köchin im umgedrehten Besen gesehen hatte, traf vermutlich Mathilde.

Die Alte war gesund und würde bald nach Hause kommen. Dann wäre es vorbei mit ihrem Schlendrian, dachte sie. Auf dem Weg zu Adeline gewann sie trotz der Gedanken Zuversicht. Arbeitskräfte waren rar und die Saison war schon so weit fortgeschritten, dass Kräfte vom Festland für die kommenden Monate kaum noch eingestellt werden konnten. Sie würde zumindest bis Oktober ihr Auskommen behalten.

Mit mehr Kühnheit, als ihr zumute war, betrat sie die Hotelküche. Bis auf die Chefin war niemand da. Vermutlich hatten die anderen sich nach nebenan in die Waschküche verzogen und würden gleich versuchen, an der Tür zu lauschen.

„Machen Sie die Tür zu und setzen Sie sich", befahl Adeline. Tonfall und Gesichtsausdruck zeigten deutlich, wie wütend sie war.

Mathilde ließ sich auf dem Rand des Stuhles sinken. Adeline holte tief Luft und Mathilde dachte, dass sie selten einen so zornigen Blick gesehen hatte. „Der Schaden, den Sie angerichtet haben", zischte Adeline Bakker „ist kaum wieder gutzumachen."

Mathilde wusste nicht, wovon die Chefin sprach. Auf keinen Fall hatte es etwas mit der Irrenanstalt zu tun.

„Ich weiß nicht, was Sie meinen. Aber wenn es um Ihre Schwiegermutter geht – Sie wissen, ich kann schweigen."

Adeline nickte, streckte den Rücken gerade und verzog den Mund. Schmerzen oder die ersten Senkwehen, vermutete Mathilde.

„Ihre Verschwiegenheit lassen sie uns ja täglich spüren." Sie klang verächtlich. „Sie haben Ihren Freibrief. Deswegen verstehe ich nicht, warum Sie so üble Gerüchte über Fräulein Flessner und meinen Schwager verbreiten."

„Habe ich nicht." Mathilde sagte die Wahrheit und fügte eine halbe Lüge hinzu. „Ihr Schwager und Hermine können sich gegenseitig nicht ausstehen."

„Hermine? Ich bin ja nicht blind. Ich weiß sehr wohl, dass Hermine Jakob nicht leiden kann. Ich rede von dem anderen Fräulein Flessner."

„Gibt es zwei?" Mathilde tat nicht nur unwissend, sie war es auch.

„Von ihrer Cousine, Bertha Flessner."

Ah! Jetzt fiel der Groschen. Die verschwundene Verwandte. War sie etwa in Jakobs Bett aufgetaucht, lag Mathilde auf der Zunge, doch sie verkniff sich den Kommentar. Doch der Name Jakob war nicht gefallen. Die Chefin hatte vier, wenn man den Schwippschwager, den Apotheker mitzählte, sogar fünf Schwäger. Da konnte es auch ein anderer Mann sein. Nicht jede Schandtat, die auf Jakob hindeutete, musste auch von ihm begangen worden sein. Wer wusste das in diesem Moment besser als sie? „Von Bertha Flessner und irgendeiner Verbindung zu den Bakkers weiß ich rein gar nichts." Wieder sagte sie die Wahrheit, was auch Adeline erkannte.

Mathilde kombinierte schnell. Wenn Hermines verschwundene Cousine die Chefin dermaßen aufregte, musste ein Fünkchen Wahrheit an der Geschichte dran sein. Und schon sah sie ihre Chance. „Soll ich für Sie herausbekommen, was …" Sie legte absichtlich eine Pause ein und ließ den Rest des Satzes offen. Adeline reagierte wie erwartet. Sie hatte gedanklich die Worte, die ihrer geheimen Sorge entsprachen, hinzugefügt.

Mathilde blickte sie herausfordernd an. Es war ein Schuss ins Blaue, das war ihr klar. Denn die Gerüchte mussten ja nicht unbedingt etwas mit Sex zu tun haben. Es gab sicherlich noch andere Dinge, womit ein geachteter Mann sich seinen Ruf ruinieren konnte. Nur fielen ihr im Augenblick keine ein.

Ehe Adeline Bakker antworten konnte, wurde die Hotelküchentür aufgerissen. Gertrud schob Dina vor sich her. „Wir müssen jetzt mit dem Kochen anfangen, wenn das Essen für die Gäste pünktlich auf den Tisch kommen soll."

Adeline wirkte erleichtert.

„Machen Sie das, Fräulein Remmers", sagte sie.

***

Die vier Männer hatten ihre Termine kurzfristig abgesagt, um auf Bakkers dringende Bitte hin pünktlich um vierzehn Uhr bei ihm zu sein. Doktor Schmidt, der Inselarzt, hatte einen Patienten, dem er ein Furunkel aufschneiden wollte, das ihn seit Langem plagte, auf den nächsten Tag vertröstet.

Pieter Klaasen Akkermann, selbstständiger Kaufmann, hatte seine Ehefrau mit einer fadenscheinigen Ausrede anlügen müssen, damit sie ihn im Laden vertrat. Dabei hatte sie mit einer Freundin das Damenbad am Südstrand, das im vergangenen Jahr eröffnet worden war, besuchen wollen. Zudem hatte er sie aus dem Haus bekommen müssen, da das geheime Treffen bei ihm stattfinden sollte.

Klaas Bakker würde für die Segeltour mit Urlaubern um vierzehn Uhr leider nicht zur Verfügung stehen. Er hatte kurzfristig den Bruder von Anje, seiner Frau überreden können, die Fahrt zu übernehmen, denn es wäre schade gewesen, dieses lukrative Geschäft mit den Touristen sausen zu lassen. Zumal nur wenige Wochen im Jahr Geld damit zu verdienen war.

Georg Köhler, neben Hotelier auch amtierender Bürgermeister der Inselgemeinde, hatte sich bei einer Sitzung im Gemeinderat entschuldigen lassen, in der es um Gas, Kanalisation und Elektrizität auf Borkum gehen würde. Zum Glück hatte er seinen politischen Stellvertreter schicken können, denn er wollte unbedingt, dass die Insel ein größeres Gaswerk erhielt. Von elektrischem Licht und einer ordentlichen Abwasserversorgung ganz zu schweigen. Jetzt mussten die Weichen für die Zukunft gestellt werden, ehe mit dem Neubau der Hotelfront vor dem Nordstrand begonnen werden konnte. „Ich hoffe, es ist wichtig. Denn ich könnte es mir nie verzeihen, dass durch meine Abwesenheit gegen den Fortschritt entschieden wird."

„Sie können ja Widerspruch einreichen", sagte Doktor Schmidt.

„Nur dass dann die ganze Angelegenheit um Monate verschoben wird. Es ist ein Graus, sich mit den ewig Gestrigen, die den Fortschritt um jeden Preis aufhalten wollen, herumzuschlagen."

„Ich bin sicher, die Opposition wird umgekehrt genauso argumentieren."

„Das ist nun mal so in der Demokratie, lieber Doktor."

Die vier Herren nahmen an einem Tisch in Akkermanns guter Stube Platz.

„Es ist schön, dass Sie so kurzfristig kommen konnten", sagte Akkermann.

„Ihr Kutscher hat mich mit einem angeblichen Notfall aus der Praxis geholt." Schmidt sah nicht so aus, als wäre er wegen der Lüge des Mannes ungehalten. „Den Karbunkel konnte ich verschieben, dennoch muss ich mir etwas ausdenken, das ich meiner Sprechstundenhilfe erzählen kann. Sie ist ein Schatz, steckt aber ihre Nase in Dinge, die sie nichts angehen."

„Seit wann haben Sie denn eine Hilfe in der Praxis?“

„Schon einige Wochen. Wir haben immer mehr Gäste. Zu meinem Glück werden die auch krank. Ich muss sagen, bei denen lohnt es sich.“

„Und ich dachte, Hannes und sein Furunkel …“

„Wie man sieht, ist es schwer, auf der Insel etwas geheim zu halten.“ Doktor Schmidt lachte und sah zu Bakker hinüber. „Apropos Geheimnis …“ Er deutete auf Georg Köhler. „Ich dachte, die Herren Köhler und Bakker sind sich spinnefeind und reden nicht mehr miteinander.“

„Was ja nicht auf den Sohn zutreffen muss“, meinte Klaas.

„Es gibt Wichtigeres, lieber Doktor“, sagte Köhler. „Geschäfte zum Beispiel.“

Pieter Akkermann schenkte Doktor Schmidt ein Augenzwinkern und noch ehe Akkermann etwas dazu sagen konnte, wurde er von Bakker unterbrochen. „Ich möchte …“, Bakker hob beide Hände als Entschuldigung, dass er das Gespräch unterbrach, „Sie nicht länger als notwendig aufhalten, meine Herren. Es ist wichtig, dass jeder von Ihnen Folgendes in seinem Angebot für die Strandgrundstücke ergänzt.“

„Hört, hört!“, sagte Akkermann. „Woher wollen Sie alle wissen, dass ich …“

„Ihre Frau ist einfach zu oft im Damenbad. Die Ladys tratschen.“

„Apropos Damen. Wie geht es denn Ihrer Frau Mutter, Bakker?“

„Hervorragend. Die Klinik schreibt, dass sie schon bald auskuriert sein wird. Wie auch immer“, kam Bakker auf den Grund der Zusammenkunft zurück, „ich möchte, dass jeder hier im Raum der Gemeinde mitteilt, dass er, sollte er den Zuschlag für eines der Grundstücke erhalten, in seinem Betrieb bevorzugt Insulaner einstellen wird."

Georg Köhler wollte etwas sagen, wurde jedoch von Bakker aufgehalten. „Ehe du dich mokierst, mein lieber Patenonkel. Ja, ich habe mit Leuten aus der Opposition gesprochen. Die wollen das zu einem grundlegenden Zuschlagskriterium machen."

„Davon weiß ich nichts."

„Darum heißt es ja auch Opposition. Genau deswegen veranstalten du und Vater ja diese kleine Finte, um nicht in den Verdacht der Vetternwirtschaft unter den Mitgliedern des Gemeinderates zu geraten. Und es funktioniert. Mir, als Sohn deines neuen Feindes, verrät die Gegenpartei einiges mehr als zuvor. Ich erfahre Kleinigkeiten, die dir als Bürgermeister und Mitbewerber verborgen bleiben."

„Aus gutem Grund. Ich bin befangen, darum erfahre ich nicht alles. Zudem möchte ich mir nicht vorwerfen lassen, Gemeindeinterna auszunutzen", versicherte Köhler und grinste schief. Jeder hier im Raum wusste, dass es erstens doch so war und zweitens hinterher so geredet werden würde, auch wenn es nicht so gewesen wäre.

„Ich hoffe, meine Herren, das bleibt unter uns."

„Die kleine Finte oder unsere Absprachen?"

„Beides."

„Selbstverständlich", sagten Schmidt und Akkermann gleichzeitig und Köhler nickte.

Pieter Klaasen Akkermann meinte: „Aber wenn die Hotels erst einmal fertig sind, bekommen wir anfänglich sicherlich Probleme, Personal zu finden. Da ist uns jeder Insulaner, der arbeiten will, doch willkommen. Wieso besteht die andere Partei …" Bakker unterbrach ihn.

„Das gilt für die Sommermonate, lieber Herr Akkermann. Das ist jedem Gemeindemitglied klar. Ich rede von den Wintermonaten und denke da an ganzjährige Anstellungen für die Insulaner. Hausmeister hätten zum Beispiel das ganze Jahr zu tun. Welchen Posten auch immer ihr angebt, der ganzjährig bestehen bleibt, es erhöht die Chance auf einen Zuschlag."

„Wird es nicht auffallen, wenn wir alle gleichzeitig unser Angebot ergänzen?"

„Lasst euch etwas einfallen."

Kapitel 9

Am Freitag bekam Hermine Post. Mutter schrieb, dass Vater versichere, es gehe ihm besser. Doch weder Hermine noch Mama glaubten seinen Beteuerungen. Mutter vertrat die Meinung, er behaupte das nur, damit sich die Familie nicht so viele Sorgen um ihn mache. Das erfüllte Hermine mit Trauer. Zum einen, weil sie Vater eine baldige Genesung wünschte, zum anderen, weil es bedeutete, weiter so viel wie möglich von ihrem Verdienst abzugeben. Nach all dem, was Mutter schrieb, konnte sie zwischen den Zeilen lesen, dass die Familie mehr denn je auf Hermines finanzielle Unterstützung angewiesen war.

„Und denk Dir", schrieb Mutter, „Tante Frieda hat eine Postkarte von Bertha bekommen. Darauf ist der Borkumer Leuchtturm zu sehen. Der ist ja wunderschön. Bitte schick uns auch eine, wenn sie nicht zu teuer ist."

Bertha verschickte Karten von Borkum? Wie war das möglich? Seit Wochen hatte sie niemand gesehen und keiner wusste, wo sie sich aufhielt. „Wenn sie auf der Insel ist, wird ihr früher oder später jemand begegnen", versicherte Köchin Gertrud. „Oder sie wird dir selbst über den Weg laufen. Länger als ein paar Tage kann sich hier niemand verborgen halten. Du hast es ja am eigenen Leib erlebt. Egal, was du tust, irgendjemand sieht dich immer."

Wenn Gertrud recht hatte, konnte Bertha unmöglich auf der Insel sein. Doch wer hatte dann in ihrem Namen die Postkarte verschickt? Vielleicht, dachte Hermine, war die Grußkarte monatelang unterwegs gewesen. So etwas war bei der Post schon vorgekommen. Sie entschied, Mutter eine Karte zu senden und Bertha einfach nicht zu erwähnen. Einen kurzen Augenblick schoss ihr der Gedanke durch den Kopf, dass ihre Cousine nach Amerika ausgewandert sein könnte. Davon hatte sie einmal gesprochen. Aber das war lange her und außerdem, was sollte sie da? Alleine? Sie kannte in Amerika niemanden, und wie hätte sie die Überfahrt bezahlen sollen? Und wenn es wirklich so wäre, warum hatte sie es dann ihren Eltern gegenüber verheimlicht? Gedanken über Gedanken. Sie schnürten ihr die Kehle zu und verdarben die Freude auf den freien Nachmittag. Trotzdem würde sie einen Bummel durch die Geschäfte machen, an den Strand gehen und auf dem Rückweg eine schöne Ansichtskarte für ihre Mutter kaufen.

„Halt!" Dirk Willems Bakker hielt sie auf der Hintertreppe auf.

So früh am Morgen war der Juniorchef selten auf den Beinen. Bakker winkte sie ins Kontor, schloss die Tür hinter ihr und ging an den Schreibtisch. Er ließ sich auf den Sessel fallen und beugte sich zur Seite, um eine der Schreibtischschubladen aufzuziehen. „Dieser Brief hier", Dirks Stimme war kaum von der seines Vaters zu unterscheiden, „ist für Ihre Cousine Bertha."

Hermines Herz klopfte wild. Also war sie endlich wieder aufgetaucht. Doch warum, fragte sie sich, hatte Georg Köhler ihr das nicht gesagt? Schließlich hatte er es ihr versprochen.

Und was in aller Welt hatte Dirk Bakker mit Bertha zu tun? Noch viel wichtiger war die Antwort auf die Frage, wo Bertha die ganze Zeit gesteckt hatte. Und noch etwas fiel Hermine ein. Warum meldete sich Bertha nicht bei ihr? Sie musste doch wissen, dass sie sie suchte.

„Aber bitte versenden Sie ihn so, dass es niemand mitbekommt", sagte Dirk Bakker.

Mit zitternder Hand nahm Hermine den Brief entgegen.

„Machen Sie nicht so große Augen, Fräulein Flessner." Hermine sah den Juniorchef zum ersten Mal, seit sie ihn kannte, lächeln.

„Es ist nur ein Brief. Er liegt schon ein paar Tage hier, aber es ist alles in Ordnung."

Hermine schüttelte leicht den Kopf. Sie hatte viele Fragen, doch ihr Bauchgefühl sagte ihr, es sei besser, keine zu stellen. Bertha würde sie alle beantworten. Hermine nahm den versiegelten Umschlag in die Hand und warf einen schnellen Blick darauf.

Da stand es schwarz auf weiß: Fräulein Bertha Flessner. Die Adresse fehlte. Sie drehte ihn um. Die Lasche war mit einem Klecks roten Wachses versiegelt worden und mit einem Petschaft war ein Siegel hineingedrückt worden. So offiziell, dass es an eine Urkunde erinnerte. Hermine wurde übel. *Bertha, was hast du angestellt, dass du so einen hochoffiziellen Brief erhältst?*

„Aber ich habe keine Ahnung, wo meine Cousine ist."

„Dann schicken Sie ihn einfach an die Familie."

Sie knickste und verließ eilig das Kontor. Die Knie wurden ihr weich. Auf dem Weg die hintere Treppe hinauf in ihre Kammer meinte sie, gleich umzufallen. Eine Scheibe Brot und ein Glas Milch würden ihr sicherlich helfen und den Magen beruhigen. Doch etwas zu essen musste warten. Zu groß war ihre Neugier, endlich Antworten auf all ihre Fragen zu bekommen. Sie ließ sich auf ihr Bett fallen und betrachtete den Umschlag. Einfach aufreißen und lesen, dachte sie. Doch sie verspürte bereits vor der Tat ein schlechtes Gewissen. Niemand wollte, dass seine Post von jemandem gelesen wurde. Sie konnte den Brief zu ihrer Tante schicken, doch ihr Verstand sagte ihr, dass sie Bertha damit keinen Gefallen tun würde. Sorgfältig untersuchte sie das Siegel, konnte aber aufgrund des Abdruckes nichts ableiten. Vielleicht eine alte Hausmarke, wie sie früher in Ostfriesland vorkam. Viele konnten weder lesen noch schreiben, aber eine Art Familienzeichen wurde von jedem erkannt oder als Unterschrift verwendet. Hier handelte es sich um ein verkehrt herumstehendes großes Z. In der Mitte mit einem Strich wie bei einer Sieben, nur dass dieser Strich wie ein Pfeil eine Spitze hatte, die nach links wies. Sie sollte Gertrud Dirksen fragen. Die Familie der Köchin lebte seit zwei oder drei Generationen auf der Insel. Vielleicht erkannte sie das Zeichen.

Dann überlegte sie es sich anders. Georg Köhler war ihr noch einen Gefallen schuldig. Als Bürgermeister und älterer Herr kannte er sicherlich auch einige Borkumer Hausmarken. Wenn nicht, konnte er im Gemeindeamt nachfragen. Die mussten wissen, wer statt einer Unterschrift eine Hausmarke setzte. Dem Bürgermeister würde man sicherlich Auskunft erteilen.

Mit schnellen Schritten verließ sie das Haus, um die zweihundert Meter bis zu *Köhlers Dorfhotel* zu eilen.

Köhlers Hausdiener weigerte sich anfangs, sie bei seinem Chef vorzulassen, und deutet mit einem Kopfnicken auf den Umschlag in ihrer Hand. Für ihn war nur das rote Lacksiegel zu sehen. „Den Brief kann ich genauso gut übergeben."

„Nein. Ich soll ihn höchstpersönlich abgeben“, schwindelte Hermine.

„Meinetwegen.“ Der Page ließ sie vorbei. „Er ist in seinem Kontor. Zweite Etage rechts. Dritte Tür.“

Hermine hatte es schnell gefunden und klopfte an Köhlers Bürotür.

„Herein.“

Georg Köhler stand am Fenster und blickte hinaus. Von hier aus hatte man einen direkten Blick auf den kleinen Friedhof rund um den alten Leuchtturm. An den Ausdruck „alter Leuchtturm“ für den viereckigen Turm mussten sich die Insulaner erst gewöhnen. Das würde sicherlich noch eine Weile dauern, denn der neue stand ja erst ein paar Jahre.

„Fräulein Flessner!“ Köhler wirkte überrascht. „Kommen Sie rein, setzen Sie sich. Sie sehen schlecht aus.“

Besser hätte Hermine es nicht umschreiben können. Mit dem Gefühl, jemand drücke ihr den Hals zu, überreichte sie stumm den Briefumschlag. Köhlers kurzer Blick darauf ließ kein Verstehen seinerseits erkennen.

„Post für Ihre Cousine“, stellte er fest.

Hermine nickte.

„Es ist keine Adresse drauf. Was soll ich damit?“

„Mir sagen, von wem er kommen könnte.“ Sie deutete auf das rote Siegel.

„Wo haben Sie ihn denn her?“

„Von Dirk Bakker. Aber ich glaube, er ist nur der Postillion und hat keine Ahnung, was drinsteht.“

„So wie Sie!“ Köhler lächelte und betrachtete erneut den Umschlag. Mit dem Finger fuhr er über das Siegel und führte es näher an die Augen. Dann schüttelte er den Kopf. „Sieht aus wie eine alte Hausmarke. Dummerweise habe ich keine Ahnung davon. Die Schrift jedenfalls stammt keinesfalls von Dirk Bakker. Die kenne ich. Leider", er wedelte mit dem Umschlag, „kann ich Ihnen nicht weiterhelfen." Er gab den Brief zurück. Und was nun?

„Öffnen Sie ihn!" Sein Tonfall ließ keinen Widerspruch zu. Hermine folgte seinem Befehl. Vorsichtig löste sie das Wachssiegel. Erst als es unter ihren Fingern zerbröselte, schalt sie sich, es kaputt gemacht zu haben. Der Umschlag enthielt zwei Stück Papier. Eine Urkunde und einen Brief.

Die Überschrift des Schreibens lautete: *Mein geliebter Sohn, liebe zukünftige Schwiegertochter.*

Das andere konnte Hermine nicht entziffern und reichte Köhler den Brief.

„Ich schicke euch die Geburtsurkunde", las er vor, *„die ihr braucht. Leider habe ich den Zettel, wo ihr wohnt, verloren und hoffe, dass der Brief doch zu euch kommt. Ich wäre gerne bei der Hochzeit dabei gewesen, aber ihr seid zu weit weg und verreisen tu ich nicht mehr. Lebt wohl und schreibt bald.*

Mutter"

„Na, wenigstens wissen Sie jetzt, wen Sie nach Ihrer Cousine fragen können."

Köhler gab die Blätter zurück. Die Geburtsurkunde lautete auf einen Harmen Hinrichs. Einundzwanzig Jahre alt und auf Borkum geboren.

„Wo finde ich die Mutter von diesem Hinrichs?"

Köhlers Gesicht verfinsterte sich. Er nahm ihren Ellenbogen und führte sie ans Fenster. Mit einem Kopfnicken deutete er hinaus. „Dort unten. Die Beerdigung war vorgestern."

Ihr wurde kalt. Es fühlte sich an, als habe jemand ihr Herz geöffnet und einen kühlen Wind hineingeblasen.

Hermine brauchte einen Platz, um in Ruhe nachdenken zu können. Sie öffnete die eiserne Pforte, die zum Walfängerfriedhof am Fuße des alten Leuchtturmes führte. Hier lagen die Walfänger und ihre Ehefrauen begraben. Zwischen den neuen Gräbern standen Grabsteine, die teilweise hundertfünfzig Jahre alt waren.

Zum Walfang fuhr kein Insulaner mehr hinaus, seit Napoleon mit seiner Kontinentalsperre diesen Einnahmezweig unterbunden hatte.

An der Südseite des Turmes stand eine Bank, auf der eine alte Frau in Borkumer Tracht saß. Es musste ihr recht heiß sein, in dem schwarzen langen Kleid und dem wollenen Schultertuch. Das Ohreisen, das wie ein nach hinten verschobenes Stirnband über den Kopf hinweg die weiße Spitzenhaube festhielt, glitzerte in der Sonne. Schweigend nickte Hermine ihr zum Gruß zu und nahm neben der Insulanerin Platz.

Bevor sie *Köhlers Dorfhotel* über den Hintereingang verlassen hatte, hatte der Hotelier ihr versichert, dass er sich umhören wolle, was aus Harmen Hinrichs geworden war. Er würde sich bei ihr melden.

Sie nahm sich vor, selbst ebenfalls Erkundigungen über Hinrichs einzuholen, da sie sicherlich eine andere Klientel als der alte Köhler befragen würde. Sie vermutete, dass er zu den jungen Insulanern weniger Kontakte hatte. Soweit sie wusste, hatte Köhler im Gegensatz zu seinem Freund nur einen Sohn und noch keine Enkelkinder.

„Kindchen!", die alte Dame legte eine Hand auf ihre. „Was ist los mit Ihnen? Sie weinen ja."

Kapitel 10

Der Juli war angebrochen und damit wurde der Umzug des Post- und Telegrafenamtes das aktuelle Gesprächsthema auf der Insel. Ein Gutes hatte es. Die Gerüchte um Hermine wurden zum Schnee von gestern. Was blieb, war die Sorge um Cousine Bertha. Was sie über Harmen Hinrichs herausfand, war wenig. Eltern beide verstorben, keine Geschwister. Ein stiller junger Mann, der sich in eine Frau verliebt hatte, die ihn abgewiesen und dennoch später in seiner Begleitung die Insel verlassen hatte. Bertha und Harmen blieben verschwunden.

Auf die Frage, wer die Postkarte von Borkum verschickt hatte, erhielt sie eine unbefriedigende Antwort.

„Mein liebes Fräulein“, erklärte ihr der Postbeamte verstimmt, „haben Sie eine Ahnung, welche Mengen von diesen Ansichtskarten durch meine Hände gehen? Sehr viele. Da kann ich mir unmöglich merken, wer wem etwas geschrieben hat. Und lesen“, seine Miene verfinsterte sich noch mehr, „tue ich die Karten auch nicht.“

Die Hauptsaison hatte fast ihren Höhepunkt erreicht. Auf der Insel war jedes Gästebett ausgebucht und es wurde viel an Veranstaltungen angeboten. Die Insulaner waren vollauf damit beschäftigt, ihr Geld zu verdienen. Schließlich musste es über die kommenden Wintermonate reichen, bis im nächsten Jahr erneut die Gäste anreisten. Sogar der Wettlauf um die geplanten Hotels am Strand interessierte im Augenblick nur wenige.

Die Hausdame, Frau Luise Menninga, fing Hermine vor der Hotelküchentür ab. „Fräulein Flessner. Wenn Sie gefrühstückt haben, gehen Sie hinüber ins *Junior*. Frau Hieltje Bakker erwartet Sie."

„Was will sie von mir?"

„Das steht mir nicht zu, zu fragen. Sie wird es Ihnen schon sagen. Ich denke, dass sie Ihre Hilfe braucht."

„Meine Hilfe?" Was könnte das wohl sein? Hieltjes Ehemann Jakob schoss ihr sofort in den Kopf und somit die Probleme, die sie mit Hieltje Bakker verband.

„Eher Ihre Arbeitskraft. Mittlerweile sollten Sie mitbekommen haben, dass wir uns mit dem Personal gegenseitig aushelfen."

Nur dass man mich noch nie von der Arbeit im Senior abgezogen hat, dachte Hermine, schwieg jedoch.

„Sei froh", sagte Mathilde, die eben mit einem Armvoll Wäsche an ihnen vorbeiging, „dass sie dich nicht zum Ausmisten in den Stall schicken."

„Fräulein Remmers macht nur Spaß." Man sah Luise Menninga selten finster gucken, doch der Blick, der Mathilde traf, ließ das Zimmermädchen schnell das Weite suchen. „Andererseits", rief sie Mathilde hinterher, „wäre es sicherlich eine gute Idee, Sie statt Fräulein Flessner hinüberzuschicken."

„Das wagen Sie nicht", rief Mathilde von der obersten Treppenstufe hinunter und schon war sie in der ersten Etage verschwunden.

„Mag der Teufel wissen", murmelte Frau Luise, „was die Bakkers davon abhält, sie vor die Tür zu setzen." Mit einem aufmunternden Lächeln an Hermine gewandt, fügte sie hinzu: „Keine Bange. Noch nie ist eines meiner Mädchen in Bakkers Fuhrbetrieben zur Arbeit geschickt worden. Obwohl es mir manchmal in den Fingern juckt." Dabei hob Frau Luise kurz den Blick gegen die Zimmerdecke. „Sie werden vermutlich die kommende Zeit im anderen Hotel arbeiten müssen. Dort ist jemand krank geworden. Wohnen bleiben Sie aber weiterhin hier. Der Weg ist ja nicht weit."

Die wenigen Meter zum *Bakker Junior* schaffte sie in ein paar Sekunden. Hermine musste nur das Haus verlassen und bis zur Straßenecke gehen. Sie umrundete den hüfthohen Pfahl, der auf dem Bürgersteig stand, *Stientje Pahle* genannt wurde und abends der Treffpunkt der Dorfjugend war. An ihm war beim Ausflug das Rad der Kutsche hängen geblieben. Hermine bog nach rechts ab, warf einen schnellen Blick in die Auslagen von *Fischers Basar*. Das einstöckige Gebäude mit Flachdach beherbergte *Fischers Laden*. Hüte, Mützen, Badeartikel, Strandschuhe und mehr. Alles, was der Badegast gebrauchen konnte. Einheimische Kunden hatte er sicherlich nur wenige. Ein Strohhut mit blauem Band und einer Schleife daran gefiel Hermine. Doch bei dem Preis musste sie es sich noch überlegen.

Ganz in Gedanken an den Strohhut versunken, wollte sie den Haupteingang des Hotels betreten. Der Page versperrte ihr den Weg.

„Guten Tag, Fräulein Flessner." Der junge Mann musste neu auf der Insel sein, denn sie kannte ihn nicht. Noch ehe sie fragen konnte, woher er wusste, wer sie war, bemerkte sie, wie er ihre Arbeitskleidung betrachtete. An der Farbe der Kleidung war sie für jedermann gut als Angestellte der Bakker-Betriebe zu erkennen. Dennoch blieb die Frage, woher er ihren Namen kannte.

„Willi?" Hermine blickte überrascht den ältesten Sohn von Adeline und Dirk an. Der Zwölfjährige, der den gleichen Namen wie sein Großvater trug, nickte eifrig. „Fast hätte ich dich in der schicken Uniform nicht erkannt."

Willi schien ein paar Zentimeter zu wachsen und ein Hauch von Rot überzog seine Wangen.

„Folgen Sie mir. Wir gehen hintenherum ins Haus."

Den Weg kannte sie, ließ sich dennoch von ihm begleiten. Er kam sich so wichtig vor, das wollte sie ihm nicht verderben.

Auf dem Weg an der Seite entlang des Hotels erfuhr Hermine, dass Willi den Pagen, Karl-Gustav war sein Name, gelegentlich vertrat. „Er ist schon sehr alt. Älter als Großvater. Und gestern Abend soll er im *Tuskulum*, das ist eine Kneipe im Strandviertel, zu lange gefeiert haben. Aber das sind Gerüchte. Wissen Sie, Fräulein Flessner, auf Hörensagen gebe ich nicht viel." Wie altklug er doch klang. „Der Karl-Gustav mag wohl mal einen über den Durst trinken, aber das sei ihm gegönnt."

„Weißt du, was deine Tante von mir will?"

Soweit Hermine wusste, trug die Verantwortung im *Bakker Junior* eine ältere Frau namens Boskamp. Sie ahnte, warum der Senior nicht Jakob und Hieltje mit dieser Aufgabe betraute. Er war von Beruf Sohn und sie seine Ehefrau, die mit sich selbst und ihren zwei Kindern und ihrer Eifersucht offensichtlich schon überfordert war.

„Nein", sagte Willi. „Tut mir leid. Ich würde es Ihnen ganz bestimmt verraten."

Kurz vor dem Hintereingang trafen sie auf Hieltje. Die Sonne ließ ihr Haar rötlich schimmern. Ihre Lippen waren voll, der geschwungene Amorbogen fett mit Lippenstift bestrichen. Das Kleid betonte ihre breiten Hüften und den üppigen Busen. Für die Tageszeit war sie viel zu elegant gekleidet.

„Liebste Tante", schmeichelte Willi, „ich bringe dir Fräulein Flessner."

Hermine knickste und versuchte über Willis lästerliches Lächeln nicht zu grinsen. Willis Abneigung gegen die Tante schienen alle zu bemerken, nur Hieltje nicht.

Ungeniert betrachtete Hieltje Bakker Hermine. Was sie sah, schien ihr nicht zu gefallen. „Nun", meinte sie gnädig, „es ist ja nur für ein paar Tage." Sie wandte sich ab.

Hermine wechselte mit Willi einen schnellen Blick. Er zuckte mit den Schultern und sie folgte Hieltje in einen Raum neben der Hotelküche, die sie durch eine offen stehende Verbindungstür sehen konnte. Eine Frau stand mit dem Rücken zu ihnen am Herd und hantierte klappernd mit den Töpfen.

Hieltje Bakker stellte sich hinter einen der Stühle, die um einen runden Tisch herumstanden. Hier wurden vermutlich die Mahlzeiten der Mitarbeiter eingenommen. Hieltje Bakker hielt sich mit beiden Händen an der Stuhllehne fest und blickte Hermine finster an. Die Frau machte keinen Hehl daraus, dass sie Hermine, die gut zehn Jahre jünger war als sie, nicht leiden konnte.

„Frau Nörder!", rief Hieltje ungehalten. Das Klappern mit den Töpfen hörte augenblicklich auf und zwei Sekunden später drehte Frau Nörder sich herum und wischte die Hände an ihrer Schürze ab. Ihrem Gesicht war keine Regung angesichts des ungehaltenen Tonfalles anzusehen.

„Frau Bakker?“ Die beiden Worte klangen rebellisch.

Frau Nörder schaute Hieltje herausfordernd an, Hermine schenkte sie keinerlei Beachtung.

„Das ist Ihre neue Aushilfe. Mein Schwager stellt sie uns für eine Weile zur Verfügung.“ Hieltje klang, als würde sie ihrem Schwager damit einen Gefallen tun.

„Sehr schön“, meinte Frau Nörder, ohne den Blick von Hieltje abzuwenden. Auf Hermine hatte es den Eindruck, als würde das Rückgrat der Köchin ein klein wenig weiter nach oben gereckt. Vor ihren Augen schien die Köchin zu wachsen. Sie war das komplette Gegenteil von Gertrud, der Köchin im *Bakker Senior*. Gertrud, groß und hager, Frau Nörder, klein und drall. „Soll sie mir als Küchenhilfe zur Hand gehen?“

„Sie sagen es.“ Ohne ein weiteres Wort verließ Hieltje den Raum.

Erst als die Tür sich hinter ihr geschlossen hatte, wandte Frau Nörder sich an Hermine. Ihr Lächeln verriet, dass sie sich gegenüber ihrer vorgeblichen Vorgesetzten durchgesetzt hatte. „Eigentlich“, sagte sie und grinste breit, „solltest du ja als Zimmermädchen aushelfen. Ich sage einfach Du, ja? Das ärgert sie.“ Nörders Daumen deutete zur Tür. „Ich bin eine geborene Teerling. Wir Teerlings kommen alle aus einem Stall, aber Madame besteht darauf, mich mit *Sie* anzusprechen. Die Gräfin, so nennen wir sie hier, ist dir nicht grün, das sehe ich. Aber das ist sie keinem Mädchen gegenüber, das jung und hübsch ist. Wie gesagt: Ursprünglich solltest du auf die Zimmer gehen, doch das macht jetzt die Maria. Gräm dich nicht, Kindchen. Glaube mir, hier in der Küche bist du gut aufgehoben, zudem ist es besser so.“

Was sollte daran besser sein? Hermine scheute keine Küchenarbeit, doch die Stellung eines Zimmermädchens war eine angenehmere Arbeit. Sie hatte sich nichts zuschulden kommen lassen, was eine Degradierung rechtfertigte. Das sagte sie Frau Nörder.

„An deinem Fleiß und deiner Arbeit liegt es nicht, Kindchen. Du bist einfach zu niedlich, um …"

Willi platzte herein. „Meine Tante hat das Angebot des Tages in letzter Sekunde geändert."

Frau Nörder griff in ihre Schürzentasche und reichte ihm ein Stück Kreide. „Willi hat die schönste Schrift von uns allen", behauptete sie. Der Junge nickte zustimmend. „Nur mit der Rechtschreibung hapert es ein wenig", fügte sie hinzu. Fragend schaute sie den Knaben an, der verlegen die Kreide in seiner Hand betrachtete. Dann schien er sich seiner Aufgabe zu besinnen. „Es soll Schollenfilet mit Krabben, grünem Salat und Bratkartoffeln geben. Und als Nachspeise Krämebrülee."

„Schreib es nur nicht so, wie du es sprichst", warnte Frau Nörder. „Es schreibt sich: C-r-e-m-e, mit einem Strich auf dem E."

„Und ein kleines B, kleines R und ein U mit einem Dach drauf, einem L und zwei E", ergänzte Hermine.

„Sie können Französisch?" Willi schob sein Pagenkäppi zurecht und hinterließ Kreidespuren auf dem Stoff.

„In Leer gibt es die *Waage,* das ist ein Restaurant. Dort kam ich auf dem Weg zur Schule immer vorbei. Die Süßspeise hatten die oft auf ihrer Angebotstafel stehen."

„Dieses vornehme Lokal an der Brücke?", fragte er. „Mit dem Kirchturm auf dem Dach? In der Nähe ist doch immer der Gallimarkt?"

„Jeden Oktober kommen die Schausteller und Viehhändler", bestätigte Hermine. „Seit 1508."

„Schluss mit der Geschichtsstunde!“ Köchin Nörder klatschte in die Hände, dann gab sie Willi Zeichen, die Küche zu verlassen.

„Halt!“, rief sie ihm hinterher.

„Der Fisch wird gleich angeliefert“, sagte Willi ihre Frage vorausahnend.

„Ich hasse es“, jammerte sie, „wenn die Gräfin vom Wochenplan abweicht. Von dem Zwist mit unserer Hausdame einmal abgesehen.“

„Es liegt ein Fischkutter vor dem Nordstrand“, informierte ein stämmiger Mann mit Vollbart und schmuddeliger Kleidung die Köchin. Er schob sich eben an den Frauen vorbei in die Küche. Er trug einen großen Korb und wuchtete ihn auf die Ablage neben dem Herd. Der Mann schien in Eile, doch Frau Nörder hielt ihn auf. „Halt, mein Freund!“, sagte sie. Für Hermine klang die Bezeichnung *Freund* alles andere als nett. Flink griff sie in den Korb, nahm die erste Scholle heraus und warf sie in die Küchenspüle. Dem toten Fisch folgten weitere, bis sie sich plötzlich mit einem in der Hand umwandte und diesen dem Bärtigen zuwarf. Der fing den Plattfisch geschickt auf und grinste breit.

„Den kannst du behalten“, verkündete die Köchin und drohte mit dem Zeigefinger.

„Hat er versucht, Ihnen einen faulen unterzuschieben?“, fragte Hermine, als Mann und Fischkorb wieder verschwunden waren. Die Köchin lachte. „Denk dir nichts dabei. Das Spielchen treiben wir beide schon seit Jahren. Einen mogelt er immer drunter, manchmal auch mehrere. Aber nun zu dir, mein Kind. Du hilfst mir in der Küche und Maria … Ah, da ist sie ja schon.“

Ein Mädchen Anfang zwanzig betrat die Hotelküche. Die mausgrauen Haare klebten ihr am Kopf, das Gesicht war hochrot, als wäre es im Laufschritt einmal um die Insel gerannt. Akne verunzierte Wangen und Stirn. Die Narben und aufgekratzten Wunden an der Nase machten den Anblick nicht schöner.

„Maria, das ist Hermine. Sie kommt vom *Bakker Senior* und hilft uns eine Weile aus. Hermine wird deine Arbeit übernehmen."

Maria schien sich über die Anordnung weder zu wundern noch sich zu fragen, was sie dann machen solle.

„Du wirst für die nächste Zeit zum Zimmermädchen befördert."

Maria nickte. Ob es sie freute, war ihr nicht anzusehen. Kommentarlos verließ sie die Küche.

„Sie kennt das", informierte Frau Nörder Hermine.

„Aber ..."

„An die Arbeit!", befahl die Köchin und deutete auf eine hölzerne Kiste, gefüllt mit Kartoffeln. Hermine verstummte. Sie hatte Frau Nörders Blick über ihre Schulter hinweg zur Küchentür wohl bemerkt. Hermine griff nach einer Küchenschürze, band sie sich um und warf einen verstohlenen Blick zur Tür. Aus dem Augenwinkel konnte sie eben noch die wunderbare moosgrüne Farbe von Hieltje Bakkers Kleid erkennen, ehe sie sich dem Schälen der Kartoffeln zuwandte.

Nach einem langen Arbeitstag in der Hotelküche erzählte sie später, als sie im Bett lag, Mathilde, was sie erlebt hatte.

„Der Fischhändler ist dafür bekannt", meinte Mathilde.

„Das habe ich mir gedacht", sagte Hermine. „Und die Gräfin?"

„Du fragst dich, was sie vorhat?" Mathilde kratzte sich am Kopf. „Ich habe da so eine Ahnung."

„Verrätst du sie mir?"

„Nur so viel: Wenn meine Vermutung stimmt und ich recht behalte, kann ich dir Informationen zu deiner Cousine liefern."

Zu weiteren Äußerungen ließ Mathilde sich nicht überreden.

„Großvater?", fragte Willi am späten Nachmittag, kurz vor dem Abendbrotessen. „Wenn ich jetzt, so wie damals dein Stiefvater, eine siebenundvierzig Jahre jüngere Frau heiraten würde, wären dann alle aus der Familie böse auf mich?"

„Du kannst keine siebenundvierzig Jahre jüngere Frau heiraten, du bist erst zwölf."

„Bald dreizehn. Das war nur ein Vergleich, Großvater." Willi zupfte an seinen Ärmeln, als wären sie ihm nicht lang genug. Großvaters Schweigen machte ihn niemals nervös, heute war das anders. Der Junge fürchtete die Antwort, das konnte man gut erkennen.

„Großvater?"

„Ja?"

„Ich liebe eine ältere Frau und habe Angst, dass die Familie … Ich meine, wenn ich sie heirate, sind sie dann alle sauer auf mich?"

„Wie viel älter ist sie denn?"

„Drei Jahre. Vielleicht auch nur zwei."

Dem Senior sah man an, dass er sich ein Lächeln verkneifen musste. „Nein, Willi. Da wären wir dir bestimmt nicht böse."

Wenn er sich da mal nicht täuschte.

Während die meisten Insulaner arbeiteten und die Gäste sich eine schöne Zeit machten, vertrieben Hieltje und Geeske Bakker sich den Nachmittag mit Einkaufen. Wie oft blieben sie im

Bekleidungsgeschäft Karsten lange genug, um sich die neueste Mode anzusehen. Beide Frauen scheuchten die Ladenbesitzerin und deren Angestellte herum, sodass für die Bedienung von Frau Behrends kaum Zeit blieb. Herr Behrends hatte erst kürzlich die Villa San Remo in der Kirchstraße erbaut. Mit vielen modern eingerichteten Zimmern, die dem neuesten Komfort entsprachen, hatten sie gut zu tun, und bereits Anfragen von Gästen für das kommende Jahr. Als Geeske der Verkäuferin einen Hut aus der Hand nahm, den sie für Frau Behrends geholt hatte, konnte diese sich einen bissigen Kommentar nicht verkneifen. „Ja, geben Sie den Hut nur den Bakkers. Wer weiß, wie lange sie sich solch einen noch leisten können. Seit wir unsere schöne, hochmoderne Villa haben, laufen ihnen die Gäste weg. Und das versetzt mich in die Lage, ein Angebot für ein weiteres Luxushotel abzugeben."

„Hört, hört!" Geeske erkannte Hochmut, war sie doch selbst damit geschlagen und bohrte sofort nach. „Sie persönlich ja wohl kaum", zischte sie.

„Selbstverständlich wird mein Hermann an den Bewerbungen teilnehmen. Schließlich haben wir tausend …" Frau Behrends verstummte und Geeske war es unmöglich, einen triumphierenden Gesichtsausdruck zu unterdrücken.

„Also stimmt es, dass Sie in der Lotterie gewonnen haben?"

Frau Behrends sah sich außerstande, jetzt noch zurückzurudern. „Ganz genau." Die Hände in die Hüften gestemmt, machte sie einen Schritt auf Geeske zu. „Und wir haben es gewinnbringend angelegt."

„Und anstatt das viele schöne Geld zu verprassen, kaufen Sie sich noch mehr Arbeit." Geeskes böses Lachen schallte durch den Laden.

„Wie man hört, steht den Bakkers finanziell das Wasser bis zum Hals.“ Und an Frau Karsten gewandt, fügte sie hinzu: „Ich an Ihrer Stelle würde nichts mehr anschreiben lassen.“

„Eine Unverschämtheit!“, rief Hieltje.

„Sie sagen es“, meinte Frau Behrends, warf den Kopf in den Nacken, nickte der Verkäuferin kurz zu und rauschte wie ein voll getakelter Dreimaster mit Rückenwind aus dem Laden.

„Die Kleider kann sie sich sowieso nicht leisten, wenn ihr Hermann noch eine zweite Villa bauen will.“ Hieltje griff nach dem Gewand, das Karstens Angestellte für Frau Behrends hergeholt hatte, um es sich vorzuhalten. „Grün steht mir sowieso besser als ihr.“ Hieltje fuhr sich mit einer Hand über den hochgesteckten Dutt und drückte leicht dagegen, als müsse sie auf ihre rote Haarpracht extra aufmerksam machen.

Keine Stunde später stand Geeske bei ihrem Vater im Büro und teilte ihm die geschönte Zusammenfassung des Treffens mit. Wichtig war ihr, Papa zu verraten, wer sich ebenfalls an der Ausschreibung beteiligen würde.

Kapitel 11

Luise Menninga war vor vielen Jahren als Borkum-Mädchen auf die Insel gekommen. Sie stammte aus Jemgum an der Ems, einem Dorf in der Nähe von Leer. In den ersten vier Jahren war sie nur für die Sommermonate von Mai bis Anfang Oktober geblieben, um gutes Geld zu verdienen. Im Herbst war sie rechtzeitig nach Hause zurückgegangen, um bei der Ernte zu helfen. Die übrigen Monate im Jahr hatte sie daheim auf den Feldern und in den Gärten geholfen, doch das richtige Geld war mit den Urlaubern zu verdienen.

Luise erinnerte sich gerne an den Jubel, den sie in der Familie bei ihrer Heimkehr stets entfacht hatte. Nicht weil sie vermisst worden war, sondern weil sie nach fünf Monaten auf der Insel reichlich bepackt zurückkehrte. Alle versammelten sich, um zu sehen, was Luise mitgebracht hatte. Die Wäschepakete für die Aussteuer, die Luise wie alle Borkum-Mädchen von den Bakkers am Saisonende als Extrabonus bekam, hatte sie im ersten Jahr für sich behalten. Im zweiten bis zum vierten Jahr hatte sie sie ihren Schwestern geschenkt. Was sollte Luise auch mit vier Aussteuerpaketen? Vermutlich ahnte sie damals schon, dass sie nie einen Ehemann abbekommen würde.

Luises Brüder hingegen lauerten stets darauf, zu erfahren, was Besonderes in ihrem Gepäck steckte. Denn Willem Dirks Bakker erlaubte seinen Bediensteten am Ende der Saison, die Fundstücke, die die Gäste im Hotel und im Restaurant liegen gelassen hatten, unter sich aufzuteilen. Einmal hatte sie ihrem jüngsten Bruder Hinrich ein Paar Badeschuhe mitgebracht. Er war der Einzige, dessen Füße klein genug waren, um hineinzupassen. Seither warteten auch Johannes und Klaus darauf, etwas ähnlich Wertvolles geschenkt zu bekommen. „Geht doch selbst im Sommer nach Borkum!", hatte sie ihnen nach ihrer zweiten Saison geraten. Die Inseln brauchten nicht nur Mädchen für die Hausfrauenarbeiten in den Hotels und der Gastronomie, auch junge Männer wurden händeringend gesucht und fanden in den fünf Sommermonaten überall Arbeit. Wenn sie sich vor keiner Arbeit scheuten. Und das war bei Luises Brüdern so der Fall. Vom Anpacken verstanden sie etwas. Es gab nur ein Hindernis: Sie mussten Frau und Kind und den Hof verlassen und für ihre eigene Arbeitskraft, die dann zu Hause fehlte, jemanden einstellen.

Luise legte einen Regenschirm ins Regal der Fundsachen und lächelte. Was hatte ihre Mutter für große Augen gemacht, als sie ihr vor Jahren einen Schirm mitgebracht hatte. „Den benutzen die feinen Herrschaften sogar bei Sonnenschein", hatte Luise erklärt. „Damit ihre Haut nicht bräunt." Kopfschüttelnd hatte die Mutter das Geschenk entgegengenommen, mit dem Kommentar, lieber die Hautfarbe eines Bauerntrampels zu haben, als mit so einem albernen Ding herumzulaufen. Luise vermutete, dass die Mutter den Schirm nicht einmal bei Regen benutzt hatte. Eine Bäuerin mit Regenschirm – lächerlich, aber aufgespannt im Stall verhinderte er, dass die Regentropfen, die ihren Weg durch das undichte Dach fanden, einer ihrer Kühe aufs Hinterteil fielen.

Luises Finger glitten über einen Seidenschal, der gestern Abend im Restaurant liegen geblieben war. Ein schönes Geschenk für Anneliese. Ihrer Nichte schenkte sie gerne besondere Dinge. Von allen aus ihrer Familie liebte sie dieses Kind am meisten.

Wie bald jeder Mensch hatte auch Luise Geheimnisse. Bei ihr waren es sogar zwei. Sie war seit Jahren unsterblich in einen Mann verliebt und genauso lange litt sie an den Folgen ihres ersten sexuellen Erlebnisses.

Frau Luise verließ die Kammer mit den Fundsachen und traf auf eine Gastdame.

„Ach, gut, dass ich Sie vor meiner Abreise noch sehe." Die Urlauberin gab Luise ein paar Mark.

„Vielen Dank! Ich hoffe, wir sehen uns im kommenden Jahr wieder. Ich wünsche Ihnen eine gute Heimreise."

Luise blickte der Dame hinterher, ehe sie das Geld in ihre Rocktasche steckte. Später würde sie es in den Trinkgeldtopf geben. Der wurde am Ende der Saison zu gleichen Teilen unter den Kollegen aufgeteilt. Ein zusätzliches Geld, das Luise sparte, um sich eines Tages einen Traum zu erfüllen. Welcher das sein würde, wusste sie noch nicht, aber dass er eines Tages da sein würde, da war sie sich sicher.

Der Gedanke an die Verteilung der Trinkgelder erinnerte sie an Hermine, die jetzt unter Hieltje Bakkers Fuchtel stand. Luise konnte nur hoffen, dass Hermine spätestens gegen Ende des Sommers wieder im *Bakker Senior* Dienst tat. Denn Hieltje veranstaltete im *Bakker Junior* jedes Mal beim Verteilen des

Trinkgeldtopfes ein großes Theater. Ihrer Meinung nach stand neben den Angestellten auch den Familienmitgliedern, also ihr, ein Anteil der Trinkgelder zu. Schließlich arbeitete sie genauso im Haus wie jeder andere. „Pah, Arbeit!", murmelte Luise. Als ob die jemals Rückenschmerzen vom vielen Bettenmachen, schrumpelige Hände vom Wäschewaschen oder stinkige Finger vom Fischausnehmen gehabt hätte.

Wenn sie an Hieltje dachte, folgte der Gedanke an Jakob auf dem Fuße.

„Du hast genug Geld", hörte sie Jakob seiner Frau gegenüber bei dieser Gelegenheit jedes Mal Kontra geben. Eine der seltenen Gelegenheiten, bei denen sich die Eheleute vor versammelter Mannschaft zankten und er als Sieger hervorging.

„Und das ist gut so", redete Luise mit sich selbst.

Die Gräfin warf schon genug für Kleider, Schmuck und unnötigen Schnickschnack zum Fenster hinaus. Nun, wenigstens passte sie in dieser Hinsicht mit Schwägerin Geeske Bakker zusammen. Was die beiden in einem Jahr ausgaben, davon hätte Luise sich vermutlich in Jemgum ein Häuschen kaufen können. Aber da wollte sie nicht wieder hin. Borkum war jetzt ihre Heimat. Seit fast zehn Jahren blieb sie auch im Winter. Vielleicht, schoss es ihr durch den Kopf, konnte das ja eines Tages ihr Traum werden. Die eigenen vier Wände auf der Insel.

Und vielleicht würde sie ihre Nichte Anneliese bitten, zu ihr zu ziehen. Spätestens dann sollte sie ihr beichten, in welchem verwandtschaftlichen Verhältnis Anneliese wirklich zu ihr stand.

***

Das schöne Wetter hatte seit Tagen angehalten. Unter den noch kleinen Kastanienbäumen vor dem Hotel summten Insekten in den Blumenkübeln. Heute war Hermines freier Tag und sie beabsichtigte, an den Strand zu gehen.

Keine zehn Minuten später schlenderte sie an braunen Strandkörben vorbei, in denen nur eine Person Platz fand. Gelegentlich sah sie Damen in blau-weißen Badekostümen mit Röckchen und Hose bis über die Knie, die an Marineuniformen erinnerten. Andere Frauen saßen im Strandkleid und mit Sonnenschirm in Liegestühlen und Männer bauten mit Schaufeln Sandburgen. Einige Urlaubsfamilien hatten ihre eigenen Kindermädchen mitgebracht, um die Buben und Mädchen zu beaufsichtigen.

Hermine wünschte, sich irgendwann einmal auch so ein Badekostüm mit großem Marine-Kragen leisten zu können. Vorerst musste sie sich, statt zu baden, weiter mit einem Fußbad im Meer zufriedengeben. Endlich hatte sie die Wasserkante erreicht. Sie wickelte ihren Rock in der Taille ein, damit der Saum nicht nass wurde, und zog die Schuhe aus. Auf dem Weg vom Hauptbadestrand in Richtung Norden suchte sie die Driftkante ab. Die auflaufenden Wellen umspülten die vielen Muscheln und hoben sie an, um sie weiter auf den Strand zu tragen. Ein winziger Strudel trug eine Miesmuschel, die beim Rücklauf der Welle ins Trudeln geriet und mit der Innenseite nach oben liegen blieb. Hermine erinnerte die silbrig glänzende Seite an die Brosche ihrer Großmutter, die sie jeden Sonntag zum Kirchgang anlegte. Hermine hob die Muschel auf, wusch das bisschen Sand mit der nächsten Welle heraus und steckte die Muschelschale in ihre Rocktasche. Einen Seestern, so groß wie ein Handteller, entdeckte sie als Nächstes. Sie nahm ihn auf und drehte ihn herum. Das Tier bewegte seine Saugnäpfe. „Armes Ding!“, sagte Hermine, ging mit ihm einige Schritte ins Meer hinein und ließ es vorsichtig ins Wasser gleiten. Eine vorwitzige Welle erwischte Hermines Rocksaum. Am Bund drehte sie den Stoff weitere zwei Mal nach innen, sodass der Rock über Kniehöhe hochrutschte. Erneut zurück an der Driftkante entdeckte sie mehr Miesmuscheln. Eine bald doppelt so groß wie die anderen und sofort dachte Hermine wieder an ihre Großmutter. Sie hatte erwartet, dass sie sie vermissen würde. „Sobald dich das Heimweh plagt, kommst du zurück“, hatte ihre Oma gemahnt und der Großvater hatte nur knapp gemeint: „Untersteh dich! Die sechs Monate auf Borkum hältst du aus.“ Hermine lächelte bei dem Gedanken und steckte die große Miesmuschel ebenfalls ein. Das glänzende Schwarz erinnerte an Opas Zylinder. Der stand immer oben auf dem Schrank. Auf Opas Kopf hatte sie ihn aber niemals gesehen. Wenige Schritte weiter lagen Herzmuscheln neben kleineren, deren Namen sie nicht wusste. Die kleinen wirkten zerbrechlich, so dünn war die Schale. Eine hatte einen Hauch von Himmelblau, eine andere trug Streifen von Rosa und Weiß. Spontan fiel ihr ihre Schwester Hildegard ein, die bei ihrer Konfirmation eine weiße Bluse getragen hatte. Hildegard war einen Tag vorher zu lange in der Sonne gewesen, sodass ihr Sonnenbrand das Weiß der Bluse besonders hervorgehoben hatte. Die zarte rosa Muschel wanderte ebenfalls in Hermines Rocktasche. Drei unterschiedlich große Schneckengehäuse kamen hinzu. Sie erinnerten an niemanden aus der Heimat, aber sie waren schön anzusehen. Hell- und dunkelbraune sowie schneeweiße Herzmuscheln, die noch zusammenhingen, also sich zuklappen ließen, steckte sie ebenfalls ein. Sogar zwei Hühnergötter fand sie. Steine, mit einem kreisrunden Loch darin. Sie kamen gleichfalls zu ihrer Sammlung. Hermine wollte sich eben von der Driftkante abwenden, als sie etwas gebogenes Schwarzes entdeckte. Sie bückte sich danach und hob es auf. Ein daumenlanger Zahn. Vielleicht von einem Wildschwein? Aber wie sollte der ins Meer kommen? Sicherlich stammte der Zahn von einem Hai. Musste zu Lebzeiten ein dicker Brocken gewesen sein. Nein, ein Haifischzahn konnte es auch nicht sein. Erst vor wenigen Tagen hatte sie bei dem Tierausstopfer in der Straße, die zum Strand führte, komplette Haifischgebisse und mehrere Zähne, die ähnlich aussahen wie dieser, im Schaufenster liegen sehen. Die stammten angeblich von einem Eisbären oder von Walrossen.

Wie auch immer. Ein schwarzer Zahn war etwas Besonderes. Hermine steckte ihn zu den Muscheln in die Rocktasche. Als der Strand einsamer wurde, machte sie sich auf den Weg nach Hause.

Verlaufen konnte sie sich nicht, wenn sie ständig auf den neuen Leuchtturm zuhielt. Sollte es sie irgendwann einmal mitten in der Nacht in diese Gegend verschlagen und sie nicht mehr wissen, wo das Dorf war, könnte sie seine Lichtstrahlen als Orientierungshilfe nutzen. Schon fast wieder in der Nähe des Ortsrandes sah sie ein Häuschen hoch oben auf einer Düne. Zuerst meinte sie, es sei das Ausflugslokal *Viktoriahöhe,* doch sie war schon näher am Ortskern, als sie gedacht hatte.

Köhlers Giftbude.

„Hermine“, rief jemand und winkte ihr heftig. An der dünnen Figur und den langen Beinen, die wie Stöcke wirkten, erkannte sie ihre Arbeitskollegin Mathilde. Hermine hob kurz die Hand zum Gruß und wäre liebend gerne weitergegangen, doch Mathilde rief weiter ihren Namen. Also ging Hermine auf sie zu. Lustwandelnde Herren mit Zylinder und Damen in langen Kleidern kamen ihr entgegen. Ihnen war anzusehen, dass sie hier ihre Ferien verbrachten. Es war keine große Kunst, Gäste von Einheimischen anhand ihrer Kleidung zu unterscheiden. Hermine hatte fast den Fuß der hölzernen Treppe erreicht, die zur Düne hochführte. Dort oben thronte *Köhlers Giftbude*.

Mathilde winkte weiter. „Nun komm schon! Wir gehen nach oben. Ich treffe mich mit ein paar Borkum-Mädchen. Die kannst du gleich kennenlernen."

„Ich weiß nicht." Hermine hob den Blick. Die *Giftbude* sah weniger gefährlich aus, als ihr Ruf es versprach. Ein schlichter Holzbau mit fünf Fenstern zur Seeseite. Mathilde folgte ihrem Blick und deutete Hermines Gesichtsausdruck richtig. „Keine Bange. Hier passiert dir nichts. Da oben bekommt man Kaffee, Kuchen und Eis. Auch Alkohol, aber den muss man ja nicht trinken. Los, sei kein Frosch!"

„Ich kenne doch niemanden."

„Das wird auch so bleiben, wenn du nicht mitkommst."

Also folgte Hermine Mathilde die über drei Absätze hochführende Holztreppe. Vierzig Stufen zählte sie. Von hier oben hatte man einen herrlichen Blick über den Strand und das Meer. Ein paar Segelboote zogen ihre Bahn und die Sonne würde eine ganze Weile brauchen, bis sie am Horizont untergehen würde.

Mathilde deutete auf einen Tisch, an dem ein Mädchen saß. „Das ist Friederike." In dem Moment hatte Friederike sie entdeckt und winkte.

„Moin!", grüßte Mathilde. „Das ist Hermine. Hermine, das ist Friederike." Die beiden nahmen am Tisch Platz. Und schon sprang Mathilde wieder auf. „Ich hole uns etwas zum Trinken. Was wollt ihr haben?"

„Ich nehme eine Fassbrause", sagte Friederike.

Hermine hatte noch nie Brause getrunken. Sie wusste nicht, ob die ihr schmeckte, deswegen entschied sie sich für eine heiße Schokolade. Mathilde rieb Zeige- und Mittelfinger gegen den Daumen und Friederike gab ihr fünfzig Pfennige. Hermine griff in ihre Rocktasche, doch da fand sie nur Muscheln. „Ich lege es für dich aus", verkündete Mathilde großzügig.

„Du arbeitest mit der wilden Hilde zusammen im *Hotel Bakker Senior*", sagte Friederike, als sie zu zweit am Tisch saßen. Es war eher eine Feststellung als eine Frage. Friederike war bestimmt schon siebzehn oder achtzehn Jahre alt, also drei Jahre älter als Hermine. Blond, die Haare geflochten und zu einem Kranz um den Kopf gebunden, darüber das Häubchen eines Zimmermädchens. „Dann müssten wir beide eigentlich Feinde sein."

Hermine sah sie entsetzt an. „Wieso? Ich kenne dich doch erst seit ein paar Minuten. Du scheinst nett zu sein. Warum sollten wir da Feinde werden?"

Friederike lachte. „So habe ich es nicht gemeint. Unsere beiden Häuser sind verfeindet." Sie deutete auf sich und Hermine, die immer noch nicht verstand, was Friederike meinte. „Hat Mathilde dir nichts davon erzählt?"

„Nein." Doch, dachte Hermine, aber nun fand sie, es sei zu spät, es zu erwähnen.

„Nun ..." Friederike schaute sich um, als ob sie sichergehen wollte, dass niemand sie hörte. „Ich war ja schon letzten Sommer als Borkum-Mädchen auf der Insel. Da war noch alles in Ordnung." Friederike fasste sich an den Kopf, um zu kontrollieren, ob ihr Zimmermädchenhäubchen richtig saß. Sowohl im *Hotel Bakker Junior* als auch im *Senior* sahen es die Herrschaften nicht gerne, wenn die Mitarbeiter in ihrer Freizeit Arbeitskleidung trugen. Außerhalb des Hauses war es nur erlaubt, wenn sie im Auftrag des Hotels unterwegs waren.

„In Ordnung?“, fragte Hermine, weil Friederike so ausschaute, als erwartete sie die Frage.

„Ja. Da waren die Herren Bakker und Köhler noch so dicke miteinander.“ Friederike legte beide Zeigefinger nebeneinander.

„Und jetzt?“, fragte Hermine.

„Jetzt sind sie sich spinnefeind. Und ehe du fragst, warum, kann ich dir nur sagen: Keiner weiß es. Man sagt, sie waren die dicksten Kumpel seit Kindertagen und nur eine Winzigkeit habe diese Freundschaft zerstört.“

„Dann können sie nicht wirklich Freunde gewesen sein“, meinte Hermine und kam sich ein wenig schäbig vor, so zu tun, als wüsste sie nicht Bescheid.

„Redet ihr von unseren Alten?“ Mathilde kam mit einem vollen Tablett an den Tisch und stellte vor jedem ein Getränk ab. Das Tablett lehnte sie auf der Fensterbank an die Scheibe und setzte sich.

„Ich wollte, du würdest sie nicht immer Alte nennen.“

Mathilde ignorierte sie. Friederike schenkte sich aus der Flasche etwas ins Glas ein. „Doch, doch. Das waren sie: die dicksten Freunde“, wiederholte sie.

„Es heißt“, mischte sich Mathilde ein, „es sei eine Kleinigkeit gewesen.“

Hermine konnte Mathilde ansehen, dass es sie wurmte, das Geheimnis noch nicht gelüftet zu haben.

„Das sagte ich bereits“, meinte Friederike und Hermine testete mit den Lippen, ob die Schokolade schon Trinktemperatur erreicht hatte. Sie war noch zu heiß.

Friederike nahm einen Schluck von ihrer Brause und beugte sich vor. „Man sagt …“, ihr Zeigefinger winkte den beiden, die sich ebenfalls vorbeugten. „Man sagt“, wiederholte sie ein wenig leiser, „der Köhler habe einen exklusiven Liefervertrag mit der Brausefirma“, sie hob ihr Glas, „abgeschlossen und seither wird das *Hotel Bakker* nicht mehr damit beliefert.“

„Brausefirma?“, fragte Hermine und Mathilde deutete in die Richtung, in der das Dorf lag. „Wirst du noch sehen, wo die ist. Du kennst dich ja auf der Insel noch nicht so gut aus. Jedenfalls wird da die Brause in Flaschen abgefüllt.“

„Zumindest“, sagte Friederike, „ist das für Bakker ganz schön peinlich. In seinem Restaurant kann er sie niemandem anbieten, denn die gibt es nur bei uns.“ In dem Augenblick kam ein junger Mann mit zwei Flaschen des besagten Kribbelwassers an ihrem Tisch vorbei. Friederike deutete darauf. „Und natürlich hier. Die *Giftbude* gehört ja dem Köhler.“

Hermine dachte an die fünf Kisten, die erst letzte Woche mit besagter Fassbrause im Hotel angeliefert worden waren. Demnach konnte Friederikes Behauptung nicht stimmen. Eine Täuschung. Vermutlich, so überlegte Hermine, war der Umzug des Postamtes auch schon lange geplant und wurde nur als weiterer Zank der beiden Parteien ausgegeben. Die alten Herren waren gute Schauspieler und Hermine hatte nicht vor, sie zu verraten.

„Und das Post- und Telegrafenamt?“, fragte sie, um zu erfahren, was darüber geredet wurde.

„Ein Punkt für euch“, meinte Friederike und nippte leicht verstimmt an ihrer Brause.

„Was wird denn aus den leer stehenden Räumen?“

„Einmal *durchgewitjet* und schon standen am nächsten Tag gemütliche Sessel, Tische und ein Klavier darin.“

Durchgewitjet bedeutete, dass die Maler da gewesen waren.

„Es heißt", Friederike machte ein Gesicht, als könne sie es nicht glauben, „dass erst letzten Monat ein Berliner etwas vorgestellt hat, mit dem man ohne Instrument Musik machen kann. Und dann singt auch noch jemand dazu, der gar nicht da ist. Grammfon oder so ähnlich heißt es. Jedenfalls will unser Chef so ein Ding so bald wie möglich anschaffen. Damit wäre *Köhlers Dorfhotel* eurem Haus wieder einen Schritt voraus." Friederikes Augen leuchteten und sie erzählte eine weitere Anekdote. Angeblich habe Köhler Bakker eine Maus in die Küche geschmuggelt, und Mathilde konterte damit, dass Bakker den Pagen aus *Köhlers Dorfhotel* mit einem Koffer, in dem sich angeblich ein Stein befunden habe, zum Strand geschickt habe. Dem Hoteldiener hätte er vorgelogen, das Gepäck habe ein Köhler'scher Hotelgast vergessen und benötige es noch vor der Ausschiffung. Irgendwie hatte Hermine das Gefühl, dass Mathilde sich diese Geschichte eben erst aus den Fingern gesogen hatte.

Die Sonne ging in prächtigen Farben unter. Das Meer schien rot, gelb, orange und lila zu glühen und die wenigen Wolken, die heraufgezogen waren, wurden zehn Minuten nach dem Sonnenuntergang farbig angeleuchtet. Es wurde Zeit, nach Hause zu gehen.

Hermine war froh, jetzt wieder im *Senior* zu arbeiten. Adeline war im Gegensatz zu Hieltje besser zu ertragen. Adeline wusste wenigstens, wie man ein Hotel führte.

***

Ein Mal im Monat, von Mai bis September, fanden im Hotel Bakker Musikabende statt. Ein einzelner Tenor und der Männergesangsverein *Liederfranz* hatten sich angesagt. Sie kamen aus Oldenburg und sangen mit Klavierbegleitung.

„Heute Abend muss alles perfekt sein. Achten Sie darauf! Nicht, dass einer vom Personal einen schmutzigen Hemdkragen hat oder ..." Jakobs Anweisungen an Frau Luise klangen herablassend. Zudem ging es ihn nichts an, was im Hotel seines Bruders geschah.

„Ach, halt doch den Mund!", fauchte Luise.

„Für Sie, Frau Menninga, immer noch Herr Bakker. Sie haben mich nicht zu duzen!"

„Wenn du mir das damals gesagt hättest, wäre mir viel erspart geblieben." Luises Augen funkelten böse und er wirkte, als habe sie ihm eine Ohrfeige verpasst. Die Erkenntnis traf ihn wie ein Schlag. Sie spiegelte sich in seinen Augen wider. Die Art, wie sein Gesicht zu versteinern schien, zeigte, dass ihn Luises Worte mehr erschütterten, als ein einfacher Widerspruch einer Angestellten es jemals hätte tun können.

Kommentarlos wandte er sich ab. Sein gehetzter Schritt wirkte, als seien nicht nur der Klabautermann, sondern alle Monster der See hinter ihm her. Bei Jakob schien endlich der Groschen gefallen zu sein, dachte Luise. Nach all den Jahren wurde es langsam Zeit. Minutenlang stand sie wie gelähmt da. Was sie sich all die Zeit in Gedanken ausgemalt hatte, war heute aus einem Impuls heraus ganz anders geschehen, als sie es sich je vorgestellt hatte. Doch das Ziel war das gleiche: Jakob endlich wissen zu lassen, was sie vor zwölf Jahren ins Hotel Bakker verschlagen hatte. Sollte seine Erinnerung an gemeinsam verbrachte Stunden jetzt und auf so profane Weise hier auf dem

Flur, quasi zwischen Tür und Angel, zurückgekommen sein? Luise hatte es sich immer ganz anders vorgestellt. Sie hatte davon geträumt, dass Jakobs Reaktion eine sanftere sein würde. Eine ohne Schrecken, Zorn und Fluchtverhalten, sondern mit Freude. Sie hätte es besser wissen müssen, doch wie hieß es so schön: Die Hoffnung stirbt zuletzt. „Aber sie stirbt dennoch", murmelte sie, weiter zur Säule erstarrt und mit einer Angst, die ihre Zukunft zerstören könnte.

Jemand klatschte in die Hände. „Von Ihnen, Frau Luise, hätte ich das nie erwartet." Mathildes tadelnder Tonfall brachte Leben in ihre steifen Glieder.

Verflucht – ausgerechnet Mathilde hatte die unglückliche Szene mitbekommen!

„Wer wird sterben?" Mathildes Blick war lauernd wie der einer Möwe, die auf eine Gelegenheit wartete, einem unbedarften Urlauber ein Fischbrötchen aus der Hand zu reißen.

„Niemand."

„Sie machen sich doch keine Hoffnungen", Mathildes Lachen klang gemein, „auf den schönen Jakob? Ihre Avancen wird er kaum erwidern. Der schaut nur jungem Gemüse hinterher."

Luise war erleichtert, weil Mathilde eine völlig falsche Schlussfolgerung aus der Begegnung gezogen hatte. Deshalb kam ihr die Gegenfrage locker über die Lippen.

„Wollen Sie damit sagen, ich sei alt?" Luise war im vergangenen November einunddreißig geworden.

„Absolut. Ich meine, für bestimmte Männer schon. An alte Schachteln verschwendet *der* keinen einzigen Gedanken. Aber keine Bange, Frau Luise. Ihr Geheimnis ist bei mir sicher aufgehoben." Mathilde machte sich auf den Weg in die Wäschekammer. Ihrem beschwingten Schritt konnte Luise ansehen, dass sie zufrieden war, etwas gefunden zu haben, wonach Luise ihr verpflichtet war.

„Wenn du die Wahrheit wüsstest!“, flüsterte Luise. *Erst dann hätte ich Grund, deine böse Zunge zu fürchten.*

Kapitel 12

Willem Dirks Bakker empfing Georg Köhler in seinem Kontor. Gegen elf Uhr war die beste Tageszeit und das Büro der sicherste Ort, um vom Personal und dem Rest der Familie ungestört zu sein. Alle waren zu diesem Zeitpunkt beschäftigt: Die Zimmermädchen werkelten in den Gästezimmern; das Küchenpersonal bereitete das Mittagessen vor; die Servicekräfte deckten die Tische ein; die Wäscherinnen waren sowieso rund um die Uhr tätig und der Page brachte das Gepäck der Gäste zum Schiff oder half auf dem Hof, die Lieferungen entgegenzunehmen. Niemand bemerkte, wie Köhler ins Haus kam. Die Zeit, da sie aller Welt vormachten, sie könnten sich aufgrund eines Vorfalles, den es nie gegeben hatte, gegenseitig nicht mehr ausstehen, würde bald vorbei sein. Nur noch wenige Wochen, dann lief die Bewerbungsfrist für die Grundstücke aus.

„Was ist so wichtig, dass du mich unbedingt sprechen wolltest?" Bakker bedeutete seinem Freund, er möge sich setzen.

Ehe Köhler Platz nahm, reichte er ihm einen Brief. Köhler schaute darauf und hob den Kopf. „Er ist an dich gerichtet."

„Schau rein."

Köhler zog das Blatt Papier aus dem Umschlag.

„Lies ihn“, forderte Bakker seinen Freund auf.

„Hundert Mark oder ich verrate, was für ein Geheimnis Sie und Köhler haben. – Erpressung?“

„Du sagst es. Jemand scheint an unserem Theater verdienen zu wollen.“

Köhler blickte auf den Umschlag. „Keine Briefmarke, also ist er persönlich abgegeben worden. Von unserer gemeinsamen Freundin?“

„Hermine Flessner?“

Köhler wiegte den Kopf hin und her.

Sie schwiegen eine Weile. Dann schüttelten beide gleichzeitig den Kopf. „Nein“, meinten sie unisono. Hermine trauten sie eine Erpressung nicht zu. Mathilde Remmers schon eher und das sagte Bakker auch.

„Wir sollten mit dem Theater aufhören.“ Köhler wedelte mit dem Umschlag. „Dann hat sich das hier von selbst erledigt.“

„Da hast du recht.“

Sie hingen eine Weile schweigend ihren eigenen Gedanken nach. „Es ist schade um die kuriosen Geschichten, die entstehen“, meinte Köhler. „Jede Kleinigkeit, die daneben geht, wird euch angehängt.“

„In meinem Haus ist es das Gleiche.“

Keinem der beiden wäre der Gedanken gekommen, dem anderen Kakerlaken in den Vorratsraum zu setzen oder gar eine Ratte in eine Mülltonne zu werfen. Die Kakerlaken waren sicherlich von der Bäckerei nebenan herübergekommen und die Ratte war ganz bestimmt von allein hineingefallen und nicht mehr herausgekommen.

„Schade, es hat mir richtig Spaß gemacht.“

„Mir auch.“

„Fast so wie damals, als dein Stiefvater uns auf seinen Seereisen mitgenommen hat." Köhler lächelte bei den Erinnerungen. „Und dann hat van Dyk so getan, als kämen die Franzosen, und wir haben alles versteckt, was herumlag."

„Er wollte nur, dass wir aufräumen."

„Bestimmt. Hat dennoch Spaß gemacht. Ich glaubte manchmal wirklich, Franzmänner gesehen zu haben."

„Ich spüre noch heute das Kribbeln im Bauch", ergänzte Bakker. „Man darf sich nur nicht erwischen lassen", fügte er Klaas van Dyks Lebensweisheit hinzu.

„Uns scheint jemand erwischt zu haben." Georg Köhler legte den Brief beiseite. „Was machen wir?"

„Abwarten, bis die zweite Mitteilung kommt, wo und wann das Geld zu übergeben ist. Dann überlegen wir weiter."

„Gut. Ach übrigens ..." Köhler grinste. „Ich habe gehört, die Kammersängerin aus Berlin hat für neuen Familienzwist gesorgt? Ich hatte sie ja engagiert, aber dein Sohn hat sie mir abspenstig gemacht. Gegen Jakobs Charme konnte ich leider nicht anstinken."

„Bist du sauer?"

„Nein."

Sie tauschten einen verschwörerischen Blick. „Wusstest du, dass es laut Aussage unserer Mitarbeiter elf zu zwölf gegen dich steht?"

Bakker schüttelte den Kopf. „So viele Streiche haben wir ja gar nicht angezettelt."

„Das mit den geräucherten Wurstwaren hat Frau Dirksen dir übelgenommen. In der Küche hat sie Zeter und Mordio geschrien, weil sie den Speiseplan und die Werbetafel auf den letzten Drücker ändern musste."

„Verzeih.“ Köhler klang, als bereue er es nicht. „Aber ich brauchte sie dringlich in der *Giftbude*.“

„Spar dir die Entschuldigung. Was gibt es Neues aus der Sitzung des Gemeinderates?“, wechselte Bakker das Thema.

„Man wundert sich, dass du ein Angebot auf ein zweites Grundstück abgegeben hast.“

„Konntest du Einblick nehmen?“

„Nein. Solange ich selbst mich bewerbe, werden mir die Zahlen, für die wir uns interessieren, vorenthalten. Aber …“

„Du hast ja Frau Wenke.“

Sie war Köhlers Spionin im Amt und würde ihm bald wieder berichten. Witwe Wenke tat alles für Georg Köhler, seit er vor vielen Jahren ihr und ihrem mittlerweile verstorbenen Ehemann geholfen hatte, nachdem sie in finanzielle Not geraten waren. Köhler hatte verhindern können, dass Familie Wenke ihr Haus räumen musste. Frau Wenke war Köhlers und Bakkers Ass im Ärmel gegenüber anderen Bewerbern. Denn so sehr sie Köhler verehrte, so sehr verachtete sie Bakker. Wie so oft – Jakob und seine Liebeleien hatten Schuld daran.

Eine Situation, die die Herren ausnutzten. Frau Wenke würde nicht zögern und Köhler Daten der Konkurrenz verraten, damit er sein Angebot in letzter Minute anpassen konnte. Das würde nur so lange gut gehen, wie sie ihren angeblichen Krach glaubhaft aufrechterhielten.

„Manchmal habe ich schon ein schlechtes Gewissen“, meinte Köhler.

„Wir müssen noch ein wenig durchhalten.“

„Und hoffen, dass wir das überstehen.“

***

Das Restaurant war voll besetzt. Die Wände waren bis auf Hüfthöhe getäfelt, darüber eine edle Tapete mit Paradiesvögeln und Palmen. Die Stühle mit rotem Leder bezogen, unter der Decke Lüster, in deren gläsernen Perlenbehang sich das Licht tausendmal widerspiegelte. Die Stirnwand war in schlichtem Weiß gehalten, damit die prunkvollen übergroßen Ölbilder, die alle Schiffe in aufgepeitschter See zeigten, zur Geltung kamen. Davor stand ein ovaler Tisch, an dem sechs Personen saßen. Die gefüllten Rotweingläser reflektierten das Deckenlicht. Gläser klirrten, Servierkräfte trugen Tabletts, leise Gespräche unterschieden sich kaum von der Lautstärke des Klavierspielers. Neben der Musik wurde den Gästen heute Abend etwas Besonderes geboten: Hummer von Helgoland.

Rechts neben ihrem Ehemann August Theilen saß Heidrun, ihre Hand lag auf seiner. Ihr gegenüber starrte der Künstler Max Liebermann darauf, als gefiele ihm das überhaupt nicht. Nervös auf seinem Stuhl, rutschte linker Hand Carl Busse, Schauspieler am Meininger Theater, auf der Fläche herum, als müsse er sich mit dem Hintern eine Kuhle graben, damit er gemütlicher säße. Der Fotograf Bernd Uden war der Einzige am Tisch, der nicht als Gast auf Borkum weilte. Er verbrachte die zweite Saison auf der Insel und beteuerte eben, wie gut die Geschäfte liefen, so dass er beabsichtige, ein eigenes Ladenlokal sowie ein Logierhaus zu kaufen und für immer zu bleiben. Er wischte sich mit dem Handrücken Rotwein von den Lippen.

Ihm gegenüber saß Sigfried Plaue. Er erzählte von seinen Fabriken und dass ihm gute Freunde die Insel empfohlen hätten. Neben ihm seine Ehefrau Viola, die sich bereits zum zweiten Mal Wein nachschenkte, den finsteren Blick ihres Mannes ignorierend. Die Sängerin aus Berlin, die in *Köhlers Dorfhotel*

Quartier genommen hatte – böse Zungen behaupteten, sie sei vor Jakobs Avancen aus dem *Bakker Junior* geflohen –, berichtete von ihren triumphalen Auftritten in Hamburg und Leipzig. Die Inseln abklappern täte sie nur, weil ihr die Luft so wunderbar bekäme.

„Das verstehe ich gut", meinte Frau Theilen, „eine Sängerin mit Atemproblemen hält sich sicherlich nicht lange in der Branche." Ihr Mann schüttelte ihre Hand ab, um einen Schluck Wein trinken zu können, und versteckte sie danach unter dem Tisch. Die Sängerin ließ sich gerade über ihr neuestes Engagement aus, das sie von Berlin nach Zürich und Paris führen würde, als der Fotograf mit schwerer Zunge sagte: „Ich möchte die reizenden Damen bitten, einmal in meinem Atelier vorbeizuschauen. Meine Fotos werden Ihnen und vor allem Ihren Ehemännern sicherlich gefallen."

Niemand reagierte darauf. In diesem Moment wurden die leeren Teller der Vorspeise, Krabben in einer Cocktailsoße, abgetragen.

Herr Plaue hatte einen Klecks Soße auf sein Hemd bekommen, was seine Frau mit einem Blick quittierte, als wolle sie sagen: „Hättest du doch dein Lätzchen umgehängt!" Um auf sein Thema zurückzukommen, verkündete Fotograf Uden, dass es schon mehr bedürfe, als einfach nur ein paar Fotos von den Urlaubern zu machen, wenn man vernünftig Geld verdienen wolle. Die Sängerin hakte nach, was das *mehr* denn wohl sein könnte, doch Uden winkte ab. Aufgrund des schweren Weines hatte er vermutlich schon zu viel verraten. Schnell lenkte er das Gespräch auf die von der Gemeinde geplanten Luxushotels, die in den kommenden Jahren am Hauptbadestrand entstehen sollten.

„Bei den steigenden Urlauberzahlen ein lohnendes Geschäft“, meinte Theilen. „Wenn ich einige Jahre jünger wäre“, er warf einen schnellen Seitenblick auf seine Ehefrau, „und mit entsprechender Partnerin, würde ich einen Prachtbau hinsetzen, den Deutschland noch nicht gesehen hat.“

„Wenn *ich* jünger wäre“, sagte seine Frau, „würde ich mir jemanden suchen, der weniger kahl und …“

Sie wurde unterbrochen, da der Hauptgang aufgetragen wurde. Eine Serviererin sammelte die restlichen Teller der Vorspeise ein und gleichzeitig wurde die freie Stelle auf dem Tisch durch den Teller mit einem halben Hummer darauf ersetzt.

„Helgoländer Hummer. Heute Morgen frisch angeliefert“, sagte die Bedienung. Die Gäste griffen nach ihren Hummerzangen. Das Knacken der Panzer ging in einem Schlussakkord des Klavierspielers unter.

„Endlich macht er Pause“, meinte Frau Plauen. „Aus dem Geklimper kann ja kein Mensch eine Melodie heraushören.“

„Wenn man von Mozart keine Ahnung hat, vielleicht“, murmelte die Sängerin und steckte sich ein Hummerstück in den Mund. Fotograf Uden war als Erster fertig und griff quer über den Tisch hinweg nach der Weinflasche. Fast hätte er dabei den dreiarmigen Kerzenleuchter in der Mitte des Tisches umgeworfen. „Verflixt!“, schnaubte er und Hermine Flessner, die eben nach seinem leer gegessenen Teller greifen wollte, meinte, angekokelte Haare zu riechen. Uden schenkte sich den Rest ins Glas und hielt die Flasche Hermine unter die Nase, in stummer Aufforderung, eine neue zu bringen.

Hoffentlich hat der Blödmann sich den Arm ordentlich verbrannt, dachte Hermine.

„Lass uns erst die Nachspeise servieren", flüsterte Oberkellner Paul ihr zu, „ehe die zu betrunken sind, um die Kochkünste unserer Küche zu genießen."

Nachdem die Teller des Hauptganges eingesammelt waren, half Hermine, den Nachtisch zu servieren. Als sie Frau Plaue einen kleinen Kristallteller hinstellte, hörte sie diese zur Sängerin sagen: „Ich hörte, dass sich der Inselarzt ebenfalls um eines der Grundstücke bewirbt. Als ob es mit Pillen und Spritzen nicht genug zu verdienen gäbe."

„Meine Liebe", mischte sich ihr Gatte ein, „wie oft soll ich es dir noch sagen: Verdienen kann man nie genug."

Den Rest des Abends verbrachte Hermine mit dem Gedanken, ob sie die Neuigkeiten Bakker Senior erzählen sollte. Sie würden ihn sicherlich interessieren. Andererseits, überlegte sie, wusste er das bestimmt schon längst.

Am nächsten Nachmittag zeigte das Thermometer sechsundzwanzig Grad an. Fotograf Uden schaute zum Himmel hoch. Seit einiger Zeit hatte es nicht mehr geregnet. Wiesen, Gärten und Dünen waren knochentrocken. Es brauchte nur ein winziges Flämmchen, und man musste mit einem Dünenbrand rechnen. Dann sollte er bereit sein, um einige Fotos von der Freiwilligen Feuerwehr zu machen. Solche Bilder ließen sich gut an Zeitungen verkaufen.

Bernd Uden ging im Schlingerschritt am Fuß der Treppe zu *Köhlers Giftbude* vorbei. In der Hand hielt er seine Kamera, die an einem hölzernen Stativ befestigt war. Hier im Schatten der hohen Düne versprach er sich die besten Fotoaufnahmen. Gelegentlich sprach er die Gäste an und sobald einer nickte, stellte er das Stativ auf, verschwand unter einem schwarzen Tuch und brachte für das benötigte Licht für die Aufnahme einen Blitzbeutel zum Explodieren. Das entzückte die Mädchen. Besonders Friederike klatschte übermütig wie ein kleines Kind in die Hände und rief mehrmals: „Das will ich auch!“

Hermine hatte den Mann, der gestern Abend im Restaurant gesessen, Hummer gegessen und zu viel Rotwein getrunken hatte, sofort wiedererkannt. Sie war nicht erpicht darauf, sich ablichten zu lassen, da ihm die Aufnahmen nach seinen eigenen Aussagen ein Vermögen einbrächten. Sie würde sich ein Bild von sich selbst kaum leisten können.

Die jungen Frauen beobachteten den Fotografen eine Weile. Es dauerte nicht lange, da waren sich die Kolleginnen einig, sich alle miteinander von ihm auf Zelluloid bannen zu lassen. So stand Hermine eingerahmt von der dicken Friederike auf der rechten Seite und der dünnen Dagmar auf der linken. Dahinter stellten sich Mathilde und Erika, Verkäuferin in einem Kleidergeschäft, sowie ein junger Mann in hellen Hosen und weißem Pullover, den Erika fest am Arm hielt. Man merkte, dass er nicht mit auf das Bild wollte. Zu ihren Füßen legten sich drei kleine Jungen, die alle in einem Matrosenanzug steckten. Der Fotograf drängte noch zwei weitere Personen dazu, mit aufs Foto zu kommen, und bat dann alle, sich aufrecht zu halten, zu lächeln und sich nicht zu bewegen. Als erneut der Blitzbeutel in seiner linken Hand explodierte, der Kopf des Fotografen steckte unter dem schwarzen Tuch, war Friederike wie aus dem Häuschen. Sie hüpfte herum, als habe sie etwas gestochen, schoss dann auf den Fotografen zu und wollte sofort das Bild sehen.

„So schnell geht das nicht, junges Fräulein.“ Bernd Uden gab ihr und allen anderen, die auf dem Bild sein würden, einen Zettel in die Hand. Darauf stand sein Name, die Adresse des

Geschäftes und das heutige Datum. „Bitte kommen Sie morgen zu mir in den Laden."

„Dann ist das Foto fertig?", fragte Friederike.

Uden nickte, griff nach dem Stativ und eilte weiter. Man hatte den Eindruck, als würde er vor Friederike fliehen.

Die Gruppe löste sich auf. Mathilde fasste Hermine an der Hand und zog sie mit sich, dem Fotografen hinterher.

„Schnell, dann erwischen wir ihn noch. Lass dich nicht so ziehen!", meinte Mathilde. „Es wäre doch schön, wenn der Mann nur von uns beiden ein Foto machen würde."

Sie erwischten ihn, bevor er anderen Touristen seine Arbeit in den höchsten Tönen anpreisen konnte.

Uden hat listige, wenn nicht gar hinterlistige Augen, dachte Hermine, als sein Kopf unter dem Tuch verschwand, um ein Foto, in der Sonne ohne Blitzbeutel, erst von ihnen beiden, dann von jeder allein, zu machen.

Hermine fühlte sich unwohl bei der Sache. Andererseits lockte die Aussicht auf ein Bild, auf dem nur sie zu sehen war, plötzlich doch.

Als Mathilde das Misstrauen in Hermines Augen sah, meinte sie: „Komm schon, Mädchen! Das wird ein Spaß! Wann bekommt unsereiner mal ein Foto von sich zu sehen?"

Als Hermine immer noch zögerte, fügte sie hinzu: „Das wäre doch ein schönes Geschenk für deine Mutter."

Das Argument zog.

***

Während die Kolleginnen sich am Strand vergnügten, saß Frau Luise im Schatten des Hotelhofes auf der Bank und grübelte.

Früher war sie eine ansehnliche junge Frau gewesen, klein und grazil, die sich im zarten Alter von vierzehn Jahren von einem Mann hatte verführen lassen. Sie sah es vor sich, als wäre es gestern gewesen. Es war beim Gallimarkt in Leer geschehen. Luises Vater hatte dort zwei Kälbchen verkaufen wollen und hatte Luise in die große Stadt mitgenommen. Sie war von den neuen Eindrücken fasziniert gewesen. Obwohl sie auf dem Land und fernab vieler Menschen aufgewachsen war, konnte sie doch auf den ersten Blick erkennen, dass der schicke junge Kerl kein Bauer war, sondern sich die Ausstellung und die Viehauktion nur aus Spaß ansah. Der schmucke, gut aussehende Mann beobachtete die Viehversteigerung und schnell hatte Luise gemerkt, dass er auch sie öfter als schicklich ansah. Nachdem Vater seine Kälbchen verkauft hatte, drückte er Luise ein paar Münzen in die Hand, damit sie sich auf dem Jahrmarkt vergnügen konnte. Karussell fahren, einen mit roter Glasur überzogenen Apfel essen. Er selbst ging in die *Waage*, ein Lokal am Fuße der Brücke, gleich am Leeraner Hafen, um mit Bier auf sein abgeschlossenes Geschäft anzustoßen. Luise sollte ihn in drei Stunden dort abholen. Im Nachhinein wusste Luise sich nicht zu erklären, warum sie sich von dem jungen unbekannten Mann hatte einlullen lassen. Fakt war jedenfalls, dass sie es genoss, von ihm beachtet zu werden. Er spendierte ihr die Fahrten im Kettenkarussell, schoss ihr an einer Bude mit einem Gewehr eine Rose aus Papier und schenkte ihr kandierte Mandeln sowie ein Lebkuchenherz. Und ehe sie sichs versah, folgte sie seinen Verlockungen, sich einmal sein elegantes Hotelzimmer mit fließendem Wasser und elektrischem Licht gleich am

Rande des Gallimarktes anzusehen. Was dort geschah, war Luise im Nachhinein wie ein wunderbarer Rausch und eine heftige Katastrophe zugleich vorgekommen. Anschließend war sie pünktlich in der *Waage* erschienen, um ihren Vater abzuholen.

Damals hatte sie noch geglaubt, den Fremden wiederzusehen, denn er hatte sich ihren Namen und ihre Anschrift extra auf einem Bogen Papier, das im Hotelzimmer auf einem winzigen Schreibtisch lag, notiert. Aber er hatte sich nie gemeldet. Eine erneute Begegnung mit ihm kam erst Jahre später zustande. Und dieses Wiedersehen traf sie wie ein Schock.

Doch zurück zu dem Oktober, an dem Luise zum ersten Mal auf dem Gallimarkt in Leer gewesen war. Wenige Wochen danach merkte sie, dass sie schwanger war. Ein vierzehnjähriges unverheiratetes Mädchen mit einem Kind galt als Schande für sie selbst und für die gesamte Verwandtschaft. Luises Zukunft war ruiniert. Wie so oft fand die Familie Menninga eine Lösung. Luises ältere Schwester Renate, sie hatte den Sohn des Nachbarbauern geheiratet, gab es als ihr Kind aus. Dem Schwager war es recht, denn die beiden waren schon einige Jahre verheiratet und hatten immer noch keinen eigenen Nachwuchs. Und obwohl sie dieses Geheimnis gut gehütet hatten, hatte es in den Anfangsjahren doch gelegentlich dörfliches Gerede gegeben.

Luise hatte weiter auf dem Hof gearbeitet, und als sie siebzehn war, war sie als Borkum-Mädchen zum ersten Mal auf die Insel gegangen, wo ihr Jakob erneut begegnete. Der erkannte sie jedoch nicht wieder und Luise hatte genügend Selbstbewusstsein entwickelt, um sich ihm nicht ein zweites Mal an den Hals zu werfen.

Jedes Mal, wenn sie jemanden aus Leer traf, so wie damals Hermine bei ihrer Ankunft, bekam sie weiche Knie und Herzflattern. Es bestand immer die Möglichkeit, dass die Person Luise oder einen aus der Familie Menninga kannte. Von Hermine Flessner war in dieser Hinsicht nichts zu befürchten, sonst hätte sie es längst herausbekommen.

Und jetzt die vermaledeite Begegnung mit Jakob, bei der sie anfangs überzeugt gewesen war, er habe in ihr endlich seine Liebschaft von damals wiedererkannt.

Seit ihrem Wutausbruch war sie Jakob nicht mehr begegnet und sie fragte sich, wie ein neuerliches Aufeinandertreffen ausfallen mochte.

***

Hermines Weg führte sie in die Strandstraße zum Fotoatelier.

Jean Baptiste Feiler, Hofphotograph, so stand es in großen schwarzen Lettern über dem Eingang des Ladens.

Und auf der Glasscheibe der Tür empfahl Feiler sein *altrenommiertes Atelier zu Aufnahmen jeden Genres. Passende Dekoration im Atelier.*

Hermine betrat den Laden. Es roch unangenehm. Beißend. Vermutlich eine Mischung aus irgendwelchen Chemikalien, die zur Herstellung von Fotografien benötigt wurden. Der Geruch schlug ihr kurz auf den Magen.

Hermine versuchte, flach zu atmen. „Guten Tag, Herr Feiler."

„Mein Name ist Uden. Der Hofphotograph Feiler ist so gut wie nie auf der Insel. Er hat Läden in Bremen, Braunschweig und Hannover, da kann er nicht überall sein."

„Ich hätte gerne die fotografischen Aufnahmen vom Nordstrand, auf denen ich und ein paar andere Mädchen abgebildet wurden, gesehen." Den Zettel, den er am Strand verteilt hatte, reichte sie ihm über den Tresen.

„Sehr schön."

„Ich würde gerne eine kaufen. Als Geschenk für meine Mutter oder als Erinnerung an den schönen Tag", sagte sie.

„Da hat die junge Dame ganz richtig entschieden", meinte Bernd Uden. Wie gestern fand Hermine auch heute sein Lächeln unecht. Vermutlich, weil er den ganzen Tag die Urlauber angrinsen und den fröhlichen Mann spielen musste, wie er es am Strand bei den Aufnahmen getan hatte. In seiner Gegenwart fühlte sie sich unwohl.

„Ich zeige Ihnen jetzt die belichteten Glasplatten. Sie müssen sie gegen das Licht halten, um zu sehen, welche der Aufnahmen Ihnen gefällt."

„Die Bilder sind nicht fertig?"

„Wo denken Sie hin, junges Fräulein? Sie wählen von diesen Platten eines aus." Er legte einen Stapel auf den Verkaufstresen. „Für die Ausarbeitung des Fotos benötige ich einen Tag. Morgen können Sie es dann abholen."

Hermine nickte und sah sich die Glasplatten an. „Es ist nicht dabei", sagte sie und blickte ihn enttäuscht an.

„Das kann nicht sein." Uden klang verärgert, so als sei es Hermines Schuld. Nervös schaute er sich um, blickte auf den Vorhang, der den Zugang zu den hinteren Räumen verschloss. So als erwarte er, dass jemand hervortreten und seine Aussage bestätigen würde.

„Es muss da sein. Schauen Sie noch einmal ganz genau nach."

Hermine tat es. „Ich habe die Glasplatten jetzt dreimal durchgesehen. Es ist nicht dabei. Kann es sein, dass ein anderer Fotograf …“, sie zögerte, „und ich habe nur den Laden verwechselt?“

„Das, mein Fräulein, ist unmöglich.“ Er schob Hermines Zettel mit dem Zeigefinger in ihre Richtung. „Ich bin der einzige Daguerreotypist auf der Insel. Auf Borkum gibt es nur unser Fotoatelier. Ich mache Ihnen einen Vorschlag.“ Uden sammelte die Glasplatten ein und legte sie hinter sich in ein Regal. Auf einem Schild waren Datum und Ort der Aufnahmen vermerkt. „Sie kommen morgen noch einmal wieder. Es ist möglich, dass meine Assistentin die fehlenden Platten mit ins Labor genommen hat. Da kann ich sie jetzt nicht stören, sonst verderben die Bilder, die sie gerade anfertigt.“

Hermine sah ihm an, dass er log. „Danke. Bis morgen.“

„Und das Gruppenbild?“, wollte später Mathilde wissen. „Was ist damit?“

„Da waren mehrere Gruppenbilder. Die Gesichter waren alle so winzig, man konnte kaum etwas erkennen. Aber es war keines dabei, auf dem Jungen im Sand lagen.“

„Und mein Foto?“

„Auch das habe ich nicht finden können.“

„Sehr sonderbar. Ich gehe morgen hin und frage selbst nach.“

***

Mittlerweile war es für Hermine nichts Ungewohntes mehr, von Willem Dirks Bakker als geheimer Postillion eingesetzt zu werden. Heute sollte sie dem Betreiber eines Fuhrbetriebs eine Nachricht überbringen.

„Ich verlasse mich auf Ihre Diskretion, Fräulein Flessner." Bakker legte kurz den Zeigefinger auf die Lippen, ehe er sich über den Bart strich. Er stellte den Gehstock, dessen silberner Griff in Form eines Seehundes Hermine bereits bei der Anreise gefallen hatte, an die Wand. Wenn sie am Ende der Saison genügend Geld übrig hätte, überlegte sie, könnte sie vielleicht ihrem Großvater so ein schönes Stück mitbringen. Nicht aus Silber. Ein hölzerner Griff täte es auch, nur die Form eines Seehundes sollte er haben.

Bakkers Hand fuhr in die Westentasche. Zuerst meinte Hermine, er wolle einen Blick auf seine goldene Taschenuhr werfen, doch dann beförderte er einen einfach zusammengefalteten Zettel zutage. Den überreichte er ihr mit dem Hinweis, wo sie besagten Fuhrmann antreffen würde.

„Und bitte erwähnen Sie nicht, dass die Nachricht von mir kommt, Fräulein Flessner." Er erklärte ihr den Weg. „Das Gulfhaus ist nicht zu verfehlen", fügte er hinzu.

Er sollte recht behalten. Die Entfernung war gering, keine zehn Minuten zu Fuß. Schon aus der Ferne sah sie das mit Ziegeln gedeckte Haus. Das Dach des Hinterhauses führte weit nach unten, wie es überall in Ostfriesland zu sehen war. Man konnte in die Dachrinne hineinsehen, ohne sich auf die Zehenspitzen stellen zu müssen. Sie erreichte die Tür zum Hinterhaus und klopfte an.

„Einfach reingehen", hatte Bakker empfohlen. Auf Borkum schloss kein Mensch seine Haustür ab. Nicht einmal in der Saison, wenn die Urlauber da waren. Doch sie zögerte und klopfte erneut. Als niemand antwortete, trat sie, wie von Bakker geheißen, ein. Würde der Eigentümer darüber erzürnt sein, konnte sie sich auf ihren Chef berufen. Die Hintertür führte zuerst zu einer kleinen Küche. Hermine kannte diese Raumaufteilung von zu Hause. In Leer und Umgebung gab es viele Gulfhäuser. Sie glichen sich alle. Die Küche war durch eine dünne Mauer vom Kuhstall getrennt. Nur dass es hier, dem Geruch nach zu urteilen, keine Kühe, sondern nur Pferde gab. In der winzigen Küche stand ein Feuerherd, es gab einen Ausguss, einen kleinen Tisch und zwei Bettgestelle. Auf dem schmalen Regal stapelten sich Kochutensilien. Vier Becher, Teller und ein wenig Besteck. Der Fußboden war mit roten Steinen gepflastert. Hermine wusste, dies war der Aufenthaltsort der Familie während des Sommers. Ebenso wie sie wusste, dass auf der anderen Seite der Küche sich ein Raum mit kojenähnlichen hölzernen Verschlägen befand, die so hoch waren, dass man nur mit einer Bettbank hineinsteigen konnte. Hermine hatte die Hausdame Luise erzählen hören, dass die weniger betuchten Insulaner diesen Raum nur im Winter nutzten. Im Sommer verdienten sie sich ein kleines Zubrot, indem sie ihn inklusive der Hauptküche an Badegäste, die sich kein Hotel oder Logierhaus leisten konnten, vermieteten. Sie bezweifelte, dass in diesem Haus viele Urlauber Unterschlupf fanden.

„Hallo“, rief sie. „Ist da jemand?“

Durch eine schmale Tür betrat sie die Stallung. An der Außenwand befanden sich die Pferdestände, sodass die Tiere mit dem Kopf in Richtung Mauer standen. Doch kein Pferd war zu sehen. Nur der stechende Geruch nach Mist und die frischen Pferdeäpfel in der steinernen Rinne verrieten, dass es noch nicht lange her war, seit sie aus dem Stall geführt worden waren. Das gegenüber den Ständen gelagerte Heu hatte all seinen

Duft verloren. Es waren die Reste der Ernte vom vergangenen Jahr. Das hier war der eigentliche Gulf, wonach die geduckten Häuser benannt wurden.

„Hallo?“, rief sie erneut.

„Was wollen Sie?“, fragte eine tiefe Stimme in ihrem Rücken. Erschrocken fuhr Hermine herum. „Herr Fisser? Entschuldigen Sie, dass ich so hereinplatze. Aber mich schickt Herr …“ In letzter Sekunde verkniff sie sich den Namen. Sofort veränderte sich der Gesichtsausdruck des Mannes. *War das ein spitzbübisches Grinsen,* fragte sich Hermine. Fisser trat auf sie zu und nickte. „Und was möchte der Herr denn?“

Hermine fummelte in ihrer Rocktasche herum und hielt ihm den Zettel hin. Fisser nahm ihn entgegen. Sonst tat er nichts, blickte sie nur an. Hermine wusste nicht, ob sie auf Antwort warten sollte, also blieb auch sie wortlos stehen und schaute zurück. Schließlich nickte er erneut, wandte sich dem Zettel zu und begann zu lesen. Das Grinsen, das eben noch spitzbübisch gewirkt hatte, war verschwunden.

„Sagen Sie dem Herrn, ich habe verstanden. Das geht in Ordnung. Ich werde kommen.“

Damit war sie entlassen. Sie wandte sich zum hinteren Tor, aus dem die Tiere nach draußen geführt wurden.

„Stopp!“, sagte Fisser. „Nicht da hinaus.“

Gab es dort etwas, was sie nicht sehen sollte? Hermine wandte sich um. Mit dem Daumen zeigte er über seine Schulter. „Gehen Sie den gleichen Weg, den Sie gekommen sind.“ Er erkannte ihren fragenden Blick und fügte hinzu: „Der Hof ist dreckig. Sie werden sich die Schuhe und das Kleid ruinieren.“

Kleid? Verflixt, sie hatte ihre Arbeitskleidung an. Vermutlich ein Fehler und die Erklärung, warum Fisser so gegrinst hatte.

Sie hatte es vergeigt. Willem Dirks Bakker hatte nicht gewollt, dass Fisser erfuhr, wer ihm diese Nachricht schickte. Andererseits schien es eine Einladung zu einer Verabredung zu sein. Die alten Herren fingen an, es mit ihrer Geheimniskrämerei zu übertreiben. Hermine ärgerte sich. Sie hätte die Nachricht lesen sollen.

Mit dem Zettel wurde Fuhrunternehmer Fisser, ein Mitbewerber der Bakker'schen Transportbetriebe, gebeten, in *Köhlers Dorfhotel* zu kommen. Für Georg Köhler hielt Fisser Augen und Ohren offen.

Vor drei Jahren hatte Fisser in eine schicke, kleine Kutsche investiert, mit der er Urlauber über die Insel kutschierte. Der größte Teil seiner Kundschaft schien ihn während der Fahrt nicht mehr wahrzunehmen. So konnte er vielen Gesprächen lauschen und hörte einige Dinge, die für seine Ohren nicht bestimmt waren. Im Laufe der vergangenen Jahre war er so zu einer Art Informationsquelle für Köhler geworden. Als Bürgermeister war Köhler stets daran interessiert, was die Gäste nicht mochten, was sie vehement ablehnten oder was sie sich wünschten. Diese Hinweise nutzten sowohl seinem Hotelbetrieb als auch seiner Funktion als vorstehendem Mitglied des Gemeinderates.

Fisser war klar, dass die Einladung eine Aufforderung zur Weitergabe von Neuigkeiten war. Keine allgemeinen Gästebemerkungen, sondern Informationen zu den Grundstücken am Strand, die er von seinen Fahrgästen aufschnappen konnte.

Beschwingten Schrittes näherte er sich *Köhlers Dorfhotel*, im besten Wissen, dass es sich finanziell für ihn lohnen würde. Köhler war niemals geizig.

Fisser fuhr mit der Hand in die Hosentasche und befühlte den Zettel. Schon als er das Mädchen sah, war ihm etwas komisch vorgekommen. Als sie gegangen war und er ihr hinterhergeschaut hatte, hatte ihn das Gefühl überfallen, etwas übersehen zu haben. Er hatte geahnt, dass ihn das den ganzen Tag beschäftigen würde. Das gleiche unangenehme Ziehen in der Magengegend hatte ihn beim Verlassen des Stalles einige Stunden später überkommen, nachdem sein Sohn die Pferde heimgebracht, sie in den Boxen getränkt und anschließend raus auf die Weiden gebracht hatte.

Die Lösung schien nah, doch er konnte den Gedanken nicht packen.

Fisser erreichte das Baugelände gegenüber des *Dorfhotels*. Wenn der Plan der Gemeinde aufginge, würden hier im kommenden Jahr Borkums Kinder zur Schule gehen. Das Fundament der Schule war bereits gelegt. Hartgebrannte rote Backsteine stapelten sich am Rand des Grundstücks.

Erst beim Blick auf Hubert, Köhlers pickeligen jungen Hoteldiener, wusste er, was ihn an der Überbringerin des Zettels stutzig gemacht hatte: Ihre Hoteluniform war eine andere. Die Deern hatte ein Kleid aus den Bakker-Betrieben getragen.

Hubert winkte ihm heftig, sich zu beeilen. „Die Herren warten schon“, rief Hubert und begleitete ihn bis zu Georg Köhlers Kontor. Er klopfte kurz an die Tür und öffnete sie für Fisser, um ihn einzulassen. Zigarrenrauchwolken hüllten den Raum ein.

„Sie haben Glück, dass *Ihre* Angestellte mich im Stall erwischt hat“, sagte Fisser zu Georg Köhler und zwinkerte mit einem Auge. Dann schüttelte er ihm die Hand. „Drei Minuten später und ich wäre auf der Weide gewesen.“ Er zog den Zettel aus seiner Hosentasche, als wäre er die Eintrittskarte, um an diesem Treffen teilnehmen zu dürfen. Erneut zwinkerte er mit einem Auge.

„Alles in Ordnung, Fisser?“ Köhler deutete mit neutralem Gesichtsausdruck auf sein Auge und zupfte ihm den Zettel aus der Hand. „Setzen Sie sich.“

Fisser nahm Platz. Zur Begrüßung der anderen Herren klopfte er kurz auf den Tisch. Gleich zu Fissers Rechten schickte Doktor Schmidt Rauchwölkchen an die Zimmerdecke. In der linken Hand hielt der Arzt einen Cognacschwenker, von dem er einen winzigen Schluck nahm. Fisser überlegte, was er in dieser Gesellschaft zu suchen hatte und ob es überhaupt um Informationen seinerseits ging.

„Bis zur Vergabe der Grundflächen bleibt nur noch wenig Zeit“, sagte Köhler und reichte ihm ein gut gefülltes Glas. „Doch die sollten wir nutzen.“

Fisser roch an dem Cognac. Mit leerem Magen würde der Alkohol direkt in die Umlaufbahn gehen. Nur nippen, dachte er, und wollte eben einen Schluck nehmen, da klopfte es an der Tür.

Zögerlichen Schrittes kam Hermann Behrends herein. Man munkelte, er habe in der Lotterie ein stattliches Sümmchen gewonnen. Wie Fisser schien auch Behrends überrascht über die anwesenden Herren zu sein und fragte sich, warum er eingeladen worden war. Behrends setzte sich neben ihn.

„Die Dinge entwickeln sich, meine Herren. Zwar nicht immer so, wie wir es gerne hätten, aber sie entwickeln sich.“

Doktor Schmidt rümpfte die Nase. Er betrachtete seine Zigarren und schaute dann auf Fissers Stiefel hinunter. „Wenigstens den Pferdemist hätten Sie abstreifen können, Herr Fisser.“

„Kann ja nicht jeder nach Kampfer und Melisse riechen, Herr Doktor.“

„Meine Herren“, verschaffte sich Georg Köhler Gehör. „Wenn ich Sie dann bitten darf, zum Thema unserer kleinen Versammlung zu kommen. Wir alle möchten ein Strandhotel bauen.“

Fisser und Behrends wechselten einen schnellen Blick. Am Gesichtsausdruck Hermann Behrends erkannte er, dass dieser genauso überrascht war wie er selbst. Auf der Insel konnte man wenig geheim halten, doch dass alle anwesenden Herren über seine Bewerbung Bescheid wussten, erstaunte ihn. Sein Blick fiel auf Bernd Uden, den Fotografen aus der Strandstraße. Schon sonderbar, dachte er, dass auch er dieser Runde angehörte. Zum einen war der Mann erst kurz auf der Insel, zum anderen besaß er weder Haus noch Hof, das der Bank als Sicherheit dienen könnte, und er schien keinen guten Ruf zu haben. Man munkelte, er habe auf dem Festland alle Zelte hinter sich abbrechen müssen. Geldprobleme, wie es hieß. Und nun sollte er flüssig genug sein, um bei solchen Objekten mitbieten zu können?

„Ich hoffe, alle hier im Raum vertreten die Meinung, dass die Gemeinde die Insulaner bei der Ausschreibung vor den Festlandbewerbern bevorzugen sollte. Da dies jedoch nicht der Fall ist, müssen wir uns gegenseitig unterstützen.“

Alle anwesenden Herren nickten. Es brauchte fast zehn Minuten, bis Köhler sie davon überzeugt hatte, wie wichtig es sei, zusammenzuhalten. Danach tauschten sie ihr Wissen über weitere Bewerber aus und was sie von deren Angeboten in Erfahrung hatten bringen können. Mit genauen Bietersummen wollte keiner herausrücken, was auch nicht notwendig sei, wie Köhler betonte. Wichtig wäre, im Bekannten- und Verwandtenkreis zu erwähnen, dass Borkum den Borkumern gehöre und man nicht den Fehler machen solle, alles an Festländer zu verkaufen.

„Nun", fasste Köhler anschließend zusammen, „jeder weiß jetzt, worauf es ankommt, damit die Grundstücke in Insulanerhänden bleiben. Sicherlich wird der eine oder andere von Ihnen sein Angebot noch ein wenig korrigieren wollen, wobei ich die Unterbringungsmöglichkeiten für das Personal hervorheben möchte. Die jungen Insulaner werden begeistert sein, ihre eigenen vier Wände von uns zur Verfügung gestellt zu bekommen. Und denken Sie daran, meine Herren, absolutes Stillschweigen über unsere Absprache zu bewahren."

Die Runde löste sich auf. Erst als Fisser das Haus verließ und er Köhlers Pagen seine Uniform zurechtzupfen sah, fiel ihm ein, wen er in der Besprechung vermisst hatte.

Bakker hatte gefehlt, obwohl sein Mädel ihm die Nachricht überbracht hatte. Er hatte es geahnt. Köhler und Bakker taten demnach immer noch so, als wären sie verfeindet, was nicht gerade förderlich für das war, was in der vergangenen Stunde besprochen worden war.

Die beiden Eigenbrötler kochten also nebenbei noch ihr eigenes Süppchen. Nun, jeder behielt irgendetwas für sich, auch die Männer, die vorhin in Köhlers Kontor saßen. Er selbst war da keine Ausnahme. Alle für einen, einer für alle und jeder für sich.

Die Erkenntnis, das Geheimnis der zwei Hoteliers entdeckt zu haben, stimmte ihn froh. Fisser liebte Mysteriöses, begeisterte sich für Ränkespiele und mochte beide Männer gut leiden. Er selbst besaß jetzt einige Geheimnisse mehr, würde sie aber nie verraten.

Endlich Regen, dachte er. Die Natur brauchte ihn dringend. Auf dem Weg nach Hause wurde der Regen kräftiger. Steife Windböen trugen ihn von Osten herüber. Er hielt mit einer

Hand den Kragen seiner Jacke zusammen. Ein Sommersturm zog auf. Er betrachtete den dunklen Himmel. Die Erfahrung hatte ihn gelehrt, dass es bald heftiger wehen würde. Dann würde das Wasser die Dünenkante erreichen. Er hatte es nicht eilig, nach Hause zu kommen, also machte er sich auf den Weg zum Strand. Sicherlich würde sein Freund Kalli Hilfe beim Bergen der Strandkörbe brauchen.

***

Am nächsten Tag schien schon wieder die Sonne. Der Sommersturm hatte nur wenige Stunden gewährt und keinen Schaden angerichtet.

Hermine machte sich erneut auf den Weg zum *Fotoladen Feiler* in der Strandstraße. Sie umrundete den Platz mit dem neuen Leuchtturm. Ihr Blick ging nach oben, wie jedes Mal, wenn sie hier vorbeiging. Von dort musste man eine fantastische Aussicht haben. Schade, dass Besucher den Turm nicht betreten durften.

Als sie den Laden betrat, schlug ihr der fiese Geruch entgegen, der ihr beim letzten Besuch des Geschäftes auf den Magen geschlagen war. Heute schien er nicht ganz so heftig zu sein. Niemand war im Laden, deshalb schaute sie sich die ausgestellten Bilder an. Es gab eine Reihe vom Bau des neuen Leuchtturmes, der in unterschiedlichen Bauphasen aufgenommen worden waren. Sie bewunderte die Männer, die hoch oben auf einem einfachen Holzgerüst standen und vermutlich für dieses Foto posierten. Hermine zählte fast dreißig Arbeiter.

„Guten Tag. Was kann ich für Sie tun?“ Eine Frau in einem grauen langen Rock und einer schwarzen Bluse trat hinter den Tresen.

„Ich war gestern schon hier. Aber meine Bilder waren nicht zu finden. Der Fotograf wollte noch einmal nachschauen, ob …“

„Wann und wo wurden Sie fotografiert?“

Hermine sagte es ihr. Wie zuvor bekam sie Glasplatten vorgelegt, die sie durchsehen sollte. Doch auch heute waren weder Hermines noch Mathildes Ablichtung zu finden.

„Es tut mir leid, mehr Glasplatten sind nicht da. Im Vertrauen gesagt, kommt das öfter vor.“

Hermine fand es ungehörig, wie sie über ihren Arbeitgeber sprach.

„Der Herr Uden“, fügte die Verkäuferin hinzu, „macht wunderschöne Bilder, aber mit der Buchhaltung und der Wirtschaft hier im Laden steht er auf Kriegsfuß. Ich empfehle Ihnen, sich erneut ablichten zu lassen. Gleich hier in unserem Atelier. Sollen wir einen Termin ausmachen?“

„Danke, ich werde es mir überlegen.“

Bei ihrer Rückkehr eilte sie in die Dachkammer, um sich für die Arbeit umzuziehen. Mathilde war nicht da, dennoch merkte sie sofort, dass etwas nicht stimmte. Im Raum hing ein unbekannter Geruch. Es roch leicht herb mit einem Hauch von Veilchen. Hermines Seife verströmte den Duft von Rosen und ihre Zimmergenossin verbreitete eher die Dünste eines ungewaschenen Körpers. Mathilde hielt wenig vom Waschen ihrer Kleidung und körperlicher Hygiene. Demnach musste jemand in ihrem Zimmer gewesen sein. Vielleicht hatte Mathilde frische Handtücher hochgebracht, doch ein Blick neben die Waschschüssel und an die Handtuchhaken verriet etwas anderes.

Ahnungsvoll und mit klopfendem Herzen zog sie ihre Nachttischschublade auf, in der sie den Wochenlohn unter einem Haufen von Muscheln versteckte, da sie noch keine Zeit gefunden hatte, ihn auf ihr neues Konto einzuzahlen. Das Geld war da. Die Briefe ihrer Mutter schienen ebenfalls alle an ihrem Platz zu liegen. Aber wer klaute schon die Post eines Dienstmädchens? Hermine ließ sich aufs Bett fallen. Ihr fiel auf, dass das Kopfkissen anders aussah als am Morgen, als sie es nach dem Bettenmachen hingelegt hatte. Sie fuhr mit der Hand darunter. Ihre Finger stießen gegen etwas, das sich wie fester Pappkarton anfühlte.

Ein Foto. Aber nicht irgendeines. Es war die Fotografie der Gruppe, die am Strand aufgenommen worden und nicht mehr im Laden des Fotografen aufzufinden gewesen war. Allerdings nur ein kleiner Ausschnitt davon. Die Jungen, die vor der Gruppe posiert hatten, und der einzelne Herr waren nicht zu sehen. Wie kam es unter ihr Kopfkissen?

Friederike konnte es gebracht haben, aber das erklärte nicht, warum die Glasplatten im Geschäft verschwunden waren. Und welchen Grund sollte Friederike haben, das Foto unter dem Kopfkissen zu verstecken?

Hermine betrachtete es genauer. Zu ihrem Entsetzen hatten alle Mädchen, auch Hermine, nur wenig bis gar nichts an. Auf der Rückseite des Bildkartons stand: „Wenn Sie nicht wollen, dass jemand das Bild zu sehen bekommt, zahlen Sie fünfzig Mark.“ So viel Geld verdiente sie im ganzen Monat nicht. Das musste sie sofort melden. Hermine sprang auf und riss Mathildes Kopfkissen hoch. Darunter lag das gleiche Bild, mit derselben Botschaft und dem Zusatz: „Sie wissen, wo Sie mich finden."

Ein Geräusch im Rücken ließ sie herumwirbeln.

„Hermine, du siehst aus, als hätte der Klabautermann dir in den Hintern gebissen."

Wortlos reichte Hermine ihr die Fotos. Mathilde warf einen Blick darauf und kicherte. Erst als sie auf die Rückseite schaute, wurde sie blass.

„Lass uns sofort zur Polizei gehen", rief Hermine.

„Warte."

„Worauf?"

„Wer weiß, ob die etwas unternehmen werden."

„Natürlich werden sie das."

„Da bin ich mir nicht so sicher. Der Fotograf könnte behaupten, dass wir uns mit Schmuddelfotos Geld nebenbei verdienen, und er wird sagen, dass er die Bilder nur auf unser Drängen hin gemacht hat. *Herr Gendarm*", klagte sie mit verstellter Stimme, „*glauben Sie mir! Normalerweise macht ein anständiger Mann wie ich keine solchen Bilder.*"

„Du meinst, es gibt Mädchen, die so etwas freiwillig tun?"

„Du bist so herrlich naiv, Minchen."

Hermine riss eines der Bilder aus Mathildes Hand. „Ich werde es trotzdem anzeigen."

„Das würde ich lassen. Denk daran, was die Herrschaften sagen werden."

„Aber wir können es beweisen. Schau mal genau hin. Wir sehen nackt ganz anders aus."

Mathilde lachte. „Willst du dich etwa vor einem Polizisten ausziehen? Nein, Hermine. Auch wenn wir nachweisen können, dass wir uns niemals so haben ablichten lassen, werden sie uns dennoch entlassen. Der gute Ruf dieses Hauses wäre ruiniert. Verstehst du?"

„Aber schau doch mal: Auf dem Foto haben wir denselben Körper. Dabei sind deine Beine viel länger und …"

„Wir unternehmen etwas dagegen."

„Aber was sollen wir tun? Zahlen? Das Geld habe ich nicht."

„Ich auch nicht. Und wenn wir erst einmal gezahlt haben, wird er vermutlich immer wiederkommen."

„Er muss uns die Glasplatte geben, dann kann er kein neues machen."

„Du vergisst, dass er uns beide auch noch allein abgelichtet hat. Wer weiß, vielleicht sind wir darauf vollkommen nackt."

Hermine brach in Tränen aus und zerriss ihre Fotografie in tausend Teilchen.

„Das hilft wenig." Mathilde legte eine Hand tröstend auf Hermines Schultern. „Überlass das mir. Ich kümmere mich darum."

„Wo willst du hin?"

„Dem Kerl gehörig in den Arsch treten."

Hermine ging an die Arbeit und wartete ungeduldig auf Mathildes Rückkehr. Sie stand auf dem Hof und hängte Bettlaken auf, als Mathilde zurückkam.

„Was hat er gesagt?"

„Er verzichtet auf das Geld."

„Und die Bilder? Hat er sie vernichtet?"

„Er hat versprochen, sie zu vernichten."

Hermine betrachtete Mathilde skeptisch. „Was musstest du dafür tun?"

„Ich? Nichts."

„Aber ohne Gegenleistung wird der Kerl wohl kaum …?“

Mathilde seufzte tief. „Wenn du es unbedingt wissen willst.“ Sie stand ihr gegenüber und drückte die Leine herunter, um ihr in die Augen zu schauen. „Irgendwann muss ich es dir ja sagen.“ Ihr Lächeln verriet nichts Gutes. „Ich habe ihm versprochen, dass er eine Nacht in deinem Bett verbringen darf.“

„Was?“ Hermine fiel ein nasses Laken auf den Boden und sie selbst wäre fast umgefallen, so mulmig wurde ihr in den Knien.

„Reg dich nicht auf, Minchen.“

„Ich soll mich nicht aufregen?“ Ihre Stimme versagte. Als Mathildes niederträchtiges Grinsen breiter wurde, schöpfte sie komischerweise Hoffnung.

„Ich habe nicht versprochen, dass du drinliegen wirst.“

Kapitel 13

Gertrud Dirksen, die abergläubische Köchin im *Hotel Bakker Senior*, würde sich immer mit einem Schaudern an diesen Tag erinnern. Ein Frösteln, das einen befiel, wenn man innerlich die ersten Vorzeichen einer Katastrophe fühlte.

Dass trotz des umgedrehten Besens ein Unglück weder über eines der Familienmitglieder noch die Hotelangestellten hereingebrochen war, hinderte sie nicht daran, erneut überzeugt zu sein. Ein Schicksalsschlag bahnte sich an.

Es geschah, als sie die Borkumer Zeitung von der letzten Woche auf dem langen hölzernen Küchentisch ausbreitete, um darauf die frisch gekochten Krabben auszuschütten. Leise vor sich hin pfeifend, ließ sie die ersten Granatleiber aufs Papier gleiten, als ihr Blick auf einen Artikel fiel. Sie unterbrach ihre Arbeit, las und dachte nach. Das musste sie unbedingt Frau Luise erzählen. Denn entgegen Luises Meinung, dass niemand ihr Geheimnis kenne, wusste Gertrud schon seit Langem darüber Bescheid. Es musste etwa neun oder zehn Jahre her sein, als Gertrud und ihr Ehemann eine Weile in Ostfriesland bei seiner Familie verbracht hatten. Es war im Oktober gewesen und Ehepaar Dirksen hatte den Gallimarkt besucht. Damals trafen sie einen alten Schulkameraden ihres Mannes. Die Herren unterhielten sich lange und stellten im Laufe des Gesprächs fest, dass sie gemeinsame Bekannte auf der Insel hatten. Unter anderem auch Luise Menninga. Frau Luise war nun kein Mensch, über den man sich lange das Maul zerreißen konnte. Sie war eine anständige, arbeitsame und eher langweilige Person, in deren Leben außer Arbeit wenig passierte. So hatte Gertrud bis dato zumindest gedacht. Bis sie aus einigen Andeutungen herauszufiltern meinte, dass es in Luises Leben, bevor sie auf die Insel gekommen war, doch etwas gegeben hatte, das einen Skandal ausgelöst hatte.

In besagtem Artikel, der nun diese Vorahnung in ihr auslöste, ging es um den Gallimarkt. Darum, dass sich die Oberen der Stadt Leer um die Moral und die daraus resultierenden Folgen gerade für die jungen unbedarften Mädchen rund um den Vieh- und Vergnügungsmarkt sorgten. Es kämen zu viele Bastarde neun Monate nach dem Jahrmarkt in Leer und Umgebung auf die Welt. Diese Unmoral, zeterten Gemeinderat und Kirche, müsse ein Ende haben.

Gertrud konnte nur hoffen, dass Hieltje Bakker, die erst gestern ihrem Ehemann eine Eifersuchtsszene gemacht hatte, den Artikel nicht gelesen hatte. Hieltje war zwar nicht die Klügste, doch wenn es um ihren Jakob ging, konnte sie überall Nebenbuhlerinnen erkennen. Es war ihr zuzutrauen, die gleichen Schlussfolgerungen wie Gertrud zu ziehen. Jeder wusste, dass Jakob seit über fünfzehn Jahren diesen Jahrmarkt regelmäßig im Oktober besuchte. Immer allein. „Viehmärkte sind Männersache", sagte er. Dass es beim Gallimarkt auch Karussells, Schießbuden, Bierzelte und jede Menge Leckereien zu kaufen gab, ließ er gerne unerwähnt.

Gertruds innere Stimme in Verbindung mit der Begegnung einer schwarzen Katze riet ihr, die Hausdame zu warnen. Die

Katze sah sie öfter, sie gehörte dem Nachbarn. Aber heute Morgen hatte sie eine Taube erbeutet, die noch mit den Flügeln schlug. Diese tierische Katastrophe in Verbindung mit dem ersten Blick in die Zeitung und auf genau diesen Artikel reichte für Gertruds Vorahnung.

„Dina, fix! Saus und sage der Hausdame, sie möge sich so schnell wie möglich bei mir melden."

Das Küchenmädchen, von Natur aus eher träge und langsam im Begreifen, musste die Dringlichkeit gespürt haben. Sie sprang vom Hocker auf. Der fiel zu Boden und Dina stolperte über eines der Beine. Fast wäre sie hingefallen, konnte sich jedoch fangen. Mit gerafften Röcken sauste sie aus der Küche und eilte die Hintertreppe zur Dachetage hinauf. Heftig klopfte sie gegen Frau Luises Tür.

Es war Mittagspause. Die Hausdame machte wohl ein tiefes Schläfchen. Dina klopfte erneut.

„Was machst du für einen Lärm?" Mathilde Remmers kam aus der gegenüberliegenden Dachkammer, dicht gefolgt von Hermine.

„Ist etwas passiert?"

„Ich weiß es nicht."

„Und warum hämmerst du wie ein Trampeltier gegen die Tür?"

„Gertrud hat es befohlen."

„Was hat sie befohlen?"

„Ich soll Frau Luise holen. Sofort."

„Die hat ihren freien Tag", maulte Mathilde, „wie jeden Donnerstag. Das solltet ihr eigentlich wissen", und ging zurück in ihre Kammer.

„Was mache ich denn jetzt?" Dinas hilfloser Blick war anrührend. „Gertrud wird mich schimpfen."

„Du kannst nichts dafür, wenn sie nicht da ist." Hermine gab ihr mit dem Zeigefinger Zeichen, sie solle ihr die Treppe hinunter folgen.

„Wenn es dir hilft, Dina, komme ich mit."

Gertrud blickte von den Krabben, die sie flink pulte, hoch. „Fräulein Flessner, was …" Dann deutete sie auf den umgefallenen Hocker. „Dina", befahl sie, „heb ihn auf, setz dich und pule die Krabben."

Mit der Handkante schob Gertrud einen Großteil des Krabbenhaufens zur Küchenhilfe hinüber. Die hatte jetzt einen doppelt so großen Haufen salziger und fischiger Krabbenleiber zu bewältigen als zuvor.

„Dina hätte dich nicht mitbringen sollen. Da du schon mal da bist, kannst du mithelfen." Sie nahm mit beiden Händen einige Krabben aus einem Eimer. Der Artikel, der ihr Magenschmerzen bereitete, verschwand unter den Tierchen.

„Du kannst doch Krabben pulen?"

„Jede echte Ostfriesin sollte das können." Hermine nahm sich einen Hocker und warf einen kurzen Blick in den Blecheimer. Wenn sie bis zum Ende der Mittagspause zu dritt die zehn Liter Granat aus ihrer Schale befreien wollten, mussten sie sich sputen.

Gertrud überlegte, mittlerweile unsicher geworden, ob sie Frau Luise gegenüber den Artikel erwähnen sollte, es lieber sein zu lassen. Schon allein deswegen, weil sie die gute Frau mit ihrem Wissen um ihr Geheimnis nicht bloßstellen wollte.

Sie konnte nur beten, dass dieses Unglück an Frau Luise vorbeiziehen würde.

Glücklicherweise las Hieltje die Zeitung ganz selten, und wenn sie einen Blick hinein warf, dann höchstens auf die Werbung und den Veranstaltungskalender. Hätte sie von Gertruds Vermutung eine Ahnung gehabt, wäre ihr der Grund ihrer heutigen Eifersucht lächerlich vorgekommen.

„Du wurdest mit einer Urlauberin im *Tuskulum* gesehen." Hieltje schaute Jakob streng an. Inständig hoffend, dass ihr Blick die gleiche Wirkung wie der ihrer Schwägerin hatte. Wenn Adeline jemanden energisch anschaute, bereitete es demjenigen von vornherein ein schlechtes Gewissen.

Jakob Willems Bakker ließ sich vom gekränkten Tonfall seiner Ehefrau und dem finsteren Gesichtsausdruck nicht von seiner Tätigkeit ablenken – dem Flicken eines feinen Fischernetzes. Jakob ging gerne an den Strand, um mit einem selbst gebauten Schieber, an dem ein Netz befestigt war, auf Krabbenfang zu gehen. Bis zu den Oberschenkeln im Wasser zu gehen und den Schieber über den Meeresboden zu bewegen, ließ ihn jede Anspannung vergessen. Die Ausbeute war gering, doch darum ging es ihm nicht. Diese Beschäftigung war für ihn die pure Entspannung.

„Von was?", wollte Hieltje ständig wissen und meuterte dagegen. Einem Hotelierssohn stände es schlecht zu Gesicht, Granat wie ein Gemeiner zu fischen.

Er griff betont langsam nach der Garnrolle, um einen längeren Faden abzurollen. Auf seinem Schoß lag ein dickeres, stabiles Seil, an dem er mit dem dünneren Garn Schlaufen mit einem Knoten um jeweils eine zusätzliche Schlaufe erweiterte.

„Im *Tuskulum*? Natürlich", knurrt er. „Auf der Insel kann man kaum einen Schritt machen, ohne von irgendjemandem gesehen zu werden. Und jeder meint, seine eigenen Schlüsse aus einer zufälligen Begegnung ziehen zu können. Die er dann auch noch lautstark unter das Volk bringt. Ich gehe mal davon aus, dass es eine deiner Freundinnen war, die mich sah? Schade nur, dass sie nicht länger hingeschaut hat, dann wäre ihr aufgefallen, dass der Ehemann besagter Urlauberin hinzugekommen ist. Und ehe du wieder herummeckerst und behauptest, ich würde mir das so zurechtlegen, wie es mir am besten passt, erkläre ich dir: Das ist die reine Wahrheit."

Immer wenn er die reine Wahrheit ins Spiel brachte, wusste Hieltje, dass ihr eine Lüge aufgetischt wurde.

„Du lügst!"

Zornig funkelten seine Augen. „Schatz, deine Hormone spielen verrückt. Das ist doch immer zu Beginn einer Schwangerschaft so. Das müsstest du mittlerweile wissen. Mir zu unterstellen, dass ich dir etwas vorflunkere, trifft mich hart. Schau, du bist wieder schwanger. Wir erwarten unser drittes Kind. Glaubst du wirklich", er legte die rechte Hand, die das Netz hielt, auf sein Herz, „dass ich da anderen Frauen hinterherschaue?"

Hieltje ließ sich von dem enttäuscht klingenden Tonfall nicht beirren, dennoch senkte sie den Blick auf ihren Stickrahmen. Er hatte es wieder verstanden, den Spieß umzudrehen und ihr ein schlechtes Gewissen einzureden. „Ich unterstelle dir gar nichts", murmelte sie. „Aber du musst zugeben, dass es für Außenstehende so aussieht, als …"

„Und was soll ich dagegen tun?" Er warf das Krabbennetz auf den Boden. „Es ist meine Pflicht, sich auch außerhalb der Bakker'schen Betriebe nett mit den Gästen zu unterhalten. Soll ich etwa nur mit den Männern reden und die Frauen links liegen lassen?" Er schob das Netz mit dem Fuß beiseite, stand auf und verließ den Raum. Sie schaute ihm mit Tränen in den Augen hinterher. Er betrog sie. Eine Frau spürte so etwas, egal ob schwanger oder nicht. Sie grollte eine Weile, verzählte sich beim

Muster, trennte es wieder auf und überlegte, ob Jakob vielleicht doch recht hatte. Es lag an den Hormonen. Sie sollte Schwägerin Geeske bitten, mit ihr für ein paar Tage zum Festland zu reisen. Ein ausgedehnter Einkaufsbummel in Emden oder Leer würde sie auf andere Gedanken bringen.

Schon am kommenden Tag verwarf sie die Idee. Ihre Eifersucht bekam neue Nahrung. Sie durfte Jakob jetzt auf keinen Fall aus den Augen lassen.

***

Die Frau, die aus der Kutsche stieg, sah aus, als hätte sie eine lange Reise hinter sich. Ihre Bluse war zerdrückt, der Mantel schmutzig und am Saum nass. Doch Letzteres kam vermutlich vom Ausschiffen. Es kam öfter vor, dass beim Übergang vom Raddampfer auf die Kutsche die Füße der Passagiere nass wurden.

Mit der jungen Frau waren zwei weitere Personen ausgestiegen, die sich dem Hoteleingang zuwandten. Sofort kam Waldemar, der Hoteldiener, angerannt, um das Gepäck der Gäste vom Kutscher entgegenzunehmen. Die junge Frau besaß nur eine abgewetzte Reisetasche. Weder der Kutscher noch Waldemar schenkten ihrem Gepäck Aufmerksamkeit. Es war zu klein für einen längeren Urlaubsaufenthalt und die Besitzerin war offensichtlich keine Frau, die sich Ferien im *Hotel Bakker* leisten konnte. Sie blieb eine Weile auf dem gepflasterten Gehweg stehen und schaute der Kutsche hinterher, deren Pferde sich durch den Sandweg quälten. Die Sonne stand hoch, dennoch blinzelte sie hinter einem viereckigen Leuchtturm hervor.

Das musste der Turm sein, der vor einigen Jahren ausgebrannt war. Ihre Tante hatte geschrieben, dass die Insulaner an anderer Stelle innerhalb von wenigen Monaten einen neuen errichtet hatten. Hätte sie beim Ausschiffen den runden Turm nicht mit eigenen Augen gesehen, hätte sie es kaum geglaubt.

Demnach keine von all den Lügen, die man ihr von Kindesbeinen an aufgetischt hatte. Bis vor Kurzem nicht weiter tragisch, da sie nicht mal geahnt hatte, dass sie angeflunkert worden war. Und dann war es ausgerechnet ihr Vater gewesen, der sich verplappert hatte. Nicht an Alkohol gewöhnt, war er von einem „Kindpissen“ in der Nachbarschaft nach Hause gekommen. Mit zu viel Branntwein mit Rosinen im Magen lallte er etwas über das Anstoßen auf die Geburt eines Kindes zu dem Zeitpunkt, als Anneliese seine Tochter geworden sei. Er brabbelte einiges darüber und da war sie raus gewesen, die ganz große Lüge in ihrem Leben. Es hatte sie vollkommen aus der Bahn geworfen. Bis dato war sie im festen Glauben gewesen, Luise Menninga sei ihre Tante. Dabei war sie ihre Mutter und die Mama war die Tante. Nach Vaters Besäufnis hatte sie die Wahrheit erfahren. Als Anneliese geboren wurde, war Luise fünfzehn Jahre alt und unverheiratet. Nachdem der Kindsvater auf Nimmerwiedersehen verschwunden war, erwartete Luise eine Zukunft als gefallene Frau mit einem Bastard. „Wir waren damals schon einige Jahre verheiratet“, gestand ihre Ziehmutter. „Und Nachwuchs wollte sich nicht einstellen. Da entschied die Familie, dich als meine Tochter auszugeben. So war allen geholfen. Und du musst zugeben, es hat dir an nichts gemangelt.“

Stimmt, gestand Anneliese sich Tage später ein. Es brauchte eben seine Zeit, sich an den Gedanken zu gewöhnen. Sie hatte eine schöne und behütete Kindheit gehabt, und dass sich ihre „Tante" immer rührend um sie gekümmert hatte, ergab heute einen Sinn.

Wie Anneliese erfuhr, schickte Luise Monat für Monat und Jahr für Jahr ihrer Schwester Geld, damit ihr es an nichts mangelte. Annelieses anfängliche Wut und Enttäuschung war schnell verraucht und sie entschloss sich, auf die Insel zu reisen, um einerseits dem langweiligen Alltag des Bauernhofs zu entfliehen und andererseits in „Tante" Luises Obhut eine Arbeit zu finden, um ihr eigenes Geld zu verdienen.

Noch wusste Luise von nichts.

„Kann ich Ihnen helfen?" Waldemar hatte die Gäste ins Hotel geleitet und war zurückgekommen.

„Frau Luise Menninga, ist sie da?"

Der Mann mit zu viel Pomade im Haar nickte. Sein Gesichtsausdruck verriet, was er dachte: *Ich wusste es!* Für einen Badegast wirkte sie zu schäbig, um am ersten Haus am Platze Unterkunft nehmen zu können.

„Anneliese, Schätzchen, was machst du denn auf der Insel?" Luise stand in diesem Augenblick mit einem Korb voll Badesachen hinter ihr.

„Tante Luise!", rief Anneliese und ließ die kleine Reisetasche fallen. Die Frauen umarmten sich.

„Was stehst du so rum, Waldemar? Los!", forderte Luise ihn auf. „Nimm das Gepäck und bring es hinauf in meine Kammer."

Waldemar nickte ergeben. Man konnte ihm ansehen, dass es ihm wenig behagte, eine winzige Tasche zu tragen, ohne ein Trinkgeld erwarten zu dürfen. Er griff danach und verschwand im Haus.

„Was machst du auf Borkum und wie geht es deinen Eltern?"

„Denen geht es gut." Anneliese beschloss in diesem Augenblick, ihr Wissen um die Familienverhältnisse vorerst nicht anzusprechen. Sie wollte einen geeigneteren Zeitpunkt abwarten. „Ich habe gehofft, dass du Arbeit für mich hast."

Sie spielte mit den Fingern an dem Medaillon. Sie hatte es von ihrer Tante bekommen, die es wiederum vor fünfzehn Jahren von Annelieses leiblichem Vater geschenkt bekommen hatte. Auch etwas, das ihr bis vor wenigen Wochen niemand gesagt hatte.

Noch ahnte Anneliese nicht, was dieser Kettenanhänger auslösen würde.

Luise blickte die Straße rauf und runter, so als befürchte sie, jemand könne sie beobachten. Dann legte sie den Arm um Annelieses Schulter und führte sie um das Haus herum zum Hintereingang. „In einem Hotel ist immer etwas zu tun. Aber ich kann dich nicht so einfach einstellen, da muss ich erst mit der Chefin sprechen."

„Ich dachte, du bist für das Personal zuständig, Tante Luise?"

„Als Hausdame beaufsichtige ich die Mitarbeiter, aber um die Einstellungen kümmert sich Frau Bakker selbst." Luise führte ihre „Nichte" durch die Hintertür ins Hotel.

„Wie bei uns daheim." Anneliese blieb an der Türschwelle stehen und deutete auf die schwarz-weißen Fußbodenfliesen. „Nur schicker." Auf dem Weg die Hintertreppe hinauf bewunderte sie die Wandmalereien. „So viele bunten Schmetterlinge, gibt es die wirklich? Oh, und da! Solche Blumen und Blätter habe ich noch nie gesehen."

Ein schwarzer Vogel, der auf einem zur Schleife gefalteten Spruchband hockte, gefiel ihr ganz besonders. Der Text lautete: „Tritt ein, bring Glück herein".

Die schlicht weiß getünchten Wände von der obersten Etage ins Dachgeschoss hinauf ließ sie unkommentiert. Luise Menninga führte sie in ihre Dachkammer. Waldemar hatte die Reisetasche vor der Tür abgestellt.

„Komm herein", sagte Luise.

In der Kammer roch es nach frisch verarbeitetem Holz. „Setz dich. Die Tasche kannst du erst einmal dort abstellen. Wissen deine Eltern, dass du hier bist?"

„Natürlich." Anneliese deutete auf die Reisetasche. „Erkennst du sie nicht? Die hat mal dir gehört. Du hast sie Mama vor Jahren dagelassen und jetzt hat sie sie mir geliehen."

„Warum hast du nicht geschrieben?"

„Habe ich", flunkerte Anneliese. „Allerdings erst vor drei Tagen. Dann wird der Brief wohl noch kommen."

„Aber sag, was ist passiert? Du wolltest doch eine Ausbildung im Schuhgeschäft anfangen."

„Die haben eine andere genommen", wich Anneliese aus. In Wirklichkeit hatte sie nicht mehr daran gedacht.

„Weißt du was? Du schaust dir Borkum an und ich kümmere mich darum, wie es hier mit uns weitergeht."

„Kann ich bei dir schlafen? Platz ist ja genug."

„Da muss ich erst Frau Bakker fragen. Hier …" Luise ging zum Schrank und nahm eine Handtasche, die an einem Kleiderbügel hing, heraus. Einem Portemonnaie, das aus Seehundfell gefertigt war, entnahm sie ein paar Münzen. „Hier, ein wenig Geld. Gönn dir einen heißen Kakao. Oder ein Eis. Im *Café Viktoriahöhe* haben sie das beste Erdbeereis auf ganz Borkum. Es ist etwas weit zum Gehen, aber es lohnt sich. Dann siehst du gleich was von der Insel. Lass dir Zeit. Und wenn du zurück bist, kann ich dir sagen, ob du hier im Haus bleiben kannst.

Später erzählst du mir, was in den letzten Monaten bei euch zu Hause los war."

***

Nach dem Streit mit Hieltje wäre Jakob gerne an den Strand gegangen, doch er hatte das Netz liegen lassen und verspürte keinen Drang, seiner Frau in den nächsten Stunden zu begegnen. Schon bald würde sie sich beruhigt haben. Wie immer.

Er verließ das Gebäude und umrundete die Ecke mit dem *Stientje Pahle,* an dem sich abends die Borkumer Jugend traf. Vor dem *Bakker Senior* sah er Waldemar mit einer kleinen Tasche im Hotel verschwinden. Vor dem Eingang stand Frau Luise und unterhielt sich mit einem jungen Mädchen. Er überlegte, wer sie wohl sein könnte, denn aufgrund ihrer Kleidung konnte sie kein Hotelgast sein. Er sah, wie die beiden Frauen zum Hintereingang gingen, und entschloss sich zu warten, bis Waldemar wieder vor dem Hoteleingang erschien. Der Page würde wissen, ob im Hotel seines Bruders eine neue Kraft eingestellt worden war.

Es dauerte eine Weile, doch Waldemar ließ sich nicht blicken. Jakob wollte eben weitergehen, da kam die junge Frau zwischen den Häusern hervor und trat auf den Bürgersteig. Sie schaute sich um, als müsse sie sich orientieren. Die Gelegenheit, sie anzusprechen.

„Kann ich Ihnen helfen?"

Er erschrak. Sie blickte ihn mit den Augen seiner Schwester an. Diese Ähnlichkeit! Die gleiche schlanke Gestalt, blonde Locken und markante Adlernase. Es schien, als stände Geeske, so wie sie vor zwanzig Jahren ausgesehen hatte, vor ihm. Sein Blick wanderte zu ihrem Hals. Sie trug ein Medaillon der Heiligen Jungfrau an einem silbernen Kettchen. Jakob starrte den Anhänger an. Die Ähnlichkeit des Mädchens mit seiner Schwester, als sie im gleichen Alter gewesen war, hatte ihn erschreckt, doch das Medaillon bereitete ihm Übelkeit. Kurz schoss ihm der Gedanke durch den Kopf, dass dieses fast erwachsene Kind seines sein musste.

Ein weiterer Geistesblitz brachte seine Überzeugung sofort ins Wanken. Erleichtert stieß er die Luft aus. Alles nur Zufall. Junge Mädchen sahen sich ähnlich und von diesen Kettchen gab es Hunderte. In seiner Sturm-und-Drang-Zeit hatte es sie überall in Ostfriesland günstig zu kaufen gegeben. Auch er hatte jede Menge davon erstanden und sie oft und gerne verschenkt.

„Können Sie mir sagen, wo das *Café Viktoriahöhe* ist?"

„Sie laufen", er musste sich räuspern, „hier die Straße entlang." Mit dem Finger deutete er die Richtung. „Dann umrunden Sie den runden Leuchtturm, biegen links ab und gehen bis zur Strandmauer hoch. Danach rechts immer dem Sandweg folgen. Es ist eine lange Strecke. Sie benötigen bestimmt eine halbe Stunde oder mehr."

„Ich habe Zeit und bei diesem schönen Wetter ist das kein Problem."

Sie dankte ihm und ging in die angewiesene Richtung. Nachdenklich blickte er ihr hinterher.

„Sie ist die Nichte von Frau Luise", sagte eine Stimme hinter ihm.

„Danke, Waldemar." Jakob war erleichtert. Er hatte im Laufe der Jahre alle drei Geschwister von Luise Menninga kennengelernt. Zwei Brüder und eine Schwester. Er konnte schwören, dass Luises Schwester, klein und drall wie Luise, überhaupt nicht sein Typ war. Auch nicht, wenn sie zwanzig Jahre jünger gewesen wäre.

Jakobs Erleichterung hielt nur ein paar Minuten an. Er selbst mochte von seiner Unschuld überzeugt sein. Doch was, wenn seiner Ehefrau oder einem anderen aus seiner Familie die Ähnlichkeit auffallen würde? Der Ärger war vorprogrammiert und das, obwohl er diesmal vollkommen schuldlos war.

***

„Hermine! Sie werden heute Abend im Restaurant aushelfen."

„Sehr wohl, Frau Bakker."

„Und beeilen Sie sich. Einige Tafeln müssen besonders dekoriert werden. Frau Kolbe soll Ihnen die Damasttischdecken geben."

Die Gesellschaft, die mehrere Tische reserviert hatte, feierte ein kleines Jubiläum. Vor zehn Jahren hatten sich die Gäste zum ersten Mal am Strand bei einem Tennisturnier getroffen. Seither reisten alle zur gleichen Zeit an und verbrachten den größten Teil ihrer Ferien gemeinsam. Jetzt standen sie in Grüppchen beieinander, bis sie zu den festlich gedeckten Tischen gebeten werden würden. Diese kleine Feier ließ sich Borkums *Badedirektor* nicht entgehen. Er hatte auch gleich den Fotografen mitgebracht.

Hermine entzündete gerade die letzte Kerze und ließ die Streichhölzer in ihrer Rocktasche unter der gestärkten Schürze verschwinden, da wurde sie von einem Herrn herbeigewinkt. „Wo bleibt der Sekt?"

„Ich hole ihn sofort."

Im selben Moment gab Waldemar Zeichen, dass die gefüllten Sektgläser bereitstanden. Einen Augenblick später stand sie mit dem Tablett in der Hand starr wie eine Puppe vor der kleinen Gruppe Männer. Eben stellte Tönjes Kieviet, von dem sie wusste, dass er der stellvertretende Bürgermeister war, einem anderen den Fotografen vor. „Er wird später, wenn ich die Urkunden der *Badedirektion* überreiche, eine Aufnahme machen."

„Ich fertige auch Porträts und Familienbilder an", meinte der Fotograf Uden in bescheidenem Tonfall.

Und unanständige Fotos, fügte Hermine in Gedanken hinzu.

„Ihre Gattin", Uden deutete mit dem Kopf auf eine dicke Matrone, „wird ganz famos aussehen."

Und du wirst anschließend einen extrem hohen Preis für das Bild verlangen, fügte Hermine in Gedanken hinzu. Am liebsten hätte sie ihm den Sekt ins Gesicht geschüttet.

Zu Udens schleimigen Beteuerungen passte nicht der Blick, den er Hermine zuwarf. So als wolle er sagen: *Ein Wort und ich blamiere dich bis auf die Knochen!* Das Blut gefror ihr in den Adern. „Man sollte ihn bei Niedrigwasser im Watt eingraben", hatte Mathilde gesagt. Hermine war derselben Meinung. Und jetzt dieses fiese, süffisante Grinsen! Es konnte nur bedeuten, dass er es ganz und gar nicht vergessen hatte, was Mathilde ihm versprochen hatte: eine Nacht in ihrem Bett. Bleich wie ein Betttuch, das zu lange in der Sonne gelegen hatte, sah sie zu, wie sich die Herren ein Glas vom Tablett nahmen.

„Fräulein Flessner!“, mahnte Adeline. Als Gastgeberin lief sie im Raum hin und her, um mit diesem oder jenem ein Wort zu wechseln. „Stehen Sie nicht rum. Die Gläser der Damen dahinten sind leer.“ Mit wackligen Knien, wissend, dass der Fotograf ihr hinterherschaute, balancierte sie das Tablett zu den Frauen hinüber. Ihre Gedanken kreisten darum, wie sie Bernd Uden und den scheußlichen Bildern, die er von ihr angefertigt hatte, entkommen könnte. Das machte sie unaufmerksam.

„Fräulein?“

„Ja bitte?“

„Ein Sekt fehlt. Bringen Sie noch ein Glas.“

„Sofort, gnädige Frau.“ Sie wandte sich um und stieß mit einem Mann zusammen. „Hoppla!“, meinte er und griff nach dem Tablett. Zum Glück stand kein einziges Glas mehr darauf. „Vorsicht, junge Dame, oder wollen Sie mich absichtlich umrennen?“

Hermine schüttelte den Kopf, die Wangen puterrot. Das Einzige, was sie denken konnte, war: *Nur weg von hier!* Der Gedanke, dass ihr dasselbe auch mit Uden hätte passieren können, ließ ihren Magen rebellieren. Sie spürte, wie ihr Mageninhalt den Weg nach oben suchte.

Egal, wie sauer die Chefin reagieren würde, sie floh in die Hotelküche.

Kapitel 14

Zwei Tage danach, in einer heißen Julinacht, schreckte Hermine aus dem Schlaf. Ein Geräusch hatte sie geweckt. Kam der Fotograf angeschlichen, um Mathildes Versprechen einzulösen? Im Licht des fast vollen Mondes brauchte sie keine Lampe anzuzünden, um etwas zu erkennen. Mathildes Bett war ungemacht wie so oft und die zweite Nacht in Folge leer. Vermutlich ahnte sie nicht einmal, was für Seelenqualen sie, Hermine, litt, weil sie jederzeit befürchten musste, dass der Erpresser kam, um Mathildes Versprechen einzulösen.

Warum musste Mathilde sie gerade jetzt in den Nächten allein lassen? Ob sie sich mit irgendeinem Mann herumtrieb? Im Stillen hoffte sie, es wäre Bernd Uden. Doch der Wunsch war zu abwegig.

Die Kammertür stand einen Spalt offen. Sie war sicher, sie geschlossen zu haben, ehe sie sich schlafen gelegt hatte. Sie schwang die Beine aus dem Bett. Die Kühle des Holzfußbodens war angenehm, deshalb ging sie barfuß. Leise schob sie die Tür so weit auf, dass sie in den Flur sehen konnte. Nichts. Im Haus war es still. Doch da! War das ein Flüstern oder bildete sie sich das nur ein? Hermine öffnete die Zimmertür ganz. Das Mondlicht reichte nicht bis zum Ende des Flures. Sollte jemand im

Dunkeln die Treppe hinaufgeschlichen sein, auf der obersten Stufe stehen und ebenso lauschen wie sie? Hermine überlegte, ob sie die Lampe anzünden und sich auf die Suche nach Mathilde begeben sollte. In dem Augenblick fiel ihr ein, dass sie Mathildes Bett gestern Nachmittag gemacht hatte, um einer Rüge von Frau Luise vorzubeugen. Demnach musste jemand darin gelegen haben, ohne dass Hermine es mitbekommen hatte. Ihr Herz schlug schneller. Ein Blick auf den Nachttopf verriet, dass er leer war. Doch zweifelte Hermine, dass Mathilde sich mitten in der Nacht die Mühe machen würde, bis in die untere Etage zu gehen, um dort für das größere Geschäft den Abort zu benutzen. *Versuche, dich zu beruhigen,* ermahnte sie sich. Sicherlich hatte Mathilde Hunger bekommen, saß jetzt in der Küche und futterte Gertruds Speisekammer leer. Das würde die angelehnte Kammertür und das Geräusch, das sie geweckt hatte, erklären. Stimmte die Vermutung, wäre am kommenden Morgen Ärger mit der Köchin vorherbestimmt, was Mathilde mit den Worten „Sie können sich jederzeit bei Frau Bakker über mich beschweren" quittieren würde.

Da, ein Flüstern! Es kam näher. Schnell schloss Hermine die Tür bis auf einen Spalt, floh zurück ins Bett und tat, als würde sie schlafen. Die Zeit verging, doch niemand betrat die Dachkammer. Sicherlich kamen die Stimmen aus einer der Kammern der anderen Zimmermädchen oder von Frau Luise und ihrer Nichte, die seit Kurzem hier schlief.

Hermine lauschte angestrengt, doch es herrschte eine vollkommene Stille. Da, eines der Dielenbretter im Flur knarrte. Einbrecher? Wohl kaum. Kein Dieb war so dumm, in Dachkammern nach Wertvollem zu suchen. Die würden eher in den Gästezimmern ihr Glück versuchen. Was, wenn es Jakob Bakker war? Es wurde gemunkelt, er jage jedem hübschen Mädchen hinterher. Aber würde er so tief sinken, es mitten in der Nacht bei einem der Zimmermädchen im Hotel seines Bruders zu versuchen? Eher nicht.

Es rumpelte, die Tür flog auf und knallte gegen die Wand. Herein stolperte Mathilde in Begleitung eines Mannes. Beide schienen dem Geruch nach Alkohol getrunken zu haben.

„Pscht!“, meinte Mathilde und schloss die Tür. Sie kicherte albern. Das Holzgestell von Mathildes Bett knarrte und kaum eine Sekunde später knackte es heftig. Unter den halb geschlossenen Lidern konnte Hermine erkennen, dass der Kerl sich hineingeworfen hatte.

Unter dem Gewicht der beiden Körper ächzte das Nachbarbett heftig.

„Wie viele Knöpfe hat dieses verdammte Kleid?“, murrte der Mann.

Erneut kicherte Mathilde und sagte, dass man es bis in den Flur hinein hören konnte: „Sei nicht so laut.“

Ich sollte schreien, dachte Hermine, um Hilfe zu holen. Doch dann würde Mathilde hinausgeworfen oder zumindest würde sie später ihren Groll an ihr auslassen. Ach was, Mathilde würde schon nichts geschehen. Kurz schoss ihr die Frage durch den Kopf, welches Geheimnis die Kollegin hütete, das sie davor bewahrte, bei all ihrem Schlendrian nicht entlassen zu werden. Die Geräusche, die die beiden machten, wurden lauter. Sollte sie weiter so tun, als würde sie schlafen?

Ehe Hermine entscheiden konnte, wie es jetzt weitergehen sollte, öffnete sich die Tür. In einem langen weißen Nachthemd stand Frau Luise, mit einer Petroleumlampe in der Hand, im Türrahmen. Hinter der Hausdame konnte Hermine einen

Schatten erkennen. Eine Hand legte sich auf Luises Oberarm und schob sie beiseite. Dirk Willems Bakker, der Juniorchef höchstpersönlich, trat ein. Hermine richtete sich in ihrem Bett auf, die Decke bis unters Kinn gezogen.

Bakker packte den Eindringling am Kragen und zog ihn von Mathilde und dem Bett herunter. Mit beiden Händen schob Dirk Willems Bakker ihn vor sich her auf den Flur hinaus. Hermine erkannte den Fotografen. Er wehrte sich nicht. Sie konnte nur vermuten, dass er zu betrunken dazu war. Mit angstvoll aufgerissenen Augen, aber stumm schaute Mathilde den im dunklen Flur verschwindenden Männern hinterher, ehe sie Frau Luise keck ansah. Hermine konnte Frau Luises Gesichtsausdruck nicht erkennen. Ihre Stimme jedoch verriet, wie wütend sie war. „Morgen packen Sie Ihre Sachen und verlassen das Haus. Und glauben Sie ja nicht, dass Sie für diese Woche Lohn bekommen werden."

An Hermine gewandt sagte sie ein wenig freundlicher: „Ich hoffe für Sie, mein Kind, dass Sie nicht eines Tages auch auf solch einem liederlichen Pfad wandern werden."

„Sicher nicht, Frau Luise", erwiderte Hermine.

„Das wäre auch besser so. Schlafen Sie jetzt." Die Kammertür schlug krachend zu.

„Was hast du dir dabei gedacht?", flüsterte Hermine, als sie sicher sein konnte, dass Frau Luise sich in ihre Kammer zurückgezogen hatte.

„Ich habe eben unser beider Probleme gelöst", entgegnete Mathilde. Sie grinste breit, wirkte entspannt und ganz und gar nicht angetrunken.

Am nächsten Morgen spürte man eine elektrische Spannung in der Luft, und das lag nicht nur an dem Sommergewitter, das heraufzog. Vor Dirk Bakkers Bürotür blieben Mathilde und Frau Luise einen Augenblick stehen. Luise Menninga hätte einen Monatslohn darauf verwettet, dass Mathilde mit dem Herrenbesuch auf ihrer Kammer endgültig den Bogen überspannt hatte. Sie sah sie bereits die wenigen Sachen zusammenpacken und das Haus verlassen. Luise würde ihr keine Träne nachweinen.

„Lassen Sie mich reden, wenn Sie wollen, dass Ihr Geheimnis bei mir sicher ist", zischte Mathilde, klopfte an die Tür und ging hinein.

Obwohl er eine Nacht darüber hatte schlafen können, zeigte Dirk Bakkers Blick unverhüllte Wut. Er schien wild entschlossen, Köpfe rollen zu lassen.

„Herr Bakker ...", begann Frau Luise, doch ihre Gedanken waren bei Anneliese. Wusste Mathilde Bescheid über ihr wahres Verwandtschaftsverhältnis?

„Frau Menninga", fiel Mathilde ihr ins Wort, „wird zu ehrwürdig sein, um den wahren Hergang zu schildern."

„Das will ich meinen!", knurrte Bakker. „Einer ehrenwerten Frau steht es schlecht zu Gesicht, darüber auch noch ausführlich sprechen zu wollen."

„Mit dem Vorfall wurde die Ehre des Hauses gerettet."

„Meine Ansichten von Ehre und Anstand sind ganz andere", polterte Bakker.

„Aber ohne diese Vorführung wäre es übel für uns alle ausgegangen. Frau Menninga hat den guten Ruf des Hauses gerettet."

Luise starrte sie entsetzt an.

„Soso." Bakker klang sarkastisch. „Hat sie das?"

„Ich ...", setzte Frau Luise an, doch Mathilde drängte sich an ihr vorbei und trat dicht an die Stühle vor Bakkers Schreibtisch heran.

„Frau Luise ist zu bescheiden, um Ihnen die ganze Wahrheit zu erzählen", betonte Mathilde mit erhobener Stimme. „Es ist ja auch zu delikat", fügte sie hinzu.

„Delikat ist der letzte Begriff, der mir dazu eingefallen wäre." Bakker rutschte nervös auf seinem Stuhl herum.

„Schamlos …" Die Hausdame versuchte, ihren Frust über die Angelegenheit loszuwerden, wurde aber erneut unterbrochen.

„Ohne Frau Luises schnelles Eingreifen wäre der Schaden für das Hotel kaum wiedergutzumachen gewesen."

Mathilde erkannte, dass Bakkers Wut sich in Neugier wandelte. Mit einem Handzeichen bedeutete er ihnen, sich zu setzen. Seine Augen ruhten auf Luise. „Nun, Frau Menninga, ich höre."

Luises Blick flog zu Mathilde. Später hätte die Hausdame nicht begründen können, warum sie das tat. Mit einem kurzen Kopfnicken erteilte sie Mathilde das Wort. „Ich wollte einfach wissen, wie Sie sich wieder einmal herausreden, Fräulein Remmers", sollte Luise Wochen später behaupten.

„Ich werde es erzählen." Mathilde legte eine Hand auf Frau Luises Unterarm, als wolle sie die Hausdame davor bewahren, das Unaussprechliche sagen zu müssen. „Alles begann mit ein paar Fotos, die am Strand von uns gemacht wurden."

Mathilde griff in ihre Rocktasche und legte ein Bild mit der Fotoseite nach unten auf Bakkers Schreibtisch. Der blickte darauf, dann zu seinen Angestellten hoch. Mit einem leichten Zögern griff er danach, um sich das Bild anzuschauen.

Die beiden Frauen hätten schwören können, dass sie ihren Chef niemals zuvor so erbleichen sahen. Frau Luise schnappte nach Luft, als er das Foto ablegte. Auch wenn es aus ihrer Sicht auf dem Kopf stand, erkannte die Hausdame, was abgebildet war.

„Das ist …“, begann Bakker.

„Eine Unverfrorenheit, ich weiß“, bestätigte Mathilde. „Und von diesen Bildern gibt es noch mehr.“

„Mehr?“, krächzte Luise und starrte Bakker mit aufgerissenen Augen an.

„Ja, es gibt einige davon. Ich habe Ihnen nur von meinem und von dem der Gästedamen aus Zimmer 7 und Zimmer 18 erzählt, Frau Luise.“ Kurz streichelte Mathilde Luises Arm, ehe sie in die Rocktasche griff und das schamlose Foto von Hermine neben das ihre legte.

„Wenn Sie genau hinsehen, Herr Bakker …“

„Gott bewahre!“, rief Luise.

„… dann“, sagte Mathilde, „erkennen Sie, dass die Körper und die winzigen Höschen exakt dieselben sind. Die Fotos, die unsere Gäste erhalten haben, sind identisch, bis auf die Gesichter natürlich.“ Mathildes Lüge bezüglich der Urlauberinnen zeigte sowohl bei Bakker als auch bei Luise Wirkung.

Mathilde nahm eines der Fotos und löste vorsichtig das Stückchen Papier, mit dem sie die Geldforderung zugeklebt hatte, ab. „Schauen Sie“, forderte sie Bakker auf.

Er las die Erpressernachricht und sein bleiches Gesicht verwandelte sich in ein puterrotes.

„Ich plante …“ Mathilde legte die Hand auf Luises Schulter. „Nein, diese mutige Frau an meiner Seite plante, den Kriminellen zu überführen. ‚Fräulein Remmers‘, sagte sie zu mir, ‚wir müssen den skrupellosen Kerl stoppen. Ein Erpresser wird nie aufgeben und immer neue Forderungen stellen.‘ Sie meinte, und dies, Herr Bakker, finde ich, ist eine hervorragende Idee gewesen, man müsse dem Mann eine Falle stellen. Bevor die ganze Angelegenheit den Ruf dieser unschuldigen Frauen und dieses Hauses ruinieren würde …"

Die eingelegte Pause nutzte Mathilde, um tief Luft zu holen. Sie ließ den beiden Zeit, den Sachverhalt sacken zu lassen und sich die Folgen dieser Straftat auszumalen. Der Schaden, den solche Fotos von Gästen dieses Hauses, von den Angestellten ganz zu schweigen, verursacht hätte, wäre kaum wiedergutzumachen.

„Der Gedanke von Frau Luises war", behauptete Mathilde, „ehe der Fotograf, Bernd Uden ist sein Name, noch mehr von den Gästen erpressen könnte, sollten wir ihm eine Falle stellen. Wir haben viele Möglichkeiten überlegt, nicht wahr, Frau Luise?"

Die Hausdame nickte, die Augen wie hypnotisiert auf die Bilder gerichtet.

„Doch es sollte eine Falle sein, die bewirken würde, dass der Kriminelle von der Insel verschwinden muss. Wir hätten ihn anzeigen können", Mathilde hob eine Hand, als wolle sie Bakkers eventuellen Einwand stoppen, „da haben Sie recht, Herr Bakker. Aber mal ganz ehrlich: Der Fotograf würde behaupten, wir hätten uns freiwillig so ablichten lassen. Wussten Sie, Herr Bakker, dass er sich von den Mädchen, die kein Geld haben, mit sexuellen Gefälligkeiten bezahlen lässt?" Als wäre sie tief beschämt, senkte Mathilde den Kopf. „Deshalb sind Frau Luise und ich auf den Gedanken gekommen, ihn einer versuchten Vergewaltigung zu überführen."

Frau Luise schlug eine Hand vor den Mund und stieß einen gequälten Laut aus.

„Bei der ich das Opfer sein musste und Fräulein Flessner sowie Frau Luise und die vielen anderen Borkum-Mädchen, die im Dachgeschoss wohnen, die frevelhafte Tat bezeugen könnten. Es war schrecklich, Herr Bakker. Ich habe mich so geschämt", log sie und blickte hoch. „Die Küsse waren ekelig und ich werde lange brauchen, um über diese Erniedrigung hinwegzukommen." Mathilde schniefte, griff erneut in ihre Rocktasche und betupfte mit einem Taschentuch Nase und Augen. „Aber jetzt wird er mit seinen liederlichen Bildern kein Geschäft mehr machen können. Er wird einpacken und die Insel verlassen müssen. Und sollte er das nicht tun, werden wir alle ihn anzeigen. Sie wissen schon, wegen …" Sie schaute Frau Luise an und erwähnte ihr zuliebe das Wort Vergewaltigung kein zweites Mal.

Die eintretende Stille, in der Mathilde den beiden erneut Zeit zum Nachdenken über die Zusammenhänge und deren Folgen ließ, unterbrach sie mit einem Schnäuzen ins Taschentuch. „Und das Gute daran …" Sie legte eine theatralische Pause ein.

„Was kann es da noch Gutes geben?", klagte Bakker.

„Dass ich dem Kerl, bevor er seine erpresserischen Bilder unseren Gästen aus Zimmer 7 und 18 zuschicken konnte, ihm diese abgenommen habe."

Bakkers Hand fuhr automatisch vor, als erwarte er, sie zu bekommen, doch Mathilde schüttelte den Kopf.

„Ich habe sie sofort vernichtet, ehe sie in falsche Hände geraten."

„Sehr gut." Bakker wirkte erleichtert und deutete mit dem Zeigefinger an, dass sie entlassen wären. Mathilde wollte nach den Bildern greifen, doch Bakker legte seine Hand darauf. Sie nickte und fasste Frau Luise an beiden Unterarmen, als benötige sie Hilfe, um vom Stuhl aufzustehen.

„Danke, Frau Menninga", rief Bakker, als die Bürotür schon fast hinter ihnen geschlossen war. „Die Familie ist Ihnen beiden zu Dank verpflichtet."

„Ich dachte, du hättest schon längst gepackt?" Hermine kam etwa eine halbe Stunde später in die gemeinsame Schlafkammer.

Mathilde bürstete in aller Ruhe ihr Haar. Sie schien es sogar gewaschen zu haben. „Warum sollte ich?"

„Du wurdest vergangene Nacht mit einem Mann erwischt."

„Richtig. Und wenn du genau hingeschaut hättest, wüsstest du, dass es der Fotograf war."

Hermine verzog das Gesicht, als müsste sie einen Schluck Lebertran hinunterwürgen.

„Was denn? Guck nicht so! Du solltest über die Entwicklung froh sein. Oder wäre es dir lieber gewesen, wenn er deine Bettlaken zerwühlt hätte? Die Familie Bakker und Frau Luise sind jedenfalls voller Dankbarkeit." Mathildes Augen leuchteten vor Hinterlist, dass es Hermine angst und bange wurde. Sie legte die Bürste beiseite und hob die Arme, um das Haar zu einem Knoten zusammenzustecken. „Würde mich nicht wundern, wenn ich die Nächste bin, die eine Pralinenschachtel geschenkt bekommt. Jetzt, da wir beide dicke Freundinnen werden, verrätst du mir, wer sie geschickt hat?"

Hermine schüttelte den Kopf.

„Auch gut. Ich werde es schon herausbekommen."

„Was ist passiert? In Bakkers Büro, meine ich."

Mathilde berichtete, was sie Bakker vorgeflunkert hatte. „Wenn du gefragt wirst, musst du die Geschichte bestätigen."

Hermine nickte. „Und Frau Luise?"

„Die hält ebenfalls den Mund. Und lass dir eines gesagt sein, Minchen: Wir sehen herrlichen Zeiten entgegen. Schwere Arbeit kann in Zukunft jemand anderes machen, ich nicht mehr. Und was das Schönste ist, unsere Geldprobleme mit dem Fotografen haben sich ebenfalls in Luft aufgelöst. Ach, ehe ich es vergesse …"

„Ja?"

„Wenn Bakker dich darauf ansprechen sollte – was er vermutlich nicht machen wird, so verklemmt, wie der ist –, vergiss ja nicht herumzujammern, wie tragisch und unerträglich das alles für dich war."

Berichte von den Geschehnissen der Nacht machten unter den Kollegen schnell die Runde. Es würde keinen Tag dauern, dann wüssten die meisten Insulaner Bescheid. Sicherlich würde die eine oder andere, die ebenfalls von Uden erpresst wurde, erleichtert aufatmen, dass dem Kerl das Handwerk gelegt wurde. Die Köchin Gertrud war die Einzige, der Hermine genügend vertraute, um ihr Mathildes Piratenstück, wie sie es später nannte, zu verraten.

„So etwas habe ich mir fast gedacht", behauptete Gertrud, „nachdem Mathilde wie eine glückliche Siegerin und Frau Luise vollkommen verstört die Treppe herunterkamen. Weißt du, Hermine, ich arbeite schon lange für die Familie Bakker. Doch in all den Jahren ist es nie vorgekommen, dass jemand sich so viel herausnehmen durfte wie Mathilde Remmers. Ich befürchte, das wird in Zukunft schlimmer werden."

„Wissen Sie, ob Mathilde vor dieser Geschichte schon mal den Bakkers einen großen Gefallen getan hat? So wie der Kutscher, der dem Juniorchef mal das Leben gerettet hat, vielleicht?"

„Ach, Hermine, du kleines Unschuldslamm! Ich denke eher, dass sie etwas weiß, was die Familie geheim halten möchte, und sie sie damit in der Hand hat."

„Ich kann mir nicht vorstellen, was es da Schlimmes geben könnte."

Köchin Gertrud fiel da so einiges ein. Mathilde habe etwas mit Jakob Bakker gehabt, was ihrer Meinung nach seitens Jakob nur eine Geschmacksverirrung gewesen sein konnte.

Oder Mathilde gehöre irgendwie zur Familie und niemand dürfte von der Blutsverwandtschaft mit den Bakkers etwas wissen und noch einige andere unschöne Dinge mehr.

Die Küchenmagd hob wie in der Schule den Zeigefinger.

„Ja, Dina?"

„Vielleicht ist Mathilde in Wirklichkeit ein Mädchen aus hohen Kreisen – eine Prinzessin oder so."

„Ach, Unsinn, Dina! Reden kann sie gelegentlich wie eine, doch bei *den* Manieren ist das kaum vorstellbar."

„Und die königliche Familie verlangt", ließ Dina nicht locker, „dass sie arbeiten gehen muss, um ihr Volk kennenzulernen. Vielleicht eine ältere und unbekannte Schwester von Prinzessin Wilhelmina von Oranje-Nassau?"

„Die Prinzessin hat keine Geschwister."

„Das weiß man nie. Unsere Lehrerin in der Schule hat mal gesagt, dass auch Könige Bastarde …"

„Stopp, stopp! Deine Fantasie möchte ich haben." Gertrud lachte. „Setz bloß keine Gerüchte in die Welt. Glaube mir, nichts davon trifft zu. Dennoch – haltet Augen und Ohren auf. Vielleicht bekommen wir es ja heraus."

Kapitel 15

Willem Dirks Bakker erfuhr bereits wenige Minuten, nachdem Luise Menninga und Mathilde Remmers das Büro seines Sohnes verlassen hatten, von der Geschichte.

Seiner Meinung nach passte die Räuberpistole nicht zu Frau Luise, doch das war im Augenblick sein kleinstes Problem. Er wusste, dass der Fotograf an Köhlers Herrenkonferenz teilgenommen hatte. Nicht gut.

Einem Kerl, der von unschuldigen Frauen Nacktfotos anfertigte, um sie zu erpressen, zudem ein mutmaßlicher Vergewaltiger, konnten durchaus noch andere kriminelle Taten zugetraut werden.

Er könnte Hilfe von den Teilnehmern der geheimen Runde einfordern. Er hoffte, dass der Kerl den Mund hielt. Sollte er die Modalitäten der Absprache ausplaudern, würden sie alles abstreiten. Das Wort vieler ehrenwerter Insulaner wog mehr als seines. Ihm würde niemand glauben. Dennoch, die Saat des Misstrauens gegen jeden einzelnen Grundstücksbewerber wäre gesät. Und es würde all diejenigen verschrecken, die ihm und seinem vorgeblichen Kontrahenten Georg Köhler Informationen zutrugen. Apropos Köhler. Jetzt, da der Fotograf aufgeflogen war, konnte man davon ausgehen, dass sein

Freund keine weiteren Geldforderungen mehr erhalten würde.

Kein Wunder, dass Uden über genügend Geld verfügte, um bei der Ausschreibung mitmachen zu können.

Ein Konkurrent weniger.

„Guten Tag, Vater", grüßte Dirk. „Hast du schon gehört …"

„Das haben Frau Luise und Fräulein Remmers gut gemacht."

„Ja, das denke ich auch. Aber das meine ich nicht."

„Was ist passiert?"

„Es heißt, der Fotograf hat die Insel auf Nimmerwiedersehen verlassen."

Hermine war froh, von Frau Luise ein paar Stunden freibekommen zu haben. Um in Ruhe über das Geschehene nachzudenken, war der Strand der ideale Ort. Am Hauptbadestrand zog sie ihre Schuhe und Strümpfe aus. Der Sand unter den Füßen war heiß und brannte an den Fußsohlen. So schnell es ging, rannte sie an die Wasserkante, um sie zu kühlen. Das Meer war angenehm und so spazierte sie mit gerafftem Rock Richtung Norden. Je weiter sie kam, umso einsamer wurde es. Gut eine halbe Stunde später erreichte sie die *Viktoriahöhe*, einen hölzernen Bau mit einer Veranda davor und einer Terrasse mit einigen Tischen und Sonnenschirmen. Hier saßen Gäste und genossen den Tag. Hermine sah, dass es einen Weg durch die Dünen bis hierher gab. Irgendwie musste das Ausflugslokal ja beliefert werden. Sie beschloss, noch ein wenig an der Wasserkante zu bleiben und auf dem Rückweg diesen Weg zu nehmen. Sie überlegte, ob sie sich nach der Aufregung im Café ein Eis mit Schlagsahne gönnen sollte. Ihren Wochenlohn erhielt regelmäßig ihre Familie, doch sie hatte noch einen Großteil des Geldes, das sie von Köhler bekommen hatte, auf dem Konto liegen.

Je näher sie der *Viktoriahöhe* kam, umso mehr war sie davon überzeugt, dass sie sich nicht trauen würde, allein an einem der Tische Platz zu nehmen.

Sie sah zwei Frauen winken und schaute sich um. Da weder hinter noch neben ihr jemand zu sehen war, konnte nur Hermine gemeint sein. Obwohl sie aus der Ferne die Gesichter nicht erkannte, winkte sie zurück.

„Hermine!" Der seichte Wind wehte ihren Namen heran. „Setz dich zu uns", rief Mathilde.

Hermine wunderte sich nur kurz, dass ihre Kollegin schon wieder freihatte. „Das ist Rosemarie. Sie kommt aus Münster und ist im zweiten Jahr ein Borkum-Mädchen."

Rosemarie war eine junge Frau, die kein Aufsehen erregte. Eine graue Maus, würde Hermines Großmutter sagen. Doch wenn Rosemarie lächelte, schien es, als würde jemand ein Licht anmachen. Sie war ihr sofort sympathisch.

„Rosemarie, das ist Hermine. Ich habe dir von ihr erzählt. Wir teilen uns die Kammer", fügte Mathilde schnell hinzu, als sie Hermines panischen Gesichtsausdruck sah.

Was mochte Mathilde Rosemarie noch alles berichtet haben? Ihr wäre es peinlich, wenn sich die Geschichte mit den Fotos herumsprechen würde.

Die beiden tauschten einen schnellen Blick. Hermine fühlte sich ausgeschlossen und trotz Einladung nicht willkommen.

„Nett, dich kennenzulernen", sagte Rosemarie.

„Ich spendiere uns", Mathilde winkte heftig der Serviererin, „allen ein Eis."

Rosemarie und Hermine schauten sie überrascht an. Jetzt waren sie beide es, die einen flüchtigen Blick wechselten. Mathilde war es wichtig, dass sowohl Hermine als auch Rosemarie blieben, besagte ihr stiller Blickwechsel. Das machte neugierig, denn normalerweise gab sie kein Geld für andere aus.

„Dreimal den speziellen Eisbecher des Hauses", bestellte Mathilde und Hermine nahm auf dem angebotenen Stuhl Platz.

„In welchem Haus arbeitest du?"

„In der *Strandvilla Hawich.*" Rosemarie klang stolz, so als wäre sie die Eigentümerin der prächtigen Villa im viktorianischen Stil, die noch allein und in bester Lage direkt am Hauptbadestrand lag. Das Hotel besaß vier Stockwerke. Eine herrschaftlich geschwungene Treppe führte zum Hoteleingang hinauf und auf einer Ecke des Daches trug es eine Art runde Kirchturmspitze mit mehreren Fenstern. Von dort aus musste man einen herrlichen Blick über den Strand und das Meer bis hinüber zur niederländischen Insel Rottum haben. Als habe Rosemarie ihre Gedanken erraten, sagte sie: „Von ganz oben aus kann man sogar die holländische Küste und die Inseln gleich gegenüber sehen."

„Ein fantastisches Haus", erklärte Mathilde. „Rosemarie hat es mir gezeigt. Na ja, nicht alles. Aber das meiste davon."

Hermine spürte einen Moment den Wunsch, ebenfalls die *Strandvilla Hawich* von innen ansehen zu dürfen.

„Rosemarie und ich sprachen eben davon, dass unser Chef", dabei deutete Mathilde auf sich und Hermine, „plant, auch so eine Strandvilla zu bauen. Ich sagte zu Rosi, dass du darüber mehr weißt."

„Ich?" Hermine war überrascht. „Was sollte ich wissen?"

„Nun …" Rosemarie nahm einen Eisbecher von der Bedienung entgegen. Erst nachdem das Serviermädchen auch Mathilde und Hermine ihr Eis gegeben und wieder gegangen war, beugte sie sich ein wenig vor und sagte mit leiserer Stimme: „In unserem Haus wird darüber geredet. Es heißt, du bist die Vertraute eures Seniorchefs."

„Vertraute? In welcher Angelegenheit?" Hermine nahm den Löffel und probierte ein wenig von der Schlagsahne und von dem Eis. Irgendwie schmeckte es fade, was sicherlich nicht am Eis lag.

„Man hat dich in *Köhlers Dorfhotel* gesehen." Rosemarie schob sich einen Happen Erdbeereis in den Mund und leckte den Löffel genüsslich ab. Sie schluckte und fügte leise hinzu: „Und dabei ging es ganz sicherlich nicht um einen Anstellungswechsel."

„Hat Hubert das gesagt?" Hermine legte den Löffel beiseite.

„Der Page? Nee. Der redet nicht über andere Leute. Aber ich weiß aus sicherer Quelle, dass bei Köhler alle Stellen besetzt sind."

Erleichtert griff Hermine nach dem Löffel. Gut zu wissen, dachte Hermine, dass Hubert verschwiegen war. Das Eis schmeckte endlich.

„Also?", mahnte Mathilde. „Was tust du bei der Konkurrenz?"

„Ich suche nach meiner Cousine. Das weißt du doch, Mathilde."

„Beim ersten Mal bestimmt. Aber du wurdest öfter dort gesehen. Erzähl uns nicht, dass es jedes Mal um Bertha ging."

Rosemarie legte die Hand, die den Löffel hielt, auf Hermines Unterarm. „Weißt du, Hermine, wir Borkum-Mädchen sollten zusammenhalten."

„Zusammenhalten? Gegen wen?“

„Die da oben. Die Reichen benutzen uns nur. Und wenn sie haben, was sie wollen, lassen sie uns fallen.“

Hermine war anderer Meinung. Einen oder mehrere Briefe abzuliefern, war in ihren Augen kein Ausnutzen. Da fiel das, was Mathilde ihren Kollegen durch ihren Schlendrian aufbürdete, schon eher in diese Kategorie. Außerdem empfand Hermine bei dem, wofür Bakker und Köhler ihre Hilfe in Anspruch nahmen, das Gegenteil. Ihr wurde Vertrauen entgegengebracht. Und die Herren verließen sich auf ihr Stillschweigen. Und mit ‚Späterfallenlassen‘ war sicherlich das Gerücht um sie gemeint. Da war nichts, was schiefgehen konnte. Da sie nie die Absicht verfolgt hatte, sich einen reichen Hotelier zu angeln, konnte sie in dieser Hinsicht auch niemand fallenlassen.

All diese Gedanken behielt sie für sich. „Ich weiß nicht, wovon ihr sprecht.“ Eine Lüge, die ihr flott über die Lippen kam. Hermine war sich sicher, dass es in den Briefen um die Vergabe der neuen Grundstücke ging.

„Es ist doch nur“, sagte Mathilde, „weil einige von den Borkum-Mädchen, die seit Jahren auf die Insel kommen, sich rechtzeitig um einen tollen Arbeitsplatz bewerben wollen. Jeder möchte in einem funkelnagelneuen Luxushotel arbeiten. Du kennst doch den Spruch: Wer zuerst kommt, mahlt zuerst.“

Sie sah Mathildes optimistischen Gesichtsausdruck und Rosemaries weit aufgerissene Augen. Sie erwarteten von ihr, die Namen der zukünftigen Strandhotelbesitzer aufzuzählen.

Das gefiel Hermine überhaupt nicht. In ihrem Magen wurde es eiskalt. Und das lag nicht am Speiseeis.

„Dann sollten sie", Hermine schob den Eisbecher von sich, der Rest schmeckte ihr nicht mehr, „wie alle anderen abwarten, bis der Gemeinderat sich entschieden hat."

***

Dirk Willems Bakker ging ruhelos in seinem Kontor auf und ab. Sein Vater und einige andere Männer saßen in diesem Augenblick mit dem Gemeinderat in einer öffentlichen Sitzung zusammen. Erneutes Thema war die Vergabe der Strandgrundstücke. Dirk fragte sich, was da zusätzlich von den Gemeindevertretern beschlossen werden musste. Schließlich ging es heute noch nicht darum, zu erfahren, wer einen Zuschlag bekommen würde. Vielleicht zusätzliche Regularien, vermutete Dirk, denn was ein Bewerber mitbringen musste, war längst vorgegeben und in der Borkumer Zeitung bekannt gemacht worden.

Die Bewerber mussten in der Lage sein, das Grundstück bezahlen zu können. Logisch. Ob nun bar oder mit einer Bankbürgschaft blieb jedem selbst überlassen. Zudem verlangte die Gemeinde einen Plan, was und wie er zu bauen beabsichtigte. Dass es ein Hotel werden musste, stand zur Bedingung. Nicht, dass sich ein reicher Industrieller aus Leipzig oder sonst woher eine private Villa hinsetzte. Dass Baupläne, Statikberechnungen und Finanzierungsunterlagen einer Bank dazugehörten, stand außer Frage.

Auf der öffentlichen Einladung zur Sitzung war unter Punkt drei der Tagesordnungspunkt zu lesen: Parzellenangabe. Die

Gemeinde hatte vermutlich in der ersten Ausschreibung versäumt, von den Kandidaten die Angabe anzufordern, an welchem der einzelnen Flurstücke sie interessiert waren. Sicherlich wollte der Gemeinderat sich vorab ein Bild machen können, wie die Strandfront später einmal aussehen würde.

Dirk Bakker überlegte, ob bei gleichwertigen Bewerbern das Los entscheiden würde. Vermutlich ja. Ihm kam der Gedanke, dass es sinnvoll sei, auf mehrere Flächen ein Angebot abzugeben. Das erhöhte die Chancen.

Er würde sich hüten, das laut auszusprechen. Adeline war gegen eine Erweiterung der Bakker-Betriebe. Er merkte, wie seine Meinung dazu ins Schwanken geriet. Einerseits sollte man mit der Zukunft gehen. Die Familie wurde größer, da war es gut, wenn man die Möglichkeiten der Kinder und Enkel auch im kommenden Jahrhundert im Blick behielt. Andererseits musste sich sofort darum gekümmert werden. Seine Kinder, Nichten und Neffen waren alle noch zu klein dazu. Kein Unternehmen florierte ordentlich, wenn man zu wenig Zeit dafür hatte.

Solange sein Vater das Oberhaupt der Familie war und den Überblick über die Betriebe behielt, sollte er sich als folgsamer Sohn fügen.

Möge er noch lange leben! Das, was Vater alles in die Welt setzte, dazu fehlte es Dirk an Talent und Nervenkraft.

„Jeder, wie er kann", murmelte er. Dennoch. Der Gedanke, selbst hoch oben in einem funkelnagelneuen Hotel direkt am Strand zu wohnen, war recht verlockend. Hochmodern sollte es werden, das hatte er Vater mehrmals sagen hören.

Papa war im Kopf jung geblieben, im Gegensatz zu ihm.

Dirk Bakker blieb vor dem Fenster stehen und dachte an die Äcker, die dem *Hotel Bakker Junior* gegenüberlagen. Nicht mehr lange, dann würde auch diese Straßenseite bebaut werden. Vielleicht sollten sie sich darum bemühen, wenn es mit den Flächen am Strand nicht klappte.

Seine Stimmung schwankte. Einerseits hoffte er, dass Vater den höchsten Grundstückspreis und das beste Konzept vorlegte, andererseits überlegte er, ob er lieber die Daumen drücken sollte, dass andere den Zuschlag bekamen.

Ihm schauderte bei dem Gedanken an die Folgekosten. Die meisten Straßen hoch zum Strand waren Sandwege. Höchstens gab es an beiden Seiten einen gepflasterten Bürgersteig. Jeder Bewerber sollte daran denken, diese Kosten in sein Konzept mit hineinzurechnen. Er hatte Vater darauf angesprochen. Der hatte den Zeigefinger gehoben und genickt.

„Gut, dass du daran gedacht hast, Sohn. Die Kosten für Kanalanschluss, Elektrizität, Gas und Wasser müssen unbedingt mit in die Planung einfließen. Das macht einen guten Eindruck und zeigt den Leuten in der Gemeindeverwaltung, dass man weiter in die Zukunft denkt und auch das Allgemeinwohl im Auge behält. Schließlich werden es die Anlieger sein, die den Ausbau einer Straße bezahlen müssen." Vater hatte ihm anerkennend auf die Schulter geklopft und wiederholt: „Gut gemacht."

Dirk seufzte und nahm seine Wanderung im Kontor wieder auf. Hin und her, hin und her. Kosten, die bedacht werden sollten. Schließlich wollte man ja einen Gewinn aus allem ziehen, und das nicht erst, wenn die Enkelkinder erwachsen und man selbst unter der Erde lag. Immer wieder holte Dirk die Taschenuhr aus der Westentasche heraus und klappte sie auf, um nach der Zeit zu sehen. Erst zehn Minuten war es her, seit er das letzte Mal darauf geschaut hatte.

Es klopfte an der Tür. Mit einem Satz war er da und riss sie auf. Vor ihm stand Fräulein Flessner mit weit aufgerissenen Augen. „Mein Gott, haben Sie mich erschreckt“, flüsterte sie.

„Was gibt es?“ Seine Stimme klang ungehalten. Er war viel zu nervös und angespannt, um jetzt auf das Befinden einer Angestellten Rücksicht zu nehmen. Sie schien weder der Ton zu kränken noch die Frage zu überraschen.

Fräulein Flessner knickste. „Ich soll Ihnen von Frau Luise ausrichten, dass die Lieferung Wein eingetroffen ist.“

„Ich komme sofort.“ Die Kontrolle, ob alles wie bestellt auch angekommen war, erledigte er gerne selbst.

Kapitel 16

Luise spritzte sich mit beiden Händen Wasser aus der Waschschüssel ins Gesicht. Sie griff nach dem Handtuch, ehe einige Tropfen ihr in den Halsausschnitt laufen konnten, und schnupperte daran. Diese fürchterlichen Waschweiber! Hatten sie doch für die Personalwäsche die teure Seife der Chefin verwendet. Luise drückte sich das Tuch auf die Nase und atmete mehrmals den herrlichen Geruch ein. Weil heute Sonntag war, würde sie auf ein Donnerwetter in der Waschküche verzichten und stattdessen den angenehmen Duft genießen. Als sich eine Hand auf ihre Schulter legte, fuhr sie erschrocken herum. Kurz überkam sie das Gefühl, bei etwas Verbotenem ertappt worden zu sein.

„Entschuldigen Sie, Frau Luise, ich wollte Sie nicht erschrecken."

„Was gibt es Wichtiges, dass Sie, ohne anzuklopfen, reinkommen?"

„Ich habe geklopft, aber …" Hermine schaute sich in Luises Kammer um. Ihr Blick blieb an einer eingerahmten Kinderzeichnung an der Wand hängen. „Das ist hübsch."

„Von meiner Nichte", sagte Luise schnell. „Ist allerdings schon einige Jahre alt. Das Bild meine ich. Meine Nichte natürlich auch. Sie ist fast erwachsen."

„Ist das die junge Frau, die vor ein paar Tagen in der neuen *Pension Staghouwer* von Ihnen einquartiert wurde? Die Zimmer dort sollen sehr hübsch sein."

Hier blieb selten etwas geheim. „Nun?" Frau Luise wandte sich brüsk ab. „Was gibt es Wichtiges?"

„Entschuldigung. Ich wollte nur fragen, was das kosten mag. Ich überlege, ob meine Eltern für ein paar Tage herüberkommen sollten. Sie haben noch nie in ihrem Leben Urlaub gemacht."

„Vierzehn Mark die Woche. Aber wenn Ihre Eltern etwas vornehmer wohnen möchten, im *Hotel Dabelstein* bieten sie eine Woche für dreiunddreißig Mark an."

„Danke." Hermine deutete einen Knicks an.

„Nur deswegen sind Sie nicht gekommen. Was gibt es Wichtiges, Fräulein Flessner?"

„Der Fotograf hat die Insel fluchtartig verlassen. Ich habe mich noch nicht bei Ihnen bedankt. Also, herzlichen …"

Frau Luise winkte ab. „Gern geschehen."

Als Hermine keine Anstalten machte zu gehen, fragte sie: „Gibt es noch etwas?"

„Eine Doppelbelegung."

„Das ist nicht meine Aufgabe. Sagen Sie es der Chefin."

„Die ist in der Kirche und die Gäste stehen an der Rezeption und warten."

„Wer ist sie?", fragte Adeline Bakker um elf Uhr, als die Glocken der kleinen Kirche am alten Leuchtturm nach Beendigung des Gottesdienstes ausklangen.

„Eine Marienerscheinung", neckte Jakob seine Schwägerin. Er war verstimmt, weil er und seine Ehefrau auf Adelines Drängen hin an dem Gottesdienst teilnehmen mussten. Ihm reichte es vollkommen, an Ostern, Pfingsten und Weihnachten ins Gotteshaus gehen zu müssen. Doch da Hieltje wieder schwanger war und das Kind später getauft werden sollte, musste er sich wenigstens einige Monate vorher mehrmals in der Kirche blicken lassen. Adelines Meinung, nicht seine. Dennoch hatte Jakob sich dem Wunsch der Schwägerin gefügt. Wusste er doch, dass er sich ihrer Zuneigung gelegentlich erneut versichern sollte, wollte er weiterhin von ihr unterstützt werden, wenn der Rest der Familie wegen seines Hangs zum weiblichen Geschlecht über ihn herfiel. Er war sich sicher, dass sie seit ewigen Zeiten heimlich in ihn verliebt war, auch wenn sie es verstand, das niemanden merken zu lassen. Nicht einmal die vor Eifersucht zerfressene Hieltje, die im Augenblick mit dem Pastor redete, hegte einen Verdacht. Ihn wunderte nur, dass Schwägerin Adeline in all den Jahren zu ihm hielt. Aber wer konnte schon sagen, was im Kopf einer Frau vor sich ging. Gut für ihn, er wusste es gelegentlich auszunutzen.

„Marienerscheinung?" Adelines Tonfall ließ ihn genauer hinschauen. Das Mädchen, das im hellen Sonnenlicht stand, den Kopf in den Nacken gelegt, um auf die Spitze des Turmes sehen zu können, sah wie ein Engel aus.

„Eher der Teufel in Gestalt einer …", zischte Adeline und hielt sich am Arm ihres Schwagers fest.

„Es ist einfach zu heiß. Du fantasierst." Jakob wandte den Blick vom Mädchen ab. Seine Schwägerin bedurfte seiner Aufmerksamkeit. Wie ein nasser Sack hing sie plötzlich an seinem Arm. Er musste sie stützen, damit sie nicht zu Boden ging. Vermutlich ein Schwächeanfall aufgrund ihres Zustandes. Die siebte Schwangerschaft machte ihr zu schaffen. Adeline versuchte, ihre Schwierigkeiten vor der Familie zu verbergen und weiter die starke Frau und Hoteliers-Gattin zu mimen, doch Jakob hatte sie durchschaut.

Er führte Adeline die Stufen vom Kirchplatz zur Straße hinunter und ließ sie auf einer Bank gleich neben der stützenden Mauer, die Turm, Kirche und Friedhof umgab, Platz nehmen.

„Wo ist sie hin?“ Adeline schüttelte seinen Arm ab.

„Wen meinst du, liebste Schwägerin?“, fragte er, wohl wissend, wer gemeint war. Aber auch er konnte sie unter den Menschen, die die Kirche verließen, und den vielen Urlaubern, die um den Turm herum lustwandelten und sich die alten Grabsteine lange verstorbener Walfänger anschauten, nicht entdecken.

„Sie kommt mir so bekannt vor“, flüsterte Adeline.

Jakob sah, wie ihr ein Schauder über den Rücken lief. Sie war aschfahl.

„Komm, ich bringe dich nach Hause.“

Am Nachmittag hatte Jakob den Vorfall vor der Kirche und den blonden Engel vergessen, da sah er sie wieder.

Diesmal im Gespräch mit seinem Vater und dem guten Geist des Hauses Bakker – Frau Luise, ihrer Tante.

Jakob beobachtete die drei aus der Ferne. Als das junge Mädchen sich mit einem Händeschütteln von seinem Vater und einem Wangenkuss von Luise Menninga verabschiedete, konnte er es an der Körperhaltung des Vaters erkennen: Papa hatte die gleichen Schlussfolgerungen gezogen, die Jakob so konsequent vor sich selbst verleugnet hatte.

Als Anneliese, ihren Namen hatte er noch am Tag ihrer ersten Begegnung herausbekommen, an ihm vorbei in Richtung Dorfmitte ging, nickte sie ihm zum Gruß zu. Er grüßte ebenso stumm zurück und sog ihren Duft, der nach Maiglöckchen roch, tief ein. Ein Kribbeln in seiner Leistengegend ließ ihn anders als gewohnt entsetzt zu Boden blicken.

„Du schaust, als habe ein Hai dir den großen Zeh abgebissen." Erschrocken fuhr Jakob herum. Sein Vater stand dicht hinter ihm. „Und soll ich dir etwas verraten, mein Sohn?"

Jakob nickte, immer noch Anneliese hinterherstarrend.

„Sie ist vierzehn", informierte ihn sein Vater. „Und du wirst dir vermutlich bald wünschen, es wäre nur der Zeh, der dir Schmerzen bereitet."

Ehe Jakob den Mut fand, um keck zu fragen, was der Alte damit meine, klopfte der ihm heftig auf die Schultern und fügte hinzu: „In deiner Haut möchte ich nicht stecken."

Keine zwei Stunden später wusste Jakob, was gemeint war.

Hieltje lauschte an der Tür und zog ihre eigenen Schlussfolgerungen.

„Selbst ein Blinder erkennt es von Weitem", beschwerte Adeline sich. „Nur Jakob verschließt vor der Wahrheit die Augen. Ehe auch andere es sehen, müssen wir es der Familie sagen. Es geht jeden von uns etwas an – vor allem aber Jakobs Frau."

Hieltje riss die Tür auf und trat ein. Erschrocken fuhren Dirk und Adeline herum. Beide wirkten, als habe man sie bei etwas Unschicklichem erwischt.

„Jakob hat eine Geliebte?" Die neuerliche Erkenntnis über die Untreue ihres Ehemannes bereitete ihr körperliche Schmerzen. Adeline, die nach dem Kirchgang einen ähnlichen Schock erlitten hatte, eilte herbei, nahm ihren Ellenbogen und führte sie zu einem der Stühle. Allein wegen dieser Hilfsbereitschaft konnte Hieltje sicher sein, mit ihrer Vermutung ins Schwarze getroffen zu haben. „Ist es die Sängerin?"

„Die trällert mittlerweile in Paris oder Zürich."

„Es ist schlimmer", maulte Dirk, „als du denkst."

„Was kann da noch schlimmer sein?"

Adeline und Dirk tauschten einen Blick. Dirk schüttelte leicht den Kopf. „Es tut mir leid." Adeline legte beide Hände auf Hieltjes Schulter und schaute über ihren Kopf hinweg Dirk an. Ihr Blick forderte ihn auf, seiner Schwägerin die Wahrheit zu sagen. „Wir haben noch keinen Beweis", sagte er. „Aber diese Ähnlichkeit kann man nicht übersehen. Dennoch sollten wir erst herausbekommen, was die Mutter dazu zu sagen hat."

„Wessen Mutter denn, um Himmels willen?"

„Wir fragen ihre Tante", erklärte Adeline und streichelte Hieltjes Oberarme.

„Jetzt weiß ich überhaupt nicht mehr, worüber ihr sprecht. Wer hat Ähnlichkeit mit wem und was regt ihr euch so darüber auf?"

Ehe sie eine Antwort erhielt, öffnete sich die Tür. Klaas, Jann, Eildert, Geeske und der Senior betraten den Raum. Jakob fehlte.

„Ich konnte ihn nirgends finden", verkündete Willem Dirks Bakker. Er trat als Letzter ein und bat Hieltje, den Raum zu verlassen. „Die Angelegenheit, die wir zu besprechen haben, betrifft in erster Linie meine eigenen Kinder."

Eine uralte Familientradition. Wenn es um etwas besonders Wichtiges ging, wurde es zuerst zwischen dem Alten und seinen Kindern besprochen, ehe der Rest der Familie seine Meinung beisteuern durfte.

Hieltje schnaufte unzufrieden, verließ jedoch das Zimmer. Sie merkte nicht, dass Adeline blieb. Heftig schlug sie die Tür hinter sich zu und wäre auf dem Flur fast in ihren Ehemann hineingerannt. In ihrem Zorn konnte sie nur sagen: „Ja, geh nur rein! Das Familiengericht sitzt schon zusammen. So wie es aussieht, hast du diesmal den Bogen überspannt.“

„Die Leute werden sich das Maul zerreißen“, klagte Geeske. Dabei sah sie ihren Vater an, als sei er an allem schuld. Doch dieses Mal gingen die Konsequenzen aus einer der Affären ihres Bruders die ganze Familie etwas an.

„Was schaust du mich dabei so strafend an, liebste Tochter?“

„Du scheinst es auf die leichte Schulter zu nehmen. Du wirkst sogar, als seist du stolz auf die Eskapaden deines Sohnes.“ Adeline traten Tränen in die Augen. Man hätte meinen können, ihr eigener Mann und nicht der Schwager hätte sie mit solchen Folgen betrogen.

„Dann lasst die Leute sich das Maul zerreißen.“ Klaas tat, als interessiere ihn die Meinung seiner Mitbürger wenig, doch alle im Raum kannten ihn gut genug, um zu wissen, dass ihn die Tatsache, plötzlich Onkel einer fast erwachsenen Nichte zu sein, berührte. Mit der Spitze des rechten Zeigefingers strich er andauernd über den untersten goldenen Knopf seiner dunkelblauen Uniformjacke. Vermutlich würde die Mannschaft auf der einmastigen Jacht *Hoffnung* jetzt ungeduldig auf ihren Kapitän warten, um betuchte Feriengäste auf die See hinauszufahren. Dabei konnte Klaas wenigstens ein bisschen seine Seefahrersehnsucht nach der großen weiten Welt stillen.

„Wir könnten alles abstreiten.“ Adeline blickte auffordernd in die Runde. Da saßen sie, die einen entsetzt, andere teilnahmslos, amüsiert oder besorgt.

„Was wollen wir abstreiten?“ Jakob betrat den Raum.

„Dass du uns ein Bastard ins Nest gelegt hast.“

„Wer behauptet denn so etwas?"

„Wir." Willem Dirks Bakker bedeutete Jakob, sich zu setzen. „Deine Schwägerin und auch ich haben es sofort gesehen."

„Die Ähnlichkeit springt einem förmlich ins Gesicht", ergänzte Adeline.

Bakker Senior ging zum Sideboard hinüber und rückte die Bilder, die dort gerahmt standen, ein wenig hin und her. Das Bild von Geeske, als sie eben zwölf geworden war, drückte er Jakob in die Hand.

Jakob starrte es an, als sähe er das schwarz-weiße Porträt zum ersten Mal in seinem Leben.

„Wenn du ehrlich bist, mein Sohn, ist es dir auch aufgefallen."

„Luise Menningas Nichte sieht genauso aus."

„Luise hat Familie?" Geeske Bakkers Stimme bekam einen harten Klang.

„Wenn du dich mehr um die Mitarbeiter unserer Betriebe als um deine Garderobe kümmern würdest, wüsstest du das." Bakker Senior ignorierte den giftigen Blick seiner Tochter.

„Und was hat das mit dieser dringlichen Familiensitzung zu tun?", wollte Jakob wissen.

„Das, liebes Brüderlein", meinte Klaas, „scheint mir das Thema zu sein, das zum Kern unseres Treffens führt. Denn solltest du mal etwas mit Frau Luises Schwester gehabt haben, ist die junge Dame, um die es sich hier dreht, ein neues Mitglied der Familie. Mit allen Konsequenzen im Hinblick auf das Erbe." Plötzlich hatte Klaas den goldenen Uniformknopf in der Hand. Verärgert blickte er seine Schwester an, die tat, als begreife sie die Folgen erst jetzt.

„Kommt überhaupt nicht infrage, dass wir alle hier für Jakobs Triebe bluten müssen."

„Halt, stopp!", rief Jakob. „Ich kenne Luise Menningas Schwester. Sie war letzten Sommer zu Besuch auf der Insel. Wenn ihr sie sehen würdet, wüsstet ihr, dass das nicht zutreffen kann."

„Was soll das heißen?"

„Dass sie ganz und gar nicht mein Typ ist: klein, dick und verlebt."

„Sie wird vor vierzehn, fünfzehn Jahren anders ausgesehen haben."

„Was sagen denn Luise Menninga und ihre Nichte zu der ganzen Angelegenheit?" Jann, den ein Hauch von frisch gebackenem Kuchen umhüllte, versuchte einen weißen Fleck auf seinem Ärmel loszuwerden.

Schweigen.

„Wir haben sie nicht darauf angesprochen, wollten erst klären, wie die Familie damit umgeht."

Willem Dirks Bakker griff nach seinem Gehstock, um mit seiner Hilfe aus dem Sessel hochzukommen. „Dann sollte ich mal mit ihr reden."

„Halt, Vater! Ehe du gehst, müssen wir entscheiden, was wir machen, falls Jakob wirklich …" Geeske brach ab.

„Ja, Vater", meldete sich Eildert zu Wort, „wie geht die Familie damit um, sollte sie wirklich deine Enkelin sein?"

„So, wie wir mit all meinen vorhandenen und zukünftigen Enkelkindern umzugehen gedenken. Ich habe vierzehn Enkel, zwei weitere sind unterwegs. Und wenn ich Geeskes Bäuchlein richtig interpretiere, wohl bald drei. Da kommt es auf eines mehr oder weniger kaum an."

„Ich habe nur zu viel gegessen", murrte Geeske und Eildert meinte: „Da bin ich anderer Meinung. Der Erbteil für Jakobs

Bastard geht auf jeden Fall von seinem Erbe ab", und klopfte Jann, der aus seiner Backstube gleich nebenan zur Familienbesprechung geeilt war, vergeblich einen Mehlfleck von der Schulter. „Das ist meine Meinung."

„Mir ist es gleich. Ich denke, wir sollten erst weiterdiskutieren, wenn wir Gewissheit haben", verkündete Jann. „Ihr entschuldigt mich, mein Sauerteig kann nicht länger warten", sagte er und verschwand.

Der Rest der Familie schloss sich seiner Meinung an. Was brachte es, sich um ungelegte Eier zu zanken? Genauso schnell gingen sie auseinander, wie sie zur Familienversammlung zusammengekommen waren.

„Jakob", hielt der Senior seinen jüngsten Sohn auf. „Du kommst mit mir."

Doch ehe die Angelegenheit geklärt werden konnte, war es Adeline, die für noch mehr Aufregung im Hause sorgte.

Mit einem Geschirrtuch über der Schulter trat Luise aus der Hotelküchentür auf den Hinterhof hinaus. Hier war es angenehm kühl. Der Juli neigte sich dem Ende zu. Er hatte sich als ein heißer Monat erwiesen und Luise war froh, in ihrer Freistunde hier im Schatten sitzen zu können. Sie ließ sich auf der Bank nieder und verschnaufte einige Augenblicke und lauschte. Ein paar Spatzen zankten sich und verstummten, weil eine Katze um die Hausecke schlich. In der Stille hörte Luise, dass jemand in die Hotelküche ging, dessen Stimme ihr bekannt vorkam, die sie aber im Augenblick niemandem zuordnen konnte. Es war entweder Bäckermeister Jann Bakker oder sein Bruder Eildert, der die komplette Bürokratie der Betriebe verwaltete. Beide konnte man anhand ihrer Stimme kaum unterscheiden.

Luise lauschte normalerweise nicht, so etwas war unter ihrer Würde, doch als sie meinte, ihren Namen zu hören, wurde sie neugierig.

Der Mann sprach mit der Köchin. Gertrud Dirksen hatte schon im Hause Bakker gekocht, als Luise ihre erste Saison hier verbracht hatte. Es wurde gemunkelt, dass die hochgewachsene dürre Gertrud vor ewiger Zeit ihren Albert dem Werben von Eildert Bakker vorgezogen hatte. Die Stimmen kamen näher. Luise, so klein und untersetzt sie auch sein mochte, konnte sich flink und leise bewegen wie ein Aal, der aus einer Reuse schlüpft. Hinter einigen Fässern, in denen das Küchenpersonal den Abfall für den Bauern aufbewahrte, ging sie in Deckung. Die Küchenreste aus dem Restaurationsbetrieb holte der Upholmbauer gerne zur Fütterung seiner Schweine ab. Zum Glück hatte er sie heute Morgen schon geleert und aufmerksam, wie Pieter Klaasen Akkermann war, lagen die Deckel ordentlich verschlossen darauf, sodass weder Fliegen rein noch allzu viel Geruch herauskam.

„Ich möchte nicht", hörte sie die männliche Stimme sagen, „dass Frau Luise davon erfährt, bevor Vater mit ihr gesprochen hat. Vielleicht ist ja nichts dran an der ganzen Geschichte und meine liebe Schwägerin macht wieder mal viel Wind um nichts."

Eine Weile blieb es still. Er musste seine Pfeife angezündet haben, denn Tabakrauch kitzelte Luises Nase. Jetzt nur nicht husten, dachte sie und daran, wie peinlich es ihr wäre, hinter den Drangtonnen hockend erwischt zu werden.

„Du weißt nichts davon?"

„Mir gegenüber hat sie kein Wort erwähnt", hörte sie Gertruds Stimme.

„Und so, wie ich dich kenne, würdest du es mir auch nicht verraten, wenn du es wüsstest." Es klang nicht, als sei er böse darüber, eher, als erkenne er Gertruds Haltung an. „Aber einen Versuch war es wert."

Luise zählte bis fünfzig. Als sie meinte, die beiden wären gegangen, kam sie hinter den Tonnen hervor.

Anneliese für einige Zeit im *Gästehaus Staghouwer* unterzubringen, war vermutlich keine gute Idee gewesen. Sie hätte wissen müssen, dass Anneliese einem der Bakkers auffallen würde.

Wurde es endlich Zeit, ihr Geheimnis zu lüften? Oder sollte sie weiter die Lüge aufrechterhalten, Anneliese sei ihre Nichte? Sie musste dringend mit ihr darüber reden. Anneliese sollte das Recht haben, selbst zu entscheiden, ob das Geheimnis bewahrt oder gelüftet werden sollte.

Die Diskussion hatte sie angestrengt. Keine Viertelstunde später saß Adeline erschöpft im Schatten des Hauses. Hier war die Sommerluft angenehm und sie konnte ihren Gedanken nachhängen. Eine leichte Brise kühlte ihre feuchte Stirn und den Nacken und trieb einen Hauch von vergammelten Lebensmitteln heran. Am Ende des Grundstücks zwischen Sanddornbüschen und Holundersträuchern war es angenehmer, doch dort brannte die Sonne.

Diese Schwangerschaft bereitete ihr große Probleme. Doktor Schmidt hatte gemeint, wenn sie noch ein wenig länger leben wolle, sollte es die letzte sein. Doch den Rat hätte er lieber Dirk gegeben. Den Kopf an die Hauswand gelehnt, starrte sie in den Himmel. Nicht eine einzige Wolke war zu sehen, dafür jede Menge Möwen, die wie Geier um etwas kreisten. Fliegende Ameisen, wusste sie und kannte die Folgen. Vermutlich würde es heute noch ein Gewitter geben. Schon meinte sie ihre Schwiegermutter und ihre Schwägerin Geeske mit ängstlich aufgerissenen Augen in ihren Sesseln sitzen zu sehen. Jede mit einer Gewitterkiste auf dem Schoß und jederzeit zum Sprung bereit, sollte der Blitz einschlagen. In der Kiste lagen Ausweise, Urkunden, Schmuck und diverse andere Kleinigkeiten, die man vor einem Brand schnell in Sicherheit bringen wollte. Seit der alte Turm vor etlichen Jahren vollkommen ausgebrannt war, war ihre Angst noch größer geworden. Obwohl die Damen sich jedes Mal bis ins Mark fürchteten, gelang es dem Schwiegerpapa nicht, sie dazu zu überreden, einen dieser neumodischen Blitzableiter zu installieren. Die Frauen irritierte der Begriff Fangeinrichtung. So wurde der Stab genannt, in dem der Blitz einschlagen sollte.

„Fangeinrichtung?", hatte die Schwiegermutter gesagt. „So ein Ding kommt mir nicht auf das Dach! Das ist ja, als wolle man den Höllenfürsten herausfordern. Außerdem verstehe ich nicht, was mit einem eingefangenen Blitz gemacht werden soll. Teufelswerk!"

Der Schwiegervater hatte versucht, es genauer zu erklären, doch mit Physik hatte die Seniorin nichts am Hut. Wie es ihr wohl ergangen war in der Nervenklinik? Bald kam sie ja zurück. Adeline war unsicher, ob es sie freuen sollte. Kaum vorstellbar, dass Schwiegermama von ihrer religiösen Besessenheit vollkommen geheilt heimkehren würde.

Sie erhob sich von der Bank und ging bis ans Ende des Grundstücks, um sich zu versichern. Ja, der Blitzableiter, der erst vor einigen Wochen angebracht worden war, war deutlich zu erkennen. Wetten, dass die Alte Jahre brauchte, um ihn zu bemerken! Beruhigt strich sie sich über den gewölbten Bauch.

Heute hatte es zu viel Aufregung gegeben. Das konnten weder sie noch ihr Ungeborenes gebrauchen. Da war es gut, dass die Schwiegermutter, die vor jedem Gewitter wie eine Irre alle verrückt machte, noch einige Tage in der Nervenklinik bleiben würde. Und Geeske, die Gott sei Dank zwei Häuser weiter über der Apotheke wohnte, ließ sich hoffentlich von ihrem Ehemann trösten und würde Beruhigungspülverchen schlucken. Adeline hielt wenig von den neumodischen Medikamenten, so wie sie sich für nichts Modernes erwärmen konnte.

„Oh, Verzeihung. Ich wollte Sie nicht stören."

Hermine Flessner kam mit Adelines jüngster Tochter, der zweijährigen Harmina, auf dem Arm in den Hof. Die Kleine liebte das Mädchen aus Leer, das sich gerne um die Bakker-Kinder kümmerte. Einerseits war Adeline eifersüchtig auf die Zuneigung ihrer Jüngsten zur Angestellten, andererseits sagte sie sich, dass sie froh sein konnte, dass ihr damit viel Arbeit abgenommen wurde. Diese verflixte siebte Schwangerschaft – sie machte so hilflos. Keine zehn Jahre war es her, da war Adelines erstgeborene Tochter Petra, damals in genau dem Alter, in dem die kleine Harmina jetzt war, gestorben. Eine Erinnerung, die sie seit Wochen täglich heimsuchte. „Das sind die Hormone", hatte Doktor Schmidt versichert. Was immer das auch sein mochte – neumodischer Kram!

„Ganz schön heiß", stellte Fräulein Flessner fest und ließ Harmina, die den gleichen Namen wie ihre Großmutter trug, herunter. Die Ähnlichkeit der Vornamen Hermine und Harmina gefiel ihrer Tochter besonders.

Adeline dachte an die patronymische Namensgebung. Ihr Ehemann wollte die Tradition durchbrechen und dem Kind einen Namen geben, der ihm gefiel. Doch Adeline hing am

Althergebrachten. Auch dieses Baby würde seine Vornamen nach altem Brauch erhalten.

Die kleine Harmina tappte, sich an Fräulein Flessners Zeigefinger festhaltend, auf sie zu. Sie konnte noch nicht gut laufen.

„Ihr fehlt der Mut loszulassen.“ Hermine Flessner lachte, als habe sie Adelines Gedanken erraten.

„Hmmm.“ Sie nickte, dann verzerrte sich ihr Gesicht vor Schmerz.

Senkwehen, sie kannte sich aus. Nicht nur ihrer jüngsten Tochter fehlte der Mut. Mit Bangen schaute sie der Niederkunft entgegen und hoffte, nach Willem, Petra, Peter, Klaas, Thomine und Harmina erneut eine Tochter zu bekommen.

„Ist es so weit?“ Hermine klang besorgt und Adeline musste sich im Stillen eingestehen, dass die Leeranerin nicht nur ein hübsches, sondern auch ein fleißiges und aufmerksames junges Mädchen war. Kurz bereute sie, Hermine am Anfang der Saison so ablehnend gegenübergestanden zu haben. Der Moment währte nicht lange, da fielen ihr die schon fast vergessenen Gerüchte um ihre Angestellte wieder ein.

„Noch nicht“, sagte Adeline. „Es sind nur Senkwehen. Aber Ruhe wäre schön. Gehen Sie mit meiner Süßen an den Strand.“

„Gerne, Frau Bakker. Soll ich die anderen Kleinen auch mitnehmen?“

„Ich bin nicht klein“, klagte der zwölfjährige Willem Dirks Bakker, genannt Willi, um ihn von seinem Opa unterscheiden zu können. „Peter ist klein.“ Willis neunjähriger Bruder Peter schlug mit der Hand nach dem großen Bruder. Der siebenjährige Klaas trug einen Eimer und einen Käscher.

„Wir gehen alle an den Strand“, bestimmte Hermine, die Klagen der Buben überhörend. „Fische und Krebse fangen.“ Unter Jubel stürmten die Jungs davon, wobei Willi ihnen gesittet folgte.

„Erzählst du uns die Geschichte von dem Meermann mit den grünen Haaren?“, fragte die fünfjährige Thomine.

„Klabautermann“, piepste Harminas zartes Stimmchen. Sie konnte schon mehr reden als Schritte alleine laufen.

„Den meine ich nicht“, korrigierte Thomine ihre Schwester.

„Aber der hat auch grüne Haare, oder Fräulein Hermine?“, krähte Klaas.

„Ihr habt beide recht. Der eine heißt Neptun, der andere ist der Klabautermann.“

„Ich bekomme die große Schaufel!“, rief Peter.

„Das glaubst auch nur du“, antwortete Klaas.

„Fräulein Flessner“, rief Adeline ihnen hinterher. „Besorgen Sie in *Fischers Basar*“, gemeint war der Laden an der Ecke, der Hüte, Souvenirs, Bade- und Strandartikel verkaufte, „eine zweite Schaufel und erzählen Sie den Mädchen kein Seemannsgarn, dafür sorgt die Köchin schon genug.“

„Sehr wohl, Frau Bakker.“

Sie waren noch keine fünf Minuten fort, da war in der Ferne das erste Donnergrollen zu hören.

„Das war's dann mit dem Strand“, erklärte Hermine auf halbem Weg dorthin. Die ersten dicken Tropfen fielen, dennoch protestierten die Kinder laut. Nur Willi zeigte Verständnis und benahm sich erwachsen. Gemeinsam mit Hermine beruhigte er die Geschwister, indem er ihnen Bonbons und eine neue Geschichte über den Meermann, der wie eine Meerjungfrau aussah, nur viel hässlicher war, versprach.

Sie erreichten das Hotel, kurz bevor das Gewitter losbrach. Die Freiwillige Feuerwehr, die hiesigen Ärzte und die Hebamme bekamen in den nächsten Stunden jede Menge zu tun.

Im Ostland schlug der Blitz in eine Scheune ein. Einige herumfliegende Dachziegel und ein abgerissener Ast verletzten drei Leute. Die Rettungsschwimmer mussten lebensmüde Badegäste, die bei Blitz und Donner im Meer schwimmen wollten, davon abhalten. Die Hebamme wurde ins Hotel gerufen.

Das Gewitter war noch nicht vorbeigezogen, da begann Adeline vor Schmerzen zu jammern. Dieses Mal schienen die Wehen sie kräftiger zerreißen zu wollen als bei allen Geburten zuvor. Die Hebamme schickte nach dem Arzt.

„Doktor Kock soll sofort kommen."

„Unser Hausarzt ist Doktor Schmidt."

„Der ist zum Ostland gerufen worden. Sie müssen schon mit Kock vorliebnehmen."

„Aber er ist so jung."

„Jeder fängt mal klein an", murrte die Hebamme. Was die Furcht der Gebärenden nur noch mehr anfachte. Auch den werdenden Vater scheuchte die Geburtshelferin fort.

Dina und Gertrud schleppten abwechselnd warmes Wasser nach oben und warteten vor der Tür auf den ersten Schrei des Neugeborenen. Viermal mussten sie wieder hinuntergehen, um erneut warmes Wasser zu holen, da das andere zum Waschen eines Säuglings zu kalt geworden war.

Das ganze Haus schien den Atem anzuhalten. Sogar die Gäste schlichen auf Zehenspitzen durch die Flure.

Der Regen hörte ebenso schnell auf, wie er begonnen hatte, ein letztes Gewittergrollen war in der Ferne zu hören. Die Sonne kam hinter den Wolken hervor. Die Luftfeuchtigkeit stieg an.

„Es ist zum Festland weitergewandert", bemerkte der Senior, als er sich zu seinem Sohn in den Hof gesellte. „Du bist ja ganz nass", stellte er fest. Dirk zuckte nur mit den Schultern. Sein Blick ging hinauf zu dem offenen Fenster, hinter dem sein siebtes Kind das Licht der Welt erblicken würde. „Ich bin jedes Mal wieder nervös", sagte Dirk.

„Verständlich."

Vater und Sohn warteten eine weitere Stunde. Sie schien ihnen wie eine kleine Ewigkeit, in der sie schwiegen und ihren eigenen Gedanken nachhingen. In der Sonne dampften Hinterhof, Büsche und Sträucher. Der Sand auf der Straße blieb an den Hufen der Pferde kleben, denn der Regen konnte den furztrockenen Boden nur wenige Zentimeter tief durchtränken. Man sah, wie viele Fuhrwerke die letzten sechzig Minuten vorbeigefahren waren. Endlich riss die Stimme von Frau Luise sie aus ihrem Zustand der Betäubung.

„Der Vater kann sich über eine Tochter freuen", rief sie in den Hof. Ein leises Babyschreien war zu hören.

Sich gegenseitig stützend, als hätten die Herren es selbst vollbracht, betraten sie das Haus.

„Es ist alles in bester Ordnung", sagte Doktor Kock. Seine Stimme klang überzeugend, doch nicht überzeugend genug für Adeline.

„Sie haben eine gesunde Tochter. Wie soll sie denn heißen?"

„Christine."

„Ein passender Name für die Kleine." Doktor Kock war der Schwiegervater von Georg Köhler Junior. Dass Köhler Senior mit Adelines Schwiegervater zerstritten war, interessierte ihn nicht. Weder der Arzt noch die Wöchnerin verschwendeten an diesem Tag nur einen einzigen Gedanken an die Zwistigkeiten ihrer angeheirateten Verwandten. Doktor Kock tauchte seine Finger in die Waschschüssel. In der zweiten Schüssel badete Frau Biel Christine.

Doktor Kock ließ sich von Luise Menninga erst die Seife und später ein Handtuch geben und trat mit dem Tuch in beiden Händen zurück ans Bett der Wöchnerin.

„Alles in Ordnung?“, fragte sie den Doktor. „Frau Bakker wirkt fiebrig.“

„Danke, mir geht es gut“, behauptete Adeline und an die Hebamme gewandt: „Ist sie gesund, Frau Biel?“

„Die Kleine ist bei guter Gesundheit und aufgeweckt“, meinte der Doktor.

„Kann ich sie halten?“

„Gleich, Frau Bakker. Ich will erst den Nabel abbinden.“ Frau Biel, die die meiste Arbeit bei der Geburt geleistet hatte, fügte hinzu: „Und ankleiden. Wir wollen sie ein bisschen hübsch machen.“

Doktor Kock trat ein paar Schritte vom Bett der Wöchnerin zurück und wäre fast in den frischgebackenen Vater hineingelaufen.

„Ist sie auch nicht kränkelnd?“, hörte Adeline Dirk den Arzt fragen. „Sie wissen, Herr Doktor, damals ist unsere kleine Petra …“

„Sie ist putzmunter. Hören Sie doch, wie sie schreien kann! Keine Sorge, Herr Bakker. Alles ist gut.“

„Gehen Sie und überzeugen Sie sich selbst.“

Hebamme Biel hatte Christine gebadet, den Nabel fest bandagiert und den Säugling in warme, flauschige Tücher gewickelt. Jetzt schob sie sich am Doktor vorbei, indem sie ihm mit ihren ausladenden Hüften einen Stoß versetzte und legte Adeline die Kleine in die Arme.

„Ich gehe mal davon aus, dass ich die Wunde versorgen soll." Sie schaute den Arzt herausfordernd an. „Oder wollen Sie das übernehmen?"

Doktor Kock hob abwehrend die Hände.

„Die Nachgeburt lässt auf sich warten", knurrte Frau Biel. „Also alle raus hier."

Doktor Kock gratulierte Dirk und wandte sich endgültig zum Gehen.

„Sie auch!", scheuchte die Hebamme Dirk hinaus.

„Auf ein Wort", sagte Doktor Kock, nachdem sich die Tür hinter den beiden Männern geschlossen hatte. „Ich fürchte sehr um die Gesundheit Ihrer Frau. Eine weitere Geburt wird sie schwerlich überstehen. Wie ich hörte, kränkelte sie ja schon vor und während dieser Schwangerschaft." Er klopfte dem frischgebackenen Vater auf die Schulter. „Kopf hoch. Sie schafft das schon."

Am Fuße der Treppe wartete der jetzt fünfzehnfache Großvater. „Ich begleite Sie hinaus, Herr Doktor", bot er an. Noch ehe die beiden Männer die Hoteleingangstür erreichten, kam ein Junge angerannt. Er wirkte wie von Haien gehetzt, als wäre er durch die halbe Nordsee geschwommen. Mit einer Hand strich er sich die feuchten Haare hinter die Ohren und blieb schnaufend vor dem Doktor stehen. Er stützte sich mit beiden Händen auf seinen Knien ab und schnaufte wie ein Walross. „Herr Bakker, gut, dass ich Sie gefunden habe. Und der Herr Doktor ist auch da. Gott sei Dank! Sie müssen beide schnell kommen."

„Was ist passiert?"

„In Ihren Stall ist der Blitz eingeschlagen. Erst hat es niemand gemerkt, bis das Heu anfing zu schwelen und …“
„Ist jemand verletzt?“
„Einen Stallburschen hat es erwischt.“

Kapitel 17

Tags darauf erhielt Hermine einen Brief ihrer Familie. Sie mussten etwas Außergewöhnliches zu berichten haben. Der Umschlag enthielt gleich mehrere Seiten.

Liebes Minchen!

Die ganze Familie ist aus allen Wolken gefallen. Ein Brief ist aus Amerika gekommen. Er stammt von Bertha. Ich frage mich, warum Du uns nicht geschrieben hast, daß sie seit langem nicht mehr auf Borkum ist. Hast Du uns die Postkarten geschickt, die von Bertha stammten? Ich habe zu Vater gesagt, das hast Du nur gemacht, damit wir uns nicht sorgen. Wegen der gefährlichen Überfahrt nach Amerika und so.

Stell Dir vor, sie lebt in Arizona. Ich mußte im Atlas nachsehen, wo das ist. Tragisch, dass Deine Cousine so wenig Vertrauen in unsere Familie hat, um nicht gleich mit der Wahrheit herauszurücken. Ich hoffe, Minchen, sollte Dir Ähnliches passieren wie ihr, weißt Du, daß Du bei mir und Deinem Vater immer ein Zuhause haben wirst. Aber ich weiche ab. Ich glaube nämlich, daß Du nicht alles über Berthas Schicksal weißt. So wie ich Bertha kenne, hat sie Dir nur von der Auswanderung erzählt und den Rest verschwiegen. Was für eine Tragödie und welche seelischen

Schmerzen das arme Kind aushalten mußte, wage ich mir gar nicht vorzustellen. Auch wenn ich die Ansichten meines Bruders, was nichteheliche Kinder angeht, weitgehend teile, so kann ich Berthas Entscheidung im Nachhinein verstehen. Mein Bruder hätte ihr die Hölle heißgemacht, und vermutlich wußte Bertha, daß er sie mit einem Bastard nicht aufnehmen würde. Die Arme! So trieb es sie nach Amerika. Deine Tante ließ mich ihren Brief lesen, und so kann ich Dir verraten, daß Bertha ihre Schwangerschaft zeitig genug dem werdenden Vater mitteilte. Im Vertrauen darauf, daß er sie heiraten würde, was der Schuft nicht tat. Im Gegenteil, er behauptete sogar, nicht der Erzeuger sein zu können, stell Dir das mal vor! Als sie dann im vergangenen Dezember hier war, hat niemand von uns gemerkt, daß sie da schon schwanger war. Sie ist dann auf die Insel gereist, um ihn zur Rede zu stellen. Da stritt er sogar ab, sie überhaupt zu kennen. Und heiraten wolle er sie auf keinen Fall, da er bereits verheiratet sei. Zudem würde er sich seine Zukunft mit dem Balg eines dahergelaufenen Zimmermädchens nicht versauen. Dieser Schuft, möge er verrotten! Na, jedenfalls wollte es der glückliche Zufall, daß alles für Bertha gut ausging. Ein Insulaner, leider habe ich den Namen vergessen, hatte sich bereits in Berthas erster Saison auf der Insel in sie verliebt. Er fand bei ihr wenig Beachtung, ließ aber in seinem Werben um sie nicht locker. Ein feiner Kerl. Ständig machte er ihr einen Antrag, den sie im vergangenen Dezember dann annahm. Natürlich hatte sie ihm von ihrem Zustand berichtet, so etwas läßt sich auch vor einem Mann nicht lange verheimlichen.

Hermine ließ den Brief sinken und starrte an die schräge Zimmerwand. Was hatte Bertha alles über sich ergehen lassen müssen. Die Arme! Und schön, dass es den jungen Herrn Hinrichs gab. Hermine hob Mutters Schreiben hoch und las weiter.

Und da der Borkumer bereits alles zur Auswanderung vorbereitet hatte, um, wie er sich Bertha anvertraute, sie sich in der Ferne aus dem Kopf zu schlagen, beschloss er, statt allein zu gehen, sie mitzunehmen.

Hermine griff nach dem zweiten Blatt Papier. Vor ihrem inneren Auge sah sie Bertha, wie sie den Erzeuger ihres Kindes anflehte, ihm drohte, es jedem auf der Insel zu erzählen.

„Damit schadest du dir selbst", antwortete der Kerl in ihrer Fantasie. „Ich werde alles abstreiten. Und wem, meine Liebe, wird man glauben? Einem dahergelaufenen Borkum-Mädchen, das nur auf die Insel gekommen ist, um sich einen Ehemann zu angeln, oder mir?"

Bei dem Gedanken kam ihr Jakob Bakker mit seinem hämischen Grinsen in den Sinn. Sie schüttelte den Kopf. Wo die Fantasie einen hintreiben konnte! Hermine versuchte weiterzulesen. Doch Bilder von Bertha, wie sie geweint haben musste und womöglich gedroht hatte, sich etwas anzutun, wollten nicht weichen. In Hermines Einbildung sah sie ihr Cousinchen von der Buhne ins Wasser springen, um sich und das Ungeborene zu ersäufen.

Aber so weit war es ja Gott sei Dank nicht gekommen. Hermine las den Brief ihrer Mutter zu Ende und in der nächsten Nacht träumte sie von Bertha. Sie sah den leiblichen Vater des Ungeborenen, der in Hermines Traum kein erkennbares Gesicht hatte, gegen Bertha handgreiflich werden. Die schallende

Ohrfeige meinte sie selbst zu spüren. Doch im Traum mischten sich Gegebenheiten, die nicht zusammenpassten.

Schweißgebadet erwachte Hermine mit Tränen auf den Wangen. Es dämmerte längst. Sie schwang sich aus dem Bett und blickte aus dem Dachfenster. Ihr Traum, wie ein Mann eine Frau geschlagen hatte, kam ihr in den Sinn. Ob Bertha wohl das gleiche Schicksal ereilt haben mochte?

Zum Anziehen war es zu früh, deshalb kroch Hermine zurück ins Bett und las den Brief der Mutter ein weiteres Mal. Unglaublich! Bertha musste jemanden auf der Insel haben, der über alles Bescheid wusste und für sie die Postkarten eingeworfen hatte. Eine gute Freundin vielleicht oder irgendeinen entfernten Verwandten aus Harmen Hinrichs Familie. Auf jeden Fall ein Mensch, dem Bertha vertraute. Eine innere Stimme verriet ihr, dass Jakob nicht der wirkliche Kindsvater war. Bertha wäre auf diesen schleimigen Kerl niemals hereingefallen. Aber es mochte ja mehr Typen seines Kalibers geben.

Hermine beschloss, den Brief vor Mathilde zu verstecken, damit die ja keine falschen Schlussfolgerungen ziehen konnte. In ihrer Reisetasche befand sich ein Geheimfach. Mutter hatte es hineingenäht. Vorsichtshalber. „Man weiß ja nie, welche Langfinger unterwegs sind."

Hermine zog die Tasche leise unter ihrem Bett hervor. Solange Mathilde schnarchte, war sie sicher, dass die Kollegin fest schlief. Sie öffnete die in den Futterstoff eingenähte Geheimtasche. Ihr Bankbuch steckte darin und jetzt auch Mutters Brief. Schritte auf der Hintertreppe und das Knarren der obersten beiden Stufen waren zu hören. Vermutlich Frau Luise, die zum Frühstück hinunterging. Schnell schob Hermine die Tasche zurück.

Bakker heftete eben die Arztrechnung von Doktor Kock in einer Akte ab. Der vom Blitzeinschlag entfachte Brand hatte den Stallburschen an der Schulter und an der Wade verletzt. Er hatte auch stark am Bein geblutet und es hatte schlimmer ausgesehen, als es war. Nach ein paar Tagen hatte er sich wieder zur Arbeit zurückgemeldet. Auch der Schaden im Stall konnte schnell behoben werden. Ohne den Stallburschen wäre vermutlich die komplette Scheune abgebrannt. Zur Belohnung hatte er vom Senior fünfzig Mark erhalten.

Es klopfte.

„Herein", sagte Willem Dirks Bakker, doch nichts tat sich. Dann klopfte es ein weiteres Mal. „Herein!", rief er so laut, dass man es bis auf die Straße hören konnte.

Vorsichtig ging die Bürotür auf. Das konnte nur Waldemar sein. Von Natur aus unentschlossen und umständlich, machte er dennoch seine Arbeit gut. Waldemar war nicht die hellste Kerze auf der Torte, aber die Familie Bakker konnte sich darauf verlassen, dass er genau und zuverlässig seine Aufgaben erledigte. Wie viele seiner Mitarbeiter wohnte auch Waldemar seit Jahren im Hotel. Die Frauen unter dem Dach, die Männer in einem kleinen Haus, das über den Hof zu erreichen war. Waldemars Eltern lebten im Armenhaus in der Süderstraße. Der Vater war dem Alkohol verfallen und die Mutter war vor Kurzem gestorben. Seit ihrem Tod, so hatte man es Bakker berichtet, hatte Waldemar seinen Vater nie mehr besucht.

Willem Dirks Bakker bekam ein schlechtes Gewissen. Seine Frau, die nach Mitteilung des Arztes bald aus der Klinik entlassen werden konnte, hatte sich immer darum gekümmert, dass es am Nötigsten im Armenhaus nicht mangelte. Die Gemeinde unterhielt die Unterkunft mehr schlecht als recht und verließ sich auf seine Harmina. Er sollte jemanden schicken, um …

„Ein Brief von dringlicher Dringlichkeit", verkündete Waldemar in der ihm eigenen Art und kam herein. „Herr Bakker, es sei ein notwendiger Notruf, sofort und unbedingt schnell zu erledigen, sagte der Mann." Mit ausgestrecktem Arm, als könne der Brief ihn beißen, trat er an den Schreibtisch heran, um die Post zu übergeben.

„Danke, Waldemar."

Waldemar machte einen Diener, rührte sich aber nicht weiter.

„Gibt es noch etwas?"

„Der Mann bestand ständig darauf, dass Sie ihn flugs sofort und gleich öffnen."

„Wartet er auf Antwort?"

„Nein. Aber die Dringlichkeit hat er mir sehr ans Herz gelegt."

„Dann sollte ich ihn öffnen." Bakker nahm den Brieföffner. Die bunten Glasstückchen am Griff funkelten im Sonnenlicht. Mit einem zügigen Ratsch schlitzte er den Umschlag auf. Bakker überflog die wenigen Zeilen und wurde blass. Ein paar Sekunden später schoss ihm das Blut zurück in den Kopf. Verdammt, er musste sich beeilen.

„Danke, Waldemar, du kannst gehen."

„Kann ich bei der Dringlichkeit helfen?"

„Nein, vielen Dank."

Waldemar wandte sich um.

„Halt! Schick mir Hermine Flessner ins Kontor."

„Das Hausmädchen, Zimmermädchen, Kinderfrau", murmelte er.

„Genau die. Und Waldemar …“

„Ja?“

„Zu niemandem ein Wort.“ Bakker wedelte mit dem Blatt Papier.

„Natürlich. Rätselhaft, geheim und geheimnisvoll. Es bleibt unser Geheimnis.“

„Sie wollten mich sprechen?“ Keine zehn Minuten hatte es gedauert, bis Fräulein Flessner an seine Tür klopfte und eintrat.

„Setzen Sie sich, bitte. Ich weiß“, Bakker schob mit dem Zeigefinger den Brieföffner ein wenig zur Seite, „dass ich es Ihnen mit meiner – nein, unserer – Geheimniskrämerei in der Vergangenheit schwer gemacht habe.“

Er blickte ihr kurz in die Augen. Es lag so viel Freundlichkeit und Klugheit in ihnen. Sie war zweifellos ein schlauer Kopf, was sie mehrfach bewiesen hatte. Und eine verschwiegene Person, was bei den Frauen selten vorkam. Ach, könnten doch all seine Schwiegertöchter nur ein wenig so sein wie dieses junge Mädchen! „Aber ich verspreche Ihnen, dass ich es wiedergutmachen werde, sobald die leidige Angelegenheit beendet ist.“

Fräulein Flessners Augenbrauen zogen sich nur für den Bruchteil einer Sekunde zusammen.

„Sie wissen, dass die Freundschaft zwischen Georg Köhler und mir nie aufgehört hat. Und ich möchte Ihnen vielmals danken, dass Sie so verschwiegen sind, auch wenn es, wie ich hörte, oft zu Ihrem Nachteil war. Köhler und ich haben alles getan, um diese schändlichen Gerüchte aus der Welt zu schaffen.“ Erneut rückte er mit dem Zeigefinger den Brieföffner ein paar Zentimeter zurecht. So offensichtlich beunruhigt zeigte er sich gegenüber Geschäftsfreunden oder Konkurrenten niemals, was ihn kurz sorgte. „Verlier nie dein Pokergesicht", hatte sein Stiefvater ihm früher immer eingeschärft, wenn es um geschäftliche Verhandlungen oder andere Dinge, oft Illegales, gegangen war, die Klaas Klaassen van Dyk wichtig gewesen waren.

„Und Sie sind intelligent genug, um mittlerweile zu wissen, warum Köhler und ich dieses Theater veranstalten." Er blickte sie erneut an. Diesmal wartete er so lange, bis sie sich genötigt sah, zu antworten.

„Es geht um die Grundstücke am Strand."

Ein Mundwinkel der jungen Frau ging nur ganz kurz nach oben, als ob sie sich ein Lächeln verkneifen wolle, dann senkte sie den Blick auf ihre Hände.

„Da haben Sie vollkommen recht, Fräulein Flessner. Ich habe eine große Bitte an Sie."

Jetzt schaute sie auf und lächelte. „Gerne, Herr Bakker." Und zwei Sekunden später fügte sie hinzu: „Ich helfe, wo ich kann."

„Dann möchte ich Sie bitten, morgen um diese Zeit wieder hier zu sein. Ich gebe Ihnen etwas, das Sie in der Gemeindeverwaltung für mich abgeben sollen. Mehr nicht. Aber …"

„… kein Wort darüber zu niemandem."

„Kluges Mädchen."

***

Hieltje hasste die Kommentare einiger Familienmitglieder zu Jakobs außerehelichem Verhalten. Sie konnte es nicht ausstehen, durch die Blume mitgeteilt zu bekommen, wenn jemand ihn in einer pikanten Situation gesehen haben wollte. Sie verabscheute die spitzen Bemerkungen und das höhnische Gerede hinter ihrem Rücken, von zweideutigen Feststellungen hinter vorgehaltener Hand ganz zu schweigen. Da tat sie lieber, als wäre sie im Hinblick auf die Untreue ihres Ehemannes blind und würde nichts bemerken. Zugegeben, kein schönes Gefühl, aber immer noch die bessere Wahl als Spott und Hohn zu ernten.

Dass ihr das nicht oft gelang, war Hieltje nicht bewusst. Und hätte sie geahnt, dass jeder, vom Angestellten über Freunde und Bekannte bis hin zur Familie, wusste, wie eifersüchtig sie war, hätte sie sich einiges verkniffen.

Vor fünf Minuten hatte sie Adeline zur Geburt ihres Kindes gratuliert. Nach ein paar schmeichelnden Worten über den Säugling wollte sie wissen, worum es bei der Familienbesprechung gegangen war.

„Bei der ganzen Aufregung hat man es wohl versäumt“, sie klang angesäuert, „es mir mitzuteilen.“

So erfuhr Hieltje von Anneliese, deren Ähnlichkeit mit Geeske, der Angst ums Erbe und was im Familienrat in Hinsicht auf die Nichte von Frau Luise mehr oder weniger beschlossen worden war.

Hieltjes Magen schien zu explodieren bei dem Gedanken, dass ihr Ehemann seine mutmaßlich eigene Tochter gierig wie eine Möwe, die ein Fischbrötchen sah, anstarrte.

„Und was hat der engste Kreis der Familie beschlossen?“

„Dass unser Schwiegervater sich darum kümmert.“

„Und was ist dabei herausgekommen?“, krächzte Hieltje, kurz davor, sich zu übergeben.

„Dass Jakob nicht Annelieses Vater sein kann. Es ist unmöglich. Luise Menninga schwört beim Leben ihrer Nichte, dass ihre Schwester niemals deinem Mann begegnet ist.“

„Und warum erfahre ich das erst heute?“

„Wir wollten jeden Kummer von dir fernhalten. Jetzt, da du wieder guter Hoffnung bist.“

„Das ist sehr nett von euch.“ Hieltjes Tonfall sagte etwas anderes.

Adeline tat, als bemerke sie es nicht. „Dennoch rate ich dir, ein Auge auf deinen Mann zu haben.“

Als ob sie das nicht ständig täte. Hätte Adeline nicht so kränkelnd und angegriffen ausgesehen, wäre Hieltje sie heftiger angegangen. So nickte sie fügsam.

***

Fast zur gleichen Stunde wie am Tag davor verließ Hermine mit einem dicken Umschlag in den Tiefen ihrer Basttasche das Hotel. Die Tasche hatte sie sich vor einigen Tagen in *Fischers Basar* gekauft. Wenn sie damit durch Borkums Straßen lief, kam sie sich sehr erwachsen vor. Gelegentlich sogar wie eine der Urlauberinnen, die sich trotz ihres offensichtlich vielen Geldes nicht scheuten, mit einer preiswerten Strandtasche gesehen zu werden.

Hoch erhobenen Hauptes und stolz darauf, dass der Seniorchef ihr den Inhalt der Post anvertraut hatte, überquerte sie die Dünenstraße. Bakker Senior hatte ihr verraten, dass angeblich im letzten Augenblick noch zwei weitere Grundstücke zur Vergabe hinzugekommen waren.

Es sickerte immer etwas durch, dachte Hermine und fühlte sich geehrt, vom Senior in das Geheimnis eingeweiht worden zu sein. Vor der Tür des Gemeindeamtes blieb sie einen Moment stehen. Sie sollte schnell hineingehen, ehe jemand sie sah, der sie kannte. Schließlich war ihr keine Begründung eingefallen, was sie hier wollte, falls jemand fragen sollte.

Im Flur war es dunkel. Ihre Augen brauchten eine Weile, bis sie etwas mehr sehen konnte. Zwei Türen gingen jeweils zu beiden Seiten ab. An keiner von ihnen stand ein Name. Wie sollte sie Frau Wenke finden, die den Umschlag erhalten sollte? Ihre Entscheidung fiel auf die zweite Tür links. Sie klopfte und trat auf ein laut gerufenes „Herein!“ ein.

„Ja bitte?“

„Sind Sie Frau Wenke?“

„Die bin ich.“

„Sehr schön. Ich möchte etwas abgeben.“ Hermine kramte in ihrer Basttasche und förderte den dicken Umschlag zutage.

„Was ist das?“, fragte Frau Wenke.

„Eine Bewerbung für eines der Strandgrundstücke.“

Die Gemeindeangestellte betrachtete sie, als wollte sie sagen, Dienstmädchen seien von der Ausschreibung ausgeschlossen. Mit verkniffenem Gesichtsausdruck nahm sie Hermine den Umschlag ab und warf einen Blick darauf. „Hier fehlt die Angabe, für welches der Flurstücke die Bewerbung sein soll.“

„Das weiß ich nicht, da muss ich erst nachfragen.“

„Dann beeilen Sie sich.“ Frau Wenke deutete auf die Uhr an der Wand. Sie stand auf kurz vor fünf. „In wenigen Minuten ist Abgabeschluss.“

Davon hatte Herr Bakker nichts erwähnt. Darüber nachzugrübeln, blieb Hermine keine Zeit. Für den Hin- und Rückweg würde sie länger als fünf Minuten brauchen.

„Nun, junges Fräulein, was ist jetzt? Ich habe nicht ewig Zeit.“ Frau Wenke hielt ihr einen Stift hin. „Einfach auf den Umschlag schreiben.“

Hermine blickte auf die Uhr. Noch vier Minuten und dreißig Sekunden, dann war Schluss.

Für welches Gelände mochte Bakker Senior sich entschieden haben, fragte sie sich. Die Front, die bebaut werden sollte, zog sich über gut einen Kilometer Länge hin. Da gab es viele Möglichkeiten. Entschied sie sich jetzt für eines in der Mitte, konnte es von Nachteil sein, an beiden Seiten Nachbarn zu haben. Die schauten einem in die Fenster, die zwangsläufig nach den Längsseiten der Gebäude hinausgingen, ähnlich wie im *Hotel Bakker*. Entschied sie sich für das südlichste, konnte es Schwierigkeiten mit dem Licht geben, das in die Gästefenster auf der Südseite hereinschien und die Zimmer im Sommer unnötig aufheizte. Nahm sie das nördlichste Grundstück, hatte die Frontseite so wie bei allen geplanten Hotels in den Gästezimmern Meerblick. Zusätzlich jedoch erhielten die Zimmer linker Hand, wenn man es von See her betrachtete, einen schönen Blick aufs kleine Kaap, ein steinernes hübsches Seezeichen, und viele Dünen. Ein Kriterium, dachte Hermine, das die Qualität des Grundstücks hob. Ein schneller Blick auf den tickenden Zeiger der Wanduhr mahnte, sie musste sich jetzt entscheiden. Der Stift in Hermines Hand schwebte über dem Umschlag. Noch zwei Minuten.

Frau Wenke ließ nicht erkennen, was sie von Hermines Zögern hielt.

„Wie viele Flurstücke sind es insgesamt?“

Frau Wenke verriet es ihr.

„So viele?“

Vielleicht wäre die Mitte, etwas weiter nördlich, Ecke Kaiserstraße/Viktoriastraße besser? Wenn ja, links oder rechts von der Viktoriastraße?

Oder doch lieber etwas südlicher? Ecke Kaiserstraße/Bismarckstraße. Und wenn ja, stellte sich erneut die Frage: links oder rechts? Oder die Eckstücke im Norden oder Süden? Sechzig Sekunden verkündete die Uhr.

„Sie sollten sich jetzt entscheiden", drängte Frau Wenke. Schon hob sie die Hand, um Hermine den Stift abzunehmen.

„Das nördlichste", sagte Hermine. „Welche Flur-Nummer hat es?"

Im gleichen Takt, in dem die Gemeindemitarbeiterin die Flur-Nummer diktierte, schrieb Hermine mit.

„In letzter Sekunde", erklärte Frau Wenke und nickte zufrieden. Vermutlich keine gute Entscheidung, was den glühenden Klumpen in Hermines Magen noch heißer werden ließ.

Hermine reichte ihr den Umschlag. Frau Wenke nahm ihn entgegen, zupfte einen Schlüssel, der an einer Halskette hing und in ihrer Bluse verschwunden war, hervor und schloss damit eine Schublade in einer riesigen Holzkommode auf. Die Länge der Laden und die ungewöhnliche Tiefe ließen vermuten, dass die Schiebefächer Bau- und Lagepläne enthielten. Hermine konnte einen schnellen Blick hineinwerfen und eine große Menge an Umschlägen erkennen. Schon war sie wieder geschlossen und Hermine war mit einem Handwedeln zur Tür entlassen.

„Sonst noch etwas?", fragte Frau Wenke, da Hermine sich nicht traute, einen Schritt zu gehen. Sie hatte Angst, die Knie würden ihr den Dienst versagen. „Nein. Auf Wiedersehen."

Und schon stand sie wieder auf der Straße. Hinter ihr hörte sie den Schlüssel, als die Gemeindehaustür von innen abgeschlossen wurde. Die Sonne blendete, Hermine zwinkerte und klemmte sich die Basttasche fest unter den Arm. Das war erledigt. Wenn es falsch war, konnte sie es jetzt nicht mehr ändern. Schlimmstenfalls würde sie entlassen werden. Doch komischerweise hatte sie das Gefühl, alles richtig gemacht zu haben. Auf dem Weg zurück ins Hotel wurde ihr Schritt mit jedem Meter, den sie dem Haus näher kam, dennoch langsamer. Was, wenn gerade auf dieses Grundstück die meisten Leute geboten hatten und Bakker, wenn sie auf ein mittleres oder ein südlicheres getippt hätte, eher die Chance auf einen Zuschlag bekommen hätte? „Das ist wie russisches Roulette", murmelte sie. Für einen war das Spiel auf jeden Fall gefährlich. Hermine erreichte den Hintereingang. Jetzt musste sie nur noch die Treppenstufen hinauf und in Bakkers Kontor laufen, um ihm zu berichten. Doch so weit kam es nicht.

Sie hob eben die Hand, um anzuklopfen, da wurde sie von Luise angesprochen.

„Da ist niemand."

„Aber ich muss Herrn Bakker unbedingt etwas Wichtiges sagen."

„Das kann warten, Fräulein Flessner."

„Nein, kann es nicht."

„Jetzt machen Sie sich nicht so wichtig, Kind. Was mag es Bedeutsames geben, was eine Aushilfskraft einem alten kranken Mann nicht auch erst dann sagen kann, wenn es ihm etwas besser geht?"

„Was? Herr Bakker ist krank?"

Hermines Magenkneifen verstärkte sich.

„Das will ich meinen, warum sonst kommt Doktor Schmidt ins Haus geeilt, als säße ihm der Klabautermann im Nacken?"

Doktor Schmidt, dachte Hermine und versuchte, sich ihre Erleichterung nicht anmerken zu lassen. Er war einer der Bewerber um die Grundstücke. Ihn trieb garantiert etwas anderes so schnell hierher. Hermine verbarg ihr Lächeln. Doch dann kam ihr ein Gedanke, der sie panisch werden ließ.

Die Gemeindeangestellte hatte schlussendlich so zufrieden gewirkt.

Angesichts der Tatsache, dass sie Minuten vorher Missfallen gezeigt hatte. Sie hatte unmöglich wissen können, dass Hermine in Bakkers Auftrag da gewesen war. Was, wenn die Frau ihr eine nicht existierende Flur-Nummer genannt hatte? Dann wäre das in letzter Minute abgegebene Angebot ungültig.

Kapitel 18

Ihr Auftritt im Amt lag jetzt ein paar Tage zurück. Bakker Senior hatte sich ihre Sorgen angehört und ihr die Angst genommen, etwas falsch gemacht zu haben. Ja, er schien sich sogar über ihre Wahl gefreut zu haben. „Und machen Sie sich keine Sorgen um Frau Wenke. Es wird schon alles seine Richtigkeit haben. Ich danke Ihnen herzlich für Ihre Hilfe und Ihr Stillschweigen."

Seelisch war Hermine mit sich im Reinen. Bertha ging es gut, und die üblen Gerüchte um sie schienen Schnee von gestern zu sein. Herr Bakker war zufrieden mit ihrer Arbeit und der Fotograf hatte die Insel fluchtartig verlassen. Er galt als mutmaßlicher Vergewaltiger und glücklicherweise ging nicht einmal der Hauch eines Gerüchtes wegen der Nacktfotos über die Insel. Auf der Arbeit gab es keinerlei erwähnenswerte Vorkommnisse und Adeline und Hieltje Bakker behandelten sie freundlich, wenn auch etwas distanziert. *Es ist fast schon langweilig,* dachte Hermine und beabsichtigte, die kommenden drei Freistunden am Strand zu verbringen.

Mit nackten Füßen stand sie an der Wasserkante. Die Hände hinter dem Kopf verschränkt, schien es, als wolle sie ihren goldgelben Haarknoten festhalten. Der Wind presste ihr dünnes

Sommerkleid fest um ihre zarten Glieder. Die Linien ihres wohlgeformten Körpers zeichneten sich scharf gegen das Licht ab.

„Die pure Versuchung", sagte eine angenehme Männerstimme neben ihr.

Hermine wandte dem unbekannten bärtigen Mann kurz den Kopf zu und nickte. „Ja, es ist herrlich." Sie blickte wieder aufs Meer hinaus. Dort waren gleich mehrere Segelboote zu sehen. Eines von ihnen war der „Lustdampfer" der Familie Bakker, mit dem Urlauber halb um die Insel und zur unbewohnten Vogelinsel Memmert gesegelt wurden. In dem warmen Wind machte der Segler schnelle Fahrt. „Wollen Sie gleich ein Bad nehmen?", fragte Hermine den älteren Herrn und deutete auf die Tasche, die er bei sich trug.

„Mit der Versuchung meinte ich etwas anderes", sagte er und lächelte. „Darf ich mich vorstellen?" Höflich zog der Mann den Hut. „Mein Name ist Wilhelm Busch. Und darin habe ich keine Badesachen, sondern Malutensilien."

„Hermine Flessner. Nett, Sie kennenzulernen."

„Irgendwo habe ich Sie schon gesehen. Ah, jetzt fällt es mir wieder ein: in *Köhlers Dorfhotel*. Arbeiten Sie dort?"

„Nein, doch gelegentlich habe ich da zu tun. Sie sind Gast auf der Insel?"

„So ist es."

„Und ein Künstler?" Hermine fielen die Worte ihrer Mutter ein und sie hörte sie sagen: „Künstler? Man weiß, was man davon zu halten hat! Alkohol, Drogen, zügelloses Leben und Verachtung für anderer Leute ehrliche Arbeit." Hermine wusste nicht, woher die Abneigung ihrer Mutter kam und ob sie überhaupt einen Künstler kannte, doch dieser freundliche Herr sah nicht so aus, als würde all das auf ihn zutreffen.

„So sagt man“, meinte Wilhelm Busch, ein Mann mit gerader, langer Nase, struppigen Augenbrauen und einem mächtigen Vollbart. „Bitte, junges Fräulein, darf ein alter Mann, wie ich es bin, Sie ersuchen, noch einmal die Arme so zu heben wie eben?“

Hermine blickte ihn verwundert an. Wollte er sie etwa malen? Hier mitten am Strand, vor aller Augen? Sollte er einen Fotoapparat dabei haben, würde sie wegrennen. Aber so ein großes Ding schien kaum in seine flache Tasche zu passen.

„Ich würde gerne eine Zeichnung von Ihnen machen“, sagte Busch.

„Ich weiß nicht recht.“ Hermine spürte bei dem Gedanken, dass man sie malen wollte, gleich mehrere Dinge. Zum einen fühlte sie sich geschmeichelt, dass jemand sie für schön genug hielt, um sie zeichnen zu wollen. Andererseits war es ihr unangenehm, vor einem fremden Mann, der ihr Vater oder gar Großvater hätte sein können, zu posieren. Zudem spukte das unschickliche retuschierte Foto durch ihren Kopf.

Sie konnte nur hoffen, dass ihr Chef die Bilder vernichtet hatte.

„Dann zeichne ich Sie anders. Geht auch ganz schnell. Wenn das gnädige Fräulein sich dort in den Strandkorb setzen würde?“

Hermine blickte zu dem leeren Korb hinüber, in dem nur eine Person Platz fand.

Busch nahm seinen Hut ab und wischte sich mit dem Handrücken über die Stirn. „Bitte!“, bat er.

Diesem Blick konnte sie nicht widerstehen. Sie deutete auf ihre Basttasche, die außer Reichweite der Wellen im Zuckersand lag, und hob sie auf. Gemeinsam gingen sie auf den

Strandkorb zu. Ehe Hermine sich hineinsetzte, drehte er den Korb ein wenig herum.

„Wegen des Sonnenlichts“, erklärte er.

Hermine setzte sich und hielt eine Weile still, derweil er einen Malblock und einen Kohlestift auspackte und mit der Zeichnung begann. Ob man während des Porträtierens reden durfte, wusste sie nicht. Andererseits fiel ihr kein Thema ein, über das sie mit einem Künstler sprechen könnte. Das Wetter? Vermutlich zu banal. Die angebotenen Veranstaltungen? Sie kannte nicht alle und hatte an keiner teilgenommen. Also schwieg sie. Als er den Bogen vom Block riss, wollte sie aufstehen, doch er bat sie, weiter sitzen zu bleiben. Erneut fuhr sein Kohlestift über das nächste Zeichenblockblatt.

„Hermine sagte mir, sie wollte, dass ich ihr mal was dichten sollte. Ich sagte ja! – Und also hüh! Fährt jetzt mein Geist per Fantasie nach Borkum, legt sich auf die Düne und dichtet was für die Hermine.“

„Wie bitte?“

„Sie inspirieren mich, Fräulein Flessner. Ich denke, es wird ein etwas längeres Gedicht werden.“

„Sie zeichnen gar nicht?“

„Doch, doch. Ich mache beides.“

Eine gute Viertelstunde später war er fertig und zeigte ihr das Ergebnis.

„Wunderschön!“, sagte Hermine.

„Sie sagen es.“

Hermine ahnte, dass Busch nicht seine eigenen Bilder, sondern sie meinte, und errötete.

„Darf ich Ihnen zum Dank eines schenken?“ Wilhelm Busch wählte ein Bild aus und überreichte es ihr. „Ich danke Ihnen herzlich, Fräulein Hermine.“ Er verbeugte sich, steckte Block und Kohlestifte in seine Tasche und verabschiedete sich.

Zurück im Hotel bat Hermine Frau Luise um ein paar Stecknadeln. Damit befestigte sie die Kohlezeichnung an der Wand gleich neben ihrem Bett.

„Das lass bloß Frau Luise nicht sehen“, mahnte Mathilde später. „Sie wird schimpfen, wenn du Löcher reinmachst. Die Tapete ist erst im vorletzten Jahr angeklebt worden.“

„Die winzigen Löcher sieht doch keiner.“

„Wo hast du es her?“

Hermine erzählte von ihrer Begegnung mit Busch. Mathilde zog ein langes Gesicht. Ihr gefiel das gar nicht. „Er soll ein berühmter Mann sein und er ist Gast in *Köhlers Dorfhotel*?“

„Das hat er gesagt.“

„Ich kann dir nur raten, niemandem davon zu erzählen. Und lass es ja nicht die Chefin hören.“

„Warum nicht?“

„Sicherlich will sie ebenfalls gemalt werden. Was, wenn der Mann Nein sagt?“

„Das Personal munkelt, unsere Angestellte, Fräulein Flessner, fraternisiert mit den Köhlers.“ Adeline senkte den Stickrahmen und steckte die Nadel zwischen Rahmen und Stoff fest, damit sie nicht herunterfiel. Ihre Stimme klang anklagend. „Und jetzt das! Nicht allein, dass der weltberühmte Künstler Wilhelm Busch bei den Köhlers logiert, statt in unserem Hotel, wo wir doch das erste Haus am Platze sind. Nein, jetzt verbrüdert sich auch noch unser Personal mit denen.“

„Wen meinst du mit denen?“ Dirk Willems Bakker hatte andere Sorgen, als sich um das Gerangel zwischen dem Vater und Köhler zu kümmern. Es reichte, dass die beiden Alten sich zu gegenseitigen Streichen hinreißen ließen und dass das dem Personal beider Häuser augenscheinlich gefiel. Er hatte von den Wetten unter den Angestellten gehört und missbilligte sie. Angeblich sollte sowohl bei seinen Leuten als auch bei Köhlers Mitarbeitern eine Liste existieren, auf der alle Intrigen gelistet wurden. Zurzeit sei Gleichstand, wie man sich erzählte. Doch dass seine Frau da jetzt auch mitmischte, gefiel ihm gar nicht.

„Köhlers Personal", verkündete sie.

„Du kannst schwerlich verbieten, dass die Küchen- und Zimmermädchen sich untereinander treffen. Das tun sie immer und werden es auch in Zukunft machen. Und nur weil Papa und Köhler sich zanken, muss das Personal …"

„Ich will dir mal was sagen, mein Lieber. Nachdem dein Herr Vater seinem ehemaligen besten Freund die Flessner ausgespannt hat, warte ich täglich auf einen heftigen Gegenschlag. Und das, mein lieber Dirk, geht uns alle etwas an."

Dirk unterdrückte ein zufriedenes Lächeln. Es kam selten vor, dass seine Adeline weniger gut informiert war als er. Nach der Abwerbung war es zu einigen Lieferengpässen und vermehrten Schwierigkeiten in beiden Häusern gekommen. Alltägliche Dinge in einem stinknormalen Hotelbetrieb, hätte man meinen können, wenn da nicht diese blöde Wette gewesen wäre. Alles, was irgendwie schiefging und normalerweise als Zufall, Unfall oder Unglück bezeichnet worden wäre, bekam jetzt einen Anstrich von gewollter Revanche vom Gegner. Dirk ärgerte es, dass er selbst in Gedanken Georg Köhler so nannte, zu dem er als kleiner Junge sogar Onkel gesagt hatte.

Adeline verzog das Gesicht. Ob vor Schmerz oder weil sie die neu eingetretene Situation mit dem Künstler missbilligte, konnte Dirk schwerlich sagen.

„Du solltest dich da raushalten und ausruhen. Du hast genug mit dem Säugling zu tun", mahnte er.

„Darum kümmert sich das Kindermädchen."

„Und der Doktor hat dich vor jeder Aufregung gewarnt."

„Mich nicht aufregen? Das sagst du so leicht daher. Um auf Wilhelm Busch zurückzukommen: Man munkelt, er habe sie nicht nur gemalt, sondern auch ein Gedicht über sie geschrieben."

Sie ist neidisch, schoss es Dirk durch den Kopf.

„Ich dachte immer, du magst keine Maler und Dichter. ‚Brotlose Kunst', waren deine Worte, wenn ich mich recht erinnere."

„Ich habe meine Meinung geändert. Kunst ist ein Handwerk. Aber das sehen die wenigsten. Da wird nicht so einfach gepinselt und Farbe auf die Leinwand gekleckst. Bei Leinwand fällt mir etwas anderes ein." Ihre Augen leuchteten böse. „Du hast mir nicht gesagt, was du mit den Fotos gemacht hast."

„Welchen Fotos?"

„Du weißt genau, wovon ich rede. Nach dem Missgeschick mit Mathilde Remmers wurde im ganzen Haus von nichts anderem gesprochen. Was ist mit den Bildern?"

„Ich habe sie vernichtet." Dirk konnte ihr ansehen, dass sie ihm nicht glaubte.

„Schade, es wäre …" Der Stickrahmen fiel zu Boden.

„Was ist mit dir?" Dirk sprang auf.

„Ich weiß nicht. Ruf den Doktor!"

***

„Wir sollten für die Chefin beten." Köchin Gertrud und die Hälfte der Hausangestellten saßen in der Küche beisammen. Das ganze Haus schien stillzustehen. Sogar die Gäste schlichen auf leisen Sohlen durch das Hotel. Alle hofften und bangten mit der Familie und warteten gespannt darauf, zu erfahren, was in diesem Moment mit Adeline in den privaten Räumen geschah. „Das siebte Kindchen war eines zu viel. Lasst uns beten!", wiederholte Gertrud.

„Woher kommt auf einmal Ihr Glaube?" Mathilde schaute von einer Zeitschrift auf. Gäste hatten sie liegen lassen. Sie war schon einige Tage alt, dennoch verströmte sie den Duft der großen weiten Welt. „Sonst ist doch der Aberglaube Ihr Glaubensgebiet und Ihre Stärke."

„Ein Gebet kann nie schaden."

„Fangen Sie jetzt bitte nicht mit diesem nervenden Gefrömmel an wie unsere Seniorchefin." Mathilde faltete die Zeitung zusammen und klatschte mit dem Handrücken dagegen. „Interessiert denn niemanden, was in der großen weiten Welt geschieht? Unser dritter Kaiser in diesem Jahr, er …"

„Nein, Mathilde. Es interessiert im Augenblick keinen. Wir alle hoffen und bangen, dass es Mutter und Kind gut geht."

„Das hat sicher etwas mit dem Tod der Tochter zu tun", sagte Dina.

„Die kleine Petra, sie war so ein süßes Kindchen." Gertrud Dirksen wischte sich mit dem Ärmel den Augenwinkel.

„Meine Mutter hat mir davon erzählt." Dina hob den Zeigefinger, als wolle sie darauf aufmerksam machen, dass sie noch mehr zu sagen habe. „Es hatte was mit Silvester zu tun."

„Sei still, du dumme Gans!"

Hermine schaute überrascht die Köchin an.

Mathilde nickte, als wüsste sie Bescheid. „Oh, unsere liebe Frau Dirksen grämt sich. Waren Sie es nicht, die damals zu Petras Geburtstag, es war die Silvesternacht 77, diese blöde Bemerkung gemacht hat? Ihr solltet es alle wissen“, Mathilde schaute in die Runde, „Frau Dirksens Aberglaube gruselt seither viele von uns.“

„Als ob das Fräulein Remmers damals schon auf der Insel gewesen wäre“, raunzte Gertrud.

„Dennoch kenne ich die Geschichte.“

Waldemar wirkte aufgeregt. „Du solltest den Mund halten und stille schweigen. Zudem ist der Säugling Christine gedeihlich und wohlauf.“

Mathilde überhörte seinen Einwand. „Sie haben damals irgend so einen Blödsinn von schlechtem Vorzeichen gefaselt, weil die Kleine wenige Sekunden vor dem neuen Jahr das Licht der Welt erblickt hatte. Das scheint ein alter Seemannsaberglaube zu sein, nicht wahr, Frau Dirksen? Dass es Unglück und ein kurzes Leben bringen soll, wenn man knapp vor Jahresschluss geboren wird.“

„Mutter sagt“, Dina vermied es, die Köchin anzusehen, „dass unsere Frau Dirksen ein zweites Gesicht hat. Und sie sagt auch, dass das etwas Gutes sein kann.“

„Danke, Dina. Da sag ich dir auf der Stelle die Zukunft voraus: Wenn du nicht gleich den Mund hältst, kannst du dir morgen eine neue Arbeit suchen!“

„Wie wird denn Silvester auf der Insel gefeiert?“, fragte Hermine. Ein kläglicher Versuch, das Thema zu wechseln.

„Wenn erst die neuen Hotels stehen, wird es sicherlich in jedem der Ballsäle ein rauschendes Fest geben.“

Die Hotelküchentür schwang auf. Adeline Bakker betrat die Küche mit festem Schritt. Ihr ging es anscheinend besser.

Energisch klatschte sie in die Hände. „Auf, auf! Keine Zeit zum Tratschen."

Kapitel 19

Private Botengänge für den Senior zu erledigen, war Hermine zur Gewohnheit geworden. Es wunderte sie nicht, an diesem Tag mit einer neuen Mission zu Borkums Tierausstopfer geschickt zu werden.

Zum Ausstopfen und Präparieren von Vögeln und Säugetieren, stand in fetten Buchstaben auf einem Werbeschild, das an der Tür hing. Und darunter in kleinerer Schrift: *In jeder gewünschten Stellung sowie Abbalgen zum Barett u. dgl. empfiehlt sich Gebrüder Bekaan's zoologisches Präparatorium. Neue Straße 38.*

Und ganz klein geschrieben: *Die Besichtigung der fertigen Tiere ist zu jeder Tageszeit möglich.*

Ausgestopfte Tiere zogen viele Menschen magisch an. So auch Hermine. Schon oft war sie an dem Geschäft vorbeigekommen und gelegentlich stehen geblieben, um sich die Auslagen im Schaufenster anzusehen. Auch Muscheln, mittlerweile wusste sie, dass es andere waren, als hier am Strand zu finden waren, gab es in vielen Farben und Größen zu kaufen. „Vermutlich aus der Südsee", hatte Hermine einmal einen Vater zu seinem Sohn sagen hören, der sich die Nase am Fenster plattgedrückt hatte, um alle Auslagen sehen zu können. Die Gebrüder Bekaan verkauften Krebse und getrocknete Seesterne, ausgestopfte Fische und mehr. Was für eine Freude, endlich einen Grund zu haben, den Laden zu betreten! Willem Dirks Bakker hatte sie gebeten, Herrn Bekaan zu fragen, ob es möglich sei, die Vogelsammlung der Borkumer Naturfreunde und Naturforscher in Bekaans Geschäft zwischenzulagern. Bakker Senior hatte erzählt, dass neben honorigen Kurgästen auch der Erbauer des neuen Leuchtturmes, Herr Schumacher, sowie Borkums Amtsvogt, diverse Kaufleute, Badeärzte, Lehrer und einige Hoteliers wie sein alter Freund Köhler Mitglieder dieses Vereines wären. Bei der Nennung von Köhlers Namen hatte Willem Dirks Bakker mit einem Auge gezwinkert. Dass Bakker selbst zur Gruppe der Naturfreunde zählte, setzte Hermine voraus. Warum sonst würde ein viel beschäftigter Hotelier sich um die ausgestopften Vögel und deren Verbleib kümmern? Jedenfalls konnten die Tiere in ihrem alten Quartier nicht bleiben. Hermine hatte vergessen, aus welchem Grunde die Viecher heimatlos wurden, oder vielleicht hatte Bakker es gar nicht erwähnt. Indessen sollte Präparator Bekaan gebeten werden, sie vorläufig unterzubringen, bis ein neues Zuhause gefunden wäre.

„Warum soll gerade ich ihn fragen?", wollte Hermine wissen. Einem so bekannten Hotelier würde der Ladenbesitzer sicherlich eher eine Bitte nicht abschlagen als einem einfachen Borkum-Mädchen. Willem Dirks Bakker zwinkerte erneut und lächelte verschmitzt.

„Weil, mein liebes Fräulein Flessner, der Herr Bekaan die Bitte eines hübschen jungen Mädchens niemals abschlagen wird. Und nicht vergessen, es handelt sich um hundertzweiundsiebzig Exemplare."

Die würden vermutlich einen ganzen Raum füllen.

Hermine öffnete Bekaans Ladentür. Der Geruch von Leder, Formaldehyd, getrocknetem Seegetier und etwas Undefinierbarem schlug ihr entgegen. Der Gestank ist kaum auszuhalten, dachte Hermine und ließ die Eingangstür offen stehen. Vorsichtig, um nicht eines der Ausstellungsstücke zu berühren, trat sie näher an den Verkaufstresen heran. Das Geschäft war vollgestopft mit wundersamen Dingen. Zwischen ausgestopften Vögeln, getrockneten Fischen, Seesternen und Krebsen und jeder Menge Körben voller Muscheln hingen unter der Decke Haigebisse neben vollkommen frisch und lebendig aussehenden Haifischen. Mehrere Krokodile von Handtellergröße bis zu über einem Meter Länge baumelten unter der Decke oder lagen mit weit aufgerissenen Mäulern in einem der Regalfächer. Ein Kugelfisch mit wie zum Kuss gespitzten Lippen wirkte, als würde er gleich platzen. Er zauberte ein Lächeln auf Hermines Gesicht.

„Komme sofort", rief eine Männerstimme. „Schließen Sie bitte die Tür, es zieht."

Hermine tat wie gewünscht. An den Geruch gewöhnte sie sich schnell. Die anfängliche Übelkeit wurde von der Neugier vertrieben. Sie wanderte durch den vollgestopften Laden und erkannte versteckt hinter einem Flechtkorb ein niedliches Gesicht, das sie mit großen braunen Kulleraugen anblickte. Zuerst dachte sie an einen lebenden Hund, doch als sie näher kam, erkannte sie, dass es sich um einen kleinen ausgestopften Seehund handelte. Hermine streckte die Hand nach ihm aus und streichelte vorsichtig über das silbergrau und schwarz schimmernde Fell. Es fühlte sich so weich und seidig an.

„Wundervoll, nicht wahr?" Die Männerstimme ließ sie erschrocken zusammenfahren. „Oh, ich bitte um Entschuldigung, mein Fräulein. Ich wollte Sie auf keinen Fall erschrecken."

Und um seiner Versicherung Rechnung zu tragen, griff er nach ein paar Schrumpfköpfen und versteckte sie hinter seinem Rücken. Nicht schnell genug. Die menschlichen Köpfe waren an ihren Zöpfen aneinandergebunden. Hermine erkannte flüchtig die zusammengenähten Lippen und Augenlider. Aus Angst vor der Antwort wagte sie nicht zu fragen, ob sie echt seien. *Die Köpfe werden mich vermutlich in meinen Träumen verfolgen,* dachte sie. Doch dann sagte sie sich, dass sie künstlich sein mussten, wenn er sie an Urlauber verkaufen wollte. Etwas anderes wäre barbarisch und sicherlich verboten.

„Was kann ich für Sie tun?" Bekaan legte die Schrumpfköpfe in einen Korb und schob ihn ins untere Regalfach, wo er nicht gesehen werden konnte.

„Ich habe ein Problem", begann Hermine, so wie Willem Dirks Bakker es ihr aufgetragen hatte. Tierausstopfer Bekaan war berühmt dafür, Probleme anderer aus der Welt zu schaffen. „Es macht dem Mann Freude", hatte ihr Bakker verraten, „und wir sollten das nutzen."

„Für Problemlösungen bin ich bekannt", entgegnete der Präparator prompt.

„Nun …", druckste Hermine herum und kam sich dabei berechnend vor. „Es ist ein heikles Thema."

„Heikle Themen sind meine Spezialität. Hat das Fräulein etwas ganz Besonderes, was von mir präpariert werden soll?"

„Wie bitte?"

„Ich denke, ich weiß, was Sie wünschen."

„Ach ja?"

„Nun, Sie müssen wissen, mein Fräulein, dass ich gerade für junge Damen der Spezialist bin."

Hermines Augen irrten im Laden umher, auf der Suche nach etwas, das Frauenherzen höherschlagen ließ. Sie wusste beim besten Willen nicht, wovon der Mann redete, und hatte den Faden verloren, Herrn Bekaan in die gewünschte Richtung zu bringen, so wie Bakker es empfohlen hatte.

„Ich rede von den ganz kleinen."

„Ganz kleinen?"

„Säugetieren, mein verehrtes Fräulein. Scheuen Sie sich nicht, wenn Sie Ihren verstorbenen und heiß geliebten Hamster oder Kanarienvogel …"

„Ich habe nichts auszustopfen", unterbrach Hermine ihn.

„Präparieren, verehrtes Fräulein, nicht ausstopfen."

„Entschuldigung, ich wollte Sie nicht beleidigen." Sie hatte es vergeigt, dachte Hermine. Bakker und seine Vogelfreunde mussten selbst nachfragen oder eine andere Bleibe für ihre Vögel finden.

„Sie haben mich nicht beleidigt. Also, was kann ich für Sie tun? Keine Bange, sagen Sie es frei heraus. Sicherlich kann ich helfen."

Hermine verriet es ihm. Herr Bekaan lächelte, als habe sie ihm mit ihrem Geständnis eine Freude bereitet. „Ich habe mich schon gefragt, wo das *Naturalistische Kabinett* abgeblieben ist. Wissen Sie, ich wollte immer Mitglied in dem Verein werden, in dem die Borkumer Tier- und Pflanzenwelt gehörig präpariert, verzeichnet und beschrieben, wie es so schön heißt, dem Publikum vorgeführt wird. Dabei ist es immer geblieben. Man sagt, dass sogar bekannte Künstler wie Wilhelm Busch im Verein der Naturfreunde von Borkum Mitglied sind."

„Herrn Busch habe ich kennengelernt."

„Oh, Sie Glückliche! Wir Künstler“, dabei machte er eine raumgreifende Bewegung, „sollten immer dafür Sorge tragen, dass das Schöne in der Welt jedem zugänglich ist. Aber ich schweife ab. Selbstverständlich werde ich die Vögel in meinem Lager unterbringen. Um wie viele Exemplare handelt es sich?“

„Hundertzweiundsiebzig.“

„Oh, so viele! Na ja. Ich tue, was ich kann. Richten Sie bitte dem verehrten Herrn Bakker aus, ich hätte das auch für ihn getan. Da muss er nicht jemanden vorschicken. Obwohl ich sehr glücklich darüber bin, Sie, mein Fräulein, dadurch kennengelernt zu haben. Verraten Sie mir Ihren Namen?“

„Flessner. Hermine Flessner.“

„Oh. Dann habe ich noch eine Bitte. Ich hoffe, die Frage ist nicht zu persönlich.“

Hermine nickte. „Fragen Sie, Herr Bekaan.“ Sie fand, es war nur recht und billig, dem Mann ebenfalls einen Gefallen zu erweisen. Dennoch blieb sie misstrauisch.

„Oh, schauen Sie nicht so skeptisch. Einem ältlichen Herrn wie mir wird so eine Frage hoffentlich gestattet sein.“

Ältlich? Er konnte höchstens Mitte vierzig sein. „Kann es sein, dass wir uns schon mal begegnet sind?“

Hermine schüttelte den Kopf.

„Aber Sie kommen mir so bekannt vor.“

„Ich habe mehrfach vor Ihrem Fenster gestanden und die Auslage bewundert“, gestand Hermine.

„Nein, nein. Auch Ihre Stimme kommt mir vertraut vor. Ach, jetzt habe ich es: Sicherlich haben Sie ein Fräulein Schwester, das Ihnen ähnlich sieht.“

„Nein“, log Hermine. „Keine Schwester.“ Weder Hildegard noch Hedwig konnte er kennen. Beide kamen eher nach dem

Vater, waren dunkelhaarig und kompakt. Zudem hatten sie Stupsnasen, kein Vergleich mit Hermines Adlernase. Und sie waren noch Kinder, zu jung, um für ein Fräulein gehalten zu werden. Und überhaupt, wo sollte Herr Bekaan ihren Schwestern begegnet sein? Da verstand sie. Der Mann sprach von Bertha. Sie beide wurden gelegentlich für Schwestern gehalten. „Sie verwechseln mich mit meiner Cousine."

„Das ist möglich. Wie ist denn ihr Name?"

„Bertha. Bertha Flessner."

„Dann war es der Name, der mir so bekannt vorkam." Herr Bekaan hob den Zeigefinger. Etwas schien ihm eingefallen zu sein. „Warten Sie einen Moment." Er verschwand im Hinterzimmer. Hermine hörte ihn rumoren, es klang, als zöge er einige Schubladen auf und schiebe sie wieder zu. „Ha, da ist es! Ich wusste es", rief er triumphierend. Und schon kam er mit etwas Felligem zurück. Seine Finger strichen liebevoll darüber.

„Wenn Sie die bitte Ihrer Cousine geben würden." Er überreichte Hermine eine Handtasche aus Seehundfell. Ähnlich denen, die im Laden zum Verkauf auslagen. Doch dieses Fell war etwas ganz Besonderes. Es war sehr hell. Grau und weiß. Herr Bekaan nahm es ihr wieder aus der Hand und trat an die Ladentür. Er öffnete sie und bedeutete Hermine, ihm zu folgen.

„Sehen Sie, wie herrlich es im Licht der Sonne glänzt."

„Ein wundervolles Stück", musste Hermine zugeben.

„Nicht wahr? Ein ganz besonderes Geschenk für Ihre Cousine."

Hermine schaute ihn erstaunt an. Warum schenkte Bekaan Bertha so eine wertvolle Tasche? „Ein Geschenk von Ihnen?"

„Nein, nein. Dennoch stammt das Stück aus meinem Laden. Es ist eine Sonderanfertigung und ich musste erst dieses schöne Fell präparieren. Aber das Warten hat sich gelohnt, nicht wahr?" Bekaans Augen leuchteten vor Stolz.

„Wann haben Sie meine Cousine denn zuletzt gesehen?"

Bekaan blickte auf. Es war nicht zu erkennen, ob er sich über die Frage wunderte. „Lassen Sie mich überlegen. Ja. Im vergangenen September oder Oktober muss es gewesen sein. Sie war in Begleitung eines Mannes. Er hatte das Tier", Bekaan deutete auf die Tasche und überreichte sie Hermine, „selbst erlegt. Aus dem Rest habe ich für den Herrn ein Paar Stiefel angefertigt."

„Wie heißt denn der Herr?"

„Nun, junges Fräulein, das sollten Sie vermutlich eher wissen."

„Cousine Bertha macht seit Langem ein Geheimnis darum", flunkerte Hermine. Herr Bekaan durchschaute ihre Lüge, das erkannte sie. Betrübt darüber verdunkelten sich seine Augen. Dann nickte er, er wusste Bescheid. Beziehungen zwischen einem Herrn, der es sich leisten konnte, auf Seehundjagd zu gehen, und einer vermutlichen Hotelangestellten gingen selten gut aus.

„Nun, ich hoffe, der Mann hat Ihrer Cousine keine Unannehmlichkeiten bereitet."

Noch ehe Hermine antworten konnte, schob sich eine Frau mit großem Sonnenhut und einem Sonnenschirm in der Hand an ihnen vorbei und betrat den Laden.

„Auf Wiedersehen, Fräulein Flessner." Bekaan deutete eine leichte Verbeugung an. „Und grüßen Sie mir den Herrn Bakker Senior. Das nächste Mal soll er sich trauen, selbst in seinen Angelegenheiten vorzusprechen." Damit betrat er wieder seinen Laden. Hermine konnte eben noch hören, wie er seine Kundin herzlich begrüßte.

Der Vater von Berthas Kind war demzufolge ein wohlhabender Mann. Ein Kurgast vielleicht. Denn wäre er ein Insulaner, würde Herr Bekaan ihn kennen. Oder es handelte sich um einen vermögenden Geschäftsmann, der auch in der trüben Jahreszeit auf der Insel seinen Geschäften nachging. Jemand, der sowohl in den Sommermonaten wie im Herbst Borkum besuchte. Ein Bauunternehmer könnte es sein, der die Tätigkeiten seiner Leute überwachte, oder einer, der die Hafenarbeiten des neuen Fähranlegers beaufsichtigte. Jemand von einer Reederei vielleicht? Es wurde darüber gemunkelt, dass in Emden eine Aktiengesellschaft für den Schiffsverkehr nach Borkum gegründet werden sollte. Wer konnte das wissen? Auf jeden Fall jemand mit Geld, denn die Seehundjagd mit anschließender Fellverwertung für eine Tasche und Stiefel konnten sich nur wenige leisten.

Müßig, sich darüber den Kopf zu zerbrechen, jetzt, da es Bertha in Amerika gut ging.

Kapitel 20

Der Sommer neigte sich dem Ende entgegen. Hermine freute sich auf den Abend in *Köhlers Giftbude*. Mittlerweile fand sie Gefallen daran, sich mit anderen Borkum-Mädchen auszutauschen, deren Geschichten zu hören und Kommentare zu den vorbeiflanierenden Gästen abzugeben. An ein gelegentliches Sich-Verwöhnen mit einem Eis, einem Halstuch und anderen Kleinigkeiten gewöhnte sie sich, ohne jedes Mal ein schlechtes Gewissen zu bekommen. Den meisten Mädchen erging es wie ihr. Sie arbeiteten, um daheim die Familie zu unterstützen. Beruhigend zu hören, wie ähnlich es bei ihnen zu Hause zuging, und spannend, welche Träume sie verfolgten und welche Erwartungen sie vom Leben hatten. Gedanken, die sich Hermine bislang nie gemacht hatte.

Viele von ihren neuen Bekannten kamen seit Jahren für die Saison von April bis Oktober auf die Insel. Die meisten in der Hoffnung, an einem Ort wie diesem, an dem hohe Herrschaften wie Barone, Kaiser und Könige, Bankiers und reiche Industrielle Urlaub machten, ihren Traumpartner zu finden. Möglichst einen mit Haus und Hof. Die Klügeren unter ihnen wussten mittlerweile, dass die wenigsten Insulaner mit Reichtum gesegnet waren und für ihr Einkommen hart arbeiten mussten.

„Was für ein Leben!“ Rosemarie, in der *Strandvilla Hawich* beschäftigt, war dümmer, als es bei der ersten Begegnung den Anschein gehabt hatte. „Den Sommer arbeiten und den ganzen Winter auf der faulen Haut liegen“, sagte sie oft, denn sie hatte immer noch nicht kapiert, dass dem nicht so war. Rosemarie schaute nur auf diejenigen Einheimischen, die es ihrer Meinung nach geschafft hatten.

Hermine hatte schnell gemerkt, dass hier auch nur mit Wasser gekocht wurde und jeder für sein Geld hart arbeiten musste.

„Hast du schon jemanden ins Auge gefasst?“, wollte Rosemarie zum wiederholten Mal wissen.

„Nein. Ich bin erst fünfzehn.“

„Höchste Zeit“, erwiderte Rosemarie.

„Lasst uns von etwas anderem reden.“

„Schaut mal, die da.“ Mathilde deutete zum Eingang. Alle starrten sie mehr oder weniger auffällig zu einer vornehmen Dame hinüber, die allein den Raum betrat. Übertrieben mit Schmuck behangen und in einem Kleid unterwegs, das besser zu einem Ball oder einer Theaterveranstaltung gepasst hätte, fiel sie zwischen den übrigen Besuchern der *Giftbude* auf.

„Im kommenden Jahr“, erklärte Rosemarie, „spätestens übernächste Saison wird Borkum von solchen Gästen überschwemmt werden.“

„Du übertreibst“, meinte Gesine. Sie arbeitete im *Frisörsalon Campen* und konnte berichten, dass sie in den Sommermonaten nur vornehme Kundinnen wie diese Dame dort hatten. Sie kämen bei der vielen Arbeit kaum hinterher, was im Winter das genaue Gegenteil wäre. „Ich glaube“, überlegte Gesine, „sobald die neuen Hotels fertig sind, mache ich meinen eigenen Salon auf.“

Und was mache ich im kommenden Jahr, dachte Hermine und schaute gedankenverloren auf das Meer hinaus. Ihr Blick folgte einer Möwe, die gegen den Wind segelnd die Strandkante nach Essbarem absuchte.

„Hermine?"

„Was?"

„Das hat Gesine dich jetzt schon das zweite Mal gefragt."

„Was denn?"

„Ob du endlich verrätst, was du im Amt zu suchen hattest?"

„Das geht euch gar nichts an."

Mathildes lauernder Blick verhieß nichts Gutes. Doch sie schwieg.

„Wenn du weiter unsere Freundin sein möchtest", erklärte Rosemarie, „rate ich dir, uns alles, was du weißt, von den neuen Hotels zu erzählen."

Die alte Leier, dachte Hermine.

„Egoisten mag keiner", fügte Gesine hinzu.

„Ich weiß gar nichts." Hermine griff in ihre Basttasche, um den Geldbeutel herauszunehmen. „Warum fragt ihr mich immer danach? Wenn all die geplanten Häuser gebaut werden, ist Arbeit genug für alle da. So viele Borkum-Mädchen können gar nicht herangeschafft werden, wie dann gebraucht werden." Die Geldbörse in der Hand, die Tasche über die Schulter gehängt, stürmte sie zum Tresen, um zu bezahlen.

***

„Kannst du ein Geheimnis für dich behalten?"

„Das fragst du mich, seit wir kleine Jungs sind. Egal, ob ich jetzt schwöre oder nicht, du verrätst es mir doch."

Dirk Willems Bakker nickte seinem jüngeren Bruder Eildert Willems Bakker zu.

Seit Eildert in finanzieller Hinsicht alle Bakker'schen Betriebe überblickte, hatte Dirk keinen Gedanken und keine Sorgen mehr an das Finanzielle verschwendet. Der Papierkram, angefangen beim Pferdestall und den Fuhrwerken über die Läden bis hin zu den Schiffen, den Hotels und den Löhnen der Mitarbeiter, lief durch Eilderts Hände. Von den verpachteten Ländereien ganz zu schweigen. Dennoch kam Eildert gelegentlich vorbei, um sich vom älteren Bruder einen Rat zu holen.

„Ich habe mit niemandem darüber gesprochen, aber ..."

Sonst war Dirk derjenige, der die meisten Sätze unvollendet ließ. Wenn Eildert das tat, war es beunruhigend. Dirk erkannte plötzlich, dass sein jüngerer Bruder in den vergangenen drei Jahren jede Menge Haare verloren hatte und der Rest grau wurde. Vermutlich war das finanzielle Jonglieren zum Haareraufen. „Geht es um die Grundstücke am Strand?"

„Du weißt immer, was mich bedrückt." Eildert ließ sich erleichtert in einen der Sessel fallen und hatte nichts dagegen, dass ihm schon am späten Nachmittag ein Glas Rum eingeschenkt wurde. Normalerweise Alkohol verschmähend, griff er hastig zu und nahm einen Schluck.

„Zigarre dazu?"

Eildert winkte ab, wartete, bis Dirk für sich ebenfalls ein Glas gefüllt und im anderen Sessel Platz genommen hatte.

„Können wir uns Vaters Zukunftsvisionen nicht leisten, wenn wir einen Zuschlag bekommen?", riet Dirk. Dabei schwebte ihm Geeskes und Hieltjes Hang zum Geldausgeben vor Augen.

„Einen Teil davon schon. Aber gestern bekam ich eine zusätzliche Rechnung vom Architekten."

„Firma Oldewurtel aus Aurich?"

„Die ist längst bezahlt. Nein, ein Büro aus Leer stellt uns Baupläne und Statik-Berechnungen für den Entwurf einer vierstöckigen Villa in Rechnung."

Dirk nickte. „Vater hat davon gesprochen. Und ehe du dich beschwerst, dass ich nichts gesagt habe …" Dirk nahm einen Schluck von seinem Rum. „Vater meint, wir hätten mehr Chancen, wenn wir zwei verschiedene Angebote mit unterschiedlichen Gebäuden und andersartiger finanzieller Gestaltung einreichen. Ich bin davon ausgegangen, du wüsstest das."

„Natürlich. Aber die Finanzierungspläne, Bankbürgschaften und so weiter sind zusätzliche Kosten", meinte Eildert und stellte verdutzt fest, dass sein Glas leer war. „Doppelte Bewerbungen bedeuten doppelte Kosten, die vielleicht alle für die Katz sind." Eildert stellte das Schnapsgläschen so heftig auf den Beistelltisch, dass man Angst um die Glasplatte haben musste. „Ich mag gar nicht daran denken, wenn wir zwei Zuschläge bekommen."

Darüber hatte Dirk sich auch Gedanken gemacht und war zu dem Schluss gekommen, dass es unwahrscheinlich sein würde.

„Dein Wort in Gottes Ohr", murmelte Eildert und erhob sich. „Apropos Gott: Mama kommt Ende des Monats zurück."

Damit kam eine zusätzliche unkalkulierbare finanzielle Sache auf die Familie zu. Beiden war klar, dass ihre Mutter ihr soziales Engagement nicht aufgeben würde. Sie spendete nicht immer zu Eilderts Freude. Denn er musste zusehen, woher das Geld kam. Wie erst im vergangenen Jahr, kurz bevor ihre

Mutter in die Klinik gekommen war. Da hatte sie angekündigt, ein neues Dach fürs Armenhaus zu spendieren. Das Gebäude gehörte der Gemeinde und die würde nach dem Verkauf der Strandgrundstücke mehr als dieses Dach vergolden können.

„Gut, dass Mutter vorher in die Klinik kam", meinte Eildert. „Klingt gemein, aber du weißt, wie ich es meine. Wie geht es der kleinen Christine?", wechselte er das Thema.

„Gut. Doch Adeline macht mir Sorgen."

„Vielleicht sollte sie zur Erholung in den Harz oder ins Sauerland fahren."

„Und das Hotel und die Familie alleine lassen? Niemals."

Eildert nickte und erhob sich. „Was machen wir in der anderen Angelegenheit?"

„Beten und hoffen."

Der Tag der Entscheidung rückte näher. Der Gemeinderat tagte und ganz Borkum fieberte der Auswahl entgegen.

„Es wird alles gut", prophezeite Gertrud.

„Woher wollen Sie das wissen?"

„Heute Vormittag saß ein Marienkäfer auf Herrn Bakkers Revers. Wie jedermann weiß, bringt es großes Glück, wenn die kleinen roten Käfer auf einen zufliegen. Es bedeutet, dass das Tierchen die Person beschützt."

„Es heißt aber auch", Mathilde verbarg nicht, wie der Aberglaube ihr auf die Nerven ging, „dass es Unglück bringt, wenn man den Käfer abschüttelt."

„Das sagst du jetzt nur", mischte sich Hermine ein, „um Gertrud zu ärgern."

„Nein, nein. Es stimmt", versicherte die Köchin, was Mathilde mit einem Verdrehen der Augen quittierte. „Aber so weit kam es nicht. Ich habe den Marienkäfer vorsichtig abgenommen und in die Freiheit entlassen."

„Dann wollen wir hoffen, dass Sie recht behalten."

Hermine und Gertrud blickten Mathilde überrascht an. Wann hatte man mal erlebt, dass die Kollegin der Köchin etwas Gutes wünschte?

„Ja, schauen Sie nicht so, Frau Dirksen. Wenn der Alte ein neues Hotel baut", verkündete Mathilde im Brustton der Überzeugung, „bekomme ich im neuen Haus den Posten der Hausdame."

„Das sollte mich wundern." Gertrud wandte sich dem Herd zu und klapperte unnötig laut mit den Töpfen.

„Wartet es nur ab, ihr werdet es erleben", prophezeite Mathilde.

„Wie lange mag es wohl noch dauern?"

Gertrud betätigte mit heftigen Bewegungen den Schwengel der Wasserpumpe. „Ich frage mich eher, wann hier jemand seinen Hintern bewegt. Das Essen kocht sich nicht von allein."

Doch Gertrud musste auf Hilfe verzichten.

„Fräulein Flessner", rief Dirk Bakker zur Küche hinein, „und Fräulein Remmers. Ich brauche Sie."

Er sah besorgt aus.

„Meiner Frau geht es schlecht. Sie kümmern sich um die Kinder …"

Hermine nickte.

„Und Sie helfen Frau Luise. Es ist Anreise. Die letzte Partie Gäste kommt."

Am späten Nachmittag hatte sich die eine Aufregung gelegt und die nächste stand bevor.

Auf dem Weg ins Raucherzimmer wurde er von Fräulein Flessner überholt. Sie trug einen Stapel frischer Tischdecken und hatte es eilig, ins Restaurant zu kommen.

„Viel Glück", wünschte sie ihm.

„Danke." Wie auch immer die Entscheidung über die Vergabe der Grundstücke in der kommenden Stunde ausfallen mochte, er durfte nicht vergessen, sich bei einigen Menschen zu bedanken. Fräulein Flessner gehörte auf jeden Fall dazu. Ohne ihre Hilfe wäre seine und Köhlers List schon längst aufgeflogen und der Schwindel hätte wesentlich weniger Spannung gehabt. Den persönlichen Schaden, den Fräulein Flessner dabei genommen hatte, würde er ihr irgendwie vergelten. Auch andere, die ihm bei dem Katz-und-Maus-Spiel behilflich gewesen waren, sollten mit etwas Besonderem entlohnt werden.

Ihm blieb keine Zeit für weitere Überlegungen. Doktor Schmidt klopfte ihm leutselig auf die Schulter. „Na, Bakker. Aufgeregt? Heute wird sich das Leben von manch einem von uns von Grund auf ändern."

Waldemar stand stramm wie ein Soldat vor der verschlossenen Tür zum Raucherzimmer. Heute Abend durfte nicht jeder hinein. Der Hoteldiener hatte eine Liste, wer eintreten durfte. Bakker nickte ihm zu. Sofort öffnete er für die beiden die Tür.

Etwa zur gleichen Zeit trafen zwei von Bakkers Kontrahenten um das Rennen der Strandgrundstücke im Restaurant des Hotels ein. Hermine erkannte Georg Köhler, der in Begleitung eines jungen Mannes, augenscheinlich seines Sohnes, war. Die Ähnlichkeit konnte niemand übersehen.

Hermine stand am Eingang zum Hotelrestaurant, um den eintreffenden Herrschaften die Jacken abzunehmen. Gegen

Abend wurde es schon richtig kühl. Sie knickste, deutete auf das Raucherzimmer und schaute ihnen hinterher. Der Jüngere musste ihren Blick gespürt haben. Mit der Hand rieb er sich den Nacken und drehte sich zu ihr um. Plötzlich machte er kehrt und eilte festen Schrittes auf sie zu. Oje! Hoffentlich war der nicht auch so ein selbst ernannter Casanova wie Jakob Bakker, dachte Hermine.

„Sind Sie Fräulein Hermine Flessner?“

Sie hatte sie den Eindruck, dass er die Antwort bereits kannte. „Ja, die bin ich.“ Hermine verkniff sich einen weiteren Knicks. Wenn der dachte, er sei ein Gottesgeschenk an die Frauenwelt, war er bei ihr an der falschen Adresse.

„Sehr erfreut, Sie kennenzulernen.“

Georg Köhler Juniors Lächeln wirkte freundlich und hatte keinerlei Ähnlichkeit mit Jakobs anzüglichem Grinsen. Dennoch fühlte Hermine sich unwohl. In aller Öffentlichkeit von einem der Herrschaften angesprochen zu werden, war nicht nur peinlich, es würde auch die verstummten Gerüchte um sie wieder anfachen.

„Ich habe schon viel von Ihnen gehört“, sagte Köhler Junior, worauf Hermine am liebsten geantwortet hätte: „Ich aber wenig von Ihnen.“ Doch sie schwieg und schaute zur Eingangstür, in der Hoffnung, dass endlich weitere geladene Besucher zur Verkündigung des Ergebnisses eintrafen.

„Sollte es Ihnen hier bei den Bakkers nicht mehr gefallen“, sagte er und beugte sich zu ihrem Ohr herab, „wartet jederzeit ein guter Posten in unserem Haus auf Sie.“

Aus dem Augenwinkel erkannte Hermine Mathildes zerknautschten Gesichtsausdruck. Sie sprühte vor Missgunst, das sah Hermine durch den langen Flur bis hin zum Hoteleingang.

Mathilde hatte die Aufgabe, den eintreffenden Herren den Weg zu weisen.

Der junge Köhler warf einen Blick über Hermines Schulter. Bakkers Schwiegertochter Hieltje stand hinter ihr. Hieltjes rötliches Haar schimmerte im Lampenlicht. Hermine fand, dass die beginnende Schwangerschaft, deren Kunde schnell unter dem Personal die Runde gemacht hatte, ihr gut zu Gesicht stand. Die weich gewordenen Gesichtszüge trübte in diesem Augenblick Hieltjes missbilligender Blick auf Hermine.

„Hieltje!", rief Köhler Junior und griff nach ihrer Hand. Er hauchte einen Handkuss darauf, der einen zarten rosafarbenen Ton auf Hieltjes Wangen und ihr ein strahlendes Lächeln auf die Lippen zauberte.

„Ist das die neueste Kreation aus Berlin?"

Köhler deutete auf das lilafarbene Kleid.

„‚Le dernier cri', wie die Franzosen sagen", kokettierte sie.

„Der letzte Schrei." Die Stimme gehörte Jakob. Georg und Hieltje drehten sich zu ihm herum. „Obwohl vermutlich ich derjenige sein werde, der schreit", fügte Jakob hinzu, „wenn die Rechnung eintrudelt."

„Das interessiert doch den lieben Georg wenig", meinte Hieltje und hakte sich bei Jakob unter. Gemeinsam verschwanden sie im Restaurant, wurden jedoch von Waldemar daran gehindert, ins Raucherzimmer zu gelangen.

„Einlass, Hineingehen und Durchkommen nur für die, die sich beworben haben."

Hermine begrüßte den Schlachtermeister aus dem Damenpfad und nahm seinen Hut entgegen. „Dort entlang, bitte." Sie deutete ihm den Weg.

Georg Köhler folgte ihm ins Raucherzimmer.

Fischer Onnen, der sein Fischfachgeschäft ebenfalls im Damenpfad betrieb, kannte den Weg. Die Jacke, die er Hermine übergab, verriet sein Gewerbe. Des Fischers Gattin rauschte an Hermine vorbei und schnappte sich zwei Gläser Sekt von dem Tablett, das Frau Luise für die Gäste, die nicht ins Raucherzimmer durften, bereithielt. Eines bot sie ihrem Ehemann an, der mit dem Kopf schüttelte, weil er vermutlich lieber Bier trank. Seine Ehefrau leerte ihr Glas, um es anschließend Hermine hinzuhalten. Sie nahm es entgegen und hätte dabei fast den Drogisten aus der Strandstraße übersehen, der sich an ihr vorbei in den Raum drückte. Dem Drogisten folgte die Dame mit dem Bademodengeschäft in der Großen Straße und der Mann, der diesen stinkenden Laden mit den vielen ausgestopften Tieren besaß. „Guten Tag, Herr Bekaan." Sein Name fiel ihr rechtzeitig ein.

„Guten Abend, Fräulein Flessner." Dem Präparator folgte eine korpulente Dame. Hermine erkannte in ihr die Frau, die im Fotogeschäft vergeblich nach ihren Bildern gesucht hatte. Vermutlich hat sie den Laden übernommen, dachte Hermine, wenn sie nicht gar von Anfang an die Chefin dort gewesen ist. Ob sie wusste, was für ein Angebot ihr Kollege Hermine und anderen Frauen gemacht hatte?

Sie alle steuerten auf die Tür des Raucherzimmers zu. Waldemar hatte Mühe, einige abzuweisen und andere hereinzulassen.

Seit wenigen Minuten traf niemand mehr ein. Gleich würde es losgehen. Die Spannung, die im Restaurant herrschte, war zu greifen. Wie mochte es da erst im Raucherzimmer sein?

Die im Hotelrestaurant Wartenden verbrachten die Zeit, bis die Entscheidung des Amtes bekannt gegeben würde, mit den

Getränken, die gratis ausgeschenkt wurden. Die Ersten griffen bereits nach dem dritten Glas, als der stellvertretende Bürgermeister mit Begleitung durch den Hintereingang eintraf. Frau Luise ließ es sich nicht nehmen, ihn persönlich ins Raucherzimmer zu führen. Dort wurde er von äußerst nervösen Herrschaften erwartet. Willem Dirks Bakker und sein ältester Sohn Klaas, die beiden Inseldoktoren Kock und Schmidt, Vater und Sohn Köhler und ein paar weitere Herren saßen in tiefen Sesseln, lehnten am Kaminsims oder standen in kleinen Gruppen plaudernd beieinander. Die meisten pafften Zigarren oder Pfeifen und alle warteten gespannt darauf, dass der stellvertretende Bürgermeister begann, ihnen den Ausgang der Bewerbungen mitzuteilen. Endlich führte Frau Luise ihn und seine Begleitung herein. Sofort herrschte absolute Stille im Raum.

Es wäre Georg Köhler Seniors Aufgabe gewesen, als Bürgermeister der Insel diesen Part zu übernehmen. Doch als Mitbewerber war er befangen und von der Auswertung sowie von der Verkündung der Ausschreibung ausgeschlossen worden.

Er schien amüsiert, wie sich sein Stellvertreter im Rampenlicht sonnte. Ähnlich einem aufgeplusterten Pfau breitete der Mann die Arme aus und drehte sich einmal um sich selbst, als erwarte er Applaus. Die gespannt wartenden Herren ließen sich nicht darauf ein und so ging Tönjes Kieviet, gefolgt von der Gemeindeangestellten Frau Wenke, in die Mitte des Raumes. Sie trug die Aktenmappe, als trüge sie eine Krone, die auf einem roten Kissen lag.

„Nun, Bakker", sagte Köhler, „bekommt vermutlich jeder hier im Raum schweißnasse Hände und rasendes Herzklopfen. Heute hat sogar deine Familie die Chance, einmal ein richtig schickes, modernes Hotel bald sein Eigen nennen zu können."

„Pass auf, dass der Schuss nicht nach hinten losgeht, Köhler", antwortete Bakker.

„Lasst endlich das Theater", rief Doktor Kock quer durch den Raum. „Jeder hat mitbekommen, dass ihr beide immer noch die dicksten Freunde seid. Oder dachtet ihr etwa, euer Geheimnis würde eines bleiben?"

Die Männer lachten. Nur einige wirkten überrascht, doch keiner schien einen Groll gegen die beiden Kontrahenten zu hegen. Nur Frau Wenke sah aus, als habe ein Seeungeheuer sie erschreckt. Den Blick, den sie Köhler Senior zuwarf, würde sogar den zähnefletschenden Klabautermann den Rückzug antreten lassen. Sie jedenfalls war auf die Maskerade hereingefallen.

Doktor Kock begann mit den Händen aufzuzählen, was Kocks eigene Spione ihm zu diesem Thema berichtet hatten. Bereits beim Anfang der zweiten Story wurde er unterbrochen.

„Das interessiert heute niemanden, Doktor Kock. Wir wollen wissen, was Herr Kieviet uns zu berichten hat."

Die Anwesenden nickten, einige legten ihre Zigarren beiseite oder stellten ihre Gläser ab, als wären sie hinderlich bei dem, was sie nun zu hören bekämen. Der stellvertretende Bürgermeister Tönjes Kieviet wandte sich Frau Wenke zu, die einen Umschlag aus der Mappe nahm. Mit hochrotem Gesicht überreichte sie ihn feierlich.

„Nun, meine Herren ...", verkündete Tönjes Kieviet mit erhobener Stimme und betrachtete die zwei Siegel auf dem festen Briefkarton. „Wir sollten beginnen." Kieviet ließ den Umschlag herumgehen, damit jeder erkennen konnte, dass er die Siegel vom Notar Altmeier aus Emden sowie des Notars Müllersohn aus Leer trug. Beide Siegel waren unversehrt. Als er den Umschlag wieder in der Hand hielt, streckte er den Arm in die Höhe wie einen Pokal, den er eben gewonnen hatte.

„Meine Herren", sagte er und legte eine längere Pause ein. „Die Würfel sind gefallen." Die Stille im Raum war greifbar. Nur hier und da stiegen ein paar nervöse Zigarrenrauchkringel in die Luft.

„Nun mach es nicht so spannend, *Bürgermeister*", rief Klaas Willems Bakker und schaute dabei seinen Vater an. Schließlich hing nicht nur seine Zukunft, sondern die der ganzen Familie vom heutigen Ergebnis ab. Bis vor wenigen Tagen hatte er im Stillen gehofft, dass sein Vater keinen Zuschlag bekäme. Heute vertrat er eine andere Meinung. Den Meinungsumschwung hatte er gleich zwei Urlaubern zu verdanken, mit denen er auf seinen Segeltouren gesprochen hatte. Dem Herrn Kommerzienrat Wittstein aus Hannover und dem Fabrikanten Bohnhorster aus Düsseldorf, die beide Vaters Ansichten vertraten.

„Borkum muss vorangehen, lieber Kapitän Bakker", hatte der Kommerzienrat gesagt. „Die Zukunft liegt im Tourismus, und wenn die Familie Bakker mithalten will, ist ein neues Hotel direkt am Strand der richtige Weg."

Endlich senkte Tönjes Kieviet den Arm mit dem Umschlag in der Hand und trat an einen der kleinen Rauchertische. Der Schlachtermeister räumte für ihn seinen Sessel. Kieviet ließ sich fallen und schnippte mit den Fingern. Während die Wartenden sich gegenseitig ansahen, einige sogar mit den Schultern zuckten, reichte Klaas Willems Bakker ihm einen Brieföffner, mit einem angedeuteten Diener, als wolle er ihn verspotten.

Kieviet, blind gegen Sarkasmus, steckte die silberne Spitze unter das erste rote Siegel, schaute auf und in die Runde.

„Trommelwirbel“, sagte Doktor Schmidt laut. Einige Herren grinsten, andere sahen aus, als fänden sie Schmidts Kommentar überflüssig. Niemand sprach ein Wort. Mit einem leisen Knack zerbrach das erste Siegel. Der Lack rieselte auf Kieviets Hosenbeine. Um es spannend zu machen, legte Kieviet den Brieföffner beiseite und wischte die Krümel fein säuberlich zusammen, um sie anschließend doch zu Boden fallen zu lassen. Dann knackte er das zweite Siegel.

„Soll ich die Fotografin holen?“, rief jemand. Einige Herren lachten.

„Nun machen Sie schon, Kieviet!“, sagten Bakker und Köhler Senior wie aus einem Mund.

Kieviet schnaubte, wischte die Reste des zweiten Siegels fort und entnahm dem Umschlag ein Blatt Papier. Aus der Ferne konnte Bakker gelistete Namen und Anschriften erkennen. Unter dem Dokument prangten zwei großzügige Unterschriften, sicherlich die der beiden Notare, sowie das Inselsiegel der Gemeinde und weitere wichtig aussehende Stempel. Kieviet ließ sich Zeit, um die Liste zu studieren. Dann schnaubte er und blickte nacheinander Doktor Schmidt, Georg Köhler Senior und Willem Dirks Bakker an.

„Nun, meine Herren. Das, was ich hier lese, ist äußerst interessant und wird sicherlich manch einen von Ihnen überraschen.“ Dabei blieb sein Blick an Bakker hängen. Dem schoss das Blut in den Kopf, was ihm seit ewigen Zeiten nicht mehr passiert war. Ihm wurde heiß, ihm wurde kalt. Seine Zigarre schmeckte plötzlich fad. Er versuchte, einen Schluck aus seinem Cognacglas zu nehmen, ehe er merkte, dass dieses leer getrunken war.

„Meine Herren, ich empfehle, dass Sie sich alle erst einmal noch einen einschenken lassen", sagte Tönjes Kieviet. Sein Gesicht verriet Besorgnis mit einem Hauch von Belustigung.

„Trinken können wir später", erklärte der Schlachtermeister. Er versuchte Kieviet über die Schulter zu schauen, um einen Blick auf die Liste zu werfen. Der drückte sie sich an die Brust. Erneut blickte Kieviet in die Runde, kurz blieb er mit undurchdringlichem Gesichtsausdruck an Bakker Senior hängen und ließ leicht die Schultern sinken.

Vater hat keinen Zuschlag erhalten, dachte Klaas Willems Bakker. Unmöglich zu sagen, was er in diesem Moment empfand. Wut, Enttäuschung oder Erleichterung? Ein schneller Blickwechsel mit dem Vater verriet, dass er das Gleiche dachte. Eben noch rot im Gesicht, war der alte Herr jetzt bleich wie eine Nebelwand.

„Bevor ich anfange, möchte ich sagen, dass diejenigen, die gleich einen Zuschlag bekommen, nicht zu fragen brauchen, für welches der Grundstücke. Das erfahren sie später von Frau Wenke. Und wenn ich später sage, meine ich das auch. Nicht, dass Sie gleich auf die Dame zustürmen. Bitte erst, nachdem alle glücklichen Gewinner bekannt gegeben worden sind. Fangen wir also an." Kieviet räusperte sich. „Ich hoffe, unser lieber Herr Doktor Schmidt wird uns als Arzt erhalten bleiben, wenn er sich in Zukunft als Hotelier versuchen wird."

Die Männer applaudierten. Doktor Schmidt grinste wie ein Honigkuchenpferd und ging fast in die Knie, weil ihm jemand heftig auf die Schulter klopfte. „Gut gemacht, Doktor. Gratulation."

„Wie soll Ihr Hotel denn heißen?", wollte Kieviet wissen.

„*Nordsee Hotel*", kam es prompt.

„Klingt nett." Kieviets Blick wanderte zu Herrn Bekaan.

„Ich hoffe doch, mein lieber Freund, in Ihrem Hotel wird es nicht so stinken wie in Ihrem Laden." Bekaan setzte an zu protestieren, da ging ihm der Sinn dieses Satzes auf. Er warf Bakker Senior einen Blick zu. Seine Lippen formten ein Danke. Der Präparator hatte die genannte Zahl der präparierten Vögel, denn die Sammlung war viel kleiner gewesen als angegeben, richtig interpretiert.

„Gratulation", sagte Kieviet. „Ich frage mal lieber nicht, wie Ihr Hotel heißen soll."

„Zur ausgestopften Möwe", rief jemand. Niemand fand das lustig.

Kieviet wandte sich an Georg Köhler. Auf dessen breiter Stirn zeigten sich Schweißperlen. „Sie, mein lieber Köhler, werden in Zukunft vermutlich kaum noch Zeit finden, um unsere schöne Insel als Bürgermeister zu vertreten. Aber keine Angst, ich übernehme den Posten gerne, denn Sie werden bald alle Hände voll zu tun haben." Auch Köhler Senior bekam Applaus, doch sein Stellvertreter hob die Hand. „Haben Sie schon einen Namen?"

„Köhlers Strandhotel", rief Georg Junior, ehe sein Vater den Mund aufbekam. „Was sonst?"

Einige Männer lachten, andere waren zu angespannt dazu.

„Sehr schön, doch das reicht mir nicht. Denn das mit der fehlenden Zeit, meine Herren, habe ich eben ernst gemeint. Unser ehrenwerter Bürgermeister wird in Zukunft nur wenig davon haben, denn er hat für ein zweites Grundstück den Zuschlag erhalten."

Den Schreck konnte man Köhler Senior ansehen, was Kieviet ein zufriedenes Lächeln auf die Lippen zauberte. „Ich hoffe nur, mein lieber Freund, Sie können so viel auf einmal stemmen!"

Ungehaltenes Gemurmel ging durch den Raum, das schnell wieder verstummte.

„Ich gehe mal davon aus", kommentierte Doktor Kock, „dass es für ein zweites noch keinen Namen gibt."

„*Kaiserhof*", erklärte Köhler Senior. Es klang, als hätte er das eben erst entschieden. Mit einem großen Taschentuch wischte er sich den Schweiß von der Stirn. Das Tuch verschwand in seiner Hosentasche. Der Hotelier schien sich über den Gedanken, auf beide Gebote den Zuschlag bekommen zu haben, zu freuen. Eine gesunde Portion Triumph war jedenfalls zu erkennen. Sein Sohn hingegen wirkte, als gefalle ihm die Entscheidung ganz und gar nicht. Doch ein schneller Blickwechsel mit seinem Schwiegervater, Doktor Kock, glättete die Falten auf seiner jungen Stirn. Sollte Kock auf sein Gebot keinen Zuschlag erhalten, gab es dennoch viel in der Familie zu feiern. Auch die Bewerbung des ehemaligen Lotteriegewinners Behrends hatte die Gemeindevertretung angenommen. Er wollte sein Haus *Ostfriesenhof* nennen.

Eines der Flurstücke ging an Herrn Stollwerk, einen Fabrikanten vom Festland.

Wohl kaum einer im Raum, der nicht mitgezählt hatte, wie viele Stücke noch übrig waren. Die erneute Stille enthielt Spannung, die man mit den Händen greifen konnte.

Niemand wagte, Willem Dirks Bakker anzusehen. Seine Chancen, jetzt, da weitere Namen von Bewerbern vom Festland fielen, tendierten gegen null. Ihr Gastgeber ging leer aus, dachten vermutlich diejenigen, die angestrengt ihre Schuhe betrachteten oder ihre Zigarre begutachteten. Keiner wollte zeigen, was er dabei empfand. Einige mochten Mitleid haben, doch es gab sicherlich den einen oder anderen, der sich seine Genugtuung darüber nicht anmerken lassen wollte.

„Nun, meine Herren …" Kieviets politisch korrekter undurchdringbarer Gesichtsausdruck ließ nichts erkennen.

„Spucken Sie es endlich aus, *Bürgermeister*", rief Doktor Schmidt, wobei er das letzte Wort deutlich betonte.

„Ich wage es kaum", zierte sich Kieviet, „auszusprechen."

„Wenn Sie in den kommenden Jahren die Gemeindesitzungen so leiten wollen", rief Hermann Behrends von Villa San Remo, „bedaure ich die anderen Gemeindevertreter jetzt schon."

„Das Beste kommt immer zum Schluss", erklärte der Schlachtermeister.

„Was auf denjenigen jetzt zukommt, geschieht lieber ihm als mir." Kieviet konnte sein Pokergesicht nicht mehr länger aufrechterhalten. Dass es ihn köstlich amüsierte, sah man deutlich.

„Ich weiß, Sie alle fürchten, die restlichen drei Strandgrundstücke könnten ebenfalls an fremde Bewerber gehen, aber …"

„Nun spucken Sie es aus, Kieviet!", wiederholte Doktor Kock die Aufforderung seines medizinischen Kollegen.

„Sofort, Doktor." Er erhob sich umständlich aus dem Sessel. Das Blatt Papier erneut fest an die Brust gepresst, sodass niemand einen Blick darauf erhaschen konnte. Er ging ein paar Schritte auf Bakker zu. Der Schalk blitzte in Kieviets Augen. „Ich hoffe doch, mein lieber Herr Bakker, Sie werden akzeptieren, was die Ausschreibung erbracht hat. Ich persönlich kann nichts dafür, die Entscheidung lag bei den Gemeindevertretern unter Aufsicht der Anwälte."

Bakker sah aus, als träfe ihn gleich der Schlag.

„Aber als Ziehsohn eines gewieften Piraten sind Sie es von Kindesbeinen an gewohnt, mit vertrackten Situationen klarzukommen. Da gibt es Höhen und Tiefen. Mal gewinnt man, mal gewinnen die anderen. Mein lieber Freund", zog Kieviet die Spannung in die Länge.

„Nun sagen Sie endlich, wer von uns die restlichen Grundstücke bekommt", rief jemand.

Tönjes Kieviet wandte sich von Willem Dirks Bakker ab und deutete mit dem Zeigefinger in die Runde, so als wolle er an einem der Herren hängen bleiben. „Leider keiner von Ihnen." Sein Finger zeigte auf den Fischer, den Schlachtermeister und den Kaufmann Akkermann.

„Aber es stehen noch drei Partien aus", ereiferte sich Hermann Behrends. Auch andere begannen ihren Ärger herauszulassen.

„So ist es. Und wenn Sie noch eine Sekunde Geduld haben, werde ich verraten, was damit geschehen soll."

Ein wenig viel verlangt, dennoch kam Ruhe in den Raum.

„Der Rest", Kieviet wandte sich wieder dem Hausherrn zu, „geht an Sie, mein lieber Bakker. Herzlichen Glückwunsch!"

Lange blieb es mucksmäuschenstill im Raucherzimmer. Je nach Charakter wirkten die Männer entgeistert, überrascht, entsetzt, wütend oder belustigt. Einige schnauften verächtlich. Andere pafften gierig an ihrer Zigarre, einer kicherte wie ein altes Weib.

Köhler Junior, auch wenn er nicht der Gastgeber war, schnappte sich die Cognacflasche und begann die Gläser der Herren mit einem ordentlichen Schluck vollzugießen. Klaas Willems Bakker stürzte seines hinunter und ließ sich sofort nachschenken. Er sah seinen Vater nur dümmlich grinsen.

„Tja, lieber Bakker, Sie haben richtig verstanden", rief Tönjes Kieviet. „Sie bekommen drei Grundstücke."

Keine halbe Stunde später erhielt Hermine von Bakker Senior den Auftrag, seinem Sohn Dirk Willems Bakker das Ergebnis der Ausschreibung mitzuteilen. „Ehe er und seine Geschwister es von anderen hören. Sie werden es für ein Gerücht halten. Eines von denen, Fräulein Flessner, das bei seiner Runde über die Insel mit jedem Mal, wenn es erzählt wird, mehr ausgeschmückt wird. Jedenfalls wird er es dafür halten."

Doch Dirk war ahnungslos, als es an seiner Bürotür klopfte. Die vergangenen dreißig Minuten hatte er hier verbracht. Neben ihm stand das Körbchen mit dem schlafenden Säugling. Komischerweise blieb die Kleine nur in seiner Gegenwart ruhig, weswegen er den Säugling zu sich genommen hatte. Seine Mutter brauchte dringend Schlaf. Sie kränkelte immer mehr, auch wenn Adeline das im Leben nicht zugegeben hätte. „Übergib sie dem Kindermädchen", hatte Adeline ihm vor gut einer Stunde geraten. „Du willst doch sicherlich dabei sein, wenn …" Darüber war sie eingeschlafen.

Die Betrachtung seiner jüngsten Tochter machte es ihm möglich, alle Gedanken an das Geschehen eine Etage tiefer aus seinem Kopf zu verbannen. Christine einfach nur anzusehen war die pure Entspannung.

Es klopfte leise.

„Herein."

„Herr Bakker? Ihr Vater schickt mich." Hermine Flessners Stimme. Statt einzutreten, blieb sie auf dem Flur stehen.

„Ich komme."

„Dann ist die Entscheidung gefallen", stellte er fest. „Kommen Sie, wir gehen in mein Büro. Bitte, Fräulein Flessner, setzen Sie sich."

Ihr scheint es unangenehm zu sein, dachte Dirk.

Zögerlich nahm sie auf der vorderen Kante des angebotenen Stuhles Platz.

„Nun?", fragte er, plötzlich sehr nervös. Ihre Haltung und der Gesichtsausdruck versprachen nichts Gutes.

Auch er rutschte auf seinem Stuhl ein wenig nach vorn. „Wie ist es ausgegangen?"

„Ich denke, gut."

„Sehr schön", sagte Dirk. Vater hat demnach einen Zuschlag erhalten. Doch warum verriet Fräulein Flessners Mimik, dass da noch etwas kam, was ihm wenig gefallen sollte?

„Wir werden also eines der Grundstücke bekommen."

„Ja."

„Sehr schön", wiederholte er. „Aber? Da kommt noch etwas?"

„Kann man so sagen, Herr Bakker." Sie senkte den Blick und betrachtete ihre gefalteten Hände und zwei nervös drehende Daumen.

Sein Vater war zu feige, um selbst zu kommen, schoss es ihm durch den Kopf. Und er kapierte auch, warum. Das Szenario, über das er mit Eildert gesprochen hatte, war eingetreten. Dirk wurde speiübel. Hatte er sich eben noch mit einem Neubau anfreunden können, überfiel ihn jetzt das Gefühl, alles um ihn herum würde zusammenbrechen. Wie sollte die Familie es finanziell und personell schaffen, zwei große Projekte gleichzeitig zu stemmen?

Er sah, wie Hermine Flessner tief Luft holte, um ihm mit den richtigen Worten die Nachricht zu übermitteln. Dirk hob die Hand.

„Ich ahne, was Sie sagen wollen, Fräulein Flessner. Es sind zwei Grundstücke, für die wir den Zuschlag bekommen haben." *Mein Gott, wie sollen wir das schaffen?* Der Alte musste eines an die Gemeinde zurückgeben. Doch im selben Augenblick wusste Dirk, diese Blöße würde Vater sich nie geben. Ein

Bakker trat niemals von einer Zusage zurück. Das tat kein ehrenwerter Geschäftsmann. Es schadete dem Ruf der Familie, von dem Gespött der Leute einmal ganz zu schweigen.

Hermine nickte, dann schüttelte sie den Kopf, blickte auf, ihm jedoch nicht in die Augen.

„Was ist schiefgelaufen?"

„Nichts. Ihr Vater scheint zufrieden zu sein."

Der Alte hatte schon immer den Leuten etwas vormachen können. Das hatte er von Kindesbeinen an von seinem Stiefvater van Dyk gelernt, der als Schmuggler oft dem Zoll ein X für ein U hatte vormachen müssen.

„Und warum kommt es mir so vor, als gäbe es da etwas, das *mir* Sorgen bereiten würde?"

„Es sind drei."

„Drei was?" Die beiden Worte waren noch nicht ausgesprochen, da wusste er es.

Fräulein Flessner nickte heftig. Sie musste ihm angesehen haben, dass der Groschen gefallen war. Am liebsten wäre er aufgesprungen, hinuntergelaufen und hätte dem Alten im Raucherzimmer vor versammelter Mannschaft den Hals umgedreht. Kein Wunder, dass er die Flessner vorgeschickt hatte. Zum zweiten Mal in wenigen Minuten dachte Dirk, dass er seinen Vater niemals für so feige gehalten hätte. „Wo ist mein Herr Papa jetzt?", brachte er krächzend heraus.

„Er feiert."

„Er lässt sich feiern, Fräulein Flessner. Das ist ein Unterschied."

Der Säugling war aufgewacht, reckte die kleinen Fäuste in die Höhe und begann zu jammern. Sofort sprang Hermine auf, um das Körbchen zu schaukeln.

„Wissen Sie zufällig, um welche Grundstücke es sich handelt, Fräulein Flessner?“ Eine wichtige Frage und eventuell der erste sich aufzeigende Weg, die Misere ein wenig einzudämmen. Statt zwei Hotels auf zwei verschiedenen Grundstücken zu bauen, ein etwas größeres Haus mittig auf zwei Parzellen zu errichten, wäre eine Lösung. Allerdings setzte das voraus, dass wenigstens zwei der drei Flurstücke nebeneinanderlagen. Er hoffte auf das Stück zwischen der oberen Strandstraße und der Viktoriastraße.

„Eines im oberen Teil der Strandstraße.“

Sehr schön, dachte Dirk. „Und welches noch?“

Er konnte erkennen, wie sie heftig schluckte, ehe sie zur Antwort ansetzte. „Eines gleich neben dem kleinen Kaap.“ Nach einer kurzen Pause fügte sie hinzu: „Und eines gegenüber der *Strandvilla Hawich.*“ Hermine ließ von dem Körbchen ab.

„Geht es Ihnen nicht gut, Herr Bakker?“

Der Säugling begann zu schreien. Hermine beugte sich hinunter, doch er hielt sie auf. „Gehen Sie. Ich kümmere mich schon um Christine.“

Die Bürotür wurde aufgerissen und knallte gegen die Wand. Adeline kam hereingestürzt. „Hast du das gehört?“

„Ja, meine Liebe. Fräulein Flessner war so nett …“

Adeline wedelte unwillig mit den Händen, als Zeichen für Hermine, sie möge verschwinden.

„Und hat sie dir auch verraten, mit wem dein sauberer Herr Papa feiert?“

Dirk ahnte es. „Mit seinem besten Freund Georg Köhler.“

„Aha. Wusste ich es doch. Es war alles nur Theater und du steckst mit denen unter einer Decke.“

Es gab Zeiten, und die kamen immer öfter vor, da konnte er den Gedankengängen seiner Frau unmöglich folgen.

„Ich sollte hingehen und …“

„Auf jeden Fall musst du dich da blicken lassen. Und mach in Gottes Namen nicht so ein langes Gesicht.“

Kapitel 21

Einen Hauch von Eifersucht verspürte Dirk Willems Bakker, als am nächsten Tag der Familienrat tagte.

Sein Bruder Klaas gab wie ein begnadeter Schauspieler jede einzelne Kleinigkeit des Geschehens im Raucherzimmer wieder. Ein Ereignis, von dem vermutlich noch die kommenden Generationen sprechen würden. Und er war nicht dabei gewesen.

Klaas' Wangen brannten vor Aufregung während des Erzählens und seine Armbewegungen erinnerten an jemanden, der einem Gehörlosen etwas mitteilen wollte. Die einzigen Male, als er Klaas so glühend Geschichten berichten gehört hatte, war gewesen, als sein Bruder von der Umrundung von Kap Horn erzählt hatte.

„Ich wüsste zu gerne …", sagte Geeske. Ihr Mann hatte eine Teilnahme am Familientreffen verweigert, mit der Begründung, er habe in seiner Apotheke genug zu tun und niemand solle auf die Idee kommen, ihn in die Hotelplanungen einzubinden.

„Vermutlich ist er sauer, dass er sich jetzt eine zweite Apotheke abschminken kann", flüsterte Hieltje.

„Das, liebe Schwägerin, wird sich noch zeigen. Es ist eine Investition, die sich rentiert." Geeske besaß ein feines Gehör.

„Ich wüsste zu gern, ob Georg Köhler weiter Bürgermeister bleibt.“ Eltje Bakker, Ehefrau des Bäckermeisters, ließ sich nur selten bei der Familie blicken. „Viel Zeit wird er dazu nicht mehr haben.“

„Von uns interessiert das im Augenblick niemanden“, meinte Jakob, griff nach Hieltjes Hand und drückte fest zu, um sie an einem weiteren Kommentar zu hindern. „Ich für meinen Teil möchte endlich erfahren, wie es zu all dem überhaupt kommen konnte.“

„Das“, Klaas schob seine Hemdsärmel hoch, sodass die Unterarmtätowierungen aus seiner Seefahrerzeit nach Batavia zu erkennen waren, „ist schnell erzählt. Vater hat zwei Angebote abgegeben, um unsere Chancen auf wenigstens eines zu erhöhen. Das dritte Grundstück ist uns praktisch in den Schoß gefallen.“ Klaas blickte zu seinem Vater hinüber. Eine Aufforderung, er solle es der Familie erklären.

Der strich sich mit der Hand mehrmals über den Bart, als müsse er ihn glätten. „In letzter Sekunde habe ich erfahren, dass die Gemeinde ein zusätzliches Grundstück verkaufen will. Und da ich das Gefühl hatte“, er wechselte einen schnellen Blick mit seiner Tochter, „dass meine anderen Angebote überboten werden könnten, habe ich die Gunst genutzt.“ Er verschwieg, dass er die Information seinem alten Freund Georg Köhler zu verdanken hatte. Auch was Frau Wenke damit zu tun hatte, würde er niemals verraten.

Was er seiner Familie aber erzählte, war Hermine Flessners Beitrag in dieser Angelegenheit.

„Papas kleine Spionin.“ Geeske zwinkerte ihrem Vater zu.

„Das nördliche Ende haben wir also ihr zu verdanken“, sagte Dirk. „Sehr vorausschauend für eine Fünfzehnjährige.

Wenn ich die Wahl gehabt hätte, wäre meine Entscheidung ebenfalls darauf gefallen.“ Es garantierte, in Zukunft nach Norden hin keinen zusätzlichen Nachbarn zu bekommen. Denn nur wenige Meter weiter stand das kleine Kaap. Ein gemauertes Seezeichen, das für die Schifffahrt unentbehrlich war und deshalb nicht rundherum zugebaut werden durfte.

„Schön wäre es, wenn die anderen beiden Grundstücke zusammenliegen würden.“ Dirk erläuterte seine Gedanken, statt zwei Gebäuden auf je einer Parzelle einfach eines mitten auf einer größeren zu errichten. „Das spart Geld und …“

„Schöne Idee, mein Sohn“, unterbrach ihn der Senior. „Aber leider nicht machbar.“

„Wir könnten versuchen, mit einem anderen den Grund zu tauschen.“

Eine Weile schwieg die Familie, jeder hing seinen Gedanken nach.

„Wir könnten aber auch eines oder sogar zwei zurückgeben.“ Bäckermeister Janns Arbeitskleidung verströmte ein Aroma nach frisch gebackenem Kuchen. Es war klar, dass er die meisten Stunden des Tages in seiner Backstube beschäftigt sein würde, weswegen mit seiner Hilfe, was den Betrieb der geplanten Hotels anging, nicht gerechnet werden konnte. Sicherlich war das ein Grund, warum er von Anfang an gegen eine Bewerbung gewesen war.

„Kommt nicht infrage“, bestimmte der Senior.

„Aber wie sollen wir das schaffen? Einmal vom Finanziellen abgesehen“, meinte Eildert. „So eine Baustelle erfordert viel Aufmerksamkeit, Arbeit, Kraft und Nerven. An die Höhe der Bankkredite mag ich gar nicht denken.“

„Mein lieber Eildert", sagte sein Vater. „Ein Schritt nach dem anderen. Es zwingt uns niemand, mit dem Bau aller drei Hotels schon im kommenden Jahr zu beginnen."

Als hätte die Familie nicht Aufregung genug in dieser Woche gehabt, verließ am Samstagabend Harmina Bakker das Dampfschiff *Augusta*. Sie trat mit helfender Hand eines der Matrosen vom leicht schwankenden Schiff auf den Kutschwagen über.

„Großmutter!", rief der zwölfjährige Willi und fiel seiner Oma um den Hals.

„*Weest versichest, mien Jung!*", mahnte der Kutscher, „sonst fallt ihr beide ins Wasser."

Willi half seiner Großmutter, auf einer der beiden Kutschbänke Platz zu nehmen, ehe er anderen anreisenden Gästen beim Verstauen des Gepäcks behilflich war. Als der Wagen keinen weiteren Fahrgast mehr aufnehmen konnte, lenkte der Kutscher das Gefährt an den Strand. Da die Seniorchefin an Bord seiner Kutsche saß, kamen alle in den Genuss, bis in den Ort und direkt vor das *Hotel Bakker* gefahren zu werden, statt an der Dünenkante das Fahrzeug wieder verlassen zu müssen.

Um Gott für den glücklichen Ausgang der Grundstücksverteilung und der gesunden Heimkehr ihrer Mutter, Schwiegermutter, Ehefrau und Großmutter zu danken, saß am kommenden Sonntag die ganze Familie Bakker in der Kirche.

Das Gotteshaus war alt und stand nur einen schmalen Spaltbreit, weniger als zwei Meter, neben dem alten Leuchtturm.

„Wo ist Pastor Mecklenburg?", fragte die Seniorin.

„Fortgezogen, Mutter. Der neue Pastor heißt Sluyter."

Am Ende des Gottesdienstes öffnete Harmina Bakker ihr Portemonnaie schon in der Kirchenbank, um für die Kollekte am Ausgang zwei Mark herauszunehmen.

Jakob schüttelte leicht mit dem Kopf. Er konnte nur hoffen, dass Mutters Wahn, alle Ideen der Kirche und des Pastors mit dem Geld der Familie zu unterstützen, ihr wenigstens teilweise ausgetrieben worden war. Spenden waren ja gut, schön und wichtig, doch man musste es nicht übertreiben. Zumindest hatte seine Mutter in der Zeit, in der sie wieder auf der Insel war, kein Wort mehr über den Neubau einer Kirche verloren. Auch schien sie von dem Wahn, der Teufel sei in sie gefahren, geheilt zu sein. Diese Vorstellung hatte noch nie einen Sinn ergeben, denn die Mutter war immer diejenige gewesen, die das Wohl aller im Blick gehabt hatte. Der Teufel, so wie er es gelernt hatte, käme niemals auf den Gedanken, sich um arme Menschen oder den Bau einer neuen Kirche zu kümmern.

Ganz in Schwarz gekleidet, als wäre sie in Trauer, saß die alte Dame kerzengerade auf der Bank. Die Kur hatte ihr gutgetan. Sie wirkte entspannt, aber auch abwesend. Vermutlich brauchte sie Zeit, um wieder richtig zu Hause anzukommen. Davon, dass die Familie drei neue Grundstücke besaß, wusste sie noch nichts.

„Wie an ihren guten Tagen", flüsterte Hieltje mit Blick auf die Hand ihrer Schwiegermutter, die das Geld für die Kollekte bereithielt. Mit den fünf Worten wollte sie darauf hinweisen, dass sie nicht die Einzige in der Familie war, die das Geld zum Fenster hinauswarf.

Zeitgleich mit den letzten Worten des Pastors knipste Harmina Bakker die Handtasche zu. Das laute Klacken war das Zeichen für diejenigen, die eingeschlafen waren, ihre Augen zu öffnen und „Wieder mal eine wunderbare Predigt“ zu murmeln.

In alter Gewohnheit wartete Harmina Bakker, bis alle die Kirche verlassen hatten. Pastor Sluyter blickte dem letzten Gottesdienstbesucher hinterher. Erst jetzt wandte der Pastor sich an Frau Bakker. „Sie haben lange keine Messe mehr besucht“, sagte er, ohne dass ein Vorwurf in seiner Stimme mitklang.

„Ich war krank. Die Nerven, Sie verstehen?“

„Das tut mir leid. Ich hoffe, es geht Ihnen wieder besser.“

„Ja. Danke.“

„Das erklärt“, fügte Pastor Sluyter hinzu, „dass Sie unbeteiligt wirkten. Lag es an meiner Predigt? War Ihnen langweilig?“

„An Ihren salbungsvollen Worten ist nichts auszusetzen, Herr Pastor.“

„Was ist es dann?“

„Nun, Ihr Vorgänger hätte es gewusst. Ihm wäre es vermutlich peinlich gewesen“, zögerte die Seniorin die schlechte Nachricht für den neuen Pastor hinaus.

„Wir sind in der Kirche, da muss einem nichts peinlich sein.“ Dennoch wirkte der Seelsorger, als erwarte er eine Beichte, die ihm die Schamesröte ins Gesicht treiben würde.

„Schämen sollten Sie sich!“, rief sie zornig. „Ich war kein Jahr fort und schon sieht es in der Gemeinde aus, als ginge alles den Bach hinunter.“

„Ich weiß nicht, wovon Sie reden.“

Der Herr Pastor verstand es, wie Gottes Unschuldslamm auszusehen. Dann dämmerte es ihm. Sein Rücken straffte sich, ein erfreuliches Leuchten erschien auf seinem Gesicht. Er hatte von ihr gehört und war froh, dass sie wieder da war. Frau Bakker Senior war in der Kirchengemeinde in den vergangenen Monaten schmerzlich vermisst worden. Ihr war es zu verdanken, dass zusätzliche Mittel, die sich die städtische Gemeinde und die Kirche nicht aufzubringen in der Lage sahen, für die Armen und Bedürftigen zur Verfügung standen. Pastor Mecklenburg hatte ihn ausdrücklich darauf hingewiesen: Sobald Frau Bakker senior wieder da sei, müsse er sie unbedingt auf das leckende Kirchendach, die holzwurmbefallenen Kirchenbänke, einen neuen Ofen fürs Armenhaus und vieles mehr aufmerksam machen. In Pastor Sluyters Schreibtischschublade lag bereits eine Liste.

„Was möchten Sie mir denn sagen, Frau Bakker?“

„Sie leckt.“

„Wie bitte?“

„Die Kuppel. Oder eher das Dach.“ Harminas Zeigefinger deutete nach oben. „Während Ihrer Predigt fielen einige Tropfen herab.“ Zum Beweis nahm sie seine Hand und legte sie auf ihren Unterarm, genau auf die Stelle, die sich nass anfühlte.

Lieber Gott, ich danke dir!, dachte Pastor Sluyter. So waren sie beim Thema, bei dem er vor Sekunden noch nicht gewusst hatte, wie er es ihr gegenüber erwähnen konnte.

„Wir benötigen ein neues Dach“, sagte er und blickte sie auffordernd an.

„Ein neues Dach? Nein, Herr Pastor. Was wir brauchen, ist eine neue Kirche.“

***

„Was ich ganz dringend brauche“, redete Mathilde mit sich selbst, „ist eine Idee.“

Jetzt, da die Seniorin wieder auf der Insel war und sich die Saison dem Ende neigte, war Mathilde klar geworden, dass sie sich etwas einfallen lassen musste, wenn sie im kommenden Jahr wieder hier im *Haus Bakker* arbeiten wollte. Ihr wurde schmerzlich bewusst, dass es kurzsichtig gewesen war, auf Dauer darauf zu hoffen, die Bakkers weiterhin mit dem Wissen, dass die Alte in einem Irrenhaus gesessen hatte, erpressen zu können. Und ihre Räuberpistole mit dem Fotografen, bei der sie vorgegeben hatte, den guten Ruf des Hauses Bakker zu schützen, würde vermutlich nicht ausreichen, um in der nächsten Saison wieder eingestellt zu werden. Komischerweise, dachte sie, machte es ihr mehr aus, als sieh erwartet hatte. Zu wissen, dass sie vielleicht kein Borkum-Mädchen mehr in einem der besten Hotels Borkums sein würde, schmerzte. Wenn die Bakkers sie nicht nähmen, würde auch kein anderes gutes Haus auf der Insel sie einstellen. Hier ließ sich wenig verheimlichen, ihr Schlendrian war jedem im Hotelgewerbe bekannt. Und der Traum, jemals in einem der neuen Hotels zu arbeiten, wäre ebenfalls ausgeträumt.

„Im kommenden Jahr wird noch keines der Häuser fertig sein", behauptete Luise Menninga. Doch was wusste die dumme Nuss von Hausdame schon vom Häuserbauen? Schließlich hatte der Bauunternehmer aus Leer es geschafft, innerhalb von neun Monaten den über sechzig Meter hohen Leuchtturm zu errichten. Da sollte so ein popeliges dreistöckiges Hotel kein Problem für den Mann sein.

Doch sie schweifte in Gedanken ab. Mathilde musste etwas finden, womit sie die Bakkers überzeugen konnte, sie in der kommenden Saison erneut einzustellen.

Mittlerweile war es Ende September und die letzten Gäste verließen Borkum. Es wurde merklich einsamer in den Straßen, den Lokalen und am Strand. Die Angestellten aus *Köhlers Dorfhotel* würden Ende nächster Woche die Insel verlassen und auch die Saisonmitarbeiter beider *Bakker-Hotels* begannen, ihre Zelte für dieses Jahr abzubrechen.

Du kannst immer noch auf einer anderen Insel arbeiten, versuchte sie sich zu trösten. Doch sie wusste, sie würde die Großzügigkeit der Bakkers, das Aussteuerpaket mit reichlich Wäsche, die Verlosung der Fundstücke und den Anteil an den sommerlichen Trinkgeldern genauso missen, wie sie ihre Kollegen vermissen würde. Alles in allem war es ein angenehmes Arbeiten in einem der Bakker'schen Betriebe, da gab es ganz andere Arbeitgeber, wie sie sehr wohl wusste.

Darum streng dich an, dachte sie. *Finde eine Lösung. Entdecke etwas, was die Bakkers veranlasst, dich wieder einzustellen.*

In diesem Moment lenkte das Gezeter einer Möwe sie vom Packen ihres Koffers ab. Sie schaute aus dem Dachfenster hinaus. Ihr Blick blieb an der kleinen Kirche gleich neben dem alten Leuchtturm hängen.

„Danke, lieber Gott!", flüsterte sie. „Etwas mit Engeln. Das ist eine großartige Idee."

***

„Und du bist wieder einmal das Unschuldslamm", schrie Jakob Hieltje an. Sie hatte bemerkt, wie ihr Ehemann einem jungen Mädchen einen Zettel zusteckte.

„Das musst gerade du sagen!", keifte er zurück.

„Was soll das denn heißen?"

„Dass ich mich frage, ob das da", er deutete auf ihren Bauch, „überhaupt von mir ist."

„Das ist so etwas von fies, und das weißt du genau!" Hieltje mochte verschwenderisch, neidisch und eifersüchtig sein. Sie hatte eine böse Zunge und nicht jeder konnte sie leiden, doch eines war sie niemals gewesen – untreu. Mit der Hand auf dem sich leicht gewölbten Bauch brach sie in Wehklagen aus.

„Hör auf zu heulen!", mahnte Jakob und wandte sich ab, um ihre Räumlichkeiten zu verlassen.

„Du bleibst hier!" Hieltje packte ihn am Handgelenk. „Das wird jetzt ein für alle Mal geklärt."

„Du kannst mich nicht ändern." Jakob gab nach, umfasste sie und drückte sie fest an seine Brust. „Im Grunde deines Herzens bist du dir doch sicher, dass ich nur dich liebe."

„Das sagst du immer."

„Weil es stimmt."

Hieltje befreite sich aus seiner Umarmung. Ihr üppiger Busen bebte vor Wut, als sie ihn anschaute. Ihre Augen waren weder gerötet noch feucht. Sie sah wunderschön aus in ihrem Zorn. Jakob strich ihr zärtlich eine vorwitzige Haarsträhne hinters Ohr. Solch schönes rotes Haar hatte er bei keiner anderen Frau gesehen.

Sie trat einen Schritt zurück, um Abstand zwischen ihnen zu schaffen und ihm den Weg zur Tür zu versperren. „Wenn ich noch einmal sehe, wie du der kleinen Anneliese nachstellst, dann …"

„Tu' ich nicht."

„Lüg mich nicht an! Ich habe es genau gesehen, wie du ihr schöne Augen gemacht und ihr hinterhergeschaut hast wie ein läufiger Köter." Ihre Hand flog hoch. „Wage es ja nicht, es auszusprechen! Ich weiß selbst, dass Rüden nicht läufig werden können."

Jakob wandte ihr den Rücken zu und setzte sich aufs Sofa. Er könnte sie jetzt ermahnen wegen der Kinder leiser zu sein, doch die waren mit dem Kindermädchen unterwegs. Deshalb gab er sich damit zufrieden, einfach nur mit hängenden Schultern dazusitzen und ihr Gezeter durchzustehen.

Im Grunde genommen hatte Hieltje ja recht. Es war die schlechteste Idee des Jahrhunderts gewesen, zu versuchen, das junge Mädchen auf eine Tasse Kaffee oder ein Eis einzuladen, von dem noch vor kurzer Zeit spekuliert worden war, ob es seine Tochter sein könnte. Doch das hatte Frau Luise Gott sei Dank aus der Welt schaffen können. Sie hatte auf die Bibel geschworen, dass ihre Schwester ihm in dieser Hinsicht niemals begegnet sei. Und das glaubte er Luise Menninga. Denn er war der Überzeugung, sich an jede Frau zu erinnern, mit der er mal etwas gehabt hatte.

Die letzten Worte von Hieltje hatte er, ganz in Gedanken versunken, nicht mitbekommen. Jetzt stand er wieder auf und trat erneut dicht an sie heran. „Du hast ja recht, mein Liebling."

Überrascht blickte sie ihn an. Dann veränderte sich ihr zorniger Gesichtsausdruck. Die Konturen wurden weich, ein kleines Lächeln glitt über ihre schwungvollen Lippen.

„Versprichst du es mir?"

Oje, was hatte sie eben gesagt? Er hatte es nicht mitbekommen. Dennoch nickte er.

„Ich verspreche es dir."

„Hoch und heilig, wie deine Mutter sagen würde?"

„Hoch und heilig."

***

Luise nahm Anneliese in den Arm. Einige Tage hatte Anneliese als Gast in der *Pension Staghouwer* gewohnt, dann hatte sie mit angepackt, da ihrer Gastgeberin die unerwartet viele Arbeit über den Kopf gewachsen war. Verständlich, denn es war Staghouwers erste Saison im Vermietungsgewerbe.

„Und grüß mir schön deine Mutter."

Aus der kleinen Reisetasche, mit der Anneliese vor einiger Zeit angereist war, war eine große geworden. „Frau Staghouwer hat sie mir geliehen."

„Das heißt, du kommst nächstes Jahr wieder." Frau Luise freute sich, wirkte aber gleichzeitig besorgt.

„Wann besuchst du uns?", fragte Anneliese. „Mama, Papa, du und ich müssen über etwas Wichtiges sprechen."

Luise nickte. *Sie weiß es,* dachte Luise. Erleichterung und Furcht ergriffen ihr Herz. „Das machen wir", flüsterte sie, küsste Annelieses Wangen und drückte sie fest an sich. „Ich liebe dich, das weißt du."

„Ich weiß. Bis bald."

***

Hermine saß auf einer Bank am Strand und betrachtete das Meer. Ihre Zeit auf Borkum ging in wenigen Tagen zu Ende. Sie würde die Insel vermissen, ebenso die Arbeit und all die Menschen, die sie in den vergangenen Monaten kennengelernt hatte.

Alles wird mir fehlen.

Ihr graute vor dem langen Winter, in dem sie zu Hause der Mutter zur Hand gehen würde, da es Vater wieder schlechter ging. Vielleicht würde sie eine Arbeit in Leer finden, doch einfach würde es nicht werden. Sie könnte eine Ausbildung als Verkäuferin beginnen, doch im Grunde ihres Herzens wusste sie, dass es ihr hinter einer Ladentheke auf Dauer wenig gefallen würde. Sie sah ihre Zukunft im Hotelgewerbe. Die abwechslungsreiche Arbeit gefiel ihr. Ebenso der Hauch der großen weiten Welt, den Frau Baronin von Wer-weiß-woher, Herr Kommerzienrat oder der reiche Fabrikant aus Leipzig und die Sängerin aus Berlin mit ihrer Ankunft ins Haus spülten.

Hermine seufzte und erhob sich, um den Rückweg zum Hotel anzutreten.

Bereits nach wenigen Schritten spürte sie ein Augenpaar auf sich gerichtet. Sie blickte sich um, konnte jedoch nicht feststellen, aus welcher Richtung es kam. Sie blieb auf halber Strecke der Bismarckstraße, so hieß die Flaniermeile, die zum Strand hinaufführte, stehen. Blitzschnell, wie wenn sie mit den Kindern Fangen spielte, drehte sie sich um. Den Fremden, der in diesem Moment so tat, als müsse er etwas an seinem Schuhwerk richten, hatte sie noch nie gesehen. Sie ging über die Kreuzung, an der mit den Arbeiten für den Bahnhof begonnen worden war, und schlenderte den Damenpfad hinunter in den Ortskern hinein. Vor einigen Schaufenstern blieb sie stehen. In der Spiegelung sah sie, dass der Mann ihr folgte. Zugegeben, es gab nur wenig andere Möglichkeiten, um vom Strand in die Ortsmitte zu gelangen, doch jetzt, da Hermine nach links in die Große Straße einbog, lief er immer noch hinter ihr her. Der erpresserische Fotograf kam ihr in den Sinn. War der Mann jemand, der Udens Schmuddelbilder übernommen hatte und sie jetzt verfolgte, um zu erfahren, wo sie wohnte? Mathilde hatte gesagt, solange nicht die Glasplatten gefunden und vernichtet worden seien, könnte man von den unschicklichen Bildern so viele Kopien machen, wie man wollte. Ein fieser Gedanke. Hinzu kam, dass es kein Geheimnis auf der Insel war, dass heute oder morgen die Mitarbeiter der beider *Bakker-Hotels* die im Sommer angesammelten Trinkgelder ausbezahlt bekamen. Dann wäre etwas Geld bei ihr zu holen. Wusste das der Kerl, der ihr folgte?

Hermine war unsicher, ob sie sich erpressen lassen oder es auf eine Bloßstellung ankommen lassen sollte. Ihre Familie brauchte das Geld dringend, um über die Wintermonate zu kommen. Kurz schmunzelte sie über sich selbst. Jetzt dachte sie schon wie eine Insulanerin. Dabei gab es auf dem Festland das ganze Jahr hindurch Arbeit.

Sie beschloss, am *Hotel Bakker* vorbeizugehen. Sie musste verhindern, dass der Mann wusste, wo sie arbeitete. Zum Glück trug sie private Kleidung, sodass er es nicht an ihrer Uniform erkennen konnte. Hermine lief bis zu *Köhlers Dorfhotel*, blieb kurz vor dem eisernen Zaun, der das Grundstück von der Straße trennte, stehen und bog dann auf die Straße zwischen Hotel und altem Leuchtturm nach links ab. Hier nahm sie die Beine in die Hand. Sie rannte den Weg hinter *Köhlers Dorfhotel* entlang und erreichte kurz darauf den Acker, der dem *Hotel Bakker Junior* gegenüber lag. Die Kartoffeln hatten welke Blätter, es hatte lange nicht mehr geregnet, und es gab jede Menge Bohnen, die unbedingt geerntet werden sollten. Hermine raffte den Rock und stieg über den niedrigen Zaun, der den Acker umgab. Als sie auf der Straße stand, blickt sie nach links und konnte eben noch sehen, wie der Fremde auf derselben Straße zwischen *Köhlers Dorfhotel* und dem alten Leuchtturm abbog. Also hatte sie sich die Verfolgung nicht eingebildet. Sie war schweißgebadet. Das Unterhemd klebte ihr am Rücken. Sie strich den Rock glatt und hob den Blick. An einem der Fenster stand Mathilde mit dem Staubwedel in der Hand. Natürlich hatte sie Hermine gesehen. Sicherlich würde sie wissen wollen, was es mit dem undamenhaften Übersteigen von Gartenzäunen auf sich hatte. Sollte sie die Wahrheit sagen? Mathilde hatte bewiesen, dass sie mit solchen Kerlen fertig wurde. Doch ein unbestimmtes Gefühl sagte ihr, es sei besser, Mathilde lieber eine erfundene Geschichte aufzutischen.

Am Nachmittag begegnete sie ihm wieder. Es brachte wenig, sich auf Dauer vor dem Mann zu verstecken. Zudem hasste sie die Ungewissheit. Das musste ein Ende haben. Hermine straffte den Körper, hob das Kinn und ging direkt auf ihn zu.

„Kann ich Ihnen helfen?"

„Ganz sicher. Indem Sie nicht noch einmal vor mir weglaufen."

„Was wollen Sie?"

„Sind Sie Hermine Flessner?"

„Warum wollen Sie das wissen?"

„Das kann ich Ihnen noch nicht verraten. Also sind Sie es?"

„Und wer möchte das wissen?"

„Auch das sage ich erst, wenn Sie mir bestätigen, dass Sie Fräulein Flessner, die Cousine von Bertha, sind."

„Bertha? Sie ist in Amerika."

In dem Blick des Fremden lag so etwas wie Mitleid. Dann blickte er sich um, als wolle er verhindern, dass jemand etwas von ihrem Gespräch mitbekam. „Gehen wir ein paar Schritte?“ Er deutete in Richtung Norden, dorthin, wo das Dorf zu Ende war und die Wiesen begannen. Keine gute Entscheidung, mit einem Fremden irgendwohin zu gehen, wo wenig Menschen waren.

Hermines Verstand sagte Nein, doch ihr Kopf nickte. Mit einer Handbewegung bedeutete er ihr, vorauszugehen. Er folgte mit einem gehörigen Abstand.

An einem Gartenzaun aus Walkinnladen, der einen Acker umgab, blieb er stehen und hüstelte laut. Sie wandte sich um und ging die wenigen Schritte zurück. Hier waren sie durch die hohen Walknochen und die Holunderbüsche vor neugierigen Blicken, die eventuell auf sie gerichtet sein könnten, geschützt.

„Warum diese Heimlichkeit?“

„Nun, es ist etwas verzwickt, Fräulein Flessner. Ich möchte auf jeden Fall verhindern, dass mich jemand von der Familie Bakker sieht.“

„Was hat Bertha mit den Bakkers zu tun?“

„So einiges, mein Fräulein. Aber lassen Sie mich von Anfang an erzählen. Zuerst möchte ich Ihnen versichern, dass es Ihrer Cousine gut geht.“

„Das weiß ich.“

„Wissen Sie auch, wo sie ist?“

„In Amerika.“

„Nun, das lässt man uns glauben.“

Hermine musste sich am Gartenzaun festhalten und wich der Hand des Fremden aus, der sie stützen wollte. „Nicht in Amerika?“, fragte sie entsetzt. „Aber wir haben Post von ihr aus Arizona.“

„Genauso wie ihre Familie Postkarten von Borkum bekommen hat. Haben Sie den Briefumschlag gesehen?“

Sicherlich meinte er die Briefmarke. Sie würde beweisen, dass der Brief in Übersee aufgegeben worden war. Hermine bezweifelte, dass ihre Mutter oder ihre Tante einen Blick darauf verschwendet hatten. Warum auch? „Nein. Aber meine Mutter schrieb …“

„Genau das, was beabsichtigt war. Bertha schrieb, was alle glauben sollen.“

„Und wo ist sie?“

„Das weiß ich noch nicht. Aber ich werde es herausbekommen. Ich möchte Sie bitten, mir dabei zu helfen.“

„Wie?“

„Halten Sie Augen und Ohren offen. Versuchen Sie, an die Post Ihrer Cousine heranzukommen. Ich melde mich bei Ihnen.“

„Aber ich verlasse die Insel.“

„Ich weiß. Ihre Anschrift in Leer ist mir bekannt. Ich melde mich“, sagte er. „Es kann jedoch einige Zeit dauern. Machen Sie sich keine Sorgen.“

Noch ehe Hermine weitere Fragen stellen konnte, drehte er sich um und eilte mit großen Schritten davon.

„Bis eben hatte ich mir keine Sorgen gemacht“, rief sie ihm hinterher. Sie wusste, ihr würde nichts anderes übrig bleiben, als seinem Rat zu folgen. Sie musste herausfinden, ob seine Behauptung stimmt.

***

Mathilde wusste, dass niemand aus der Familie der Seniorin berichtet hatte, dass sie Harmina Bakkers Klinikaufenthalt als Druckmittel verwendet hatte. Um auch in der kommenden Saison eine Anstellung zu bekommen, plante Mathilde, die Alte davon zu überzeugen, sich für sie einzusetzen. Harmina Bakkers Hang zum Göttlichen hatte Mathilde auf den Gedanken gebracht. Mathilde blieb ein einziger Versuch. Die Idee war gut, nun musste sie nur noch ihre Geschichte der Verrückten, wie sie Harmina Bakker im Stillen nannte, auf die Nase binden. Harmina war aus zweierlei Gründen die geeignete Person. Zum einen, weil sie den Kram, den Mathilde sich ausgedacht hatte, glauben wird. Zweitens: weil ihr Ehemann ihr keinen Wunsch abschlagen konnte. Wenn Harmina für sie eintreten würde, bekam Mathilde die Chance, auch im kommenden Jahr als Borkum-Mädchen in diesem Hause zu arbeiten.

Vor den privaten Räumen der Senioren blieb sie stehen und zupfte ihre Zimmermädchenuniform zurecht. Einmal holte sie tief Luft, dann klopfte sie an die Tür.

„Herein!"

„Haben Sie einen Moment Zeit für mich, Frau Bakker?"

„Was gibt es denn, Fräulein Remmers?"

Mathilde trat ein und schloss sofort die Tür hinter sich. „Es ist eine persönliche Angelegenheit." Mathilde knickste und trat näher an den Sessel heran, in dem Harmina Bakker saß. Eine Bibel lag aufgeschlagen auf ihrem Schoß, die Lesebrille steckte auf ihrer Nasenspitze und man musste befürchten, dass sie gleich herunterfallen würde.

„Meine Schwiegertochter ist für die Angelegenheiten unserer Mitarbeiter zuständig", sagte Harmina. Dennoch war sie neugierig genug, um die Bibel zu schließen. Sie ließ jedoch einen Finger zwischen den Seiten stecken, damit sie die Stelle, die sie eben gelesen hatte, sofort wiederfand.

Mathilde senkte demütig den Kopf. „Ich weiß, Frau Bakker. Aber in dieser Angelegenheit können nur Sie mir helfen." Mathildes Blick fiel auf das Kreuz, das zwischen zwei Fenstern an der Wand hing. Sie bekreuzigte sich, so wie sie es in der Vergangenheit schon oft bei ihrer eigenen Großmutter gesehen hatte, und hielt den Blick über Frau Bakker hinweg auf den hölzernen Jesus gerichtet. „Denn ich hatte eine Vision."

Harmina Bakker starrte sie einen Moment an. Dann legte sie die Bibel auf einem Tischchen gleich neben dem Sessel ab. „Versündigen Sie sich nicht vor Gott." Ihre Stimme klang hart.

„Das würde mir niemals einfallen, Frau Bakker." Demütig blickte sie auf ihre Schuhe. „Am vergangenen Sonntag zur Zeit der Messe…"

„Sie habe ich nicht in der Kirche gesehen."

Verflixt, da habe ich einen Fehler gemacht, dachte Mathilde. „Ich bitte um Vergebung." Sie knickste erneut. „Aber ich wurde von einer ungewöhnlichen Unrast erfüllt. Es war mein freier Tag. Also spazierte ich über den Strand, um in der freien Natur und bei dem schönen Wetter einen klaren Kopf zu bekommen. Ich wanderte auch durch die Dünen und mit einem Mal hatte ich das Gefühl, als müsste ich mich auf einer Düne niederlassen. Mein Blick schweifte über das Meer und da sah ich sie."

„Wen?"

„Zwischen zwei Wolken. Als ob die Sonne ihre Lichtstrahlen gebündelt hindurch schicken würde. Da war sie. Eine lichtumflutete Gestalt.“ Mathilde deutete mit dem Zeigefinger zu einem der Fenster.

Frau Bakker wandte kurz den Kopf zum Fenster. Bis auf die Bäckerei nebenan war nichts zu sehen. Mit heftiger Bewegung nahm sie die Lesebrille ab.

„Vielleicht ein Engel? Sie blieb nur wenige Sekunden, und als sie verblasste, sah ich drei dunkle Fischrücken aus dem Wasser auftauchen und wieder verschwinden.“

„Schweinswale, die sieht man hier öfter.“

„Stella Maris, die Schutzpatronin der Seeleute“, flüsterte Mathilde.

Frau Bakker Senior starrte sie mit aufgerissenen Augen an. „Der heilige Nikolaus ist der Schutzpatron der Seefahrer. Er…“

Mathilde redete unbeirrt weiter. „Eine innere Stimme verriet mir, dass es die Jungfrau Maria sei. Und sie sprach mit mir.“

Selbst in Mathildes Ohren klang es, als könne sie das Wunder kaum fassen. „Die Jungfrau Maria sagte, dass nur ich es schaffen könnte, den Machenschaften, die über die Familie Bakker hereinbrechen werden, Einhalt zu gebieten. *Was für Machenschaften?*, fragte ich die Jungfrau Maria und sie antwortete: *Die, die ab dem kommenden Mai hereinbrechen werden.*“ Mathilde holte tief Luft und fasste sich mit der rechten Hand ans Herz. *Aber wie kann ich das?* fragte ich. *Ich bin ein kleines unbedeutendes Zimmermädchen. Soll ich etwa zu den Sündern hingehen und sie zur Rede stellen? Wer bin ich, dass ich mir so etwas erlauben darf? Du findest einen Weg,* flüsterte die liebliche Stimme.“ Mathilde seufzte. „Und so habe ich den Weg zu Ihnen gefunden.“ Erneut senkte Mathilde in Demut den Kopf. Dann fingerte sie ein Taschentuch aus ihrer Rocktasche heraus und tupfte sich die Nase. „Was soll ich nur machen?“

„Nun“, sagte die Seniorin und es klang streng. „Vorerst wird es angebracht sein, dass Sie in Zukunft regelmäßig die Kirche besuchen, denn Sie scheinen mir eine gläubige Person geworden zu sein.“

„Das tue ich, Frau Bakker. Ich besuche die Katholische Kirche und für mich spielt die Jungfrau Maria eine große Rolle.“

Harmina Bakker wedelte mit der Hand, als wollte sie etwas wegwischen. Dann griff sie nach ihrer Brille und dem Buch der Bücher. „Ich werde darüber nachdenken müssen. Ab mit Ihnen. Die Arbeit macht sich nicht von alleine.“

Mathilde knickste zum dritten Mal. Hatte die Alte ihr geglaubt und würde sie in der nächsten Saison wiederkommen können, um „Ungemach“ abzuwenden, oder würde sie auf einer anderen Insel Arbeit suchen müssen?

Statt aus dem Raum zu eilen, zwang sie sich gemessenen Schrittes und mit hängenden Schultern zu gehen.

Als sie die Tür leise hinter sich schloss, hörte sie Frau Bakker flüstern: „Ich wünschte, Gott würde mir auch ein Zeichen senden.“

Mathilde lächelte zufrieden, dabei überfiel sie kurz das unangenehme Gefühl, als hinterließe sie einen Hauch dünnen Gestanks nach Schwefel, mit dem der Teufel sich umhüllte.

„Du hast was gesagt?“ Hermine wollte es kaum glauben.

„Irgendwie musste ich ja sicherstellen, dass sie mich im kommenden Jahr wieder einstellen werden. Reg dich ab, Minchen. Das meiste davon stimmt“, behauptete Mathilde. Sie zog ein Bettlaken im Gästezimmer 15 glatt. „Da war wirklich ein Sonnenstrahl und da waren diese Viecher im Wasser. Was denn? Schau mich nicht so strafend an. Hauptsache ist doch, dass es gewirkt hat."

„Eines Tages", prophezeite Hermine, „werden dir deine erfundenen Geschichten das Genick brechen."

„Hoffentlich nicht so bald." Mathilde blickte Hermine herausfordernd an. Dann fiel ihr Augenmerk auf eine geöffnete Schachtel Pralinen, die auf dem kleinen Tisch unter dem Fenster lag.

„Das wagst du nicht!", sagte Hermine.

„Heute ist mein Glückstag." Mathildes Finger kreisten über der offenen Schachtel. Dann stieß ihre Hand nieder wie eine Möwe, die einem Badegast das Fischbrötchen stehlen will, und sie fischte sich eine Praline heraus. Ehe Hermine sie davon abhalten konnte, verschwand die Süßigkeit in Mathildes Mund.

„Das ist Diebstahl."

„Stell dich nicht so an."

„Wenn das rauskommt", warnte Hermine und drohte mit dem Zeigefinger. „Dann hilft dir keine noch so heilige Ausrede weiter, das schwöre ich dir."

„Wie ist es mit dir? Wirst du im nächsten Jahr wieder hier arbeiten?"

„Liebend gerne. Nur…"

„Ich weiß, was du meinst. Bakkers Schwiegertöchter werden sich gegen dich aussprechen. Aber ich bin mir sicher, der Alte wird sich durchsetzen. Du wirst sehen, spätestens zu Weihnachten wirst du Post bekommen. Die wären ganz schön blöd", Mathilde deutete mit dem Finger nach oben, „wenn sie so eine fleißige Kraft wie dich nicht wieder einstellen würden."

Um Hermine von dem trüben Gedanken abzulenken, tat Mathilde, als wolle sie eine weitere Praline stibitzen. Hermine schlug ihr heftig auf die Hand.

„Aua!"

So nahm der Herbst seinen Lauf und der Winter kam dieses Jahr recht früh. Der große Schneesturm in Amerika vom vergangenen März wurde Gesprächsthema Nummer eins, als es immer heftiger zu schneien begann und nicht wieder aufhörte. Vor fast einem Jahr hatte es dort Schneeverwehungen von über fünfzehn Meter Höhe gegeben und zweihundert Schiffe waren auf Grund gelaufen, wobei mindestens hundert Seeleute gestorben waren. Ob solch eine Naturkatastrophe den Küsten- und Inselbewohnern bevorstand oder ob sie auch dieses Mal ungeschoren davonkämen, lag allein in Gottes Hand.

Um die Familie von den Sorgen um die Cousine in Amerika abzulenken – in Arizona gab es angeblich einen fürchterlichen Wirbelsturm –, erzählte Hermine gerne von dem, was sie auf der Insel erlebt hatte. Sie verschwieg jedoch die Begegnung mit dem Fremden und dessen unheimliche Behauptung. Endlich kam ein weiterer Brief von Bertha. Leider gelang es Hermine nicht, einen Blick auf den Umschlag zu werfen. Speziell danach zu fragen, wagte sie nicht. Ein plötzliches Interesse an Briefmarken hätte Misstrauen erwecken können. Auf jeden Fall erkannte sie Berthas Schrift. Sie schrieb, es ginge ihr gut. Was wollte man mehr? Nur gelegentlich kam ihr der Fremde in den Sinn und sie sagte sich immer wieder, es reiche vollkommen, wenn sie sich sorge. Ihre Mutter war von der Aussteuer, die sie heimgebracht hatte, begeistert. Hermine brauchte Tage, um ihr begreiflich zu machen, dass die Handtücher, Bettwäsche und Tischdecken sofort verwendet werden sollten. Es würde schließlich noch Jahre dauern, bis sie ans Heiraten denken konnte. Zudem plane sie, erneut eine Saison auf Borkum zu verbringen. Dann würde sie im kommenden Herbst wieder etwas mitbringen. Hermines Anteil an den Trinkgeldern reichte, um die Familie drei Monate über Wasser zu halten. Ihr Vater erholte sich endlich und konnte wieder halbe Tage als Bürovorsteher arbeiten. Je weiter der Winter fortschritt, umso mehr war Hermine sich sicher, erneut als Borkum-Mädchen auf die Insel zu gehen. In einem der Bakker'schen Hotels würde sie immer Arbeit finden, das hatte nicht nur Frau Luise, sondern auch der Senior ihr mehrmals versichert. Und wenn die sie nicht haben wollten, würde sie Köhlers Versprechen auf eine Arbeit einlösen.

Anfang März 1889 vermisste sie die Insel, die Menschen und die Abenteuer so sehr, dass es weh tat.

„*Ich muss an die See*", sagte sie sich selbst. „*Wenn ich in Leer hocken bleibe, werde ich verrückt.*"

Mitte März erhielt Hermine einen Brief. Darauf klebte in der rechten oberen Ecke eine wunderschöne Briefmarke. Blauweiß mit einem Adler. Über dem Kopf des Vogels eine Krone, auf seiner Brust ein Wappen. Hinten auf dem Umschlag war der Absender aufgedruckt. *Hotel Bakker.*

„Jetzt ist unsere Kleine erwachsen", sagte die Mutter.

„Warum?", wollte der Vater wissen.

„Weil sie Post bekommen hat und …" Ein weiterer Grund fiel ihr nicht ein. „Dein erster Brief", sagte die Mutter, „wenn man von meinen absieht." Es klang, als wäre ein Wunder geschehen.

Hermine lächelte und sah sich von ihren Geschwistern umringt.

„Von wem ist er?“, fragte ihr Bruder Heinz.

„Lass mal sehen“, verlangte ihr jüngster Bruder Hinrich.

„Kann ich die Marke haben?“, bat Heinz. „Die sammle ich.“

„Das ist das Erste, was ich höre“, meinte Hermines Schwester Hildegard. „Wie viele hast du denn schon?“

„Die da wird der Anfang sein. Bitte, Hermine, darf ich sie haben?“

Hermine nickte.

„Ha“, rief Heinz und schaute Hildegard triumphierend an.

„Du solltest Tante Frieda bitten, dir die Marke aus Amerika zu geben“, schlug Hermine vor.

„Das ist eine gute Idee.“

„Nun lasst Hermine in Ruhe ihren Brief lesen“, verlangte Mutter und machte den Familienmitgliedern ein Zeichen, dass sie sich alle um den Tisch herum hinsetzen sollten.

Hermine hätte den Umschlag gerne in Ruhe geöffnet und den Brief allein gelesen, doch konnte sie unmöglich den erwartungsvollen Blicken widerstehen.

„Vorsichtig!“, mahnte Heinz, als sie den Brief öffnen wollte. „Mach die Marke nicht kaputt.“ Er sprang auf, nahm ein Messer aus der Besteckschublade und reichte es seiner Schwester.

„Schön vorsichtig.“

Hermine tat, worum er sie gebeten hatte, schlitzte den Briefumschlag auf, nahm das Blatt Papier heraus und gab den Umschlag an Heinz weiter.

„Juhu!“, jubelte er, sprang auf und verließ den Raum. Welche Nachricht Hermine bekommen hatte, interessierte ihn nicht.

„Nun?“, wollte ihre Mutter wissen, nachdem Hermine den Brief gelesen hatte.

„Man fragt an, ob ich in der kommenden Saison wiederkomme. Sie würden mir die Stelle freihalten. Bis Ende März soll ich ihnen Bescheid geben."

„Meine Tochter!" Ihre Mutter legte die rechte Hand auf ihr Herz und es schien, als würde sie ein paar Zentimeter wachsen.

„Potz Blitz!", meinte der Vater stolz. „Da wirst du ja einen ordentlichen Eindruck hinterlassen haben."

„Wirst du gehen?", fragte Hildegard. Die Neunjährige blickte ihre große Schwester erwartungsvoll an.

„Natürlich geht sie", sagte ihre Mutter.

Nachwort
Für alle, die es genau wissen möchten

Ich gebe zu, ich habe geschummelt. Um die Geschichte spannender zu gestalten, habe ich die Jahreszahl der tatsächlichen Errichtungen der *Bakker'schen Hotels* an der Strandpromenade geändert.

Das *Strandhotel Bakker* wurde bereits 1885 gebaut. Das Hotel steht in der oberen Strandstraße. Später hieß es *Deutsches Haus*, danach *Hotel Rheinland*. Heute ist es der *Inselhof Borkum*.

Bei *Bakkers Logierhaus* erfolgte die Grundsteinlegung 1891. Später hieß das Haus *Bakkers Strandvilla*. Heute ist es das *Strandhotel Vier JahresZeiten*.

Im Jahr 1898 wurde das *Hohenzollern* fertiggestellt. Die Kosten dieses 50-Zimmer-Hotels gingen weit über den Kostenvoranschlag hinaus. Nicht nur das Gebäude war großzügig gebaut, auch die Inneneinrichtung war kostenintensiv, wie aus den Schuldscheinen der Ostfriesischen Sparkasse Aurich zu ersehen ist. Nach dem Verkauf wurde es zur Jugendherberge umfunktioniert. Heute ist es erneut eines der besten Häuser am Platz und trägt weiter den Namen *Hohenzollern*. Nach wie vor ist es das nördlichste Hotel auf der Promenade. Zur Seite hinaus – der unverbaute Blick auf das Kaap und die Dünen.

Die erwähnten Gebäude *Bakker Senior* und *Bakker Junior* haben die vorletzte Jahrhundertwende gut überstanden. Leider wurde das *Hotel Bakker Junior* 1969 abgerissen. An seiner Stelle finden wir heute einen hässlichen Parkplatz.

Das *Hotel Bakker Senior* (eröffnet im Jahr 1850) gibt es bis heute. *Arthotel Bakker* heißt es. Die alte Fassade ist teilweise gut erhalten, neue Anbauten sind hervorragend integriert. Im Jahr 2022 komplett saniert, gehört es zu den Tophäusern der Insel.

Auch die Villa, die ehemals Klaas Willems Bakker bewohnte, hat die beiden Jahrhundertwenden gut überstanden. Sie steht im Rektor-Meyer-Pfad und ist prächtig anzusehen.

Die *Apotheke Bakker,* Ecke Neue Straße/Wilhelm-Bakker Straße, wurde im Jahr 1883 erbaut. Die Fassade ist unverändert geblieben. Sie trägt seit alters her die Bezeichnung *Nordsee-Apotheke.* Die vormals Große Straße wurde damals umgewidmet und trägt heute seinen Namen. Wilhelm Bakker hat sich als Badedirektor, eine Tätigkeit, die er neben dem Betrieb seiner Apotheke ausübte, hervorgehoben.

1884 übernahm Jann Willems Bakker die Bäckerei, die zwischen dem *Hotel Bakker Senior* und der Apotheke lag. Er stockte das Gebäude auf und richtete einen neuen Verkaufsraum ein. Seine Nachfahren betrieben die Bäckerei für eine lange Zeit.

2022 wurde sie an den Eigentümer des *Arthotel Bakker* verkauft. So kam wieder zusammen, was einst zusammengehörte.

Es kann unmöglich die Hermine Flessner aus meiner Geschichte gewesen sein, der Wilhelm Busch ein schönes Gedicht gewidmet hat. Der Dichter verbrachte seine Urlaubstage zu einem früheren Zeitpunkt auf Borkum. 1876 und 1879. Dennoch habe ich mir die Freiheit genommen, es zu behaupten. Es entspricht aber der Wahrheit, dass er damals in *Köhlers Dorfhotel* logierte. Seine Eintragung ins Gästebuch kann man sich im Borkumer Heimatmuseum ansehen.

„Hermine sagte mir, sie wollte, dass ich ihr mal was dichten sollte. Ich sagte ja! – Und also hüh! Fährt jetzt mein Geist per Fantasie nach Borkum, legt sich auf die Düne und dichtet was für die Hermine." Dieses Zitat stammt aus einem Gedicht von Wilhelm Busch, das er während eines seiner Aufenthalte auf Borkum geschrieben hat.

„Jede Geschichtsschreibung ist Fiktion." Das haben schon mehrere Schriftsteller gesagt und so ist es auch in dieser Geschichte. Was ich über die Charaktere der Familienmitglieder berichte, könnte so gewesen sein, denn niemand, auch nicht die zahlreichen Nachfahren, vermag mit Bestimmtheit zu behaupten, die persönlichen Eigenarten seiner Ahnen wären anders gewesen.

Zwei Nebengeschichten bleiben ungelöst: Ist Hermines Cousine Bertha in Amerika angekommen oder lebt sie – wie der fremde Mann behauptet – irgendwo anders? Das wird sich in Band 2 herausstellen. Auch das Geheimnis um die leiblichen Eltern Annelieses bleibt vorerst ungelüftet. Anneliese könnte Anspruch auf ihr Erbteil erheben, auch das wird sich in Band 2 aufklären.

Daten wie Namen und Geburtstage sind dokumentiert. Ebenso die Geschichtsdaten rund um die Insel. Cafés, Restaurants,

Logierhäuser wie *San Remo* oder *Staghouwer* und Ladenlokale wie die *Giftbude* gab es wirklich, teilweise gibt es sie noch heute.

Große Teile der Vogelsammlung der Borkumer Naturfreunde und Naturforscher, das *Naturalistische Kabinett,* kann man sich heute im Heimatmuseum ansehen. Alles andere, was das menschliche Miteinander angeht, ist erfunden.

Ob Geeske Bakker, die jüngste Tochter von Willem Dirks Bakker, verschwendungssüchtig war, wissen wir nicht, aber alte Fotos von ihr zeigen, dass sie eine schicke Frau war und mit der neuesten Mode ging. Ebenso wenig ist nachgewiesen, ob Harmina Bakker nervenkrank war und sich für das Armenhaus mehr als üblich eingesetzt hat. Das Armenhaus in der Süderstraße hat es jedoch gegeben. Mitte des 20. Jahrhunderts stand dort der städtische Kindergarten, heute stehen auf dem Grundstück mehrere Ferienhäuser.

Das Gebäude *Köhlers Dorfhotel* hat ebenso fast unverändert seit damals die Zeit überstanden. Nach Köhler von der Familie Stindt betrieben, beherbergt es heute den Evangelischen Kirchenkreis Lüdenscheid-Plettenberg (Haus Alter Leuchtturm).

Köhlers Strandhotel war und ist ein riesiges Gebäude. Später hieß es *Haus Europa.* Heute logiert dort das Fachklinikum Borkum.

Köhlers Giftbude gibt es leider nicht mehr. In einer Sturmnacht wurde sie fortgeschwemmt. Die *Viktoriahöhe* ist heute das Ausflugslokal *Sturmeck.*

Hermann Behrends ist der Erbauer des *Ostfriesenhofes.* Damals hieß das Hotel *Strandvilla Behrends.* Er soll wirklich 1.000 Mark in der Lotterie gewonnen haben. Er verkaufte die *Villa San Remo* an seinen Bruder und baute den *Ostfriesenhof.* Dessen Originalfassade ist heute immer noch zu bewundern.

Auch das *Nordseehotel,* bis zum heutigen Tage im Besitz der Familie Schmidt, hat im Laufe der Jahrzehnte glücklicherweise sein Gesicht nicht verändert.

Die *Strandvilla Hawich* wurde leider in der zweiten Hälfte des zwanzigsten Jahrhunderts abgerissen. Heute steht dort ein hässliches Apartmenthaus. *Geffah-Haus,* wie die Insulaner dazu sagen.

Und die *Villa Ines,* erbaut vom Fabrikanten Stollwerk, brannte in den Fünfzigerjahren vollkommen ab. Heute steht dort die Nordseeklinik Borkum.

Die in Ostfriesland gegenwärtig nur noch teilweise angewendete patronymische Namensgebung macht es schwer, die Personen in den Familien auseinanderzuhalten. Sie tragen alle den gleichen Namen. Um den Großvater von den Enkelsöhnen zu unterscheiden – von Willem Bakker hießen gleich vier seiner Enkelsöhne ebenfalls Willem Bakker –, gab und gibt es heute noch Spitznamen. Wie sonst soll man sie auseinanderhalten?

Das Post- und Telegrafenamt wurde bereits zum 1.4.1884 von *Köhlers Dorfhotel* in die neue Apotheke von Bakker verlegt. Auch hier habe ich mit der Jahreszahl geschummelt, da der Umzug gut in meine Geschichte passt.

Borkum ist heute ein Familienbad, doch damals war die Insel ein bevorzugter Urlaubsort der Großen, Reichen und Berühmten Deutschlands. Man reiste zu jener Zeit mit dem ganzen „Hofstaat" an. Ob Carl Busse und Max Liebermann dazu gehörten, kann ich nicht sagen. Es ist frei erfunden.

Das lukrative Geschäft des Tierausstopfers hat Herr Lübberstedt von Herrn Bekaan übernommen. Lübberstedts Laden, in dem ich als Kind oft gewesen bin, befand sich in der *Strandvilla Hawich,* in der oberen Bismarckstraße. Die Villa gibt es leider nicht mehr. Noch heute habe ich den Geruch in der Nase und die (echten!) menschlichen Schrumpfköpfe vor Augen.

Die Straßen, die angegeben sind, tragen heute teilweise andere Namen. So wurde aus:

Damenpfad – Franz-Habich-Straße
Große Straße – Wilhelm-Bakker-Straße
Kaiserstraße – Jann-Berghaus-Straße

1885 betrug die Zahl der Einwohner 898 Personen. Wenige Jahre nach dem Bauboom, dem Bau der Gleisanlagen, des Hafens und des Bahnhofs hatte sich die Einwohnerzahl fast verdreifacht.

Johann Fischers Basar war ein hölzerner Flachbau, den der Händler Johann Fischer von der Gemeinde gepachtet hatte. Hüte, Mützen, Badeartikel, Strandschuhe und mehr gab es zu erwerben. Heute steht dort das Rathaus.

Der Pfahl *Stientje Pahle,* an dem sich die Dorfjugend traf, ist Geschichte.

Im Verlag CW Niemeyer bereits erschienen ...

Konrad Georg Brichtner stolpert am Duhner Strand in Cuxhaven über eine Leiche. Das Opfer hält einen mysteriösen Gegenstand in der Hand – eine Petrischale mit Nährboden für Bakterien. Das Bizarre: Die Bakterien wachsen in Form einer numerischen Reihenfolge. Konrad beschließt, eigene Nachforschungen anzustellen, als er erfährt, dass das Opfer ein ehemaliger Kollege seines Onkels und Ziehvaters ist. Alles deutet darauf hin, dass der Mord etwas mit einer früheren BKA-Ermittlung zu tun hat, in die sein Onkel eingebunden war. Dann werden weitere Leichen mit ähnlichen Bakterienschalen aufgefunden …

Markus Rahaus. Mordlinie
416 Seiten. Klappenbroschur. ISBN 978-3-8271-9335-3
E-Book 978-3-8271-9783-2 (Epub)

#niemeyerbuch

Jetzt kein Buch mehr verpassen